Managing the Public Sector

The Dorsey Series in Political Science

Consulting Editor   SAMUEL C. PATTERSON
University of Iowa

Managing
the
Public
Sector

GROVER STARLING
Director of Programs in
  Public Affairs
University of Houston at
  Clear Lake City

1977

The Dorsey Press Homewood, Illinois 60430

Irwin-Dorsey Limited   Georgetown, Ontario   L7G 4B3

First Printing, March 1977

ISBN 0-256-01936-3
Library of Congress Catalog Card No. 76–47735

Printed in the United States of America

To my wife,
Yolanda Blandón Starling

Preface

The whole secret of the brain's ability to learn by experience, some researchers say, is the acquisition of special influence by one neuron over another across a connection called a synapse. Because of these cooperative reactions, we can say that our brains over time acquire deep "grooves" through which our thoughts tend to flow. The study of public administration is not without its own deep grooves. As a result, most textbooks on the subject tend to be variations of the same themes. Not so with this volume.

The title itself, *Managing the Public Sector,* reveals much about what new circuits might open in the pages ahead. The operative word in the title is *managing,* for this is a book, first and last, about the practice of management. To many authorities and surely most of the American public, the most acute need facing government in the decades ahead will be better management. But "better management" means more than the doxy of basic personnel, budgeting, and administrative practices. The call for better management, as I interpret it, means greater attention to modern analytical, behavioral, and informational techniques that are required to successfully manage any large-scale enterprise.

But an introduction to public administration must provide more than an exposure to such business school topics as management by objectives, accrual and cost accounting, microeconomic analysis, decision theory, and job redesign. Otherwise, this book would hardly be necessary—after all, a clutch of business school textbooks are available on all of these topics. No, an introduction to public administration must in at least two ways go beyond an inventory of management techniques. It must, first, place these techniques in the context of the public sector. And by *public sector,* I refer not only to governmental jurisdictions but also to other nonprofit institutions such as hospitals, foundations, and universities. Second, an introduction must make crystal clear the highly political environment of American public administration. While quite sympathetic to the notion that the environment of private sector management is becoming increasingly like that of the public sector management, I still see fundamental, perhaps irreducible, differences. To cite only one: In the private sector, objectives are usually given; they become, as it were, problems to be solved. In contrast, the public sector's objectives are far less certain, far more debatable. Indeed, the public administrator often participates in the process of determining those objectives. In finding a place for the management expert, we cannot afford to toss out the political scientist.

Besides the strong, though not exclusive, emphasis on management, what else is new about this book? Most introductions tend to provide potted summaries of what individual scholars have said. What they generally have not done is what an introductory textbook in a major field of study ought always do: provide organizing assumptions, concepts, and definitions that underlie any systematic inquiry and that give a field coherence (Landau, 1962: 178). To provide this coherence, the book builds around four major themes: the sociopolitical environment of public administration (Part I); the management of governmental programs (Part II); financial management (Part III); and the management of people (Part IV). But, and this is important, the quartet forms an integrated whole—one that attempts to reconcile the current thinking on administrative theory.

Now we come to the deepest groove in the cerebellum of public administration, namely, the tendency to ignore the practical for the theoretical. By 1950, it had incised enough to prompt Simon, Smithburg, and Thompson (viii) to write:

> Excessive preoccupation with "ideal" or "desirable" administrative arrangements may be seriously misleading (since final truths are still a long way off in this field) and may leave the student unprepared for the realities of administration as he later finds them. In training students to advise the President, universities have not always trained them to discharge the first modest responsibilities that are placed upon them in government employment. The disillusioning shock that students of public administration have so often experienced in the past should warn us against this danger.

The main body of this book differs from most of the literature in that it provides how-to-do-it techniques that can be applied immediately in any organization at any level. In order to insure that the content of *Managing the Public Sector* accurately reflects what goes on in the real world of government and that the most relevant knowledge and techniques are introduced, I consulted a number of surveys and studies. (See, for example, F. Cleaveland, 1973; Grode and Holzer, 1975; National Training and Development Service, 1975; and National Association of Schools of Public Affairs and Administration, 1974.)

A collateral but more subtle problem concerns how to convey this information in such a way that the reader can see how the techniques can apply in organizational settings. Whenever possible, I have tried with examples drawn from actual experience to illustrate the techniques and generalizations and thereby make them come alive for the reader.

Taking this tack forces the introduction of concrete problems of public policy. This is good. Most introductory treatments of public administration tend to focus almost exclusively on describing the structures and functions of agencies. But the study of public administration has a policy dimension as well: What is the best transportation system for Seattle? What approach should Florida take to managing its coastal zone? Who really benefits from the current federal tax structure? What should be done about the projected imbalances in the financing of the social security system? Because the public administrator cannot duck these questions, this book does not. Rather, discussion of public policy issues is closely integrated with description of structure and function.

In this preface, I have thus far dealt exclusively with the major objectives of *Managing the Public Sector.* These were:

To discuss the latest analytical, behavioral, and information techniques, which are required to successfully manage any large scale enterprise, in the context not merely of government but of the public sector.

To provide the organizing assumptions, concepts, and definitions that underlie the study of public administration and that give the subject coherence.

To introduce techniques that can be applied immediately in any organization at any level and to illustrate their application with concrete problems of public policy.

I should like to conclude on a brief pedagogical note. To ease the reader's journey into what may be entirely unfamiliar territory, I have taken several steps. Chapter titles and formats were carefully drawn to provide a clear and balanced view of the subject. Lists of new terms were placed at the end of each chapter; connective summaries, throughout. I have attempted to make the theoretical parts as clear-cut, short, and important as possible.

The philosopher and mathematician, Alfred North Whitehead (1929:13) once said, "A merely well-informed man is the most useless bore on God's earth." He added: "above all things we must beware of what I will call 'inert ideas' — that is to say, ideas that are merely received into the mind without being utilized, or tested, or thrown into fresh combinations." To battle the pestilence of inert ideas, I have added to the end of each chapter a set of problems designed not for review but for critical, analytical thinking. These problems, then, are an integral part of the book. They help in the attainment of what surely must be our ultimate objective: to improve the quality of thinking about the management of the public sector.

February 1977   GROVER STARLING

Acknowledgments

As the Director of a relatively large Program in Public Affairs at a university with a strong commitment to local, regional, and state problems in one of the most rapidly growing areas in the world, I had the good fortune—and indeed, great pleasure—of meeting with literally hundreds of practicing managers in virtually every facet of public sector management. Through these meetings, I was able to test out my own ideas and to discover new avenues for further investigation. While I cannot begin to acknowledge each of these practitioners by name, I can at least acknowledge the prescience of those that layed the groundwork for the Public Affairs Program at the University of Houston at Clear Lake City: Alfred Neumann, Louis J. Rodriguez, and June Hyer.

But I have been doubly fortunate. The nearby Johnson Space Center provided me with a laboratory for testing my ideas against the concerns of managers in a federal agency. As a consultant to NASA for the past two years, I probably learned at least as much as I taught. While I cannot begin to acknowledge this most capable group of managers by name, I must at least mention one—Philip Whitbeck, Director, Administration and Program Support. Phil not only started my involvement in the activities of this highly touted agency but also proved a most demanding critic of my writing.

For a thorough reading of the entire manuscript and for valuable suggestions too numerous to mention, I would especially like to thank Brian R. Fry of the University of South Carolina. I would also like to express my appreciation to Samuel C. Patterson, consulting editor, and to the following reviewers: Michael King, Pennsylvania State University; Perry Moore, Wright State University;

and Dean L. Yarwood, the University of Missouri, Columbia. For a review of the entire manuscript and collaboration on parts of Chapter 11, I would like to thank my good friend James I. Scheiner of Booz, Allen & Hamilton. For reviewing various parts of the manuscript, I would like to thank the following colleagues at the UH/CLC: Les Sartorius, Norman Weed, Walter Natemeyer, Kim Hill, and Jay Shafritz.

Administering a rapidly developing academic program and writing a rather lengthy book do not go together smoothly. Two people, however, helped prevent this misalliance from becoming an outright ordeal. First was Rosemary Pledger, Dean of the School of Professional Studies, as understanding a supervisor as one is likely to find anywhere. Second was Jean Sherwood, my secretary, who freed me from many of the details of my own administrative responsibilities. Over the past two years, a number of typists were involved with the manuscript. Among those most involved were Betty Frels, Kandie Easterling, and Marcia Morris.

Two people deserve special acknowledgment. First is my wife, Yolanda, for ineffable support. And second is my former professor, Emmette S. Redford—a man from whom I learned more than public administration.

G. S.

Contents

Even more important than winning the election is governing the nation. That is the test of a political party—the acid, final test. When the tumult and the shouting die, when the bands are gone and the lights are dimmed, there is the stark reality of responsibility. . . .

Adlai Stevenson, 1952

Public Administration: The Accomplishing Side of Government

In this introductory chapter, the fundamental questions of who public administrators are and what they do are answered. To give the reader perspective in dealing with the enormous scope of public administration, five basic subject areas of public administration are identified and discussed. Finally, we consider the professional— as opposed to scientific—nature of public administration as a field of study.

AFTER THE CHEERING

Public administration concerns the accomplishing side of government. It comprises all those activities involved in carrying out the policies of elected officials and some activities associated with the development of those policies. Public administration is, in short, all that comes after the last campaign promise and election night cheer. To make the term as clear and concrete as possible, let us begin by considering two basic questions. Who are public administrators and what do they do?

Who Public Administrators Are

In Stockton, California, a man sits behind his desk in a tan business suit. He talks of computers, multimillion dollar budgets, in-service training requirements, and management by objectives. He is not an advertising executive, an investment counselor, or a production manager; he is a sheriff.

Sheriff Michael N. Canlis oversees law enforcement in San Joaquin County, a sprawling, 400 square miles of city and farm land with a population of 300,000. On one recent day, he monitored a continuing labor conflict between the International Brotherhood of Teamsters and the United Farm Workers, delved into parts of his $6 million budget, consulted the governor's office, participated in a helicopter crash inquiry, met with militant pickets, checked the installation of his department's new computerized communication system, consoled the relatives of an injured deputy, and chatted with countless friends and petitioners in the hallway. (Malcolm 1974) Sheriff Canlis is also a public administrator, one of a new breed of men, and a growing number of women, effecting fundamental changes on some of the oldest governmental institutions in the English-speaking world.

Across the country, in Washington, Carla Anderson Hills, the Secretary of Housing and Urban Development, is charged with administering a new and complex housing-subsidy program whose implementation had fallen far behind schedule. As she assumes her post, the department is saddled with a huge load of property that has to be taken care of and ultimately disposed of. Morale is low, scandals rampant, the home building industry depressed. Through no housing expert, she takes firm hold of the department in a remarkably short time. She gets programs moving that had languished months under her predecessor.

The adjective most frequently applied to her is "tough." Few of Ms. Hills's staff escape her pointed cross-examination of their proposals. She uses the same technique when something goes wrong, pursuing the cause of error through layers of rationalization and double-talk.

Her speed and decisiveness dazzle her staff, some of whom are old Washington hands long accustomed to bureaucratic delay. One of her deputy assistant secretaries recalls bringing to her a large packet of materials that had to be issued quickly. As he prepared to brief her, Mrs. Hills asked:

> "Have you reviewed this package personally?"
> "Yes."
> "Are you satisfied with it?"
> "Yes."
> "Do I have any personal knowledge to contribute?"
> "No."
> "Do you recommend that I sign it without going over it?"
> "Yes."
> Exit assistant with her signature. (Roos 1975)

Hills and Canlis illustrate at least one important thing about who public administrators are; namely, individuals who are found at all levels of government — urban/local, state/regional, national, and international. But as used in this text, the term has an even broader meaning. Specifically, public administrator refers to those individuals employed not only by government but also by service institutions, such as hospitals and universities. It also refers to individuals employed by the many quasigovernmental institutions that have proliferated in the last 10 or 15 years. Among these quasigovernmental institutions, we might include research institutes (e.g., RAND), foundations (e.g., the Ford Foundation), and federally chartered corporations (e.g., Amtrak). We shall refer to this broad spectrum of institutions — governmental, service, and quasigovernmental — as the *public sector.*

One final point concerning who today's public administrators are: it would be a great mistake to ignore the administrative responsibilities of elected officials. In the next chapter, we shall examine a debate that characterized the earlier stages of the development of public administration as a field of study. Roughly speaking, the debate centers on the question of whether administration could be divorced from politics, whether the administrator could effectively carry out his duties oblivious to politics. Fortunately, that question has finally been laid to rest by a firm negative. Less fortunately, however, is the fact that few thought to ask — or, much less, press home — the converse question: Could the elected official efficiently carry out his duties oblivious to the complexities of administration? Significantly, when John Lindsay (1973) was asked what his best moment was in eight years of mayor of New York City, he replied: "Curiously, the thing I will take away with me — that I'm happiest about, is the most mundane of all, and that is just straight management and administration. It's the hours and hours spent on the production line, on the process of even hiring and bringing into government analytical people and project managers and computer people. I had a lot of frustration over it, but we got a thousand men and women now in the middle management ranks." Clearly, then, elected public officials have administrative as well as political responsibilities and the former can be every bit as important as the latter.

What Public Administrators Do

Again, the cases of Sheriff Canlis and Secretary Hills are illustrative, for they at least hint at the wide variety of functions performed and roles fulfilled by today's public administrators. Indeed, in addition to criminal justice and housing, public administrators are involved in such functional areas as community development, business regulation, educational administration, environmental management, international development administration, manpower and employment, national security and arms control, space law, personnel, health care service administration, medical research, public works administration, and transportation planning. The roles they might follow are equally varied. (Cf. Caiden 1971:290–1):

Crusading reformer, transforming some aspect of community life.

Policy formulator, developing strategies to meet the unknown future.

Three Public Administrators At the Top in Washington, 1976

The rapid rise of Carla Hills was a tribute both to talent and to the happy accident of being the right sex at the right time. Her first government post in Washington was as assistant attorney general in charge of the Justice Department's civil division.

John Reed, while still in his 20s, was appointed Assistant Secretary of Labor. Before that he served as executive assistant of the secretary. Despite minimal training in economics and virtually none in labor affairs, Reed was not overwhelmed. "Experience within the department in which you work," he says, "is not the most important criterion for the job of executive assistant. The ability to ask questions and to say 'I don't know' is probably more important than any other in this job. You have to be smart enough to admit when you don't know something and not go off in the wrong direction just because an executive assistant has to seem that he knows what he's doing."

William Taft, at age 30, was appointed General Council for the Department of Health, Education, and Welfare. He has also worked as a Nader Raider and executive assistant to the HEW secretary. Taft finds "it isn't surprising that young people can move rapidly into high government posts, given the needs of cabinet officers for executive assistants and the kinds of jobs they must do. It's difficult to get someone who is 50 years old and who has had a long career in the bureaucracy to function efficiently as an aide."

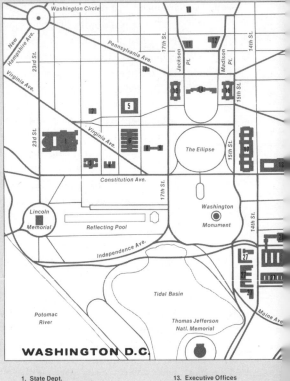

WASHINGTON D.C.

1. State Dept.
2. American Red Cross
3. Federal Reserve Bldg.
4. Bureau of Indian Affairs
5. General Services Admin. Bldg.
6. Interior Dept. Bldg.
7. U.S. Information Agency
8. Constitution Hall
9. Continental Hall
10. Commonwealth Bldg.
11. Chamber of Commerce (U.S.)
12. Veterans Admin.
13. Executive Offices
14. White House
15. Treasury Dept.
16. Board of Education
17. Commerce Dept.
18. Interstate Com. Comm. and Labor Dept.
19. Internal Revenue Bureau
20. F.B.I. Bldg.
21. Justice Dept.
22. Tariff Comm.
23. Archives
24. Federal Trade Comm.

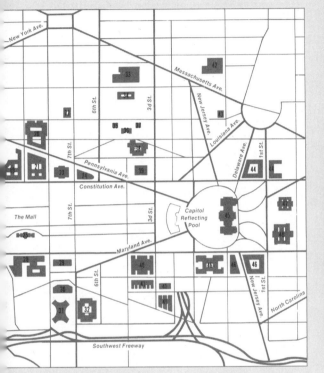

25. Smithsonian Institu
26. Dept. of Agriculture
27. Bureau of Engraving and Printing
28. Forrestal Bldg.
29. Federal Aviation Agency
30. G.S.A. Regional Office
31. Housing and Urban Development
32. Dept. of Transportation
33. General Accounting Office
34. Pension Bldg.
35. Court of Military Appeals
36. Court House

37. Juvenile Court
38. Municipal Bldg.
39. District Court (U.S.)
40. Health, Education and Welfare
41. F.B.I. (Identification Division)
42. Govt. Printing Office
43. Securities and Exchange Comm.
44. Senate Office Bldgs.
45. The Capitol
46. House Office Bldgs.
47. Supreme Court
48. Library of Congress

Social-change agent, accepting new ideas and pushing others to accepting them.

Crisis manager, acting quickly but calmly.

Program manager, shaping new courses and adapting ongoing arrangements.

Humanitarian employer, treating staff with respect and meting out even-handed justice.

Competent administrator, ensuring effective performance with minimum political embarrassment.

Interest broker, choosing among competing interests and reconciling all parties to the outcome.

Public relations expert, building support.

Decision maker, assuming responsibility and giving clear instructions.

Leader, commanding attention and stimulating subordinates.

In sum, the challenge of a career in public administration today is as broad and exciting as contemporary life itself.

But our second question raises a third: What basic knowledge and skills must public administrators have to perform the functions and fulfill the roles outlined above? Mark the question well, for it points us squarely in the direction of the subject of this book.

THE BASIC KNOWLEDGE AND SKILLS OF PUBLIC ADMINISTRATOR: A PREVIEW

In providing a preliminary yet systematic answer to this question, we are in the fortunate position of being able to draw upon an authoritative report by the National Association of Public Affairs and Administration (NASPAA). Recognizing that the quality of government would suffer if the study of public administration could not be more effectively delineated, NASPAA decided at its 1973 annual conference to move toward the establishment of standards and guidelines for education and training programs. Accordingly, a committee on standards was established; during the year 1973–74, it conducted a study in close cooperation with a number of professional associations and public employing agencies. The initial product, *Guidelines and Standards for Professional Masters Degree Programs in Public Affairs/Public Administration,* was unanimously adopted by the delegates to the 1974 NASPAA Conference.

The heart of the guidelines and standards is a matrix that sets forth the competencies in knowledge, skill, values, and behavior to be attained by public managers. Basically, the committee recommended that public administration programs in colleges and universities cover five subject matter areas: (*a*) the political, social, and economic environment; (*b*) policy analysis; (c) managerial processes; (d) analytical tools; and (e) individual, group, and organizational behavior.

The Environment

The first axiom of administration might be that organizations do not operate in vacuums. And this axiom applies not only to public sector but also to the private. For that reason, few graduate level business curriculums today fail to require courses such as "business environment" or "business and society." Nevertheless, it is in the public sector that the axiom become the most crucial to competent administration.

To say that organizations do not operate in vacuums implies much. Public administrators should have, for example, knowledge of the cultural and social mores and patterns of the locale within which their organization operates. And more: they should have tolerance for this diversity. Public administrators should also have knowledge of the physical environment, particularly when their organization has responsibility for technological projects. Further, they should have knowledge of economic processes and institutions. In an era of increasing concern about pollution and the quality of life, the last two requirements should be obvious enough. As Kenneth Boulding (1966) pointed out: today's economy differs from yesterday's.

The open economy of the past was the "cowboy economy." Boulding uses the expression cowboy because it is symbolic of the illimitable plains and of reckless, exploitative, romantic, and violent behavior. In characterizing today's economy, Boulding is equally picturesque—"spaceman economy." The conditions in the latter are of course quite different: "the Earth has become a single spaceship, without unlimited reserves of anything and in which, therefore, man must find his place in a cyclical ecological system. . . ."

What else does the competent public administrator need to know about the environment? Perhaps the most obvious thing of all: knowledge of governmental institutions, powers, processes, and relationships. The last named item can be especially vexing, for the United States is a political system composed of not one but thousands of jurisdictions. Unfortunately, political knowledge alone is not enough; good administrators must also have political skills—skills to analyze and interpret political, social, and economic trends; skills to evaluate the consequences of administrative actions; and skills to persuade and bargain and thereby further their organization's objective. To put it bluntly: it behooves those people who possess great technical and managerial talent to be sufficiently skilled politicians. Society suffers a great loss, I think, when outstandingly talented people are so inept in their political skills that they can only contribute a small fraction of their talents.

Finally, administrators cannot—must not—ignore the political values of society. In the United States, at least, among these values we would include the democratic tradition, constitutionalism, the rule of law, citizen participation, and responsiveness (i.e., prompt acquiescence by government to popular demands for policy change).

Policy Analysis

The term responsiveness suggests that public administrators are, like elected officials, very much involved in the process of making policy (that is, deciding on broad courses of action). This is quite true. Therefore public administrators need to be able to think through, to analyze as carefully as possible their alternatives. Policy analysis is a relatively new approach and method, drawing on both political science and economics for doing just that.

What exactly, does the policy analyst look for? One item is conflict among policies. Consider, for example, subsidies to farmers to decrease agricultural output. Can that policy be reconciled with other governmental actions such as research grants to universities and land reclamation projects to increase output? Another important item concerns the costs and benefits of a policy: What is the distribution of the costs and benefits of a policy? Do the benefits exceed the costs? What effect, if any, will the contemplated action have on the environment? Further, the analysis should look for internal consistency in, and establish priorities among, the objectives of the policy.

The foregoing provides only a glimpse at a few of the many components of policy analysis. Nonetheless, the reason why the NASPAA committee chose to include this subject on their list should be clear enough. The days when government could launch expensive, new policies with little or no regard to consequences and feasibility have past. Today administrators as well as their political leaders must think before acting. At least on this point, public opinion seems unequivocal.

Managerial Processes

The third subject area, administrative process, probably requires less explanation than the preceding two.[1] After all, it is fairly self-evident that after a policy has been decided upon somebody must be concerned with carrying

---

[1] The NASPAA Committee uses the term "administrative processes" along with "managerial process." Unfortunately, a quick trip to the dictionary will do little to untangle the two terms. But administration does seem to have a more subtle and extended series of meanings than management." It is more usually found in the public sector than the private and, in general, carries an implication, not of ultimate sovereign control, but of directing and coordinating things on behalf of other people or authorities." (Baker 1972:12) The term "management," on the other hand, usually carries a rather different flavor. Drucker (1973) views management primarily in terms of a fairly specific set of tasks: to perform the function for the sake of which the institution exists; to make work productive and the worker achieving; to manage the institution's social impacts. But in coordinating complex situations where no criteria really exists, administration is probably a more appropriate word. It is also slightly more embracing in that it includes a lot of preparatory and supportive work for higher-level decision making (for example, all those activities referred to as "policy analysis" above). For consistency, we shall use the term administrator when refering to public sector managers.

it out, making it work. This means that organizations must be designed, work assigned, progress monitored, efficiency maintained, and money spent.

To dismiss these activities as mundane would be a grave mistake. Today we see a growing concern over the managerial process of the public sector. Thus the best clients of large American management consulting firms these last 10 or 15 years have been governmental agencies such as the Department of Defense and the city of New York. Peter Drucker (1974: 8), a distinguished management consultant himself, thinks that managing the service institution is likely to be the frontier of management for the rest of the century. "The management of the nonbusiness institutions will indeed be a growing concern from now on. Their management may well become the central management problem — simply because the lack of management of the public-service institutions is such a glaring weakness, whether municipal water department or graduate university."

While this line of thinking is a cornerstone of *Managing the Public Sector,* its hue is entirely negative. This need not be. Positive justifications for the importance of management to the public sector are not hard to make. Indeed, to Jean-Jacques Servan-Schreiber, a French journalist, "Management is, all things considered, the most creative of all arts. It is the art of arts. Because it is the organizer of talent."

Now, no one can "prove" such a statement right or wrong. But consider at least this:

One of the most striking things about the science fiction of the pre-Apollo era is virtual absence of any reference to, or appreciation of, the purely managerial complexities involved in a moon landing. Robert A. Heinlein's *Destination Moon,* a 1950 milestone in the history science fiction motion pictures, is an obvious — and by no means isolated — example. Space flight seemed to require only two ingredients, a dauntless protagonist and a brilliant scientist. (Three ingredients if one counts the latter's pulchritudinous daughter.)

Yet the most important thing about the Apollo mission was not the technology, which had been in existence for some time, but the extraordinary organizational structure. What was this structure? In reporting on their four years of intensive study, Sayles and Chandler (1971) pointed out that, at its peak, NASA sought contributions from 20,000 different organizations. The key to making NASA's structure work rested upon creating an effective communications network that engulfed anyone who could conceivably influence or implement the decision and that contained various "management councils" composed of co-equal associates to share progress and problems.

Why did science fiction writers fail to see the emergence of management as one of the pivotal events of our time? I think the answer is that rarely, if ever, has a human activity developed as rapidly as management. But the rate of development should not be surprising, for today every developed country has become a society of institutions and institutions require management. Indeed, every major social task — economic performance, health care, education, conservation, scientific research, etc. — is today entrusted to big organizations, managed by their own managements. This situation contrasts sharply to society at the turn of the century. The emergence of big government and big business hardly needs elaboration, but interestingly, other institutions have grown much faster. Before 1914, no university in the world had much more than 6,000 students; today the State University of New York has well over 200,000. Similarly, the hospital has grown from a marginal institution for the poor to the center of health care and a giant in its own right.

Analytical Tools

In carrying out the managerial tasks noted above, the competent administrator uses, when possible, analytical tools. The idea here is not to make every general administrator a "computer expert" or "management science expert" but to introduce him or her to the bare essentials necessary to make effective use of these tools. The focus needs to be upon the role of analysis in managerial decision making, upon the strengths and limitations of the quantitative approach, and upon the systems aspects of decision making.

While analytical tools really became installed and refined in government during the McNamara dynasty at the Pentagon, the idea of using analytical tools to improve management is hardly new. Peter Drucker reminds us that double entry bookkeeping actually began in the Renaissance. Today, however, the number and sophistication has—to understate considerably—grown. And that long forgotten Italian who developed double entry bookkeeping would surely be awed—though few of the modern tools could compare in simplicity, elegance, and usefulness with his. Roughly, we may divide these modern tools into three classes: first are quantitative and logical approaches to decision making; second, systems and procedures analysis; and, third, computer based management information systems. When judiciously used, these tools can provide the public administrator with a better understanding of the risks involved in a certain decision, of the most economical way to use resources, and of exactly what resources are available.

Individual, Group, and Organizational Behavior

Lastly, the committee recommended that public administrator have some knowledge about how individuals behave in an organizational setting. In particular, competent administrators should be able to motivate and lead. They also must be able to interact effectively with superiors and peers. It is in this subject area that public administration has drawn most heavily upon behavioral sciences such as psychology. Like the analytical tools noted above, the behavioral sciences can improve the performance of an administrator in managerial process.

The Approach of this Book

These five subject areas—environment, policy analysis, managerial processes, analytical tools, and behavior—not only answer the question of what public administrators need to know but also highlight what lies in the chapters ahead. But we shall not follow the NASPAA committee in lockstep; considerable rerouting will be necessary. To see why this is so, let us consider just one change.

The chief reason why policy analysis and analytical tools have not been more widely used in the public sector is that public administrators, by and large, have failed to take managerial responsibility for them. They have not done so because they have viewed policy analysis and analytical tools not as *a part of the task of managing* but as separate bodies of knowledge, perhaps best left to the experts. As a partial solution to this state of affairs, I have tried to fold both subjects into the chapters of the book that deal with the management of governmental programs. The chart below attempts to show at a glance how the four major parts of this book relate to NASPAA's five subjects.

This part of Managing the Public Sector	Covers these parts of the NASPAA matrix
I. Environment	1. Political, social, and economic context
II. Management of governmental programs III. Financial management	2. Policy analysis 3. Management processes 4. Analytical tools
IV. The management of people	5. Individual, group, and organizational dynamics

As shown in the Table, this book builds around four major themes: (1) the sociopolitical environment of public administration, (2) the management of governmental programs, (3) financial management, and (4) the management of people. Ultimately, what it attempts to accomplish is two-fold: (a) to reconcile the current thinking on administrative theory and then (b) to reconcile that thinking with the everyday problems of the administrator who stands on the firing line. The operative word is to reconcile and it merits emphasis.

To reconcile, as used in (a) does not mean merely to tie together — in a more or less neat package (usually called a survey) — all the facts, hypothesis, and opinions that happen to be in good currency among the theoreticians of administration. No. It means instead to inventory systematically the current state of the art; then, to eliminate mercilessly all that is dated, mediocre, irrelevant, or redundant; and, lastly, to present the balance in as clear, concise, and consistent a manner as possible.

But how does one know what particular knowledge or skill is of use to the practitioner? Clearly no single individual is competent to make such a determination. Fortunately, a number of studies and surveys are available to help construct a fairly accurate picture of what an administrator, in general, needs to know. (See, for example, N. Cleaveland 1973; Grode and Holzer 1975; National Training and Development Service 1975; and NASPAA 1974).

Moreover, some of the surveys actually give us an idea of the relative emphasis to place on the topics.

How then does one present this knowledge and these skills with clarity and concision? An especially good answer is through the use of *models,* which are no more than simplified representations of how the real world works. Models can be expressed by mathematical equations, geometric graphs, or simply stated in words. *Managing the Public Sector* makes frequent use of them.

What is lost by taking the essentially pragmatic approach in designing an introduction to public administration? Only the pretense that public administration can be a science. Admittedly, an important assumption is being made here, namely, that public administration cannot be a science like physics or chemistry. And before proceeding any further, we must pause to make the implications of this assumption crystal clear.

PARADIGMS AND PROFESSIONS

The Concept of Paradigm

In a groundbreaking study of the history of science, *The Structure of Scientific Revolutions,* Thomas S. Kuhn argued that the development of a science can be best understood in terms of *paradigms* (PAR-a-dimes). Normal, everyday science is conducted within the conceptual framework provided by the paradigm. Eventually, however, results from experiments begin to appear that cannot be explained in terms of the paradigm; these results Kuhn calls anomalies. If the number of anomalies continues to increase and to remain unexplained, a scientific revolution occurs and the old paradigm is replaced by a new one; thus, in physics, the Newtonian world view was replaced by the Einsteinian.

The relevance of Kuhn's work to the study of public administration becomes apparent with the introduction of the concept of the "preparadigm" stage—a kind of twilight period in which hypothesis, facts, and opinions float about but do not really hang together. Suddenly, a Newton appears, proffers the paradigm, and a new science is born. To not a few scholars public administration is at the moment considered to be in such a stage, waiting patiently (and sometimes not so patiently) for its Newton.

Attempts to make administration a science have a venerable tradition, now almost a century old. In the 1880s Frederick Taylor, a self-taught American engineer, began to study work systematically. The *scientific management* concepts, which Taylor pioneered, was based on the notion that, in any undertaking, scientific analysis would lead to discovery of the "one best way" of carrying out each operation. In this way, the scientific management of work became the key to productivity. Taylor's aim, however, was not merely to increase of productivity for higher profits but actually to free the worker from the burden of heavy toil—a point often forgotten when Taylor is mentioned today.

The mood of "Taylorism" helped to create the *administrative science movement.* The idea of this movement was that if you look coldly at the "facts" for a long enough time, soon you will begin to see "principles" that tell you how to administer. The origins of this approach could be, perhaps, traced as far back as 1908, the year in which Henri Fayol's classic *Administration Industriaelle et Généralé* appeared. Fayol, who had a long and successful career as a general manager in French mining and engineering, argued in a lofty, almost Napoleonic vein that the administrative function may be subdivided into five elements or processes—foresight, organization, command, coordination, and control.

In the United States, Luther Gulick began to develop Fayol's analysis of administrative functions and in 1937 put forth the POSDCORB formula. This snappy anagram stood for the seven principles of administration: planning, organizing, staffing, directing, coordinating, reporting, and budgeting. As Gulick (1937: 191 and 195) put it: "At the present time administration is more an art than science; in fact there are those who assert dogmatically that it can never be anything else. They draw no hope from the fact that metallurgy, for example, was completely an art several centuries before it became primarily a science . . . [Several] factors played their part in the conquest of the natural world by exact science, and may be counted upon again to advance scientific knowledge and control in the world of human affairs."

The problem with the view that public administration can and should have a paradigm and thus take its place among the other sciences is, in the author's opinion, two-fold. Of most immediate consequence, it tends to direct the efforts of scholars away from the resolution of pressing administrative problems to the study of arcane theoretical puzzles.

But a longer term problem with this view is exclusivity. That is to say, once you adopt a particular paradigm, as Kuhn shows so well, the paradigm begins to dictate the important subjects of inquiry; scholars work, so to speak, inside the paradigm. Kuhn documents for science the deleterious effects of excluding certain questions. It would hardly be unreasonable to expect the same for public administration operating within a paradigm.

The Concept of Profession

A more satisfactory analogy than disciplines such as physics and chemistry appears to be professions such as law, business, and medicine. Furthermore, much is to be gained by making the assumption that public administration is not a science but a profession. Unlike a science, which is systematic and internally consistent, a profession is an admixture of many ingredients, including the findings of many sciences. In the context of this book, we are not shackled to any particular approach but are free to roam wherever necessary. Thus, the reader is exposed to the investigations of psychologists and sociologists in Chapter 12; to the techniques of systems analysts and operation researchers in Chapter 6; to the writings of philosophers and statesmen in Chapter 4; and to the experience of top administrators and policy analysts throughout.

From the foregoing discussion, it should not be inferred that public administration is no more than a kit bag into which remnants of other disciplines are tossed. Much to the contrary, considerable intellectual effort must be put forth to achieve a useful, consistent blend of the best of other fields of study. No scholar has better highlighted the challenges that the analogy of the medical professions offers than Dwight Waldo (1975:223–24):

> The hardness of medicine can easily be exaggerated or idealized: There is no single, unified theory of illness or health, theories and the technologies based on them constantly change, there are vast unknowns, there is bitter controversy over medical questions of vital importance, the element of "art" remains large and important. "Health" proves, on close scrutiny, to be as undefinable as "good administration." While the prominence of the M.D. suggests at first blush a single, uniform, definable product for medical education, that is illusory. By "medicine" I mean the medical professions, the many specialties and career lines of the health services.

Professor Walso continues:

> To think of preparation for public administration as roughly comparable to preparing for careers in health care is liberating and challenging. It frees public administration from second-class citizenship in the college of liberal arts. It frees us from guilt because we don't have a paradigm in some strict sense. (American medicine has a wide variety of "paradigms.") It gives us a license to seek what we need wherever it may be located, whatever the name of the source, and whether in or out of academia. It gives us an opportunity to experiment with diverse combinations of knowledge, different degrees for different purposes, and varying educational arrangements.

Two Caveats

To repeat: this book builds around four major themes: (1) the sociopolitical environment of public administration; (2) the management of government programs; (3) financial management; and (4) the management of people. Under each theme, a considerable amount of information is introduced. But the mastery of this information is not the most important thing. It is this: to comprehend the few general principles that are associated with each of the four themes and to learn thoroughly the way these principles apply to a variety of situations.

One final caveat. The four themes listed above should not be thought of as a separate, watertight compartments; they overlap considerably. For example, in the chapter after next, which deals with the relationships between governments (e.g., federal and state), this overlap is readily apparent. Nominally, the chapter comes under theme number one, the sociopolitical environment of public administration. But when we begin to examine the difficult political problems of administering federal programs at the local level, it might seem we are actually in the realm of theme number two (the management of government programs); when we begin to examine revenue sharing, in the realm of theme number three (financial management); or when we begin to examine intergovernmental conflict, in the realm of theme number four (the management of people).

Despite this limitation, the four themes do tend to emphasize nicely the great importance of public administration as a subject. Though we need not acquiesce in the political heresy of Alexander Pope, who said;

> For forms of government let fools contest
> That which is best administered is best

yet we may safely pronounce that a true test of good government is its aptitude and tendency to produce an administration that is (1) upright in its politics and ethics, (2) effective in its treatment of societal problems, (3) equitable and efficient in its spending, and (4) fair and humane to its own employees.

NAILING DOWN THE MAIN POINTS

1 Public administration concerns the accomplishing side of government; that is, all those activities involved in carrying out the policies of elected officials and some activities associated with the development of those policies.

2 Public administrators are found at all levels of government as well as in a wide variety of nonbusiness institutions.

3 The National Association of Public Affairs and Administration recommend in 1973 that the study of public administration cover five basic subject areas: (a) the political, social, and economic environment; (b) policy analysis; (c) managerial processes; (d) analytical tools; and (e) individual, group, and organizational behavior.

4 Competent administrators are sensitive to the environment of their organization and are able to analyze problems. For the latter, policy analysis and many new analytical tools are proving to be quite useful.

5 In the decades ahead, the management of public sector institutions will likely become the central management problem facing society.

6 This book builds around four major themes: (a) the sociopolitical environment of public administration, (b) the management of governmental programs, (c) financial management, and (d) the management of people.

7 According to Thomas Kuhn, sciences are characterized by conceptual frameworks known as paradigms. Efforts to turn the study of public ad-

ministration into a paradigm have not, however, been altogether successful.

8 As a consequence for public administration, a more satisfactory analogy than sciences such as physics and chemistry appears to be professions such as law and medicine.

CONCEPTS FOR REVIEW

public administration	model
public sector	paradigm
policy analysis	scientific management
managerial processes	administrative science movement
analytical tools	profession

PROBLEMS

1. O. W. Markley, a senior policy analyst for the Stanford Research Institute, argues that a new image of man is emerging. Though not fully shaped as yet, this new image of man tends to do the following: (*a*) entail an ecological ethic, emphasizing the total community of life as well as the oneness of the human race; (*b*) involve a self-realization ethic, placing the highest value on development of the individual; (*c*) balance and coordinate satisfactions along many dimensions rather than overemphasizing those associated with status and consumption; and (*d*) be experimental and open-ended, rather than ideologically dogmatic. Assuming this vision correct, at least in part, discuss its implications for the theory and practice of public administration.

2. What dangers, if any, do you see in the drift toward a totally managed society?

3. Which of the following fields of study do you think Kuhn would say are in the preparadigm stage of development? Why? Accounting, anthropology, biology, history, political science, psychology, and sociology.

4. List some of the events or forces you think have helped to bring about the management revolution.

5. How separate do you think politics is from administration? In what ways does the job of public administrator differ from that of the business executive? How are they alike?

6. Do you agree or disagree with the Servan-Schreiber quote on page 9?

PART I

The Environment of Public Administration

INTRODUCTION

Today's administrators can not ignore the political environment of their agencies. In the first place, these administrators are involved both in the formulation and implementation of public policy. Because policy decisions so profoundly influence who gets what, this involvement in policy inevitably involves them in politics. In the second place, they must deal on a day to day basis not only with their immediate supervisors but also with all kinds of external groups and publics. As a result, administrators find themselves in a kind of political force field. Competent administrators do not, however, turn their backs on these matters. "The lifeblood of administration is power. Its attainment, maintenance, increase, dissipation, and loss are subjects the practitioners can ill afford to neglect." (Long 1949:257)

In this chapter, we begin with a case study designed to show how difficult it is for an urban manager to ignore the political realm. We then see how the issue of separating politics from administration was debated among the early students of public administration.

That brings us to the heart of the chapter, which can be highlighted with three questions: How is the public administrator involved in the policy making process? What are the relationships between the administrator and external political forces? And, how can the administrator be more skillful politically?

2

The Politics of Administration

Politics and Administration: A Case Study

In the 1960s, the voters of St. Louis twice elected as mayor a successful insurance executive. His name was A. J. Cervantes, and his message to the voters was plain: "Put government back into the hands of men who know the meaning of the tax dollar, the balanced budget, business methods, and a successful city."

In retrospect, what does Mr. Cervantes (1973:19–20) think about this notion—still quite popular—that businessmen can restore life to American cities? "As one becomes more involved in governing a large city, one learns that in many cases business methods can not be translated into political reality." To take a word from business, let us consider a few of his "practical" examples:

St. Louis has two city hospitals, one traditionally serving black patients and one traditionally serving white patients. Good management calls for a merger: But that would require that one or the other be closed. And in a city one half black and one half white, each racial group refuses to allow "its" hospital to close.

St. Louis has a number of recreation programs operating in school play-grounds and parks. Some programs have many participants, others few. Again, good management would say close those programs that have rela-tively few participants: But this would mean that some neighborhoods would have no programs for those who would use the facilities. Recreation centers must be reasonably close to everyone, so all of them stay open.

St. Louis needs a new, modern airport suitable for the needs of the 21st century. Federal officials and airlines agree that the best location would be in Illinois, just across the river from St. Louis. Jobs would be created, the area's economy given a boost, and the city's tax base improved: But Missouri interests—union and business—want the contracts and jobs that would flow from the new airport. Even though Missouri does not have a site or funds for the land, they would block the Illinois airport. Would a good manager turn down an investment opportunity because one group of workers or subcontractors received the benefits rather than another? Not one who wanted to survive. Yet political reality forced other government leaders to oppose the Illinois site.

POLITICS AND ADMINISTRATION: AN HISTORICAL PERSPECTIVE

Cervantes's new message reads: Purely administrative matters can sel-dom be separated from politics. Yet, interestingly enough, this view, which Cervantes now articulates with such verve, could not always be found in the literature of public administration. In fact, for several decades, its antithesis prevailed.

"The field of administration is a field of business," a young academic in the Progressive Movement of the 1800s once argued. "It is removed," he continued, "from the hurry and strife of politics." An incredible observation, perhaps; but its author, who was named Woodrow Wilson (1887), did not stand alone. For example, F. Goodnow, often termed the "father of American public administration, and W. F. Willoughby, an earlier director of the Institute of Government Research (The Brookings Institution), also had little trouble in dividing government into two functions: political decision and administrative execution. Unlike Wilson, however, they had the good fortune of never having to carry such views into the White House.

To be sure, a handful of dissenters could be found. And few of them stated the problem more cogently than L. D. White (1927:230):

> If city managers follow the strict theory of the manager plan and conceive themselves primarily as professional-technical administrators, they achieve the prerequisites of permanence in their position and lay the foundation of city administration of an order of excellence hitherto unequaled. But they do this at the cost of being forced to observe the needs of the city ignored, or misrepresented, or so ineptly set before the voters that they are defeated at the polls. If they set themselves the task of supplying the deficiencies of the council and directly or indirectly attempt to direct public opinion in favor of the needs of the city, they may easily achieve the temporary leadership of their community, but only at the serious risk of becomming involved in politics and of forfeiting the privilege of giving uninterrupted technical service of a high order of excellence.

Unfortunately, it was not until the end of World War II that these difficulties in politics-administration separation began to be widely recognized. Fritz Morstein Marx's *The Elements of Public Administration* (1946) pointed out the involvement of administrators in policy formation, in the use of discretionary power, and in the general political process. The following year, Waldo (1947:121) put the debate into sharp focus: "The disagreement is not generally with politics-administration itself; only with the spirit of rigid separatism. In some measure, this is an advance into realism. In some measure, it flows from a feeling of strength and security, a feeling that the processes and the study of administration have matured, that they no longer need be isolated from the germs of politics. Administration can even think about invading the field of politics, the field of policy determination."

Feelings of strength and security, invasions into fields of politics and policy determination—all heady stuff indeed. But has the debate, which we have quickly traced from Wilson, been ended by venial rhetoric or, as Professor Waldo suggests, increased realism? The next two sections address this question.

Our approach will be analytic in that we divide the issue into two components. First, we consider the degree to which administration has entered the field of policy determination; and, second, we consider the degree to which it has entered the field of politics.

ADMINISTRATION IN THE FIELD OF POLICY DETERMINATION

We all recall the neat textbook diagrams in Government 101 outlining "how a bill becomes a law," that very logical process by which legislative bodies make *policy*. (By policy we mean here simply laws that are, in scope and impact, major attempts to solve problems or to seize opportunities.

Chapter 5 will provide a more rigorous—but not dissimilar—definition of policy.) In the process, we were told, the chief executive is the chief legislator, since most major policy—roughly 80 per cent over the last two decades—originates with him. Further, we learned that congressmen submit bills, which must pass through committee, on to the floor and the other chamber, and (prior to a presidential signature) probably to a conference committee. Things were so simple.

The foregoing interpretation of the policy-making process is not so much wrong as it is misleading. In the first place, administrators frequently participate in the process. Chief executives rarely make decisions about issues not presented to them. The issues and solutions, therefore, sometimes bubble up from the echelon of planners just above the career administrators and just below the political appointees of the cabinet and subcabinet.

In the second place, administrative decisions may in effect produce policy. For example, the choice of new weapon systems, of new state highway routes, of solar energy programs, of level of price support for agricultural commodities are all choices likely to be influenced greatly by administrators. In sum, administrative agencies are influencial in both the formulation and implementations of public policy. This fact is quite important. And at least one political scientist (Boyer 1964) suggested a redefinition of public administration in terms of policy making: "Public Administration is that organized and purposeful interactions of society which, within law, systematically formulates and applies policies of government agencies." Without necessarily subscribing to this definition, we might at least take a closer look at what the formulations and implementations of policy involves.

Formulation of Policy

More than is realized, agencies themselves provide a productive source of new ideas. In some instances, an administrative agency may conceive of its function largely as accommodating the needs of some interest group representing its specialized clientele like farmers, truckers, bankers, and wage earners. Thus the policy proposal is really designed to further those interests.

Such is not always the case, however. NASA alone proposed to go to the moon long before such plans were made national policy. "Operating pretty much in a political vacuum in terms of policy guidance, and basing their choice on what constituted a rational technical program of manned space flight development, NASA planners chose a lunar landing objective fully two years before President Kennedy announced his choice of the lunar landing as a national goal." And without the Kennedy decision in 1961, NASA no doubt would have continued pressing for the lunar decision. In fact, NASA's Sustaining University Programs, which was a major contribution to U.S. science policy, had no specific legislative authorization at all. (See Lambright 1976:195.)

Can you identify these 19 federal agencies? Anyone outside the Washington, D.C., area who can name 15 of them rates a Ph.D. in Bureaucracy.

Perhaps a more typical pattern of policy formulation can be seen in the War on Poverty. The initial work in formulating the antipoverty policy was handled in 1963 by a task force drawn from the Council of Economic Advisors and the Bureau of the Budget (now the Office of Management and Budget). No attempt was made to devise specific programs. Then, in early November, the chairman of the council requested the major departments and agencies to submit suggestions for a legislative program. "The result was a veritable flood of proposals, featuring many of their favorite ideas—job training and employment programs from Labor, rural development from Agriculture, education and welfare services from Health, Education and Welfare, and so on. The council-bureau task force was now confronted with the necessity of selecting from among the many proposals presented concerning how to do this and develop an integrated war on poverty for $500 million." (Anderson 1975:73)

About this time, the council-bureau began favoring a program featuring a limited number of general purpose grants to help localities develop their own antipoverty program. Not surprisingly, the departments and agencies were unhappy about this proposal that would mean loss of control over their own funds and programs. The situation changed suddenly in early February 1964, when President Johnson appointed Sargent Shriver to plan the war on poverty. Recognizing that the broad-based and multifacited war on poverty enjoyed wide support among the administrative agencies, "Shriver assembled a new task force of volunteers and others on loan from their departments and agencies. Included were people from the Departments of Labor, Agriculture, Defense, and HEW, the Bureau of the Budget, the Small Business Administration, and other agencies. Some concerned intellectuals were involved. All ideas and proposals were reconsidered. Scores of businessmen, union officials, mayors, welfare officials, and others were consulted or asked for suggestions." (Anderson 1974:74) Within a few weeks a legislative proposal was developed and by March President Johnson was able to submit to Congress his bill for the Economic Opportunity Act.

Agencies also become involved in policy formulation when they recommend to the legislature amendments to existing laws. A large part — perhaps the major portion — of modern legislation is proposed by administrative agencies. This should not be surprising. Agencies are closest to where the action is and therefore are more likely to see imperfection and incompleteness in the laws. Indeed, legislatures *expect* that those who deal continuously with problems will suggest improvements.

In concluding this discussion of the role of the administrator in policy formulation, we ought to note its negative aspect. Bureaucracy *stops* far more policy than it formulates. Is this a bad thing? One close observer of Washington thinks not:

> As an entity the bureaucracy is no better equipped to manufacture grand designs for government programs than carpenters, electricians, and plumbers are to be architects. But if an architect attempted to build a house, the results might well be disastrous. What the White House identifies as bureaucracy's inherent deficiencies are often its strengths. Effective functioning of the governmental machine requires a high degree of stability, uniformity, and awareness of the impact of new policies, regulations, and procedures on the affected public. If the Post Office at the outset refused to handle mail which did not include the zip code, the Department of Defense each year revised its procurement regulations, the Department of Health, Education and Welfare discarded all previous standards applicable to grants-in-aid, the public outcry against innovation would shake the Congress and the White House. (Seidman 1970:76)

Implementation of Policy

The formulation of policy ends when the policy becomes law. The annual product of Congress appears in the *Statutes at Large* and the collection of all statutes of the nation still in force appears in the U.S. Code.

Now, the implementation begins. In Chapter 9, we shall look at this process from a management perspective, but here our perspective is political. Our aim: to lay bare the ways in which administrative decisions may implement policy. We shall note four: (1) rule-making, (2) adjudication, (3) law enforcement, and (4) program operations.

1. Administrative rule-making is the establishment of *prospective rules;* that is, agency statements of general applicability and future effect that concerns the rights of private parties. These guidelines have the force and effect of law.

Under the requirements of the Federal Administrative Procedure Act (APA), general notice of proposed rule-making must be published in the Federal Register. Figure 2–1 shows the cover of one issue. The *Register,* published five days a week, also contains the latest presidential orders and

FIGURE 2-1

Vol.41—No.84
4-29-76
PAGES
17871-18051

THURSDAY, APRIL 29, 1976

highlights

■ CONTINUED INSIDE

The *Federal Register,* widely considered to be one of Washington's most unreadable publications, has recently been made more readable and useful to ordinary citizens. Its front pages now feature brief highlights of the day's contents. Further, agencies have been required to summarize their rules in language that nonexperts can understand.

rules adopted by agencies, and a great variety of official notices. Recent items have ranged from the results of mileage tests on 1976 model autos to a notice that the Mississippi conservation director was granted a federal permit to "capture and transport alligators" in that state and move them "to more advantageous locations."

Notices of proposed rules must indicate clearly where the proceedings are to be held, under what legal authority rules are being proposed, and the substance of the proposed rules. After such notice is given, interested parties are to be provided with the opportunity to participate in the rule-making proceedings through the presentation of written data. At the discretion of the agency, oral presentation may be permitted. Unless notice or hearing is required by the statutes governing the agency's operation, notice of rule-making can be withheld if the agency considers it to be "impracticable, unnecessary, or contrary to public interest." While this could potentially exclude many proceedings from public participation, agencies do in practice attempt to conform to the spirit of the APA.

A typical hearing might involve an Environmental Protection Agency official discussing proposals to curtail hydrocarbon emission in a city. These might range from controversial (e.g., gasoline rationing and limiting car travel) to mild (e.g., establishing car pools and installation of vapor recovery systems at service stations). In any event, the agency comes up with the final proposals.

Those who wish to change or repeal rules are given the opportunity of petition by the Administrative Procedures Act of 1946, although changes and repeal rules on this basis have been extremely rare. Actually, no effective way to compel an agency to alter its policies exists—short of recourse to a superior agency, to the courts, or to the Congress. Despite this wide latitude of administrative rule-making power, complaints of abuse are uncommon. Most rules are created by one of the large, generally impartial corps of lawyers, engineers, accountants, or scientists concerned primarily with the implementation of a target policy.

In sum, rule-making by more than 100 agencies is a continual national activity. Collectively, the volume of rules to a substantial extent is policy. Rule-making involves modifying existing policies as well as adopting new ones: The Department of Agriculture describes the labeling requirements for pesticides one day; the Food and Drug Administration prescribes safe levels of pesticide residues on plants the next; and an agency in the Interior Department sets a different standard of pesticide toxicity for fish and fowl on another occasion. Moreover, as we shall see in the next chapter, these vertical negotiations with Washington are crisscrossed with horizontal negotiations at the state and local levels. Not without reason did Bailey (1966:17) once refer to this process of policy refinement, communications, and compliance as kaleidoscopic.

2. Another important way in which agencies implement policy is through their adjudicative powers, granted to them by Congress. Adjudication differs from rule-making in that it applies only to the specific parties involved in a

Agencies may also influence public policy by the vigor or laxity with which they enforce the law.

"So that's where it goes! Well, I'd like to thank you fellows for bringing this to my attention."

Drawing by Stevenson; © 1970 The New Yorker Magazine, Inc.

controversy before the agency. Administrative orders have retroactive effect, unlike prospective rule-making. In other words, the parties involved do not know how the policy is going to be applied until after the order is issued, giving the agency decision a retroactive effect like a court room decision. Deciding policy through adjudication necessarily means that it will be decided on a case by case basis. And while the rule of *stare decisis* (i.e., requiring precedent to be followed) does not prevail, over time these cases can mark out public policy and indicate the kinds of practices prohibited.

3. Agencies may also implement policy by the vigor or laxity with which they enforce the law. The obvious example is, of course, whether the highway patrol gives you a ticket or warning. Less obvious, but more relevant to policy making, is the following.

The Hepburn Act of 1906 authorized the Interstate Commerce Commission to regulate rates charged by pipeline companies, but the commission took no action by itself until 1934. It did not complete a pipeline rate proceeding until 1948 and even then no action resulted. "Since then, the ICC has continued to do little to carry out this authorization, essentially substituting a policy of no regulation for the legislatively declared policy of regulation." (Anderson 1975:117)

4. Much of an agency's day to day operations is not *directly* concerned with rule-making, adjudication, or law enforcement. The agency simply administers a program, which means it distributes certain benefits and services, makes loans, provides insurance, constructs dams, and so forth.

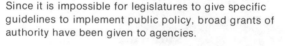

Since it is impossible for legislatures to give specific guidelines to implement public policy, broad grants of authority have been given to agencies.

"Isn't it about time we issued some new guidelines for something?"

Drawing by Alan Dunn; © 1968 The New Yorker Magazine, Inc.

But the kinds of decisions an agency makes in administering the programs for which it has been given responsibility can, over time, help determine policy. And the more general the language the more this is true. Indeed, some legislative grants of authority to administrators are very broad, e.g., the delegation of authority to agencies to make "reasonable" policies for the protection of public health or to eliminate "unfair" trade practices. (What is reasonable? Unfair?) To get a better idea of just how much delegation can be contained in certain legislation, consider the case below (Blumenthal 1969:128–79).

Maximum Feasible Misunderstanding

The Community Action Program was contained in Title II of the Economic Opportunity Act of 1964, commonly known as the Poverty Program. The provision that subsequently caused the most controversy was the requirement that community action plans be "developed and conducted with the maximum feasible participation of the residents of areas and members of groups" affected. Apparently, neither the drafters nor Congress foresaw the uses to which *lower level administrators* would put these words.

Recalls James Sundquist, then Assistant Secretary of Agriculture and drafter of Title III: "Nobody listened much. If you have a program for somebody, you want him to participate, you want the maximum number of people to be affected. It seemed very obvious, very innocuous." Likewise, the rest of Title II was very general. A community action program designed to eliminate poverty was "one which mobilizes and utilizes resources by providing services, assistance, and other activities . . . of sufficient variety, size, and scope to give promise of progress toward the elimination of poverty. . . ." The definition of the geographical areas set virtually no limits in size or character on the prospective region to be served. The description of the community action organization furnished only clues, at best, as to structure and function. Charged with "conducting, administering, or coordinating" the program, the agency could be either public or private nonprofit as long as it was "broadly representative of the community." At every point, the drafters left the future director broad discretion to "prescribe such additional criteria as he might deem appropriate." Heeding the wishes of the White

House, they avoided any reference to planning and dealt only with action aspects. Yet even here they left loopholes. They wrote the bill to allow spending in limited amounts on "research, training, and demonstration" and to imply that community action agencies would be forced, after a "limited period of funding, to present a comprehensive strategy."

Congress was equally negligent. On August 2, 1964, barely one week before the antipoverty bill passed by the House, Phil Landrum (D., Georgia), the manager of the bill, was asked by a freshman colleague for an explanation of the Community Action Title. Landrum reached in his desk, and tossed across a copy of the *Congressional Presentation.* "That pretty much says it," he told the congressman. "Of course, you know" — he leaned forward now — "this bill was written over there." He then pointed out his window toward the White House and the federal departments, shimmering in the noonday sun.

The upshot of all this was that in many communities the bureaucracy decided that a key part of the program should be organizing the poor to take political and legal action against local government or private parties with whom they had grievances. Further, because the act called for the "maximum feasible participation" of the poor, the community programs were administered by persons who had no prior experience.

This story is not typical. And its moral can be stated simply: Although nominally neutral, public bureaucracies, thanks to the haziness of national policy, enjoy considerable freedom to propose their own public policies and to promote their adoption.

ADMINISTRATION IN THE FIELD OF POLITICS

In the preceding section, we saw how profoundly administrators can influence the formulation and implementation of policy. In this section, we see how an agency's top administrator interacts with the external political environment in order to build adequate support (financial and otherwise) for agency programs. The iron cross in Figure 2–2 attempts to give a bird's-eye view of what that environment looks like.

Essentially, what Figure 2–2 shows is the top administrator at the apex of four *hierarchies.* The concept of hierarchy is based on the distinction between the role of superior and subordinate. The former is expected to exercise *authority* over the latter. In other words, the superior has the power to make decisions that will guide the actions of the subordinate. In most organizations, of course, this relationship is carried much further by making one subordinate the superior of another subordinate. The resulting configuration is often shown as a pyramid. The tremendous potential of the pyramidal form for bringing larger numbers of subordinates under central authority should not go unnoticed. Consider a pyramid with only nine levels of administrators and six subordinates for each administrator at the upper eight levels. Under such an arrangement, one executive could exercise formal authority over 2,015,539 people.)

In recent years, as observations and insights increased, it became apparent that the single hierarchical picture, especially when applied to public agencies, was inadequate. Why? It is based on the assumption that each subordinate has only one direct supervisor. At the national level, for example,

FIGURE 2–2
The Administrator's Political Environment

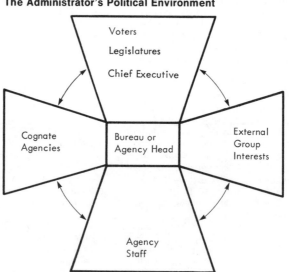

Sources: Adapted from Bailey (1968) and Gross (1968:223).

the president is certainly subject to the authority of both the voters and Congress. In that sense, there is an overhead hierarchy.

This phenomenon of multiple subordination, notes Bertram Gross (1968:227), is even more widespread at levels below the chief executive offices. Thus, Figure 2-2 shows the top administrator with not only an overhead pyramid but also two lateral pyramids. The next four subsections elaborate these linkages at the national level. Before turning to these linkages, three additional though briefer points regarding Figure 2-2 need to be made.

First, technically speaking, what we have in Figure 2-2 is *model,* a term defined in Chapter 1. A model, it will be recalled, is a simplified representation of some part of reality. It is usually simplified because reality is too complex to copy exactly and because, for the modeler's purposes, much of the complexity is irrelevant. On the other hand, no model can cover satisfactorily as many specific cases as the modeler might wish. For example, several agencies have more independence than suggested by our model in Figure 2-2. The Veterans Administration is such an agency. Veterans organizations, such as the Veterans of Foreign Wars and the American Legion, feel their interests are best served by not subordinating the VA within an executive department. For similar reasons, the Civil Rights Commission is independent of the biases and red tape of other departments. The National Aeronautics and Space Administration is independent largely because President Eisenhower sought to highlight his concern for acceleration the United States commitment to the space race.

Second, as drawn, the model refers explicitly to the governmental administrator, but it could be easily redrawn for the university president or hospital administrator. Let us consider for a moment the former. When asked to reflect on how their jobs have changed, university presidents invariably reply that they must woo and satisfy new external constituencies. State legislators and federal bureaucracies are becoming increasingly important sources of money for private as well as public institutions. And along with public money comes new requirements, such as federal affirmative action plans (discussed in Chapter 14). As a former executive of International Business Machines—who now runs a college—puts it: the college president's job is now closer to that of a big city mayor than a business executive. "He has a lot of shared power arrangements. It's like getting people to agree on the need to revive the downtown area." (Fiske 1975)

Third, the alert reader might note several omissions from Figure 2-2. The courts, to be sure, influence agencies, especially in assuring they behave in a responsible manner; accordingly, their role is best examined in the context of administrative responsibility in Chapter 4. The public, too, influences agency behavior and, conversely, agencies sometimes try to influence the public. Chapter 4 also examines this dialectic. The administrator must concern himself as well with other levels of government. The city manager, for example, must be sensitive to the political currents flowing from Washington, the federal regional office, the state capital, the area council of government, and the county. Chapter 3 attempts to sort out some of these vertical relationships.

Agencies and Congress

One important means by which Congress exercises formal authority over agencies is by setting policy, a process already discussed in this chapter. To that earlier discussion, one point might be added: to the extent congressional power is fragmented, the programs administered by a federal agency are fragmented. One former Secretary of Health, Education and Welfare (Richardson 1973) traces the chaotic character of social programs and their administration to essentially political sources, specifically, the conflicts between congressional authorization and appropriations committees, the desire of congressmen to author their own pet bills regardless of the narrow structure of the categories found in each. the tendency to legislate redundant programs in order to remain popular with constituents, and the popularity of latching onto faddish ideas that seem popular to the public at the expense of more essential programs that are not currently in vogue.

A second means by which Congress exercises control over agencies is the appropriations process. A case study in the extent to which the power of the purse can undermine attempts to cope with major national problems such as hunger is provided by Nick Kotz's (1969) vivid portrait of Jamie Whitten, Chairman of the House Appropriations Subcommittee on Agriculture. Whitten exercises his power shrewdly. His appropriations subcommittee doles out funds for every item in the department's $7 billion budget, and it does not take long for Washington bureaucrats to realize that the chairman's wrath can destroy precious projects and throw hundreds of people out of jobs. Consider just a couple of Kotz's observations and examples:

> The key to this phenomenal power—which goes beyond that of budget control—lies in Whitten's network of informants within the department and his skills in directing their activities and operations. Executive branch officials learn to protect their own jobs, adjusting their loyalties to the legislative branch in a way never the Founding Fathers may never have envisioned.

> Whitten's opposition to any program resembling social welfare contributed to the failure of War on Poverty programs for rural America. When President Johnson signed an executive order giving the Agriculture Department responsibility for coordinating the rural war on poverty, Secretary Freeman created a Rural Community Development Service. Within a year, the Rural Community Development Service was dead. "Whitten thought the service smacked of social experimentation and civil rights," a Department of Agriculture official said. Whitten

Fighting Waste and Secrecy: Four "Watchdogs"

Proxmire   Leahy   Moss   Aspin

If Congress as a whole generally does a poor job of keeping tabs on federal laws and bureaucrats, the same can't be said about every congressman. Here are four Capitol Hill "watchdogs."

Persistent Gadfly. Senator William Proxmire, labeled a liberal when he entered the Senate in 1957, has been battling for years for elimination of waste.

His targets have been both large and small: the supersonic transport plane, federal limousines, allegedly frivolous National Science Foundation grants.

Each month, Senator Proxmire gives his own "Golden Fleece Award" for what he feels is a waste of taxpayers' money.

Among recent winners of his award is the Federal Aviation Administration, for spending $57,800 on a study of the measurements of airline stewardesses to help in the design of safety equipment.

New Breed. Like many of the new Democrats who entered Congress this year, Senator Patrick J. Leahy believes the federal bureaucracy could stand some whittling.

One small victory for the Vermonter came last summer when the senator blew the whistle on the Federal Fire Council, which was doing next to nothing and spending $67,000 a year in the process.

Mr. Leahy is now plumping for creation of a special Senate committee to weed out overlapping programs and agencies. And he thinks that before Congress approves any new program, it should be required to get a full report from the General Ac-

counting Office on the program's workability.

Secrecy Fighter. Representative John E. Moss has spent much of his 22 years in Congress trying to pry information out of bureaucrats. He recently roared at a recalcitrant Cabinet member: "When I want information, all the forces of heaven and hell could not stop me."

The chairman of the Oversight and Investigations Subcommittee of the House Commerce Committee hasn't always had success. But he made considerable headway when the Freedom of Information Act was passed by Congress.

Only if "the cult of secrecy" is broken, says the California Democrat, can Congress and the public determine whether laws are being carried out properly.

Scourge of the Pentagon. Representative Les Aspin (Dem.), of Wisconsin, is widely regarded as the most effective critic of the military on Capitol Hill.

A former Pentagon official himself, Mr. Aspin and his staff function as a kind of unofficial inspector general's office—churning out several carefully researched broadsides against the Pentagon each week. The targets: cost overruns, arms sales abroad, costly new weapons—whatever strikes Mr. Aspin as waste or bad judgment.

Source: *U.S. News & World Report,* Nov. 10, 1975.
Copyright 1975 *U.S. News & World Report, Inc.*

simply cut off the funds, and pigeonholed the coordinating powers of RCDS by placing the responsibility with the docile, conservative Farmers Home Administration. Freeman never fought the issue.

A third means by which Congress controls agencies is *oversight*. At its best, oversight involves continuing, systematic congressional checking on the performance of the executive branch — how well government programs are working, how honestly or efficiently or faithfully the laws are being administered. By and large, though, oversight has been infrequent and slipshod. The reasons are political: there is just more political mileage in running errands for constitutents and more satisfaction in passing new laws. Tough oversight, on the other hand, can make enemies among congressional colleagues or powerful interest groups. "Everyone recognizes the need for oversight," said Sen. Edmund Muskie (1975), "but other things come along, and it gets pushed farther and farther down the ladder until it disappears."

But, the situation appears to be changing. Increasingly, oversight is seen

Courtesy Creative Photographic Communications

The GAO is Congress's most potent "external" investigative tool. To a great extent, its successes can be credited to its director, Comptroller General Elmer B. Staats, a redheaded Kansan with a Ph.D. in public administration from the University of Minnesota. Above, Staats and Assistant Comptroller General E. H. Morse, Jr. testify before a congressional committee.

as one tool Congress can use to reassert its authority over a post-Vietnam, post-Watergate executive branch. By the mid-1970s, at least a dozen committees and subcommittees were scheduling close-up looks at a wide variety of agencies and programs. These range from the well-publicized investigations of the government's intelligence apparatus to less well-publicized studies of how well banks and utilities are regulated, how science grants are awarded, why the new towns programs did not work, and whether the tax laws are fairly administered.

Any movement toward greater legislative control is, of course, strengthened by the General Accounting Office, an operating staff arm of Congress created in 1921 and originally disguised to post-audit government expenditures. Since 1950, the GAO has been moving into what might be called management audits. These audits are policy oriented, seeking to determine what the basis for agency decisions and actions were. (See Chapter 9 for fuller discussion of the GAO's new role.)

Agencies and the Presidency

For a number of reasons, national administration tends to be, as Stephen K. Bailey once observed, "a many splintered thing," Three reasons might be given for this lack of cohesion. In the first place, agencies form alliances with legislative subcommittees and outside interest groups; this enables, and indeed encourages, them to pursue independent policy courses. We shall discuss these triple alliances later. Second, if the president and agencies can be at cross-purposes over the ends of policy, so too can they be over the means. For example, in attempting to attain policy goals, presidents are often driven to economize and to reorganize—two activities that invariably upset some agency interests. Finally, agencies have a tendency to become resistant to change due to strong ties to traditional policies and professional orientation of careerists.

The upshot of all this is that presidents wanting to be effective have increasingly circumvented large bureaucracies either by using their own staffs or setting up new agencies. Arthur M. Schlesinger, Jr. (1965:406) reports that President Kennedy well understood the difficulty of converting a tradition ridden bureaucracy into a mechanism for providing information and making decisions. Nevertheless, it was a constant puzzle to him that the State Department remained so formless and impenetrable. He would say, "Damn it, Bundy and I get more done in one day in the White House than they do in six months in the State Department." Giving State an instruction, he remarked, is like dropping it in the dead-letter box. "They never have any ideas over there," he complained, "and never come up with anything new." "The State Department is a bowl of jelly," he told *Time* in the summer of 1961. "It's got all those people over there who are constantly smiling. I think we need to smile less and be tougher."

Yet the president does not stand helpless. In addition to his formidable command over the public attention (discussed later in this chapter) and his power to appoint key administrators (discussed in Chapter 13), the president has the Office of Management and Budget (OMB). The largest of the executive office components, the OMB has two main functions. The first is preparation of the budget, a process examined in detail in Chapter 11. The second is *legislative clearance.* Before an agency can submit new legislation to Congress it must be cleared by OMB to ensure that it is consistent with the goals and policies of the administration. In recent years, OMB has begun to take on a third function: the coordination and evaluation of executive branch programs. Chapter 9 will be devoted to a few of the management techniques executives at all strata of government have available to gain better control over the bureaucracy.

Agencies and Client Interests

We have already seen one important way in which interest groups interact with agencies, namely, by contributing members to the advisory groups used during the policy-making process. And, given the functional basis upon which federal agencies are established, which gives them a built-in representative character, one might suspect that interaction between agencies and interest groups involves more than advising.

One would be right. Top administrators are quite sensitive to the dominant interest groups they represent. Nowhere is this more evident than with the federal regulatory agencies. As one Justice Department deputy assistant attorney general put it: in general, there are "incredible love affairs going on between the regulators and the regulated." As a result, critics say, the agencies often condone or even champion monopolistic practices and rubber-stamp higher prices for everything from airline tickets to natural gas and to telephone calls. Regulators, on the other hand, say that they are not unduly influenced and that they can not be insulated from them if they do their jobs right.

To find an explanation for such cozy ties is not hard. As already indicated, agencies need outside support for their programs; thus, a symbiotic relationship emerges. How does it work? Say an agency develops a long range plan that would, among other things, bring certain benefits to a particular industry. Given this set of circumstances, it would hardly be surprising to find some private industry, say, to sponsor a conference to promote the plan. Another obvious reason for friendly relationships is that some administrators come from the industry they regulate or support. Moreover, commissioners and top administrators often need interest group support to get and keep appointments, and, once in office, they sometimes feel it necessary to curry favor with interest groups to help win renomination.

One final point about interest groups. In the last few years, a new type of interest group has emerged. Instead of seeking to convert government to its cause, the *public interest group* seeks to convert the public to a cause that has yet to attract enough support to challenge private interest groups. The best illustrations of these groups are the environmental groups, consumer groups, Ralph Nader's Public Interest Research Group, and John Gardner's Common Cause.

Agencies and Cognate Agencies

According to the *Oxford English Dictionary*, cognate means "kindred, related, connected, having affinity." In considering how government goes about attacking national problems (e.g., decay of city, pollution, regional economic development, and manpower development), the expression "cognate agencies" seems a handy way of indicating that seldom will only one agency—or even one government, since we do have a federal system (see Chapter 3)—be involved.

> The problem of the cities belongs in the Federal Housing Administration because of its special concern with urban housing. It belongs to the Department of Commerce because of the rule of the cities in economic development. It belongs in the Department of Health, Education and Welfare because of the city as a focus for health, education, and welfare services. It belongs in the Department of Agriculture because the city consumes the nation's agricultural products. It belongs in the Department of Interior because the city is a center for the consumption, distribution, and the use of natural resources." (Schon 1971:166)

Such a situation breeds not only management problems (e.g., interagency coordination) but also political ones. Agencies compete for specific programs: the Bureau of Reclamation versus the Army Corps of Engineers, the Federal Reserve Board versus the Treasury Department, the air force versus the navy, the Soil Conservation Service versus the Agricultural Extension Service, etc. Table 2–1 shows how in the area of solar energy policy no less than 15 agencies compete. Similarly, as each agency becomes attached to particular programs, efforts at reorganization become politicized. This reaction is, of course, quite predictable, since reorganization almost invariably requires a reallocation of existing programs. In Chapter 8, we take a detailed look at the politics of reorganization.

But is all this jurisdictional and mission overlap, which breeds so much interagency conflict, entirely bad? The problems are clear enough. Agencies become rigid and uncompromising. The results, at best, can be wasted time and money—at worst, policy stalemates in the face of critical problems. Careful. More might be involved here than economy and efficiency. Does not this duplication and overlap provide greater access and representation of different views and interests? Further, Martin Landau (1969) argues that, from a purely administrative point of view, the duplication of mission management and information gathering by cognate agencies provides backups, compensations, and corrective forces for errors and bad judgments.

Landau's argument is compelling. Agencies should have not one but several paths through which policy may be formed and then implemented.

TABLE 2–1
Federal Areas of Responsibility, Solar Energy

	ERDA	FEA	HUD	NASA	NSF	State	DOD	DOC	USDA	GSA	USPS	HEW	FPC	FTC	Treasury
Direct thermal applications															
Solar heating and cooling of buildings	X	X	X	X	X		X	X		X	X	X			
Agricultural and process heating	X				X			X	X						
Solar electric applications															
Wind energy conversion	X		X	X	X		X								
Photovoltaic energy conversion	X		X	X	X		X	X							
Solar thermal-electric conversion	X				X		X								
Ocean thermal energy conversion	X				X		X								
Fuels from biomass	X				X		X		X						
Technology support and utilization															
Solar energy resource assessment	X		X	X	X		X		X						
Solar energy research institute	X														
Technology utilization and information dissemination	X		X	X	X	X	X		X	X	X	X	X	X	
Regulation of energy	X	X											X	X	X
Energy policy analysis and development	X		X		X			X	X						
Program definition	X		X	X	X									X	X
Manpower and training	X				X							X			

Source: Energy Research and Development Administration (1975: IV–10).

Like an electric current in a parallel circuit, formulation and administration of policy in an agency should be able to flow through more than one branch. Thus, the chance for error to be fatal to an agency's policy and administrative responsibilities is lessened. The agency is far less vulnerable to administrative sabotage, while far more capable of policy initiation.

POLITICAL COMPETENCY

Our discussion has ranged far beyond the pleas of Woodrow Wilson and others for a separation of politics and administration. As we have seen, the administrator is placed squarely in the policy-making process. Further, day to day events force administrators to operate in a field crisscrossed by political forces generated by overhead authority (Congress and president), client groups, and cognate agencies.

What follows is neither an essay on realpolitik nor revelations on the political art—the former would be outré, the latter presumptious. The following section only attempts to introduce a few basic political concepts that are highly pertinent to good administration. And by good administration, we simply mean administration that can mobilize support for its programs and, in short, get things done. "There is no more forlorn spectacle in the administrative world than an agency and a program possessed of statutory life, armed with executive orders, sustained in the courts, yet stricken with paralysis and deprived of power. An object of contempt to its enemies and of despair to its friends." (Long 1949:257)

But what are these concepts so pertinent to good administration? Recall for a moment the case of Mr. Cervantes, the former mayor of St. Louis, cited at the start of this chapter. If he had decided to attempt to get the airport built in Illinois, then what basic *political* considerations would have been involved? First, he probably would have wanted to assess his strength—or, to put it in the political vernacular, his clout—to see if he should even try. Assuming he did have sufficient political strength, he would then probably ask himself: Does my objective really merit such an expenditure of political capital?

Let us be clear on the meaning of this second question. If it is financially possible for me to buy a Mercedes 450 SEL, it does not necessarily follow that I should. What else could I have invested my limited capital? How much would I have left for future contingencies?

But we shall assume Cervantes is in better position than the author. Therefore, he decides that he has the political capital *and* that the price (in terms of allies lost, etc.) is not too high. Now he must consider the specific strategies and tactics he must use to attain his objective. In sum, what we have done in this example is simply suggest that the administrator must sometimes think through three political questions concerning resources, costs, and strategy.

Resources

Essentially, the administrator's power flows from three sources: external support, professionalism, and leadership. The prudent administrator assesses each before attempting any major political act.

1. One of the more enduring sources of bureaucratic power is the phenomenon of the *subsystem* or *triple alliance.* Agencies ally themselves with congressional committees and interest groups. Examples are legion: agriculture committees, the American Farm Bureau Federation, and agencies within the Department of Agriculture; subcommittees on Indian Affairs, the Association on American Indian Affairs, and the Bureau of Indian Affairs; the House Agriculture Committee, the sugar industry, and the Sugar Division of the Department of Agriculture; etc. The most immediate consequence of the alliance is that agencies are able to take less seriously supervision by superiors in the executive branch. The two examples below highlight other aspects of the alliances — how it can work and how it can fail to work:

> In the early 1960s, both the President's Science Advisory Committee and the air force were unhappy about the amounts of money NASA was receiving. The basic scientists, who were on PSAC to advise the president, were unhappy because so large a proportion of the nation's scientific talent was being devoted to a spectacular political purpose rather than basic research. Similarly, the air force (a cognate agency in this case) was unhappy because it would have preferred rocket development to be kept as means toward air force ends. But, and this is the crucial point, the members of the alliance of applied (as opposed to basic) scientists and congressional committees responsible for NASA were pleased. This alliance, reports Don K. Price (1965:223) had its effects; in fact, the congressional committees that watched over NASA undertook to protect its jurisdiction as their own. For example, the House Committee on Science and Astronautics intervened to make sure that NASA, rather than the Weather Bureau, would put a weather satellite into orbit and vigilantly protected NASA against the jealousy of the air force.
>
> In 1952, Samuel P. Huntington (1952: 461–509) analyzed the causes of the decline of the Interstate Commerce Commission in terms of its alliance with the railroads. Huntington concluded that the commission had tied itself too closely with the railroads; consequently, nonrailroad interest groups (water, motor, and air carriers) blocked the extension of commission power into their field. The ICC was thus unable to expand its basis of support. Second, Professor Huntington found that with some agencies, such as Department of Agriculture and the Maritime Commission, estrangement developed because these bodies were closely affiliated with interest groups alienated from the commission. More frequently, however, the commission lost support from other agencies because its advocacy of railroad interests conflicted with the responsibility other agencies felt toward broader based interest groups.

Thus the administrator in assessing his own strength must at the same times assess the strength of his support. But the size alone is not enough: also important are the dispersion and unity of his constituency. For example, the strength of the Secretary of Interior increased with the establishment of the Bureau of Outdoor Recreation, which broadened his base from just the Western states to the urban Northeast (Rourke 1969:65). For similar reasons state university systems try to establish satellite campuses in as many state senatorial districts as possible. Regarding the importance of unity, one need only compare the influence of the large, loosely knit consumer movement with the relatively small, tightly knit American Rifle Association.

2. The second source of agency power is *professionalism.* In defining a profession, we shall follow Frederick G. Mosher (1968:106): a reasonably clear-cut occupational field that ordinarily requires higher education at least through the bachelor's level and offers a lifetime career to its members. As society becomes more specialized and dominated by technological concerns, we can surely expect to see more individuals fitting this description in government agencies. The consequences of this trend are two-fold.

Professionals within an organization are obviously in excellent position to mobilize the support of relevant external professional organizations. Actually, the arrangement is reciprocal: Each profession tends to stake its territory within the appropriate government agency; e.g., medical profession in the Food and Drug Administration and the National Institutes of Health and the legal profession in the Justice Department.

Another consequence of professionalism is that within the agency the professionals tend to form a kind of elite with substantial control over operations, despite nominal political control from above. At least three elements form the base of expert power. (For a more complete analysis, see Benveniste 1972:Chapters 2 and 7.)

Full-time attention to a problem assures complete information about the ramifications. This is an advantage, vis-à-vis political authorities, in framing policy questions.

Subpart specialization develops expertise by breaking the function, issue, or problem into subparts.

Monopolization of information allows the agency to develop and determine the facts of a case and to control timing of information releases.

3. The last sources of agency power, leadership, is perhaps the most difficult to distinguish, for it is really a mixture of a number of intangibles — vitality, drive, energy, and courage. Although we can not offer a rigorous definition, we can, I think, recognize it when we see it. George C. Marshall, who, as Secretary of State, proposed and directed the Marshall Plan, had it. Hyman Rickover, who, while in the Bureau of Ships, developed and delivered early the nuclear-powered Nautilus, had it. And, from all accounts, Eliot Richardson, who has served in numerous cabinet level positions, had it. Conversely, we can, I think, note its loss, as did Professor Huntington in his study of the ICC.

The Good, the Bad, and the Ugly: Three Approaches to Political Competency

Rickover   Waterman   Hoover

Wide World

Always Getting His Way

Since the death of J. Edgar Hoover, probably no other administrator in Washington has exerted the influence over individual members of Congress as has Vice Admiral Hyman G. Rickover. A seemingly inexhaustible sexagenarian, Rickover knows that Congress can be an important ally in his struggle to drag a conservative navy into the nuclear age.

This is how it works. Rickover wants a $60 million down payment for a nuclear powered cruiser that will cost $1.2 billion amended to the 1975 budget. He goes to his congressional friends such as Rep. Melvin Price, Democrat of Illinois, the Chairman of the House Armed Services Committee and Rep. Charles E. Bennett, Democrat of Florida, Chairman of the Seapower Subcommittee. They, in turn, take the admiral's case to the president, who agrees with his former associates. "No matter that the nuclear cruiser was opposed by the Defense Department and the president's own budget office. No matter that in a time of fiscal restraint proclaimed by the president the project would add over $1 billion to the next year's defense budget. No matter that it would absorb funds urgently needed by the navy for other ships. What Admiral Rickover wants, he usually gets." (Finney 1975)

Administrative Self-Restraint

Alan Waterman was the first director of the National Science Foundation (NSF), serving from 1950 to 1963. To him the agency's supreme objective was to serve the needs of the scientific community. The single-minded pursuit of this objective led Waterman largely to ignore national bureaucratic politics. In a word, Waterman followed a strategy of self-restraint.

NSF was born when a number of federal research organizations already existed. In addition to the Office of Naval Research, already a major source of funds for the scientific community, the National Institutes of Health were entrenched in life sciences, and the navy, the air force, and Atomic Energy Commission were active in the physical sciences. Where would NSF fit in? To Waterman the answer was obvious: Where others are not. As a result NSF was placed in the position of supporting research that was least relevant to any mission-oriented goal. "NSF avoided expansion of jurisdiction into applied areas, even when there was little competition from other agencies." (Lambright 1976: 143)

Since NSF under Waterman did not want to enlarge its jurisdiction, it could hardly hope to enlarge its constituency. But "by moving into applied areas, NSF might have built a broader, more applied constituency to go along with the performers. It might have used its direct access to the president as a means to gain his support and that of his broad national clientele." As for Congress, NSF "might have enlarged its legislative constituency by distributing grants with an eye to geographical spread and congressional support. (144)

The Truth About Hoover

Above we compared Hoover with Rickover in the way they both acquired and held their influence in Congress. There is, however, one important difference. Admiral Rickover's influence was obtained "by dint of success and a tongue sometimes tart and sometimes flattering" (Finney 1975). Mr. Hoover, on the other hand, seemed to benefit from the general suspicion in Congress that he knew some skeletons in the closet.

Apparently, these general suspicions were not without foundation. For only three years after his death, congressional and journalistic scrutiny, as well as the writings of his once fearful agents, began to reveal a rather dark picture of the man who built the Federal Bureau of Investigation into one of the world's most reputable police organizations through 48 years as its director. In the new picture, Hoover is seen as a "shrewd bureaucratic genius who cared less about crime than about perpetuating his crime-busting image. With his acute public relations sense, he managed to obscure his bureau's failings while magnifying its sometimes successes. Even his fervent anti-Communism has been cast into doubt; some former aides insist that he knew the party was never a genuine internal threat to the nation but a useful, popular target to ensure financial and public support for the FBI." (*Time* 1975)

In a 1975 cover story, *Time* reported that Hoover did in fact use information compiled by his agents to built political support for the bureau. For example:

> ". . . Hoover went to one senator with the revelation that his daughter was using hard drugs. Hoover agreed to keep the matter quiet—and thereby earned the senator's lasting gratitude."
> ". . . when Hoover discovered that one Congressman was a homosexual, he visited the legislator to assure him that this news would never leak from the FBI—and this made a new friend for the bureau."

Costs

Since cost is an economic term, we might do well to discuss political cost in essentially economic terms and, in so doing, perhaps achieve a little more rigor.

Virtually every important administrative action has an indirect impact; the economists call such indirect or secondary impacts *externalities* or spillovers. David Halberstam (1969:302–3) a Pulitzer Prize winning journalist, provides the following incident from the Kennedy years:

> In 1962 McNamara came charging into the White House ready to save millions on the budget by closing certain naval bases. All the statistics were there. Close this base, save this many dollars. Close that one and save that much more. All obsolete. All fat. Each base figured to the fraction of the penny. Kennedy interrupted him and said, "Bob, you're going to close the Brooklyn Navy Yard, with 26 thousand people, and they're going to be out of work and go across the street and draw unemployment, and you better figure that into the cost. That's going to cost us something and they're going to be awfully mad at me, and we better figure that in too.

I believe it was Paul Applebey who remarked that the four questions every administrator should always ask prior to an important decision are: Who is going to be glad? How glad? Who is going to be mad? And, how mad?

Now we come to little more complicated economic concept. Virtually every important agency action involves an *opportunity cost.* Every one recognizes costs that are actual cash payments (e.g., $200,000 for a new city park). But the administrator must go further; he must realize that some of the most important costs attributable to doing one thing rather than another stem from the foregone opportunities that have to be sacrificed in doing this one thing. Thus, as Richard Neustadt (1960:31) suggests, when Truman dismissed MacArthur he "exhausted his credit"; as a consequence, he was unable to make his case with Congress, court, and public in a steel strike that came the next year.

Agency administrators can also go into debt. If they use top level support, it is quite likely that higher officials will demand bureau backing for other administration programs or demand influence in bureau policy in return for support. And, as we saw in the case of Congressman Whitten and the Department of Agriculture, these political debts can be high indeed.

Strategies

Top administrators have a wide range of strategies available for dealing with the agency's environment. And all administrators may safely assume that, either voluntarily or otherwise, they will become involved in these strategies. To ignore them is, therefore, to ignore a very big part of day-to-day administration. For purposes of discussion, we shall classify them rather broadly as (1) cooperation, (2) competition, and (3) conflict.

1. Cooperation is based on the idea that organizations and groups can share compatible goals without having to give in or defer to the other. Thus, all parties can be winners, though some more than others. Put in mathematical terms, a cooperative strategy means the parties are engaged in a *variable-sum game.*

Cooperative strategies come in many varieties. *Persuasion,* for example, is a variety of cooperation and its essence was stated precisely by Richard Neustadt (1960:46) as follows: to induce someone to believe that what you want of them is what their own appraisal of their own responsibilities requires them to do in their own self-interest. As one Eisenhower aide put it:. "The people on the Hill don't do what they might *like* to do, they do what they think they have to do in their own interest as they see it."

Another variety of cooperation is *bargaining,* that is, the negotiation of an agreement for the exchange of goods, services, or other resources. Universities bargain the name of a hall in return for the donor's contribution. The Attorney General's Antitrust Division signs consent decrees with firms which promise not to pursue actions further without admitting guilt.

In an attempt to add precision to our analysis, we shall distinguish two bargaining techniques. *Compromise,* the first, usually results from bargaining over a single isolated issue when the outcome is one of more or less. Examples would include such matters as bussing distances or boundaries, hiring and promotion requirements in government employment, amounts of public housing for ghetto areas, and types of learning programs for un-employed. Quite clearly, compromise is widely regarded as a positive value in the American political system, but it can lead to ludicrous solutions. In 1961, the Director of Defense Research and Engineering had to negotiate between the air force and navy the requirements for fighter to be used by both. The navy argued for 56 feet; the air force, 90 feet. Solution? Seventy-three feet, of course.

With the other bargaining technique, *logrolling,* we are concerned with more than one issue. Logrolling, therefore, involves reciprocity of support for different items of interest to each bargainer. For example, in 1969, the Urban Affairs Council, in return for then presidential counsellor Arthur F. Burns's support of their Family Assistance Plan, was willing to let Burns's group develop a legislative version of a revenue sharing plan, although the plan properly belonged with UAC. Consider interdepartmental negotiations: when a top administrator from the Department of Labor concedes something to a representative of the U.S. Treasury, he can often expect a concession at some later date. Observes Charles Lindblom (1968:96), ''he has stored up a stock of goodwill on which he can later draw.''

In addition to persuasion and bargaining, we might consider the coalition as a variety of cooperation. *Coalition* involves a combination of two or more organizations for a specific purpose. A good example is provided by the ''Mohole'' project, which sought to develop new technology that would al-low an anchored drilling ship to penetrate the Earth's mantle (See Green-berg 1967:Chapter 9). The original group of sponsoring scientists were con-cerned with maximizing the scientific returns from the drilling. The contractor understandably sought to confine the project as nearly as possible to a straightforward engineering task. Meanwhile, the President's Office of Sci-ence and Technology was concerned over the international and prestige aspects of success or failure of the project. The National Academy leadership was concerned to preserve the prestige of science, free from controversy. The National Science Foundation sought to sustain the impetus of an im-portant project in earth sciences, but at the same time to support orderly progress in all other fields of science it was sponsoring. Similarly, today we see a coalition of NASA, air force, and contractors backing the space shuttle program.

What do we know about the art of coalition building? The first thing good administrators have learned is that, because of the speed of communication, a proposal can be tested by feinting. The proposal is released by a ''reliable source'' as a trial balloon before it is officially made. This gives the agency an opportunity to test the different responses that might occur if such a proposal is actually made. Then, if opposition develops or support fails to develop, it can either be modified or dropped.

Good administrators have learned too that clarity—sometimes but not always—is essential; in other words, if a coalition is to form around a pro-posal, then that proposal must be as unambiguous as possible. One of the central difficulties of the negative income tax proposal, for example, lay in communicating not only to the public but also to mature editorial writers and legislators exactly how it worked. The National Institutes of Health were not, however, confused on this point. In 1955, the NIH National Microbiological Institute was renamed the National Institute of Allergy and Infectious Diseases. No longer would they be handicapped because "no one died of microbiology" (Seidman 1970:35).

Good administrators have learned the advantage of linking their agency's proposal with the goals of other agencies and political authorities. Advocates of the nuclear plane in 1953 were successful in linking this proposal in an unmistakable way to a high-priority defense need (Lambright 1967). Similarly, President Johnson increased the coalition backing the Elementary and Secondary Education Act of 1965 by linking the proposal of federal aid to public school to his antipoverty program. And by the late 1970s, NASA was linking programs to environment and energy. (Lambright, 1976:53, calls this "repackaging.")

2. For the last few pages, we have discussed the various forms that a cooperative strategy might take. Now we turn to the second classification of strategy, competition. Competition may be defined as a struggle between two or more parties with a third party mediating.

The occasions in government for intergroup competition are not hard to find; for example, the Labor Department competes with the Bureau of Land Reclamation over proposals to restore wasteland. Often, in competitive situations, the winnings of one competitor are equalled by the losses of the other; a simple example is when a project is transferred from one agency to another. Game theorists call these kinds of competitive situations and their pay-offs, *zero-sum.*

What can an administrator do in a zero-sum situation? While the alternative are no doubt many, we shall consider only two examples. In the early 1960s, it became apparent to the air force as well as the navy that the new defense secretary, McNamara, was going to choose a single plane to serve, with certain modifications, both services. The plane would be a modification of either the air force's TFX or the navy's F-4. Under these conditions, the air force immediately, and successfully, launched a campaign of emphasizing the flexibility of *its* plane; at the same time, it glossed over how well it would suit its special needs. (Coulam 1975:1–38)

Administrators sometimes can co-opt their adversaries. The classic example of co-optation is the way in which the Tennessee Valley Authority (TVA) adapted its goals to survive. Philip Selznick (1949) defines it as "the process of absorbing new elements into the leadership as policy determining structure of an organization as a means of averting threats to its stability or existence." Co-optation deliberately seeks participation as a means to gain public agreement to agency programs. In his study of TVA strategy, Selznick tells how potential opposition from the community and regional groups were brought into TVA's decision-making process. In much the same way, some university administrations have co-opted campus radicals. For once the radical becomes a part of that world of gluten, the twilight of radical ardor is near.

Finally, awarding lucrative government contracts can provide an enormously flexible way for an agency to co-opt legislators. Companies are simply selected in the districts of key legislative constituents. "Locational politics can be used by the agency to enlarge the program's geographical, legislative clientele" (Lambright 1976:48–49). Similarly, certain federal agencies seek to co-opt the scientific community by appointing scientists to advisory boards and giving research grants.

3. While cooperation and competition are essentially peaceful and governed by formal rules and informal normative constraints, *conflict* involves situations where actors pursue goals that are fundamentally incompatible. It also can involve attitudes not unlike that of Metternich at the Congress of Vienna. Upon hearing of the death of the Russian ambassador, Metternich is said to have asked, "What could have been the motive?" While these situations and attitudes do not flourish in the American political system, they nonetheless exist.

Consider the case of Kennedy and U.S. Steel. On Tuesday, April 10, 1962, President Kennedy was surprised to note that his appointment calendar included a 5:45 P.M. appointment with Roger Blough, U.S. Steel chairman. The purpose of the Blough visit was to hand the president a press release announcing a $6-a-ton price increase. The president was stunned. He felt his whole fight against inflation was reduced to tatters. Above all, he felt duped. The man seated on the sofa next to his rocking chair had personally, knowingly, accepted his help in securing from the workers a contract that would not lead to an increase in prices. Although being challenged in an area where he had few weapons, the president would not accept this *fait accompli* without a fight. His main line of attack was divide and conquer; more specifically, he focused his efforts on the Inland Steel Company of Chicago to obtain an agreement that they would not follow U.S. Steel's lead. In addition, he followed other courses of action. In brief, he got Senator Kefauver and the Justice Department to begin investigating steel activities; used a press conference to mainstream public opinion; and made implied threats to cancel certain defense contracts.

Within a period of 72 hours, Blough capitulated before the onslaught. What this event had shown was the ability of the chief executive "to mobilize and concentrate every talent and tool he possessed and could borrow to prevent a serious blow to his program, his prestige, and his office" (Sorensen 1965:516).

Conflict, of course, occurs not only at such lofty levels; nor does it always end in a government victory. Journalist Tom Wolfe (1970: 22–23) gives us a vivid picture of how ghetto youth and militants can intimidate the bureaucrats at city hall and in the local Office of Economic Opportunity. Wolfe calls the practice mau-mauing. One man named Chaser, Wolfe relates, almost gave classes in mau-mauing.

> Then Chaser would say, "Now when we get there, I want you to come down front and stare at the man and don't say nothing. You just glare. No matter what he says. He'll try to get you to agree with him. He'll say, 'Ain't that right?' and 'You know what I mean?' and he wants you to say yes or nod your head . . . see . . . it's part of his psychological jiveass. But you don't say nothing. You just glare . . . see . . . Then some of the other brothers will get up on that stage behind him, like there's no more room or like they just gathering around. Then you brothers up there behind him, you start letting him have it . . . He starts thinking, 'Oh God! Those bad cats are in front of me, they all around me, they behind me. I'm surrounded.' That shakes 'em up.
>
> "And then when one of the brothers is up talking, another brother comes up and whispers something in his ear, like this," and Chaser cups his hand around his mouth like he's whispering something. "And the brother stops talking, like he's listening, and the man thinks, 'What's he saying? What kind of unbelievable s--- are they planning now?' The brother, he's not saying anything. He's just moving his lips. It's a tactic . . . you know . . . And at the end I'll slap my hand down on the desk — whop — and everybody gets up, like one man, and walks out of there. And that really shakes 'em up. They see that the people are unified, and disciplined, and mad, and tired of talking and ready for walking, and that shakes 'em up." (Reprinted with the permission of Farrar, Straus & Giroux, Inc., from *Radical Chic & Mau-Mauing the Flak Catchers,* by Tom Wolfe. Copyright © 1970 by Tom Wolfe.)

In conflict situations, the astute administrator needs to keep several things in mind. First is the ever present danger of *escalation.* This process is characterized by each side in the conflict repeatedly increasing the intensity of the conflict; if continued with a constant rate of increments, the process is likely to run out of control, ending in violence. Suppose that a minor incident occurs in which a black citizen is challenged or wronged by a white policeman and a fracas results. Black witnesses spread the word. As the rumors circulate, the hostilities involved become exaggerated. Reactions of anger and demonstration take place, leading to looting and destruction. The police are ordered to contain the riot; this attempt at control increase the anger of the blacks. Snipers begin to fire at the police and firemen. The national guard is brought in and shoots into the crowd. There are 34 dead, as in the Watts riot in Los Angeles. As a result, great resentment spreads, which, in turn, results in more clandestine attacks, more arson and rioting, and more attacks against the police. The police respond with armored trucks patrolling the streets and more heavy handed repression. In short, we have a spiral of bloodshed.

Besides attempting to spot the escalation process before it gets out of hand, the administrator should remember in conflict situations to avoid humiliation of the interests that lose out in the clash of policy. Where one's adversary has no honorable path of retreat, conflict can become quite protracted.

Timing and forbearance are also important. In the steel price dispute,

Kennedy realized that he had to act swiftly, before a parade of companies, rushing to imitate U.S. Steel's increase, began. But one must also know when to stop pressing the attack, how to avoid overkill. Benjamin Disraili recognized this factor when he said, "Next to knowing when to seize an advantage, the most important thing in life is to know when to forego an advantage."

Lastly, and most importantly, I think, the administrator needs to know that conflict situations do not require backroom politics; rather they can be managed with forthrightness and even a certain dignity. Indeed, even in the ultimate of conflicts — war — men and women still have this option. The following letter to the Japanese ambassador illustrates my point.

> Sir,
>
> On the evening of December 7th His Majesty's Government in the United Kingdom learned that Japanese forces without previous warning either in the form of a declaration of war or of an ultimatum with a conditional declaration of war had attempted a landing on the coast of Malaya and bombed Singapore and Hong Kong.
>
> In view of these wanton acts of unprovoked aggression committed in flagrant violation of International Law and particularly of Article I of the Third Hague Convention relative to the opening of hostilities, to which both Japan and the United Kingdom are parties, His Majesty's Ambassador at Tokyo has been instructed to inform the Imperial Japanese Government in the name of His Majesty's Government in the United Kingdom that a state of war exists between our two countries.
>
> I have the honour to be, with high consideration,
>
> Sir,
>
> Your obedient servant,
>
> WINSTON S. CHURCHILL

As Churchill (1959:508) noted in his *Memoirs,* "some people did not like this ceremonial style. But after all when you have to kill a man it costs nothing to be polite."

NAILING DOWN THE MAIN POINTS

1 Public administrators have learned that to separate administration from politics is impossible; the two are inextricable intertwined. Specifically, today's administrators are intimately involved in policy making as well as the day to day play of politics.

2 Administrators frequently participate in formulation of public policy by making proposals that further their client's interests, originate entirely with the agency, or suggest improvements on existing legislation. Nevertheless, bureaucracy *stops* far more policy proposals than it starts.

3 Implementation of policy begins where formulation ends. Administrative decisions can be crucial in this stage of the policy making process.

4 Legislative bodies exercise authority over agencies by establishing the programs the agencies must administer, by appropriating funds for those programs, and by checking on the agencies performance (oversight).

5   Control by the chief executive officer is made difficult by the alliances the agency may form with legislators and clients. Nonetheless, at the national level, the president possesses formidable tools to control agencies: public opinion, appointment, budget preparation, and legislative clearance. In recent years, presidents have used the Office of Management and Budget for coordination and evaluation of agency activities. Significantly, many governors have adapted this approach.

6   In addition to the varying degrees of control exercised over the agency by legislatures and chief executives, agencies need to consider two other external political bodies: clients and agencies. While agencies supposedly regulate these clients, critics charge that, in reality, the relationships become too cozy. Since several agencies can become involved in one policy area, administrators need to consider these cognate agencies when surveying their own political environment.

7   The political resources available to an administrator flow from three chief sources: external support, professionalism, and leadership. In assessing the political consequences of their actions, administrators need to consider, in addition to the resources available, the *political* costs involved.

8   In dealing with the environment, administrators have three broad strategies available: cooperation, competition, and conflict. While a cooperative strategy might be the preferred, administrators should recognize that they can frequently become embroiled in competition or conflict.

CONCEPTS FOR REVIEW

politics-administration debate
policy
policy making, policy formulation, and policy implementation
rule-making, adjudication, law enforcement, and program operations
prospective rules
Federal Administrative Procedures Act
Federal Register
stare decisis
hierarchies
authority
multiple subordination
congressional oversight
General Accounting Office
legislative clearance

clients
public interest groups
cognate agencies
subsystem politics or triple alliances
professionalism
externalities
opportunity cost
cooperation, competition, and conflict
variable-sum game and zero-sum game
persuasion
bargaining
logrolling
coalition
co-optation
escalation

PROBLEMS

1. "The Watergate scandal clearly reveals the value of a semiautonomous bureaucracy." Discuss.

2. Discuss the possibility and implications of citizens participation being overwhelmed during hearings on controversial issues by expert testimony from government and industry representatives. Can you find examples in the local newspapers?

3. Look up a major national act in either the *Statues at Large or* the *Congress Quarterly Weekly Report* and then attempt to find applicable executive agency decrees relevant to it in either the *Federal Register* or the *Bureau of National Affairs Reports.* Do you think the law has been perverted to serve the goals of those who enforce them?

4. "The successful executive will readily accede to congressional participation in areas where its committees or members have a proper concern," writes former NASA chief, James E. Webb. Is Mr. Webb naive?

5. "TVA has lost much of its national constituency," said Sen. Howard H. Baker recently. Using recent periodicals, analyze the authority's political position and outline a plan to rebuild it.

6. Given the prevalency of logrolling, why might an administrator want to keep his preferences unclear? What do you think the effect of a ban of logrolling would be?

7. Assess the possibility of the adoption in your city of free-fare bus service. Consider the possibility in terms of (a) possible allies, (b) probable opponents, (c) distribution of resources among the actives, (d) legal constraints, and (e) alternative strategies for achieving it.

8. What externalities were involved in the three decisions faced by Mayor Cervantes?

9. "Expertise," said Harold J. Laski, "sacrifices the insight of common sense to the intensity of experience." Discuss.

10. Write an essay that compares the strength of professionalism to mobilization as a means by which an agency might exercise its power.

11. Can you see any link between the American party system, which is fairly weak in comparison to other Western nations, and the political activism of administrators?

12. "Vote trading and arm twisting are effective when the issue is not that big, when it isn't a glaring national issue. But it doesn't work when you've got the full focus of national attention on it." Do you agree or disagree? Support your answer with examples.

13. Historians Richard Hewlett and Francis Duncan (1974:191) write: "Rickover's tactics were to approach his assignment with ruthless determination and as a project manager to fight to the last for everything he needed to attain his goal. These tactics, admirable in a project manager, were precisely what appeared to many to disqualify Rickover for broader responsibilities." Why?

14. Redraw Figure 2–2 with a college president in the center. Can you redraw it for a union leader as well? A hospital administrator? What do you think it would look like for the chief executive of a multinational corporation?

15. The PRINCE Political Accounting System has been used in a variety of public administration programs to teach political strategy skills. See if you can apply the system to a current policy issue. (See William D. Coplin and Michael K. O'Leary *Everyman's PRINCE: A Guide to Understanding Your Political Problems* and, for

a briefer introduction and valuable insights on classroom use, their "Teaching Political Stretegy Skills with PRINCE," *Policy Analysis* (Winter 1976), 145–60.) Below are shown two examples of how the system works. Salience refers to the *importance* each political actor attaches to the issue. What are the implications of each in terms of possible political strategies?

ISSUE: The U.S. Government Will Pull Out of Vietnam in the Next Six Months

Actors	Issue Position	× Power	× Salience	= Total Support by Actors
President Nixon	−3	3	2 =	−18
Secretary Kissinger	−3	3	1 =	− 9
State Department officials	+1	1	3 =	+ 3
Department of Defense	−3	2	3 =	−18
Congress	+2	1	2 =	+ 4
Total of actors' scores				−38

ISSUE: A Neighborhood Health Center Will Be Established

Actors	Issue Position		Power	Subtotal (IP × P)		Salience		Total Support by Actors
Dr. Goodguy	+3	×	1	+3	×	3	=	+ 9
Dr. Esteem	+2	×	2	+4	×	1	=	+ 4
Chairperson, Citizens' Committee for Human Development	+3	×	1	+3	×	3	=	+ 9
Chairperson, County Medical Society	−1	×	3	−3	×	2	=	−6
Chairperson, Black Medical Society	−1	×	3	−3	×	2	=	− 6
Dean of Medical School	−2	×	3	−6	×	3	=	−18
Director, City-County Public Health Department	−1	×	2	−2	×	2	=	− 4
Total	+3			−4				−12

16. Another approach to increasing political strategy skills was suggested by Arnold J. Meltsner in "Political Feasibility and Policy Analysis," *Public Administration Review,* November–December 1972, 859–67. As a way of getting started, Meltsner suggested the following broad categories about which the analyst should gather information for the policy issue under consideration: (1) actors, (2) motivation, (3) beliefs, (4) resources, (5) sites, and (6) exchanges. Read this article, select an issue, and try to apply his approach. How does it compare with PRINCE?

INTRODUCTION

In Chapter 2, we began sketching the environment of American public administration. Now we add to our palette and attempt a brighter, truer sketch of that environment. For contrary to the impression Figure 2–2 gives, today's administrator works in a context of intergovernmental relations (IGR) as well as interagency ones. And by intergovernmental relations, we mean all those activities occurring between governmental units of all types and levels within the United States.

Because the subject of our investigation is so vast, the temptation is simply to plunge in and swim indescriminately from one island of fact to another, until we emerge at the end dripping with irrelevant details. Let us, therefore, resolve to set an objective and then plot as straight a course as possible toward it.

Simply stated, the aim of this chapter is to explain how intergovernmental relations affects the job of managing the public sector. But before we can deal directly with that topic, two preliminary steps are essential. First, we must be clear on what intergovernmental relations means and how that meaning has changed over the years. Second, we must examine a few of the kinds of cooperative relations that today exist among the thousands of jurisdictions in the United States.

THE MEANING AND DEVELOPMENT OF IGR

Federalism and IGR Compared

Not all authorities would use the term intergovernmental relations in titling a chapter such as this one. Some, in fact, would say that IGR is *au fond* federalism. Fortunately, this line of thought

3

Intergovernmental Relations

is today trading sluggishly, mostly under the counter. And before we go any further with IGR, it merits consideration.

In its most formal sense, a federal system (such as the United States, Canada, Switzerland, and West Germany) stands in contrast to a unitary or centralized system (such as France or Great Britain). The former divides power between the central government and regional governments (states, provinces, cantons, and lands); each government, central or regional, is legally supreme in its own area of jurisdiction. In the United States, for example, the federal government controls external affairs, regulates interstate commerce, and establishes rules for immigration and naturalization. On the other hand, the Constitution reserves certain powers for the states: control of elections, local governments, public health, safety, and morals. And though some powers are shared between governments—taxing and spending for the general welfare, defining and punishing crimes, and so forth—the traditional or "layer cake" theory still assumes that functions appropriate to each level can be defined with reasonable precision and should be kept distinct from and independent of each other.

Morton Grodzin and Daniel J. Elazar (1966) reject this model of the federal system, preferring a *marble cake model.* According to Grodzin and Elazar, separation of functions is both impractical and undesirable when governments operate in the same area, serve the same clients, and seek comparable goals.

"Layer" and "marble" are, of course, crass shorthand. In the first place, these models of federalism do not tell us very much about the policy component in the relationship between levels of government. What I mean by policy component is this: In several important areas of public policy (e.g., health services, housing, agriculture, higher education, and welfare), we have self-governing professional guilds or "vertical functional autocracies" (Seidman 1970:138). Former governor of North Carolina, Terry Sanford (1967:80), sees these "vertical functional autocracies" as forming a kind of picket fence: "The lines of authority, the concerns and interests, the flow of money, and the direction of programs run straight down like a number of pickets stuck into the ground. There is, as in a picket fence, a connecting cross slat, but that does little to support anything. In this metaphor, it stands for the governments. It holds the pickets in line; it does not bring them together. The picket-like programs are not connected at the bottom." Thus we might replace the old marble and layer cake models with one that looks something like Figure 3–1 (adapted from Wright 1974:15).

Within each picket, or "vertical functional autocracy," relationships become as crowded as Leonardo's drawings of the braids and spirals of live water. Figure 3–2 attempts to give some sense of this complexity for just one area of public policy—health services which are managed by eight agencies of the Department of Health, Education and Welfare.

The boxes at the top of the chart describe the 30 basic "statutory authori-

FIGURE 3-1

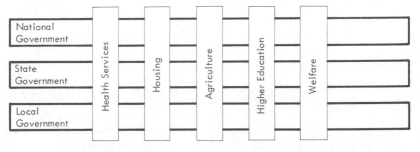

ties" for the programs. Moving down the chart, however, things began to get more complex. Lines of authority begin to move back and forth as they flow downward through 20 bureaus and 50 programs. Soon the lines begin to intersect and merge until they form broad and turgid series of money and authority, sometimes augmented and rechanneled by state agencies. (In a nearly futile attempt to keep the lines distinguishable on the chart, they are rendered in eight varieties—including dots, diagonals, dashes, and dashes and dots.) At the bottom, where the confusion is such that arrows are necessary to direct traffic, await the beneficiaries of the programs voted by Congress.

Remember, the chart shows only the programs managed by one division of HEW and its counterparts at the state and local levels. Since HEW runs more than 400 programs, other charts for other vertical functional autocracies could just as easily been presented. In any event, the point should be clear why some argue, along with Governor Sanford, that the crucial division between federal, state, and local is not between *levels* of government as the two cake models of federalism would have it.

A second deficiency of federalism as a discriptive model is that it tends to recognize mainly national-state and interstate relations but to ignore national-local, state-local, national-state-local, and interlocal. In contrast, "IGR includes as proper objects of study all the permutations and combinations of relations among the units of government in the American system." (Wright 1974:2) And local, as used here, means not only the 3,044 counties; 18,517 cities, villages, and boroughs; 16,991 townships; but also the paragovernments for special purposes. Among these paragovernments are 15,781 school districts and 23,885 other special districts (for sewerage and water supply, natural resources, health, utilities, and the like).

To sum up: While the term federalism perhaps helps us distinguish between one general class of governments and another class (called unitary), it does not provide the best approach to understanding the kinds of knowledge highlighted earlier. For the public administrator at least, the preferable term then is intergovernmental relations.

FIGURE 3–2
Picket Fence Federalism: A Close Up

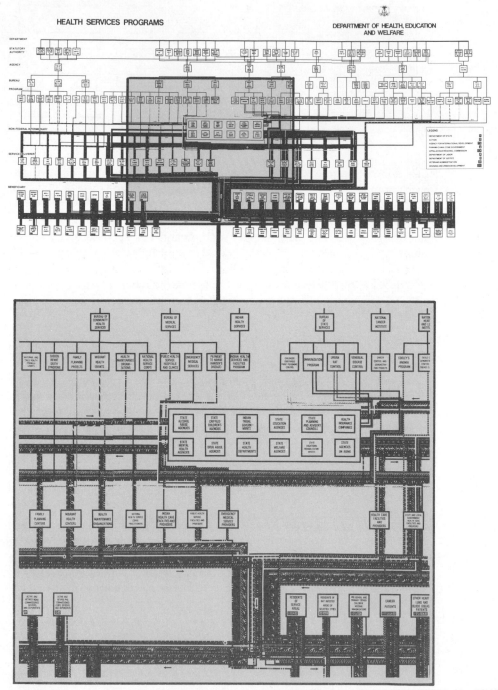

Source: HEW.

IGR since 1945

Definitions first. Federal grants to states or localities to be used for specific purposes are *grants-in-aid* (also known as *categorical grants*). Federal grants are of two types, *project* and *formula based.*

Project grants, a relatively new development, are awarded on an individual basis to solve specific problems; e.g., the Head Start program aimed at the intellectual enrichment of preschool children in the central city. But most legislation provides that grant funds be allocated on a formula basis, that is, monies are distributed to all eligible communities on the basis of some formula such as population, the wealth of the community, or the number of poor people. For example, under the Elementary Secondary Education Act of 1965, funds were available to states on the basis of the number of school children in low-income families (see Heller 1966:142). With these distinctions in mind, we can begin our story.

Prior to the depression of the 1930s Congress provided grants to states for agricultural education, roads, and conservation and performed other functions traditionally regarded as state rather than national. During the depression, 14 programs were added to cover such new services as welfare, employment assistance, public and child health care and public housing. This period was important because "substantial and significant fiscal links were firmly established. These established conduits were harbingers of more to come." (Wright 1974:7)

From 1946 to 1960 major new grants-in-aid programs were established. Accompanying this growth were corps of program professionals in each of the specialized grant fields, such as airport construction, hospital construction, slum clearance and urban renewal, urban planning, and waste treatment.

The decade from 1958–68 is usually termed the period of *creative federalism.* And the reasons are clear enough: Faced with demands from local communities, especially big cities, Congress responded with a plethora of programs. In 1961 the Advisory Commission on Intergovernmental Relations (ACIR), a bipartisan federal commission of 26 members, identified approximately 40 major grant programs in existence that had been enacted prior to 1958. By 1969 there were an estimated 160 major programs, 500 specific legislative authorizations, and 1,315 different federal assistance activities, for which money figures, application deadlines, agency contacts, and use restrictions could be identified. The ACIR also found that the number of grant catalogs being issued about federal programs was proliferating to the point that it published a catalog of catalogs, covering nine single-spaced pages. (ACIR 1970:3)

Most of the programs launched since 1960 do not distribute funds to states automatically according to a set formula. Rather they establish project grants—an approach under which state or local agencies applying for federal assistance prepare applications, submit them to the nearest federal regional office—"and hope for the best." Eligibility to receive a federal grant can extend to nongovernmental agencies, thus permitting Congress and the national administration to bypass state governments and place the money directly "on the target." (U.S. Advisory Commission on Intergovernmental Relations 1970:3)

The creative phase was important for other reasons. Planning requirements were attached to 61 of the new grant programs enacted between 1961 to 1966. We shall have more to say about these requirements later. Second, public participation requirements were tied to some grants — an action that "increased the complexity, the calculations, and occasionally the chagrin of officials charged with grant allocation choices." (Wright 1974:11) The Community Action Program, discussed in the preceding chapter, serves as an example of this public participation emphasis.

This proliferation of grants created what some called a management mess. What was the answer? In the mid-1960s, Walter Heller (1966) devised a plan through which federal monies could be channeled to localities. Entitled *revenue sharing,* it called for the federal government to distribute a portion of the income tax to the states each year on a per capita basis "with next to no strings attached." Three years later, using the rhetoric of the radical left, President Nixon formally recommended his general revenue sharing plan as a way of returning "power to the people." Intergovernmental relations had crossed another meridian. How well revenue sharing works is a question to which we now turn.

THE NEW FEDERALISM

Actually, revenue sharing is only a part — though a key part — of a larger innovation called the *new federalism.* It may be helpful for understanding the doctrine of the new federalism to discuss it in terms of the four *D*s that constitute its basic framework: dollars, discretion, decentralization, and delivery.

Dollars

Since it was passed in 1972, revenue sharing provided $6 billion a year for five years to supplement federal grant programs and give state and local governments the chance to spend federal money without bureaucratic interferences (see Figure 3–3). Today revenue sharing touches almost every community — big or little, rich or poor. Checks are distributed quarterly to 39,000 counties, cities, towns, townships, Indian tribes, and Alaskan villages as well as to the 50 states (which get about one third of the money).

The chief argument for revenue sharing centers on the apparently inadequate revenue sources of state and local governments. Traditionally, the federal government has been in a much better position to collect revenues. Yet, the state and local governments are the ones facing most directly the urgent demands for more and better education, welfare, urban transportation, and crime control.

In the past, the upshot of these conditions was a tendency (noted earlier) for the federal government to provide more and more conditional grants and assume direct responsibility for more and more functions. In other words, the federal government took over much of the decision making, which had been reserved for the states and cities. Naturally, this trend creates an increasingly complex network of grants and rules. In this context, sharing revenues seemed a clear cut way out.

But not to everyone. Some critics argue that many states have substantial unused fiscal capacity and could easily raise substantial additional sums. (Musgrave and Polinski 1971) Others argue that states do not use the money to meet the most pressing needs and, in some instances, waste the money. A particular complaint is that too much of the money has been used to pay for new construction or equipment, to balance state and local budgets, or to cut taxes and that not enough has gone to aid the poor, the elderly, and minorities. They point to cases like St. Louis County, Missouri, where officials decided to spend $4 million on public golf courses and ice skating rinks. This line of criticism was predictable. One reason for the New Deal's preference for categorical programs was a distrust of the competence of local gov-

FIGURE 3–3
Where Revenue Sharing Fits in the Flow of Federal Aid

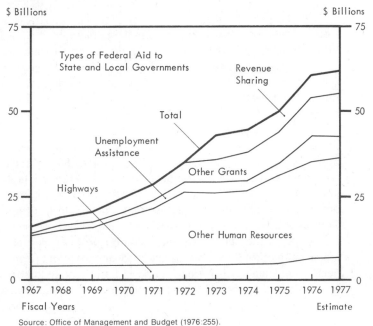

Source: Office of Management and Budget (1976:255).

ernment. During the civil rights movement of the 1960s, many more categorical grants were spawned in response to demands from blacks for federal aid because they were discriminated against at the state and local levels.

What are the facts? According to the Treasury Department (cited in Shafer 1975), the majority of the money—60 percent of $9.5 billion spent through June 1974—has been used for public safety, education, and transportation. Cities have put the biggest chunk, 46 percent, into police and fire protection. Further, only 1.6 percent of the revenue sharing funds went for social service and only 1.5 percent went for health care, according to a study done in 1974 by the tax foundation, a nonprofit, nonpartisan research organization based in New York City. Most of the states' shared revenues have aided education. Therefore, the critics are correct at least in this respect: the net effect has not been to further programs designed primarily for the disadvantaged. Whether this effect was intended or unintended by the architects of revenue sharing is the harder question to answer.

A third complaint is that the formula used in allocating revenue-sharing funds fails to give adequate help to poor cities and rural communities. Opponents also charge that there has not been enough accountability about how revenue sharing money is spent and that public participation in the spending choices is lacking.

Discretion

The new federalism also drastically shifted the federal grant system away from detailed categorical grants, which stipulate in detail how the funds will be used, to programs that give more discretion to state and local officials.

The most unconditional type of grants are called *general revenue sharing grants,* where Congress merely turns over tax dollars to state and local governments with few or even no strings. *Special revenue sharing grants* consolidate existing programs into broad areas; for example, urban community development, education, manpower training, law enforcement, transportation, and so on. *Block grants* are somewhat narrower in focus but still bring together detailed categorical grants into larger units that give state and local units more discretion in their use. Early examples of the block grant were the Partnership and Health Act of 1966, which merged some 16 previously small separate health grants, and Title I of the Omnibus Crime Control and Safe Streets Act of 1968.

Implicit in the special revenue sharing program is that strings must be loosened in order for the states and local government to determine what their needs are. Richard P. Nathan (cited in Farrell 1976), a senior fellow at the Brookings Institution and a Republican architect of general revenue sharing, feels that block grants open "the window on tens of thousands of local governments previously little affected by federal policies." The existing block grant programs, he said in an interview, are an implicit statement by the federal government that it now has greater trust in state and local govern-ments than it did before. "Ours is still a nation of small governments."

Decentralization

New federalism attempts to come to grips with a strange paradox in American political life: most Americans want the federal government to make sure that there is more fairness in life but, at the same time, they want the faceless monster of Big Government to get out of their lives. Writes William Safire (1973): "What dawned upon the New Federalists was *'selective decentralization,'* which held that the ship existed only for the sake of the passengers. The level of government that dealt with a problem should not depend upon which system, nationalized or decentralized, was in fashion, but upon which level of government worked best to solve that specific problem."

Safire continues: "Therefore New Federalists say, power should seek its own level: The decision about whether city or state or federal government 'handles' a problem should be determined by which delivers the most fair-ness with the least offensive administration.

"On that principle, and with absolute consistency, new federalists can say: (1) welfare should be centralized and standardized, since this serves the cause of fairness best and the feds are the most efficient at sending out cash; (2) unemployment insurance should remain at the middle, or state, level, pro-viding enough administrative diversity to reflect regional conditions; and (3) manpower training should be gradually turned over to states and lo-calities because this type of face-to-face service is more responsively handled 'closest to the people.'"

Federal decentralization is further exemplified by the ten uniform federal regions (see Figure 3–4). Before standardization of regions for the major domestic agencies, officials in Boise, Idaho, for example, had to deal with three federal regional offices, including one located in Kansas City.

In 1972 an executive order established within each region a *Federal Regional Council*. They are made up of the chief regional offices of nine federal domestic agencies, and are designed: (1) to facilitate interagency program coordination (2) to deliver services that are unique to a region or areas within the region and (3) to serve as a point of contact for state and local governments with the federal government and to link Washington more closely to the views, needs and interest of state and local governments. So far, however, the councils have been handicapped by their lack of permanent chairpersons, inadequate staff and funding, and withdrawals from participa-tion by certain agencies, thus detracting from their representation of the full spectrum of federal domestic programming. While they have helped to improve interagency coordination, they have not attempted major, ongoing intergovernmental coordination between local priorities and federal program needs. (U.S. Office of Management and Budget 1975:14)

FIGURE 3–4

Map of the United States, Showing Federal Administrative Regions

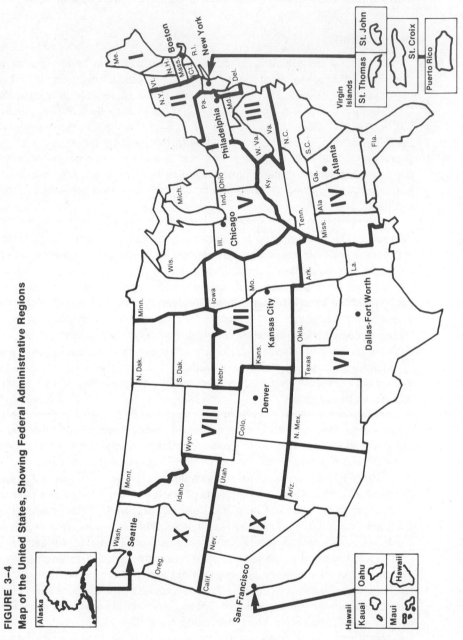

Source: U.S. Bureau of Census (1974).

Delivery

The last *D* raises the concept of state and local responsibility. James S. Dwight (1973:19) reports that in 47 identifiable federal programs, state and local participation has been increased substantially.

For the new federalism to be entirely successful, each jurisdiction must develop the capability to identify and delineate what is a federal responsibility, a state responsibility, and a local responsibility. "Where there are mutual interests and participation requirements, all must be able to divide properly those duties and bear respective responsibility in carrying them out. Administrators must understand this and discard the idea of a scapegoat in each case of delivery failure. Too often the federal employee blames the state or local employee, and vice versa."

Revenue sharing is a case in point. "The reaction at the federal level is 'Ho-hum, I'm not sure how it affects me.' At the state and local levels, there seems to be a lack of awareness of the nature of the opportunity presented or a reluctance to accept the responsibility that goes with revenue sharing. To achieve their true potential, state and local officials must recognize the opportunities and responsibilities that revenue sharing and other reforms bring. For the federal establishment, it means reducing the magnitude of operations and a decreasing of options in terms of framing the delivery of services." (Dwight 1973:18)

The aim of this chapter, it will be recalled, is to explain how intergovernmental relations affects the public administrator's job. But before we can deal directly with that topic, two preliminary steps are necessary. The first step, to explain what intergovernmental relations is and how its meaning has changed, we have just taken. Now we must take the second step—which is to sample a few of the kinds of specific relationships that exist among the thousands of jurisdictions in the United States.

PERMUTATIONS AND COMBINATIONS

It would perhaps be useful to set forth schematically the kinds of general relationships this section examines. To simplify greatly, let us think of Washington, D.C., as the top circle in the accompanying diagram. The three circles below the top one we shall let stand for the states and the bottom row of nine circles, for the cities. This diagram serves two purposes. First, with the addition of connecting arrows, it shall help us visualize what spe-

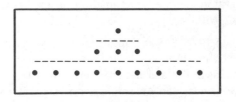

cific relations we are concerned with in each of the four subsections that follow. Second, and perhaps more important, it can give some hint of the astronomical number of possible intergovernmental relations in the American political system. As an exercise, count the number of connections possible between all the points. Now imagine the number on a more complete diagram—one that showed *all* of the thousands of jurisdictions in the U.S., including federal administrative regions. But accuracy must pay the fare of clarity in our diagram.

One final point worth keeping in mind when gazing upon the 13 circles: "It is human beings clothed with office who are the real determiners of what the relations between units of government will be. Consequently, the concept of intergovernmental relations necessarily has to be founded largely in terms of human relations and human behavior." (W. Anderson, 1960:4) In this sense, there are no intergovernmental relations—only relations among officials in different governing units.

Federal Governmental Relations with State and Community

No longer can governors, big city mayors, or even university presidents ignore Washington. The race among states, cities, and universities for the proposed Federal Solar Energy Research Institute (SERI) illustrates this new reality.

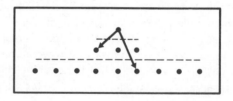

In 1975, states from New England to California entered competition for the site of the institute which could build up to a $50 million annual budget three years after its establishment in 1976. The sweepstakes have been compared by some to the 1954 search for a home for the U.S. Air Force Academy. In the contest, some states stressed how much sun shines on them, while others emphasized their intellectual and industrial resources for a large laboratory. Writes Victor K. McElheny (1975): "The scramble preceding the site selection was regarded as the most widespread, public, and intense competition up to that time for a federal scientific installation. The competition for the solar institute is expected to rival that for the accelerator." Witness:

In late 1974, El Paso put in an application for SERI proposing a regional institute that would include scientists from both the University of Texas at El Paso and the University of New Mexico. Meanwhile, Henry B. Gonzalez, San Antonio's congressman, works with the mayor and city manager to push his home town as the site.

In February 1975 Governor Jerry Apodaco, Senator Joseph M. Montoya, and a consortium of science laboratories present a proposal to place the solar center in New Mexico.

In June 1975 universities and industries on Long Island form a similar consortium.

In October 1975 Governor Carey designates Dr. William E. Seymour of the New State Department of Commerce to coordinate proposals for the center from various regions in the state.

In the same month the governors of six New England states, sitting on the New England Regional Commission, vote to "work as a regional force" to attract the center to New England.

Fortunately, not all interaction with Washington is so feverish. To help public officials at the state and local community level keep informed concerning available assistance and newest regulations are the federal government's own information service (*Area Reports and Record Service*) and the Council of State Governments. Actually, the Council, formed in 1925, does more: it helps state officials share their experiences related to common problems. It does this by publishing a monthly magazine (*State Government*) and, in conjunction with its affiliate organizations (e.g., the Governors' Conference), conducting meetings.

Actually, the variety of services provided by the federal government to states is enormous. Rather than to try to record them with talmudic thoroughness, as did the U.S. Senate Subcommittee on Intergovernmental Relations (cited in Adrian 1976:62), we only sample:

Collates facts about fields of state legislation and publishes them.

Supplies advisory leadership, as in the drafting of model milk ordinance by the Public Health Service.

Helps to improve local building codes through the technical work of the National Bureau of Standards.

Assembles comparative information about state and local governments, as in the Governments Division of the Census Bureau.

Trains state and local personnel.

Lends federal employees to the local levels. (Ordinarily there is no statutory basis for these personnel arrangements. The Natural Gas Act, however, authorizes the loan of rate, valuation, and other experts as paid witnesses to state regulatory bodies. Some types of federal employees become incidental agents of the states. A federal law has long provided that Forest Service officials shall "aid in the enforcement of the laws of the states and territories with regard to stock, for the prevention and extinguishment of forest fires, and for the protection of fish and game." State laws frequently endow federal employees with the powers of peace officers.)

Furnishes local personnel agencies with information on examination techniques.

Makes a great deal of technical information available to states and their subdivisions concerning commodity specifications (a valuable service since not many of the governments could afford to operate testing bureaus).

Gives technical advice on air pollution problems.

Furnishes advice on sanitation problems.

Arrests local law violators who have left the state.

Interstate Relations: Competition and Cooperation

The Constitution deals with many of the issues involving the relations between the states — for example, privileges and immunities, full faith and credit, extradiction, and economic competition. Since a standard American government text should cover most of these issues, the following discussion focuses on only one, interstate compacts.

Because interstate agreements can improve the allocation of resources, administrators have keen interest in them. For example:

Through the Crime Compact of 1934, parole officers in all states are able to cooperate across state lines with minimum red tape.

Sparsely settled states, lacking requisite facilities may make arrangements with other states to help them with professional education, welfare, tuberculosis, and mental illness.

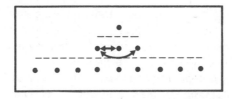

Increasingly, states are entering compacts to coordinate planning, transportation, and environmental control.

State Relations with Local Governments and Special Districts

All units of local government are public corporations created under the authority of state law, to provide services that, presumably, could not adequately be provided by the private sector. *Dillon's rule*—which declares that local jurisdictions are the creatures of the state and may exercise only those powers expressly granted them by the state—has been a guiding doctrine for more than a century. But after creating local units, states tenaciously try to keep them under control. Three types of oversight are available: judicial, legislative, and administrative.

Judicial oversight comes into play because of Dillon's rule. If a local government's standing is roughly that of a private corporation, then it must from time to time prove in court that it has the power to do what it seeks to do. Legislative oversight, however, has dwindled in recent years. Because of the increasing complexity of urban operations, legislators reluctantly but inexorably have transferred increasing amounts of supervision to the administrative branch of state government. (The following discussion borrows from Adrian 1976:69–75).

Although some states have departments to coordinate state and local affairs, administrative relations between the city and the state are generally on a functional basis. Thus, the state department of education supervises the activities of local school districts and the state department of health, the activities of local health departments. According to Adrian (ibid.:69–70) state government is especially watchful of local activities that involve (1) the expenditure of state grants-in-aid (e.g., in education, health, welfare, highways); (2) those areas of federal grants-in-aid that are administered through

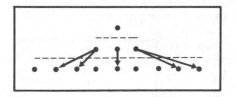

the states but under conditions requiring state supervision of the expenditures (e.g., the building of airports in some states); and (3) those activities in which the state as a whole has a particular interest (e.g., the spread of communicable diseases, law enforcement, finances.)

State bureaucracies have several techniques of supervision. First, they can simply require reports from local communities. Reports warn the state agency when trouble spots (e.g., excessive debts) begin to appear. Second, state agencies can, as the federal government does for them, furnish advice and information. Third, with larger budgets and more specialized equipment and personnel, the state can provide technical aid. Finally, if all else fails, the state can use its coercive power. For example, it can:

Grant or withhold permits for certain things, e.g., to dump raw sewage into a stream under prescribed conditions.

Issue orders, e.g., to build a sewage-treatment plant; or issue rules and regulations that are technically called ordinances, e.g., to prescribe the standards for water supply purification.

Withhold grants-in-aid if standards prescribed by state, or sometimes federal law, are not complied with.

Review decisions of local agencies, e.g., the power of the state tax equalization board to review the determination of local boards and perhaps to order reassessment in extreme situations.

Require prior permission from a state agency, e.g., the power of some state health departments to pass upon the qualifications of local health officer nominees.

Appoint certain local officials or remove them, e.g., the local police chief or sheriff.

Apply substitute administration, and in extreme cases, suspend local self-government altogether.

Interlocal Relations

Given (a) the interrelationship of society due to modern transportation and communication technology and (b) the great number of local governments, it is no surprise to learn that local administrators are meeting with increasing frequency. This subsection examines two ways in which these administrators can work out their problems together: cooperative arrangements and regional councils.

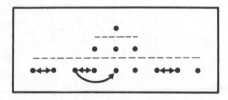

One of the oldest forms of interlocal cooperation is an agreement between two or more adjacent units. A 1972 national survey of nearly 6,000 incorporated municipalities revealed that, of the 2,248 responding, 61 percent had entered into formal or informal agreements for the provision of services to their citizens by other government units or private firms. As population increases, local governmental units—especially the smaller ones—will surely tend to turn over the administration of some of their programs (e.g., water supply) to other local units on a contractual basis.

The basis of informal arrangements, unlike contracts, consists of personal relations among operating officials. Just as the Council of State Governments helps bring state officials together, state associations of municipal officers, facilitate discussion of and cooperation on common problems.

Efforts to merge the government of the central city with surrounding governments—and thereby put government on a more rational administrative basis—have a long, intricate, often checkered history. These efforts seldom end in success. Yet the need for a more regional basis of administration remains.

As a partial solution to the so-called Balkanization of metropolitan areas, the early 1970s witnessed the rapid growth of regional councils. These councils include councils of government, regional planning commissions, and economic development districts. The 1972 Membership Directory of the National Association of Regional Councils lists more than 600 such councils —up 142 from only three years earlier.

Much of the pressure for the creation of this fourth layer of government, as some refer to it, comes in part from federal legislation that recognizes that in metropolitan areas everything connects with everything else, that an action in one community affects another community. In consequence, applications for federal grants and loans under either Section 204 of the Demonstration Cities and Metropolitan Government Act of 1966 or Title IV of the Intergovernmental Cooperative Act of 1968 must be first reviewed by some *areawide* agency. To help regional councils in accomplishing their review, Section 701 of the Urban Planning Assistance Act of 1954 was in 1965 expanded to include these subnational planning agencies as eligible recipients of funds.

Then, in 1969, the Office of Management and Budget published its Circular A-95, which encouraged this kind of intergovernmental planning for an even wider variety of federal programs. Now regional councils would serve as "clearinghouses" for the review of proposed projects within the region. Among the possible improvement projects that a council might first review and then comment upon are airports, water supply and distribution systems, sewage and waste treatment plants, highway and transportation facilities, manpower programs, education systems, and criminal justice systems. For prospective applicants, councils generally maintain catalogs of federal and state assistance programs and help applicants fold their local plans into region wide planning. Figure 3–5 shows the clearance process for the Houston-Galveston Area Council.

FIGURE 3–5
Example of COG Review and Comment Process

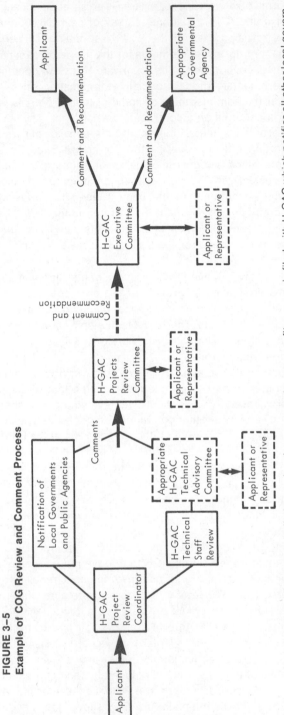

A complete application, usually from a local government or nonprofit agency, is filed with H-GAC which notifies all other local governments and concerned public agencies of the proposal, so that they can gauge its possible effect upon their own plans. Meanwhile, H-GAC technical and advisory committees and staff examine the project for its consistency with overall regional planning, and, if appropriate, confer with the applicant. All comments are presented to the H-GAC project review committee which finally reviews the project subject to any final review by the H-GAC executive committee. An applicant may elect to appear before any of these H-GAC groups. These comments and recommendations are then returned to the applicant and forwarded to the funding agency which makes the ultimate decision on funding. The H-GAC review process itself usually takes 30 days, from the time a completed project application is "logged in" to final review by the H-GAC project review committee.

Source: Houston-Galveston Area Council (1975:4).

ADMINISTRATIVE IMPLICATIONS

It takes no long-run patience or spinning of fine webs to capture and assess the consequences of the complex relationships described in this chapter for administration. In this closing section, therefore, we shall do no more than highlight a few of them.

1. From the standpoint of the public administrator, the picket-fence relationships shown in Figure 3–1 have certain advantages. Professional technicians feel more at ease and have less of a feeling that they will be exploited when they deal with other professionals in the "vertical functional autocracies" rather than with the political leaders at each level. A smoother, more confident relationship results.

Sources of conflict, therefore, are not necessarily between levels of government but rather between professional program administrators and elected policy makers. The public interest groups represent, in Deil Wrights's words, "a reassertion of the executive leadership doctrine and a challenge to the program professional's doctrine of neutral competence." (1974:14) This observation especially applies to the so-called Big Seven: National Governors Conference, Council of State Governments, National Legislative Conference, National Association of County Officials, National League of Cities, U.S. Conference of Mayors, and International City Management Association.

2. Unlike a unitary system, the American intergovernmental system outlined in this chapter provides probably a higher capacity for experimentation and innovation in policy as well as administration. Much of the domestic policy enacted by Congress reflects the pioneering legislative experience of particular states. Similarly, the larger cities and counties of a state can be important innovators of policies later applied statewide.

And this cross-fertilization applies to administrative practices as well as to policy. In Chapters 9 and 11, we shall discuss two management techniques, management-by-objectives and program budgeting. The Office of Management and Budget has attempted to aid states and local governments in their adoption of each. Examples could be multiplied.

3. What are the implications of IGR for the administrator in the federal government? To say that the United States is a large and diverse nation surely must be one of the hoariest platitudes around. Yet federal administrators can not ignore it. In the first place, when a federal agency suggests legislation (as discussed in Chapter 2), it must be sensitive to the unfriendly biases in Congress. Assuming passage, the agency then must be sensitive to the different claimants within state boundaries when administering the policy.

Daniel Elazar (1972:106–7) captured some of this diversity by mapping the United States in terms of three political cultures. He identified three pure types: moralistic, individualistic, and traditionalistic. Moralistic political culture views government as a positive instrument with which the general welfare is secured and politics is seen as righteous activity. The individualistic culture stresses limitations on government and the centrality of private concerns. Traditionalistic culture desires government to maintain existing relationships, and politics becomes the caretaker of established interests. Figure 3–6 shows Elazar's distribution of political cultures within the states. The administrative implications of these political cultures are shown below:

Political Cultures	Possible Implications
1. Moralistic culture	Views bureaucracy as extensive corps at all levels of government;
	Welcomes public services for the good of the commonwealth;
	Coincides with high levels of taxation and government expenditure and generous levels of public service.
2. Individualistic culture	Views governmental bureaucracy as a fetter on private affairs, but also as a resource that public officials can use to further their own goals;
	Supports political machines that carve up public resources and distribute them as payments to individuals;
	Minimizes public services to permit a balance of satisfaction from activities in the private and public sectors;
	Coincides with low levels of taxation, expenditures, and services.
3. Traditionalistic culture	Is most opposed to the growth of bureaucracy as a restraint on the traditional elite;
	Should have smaller and less well paid administrative staffs;
	Opposes all governmental activities except those necessary to maintain the existing power structure;
	Promotes low levels of taxation, expenditures, and services.

Source: Adapted from Sharkansky (1972:197–200) and Morrow (1975:128 and 132).

4. If the federal administrator must seek accommodations with these various interests at the state and local level, then the reverse is just as true. Consider, for example, the proliferation of federal grants, which gave rise to the grantsmanship perspective.

Buried in hundreds of spots all over Washington are piles of money—federal grants that cities can use to buy buses, to repair streets, or to establish health clinics. To obtain it, writes Shafer (1976), a "locality must learn where the money is and then figure out how to qualify for it. None of that is easy, for the federal aid system has grown into an overlapping and confusing maze of more than 1,000 grant, loan programs, and subsidy arrangements."

FIGURE 3–6
The Distribution of Political Cultures within the States

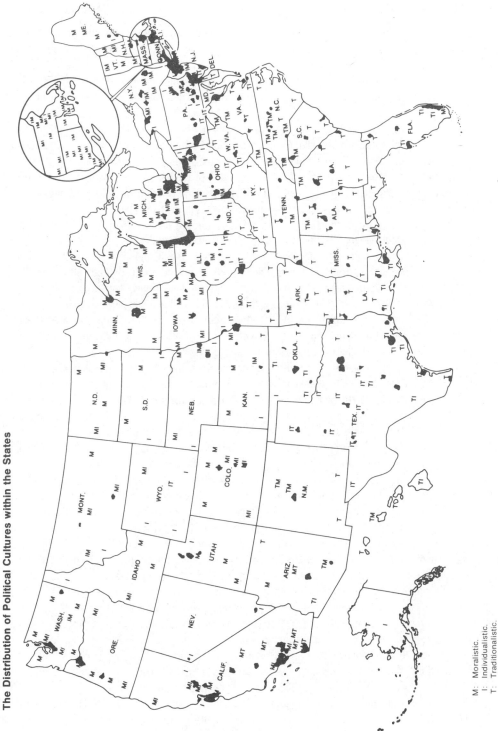

M: Moralistic.
I: Individualistic.
T: Traditionalistic.

Note: Two letters juxtaposed indicates either a synthesis of two subcultures or the existence of two separate subcultural communities in the same area, with the first dominant and the second secondary.

Source: Elazar (1972:106–7).

"Many state and local officials don't learn about the assistance available or learn of it too late to apply," according to a report by the General Accounting Office.

Shafer reports that about 20 states and more than 50 cities have Washington representatives. The cities pay $15,000 to $60,000 a year, depending on whether they want a full-time or part-time representative. "A key assignment, of course, is to sniff out federal grants. Last year, Buffalo hired a man to find more federal funds to help the city with its economic development program. When Buffalo was forced to cut back on some projects last year because of rising borrowing costs, it was able to fill the gap partly with grants ranging from a $440,000 award for a downtown beautification project to a $60,000 grant to hire sculptors to create civic statues."

Not only do individual states and cities have lobbyists in Washington but many special organizations lobby collectively. The Council of State Governments, for instance, speaks for many state positions in Washington. The National Governors' Conference, the National Conference of Chief State School Officers, and National Association of Attorneys General are also important. For cities, the United States Conference of Mayors and the American League of Cities lobby. At the local level, similar agencies exist for collective lobbying of state government. Of course, individual cities can still have their own lobbyists in the state capital.

5. Jurisdictional fragmentation obstructs delivery of services. A private organization has few restrictions on the scope of its operations other than the logic of profit or survival. Not so in the public sector.

A Standard Metropolitan Statistical Area (SMSA) is defined as an integrated economic and social unit with a large population nucleus. Generally consisting of a central city with a population of at least 50,000, and the metropolitan area around it, it may include two or more central cities in one area, although generally within one state. (See Figure 3–7). In any case, "an integrated economic and social unit" does seem to imply a certain commonality of interest between the central city and the suburbs around it. In short, the SMSA provides a logical basis for administration.

In reality, however, the SMSAs are incredibly fragmental. In 1971, the 243 SMSAs harbored some 20,000 units of government. (In 1975, the census bureau reported 272 SMSAs.) To bring the problem into sharper focus, the Chicago metropolitan area may be taken as an example. As of the early 1970s, it was composed of six counties, 114 townships, 250 municipalities, 327 school districts, and 501 special purpose districts. For this metropolitan area, there were 1,198 separate units of government. This represented one local government for every three square miles or one for every 5,550 inhabitants. Not surprisingly, some of these governments have quite limited functions such as mosquito abatement or street lighting.

The Houston SMSA might be given as a second example. There eight governmental agencies try to enforce protection programs for the environment. The eight agencies in Table 3–1 are involved only in monitoring,

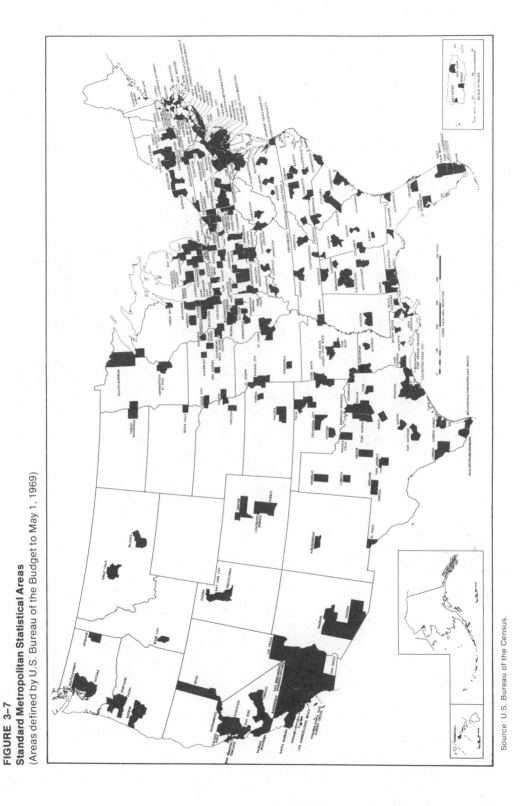

TABLE 3–1
Environmental Control Agencies, Houston

Agency	Function	Staff	1975 Budget
Federal			
Environmental Protection Agency	Administers and enforces federal law and regulations in areas of air and water pollution, solid waste, noise, pesticides, and radiation; formulates control strategies for states and localities; issues permits for waste water discharges; Houston office is surveillance and analysis lab only, with other functions performed out of Dallas regional office.	300* 19† (budget not available)	$ 7,500,000*
State			
Texas Water Control Board	Created by Texas Water Quality Act to develop general overall water quality plan for state; establish standards, requirements, and regulations consistent with federal requirements; research and monitor pollution levels; hold hearings, issue permits for waste discharge, and enforce compliance with these permits.	401 37†	$ 7,300,000 $ 560,000†
Texas Air Control Board	Created by Texas Clean Air Act to develop a general plan for proper control of air resources of state; to formulate regulations for air pollutants in the state; issue permits to new industries regulating emissions; hold hearings; conduct research and monitoring programs.	345 25†	$ 6,500,000 $ 1,700,000†
Local			
Gulf Coast Waste Disposal Authority	Legislatively created to combat water pollution in Harris, Galveston, and Chambers counties; operate regional waste treatment plants for industries and municipalities; issues bonds to help industries acquire pollution control equipment.	110	$ 4,200,000
Harris County Pollution Control Department	Enforcement arm of State Water Quality Board and Air Control Board; samples emissions and effluents from county industries to gather evidence for legal action against violators; takes action as result of outside complaints mostly, although some patrolling done.	42	$ 787,000

City

Air Pollution Division, Health Department	Enforcement of Clean Air Act and city incinerator ordinance; air quality monitoring; review construction permits.	63	$ 746,000
Water Pollution Control Division, Health Department	Enforcement of Water Quality Act within city limits and in the Ship Channel; review discharge plants for construction plans and enforcement of sewer permits; maintain routine network of sampling points for surface water; file annual reports with Water Quality Board.	40	$ 528,000
Waste Water Treatment Division, Public Works Department	Provides treatment of waste water; initiates applications for water board and federal waste discharge permits; reviews requests to add to waste loads; issues industrial permits; sets charges for permit holders; plans new sewer lines, septic tank requirements, and treatment facilities; review city planning plans for proposed developments.	500	$13,846,000

* Data is for all of Texas, except as noted.
† Houston only.
Source: Houston Chronicle (May 26, 1975).

regulating, and carrying out pollution abatement programs; but a swarm of additional agencies have an interest and some authority in environmental programs. Among these we might include U.S. Corps of Engineers, the U.S. Coast Guard, the attorney general's office, the department of health, the parks and wildlife department, the general land office, the agricultural departments of the state, various river authorities, the Harris County district attorney and county attorney, and planning agencies such as the Houston Galveston Area Council and the Houston City Planning Division.

Administratively, this overlap and fragmentation is expensive, confusing, and inefficient. But more macabre examples are available — firemen watching houses burn just outside their jurisdiction and police from one town arresting the plainclothes detectives of another. We need not go on.

In sum: the complexity of intergovernmental relations, like the forces of politics, makes the task of managing the public sector a little more arduous. And, despite major innovations such as the new federalism, I suspect that this will remain true. In the first place, innovations are by no means permanent — indeed, as this is written, new federalism faces an uncertain future.

But, setting aside for a moment innovations such as the new federalism, consider this reality: Whenever any state and local unit participates in activities over which the federal government has final jurisdiction, they become manacled by increasingly stringent federal regulations. (See article.)

Thus, in order to get federal funds for a new library, university presidents must struggle with lengthy applications. Among other things, HEW might want to know how the proposed project "may affect energy sources by introducing or deleting electromagnetic wave sources which may alter manmade or natural structures or the physiology, behavior patterns, and/or activities of 10% of a human, animal or plant population." The questions go on and on, but you get the idea.

Mud and Debt: Village of Walton, N.Y., Is Fed Up With All the Expert Planners and Federal Strings

By Barry Newman
Staff Reporter of The Wall Street Journal
WALTON N.Y. — Memo to the federal government from the people of Walton:
GET OFF OUR BACK!
Walton isn't interested in your paperwork. Walton doesn't want a lot of expert planners. Walton doesn't even want your money — unless you're willing to just hand it over, no strings attached.

Walton doesn't mind some of your less irritating representatives, like the postmaster. But Mayor Charlie Stevens is tired of your meddling: "They tell you what to do about everything. You've got to do this, you've got to do that." Town Supervisor Bruce Budine is fed up with your demands: "It ain't what you want; it's what they dictate to you."

It all comes down to this, says newspaper editor Al Peake: "Most people around here like to do things by themselves."

Walton is 250 miles from Washington as the crow flies and light years away as the bureaucracy trudges. It is a village (pop.

3,744) under a maple canopy, and it is a surrounding town of woods and fields deep in the green valley of the Delaware River's west branch. Walton hasn't grown any bigger or any smaller in anybody's memory The changes that have come here have come, often as not, from the outside.

Like the sewers.

Mud and Debt

Mandated by the federal government, and the biggest construction project Walton has ever seen, the sewer system has left the Victorian village caked in mud and ankle deep in debt. Total every scrap of real estate in the village and you get a value of $21 million. The sewers are costing Walton, Albany and Washington $9 million. It's as if New York decided on a capital project for a neat $20 billion. "We're spending $9 million to cover 3,700 people," Mayor Stevens says. "You have to throw up your hands and just wonder."

As the presidential candidates have been saying, there doesn't seem to be much love for Washington in places like Walton. The feeling here doesn't appear to be rooted in Vietnam or Watergate or the economy. Walton's problem is that the federal govenment can't deal with the kernel of American culture—the small towns and small cities where 65 million people still make their homes.

Walton's personal link to the federal government, theoretically, is something called the Southern Tier East Regional Planning Development Board, 50 miles west of here in Binghamton. (The Southern Tier is the area of New York along the Pennsylvania-New Jersey border.) The board consists of six professional planners, one secretary, one typist and a $125,000 budget from the federal Department of Housing and Urban Development and the Appalachian Regional Commission. Walton, in the foothills of the Catskills, is considered part of Appalachia.

The Arrangement Doesn't Work

The board is one of 12 in New York State that Washington finds a convenient size for parceling out money. But the size isn't quite convenient for Walton. There are eight counties in the Southern Tier East, 150 units of government and 460,000 people. The planners are supposed to furnish the bureaucratic know-how that all those little governments need to get hold of federal grants. Unfortunately, the arrangement doesn't seem to work.

Stan Hayes, the board's director, says the towns and villages in his territory don't know what grants are theirs for the asking, aren't interested in finding out and wouldn't have the capacity to make the programs work anyway. He says the small governments are mainly concerned about remaining independent and don't like the strings attached to most federal dollars. Mr. Hayes likes small towns, but he wonders about them: "It's just a case of whether it's really manageable to maintain any sort of administrative governmental framework at these levels."

A state official, who would rather not be identified, thinks this is how those anti-Washington sentiments are spawned. "The federal government wants to view the country in terms of substate districts," he says. "They don't want to come to New York and look at 1,600 units of government. They can't deal with 1,600 governments."

Mr. Hayes says he rarely has any contact with a village the size of Walton; he talks to county representatives. Walton couldn't care less. "We never have gone out and looked for funds," says Mayor Stevens, a retired A&P manager whose duties include hanging the flag out in front of the village clerk's office. "There's thousands of programs from what I hear. All different types. We feel by the time you got through with them, it would be costing the village more than it should."

It's News to the Mayor

The village budget this year is $575,137. It includes $44,912 in federal revenue sharing. That is as much federal financing as Charlie Stevens would like to see. What about the Southern Tier East Regional Planning Development Board? The mayor never heard of it.

Much of the federal money that does filter into Walton (mainly for welfare and social services) comes through the Delaware County seat of Delhi (pronounced DELL-high), 15 miles away. Walton's first line of defense against the federal bureaucracy, therefore, is to evade the clutches of county bureaucrats. This is the job of Mr. Budine, the town supervisor who is also distribution manager of Walton's Breakstone dairy, where sour cream and cottage cheese are concocted in stainless-steel tanks.

Mr. Budine represents Walton on the county board of supervisors, which runs the county. The part-time board has always gotten along without an elected county executive who, Mr. Budine worries, might take it to mind to tell the towns what to do. County government at the moment is just a loose collection of agencies overseen by the supervisors. "The board has served its purpose very well so far," says Mr. Budine, who is currently resisting the county's efforts to take over Walton's dump.

There is one presence in the county that irks Mr. Budine: the county planner. "That's a bad name in my book," Mr. Budine says. "Maybe the town of Walton don't want to participate in any plans." The planner's name is David Fonseca. He has been in Delhi since 1973 trying to help Delaware County see the future more clearly and trying to help towns apply for money from the federal government. Mr. Fonseca has another project going. Here is how he describes it:

"We are instituting a town-planning advisory program to provide ongoing technical data-gathering and analysis services . . . to create the technical framework for self-realized community development."

Eight of Delaware County's 19 towns are participating in this program. Walton is not. A few weeks ago, the Walton Reporter had a front-page story about Mr. Fonseca; it said there was a move on to "oust" him because of his "arbitrary nature" and because he had spent $64 on retirement presents without getting permission. "At times I get the feeling that people in the area don't think I serve a useful function," Mr. Fonseca says.

The federal government itself does have a few representatives in Walton. There is the postmaster (who will put a Walton postmark on your envelope instead of a bunch of numbers if you want him to) and there are some people with the Agricultural Extension Service, who help out dairy farmers with things like feed tests. This seems to be a sufficient federal presence for most Waltonians, whose contacts with Washington otherwise are limited to filling out forms or contending with an occasional inspector.

Popular Congressman

There is one federal official that nearly everyone in Walton, surprisingly enough, would like to have stop by for a visit, even though the official, Congressman Matt McHugh, is from far-away Ithaca. There are hundreds of towns in his district, but the first-term Democratic congressman has somehow found a way to meet with people in the village of Walton and to chat with farmers in the fields around it.

He even went all the way to the Secretary of the Navy several months ago to complain about the drafting of the town's only obstetrician. The gesture was appreciated, even though it didn't do any good.

"I've been trying to personalize government," Mr. McHugh says. "I realize the people feel a distance. I think it makes sense for the local governments to make decisions. I don't sound like a Democrat, but that's the way I feel."

Nothing Matt McHugh does for Walton, however, could ever bring the federal government closer (or move decision making farther away) than the Water Pollution Control Act of 1972. This is the federal law that says Walton and thousands of villages like it have to put in sanitary sewers by 1977.

There aren't many culprits in Walton dumping waste into the Delaware—only the Breakstone plant (owned by Kraftco Corp., one of the food industry's bigger companies) and the 10% of Walton's homes and businesses that lack septic tanks. If the cleanup had been left to Walton on its own, Mayor Stevens figures the village could have come up with a simple answer. "We would probably have passed an ordinance that would have said, 'Here, all you people that don't have a septic tank or a cesspool, you're going to have to put one in.'"

But the 1972 bill doesn't provide any money for septic tanks or for other individual devices that are fairly inexpensive. The money—and a lot of it—was for sewage-treatment plants. Walton would have to clean up its sewage the government's way. The plant would cost $5.8 million. The federal government would pay $4.35 million and the state $725,000. The village would also kick in $725,000.

Village Pays for Pipes

There was a slight catch: The federal and state governments help pay for the plant, not for the pipes that carry the sewage to it. The village is paying for the pipes. They cost $3.2 million.

Walton has raised the money. The village has never been in debt before. It is in debt now. The pipe is being laid in trenches along every peaceful street. In front of each house the word "sewer" has been written in iridescent paint on the old slate sidewalk where the connecting line will go in. The connecting lines will cost each owner $200. When the plant is finished, in 1978, the village will hire eight people to run it. That's more people than there are on the village police force. Operating the plant and paying off the village debts will cost each home owner $190 a year. The median family income in Walton is under $9,000 a year.

In the Western Auto store on Delaware Street, owner Charles Fiumera says the sewers are a federal "gift" that Walton could have done without. "We needed a sewer system," he says. "We didn't need the one we got." Mr. Fiumera thinks there are people in Walton who can't afford to pay for their sewers. "My mother can't make it," he says. "She can't even start to make it."

Rachel Fiumera came to the United States from Italy in 1908, traveling in steerage aboard a crowded ship. Her father had found a job in Walton, and she has lived in the same house here for 55 years. Mrs. Fiumera is an independent woman. "I pay my own way," she says. But as her son says, she can barely pay her village tax bill on her income from Social Security. Money for her sewer, she says, will be hard to come by.

So she has taken a job. She works 24 hours a week for $2.30 an hour at the Neighborhood Service Center, a store that sells afghans and baby sweaters, stuffed dolls and fresh bread, all made by local women. The store is part of a program to help people like Rachel Fiumera survive in a world of $9 million sewers for places like Walton, N.Y.

The money to support the program comes from the U.S. Department of Labor, in Washington.

Source: *The Wall Street Journal*, July 26, 1976.

NAILING DOWN THE MAIN POINTS

1 Intergovernmental relations is a more satisfactory term than federalism to describe the complete governmental structure in the United States. Federalism places too much emphasis on separation of federal, state, and local government and not enough on the intermediate levels of government.

2 Federalism also obscures the "vertical functional autocracies" that exist in many areas of public policy. In Terry Sanford's view, these "autocracies" form pickets, while the three levels of government form the cross slats. Figure 3–1 provides a close up for the "picket" for health services policy. In this figure we see the various participants at all levels of government who serve to link federal programs with local beneficiaries of the programs. The figure further shows the incredible, though typical, complexity of relationships between governments.

3 Federal grants to states take many forms. Many programs since 1960 establish project grants, rather than distribute funds to states automati-

cally according to a set formula. This approach, most popular during creative federalism (1958–68), leads to a management mess, as the number of grants begins to increase.

4   To alleviate some of this management mess, the federal government began to distribute a portion of the income tax to the states each year with little restriction on how it might be spent.

5   This approach was called revenue sharing and it formed a key part in a broader innovation in intergovernmental relations—new federalism. Other elements in this innovation were: greater discretion to states and local officials, selective decentralization, and greater local responsibility and efficiency.

6   Given the thousands of jurisdictions in the United States, the number of possible and actual intergovernmental relationships is staggering. States and communities constantly vie for grants. States form compacts among themselves. States tenaciously try to keep their cities under control. And cities try to work out their mutual problems through a myriad of cooperative arrangements and some 600 regional councils.

7   These complex relations, not surprisingly, affect the job of the public administrator. The picket fence relationships, for example, lead to smoother relations among like-minded professionals *within* the picket but often to conflict between these professional program administrators and the elected policy makers on the outside. The variety of governments in the United States leads to increased opportunity for experimentation and hence cross-fertilization. But the variety of political cultures and the jurisdictional fragmentation within the U.S. can lead, especially at the national level, to greater complexity in program design and administration. Meanwhile, at the local level, administrators find that accepting federal grants can mean more red tape.

CONCEPTS FOR REVIEW

intergovernmental relations
federalism
layer cake, marble cake, and picket
   fence models
vertical functional autocracies
grants-in-aid, categorical, project,
   and formula based grants
creative federalism
new federalism
general revenue and special revenue
   sharing grants
block grants

selective decentralization
federal regions
federal regional councils
interstate compacts
Dillon's rule
cooperative arrangements
regional councils
circular A-95
political cultures
Standard   Metropolitan   Statistical
   Area

PROBLEMS

1. "Ultimately, the new federalists realized that in order to decentralize they would first have to centralize." What does this statement mean?

2. Some observers think that the policies coordinated by circular A-95 have established the potential for evolving a new level of government. Why do you think they think that? Assuming they are correct, do you view this new level as a good or bad thing? Why?

3. In his seminal study of federalism, Morton Grodzins (1966) concludes that a little chaos is a good thing. What good do you think Professor Grodzins sees in chaos? Is he an anarchist?

4. Write an essay on whether revenue sharing should be continued.

5. Actually, the areas of federal control are, relatively to those of states and their subdivisions, few. List those areas in which you think federal policy control is essential. (For example, some would argue that state and local radio stations could not operate effectively unless they were coordinated with commercial stations.)

6. Some of the major social and economic innovation in the United States have begun with small-scale experiments on the state level. Wyoming, for example, permitted woman suffrage 50 years before the 19th Amendment. Can you think of others? What current state experiments might one day be taken up by the federal government?

7. Discuss further the administrative implications of Elazar's map of political cultures. What shortcoming, if any, do you find in his research?

INTRODUCTION

The last two chapters considered major environmental influences on the public administrator, political processes and intergovernmental relations. This chapter considers a third and final influence, the dominate values of the society in which the administrator works. By values *we mean things or relationships that people would like to have or to enjoy. Obviously, we can not—and fortunately we need not—consider the entire complex of values held by American society.*

Actually, we need concern ourselves only with those values that are relevant to administration. What might these be? Most Americans would agree, I think, that government should be, among other things, responsive, flexible, consistent, stable, honest, prudent, lawful, and accountable. In this chapter, we shall use the word responsibility *as a collective term for values like these, for qualities people would like to see in their government.*

In the first section we shall attempt to spell out how several of these values relate to public administration. In doing so, we should, in effect, be helping to explain what the ideal of responsibility has come to stand for in the literature of public administration. To speak of an ideal *implies an existence not in the actual world but in the mind; it suggests a perfection exceeding what is possible in reality. So it is with the ideal of administrative responsibility. Our discussion, therefore, would be quite incomplete if we did not consider a few of the pitfalls on the road to administrative responsibility in the actual world of governmental administration. Among those discussed in the second section of the chapter are coercion, collusion, distortion, and elitism.*

James Madison knew that administrative respon-

4

Administrative Responsibility

sibility could not be assumed. He knew too that some thought must be given to its protection. "If men were angels, no government would be necessary. If angels were to govern men neither external nor internal controls on government would be necessary. In framing a government which is to be administered by men over men, the greatest difficulty lies in this: you must first enable the government to control the governed; and in the next place to oblige it to control itself. A dependence on the people is, no doubt, the primary control on the government; but experience has taught mankind the necessity of auxiliary precautions" (Federalist Paper No. 51). *Going on the assumption that angels still do not govern, we shall conclude this chapter by giving some thought to external and internal controls designed to help insure administrative responsibility.*

THE IDEAL OF ADMINISTRATIVE RESPONSIBILITY

While neither exhaustive nor definitive, the following subsections do probably cover most of the values implied when the term administrative responsibility is used. (For this approach to defining responsibility, I am indebted to Gilbert 1959.)

Responsiveness

This is the prompt acquiescence by an organization to the popular demands for policy change. Responsiveness can also mean that government does more than merely react to popular demands: in some cases, it can mean that government takes initiatives in the proposal of solutions for problems and even in the definitions of problems.

Organizations might even be classified according to their level of organizational responsiveness. Philip Kotler (1975:40–43) finds four types. First is the unresponsive organization that (a) does nothing to measure the needs, perceptions, preferences, or satisfaction of its constituent publics and (b) even makes it difficult for them to place inquiries, complaints, or suggestions. The prevailing attitude seems to be "we know what is best." Organizations facing a high and continuous demand for customer needs (such as hospitals) often fall into this category.

Second is the casually responsive organization that *does* show an interest in learning about constituent needs and complaints. Thus, as American universities began to experience a decline in student applications in the early 1970s, they began to listen more to students and to encourage faculty-student committees.

Third is the highly responsive organization that uses systematic information collection procedures (e.g., formal opinion surveys and consumer panels); creates formal systems to facilitate complaints and suggestions (e.g., comment cards); and where called for, takes steps to adjust services and procedures. Kotler reports that large firms such as Sears, Procter &

Gamble, General Mills, and General Electric have gone furthest in adopting these characteristics. Sears, for example, uses information from its surveys to chart an attitude index to see if there are *developing* problems requiring attention. Universities, municipalities, and hospitals tend to be rather casual about these matters, although in later chapters a few exceptions are noted. (See Figure 11–3, for example).

Fourth is the fully responsive organization that overcomes the "us" and "them" attitude of most organizations by accepting its publics as voting members. Examples of organization that are seen, in principle at least, as existing for and serving the interest of the constituents are churches and trade unions. Kotler thinks that once the principles of a fully responsive organization are fulfilled, then the members will be ready to lend their support and energy. Consider the recent case of a Canadian university that was searching for ways to build a more active alumni association. "Just sending out newsletters about the school did not suffice to build up alumni pride or interest. It developed the idea of conferring membership status to its alumni, with certain privileges and voting rights on certain issues. Suddenly this group became alive with interest in the school. This gesture proved very meaningful to the alumni, who had hitherto felt that the university was simply using them for their money." (Ibid.:43)

Regarding the overall responsiveness of the federal government, what might be said? Contrary to cliché, a 1975 University of Michigan research team reported that it is reasonably responsive. After surveying 1,431 persons, the team concluded, "Americans like the bureaucrats they deal with pretty well." Table 4–1 shows that for seven major federal programs, in almost every instance, the most frequent rating by the clients was "very satisfied."

TABLE 4–1
National Survey of Quality of Federal Services

	Rating			
	Very Satisfied	*Fairly well Satisfied*	*Somewhat Dissatisfied*	*Very Dissatisfied*
Job Finding	35	26	16	20
Job Training	51	23	19	6
Workmen's Compensation	53	23	5	10
Unemployment Compensation	35	36	14	12
Welfare	27	34	18	10
Hospital/Medical	49	9	24	18
Retirement	64	24	4	3
Total	43	26	13	14

Source: Kahn (1975:69).

Flexibility

In the formulation and implementation of policy (see Chapter 2), administrators should not ignore individual groups, local concerns, or situational differences relevant to the attainment of policy goals.

FIGURE 4-1
Different Approaches to Market Segmentation

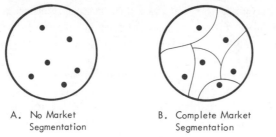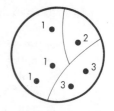

A. No Market
   Segmentation

B. Complete Market
   Segmentation

C. Market Segmentation
   by Income Classes
   1, 2, and 3

Source: Adapted from Kotler (1975:101).

One of the first steps facing an organization is to define the boundaries of a policy's market. "Any market consisting of more than one member will have a structure insofar as the members have different needs, perceptions, and preferences. In most cases, the organization cannot serve the whole market with equal facility and must make a choice among the parts it will serve." (Kotler 1975:94) In certain cases, such as poverty or public health programs, then choices become exceedingly difficult, analytically as well as politically.

Figure 4-1 attempts to illustrate some of the difficulty involved. Figure 4-1A shows a hypothetical market consisting of six persons who share some need in common; no segmentation is required. Figure 4-1B shows the opposite case: here the organization has decided to see each of the six members of this market as being different. But few organizations find it worthwhile to study every individual member and then customize the service to each member's need. Instead, organizations generally search for broad groupings that can be approached as segments. The organization can then choose to deal with all these segments or concentrate on one or a few of them (ibid.:101-2). In Figure 4-1C, the organization has taken this approach and used income class as the basis for segmentation.

Of course, many other variables could have been used other than income. The most important fall into three major classes: geographic (by region, county size, climate, etc.), demographic (by age, sex, race, etc.), and psychographic (usage rate, benefits sought, life style, etc.). When governments ignore these kind of complexities in the formulation and implementation of policy, they tend to fail the standard of flexibility and thereby become a little less responsive.

Competence

Administrative responsibility also requires that the formulation and implementation of public policy should be guided by recognized objective standards, where they are available. Administrative action should be prudent rather than hasty and should display care for the consequence rather than negligence. Competence also requires that appropriate expertise should be sought whenever necessary. One character in the film *Electric Blue-Glide* capsulated this value when he said, "The worst form of corruption is incompetency."

Like flexibility, competence can often be a difficult value to realize. Do "objective standards" of performance even exist in the more controversial areas of public policy? Further, how does the government use fully the knowledge of experts without allowing these specialists to set policy itself? Experts, as a popular saying goes, should be "on tap but not on top." Finally, given the incredible fragmentation of U.S. government at all levels, how can contradictions in policy be avoided. As one garrulous observer puts it: "The priorities of the bureaucracy are sometimes difficult to figure out. It spends millions of dollars building roads through parks and forests that other federal agencies are spending millions allegedly to preserve. When the Indians rebelled at Wounded Knee in 1973, more than 400 federal officials showed up at that tiny village. But when it was discovered that traders licensed by the Bureau of Indian Affairs were cheating and defrauding the 130,000 reservation Navajos not one bureaucrat could tear himself away from Washington to look into the matter." (Sherrill 1974:200)

Due Process

To the lawyer, due process connotes something sufficiently special that it can not properly be exhausted in any other value, though it does overlap some of them. The concept of due process is stated for the federal courts in the Fifth Amendment and for the state courts in the Fourteenth. It assumes that no citizen shall "be deprived of life, liberty, or property without due process of law." In short, it is an assurance that the government will be administered by laws, not by the arbitrary will of people who condemn without a public hearing.

While the concept of due process originally had to do with criminal law, it was later extended to administration. Today it serves as a major limitation on administrative discretion. Indeed, the courts have evolved a set of rules to govern the procedures of agencies. Such agencies must have jurisdiction over the matters with which they deal; must give fair hearings to all persons affected by their rulings; must give adequate notice of such hearings well in advance of the dates when they are held. Their officers must be impartial, with no personal interest in the questions upon which they are called to pass. Their decisions must be based upon substantial evidence. In the orders they issue, specific findings of the law and fact must be set forth. The persons affected by such orders must be given an opportunity to appeal. This is due process, in the *procedural* sense of the term.

While such safeguards against arbitrary administrative action are clearly in the public interest, administrative agencies still might become so bound by procedural requirements that operations would be impaired. This danger is illustrated by two decisions handed down by the U.S. Supreme Court.

> In *Morgan* v. *U.S.* (1936) where the Secretary of Agriculture had issued an order on the advice of a trial examiner, following extensive hearings, the Court complained that the secretary had not himself read each of the 13,000 pages of testimony and 1,000 pages of exhibits in the transcript.
>
> In *Morgan* v. *U.S.* (1948) the Court invalidated one of the secretary's orders on the grounds that the respondents had not received a copy of the trial examiner's intermediate report in time to use it in preparing their final brief.

In the name of due process, the courts have gone on to interest themselves not only in form but also in *substance*. Instead of confining themselves to determining whether administrative orders were based upon sufficient evidence, they have arrived at independent judgments by going into evidence themselves. In recent years, however, substantive due process has gradually been abandoned.

Accountability

A good synonym for this term is "answerability." The organization must be answerable to someone or something outside themselves. When things go wrong, someone must be held responsible.

A frequently heard charge is that the bureaucracy is faceless and that, consequently, affixing blame is difficult. As the chairman of a special presidential task force put it, "Everybody is somewhat responsible for everything, and nobody is completely responsible for anything. They spend their time coordinating with each other and shuffling paper back and forth, and that's what causes all the red tape and big staffs in the department. Nobody can do anything without checking with seven other people." (*Wall Street Journal,* September 30, 1970)

Accountability can also refer to the managerial processes of "direction and control." Perhaps the best known quote to illustrate the level of control in the federal bureaucracy came from Pres. Franklin D. Roosevelt. Roosevelt reportedly had this exchange with one of his aides (cited in Sherrill 1974:203):

> When I woke up this morning, the first thing I saw was a headline in the *New York Times* to the effect that our navy was going to spend $2 billion on a ship-building program. Here I am, the commander in chief of the navy having to read about that for the first time in the press. Do you know what I said to that?
>
> (Aide): "No, Mr. President."
>
> I said: "Jesus Chr-rist!"

Honesty

When the values of Americans are surveyed, honesty inevitably ranks either at the top or quite close to it. Not surprisingly, governments have devoted considerable effort to enforcing it—although disagreeing widely on the means. In light of the war in Southeast Asia, the resignation of a president, and the investigations of the FBI and CIA, I suspect ethics-in-government will continue to be a major concern.

One dimension of honesty is candor, which, as used here, refers to the notion that policy making and administration should be at some stage open to public scrutiny. Gilbert (1959:376) elaborates: "the political and governmental system in general should reach and decide the merits of issues rather than obscure them through personal or procedural obfuscation. A further requirement might include that of reasoned justification of governmental decisions. Though logically three separate notions, they are lumped together here since they all have presumed value for public discussion, education, and the sense of individual 'responsibility' for public policy."

Some theorists believe that total candor can "overheat" the political system. Certainly, many of the newer rational, analytical tools (see Chapter 6) used in governmental planning require that the merits of an issue be made explicit and that the preferred alternatives be justified. To that extent, they can tend to increase the probability of open conflict. In an earlier age, these kinds of questions were lost in a murky sea of political wheeling and dealings; then it was harder for outside groups and individuals to see exactly how they would be affected by the outcome of the process. This line of reasoning may or may not be valid (cf. Bell 1967). In either case, greater candor in government seems worth a little political conflict.

PITFALLS ON THE WAY TO RESPONSIBILITY

In the opening section, we distinguished five values or concerns generally linked to the term administrative responsibility. They were responsiveness, flexibility, competence, due process, accountability, and honesty. But as T. S. Eliot reminds us: "Between the idea / and the reality / Between the motion / and the act / Falls the Shadow." In this section, therefore, we must pause to consider how far the practice of public administration is from realizing the theory of administrative responsibility. Our discussion centers around four major shortcomings: collusion, coercion, distortion, and elitism.

Collusion

In Chapter 2, we saw much policy making taking place in the political subsystems composed of congressional subcommittees, relevant agencies, and special interest groups. All too often these subsystems are impervious to higher political officials such as the president or the entire Congress, who would appear to have a broader perspective and more clearly represent more the public interest.

Collusion in some instances might be too strong a word, since frequently agencies, over time, come to see certain special interest as their "clients." Hence, the agency comes to feel it has a *legitimate* responsibility to protect that interest. This pattern, unfortunately, is particularly likely to be found in regulatory agencies.

Possibilities for collusion, however, are not limited to national government. In fact, one can identify a number of areas that have potential opportunity for corruption and that should be carefully watched by local officials: zoning contracting out of municipal services, purchase of supplies, liquor licenses, and building and construction permits.

Courage in government takes many forms. President Kennedy's *Profiles in Courage,* for example, dealt with a rather dramatic form: abiding by principle in an unpopular cause. In public administration, however, courage is more frequently required to avoid small favors. Paul Appleby (1952:130) relates a relevant story about George Washington. Washington told a friend seeking an appointment: "you are welcome to my house; you are welcome to my heart . . . my personal feelings have nothing to do with the present case. I am not George Washington, but president of the United States. As George Washington, I would do anything in my power for you. As president, I can do nothing."

Exactly how much collusion exists today is a question I am not prepared to answer. But the following exchange between Senator Proxmire and the former head of the Federal Energy Administration is revealing. Moreover, it has what I miss in much contemporary writing on the subject of collusion — a sense of self-qualification.

SENATOR PROXMIRE: Mr. Sawhill, to clear the air, I am going to ask a question which I think is in the mind of many, and it might be useful for you to say whatever you would like to say in connection with that.

There have been many statements I suppose some true and some false, that your resignation was caused, at least in part, by pressures from the oil industry. Many of us in the past have been concerned that in all administrations, Democratic as well as Republican, the oil and gas industry has had too much power in industry. They run the office of oil and gas. They have a powerful influence over the regulatory agencies and tax-writing committees in Congress.

Let me ask two questions. First, do you believe the oil industry exercises undue influence in government?

MR. SAWHILL: Well, it certainly does exercise a lot more influence than I realized when I came down here as a businessman to work in the government. There is no question that there is a tremendous oil lobby here in Washington that I had not previously been aware of. Whether that constitutes undue influence or not is a little difficult for me to say, but it is a very considerable influence and something that I think should be watched carefully.

SENATOR PROXMIRE: Would you like to say a little bit more about how considerable it is, in view of your experience, what effect it had on your ability to do what you feel is in the public interest?

MR. SAWHILL: I felt very strongly that FEA had to be a very open agency, and from the beginning we adopted policies to insure that we could regulate in the public interest, not in the interest of any particular group. We developed freedom-of-information regulations, for example, which were among the most stringent in the government. We developed conflict-of-interest regulations and standards of conduct for our employees, which went so far as to require that our employees not be permitted to have lunch with anyone connected with an industry that our agency was regulating and to have that person pay for their lunch.

We developed lobbying regulations which required lobbyists to register with the FEA and required all top management of FEA to record any contacts they had with people that had regulatory matters before the agency and to make those contacts and conversations public.

Finally, I published my financial statement which turned out to be not very interesting and said that I would not go to work for the oil industry when I left the government, purely to try to set the tone and pattern for the agency. And we, incidentally, in forming advisory committees, were careful to include not only industry members, but consumer and environmental groups on these committees so that we could have an open and public discussion of issues before the agency with all groups represented.

I feel very strongly that a regulatory agency regulating something as sensitive and as important to the lives of every American as energy has got to be run in this fashion, and I hope that at least I will leave a legacy of this kind of management in the FEA because I think it would be very unfortunate if we lost this, and I would hope that the Congress would continue to encourage this kind of open decision-making. We certainly made a lot of mistakes, but they were not mistakes or errors that were committed because we were being unduly influenced by one group or another. They were frankly simply administrative errors and problems that are always encountered in starting a new agency.

But I think it very important that the Congress pay careful attention to a regulatory agency like FEA, particularly one that is not independent of the executive branch, but resides in the executive branch because there is always a danger that one group or another can capture the agency and exercise undue influence.

SENATOR PROXMIRE: Well, I think that is

excellent advice, and I certainly commend you on your conduct. I think there has been a pattern which Dean Landis of Harvard Law School observed in 1960 when Landis was asked by President-elect Kennedy at that time before Kennedy took office to study the regulatory agencies, and Landis found that when they were first started, they often operated with considerable force and in the public interest, but quite regularly they were taken over by the industries that they were designed to regulate.

At the same time, there has been talk, and there has been some documentation, that a large number of the people who make policy in the energy agency are from the industry, and that most of them go back to the industry after they leave the agency. Is that not the case?

MR. SAWHILL: We have not had anybody that I know of that has left the agency and gone back to the industry. Of course, I publicly said that I would not do that and tried to set a standard of conduct for the other employees in the agency.

We have some employees that have come from the industry, but we have employees that have come from consumer groups and environmental groups and all other——

SENATOR PROXMIRE: In proportion, though, in positions of the most significance, does the industry not have a very considerable influence in this way. Are not many of the people in the top levels from the industry?

MR. SAWHILL: No; I would not say that. Of the senior management in the agency, of the ten to fifteen people that most closely work with me, there are two or three that are identified with the industry, but most of the rest have varied backgrounds. Some are economists; some are engineers; some are lawyers. I do not think there is an undue industry influence, but I think it is something that we have to continue to watch carefully.

SENATOR PROXMIRE: Now you said, in response to my initial question on this, that you were surprised at the power and force of the oil lobby. How did it demonstrate itself? Can you give us two or three examples of how they were able to make their will effective?

MR. SAWHILL: In our agency they were not able to make their will effective, but I was just surprised at the tremendous number of people here in Washington that were connected in one way or another with the oil industry?

SENATOR PROXMIRE: In your agency they were not able to make—well, certainly some of the decisions were made with respect to, for example, the price of old oil, et cetera.

MR. SAWHILL: That was not made by our agency, initially anyway.

SENATOR PROXMIRE: Well, there was one in which your agency had an interest and could have had a considerable influence in?

MR. SAWHILL: Yes; but that decision was made by the Cost of Living Council, and as you will recall, President Nixon——

SENATOR PROXMIRE: Were you not consulated in that?

MR. SAWHILL: I was not, no, on that decision. That was made prior to the time our agency was formed.

SENATOR PROXMIRE: Then I would like to ask you, did the oil industry have any influence in your resignation?

MR. SAWHILL: Well, I do not know. I know that various newspaper people around town have told me that the oil industry lobbied heavily against me. No question I took a lot of actions that were particularly counter to the interests of the major oil companies. Some of the independent oil companies, I think, actually supported me, because we were trying very hard to protect that independent sector of the industry, so I have no direct knowledge that this was done. I only have indirect knowledge that there may have been——

SENATOR PROXMIRE: What indirect knowledge do you have?

MR. SAWHILL: Well, as I say, there were a number of newspaper reporters, for example, that told me that they had understood that there was heavy lobbying against me.

Source: U.S. Congress, Joint Economic Committee (1975:22–24).

Coercion

A second pitfall on the road to administrative responsibility is coercion. And how it emerges is itself interesting. Democracy can not exist without a modicum of consensus, for the modern administrative state has yet to adopt the principle of George Barnard Shaw's friend: do whatever you want, as long as you don't scare the horses. Consequently, the administrative state has what some observers might call an alarming number of programs and techniques for dealing with those who fail to share in the consensus, who dissent from it, and who, in some instances, advocate covertly as overtly its destruction. Among these sometimes coercive programs and techniques, we might include loyalty oathes, restriction on speech and assembly, lie detector tests, wire tapping, data banks, and behavior modification drugs. These activities are not always easily reconciled with the value of due process.

This quest for consensus also goes on *within* government. The resulting pressures sometimes require that the administrator ask whether he or she is ultimately accountable to the political executive or the Constitution, laws, and the people when the two are not compatible.

Distortion

The purposes of an agency's public relations program are (1) to inform and (2) to constructively influence the public. And with both, the risk of distortion needs to be recognized.

1. The importance of keeping the public informed can not be overemphasized; and an informed public is an essential ingredient of democracy. James
Madison put it eloquently: "A popular government without popular information, or the means of acquiring it, is but the Prologue to a Farce or a Tragedy:
or perhaps, both. Knowledge will forever govern ignorance: And a people
who mean to be their own Governors, must arm themselves with the power
which knowledge gives."

Yet, in practice, some policy makers have found an easy justification for
both secrecy and deception. Ordinary citizens, they believe, cannot understand complex decisions like the following:

Do aerosol cans affect the ozone content of the stratosphere?

Does underground nuclear bomb testing produce serious earthquakes
and tidal waves?

Are we spending too much on nuclear energy research and not enough
on solar energy?

Is our level of defense spending really adequate in comparison with the
Soviet Union?

What should we do about the economy? What is the proper trade-off
between inflation and unemployment?

The apparent inability of the people to understand these complex problems gives the policy makers—so the argument runs—a kind of "right to
deception." Consider the case of the Atomic Energy Commission, which
for at least ten years repeatedly sought to suppress studies by its own scientists that found nuclear reactions were more dangerous than was officially
acknowledged. The details of the commission's efforts to avoid publishing
reports on potential hazards emerged in 1974 from an examination by the
New York Times of hundreds of memos and letters written by commission
and industry officials since 1964. One key study, which was suppressed,
found that if a major reactor accident did occur, nearly 45,000 persons
could be killed and the disaster could cover an area possibly the size of
Pennsylvania. (Burnham 1974) But as Walter Lippmann noted many years
earlier, it is sophistry to think that in a free country certain men have some
sort of inalienable or constitutional rights to deceive their fellow men like

this. "There is no more right to deceive than there is a right to swindle, to cheat, or to pick pockets."

2. The second objective in a public relations program, besides simply providing information, is to influence the public. As we said in Chapter 2, the effective administrator is the one who can attain his agency's goals and this task, in turn, frequently *requires* the mobilization of public support. And in a few instances, the agency must actually *persuade* the public to take certain action; e.g., participate in immunization programs, use seat belts, and stop smoking.

No official of the federal government has the words "public relations" in his or her title. So measuring the scope of the government's public relations activities becomes difficult. Nevertheless, in 1970, using a fairly narrow definition of public relations, the Office of Management and Budget sent out questionnaires to departments and agencies, asking them to report back the cost and scope of their information programs. From the replies, OMB estimated that the executive branch employed 6,144 people at a cost of $161 million a year. (Three years earlier, however, an Associated Press team estimated public relations costs at $425 million a year, but this figure included $200 million spent by defense contractors and $125 million in government printing costs.)

According to a former press secretary to Attorney General Robert F. Kennedy, government public relations personnel can be divided into three categories. First in the policy-level advisor, who advises his boss on the public information consequences of policy. Second is the "faithful mechanic," who gets the news out, handles the press, leaks stories, and builds good relations with interest groups. Last is the "defensive PR" man. He does nothing but answer questions. . . . He gives minimal answers, tries not to be quoted, and speaks on background. He is evasive and doesn't return telephone calls. He does the worst job for his boss" (cited in Wise, 1973:304).

William Baroody is a good example of the second type. In 1975, he was in charge of the White House Office of Public Liaison, a "little-noted but extremely sophisticated operation designed to sell Gerald Ford's policies to the people with clout: leaders of special interest groups." Each month Mr. Baroody brought top administrative officials face-to-face in closed door dialogue with more than 1,000 interest group leaders — "everybody from environmentalist and welfare-rights activists to industrialists and labor leaders." These groups were also offered the chance to influence, as well as hear, White House policy makers. (Farney 1975)

Public relations operations at the local level, while obviously smaller in scope, are basically no different. Consider, for example, the following objectives established for the community information offices in Saginaw, Michigan: (1) to assist in the translation of public opinion into concrete programs by passing on to the city administration and city council citizen opinions, suggestions, and complaints, so that they may become the basis for building realistic new programs and for making necessary modifications

in ongoing programs; (2) to clarify and explain the policies of the city government; (3) to make information available to citizens about various services provided by the city so that they may fully utilize and gain the greatest benefit from the services; and (4) to educate citizens by providing them with the facts relating to the government activities, policies, and procedures, as well as with an understanding of those facts. (Fowles, 1974:280)

Public relations at the local level is not, however, the sole responsibility of such community relations officers. The chief administrator certainly has an important role. As Desmond L. Anderson put it: "The city manager has an inescapable obligation for public relations, an obligation that is just as compelling as his responsibilities for sound public finance, effective personnel systems, and other areas of management. He must instigate training for employees in all areas of public relations. . . . It is the city manager's job, using all means available to fashion improvement in the image of the city. He sets the pace for the entire municipality" (ibid.:282).

Like the chief administrator, the employee in municipal government has a public relations role. Accordingly, supervisors should make sure that the rank and file are given a preliminary orientation and then keep up to date about the activities of their government. If not, it is unlikely they will be able to answer accurately questions from the public and thus avoid the negative feelings generated by the dreaded runaround.

But regardless of the level of government, when improperly used, public relations becomes a threat to the ideal of administrative responsibility. For example, it can be used as a substitute for failed policy. While the Vietnam War abounds with examples of such misuse, let us consider a domestic example.

Our story begins in 1971, when Harry Treleaven, Jr., a highly successful public relations man, was hired by the new Secretary of Interior, Rogers Morton, to use his Madison Avenue expertise to "streamline" and "improve the image" of the department. (Wise 1973:295–301) Subsequently, Treleaven turned in an 85-page report, which, among other things, described the goals of the Office of Information of the Secretary of Interior. Among the objectives listed were: "to head off or conteract adverse publicity resulting from events and activities that could put the department in a bad light (such as mine disasters, accidents in National Parks, etc.).''

Treleaven's reference to mine disasters was a hint of his next project: a full-scale all-media communications program to convince coal miners that their own carelessness is a major cause of mine disasters and deaths. Observes Daniel Wise (1973:300): ''While mine owners like to promote the theme that carelessness causes disasters, negligence by the mine operators and failure of the Bureau of Mines to enforce federal safety standards are much more important causes. On the floor of the House, Rep. Ken Hechler, the West Virginia Democrat, ripped into the Treleaven proposal. Hechler noted that the head of the General Accounting Office, the congressional auditor of government spending, had estimated that about 90 percent of coal mine accidents ''are due to failures of the mine operators rather than to the failure of the miner himself.''

Another questionable use of public relations is to insure a long life for an agency by drumming up more jobs to do. For example, in 1976, 1.7 million American third graders were busy coloring pictures of a bug-eyed cartoon character named Energy Ant. The coloring books had been provided to schools by Energy Ant's creator, the Federal Energy Administration. Although the Arab oil embargo is long gone, the agency is still around—big and getting bigger. Reports the *Wall Street Journal* (House 1976): ''Coming soon is a second cartoon book. There are plans to put Energy Ant into television commercials and onto cereal boxes. The agency even is seeking trademark protection for him.''

''The agency spends much time and, well, energy, in such self-promotion. Among other things, its 112 publicists have cranked out nearly 1,000 press releases—all computerized for speedy retrieval. It also has a growing constituency, including many oil companies supposedly regulated by the FEA—companies that would hate to see it abolished.''

Elitism

In addition to the pitfalls of collusion, coercion, and distortion, there is yet a fourth on the road to the democratic morality ideal. And its recognition here is no revelation, for a number of observers have pointed to the omnipresent possibility of the emergence of a faceless, amoral elite of experts who run the government. The threat such a group poses to the ideal of administrative responsibility comes in many guises.

In 1954 the French sociologist, Jacques Ellul (1964:275) was arguing the use of technique—i.e., any complex of standardized means for attaining predetermined results—subverts democracy and tends to create new aristocracy. ''In the administrative domain, the intervention of a technique of organization and mechanization results in the creation . . . of two classes very far removed from one another. The first, numerically small, understands the means to conceive, organize, direct, and control: the second,

infinitely more numerous, is composed of mere executants. The latter are hacks that who understand nothing of the complicated techniques they are carrying out. It is not conceivable that the normal operation of democracy would be acceptable to those who exercise this technical monopoly; which, moreover, is a hidden monopoly in the sense that its practitioners are unknown to the masses."

Joining into the spirit of things, Theodore Roszak (1973:35–36) argued that technology is an "extraordinarily potent means of subverting democracy from within its own ideals and institutions. It is a citadel of expertise dominating the high ground of urban-industrial society, exercising control over a social system that is utterly beholden to technicians and scientists for its survival and prosperity." Similarly, another American, Bertram Gross (1970), sees the rise of a new form of totalitarianism which he calls "Techno-Urban Facism, American Style." More specifically: "A managed society rules by a faceless and widely dispersed complex of warfare-welfare-industrial-communications-police bureaucracies caught up in developing a new-style empire based on technocratic ideology, a culture of alienation, multiple scapegoats, and competing control networks."

One need not really strain to such Orwellian lengths to make the simple point that expertise and elites can threaten the values of administrative responsibility. The emergence of professionalism in government and the insensitivity of bureaucratic elites to minorities are issues of today not tomorrow.

Specifically, the growth of professionalism raises at least four major concerns. First, certain elite professions (e.g., law, medicine, and science) tend to dominate the governance of many bureaus and other public agencies. Second, at the expense of general government agencies such as the civil service, professional groups dominate in matters of recruitment, selection, and advancement (see Chapter 13). Third, professional specializations are becoming narrower. Fourth, organized public employees in professional and subprofessional fields increasingly press for changes in public policy related to their particular fields of endeavor and thereby infringe upon the prerogatives of elective and appointed officials.

According to Fredrich C. Mosher (1968:132–33), the trend toward professionalism inside or outside of government will not soon be reversed or even slowed. The best check on professionalism, therefore, appears to be the educational process through which the professionals are produced and later refreshed (in continuing educational programs). This process can, Mosher suggests, be studied and conceivably changed. "The needs for broadening, for humanizing, and in some fields for lengthening professional education programs may in the long run prove more crucial to governmental response to societal problems than any amount of civil service reform."

The litmus test of the responsiveness and flexibility of a government might be how well it treats those at the bottom of the social order. To survey the contemporary circumstances of minorities and to examine the minority-related program of the 1960s and 1970s are objectives beyond the scope of a work of this kind. But to consider briefly how the cultures of chicanos and blacks differ from that of the dominant society could be fruitful if it lead to a little better appreciation of the many viewpoints of the various segments of the chicano and black population in the United States (see box).

Unfortunately, too many administrators for various reasons have not given consideration to these matters. They tend to view other groups strictly in terms of their own culture, a tendency sociologists call *ethnocentricism*. Regardless of the label, it smacks of insensitive elitism and retards the values of responsiveness and flexibility, since the thrust for racial identity in certain segments of the population is ignored.

Elitism, Ethnocentricism, and Administration

Roughly, the world-view of nearly all nonminority Americans has the following values, assumptions, and preferences:

Individualistic: It is natural for individuals to compete and to seek to satisfy themselves through material gain.

Faustian: It is natural for man to struggle against and master nature.

Objective: Problems and situations are to be analyzed by means of tangible evidence ("hard facts") and the scientific method.

In contrast, the chicano world-view has origins in the Indian world-view that places individualism on a social rather than economic basis and considers human life inextricably bound up with nature. In addition to this affinity with their Indian forbearers, chicanos want to recapture their unique Spanish-Indian heritage and

thereby making *"la Raza"* an effective political force. Writes Armando Rendon in *Chicano Manifesto* (1971:46): "Our ideals, our way of looking at life, our traditions, our sense of brotherhood and human dignity, and the deep love and trust among our own are truths and principles which have prevailed in spite of the gringo, who would rather have us remade in his image and likeness: materialistic, cultureless, colorless, monolingual, and racist. Some Mexican-Americans have sold out and become agringados . . . like the Anglo in almost every respect. Perhaps that has been their way of survival, but it has been at the expense of their self-respect and of their people's dignity."

Unlike the chicanos, who tend to envision a multiminority cultural pluralism, the blacks emphasize black culture as a prelude to a more far reaching social change. Blacks, however, are equally sensitive to the necessity of maintaining one's identity. As Stokely Carmichael (1971:351) put it: "We will no longer accept the white man's definition of ourselves as ugly, ignorant, and uncultured. We will recognize our own beauty and our own culture and will no longer be ashamed of ourselves, for a people ashamed of themselves cannot be free."

While several black writers such as James Baldwin and Ralph Ellison have brilliantly captured the ambiance of the black in urban America, at least one white writer, Norman Mailer (1959), has come close, "Any Negro who wishes to live must live with danger from his first day, and no experience can ever be casual to him, no Negro can saunter down a street with any real certainty that violence will not visit him on his walk. The cameos of security for the average white: mother and the home, job and the family, are not even a mockery to millions of Negroes; they are impossible. The Negro has the simplest of alternatives: live a life of constant humility or ever-threatening danger. In such a pass where paranoia is as vital to survival as blood, the Negro had stayed alive and begun to grow by following the need of his body where he could. Knowing in the cells of his existence that life was war, nothing but war, the Negro (all exceptions admitted) could rarely afford the sophisticated inhibitions of civilization, and so he kept for his survival the art of the primitive, he lived in the enormous present, he subsisted for his Saturday night kicks, relinquishing the pleasures of the mind for the more obligatory pleasures of the body, and in his music he gave voice to the character and quality of his character and quality of his existence, to his rage and the infinite variations of joy, lust, languor, growl, cramp, pinch, scream, and despair."

For more than 40 years, anthropologist Edward T. Hall (1976) has interpreted other cultures for business and government. According to Hall, some cultures are high-context, others low-context. In the former category, Hall includes Chinese, Japanese, Arab, and American black cultures; in the latter, white western cultures, which certainly includes middle class America. One of the most salient differences between the two is found in communication: In high context cultures, less information is carried in the verbal part of a message since more is in the context (e.g., social status of sender). In low context cultures, *words* carry most of the information; messages are quite explicit.

"Since much of culture operates outside our awareness, frequently we don't even know that we know. We pick them up in the cradle. We unconsciously learn what to notice and what not to notice, how to divide time and space, how to walk and talk and use our bodies, how to behave as men and women, how to relate to other people, how to handle responsibility. . . . What we think of as 'mind' is really internalized culture." These different assumptions work to make misunderstanding between people likely and destructive. Hall gives specifics:

". . . take the matter of the way we listen or show that we are paying attention when someone is talking. I once got a young black draftsman a job with an architectural firm, where he almost got fired. He did his work well but his employer complained about his attitude. This mystified me until once when I was talking to him and noticed I wasn't getting any feedback. He just sat there, quietly drawing. Finally I said, "Are you listening?" He said, "Man, if you're in the room, I'm listening. You listen with your ears." In their own mode, interacting with each other, ethnic blacks who know each other don't feel they have to look at each other while talking. They don't nod their heads or make little noises to show that they're listening the way whites do" (ibid: 74).

"Blacks also pay more attention than we do to nonverbal behavior. I once ran an experiment in which one black filmed another in a job interview. Each time something significant happened, the watching black started the camera. When I looked at those films, I couldn't believe my eyes. Nothing was happening! Or so I thought. It turned out that my camera operator was catching — and identifying — body signals as minor as the movement of a thumb, which foreshadowed an intention to speak. Whites aren't so finely tuned" (ibid: 97).

Administrators are apt to mark high-context ethnic neighborhoods as slums, and classify them for renewal because they do not see the order behind what appears to be disorder. "Live, vital, cohesive ethnic communities are destroyed. To make way for a university in Chicago, planners wiped out a Greek and Italian neighborhood, over strong protests. The scars haven't healed yet. It is important to stress that when you scatter such a community, you're doing more than tear down buildings; you're destroying most of what gives life meaning, particularly for people who are deeply involved with each other. The displaced people grieve for their homes as if they had lost children

and parents. To low-context whites, one neighborhood is much like the next. To high-context people, it is something else again" (ibid.).

And what does all this mean for the public administrator? First, most governmental programs designed to aid minorities are based on the dominate world-view. To participate in these programs as a route to progress, minorities must perforce cast aside part of their very identity. Thus they are placed in a dilemma—the implications of which can be fully measured by income and employment statistics. While it is unlikely that public administrators can easily resolve the dilemma, it is inexcusable for them not to recognize it.

EXTERNAL AND INTERNAL CONTROLS

A multitude of measures have been taken to avoid the pitfalls of collusion, coercion, distortion, and elitism. As a simple framework for discussion, these measures are divided into four main categories: internal formal, internal informal, external formal, and external informal. No writers advocate exclusive reliance upon any *one* of these four. There is, then, no school of thought to be found *entirely* within any one of the cells in the diagram or in either the vertical or horizontal columns (Gilbert 1959:382):

	Internal	*External*
Formal	Chief executive officer	Legislature Courts
Informal	Professional codes Representative bureaucracy Public interest Moral philosophy	Interest group representation Citizen participation

Of course, use of the four descriptive categories entails difficulties of definition and classification; but, on the balance, it does seem a helpful means of distinguishing and analyzing various institutional approaches and proposals for insuring administrative responsibility. The distinction between formal and informal, though not always easy to draw, is roughly this: informal relationships are those not explicitly provided for in the Constitution. The distinction between internal and external is that between the executive branch of government and the top executives who head it up on the one hand

and the rest of society and its political apparatus on the other. As Gilbert notes, it is similar to Barnard's distinction between the organization proper and its "consumers."

Since the internal formal measures available to a president were touched on in the previous chapter and will be further developed in Chapters 8 and 9, nothing need be said here. Likewise, the external formal measures available to Congress (e.g., oversight) and the external informal influence by interest groups were noted in Chapter 2 and should require no reinteration. This leaves us with six topics to consider: the courts, citizen participation, professional codes, representative bureaucracy, public interest, and moral philosophy. The last named control we shall consider in some detail.

Judicial Control

Many, particularly members of the legal profession, hold that one of the principal arrangements designed to monitor administrative decisions that affect individuals, private organizations and local communities, is the national court system. After exhausting administrative remedies, individuals in many cases have the opportunity to obtain a *judicial review* of the administrative decision.

The Administrative Procedure Act of 1946, in fact, provides that every executive agency action for which no adequate court remedy is provided, shall be subject to review by an appropriate national court. The court, in turn, may set aside any agency action that entailed abuse of discretion, excess of statutory or constitutional authority, or improper proceedings; or that was unwarranted by the facts. To see how the judicial review process can work, see the article, "The Hunger Lawyers."

The Hunger Lawyers

Ron Pollack's small New York City law firm consistently wins the biggest money judgments in the nation. Yet Pollack and the four other young lawyers (average age: 31) who work with him do not handle the traditionally lucrative kinds of cases— personal-injury litigation, treble-damage civil antitrust suits, defending giant corporate clients. Ron Pollack is into food for the poor. For the past six years, his Food Research and Action Center has successfully fought administration efforts to cut back federal spending on food for those who would otherwise have to do without. In the process, Pollack and FRAC (as the center is acronymously known) have forced the government to free hundreds of millions of dollars' worth of congressionally approved food benefits that the White House had sought to eliminate by executive fiat. Says Pollack: "Our function is to use the law to feed people."

He uses it with devastating success. Of 150 suits filed in the past half-dozen years, FRAC has won all but four—and three of those losses generated legislative changes in favor of FRAC's causes, while the last may yet be won on appeal. The past few months have been especially rewarding for Pollack and his team. In May FRAC got a judicial order directing the Department of Health, Education and Welfare to stop blocking $37.5 million in food benefits for 63,000 elderly citizens. Then came a $125 million victory over the Department of Agriculture, which had been holding back congressionally appropriated food funds for pregnant women, nursing mothers, and young children. The topper was last month's stunning blow to the Ford administration's bid to eliminate $1.2 billion in food stamps. Ruling that the proposed action was probably illegal, federal judge John Lewis Smith Jr. blocked the food-stamp cut until the case is finally resolved. Said Smith: "Hunger and deprivation might result, which could hardly be cured through any retroactive relief."

Bad Policy

The New York City-born attorney, now 32, was a student civil rights activist who went to Mississippi in the mid-'60s, where he "saw in the starkest terms people who were extraordinarily hungry and needed government assistance." Only five months out of law school (New York University, class of '68), Pollack filed 26 suits in a single day against foot dragging on food programs by 26 states and the Agriculture Department. "I was arrogant," he now concedes. But, proceeding with careful research and thorough preparation, he won 25 of the 26. These legal triumphs helped him get a $250,000 federal grant in 1970 to start FRAC, which is now supported by a host of religious and foundation sources. Pollack's work has won him respect from supporters and opponents alike.

Justice Department attorney Mack Norton, who has faced him in court and lost, says, "With Ron, we have to work a little harder." Adds Marshall Matz, general counsel of the Senate Nutrition Committee, "He argues congressional intent better than anyone else I've seen."

That is almost always Pollack's key argument—that the intention of the lawmakers is being subverted or ignored by executive actions. But the young lawyer wishes that the adversary relationship were not necessary. The government's problem, he explained to *Time* magazine's correspondent Don Sider, "is constant pressure to minimize spending. The areas that are most vulnerable are the ones with the weakest political constituencies." Thus in recent years, despite congressional appropriations to help the poor, the administration has often withheld the money, prompting FRAC lawsuits on behalf of the deprived beneficiaries. Says Pollack: "It's almost an institutionalized thing and it's not a good way to make public policy."

Even with a friendlier White House attitude, Pollack would still have plenty of work just making sure that his victories stuck. Two months after winning one lawsuit, he called the appropriate federal administrator, who admitted with shock that he had never done anything about the court order because he had never been told about it.

Source: Reprinted by permission from *Time,* The Weekly News magazine, Aug. 2, 1976; Copyright Time Inc.

In addition to the right of appeal, the act of 1946 attempts to provide more uniform procedures in executive agencies through the following requirements:

1. Every executive agency must give full publicity to its formal procedures so that interested persons may know how to use its facilities.

2. Ample notice of the contemplated adoption of rules must be given, either personally or through the *Federal Register* (see Chapter 2), to interested individuals or corporations so that they may have time to protest.

3. Officials engaged in investigating and presenting cases for adjudication should have no part in deciding them.

4. Any interested person must be allowed to appear before any agency for presentation of any issue, request, petition, or controversy.

5. Persons compelled to appear must be permitted counsel.

In short, the requirements say that a citizen has the right to know, the right to access, and the right to a fair forum.

In 1966 the Freedom of Information Act gave *any* person the right to request information from agencies and to file action in federal court if the request was denied. With an estimated 6 billion files, the U.S. federal government is the largest single creator and collector of information in the world. This vast storehouse includes the well-known files of the FBI and CIA, information on almost every type of product and service the government purchases, safety reports on products it regulates, compliance reports on laws it administered, and written records of official communication and action. The purpose of the 1966 act was, in brief, to give the public the right to know what their government knows (with certain specific exceptions such as national security and law enforcement investigatory records) and to have the data upon which decision making is based. In 1975, over a presidential veto, Congress passed a number of changes to the act to make it more effective; in particular, they required a reply by agencies to any request within ten working days and limited duplicating charges to actual costs. Further, the new provisions call for *in camera* (i.e., in the privacy of the judge's chambers) review by judges of national security claims.

Senator Lawton Chiles has recently introduced a bill that, by opening meetings of 47 federal agencies to scrutiny by the public, would also attempt to insure administrative responsibility. Chiles, no doubt, would agree with Justice Louis Brandeis's homily: "Publicity is justly commended as a remedy for social and industrial disease. Sunlight is said to be the best disinfectant and electric light the most efficient policeman." Already 49 states have "government in the sunshine" laws. Florida, Mr. Chiles's home state, is the most stringent, and Gov. Reubin Askew testified before Congress that it works: "Predictions that too much sunshine would lead to unnecessary embarrassment of public employees, costlier land acquisitions and other problems haven't been borne out by the Florida experience." (Large 1975)

What are the limitations to judicial control? The first point to recognize is that responsibility is always after the fact; that is to say, all that courts can do is alleviate or punish wrongs that have already occurred. As a remedy, some have recommended the use of *declaratory judgments proceedings.* These proceedings would enable disputes to be determined at their inception; in effect, courts would determine the validity of an agency policy *before* its violation. But as William W. Boyer (1964:132) notes: "Little information . . . is available concerning how much the declaratory proceeding, where permitted, is utilized."

A second point about judiciary control comes from a study of U.S. Supreme Court decisions with respect to ten executive agencies from 1947 to 1956 (Tanenhaus 1960). The study concluded that "the Court and its individual members favor federal agencies more frequently than they oppose them to a statistically significant degree." In other words, it would appear that the outlook is not altogether promising for individuals who choose to

control agency action in court. Of course, it is unlikely that at state and local levels, where judges tend to construe the powers of government more narrowly, that this pattern would hold.

Our third point is speculative. The rise of public interest lawyers, such as Ron Pollack (see the boxed article "The Hunger Lawyers"), and a post-Watergate climate of "litigious paranoia" have probably brought the courts into public administration more than any other time in U.S. history. Harlan Cleveland suggested that the ultimate effect this event might be to cause every public agency to write down all its procedures, to put greater power in the hands of lawyers, and to generate in consequence jerky and arthritic administrative procedures.

Nor are the Freedom of Information Act and the proposed sunshine laws without certain limitations. As a result of the former, federal agencies have been swamped with demands for information. The FBI, for example, handled 1,789 requests for information in April 1975 alone. Meanwhile, the CIA has had to establish a freedom of information office, staffed by 50 full-time employees. Reporters and public interest groups, who were first thought to be primary beneficiaries of the act, have only accounted for a small percentage of the requests. Most have come from individuals seeking to find out if the government has a secret file on them and, ironically, from businesses seeking information given to the government by competitors and indications of forthcoming actions by regulatory agencies.

Requiring government agencies to open all their meetings to the public could have in some cases, similar unintended consequences. First, if an agency like the Civil Aeronautics Board is forced to make its deliberations public, the room might just fill not with public interest groups but with airline lobbyists. Similarly, public discussion of, say, government personnel policies could invite not lively and informed public debate but intensive lobbying and pressure on Civil Service Commission members. Second, officials might be reluctant to request information lest they create a public image or ignorance. Third, few might take advantages of the new openness. The student movement of the 1960s is illustrative: Although the movement achieved much opportunity for participation in university decision making, it is questionable today how interested students are in committee meetings on the budget and curriculums. Fourth, some have suggested that open meetings would become a sham, since the real decisions would probably be made elsewhere. Washington would become a city of long lunches and hushed voices.

Institutionalized Citizen Participation

When William F. Buckley, Jr., wrote that he would rather entrust his governance to the first hundred persons listed in the Cambridge telephone directory than to the faculty of Harvard College, he was simply stating the basic philosophy behind including the citizenry in the public decision-making process. Other observers maintain that citizens as customers of government are naturally more responsive to public needs than government officials. It might even be put forth as a tentative proposition that the poorest moral performances and the least accountability by government are generally associated with conditions in which few citizens have any influence. For these reasons, among others, it is not surprising to see governments at all levels trying to formalize the participation of citizens in the administrative process.

The most common forms that citizen participation assumes are the citizen committee as an advisory group, the citizen group as a governing group in a specific policy area, and the idea of neighborhood government, where citizens have direct responsibility in a number of policy areas. Citizen's advisory committees often play important roles in the policy making process described in Chapter 2.

Advisory groups, as used here, refer to the over 1,200 boards, commissions, and committees found within federal executive departments, their regional or district subdivisions, and within units of local government. These advisory committees involve more than 20,000 people and cover nearly every imaginable topic—from the President's Council on Energy Research and Development to the Agriculture Department's committee on hog cholera eradication.

Unfortunately, these committees are often influential to the point that they have served to minimize the possibility of real federal control and have buttressed the old system of local control. For example, a *New York Times* survey (Hill 1970) of boards in 35 states organized to advise on grazing allotments and privileges on federal land revealed that they were "dotted with industrial, agricultural, municipal, and county representatives whose own organization or spheres of activity are in many cases in the forefront of pollution." The same study reported that a Colorado commission examining the pollution of streams by a brewery was chaired by the pollution control director of the brewery and that in Indiana the governor dismissed members of a pollution board because their firms had been indicted as polluters.

Although prohibited by law from making policy decisions, critics charge that the advisory committees exercise tremendous influence over many government actions, particularly the areas of health, commerce, and energy. Officials in agencies such as the National Institute of Health and the National Science Foundation seldom overrule expert panels in awarding research grants. Foreign trade regulations are based largely on recommendations from committees of industry leaders. And for almost 30 years, the 150 member National Petroleum Council "has dominated federal energy policies as the major source for government data on oil and gas reserves" (Atcheson and Newbauer 1975). Proponents of the advisory committee system argue that the groups provide government with a necessary sounding board for ideas, far-reaching view points, and uninhibited outside opinions.

Local governments create advisory committees on subjects ranging from community planning and police reform to mass transit and air pollution control. Administrators use these bodies to obtain information, advice, and opinions from representatives of affected interests. This input may aid administrators in making informed policy decisions.

What other limitations to citizen participation might we note? First, it could be argued that some public administrators see the participatory movement as a way to rid themselves of insoluble problems: given an intractable problem one need only hoist the banner of participatory democracy while transferring responsibility elsewhere. Second, by bringing highly dissatisfied groups into the administrative process, administrators may be able to pacify (or co-opt) them. For example, the citizens participation in local programs of the Housing and Home Finance and Community Action agencies, upon careful examination, appears to serve much more the interest of the administrators and local businessmen than the interests of the citizen participants (here, the poor). (Krause 1968) Third, citizen participation can be used as a vehicle by which a bureaucracy builds a clientele. This technique could be used for instances with environmental programs, which have no natural interest group. An enterprising administrator would need only to form a task force, composed of highly influential citizens, and he would have the nucleus of an effective citizens lobby for his pet programs.

We might conclude our discussion of citizen participation with another speculation by Cleveland (1975:6): "It is no accident that so many memorable public policy initiatives (in foreign policy, I think of the Marshall Plan, Point Four, Open Skies, The World Weather Watch, and The Nuclear Test Ban) began as the products of hunch and thinking-out-loud rhetoric, with most of the professional staffwork and the domestic and foreign consultations following after. If the statesmen involved *had consulted widely* before launching them, some or all of these great ideas might have died in the womb."

Professional Codes

The remainder of this chapter devotes itself to consideration of the so-called internal informal controls to insure administrative responsibility. The first of these is the use of professional codes—a devise that can be traced back at least to the Hippocratic oath, which has guided the practice of medicine for more than 20,000 years. Interestingly, with few exceptions the Watergate culprits were all lawyers. Yet, next to physicians, lawyers probably have the most stringent set of professional requirements to be found. Nevertheless, it appeared that these men had no guiding ethic—except loyalty to their boss.

A number of reasons might be suggested for why codes have such limited usefulness. First, the scope of activities of an administrator seldom limits itself to the bonds of one profession; inevitably, questions arise outside the code's purview. Similarly, the administrator often finds his code in conflict with other loyalties, such as to a particular client or geographic region, political party or political leader, social class or union.

A second reason for the limitations of professional codes derives from the wording of these guidelines. If too general, they are useless as a guide to action. If specific enough to serve as a guide to action, they might be so numerous, so detailed as to be unworkable on a day-to-day basis.

Third, to the extent many codes posit obedience to authority in one form or another, it could be argued that they are inherently weak, possibly even dangerous. Fortunately, we need not rehash the Watergate affair to make the point that obedience to authority can be a self-defeating component in a code of ethics. Rather let us consider the famous series of experiments on human beings begun in 1960 by Stanley Milgram (1974) at Yale University. The experiments themselves are worthy of Kafka.

The participants were led to believe that the purpose of the research project was the "scientific study of memory and learning." By a series of manipulations the participant was chosen to be the "teacher." Next, a fake "learner" was then taken to an adjacent room, strapped into a chair, and manacled with electrode. Enter a supervisor dressed in a gray technician coat who tells the "teacher" to administer a verbal learning test to the man in the next room. Whenever an incorrect answer is given, the "teacher" is to give the other an electric shock from the "shock generator."

The results of this experiment were surprising and disturbing, for no one refused and walked out of this "Eichmann experiment ' In fact, nearly two thirds of the "teachers," who represented a broad cross section of the occupational community, kept pressing away to 450 volts—despite the well rehearsed shouts and screams of the "learner." The results, to state the obvious, were not what was expected: The autonomy of human beings proved astoundingly low. (Another interesting aspect of this experiment, which we can only mention parenthetically, concerns the professional ethics of a psychologist who, like Milgram, manipulates and deceives his sub-jects.)

Representative Bureaucracy

A representative bureaucracy is, roughly speaking, one that represents its society, that is, the percentage of each minority group in the government approximates the percentage of that group in the entire population. The assumption is, of course, that, by hiring more members of some ethnic group, the representation of that group's attitudes within the bureaucracy is en-hanced. This representation can be either active or passive (the distinction is Mosher's; 1968:12) The former focuses on the source or origin of civil servants and the degree to which their backgrounds mirror the total society. The latter denotes situations where the administrator presses for the in-terests and desires of those whom he or she is presumed to represent, whether they be the whole people or some segment of the people.

In the United States, representative bureaucracy has become an issue of great moment, as nonbinding targets and timetables for hiring members of certain groups has become standard practice. We shall discuss the pro-cedural aspects of these activities in Chapter 14, but here our concern is with the theoretical: does ethnic representation lead to active representation of that group's interest in the bureaucracy. Frank Thompson (1976:576–601), after a rather thorough review of studies on the question, concludes probably not, although the data are quite inconclusive.

Consider:

One study of black and white police in 15 core cities found that the black police viewed ghetto dwellers more positively. They more readily per-ceived ghetto residents as honest, industrious, respectable, and religious. Other data reveal that black police are more likely to view black citizens as mistreated by the police.

A study of Model City workers in Atlanta revealed that black profes-sionals and paraprofessionals were more likely than white co-workers to perceive their clients as having "positive attitudes." But black welfare workers in 15 cities concluded—to a greater degree than their white colleagues—that black clients did not do enough to improve themselves and that black clients were especially arrogant.

Similarly, another study of law enforcement personnel in core cities showed that race had little effect on whether police engaged in such potentially controversial practices as searching without a warrant, breaking up loitering groups, and stopping and frisking. Indeed, an analysis of black police in New York City uncovered a "Cossack" disposition. When black police worked with white ones, some of them tended to view black offenders as an embarrassment and treat them harshly. In the words of one black officer, "I have treated many Negroes in a way I wouldn't treat a dog. I am harder on a Negro that commits an infraction than a white person." (Cited in Thompson 1976:591)

Anthony Down (1967:233) offers this explanation for the weak link between ethnic representation and substantive representation: "Officials . . . have no strong incentives to employ representative values in making decisions. The pressure on them to seek representative goals is much weaker than the pressure of their own personal goals or those of their bureaus. . . . Neither do officials face reelection, thus having to account for or justify their policies. This lack of any enforcement mechanism further reduces the probability that officials will behave in [a] representative way."

A number of other explanations might be offered: officials may lack authority to do very much; formal organizational sanction and peer group pressure may reduce gestures of sympathy by public servants from a certain ethnic groups (one "gets ahead by going along"); and uncertainty may exist regarding just what the "proper ethnic perspective" is. (Thompson 1976: 589–90)

Public Interest

Given the limitations involved in professional codes and representative bureaucracy as internal informal approaches to administrative responsibility, some posit the concept of the *public interest* as a guide to making administrative decisions. According to this view, the administrator should make decisions based on the best interests of some collective, overarching community or national good rather than on the narrower interests of some small, self-serving group.

To discern clearly the public interests is no easy task. Walter Lippmann (1955:42), as lucid a thinker as one is likely to encounter on the subject, could give no better answer than this: "There is no point in toying with any notion of an imaginary plebiscite to discern the public interest. We cannot know what we ourselves will be thinking five years hence much less what infants now in the cradle will be thinking when they go into the polling booth. Yet their interests, as we observe them today, are within the public interest. Living adults share, we must believe, the same public interest. For them, however, the public interest is mixed with, and is often at odds with, their private and special interests. Put this way, we can say, I suggest, that the public interest may be presumed to be what men would choose if they saw clearly, thought rationally, acted disinterestedly and benevolently."

Quite a tall order. But even if the public official could see with this clarity, rationality, and objectivity, would it really be enough? How does one distinguish qualitatively between aggregated private interests (e.g., public opinion polls) and genuine common concerns? How does one distinguish between the various types of public: reasonable and long-range versus passionate and temporary? Above all, does focusing on the public interest somehow restrict political discussion? Is bargaining substituted for real thought?

It is not surprising therefore to find Glendon Schubert (1962:176) concluding, after a careful study of the literature: "if the public interest concept makes no operational sense, notwithstanding the efforts of a generation of capable scholars, then political scientists might better spend their time nurturing concepts that offer greater promise of becoming useful tools in the scientific study of political responsibility." This is a challenge to which we now turn.

Moral Philosophy

Taking what has been said in the chapter about judicial control, citizen participation, professional codes, and the public interest, along with our earlier reflections on executive and legislative control of the bureaucracy and interest group activities in administrative policy making, one tentative conclusion is possible. The quest for more responsible administration is a never-ending one. We need to press our inquiry further. Specifically, in this section and the next, we draw on some recent ground-breaking work in the field of moral philosophy. Our immodest goal: to develop a more workable framework of moral choice for the public administrator.

Moral rationalism claims that purely rational procedures can show the individual what one ought to do. The beauty of this approach, its proponents maintain, is that one need not choose between different ideals or goals. In the place of tragic, difficult choices, we find a kind of moral geometry. The example par excellence of this approach is John Rawl's *A Theory of Justice* (1971). Rawls begins, much like Lippmann, by imagining rational, mutually disinterested individuals meeting. But in this hypothetical situation, rather than making specific decisions, people choose the first principles of a conception of justice. And these principles are operational; that is, they can serve to regulate all subsequent decision making.

But what are these principles they agree to? Rawls maintains that persons in this initial situation "would choose two rather different principles: The first requires equality in the assignment of basic rights and duties, while the second holds that social and economic inequalities . . . are just only if they result in compensating benefits for everyone, and in particular for the least advantaged members of society. These principles rule out justifying institutions on the ground that the hardships of some are offset by a greater good in the aggregate. It may be expedient but it is not just that some should have less in order that others may prosper. But there is no injustice in the greater benefits earned by a few provided that the situation of persons not so fortunate is thereby improved." (ibid.: 14–15)

According to Rawls, these principles are, in essence, a rigorous statement of the traditional Anglo-Saxon concept of fairness, but according to his critics, his principles are more the application of the handicapper's art to humanity. Compensatory equalization of this sort was the theme of Aristophanes' *Ecclesiazusae,* a play in which the dirty old men of Athens are compensated for their natural handicap by going to the head of the line for access to girls. At the same time, crones have first call on young men— the most cronish first of all.

The crucial question is whether this notion of justice-as-fairness can be applied as a theoretical framework for public administration? As an exercise, consider the issue of hiring members of socially disadvantaged groups into the public service (the example is suggested by Henry 1975:39–40). Following the logic of justice-as-fairness, what position would you take: (*a*) make special efforts to hire these individuals or (*b*) refuse to lower the entrance standards?

Autonomous Morality: Walter Kaufmann

A fundamental problem with Rawl's theory of justice, at least from the standpoint of the public decision maker, is that it is inflexible and, as such, reduces autonomy. This objective is raised with particular eloquence by Walter Kaufmann (1973), who like Rawls, is a professor of philosophy capable of highly original thought.

"Invocations of justice," he writes, "help to blind a moral agent to the full range of his choices. Thus they keep people from realizing the extent of their autonomy." Kaufmann continues: "We can point two examples of love and honesty, courage and humanity. We do not know in the same way what justice is, as a quality of punishments and distributions. We cannot point to concrete examples. Solomon's celebrated judgment illustrates his legendary wisdom rather than his justice. What made his judgment so remarkable was that *he managed to get at the facts. . . .*" (*Emphasis added.*)

To return to the question about hiring the disadvantaged, it seems fairly certain that the Rawls solution would be to hire—for not to hire would be further deprivation of societies most deprived group for the sake of efficiency and hence the whole society. Kaufmann would, I think, object on the grounds that this procedure is simply too pat: it ignores the subtleties of the question and considers the present at the expense of the future. For example, what happens if the minority applicant is applying to a governmental agency designed to end discrimination? Thus to hire him, instead of a more qualified applicant, could very likely result in a set back to the overall goal of ending discrimination. While this result is by no means inevitable, the point remains: the Rawls approach appears to reduce autonomy.

Where does this leave us in our search for a workable framework of moral choice for public administrator? Certainly not in a hopeless position, for Kaufmann has put forth a most useful concept which he calls the "new integrity."

As Kaufmann sees it, in our time one concept of integrity, closely linked with justice, is being replaced by another, associated with individual autonomy and honesty. Honesty, however, as used here, is not merely sincerity, credibility, or frankness; rather, it is as justice was to the Greeks, the *sum* of the virtues. Surely, says Kaufmann, that is what we mean when we refer to Abraham Lincoln as "Honest Abe"—not that he could never tell a lie (that was George Washington) but that he was virtuous.

Again Kaufmann: "High standards of honesty mean that one has a conscience about what one says and what one believes. They mean that one takes some trouble to determine what speaks for and against a view, what the alternatives are, what speaks for and against each, and what alternatives are preferable on these grounds. This is the heart of rationality, the essence of the scientific method, and the meaning of intellectual integrity." (Ibid.:178)

But the new integrity requires one additional quality: Practice must be integrated with theory. To live in accordance with the new integrity thus requires self-confidence and courage; one must be able to *apply* the canon to the most important questions he faces. "He does not bow to authority; he decides for himself."

A final question: Is the canon of the new integrity workable? The question can only be answered by cases drawn from the world of administration. Below we consider three. (These illustrations are drawn from Lewis 1975; Karr 1975; Broder 1975; and H. Cleveland 1972.)

Early in 1975 William T. Coleman Jr., became Transportation Secretary. As his style of decision making began to emerge, it became obvious that Coleman was a post-Watergate example of a man of independence, accepting responsibility. He approaches decisions like a judge; that is, he tries to get all the facts and then actually writes an opinion explaining his decision in an open way. For example, when deciding on a proposed superhighway through the Virginia suburbs, he took the unusual step of personally holding a four hour public hearing in which both sides give their arguments. The following year, he faced an even tougher decision: whether the controversial Concorde airplane should be allowed flights into the United States. Taking careful measure of the complex—often conflicting—values of technology, the environment, and world politics, he reached a cautiously balanced decision that established a limited test period for the flights under carefully controlled conditions. Typically, the decision was accompanied by a cogently reasoned explanation. In his 61-page decision, the secretary wrote: "It may well be that further development of this technology is not economically sensible in the energy—and environmentally—conscious period in which we live. If so, then the Concorde will fail because it is an anachronism and its failure will be recognized as such rather than attributed to an arbitrary and protectionist attitude of the United States out of fear that our dominance of the world aeronautical manufacturing industry is threatened." (*New York Times,* February 15, 1976.)

William T. Coleman Jr., Transportation
Secretary, holding a copy of his opinion
on the Concorde in Washington.

The New York Times/Teresa Zabala

Also early in 1975, Edmund G. Brown, Jr., took office as governor of
California. "The central principle that guides me," he says, "is an attempt to restore confidence in government, and that means taking the
most honest approach possible. That sounds trite, but there's a lot of
sloppy thinking in government, even where there isn't deliberate deception. The most certain way to restore confidence is to insist on a relentless honesty in every step. That is more important to me than any
program." It appears that this principle of "relentless honesty" results
in a different manner and method in government. The most striking
characteristic is his skeptical, inquisitor-general attitude regarding any
policy issue brought to him. Reports the *Washington Post:* "Dissatisfied
with the evidence presented by scientists in 35 hours of hearings in his
office on the effects of an automobile antipollution device, the governor
ordered new field tests made. When they showed only marginal impact,
far short of the original promise, he reversed his campaign posture and
killed the program."

Harlan Cleveland has had a rich experience as a public executive—
foreign aid administrator, magazine publisher, university president, political executive in Washington, and ambassador abroad. His reflections
on public administration, therefore, are worth considering. First, he
disposes of the notion that any one set of principles is going to be much
of a guide: "Wise sayings from Mencius and Aristotle, the Bible and the
Founding Fathers, not to mention our own parents, may likewise be

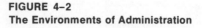

FIGURE 4–2
The Environments of Administration

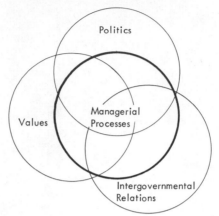

The three environments of public administration, the subject of the first part
of the book, permeate the traditional
managerial processes, the subject of next
two parts. Sometimes the administrators
find themselves operating in the eye of
the diagram. There the management
concerns become, as it were, pasted over
with concerns about politics, intergovernmental relations, and values. These
are the times administrators may wonder
why they did not become businessper-
sons.

useful but hardly controlling: with a little help from a concordance of
the Bible or Bartlett's *Familiar Quotations,* it is all too easy to find some
pseudoscriptural basis for whatever one really wants to do." Having
cleared the brush, he then gives the key question that he asked himself
before getting committed to a line of action. The question is not "Will I
be criticized?" (After all, operating in the public sector, the answer to
that question is frequently "Yes.") Rather, it is this: "If this action is held
up to public scrutiny, will I still feel that it is what I should have done,
and how I should have done it?"

NAILING DOWN THE MAIN POINTS

1 Administrative responsibility is a collective term that covers those values
people generally expect from government.

2 Responsiveness in organizations, one such value, comes in various forms: unresponsive, usually responsive, highly responsive, and fully responsive. The fourth type overcomes the "us" and "them" attitude by accepting its publics as voting members.

3 Another value associated with responsibility is flexibility, which simply means that administrators do not ignore individual groups, local concerns, or situational differences in formulating and implementing policy.

4 People also expect that government will perform competently, follow due process, remain accountable (not "faceless"), and, perhaps above all, be honest.

5 Administrative responsibility is, therefore, an ideal — a castle in the sky. Not surprisingly, a number of pitfalls face any government in attaining it. First is the omnipresent possibility of collusion, for example, between an administrative agency and the group it is supposed to regulate. With massive law enforcement apparatuses, governments also run the risk of letting their zeal for consensus and public order become coercive. Or, zeal for the mission of the organization can transform the public information programs from its legitimate function of keeping the public informed into outright deception. More gently put, truth becomes distorted.

6 While the emergence of an amoral elite of experts does not seem imminent, the growth of professionalism raises four causes for concern: elite professions tend to dominate many agencies; they also dominate in matters of recruitment, reelection, and advancement; they are becoming more specialized; and they can infringe upon the prerogatives of political leadership. Another concern for those interested in administrative responsibility is the ethnocentricism of some public administrators.

7 The measures that have been taken to avoid the pitfalls outlined under points 5 and 6 can be discussed within a framework of four categories of control: internal formal, internal informal, external formal, and external informal. No writers advocate exclusive reliance upon any *one* of these four, however.

8 Furthermore, even in combination, measures such as the following each have distinct limitations in making the ideal of administrative responsibility a reality: executive, legislative, and judicial control; interest group representation; citizen participation; professional codes; representative bureaucracy; and public interest. The recent work in the field of moral philosophy has, however, sparked renewed interest in finding more effective measures. For example, work by John Rawls and Walter Kaufmann does suggest a couple of internal informal controls — justice-as-fairness and autonomous morality. The latter, while no more foolproof than the other measures, does at least seem workable.

CONCEPTS FOR REVIEW

responsibility
responsiveness
flexibility
market segmentation
competence
procedural and substantive due
  process
accountability
public relations
elitism
professionalism
ethnocentricism

external and internal controls
judicial review
Administrative Procedures Act
Freedom of Information Act
sunshine laws
declaratory judgments proceedings
institutionalized citizen participation
professional codes
representative bureaucracy
public interest
justice-as-fairness
new integrity

PROBLEMS

1. "Loyalty is the virtue of a dog."—H. L. Mencken. Do you think loyalty to political executives is overrated in the United States? How far should loyalty extend? If you think it even possible, how would you rank that loyalty in comparison with the following: humanity, U.S. Constitution, public interest, political party, social class, religion, profession, union, and client?

2. President Franklin D. Roosevelt once said to an aide: "Tell that man to go see Dean Acheson to learn how a gentleman resigns." In 1933, as Under Secretary of the Treasury, Mr. Acheson was asked to do something he believed illegal. He left the government, but without public complaint, demonstrating his deference to the norm of team loyalty that qualified him to rejoin the Roosevelt administration eight years later as Assistant Secretary of State. Is this the way resignations should take place or should an individual either stay and fight or resign and fight? (See Weisband and Franck 1975 for a full discussion of resignation in protest.)

3. Write an essay on ethical and legal issues of social experimentation. (This topic looks forward to Chapter 9.)

4. Generally, the public accepts the right of business to publicize and advertise, even though the customer pays for it in the long run, but it often regards a similar expenditure of funds for government information as frivolous or a waste of the taxpayer's money. Would you conclude therefore that the public tends to apply a double standard? Why or why not?

5. Write a paper on the various proposals for a national databank.

6. The aim of the ombudsman, a Swedish idea, is to create a representative or agent of the legislation to protect citizens' rights against bureaucratic abuse. More precisely, the ombudsman is available to hear complaints of any citizen against erroneous, unfair, or even impolite action by government officials; and then, if necessary, investigate the complaint, publicize any abuse, and recommend corrective action. Research this idea further and then report on whether the United States should have the ombudsman.

7. "The ethical behavior of public servants . . . is higher than in most sectors of American society, but it can never rise much above the standard of its environment. It is rather difficult to build and maintain integrity in the administrative agencies of government when legislators and private interests connive to commit far greater damage to the general welfare than any bureaucrat has ever been accused of. As long as millionaires can get by without paying income taxes, as long as depletion allowances can help to create a culturally shabby 'nouveau riche' in the oil states, as long as factories can get away with shoddy or unsafe products and pollute our streams and our air with impurity — as long as these big thefts within the public weal are permitted, I cannot get too excited about the relatively minor graft that may occasionally crop up in the bowels of the bureaucracy." (Stahl 1971) Do you agree or disagree? Discuss.

8. Toward the end of the 18th century Edmund Burke said: "Constitute government how you please, infinitely the greater part of it must depend upon the exercise of the powers which are left at large to the prudence and uprightness of minister of state." Which ideas expressed in this chapter do you think Burke would be most comfortable with? the least?

9. Write an essay on how the history and culture of black Americans has resulted in the many viewpoints of the various segments of the black population in the United States. What effect have these experiences had on black-white relationships today? (This problem really presupposes some previous work in the area of black studies.)

10. Write a memo outlining a strategy for reducing ethnocentricism in domestic program for the American Indian. (See Laura Thompson's *Culture in Crisis: A Study of Hopi Indians.*)

11. In a few paragraphs discuss Carlos Castaneda's explanation of ethnocentricity. (See *Journey to Ixtlan.*)

12. Select one of the following plays to discuss in class in terms of the ethical or value questions it raises for public administration:

    Anouilh, *Antigone.*
    Anouilh, *Becket.*
    Arden, *Left Handed Liberty.*
    Arrighi, *An Ordinary Man.*
    Bolt, *A Man for All Seasons.*
    Boyer, *Don Juan in Hell.*
    Brecht, *Galileo.*
    Camus, *Caligula.*
    Ibsen, *A Doll's House.*
    Ibsen, *Enemy of the People.*
    Kippardt, *In the Matter of J. Robert Oppenheimer.*
    McLeish, *J.B.*
    Shaw, *Mrs. Warren's Profession.*
    Stone and Edwards, *1776.*
    Vidal, *The Best Man.*

13. A. A. Berle (1968:10) maintains that a set of guidelines by which to assess the advisability of administration actions and based on common sense is not all that difficult to construct. Consider this list of values:

    a. People are better alive than dead.
    b. People are better healthy than sick.
    c. People are better off literate than illiterate.
    d. People are better off adequately than inadequately housed.
    e. People are better off in beautiful than in ugly cities and towns.

    f. People are better off if they have opportunity for enjoyment—music, literature, drama, and the arts.

    g. Education above the elementary level should be as nearly universal as possible through secondary schools, and higher education as widely diffused as practicable.

    h. Development of science and the arts should continue or possibly be expanded.

    i. Minimum resources for living should be available to all.

    j. Leisure and access to green country should be a human experience available to everyone.

How useful do you regard this: More useful than a professional code of ethics? Do you agree with all the points?

14. "... in governing boards (of regents, trustees, or directors), in regulatory commissions, in regular government departments, or in corporate executive suites, there must always be provision for talking out in private the most controversial issues, for compromise and face-saving and graceful backing down. If all boards were required by law to have all their meetings in public, that would just increase the frequency of lunches and dinners among their members, as they negotiate in informal caucus the positions they are going to take in the formal meetings." (Cleveland 1972:119) Do you agree with this statement? If yes, what are its implications for "sunshine laws"?

15. How effective do you think Kaufmann's ideal of autonomous morality would be in alleviating the four quandaries of democratic morality discussed earlier in the chapter (namely: coercion, collusion, distortion, and elitism)?

16. Write an essay on Daniel Ellsberg and the moral obligations of government service. To get Mr. Ellsberg's side of the story, see the two interviews appearing in *Rolling Stone* on August 9 and December 6, 1973.

PART II

The Management
of Governmental
Programs

5

Planning

INTRODUCTION

Planning is the keystone of the arch of program management, and government success is often synonymous with planning success. Quite properly, then, Part II of this book on managing the public sector begins with planning.

As will be explained shortly, planning covers a far wider spectrum of meanings that can be encompassed in this chapter. Indeed, many of the things said in Chapter 2 about policy making apply to planning, which we interpret in this chapter quite broadly: reasoning about how an organization will get where it wants to go.

The essence of planning is to see opportunities and threats in the future and to exploit or combat them by decisions taken in the present. It is therefore hardly an overstatement to say that planning, as defined here, shapes the whole field of public administration. It determines the limits of government responsibility, the allocation of resources and the distribution of costs, the division of labor, and the extent of public controls. Nor is it an overstatement to say that the magnitude of current problems—such as pollution of air and water, exploitation of natural resources, and decline in the quality of urban life—are related to our inability to plan effectively.

If planning is an important area of public administration, it is also a relatively neglected one. The situation, moreover, is especially perplexing when one considers the several significant changes in the practice of planning that have taken place in the last 50 years: (Gross 1971)

The steady growth of long-range, corporate planning over the entire period from the 1920s to the present.

The fumbling efforts of the New Deal to develop a planned escape from the Great Depression.

Large-scale World War II planning of economic production and military operations.

The sequence of Fair Deal, New Frontier, and Great Society plans for full employment and social welfare.

The developer-speculator planning of the "march to the suburbs" and of inner city "urban renewal."

The growth of so-called "systems planning" in the industrial-military complex and its attempted extensions to welfare programs.

The fascinating sequence of calculational techniques designed to assist in various tactical aspects of planning and control, particularly those associated with emerging computer technology.

Recent attempts to remedy this neglect of planning in the literature of public administration have yielded almost as much confusion as progress. For this reason, we begin our discussion by attempting to clarify what we mean, and what we do not mean, by planning. Then, we shall examine one conceptual model of the planning process. The importance of this model cannot be overemphasized: it sets a framework for organizing thinking about the planning process. This chapter then examines a few selected elements of the model, such as premises, goals, and alternatives. It concludes by foreshadowing the chapters that follow. In these chapters, we shall consider additional elements of the planning model—namely, decision making, organizational structure, organizational design, implementation, and evaluation.

One final and crucial point. If, and only if, we keep the themes of the last three chapters firmly in mind can we hope to develop a balanced view of American public administration. I therefore warmly encourage the reader to test continually the crisp and, at times, cooly logical ideas that follow against the messy and seemly irrational forces of politics, intergovernmental relations, and values. The perennial question, in short, must be this: Given the environment of administration, how well will this or that management concept work? Worlds of certainty do not lie ahead.

CRITICAL DEFINITIONS

It would no doubt be helpful to both scholar and practitioners of planning if a common vocabulary, accepted by all, were available. Such however is not the case. So, from the start, we find ourselves in a position uncomfortably close to that of Humpty Dumpty in *Through the Looking-Glass*. There, it will be recalled, Humpty defines "glory" as "a nice knock-down argument." To Alice's reasonable objections, he says scornfully, "when *I* use a word, it means just what I choose it to mean. . . . The question is which is to be the master. . . ."

Actually, our situation is not quite that bad. In the first place, while Humpty is merely being capricious, we can give solid reasons for defining planning a certain way. And, second, the definitions offered below — unlike Humpty's unique definition of "glory" — are supported by an increasing number of scholars.

A Variety of Meanings

Before offering a "common vocabulary," it might be useful to consider a few of the alternative ways of viewing planning.

To some its meaning is virtually synonymous with *city planning* and thus stands for little more than development of *land-use plans.* These plans are concerned primarily with physical location and design: they include rules and regulations for subdivisions, building codes, and *zoning laws* (i.e., the principal tool for enforcing use of private property as prescribed by the municipality.)

But not all planning at the local level has so narrow a focus. A *comprehensive plan,* for example, is an official document adopted by a local government as a guide to decision about the physical development of the community for the next 20 to 30 years. "Comprehensive" means that the plan encompasses all geographic parts of the community and all functional elements that bear on physical development. According to Alan Black (1968:350), three technical elements are commonly included in comprehensive plans: the private use of land, community facilities, and circulation (i.e., transportation). "Comprehensive plans may cover other subjects, such as utilities, civic design, and special uses of land unique to the locality. Usually there is background information on the population, economy, existing land use, assumptions and community goals." "Among most city planners, the preparation, adoption, and use of a comprehensive plan are considered to be primary objectives of the planning program."

In the last few years, many cities that once thought the population explosion the next best thing to sunshine have embarked on a "grow slow" campaign to protect their way of life. A study by the Council of Environmental Quality's Task Force on Land Use and Urban Growth identified this new mood in the nation: increasingly, citizens are asking what urban growth will add to the quality of their lives; they are measuring new development proposals by the extent to which environmental criteria are satisfied — by what new housing or business will generate in terms of additional traffic, pollution of air and water, erosion, and scenic disturbance. In sum, comprehensive planning has become a logical vehicle to achieve agreement on growth management. Its scope, moreover, is much broader than earlier planning attempts, since it considers social and economic ramifications of development in addition to the traditional physical factors.

Petaluma, California, took the lead in this direction in 1972 when its city council decided that the city was too crowded, the sewers overflowing, garbage collectors overworked, and other city services suffering. The council adopted a five year plan that restricted new home construction to 500 a year. Developers and local merchants promptly challenged the plan, but a lower court decision upheld the growth control plan and subsequent appeals failed all the way to the Supreme Court. The Court's decision in February 1976 was a landmark: communities *did* have the power to curb growth.

But not everyone wants to curb growth. In particular, the governments of the developing nations of Asia, Africa, and Latin America attempt to set out the chief measures they need to take in order to raise national output per person. This is *development planning.* The typical plan will include most of the following: a survey of current economic conditions and the current social situation, an evaluation of the preceding plan, a statement of objectives, estimates of growth, suggested measures to raise growth rate, and a program of government expenditures. (See Lewis 1968: IX, 118–24)

Interestingly, on May 21, 1975, Senators Hubert Humphrey and Jacob Javits introduced the Balanced Growth and Economic Planning bill. In brief, the bill would establish within the executive branch a three-person economic planning board with broad responsibilities including forecasting, goal clarification, policy coordination, and the submission of a "rolling" six-year plan; a council on economic planning, made up of department heads and other cabinet-level officials; a division of economic information to coordinate federal statistics; a division of economic planning in the Congressional Budget Office; review of the National Economic Plan by the Joint Economic Committee; and its adoption by concurrent resolution of Congress. The six-year plan would not be binding upon the private sector, and in this respect resembled indicative planning on the French model. But it would be binding upon the government. (In 1976 the bill has, in effect, replaced by the Humphrey–Hawkin bill.)

A final connotation of planning we may note is *fiscal policy making,* that is, governmental tax and expenditure policies, budgetary deficits and surpluses. This brand of planning is explored in detail in Part III.

Since the thrust of this book is toward the integration — not the fragmentation — of thought, none of these interpretations of planning will be emphasized. Instead, planning will be treated as a general process, recognizable in a great number of human situations. The definition of planning that opened this chapter reflects this more general approach:

Planning is reasoning about how an organization will get where it wants to go. Its essence is to see opportunities and threats in the future and to exploit or combat them by decisions taken in the present.

To really grasp the dynamics of this process, it is of course necessary to understand its components. What, for example, is a "plan"? How does a plan differ from a "policy"? From a "program"?

Policy, Plans, Programs

For our purposes, a policy is a statement of goals and of the relative importance attached to each goal. It is translated into a *plan* by specifying the objectives to be attained. A proposed set of specific actions intended to implement a plan is called a *program.*

A simple example will perhaps do much to clarify these terse terminological stipulations (cf. Helmer 1968: 14–16). Assume that the mayor of a city has among his goals an increase in the physical safety of the city's inhabitants and improvements in housing conditions. He might then announce a policy that these goals, in the order stated, are to have priority over all other goals. A plan to implement this policy might specify the objectives of (a) reducing the rate of crimes of violence in the city as well as the death rate from traffic accidents by 25 percent and (b) providing an additional 10,000 housing units. A program would spell out in detail the actions to be taken to achieve these

FIGURE 5–1
Objectives Fiscal Year 1975, Charlotte, North Carolina: Law Enforcement Administration

Provide leadership and management of all human and fiscal resources allocated to the police department so as to elicit high morale and interteam cooperation, enhance community relations, and deliver high quality, effective law enforcement services. Responsibilities include administration, planning and research, personnel, inspection and internal investigations and the training bureau.

1. Institute an active minority recruitment program so that their representation in the police force as ordered by the U.S. District Court will be accomplished at an early date. During FY '75 fill patrolmen vacancies at an average rate of over 40 percent with minorities, and sergeant vacancies at an average rate of over 30 percent with minorities. Investigate the possibility of filling at least one higher rank position with a minority member by arranging a one- to two-year intergovernmental transfer with a metropolitan city;
2. Investigate and report to city manager results within three weeks for 75 percent (and eight weeks for 100 percent) of all complaints concerning alleged police misconduct or misuse of force;
3. Report on findings within one week for 85 percent (and four weeks for 100 percent) of all accidents involving police equipment;
4. Promote an atmosphere of community safety and security through increased citizen involvement in police efforts and establish measurements that will indicate the degree of success attained.
5. Report monthly progress on implementation of the LEAA funded program to reduce robberies, and on available results or indications found;
6. Increase the cost-effectiveness of the police department by reduction or elimination of less productive activities and simplification of procedures so as to reduce the operating budget by 2 percent in FY 75;
7. Increase in-service training hours by 3 percent to improve performance in areas such as those where a high incidence of officer injuries is occurring or where clearances/apprehensions can be improved.

Source: Budget and Evaluation Office, Charlotte, N.C., *Objectives FY 75.*

objectives; e.g., increasing the police force by 1,000 and providing city-backed, long-term loans to construction firms.

Figure 5–1 provides a more detailed example of this approach. At the top of the exhibit, the city of Charlotte, North Carolina, stated its goals in the area of law enforcement. Note how general these are. But below are listed seven rather specific objectives to attain these goals. What specific actions would you recommend for each objective?

The crucial difference between the terms policy, plan, and program is level of generality. More specifically, an increasing number of writers suggest the term policy should be reserved for statements of intention and direction of a relatively high order. Harold Lasswell (1951:5–8) puts it succinctly: "The word 'policy' is commonly used to designate the *most* important choices made either in organized or in private life." The emphasis, then, is not upon the topical issues of the moment but upon the fundamental problems of man in society.

As we shall see below, these terminological stipulations are more than mere academic hairsplitting: they help to make better policy. Possibly Confucius had something like this in mind when he said that, because actions follow words, he would, if ruler of the world, fix the meaning of words.

THE BASIC MODEL

To provide a meaningful and systematic framework for understanding the planning process, the now familiar and well established model of the rational planning process is presented. According to this model, a planner would be acting rationally if he or she undertook five interrelated steps:

1. Identify the problem or problems to be solved and the opportunities to be seized upon.
2. Design alternative solutions or courses of action (i.e., policies, plans, and programs) to solve the problems or seize upon the opportunities and forecast the consequences and effectiveness of each alternative.
3. Compare and evaluate the alternatives with each other and with the forecasted consequences of unplanned development, and choose the alternative whose probable consequences would be preferable.
4. Develop a plan of action for implementing the alternative selected, including budgets, project schedules, regulatory measures, and the like.
5. Maintain the plan on a current basis through feedback and review of information.

Although these steps are treated separately, and in linear sequence, in actual practice they represent a cyclic process. Evaluation procedures, for example, enter into the process at the outset in the identification of problems and opportunities; they also influence the design of alternative solutions. Likewise, the problems of implementation enter into the design stages as

FIGURE 5–2
Basic Planning Model

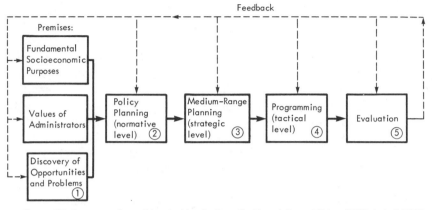

Source: This is a composite model, embodying the theoretical formulations of Steiner (1969), Jantsch (1969), and Ozbekan (1965) as well as the author's own work in forecasting and systemic planning.

constraints that must be taken into account. For this reason, it is probably preferable to present the model not as a list of steps but as a dynamic and iterative process. In this model, shown in Figure 5–2, the five steps have been rearranged in the form of a dynamic model and are indicated by the circled numbers.

Premises

At the left of the model are three underlying foundations of any government planning effort. The first, fundamental organizational socioeconomic purposes, refers to those underlying ends that society expects of its governmental institutions. Basically, this means that society demands that governments utilize the resources at their disposal to satisfy the wants of society. It is important for administrators to keep in mind this underlying reason for the existence of government. It explains why, as governments become larger and society becomes more complex, the things society wants from government become more numerous and sometimes contradictory.

The second fundamental set of foundations for planning are the values the top administrators hold—for example: "the private sector should be used as much as possible." Included here too would be the values of the elected officials, both executive (e.g., president, governor, and mayor) and legislative (e.g., Congress, legislature, and council). In fact, in the earlier stages of the planning process, where policy decisions are made, the influence of this group—especially through legislation—is usually decisive. Needless to say, their values do not always coincide with those of the administrator.

We now come to the final foundation of any government planning effort. A cardinal purpose of planning is to discover future opportunities and make plans to exploit them. Likewise, basic to planning is the detection of obstructions or problems that must be removed from the road ahead. The most effective plans are those that exploit opportunities and remove obstacles on the basis of an objective and systematic survey of the future. There is, in short, an enormous payoff to the skilled probing of a future and relating it to an unbiased study of an agency's strengths, weaknesses, and purpose. Today's administrator is not alone however in his efforts to forecast. The formal study of the future has, in fact, become an industry. In the United States a burgeoning network of future-oriented research institutes stretches from the Institute for the Future on the west coast to the Hudson Institute on the east, and the RAND Corporation has branches on both. Further, Congress, by establishing a Technology Assessment Board in 1972, evidenced concern with the future. How might these studies be used?

If a city is planned for orderly community development, then the regular forecasting of changes becomes vital. What should such a forecast include? At least such factor as number of people, number of school children, number and types of new residential and other buildings, and number and location of automobiles. Whenever possible, the forecast should include changes in the characteristics of the population, of land use, of the economic conditions, and of transportation patterns. The Houston-Galveston Area Council, one of many voluntary associations of local governments and local elected officials, is a pioneer in linking forecasting to planning. Through its coordinated regional approach to the usage of electronic data processing, the area council's comprehensive, detailed information system can provide area governments with facts and forecasts with exceptional precision and swiftness.

Obviously, the relevance of forecasting is not restricted to urban and regional planning. The analysis done, for example, by Dennis Meadows and his coauthors in *The Limits to Growth* (1972) purports to give advice not only to national but also to global planners. The argument, in a nutshell, runs like this: Continued growth will lead to increases in pollution, exhaustion of natural resources, and decline in per capita real incomes. To avoid this disaster, we must begin to undertake *immediately* some drastic measures— abolition of all population growth; abolition of all net capital formation and production growth; and concentration on food and services and recycling of resources.

While the methodology of this study has been severely criticized, we can nonetheless draw one important lesson from it. The essence of planning is to make *present* decisions with the knowledge of their future consequences. Hence planning requires knowledge of the future: What do we have to do today if we want to be in a particular place in the future?

The third foundation of planning, however, implies more than good forecasts. The effective planner must also be able to discern clearly and accurately what the problem is. As the French novelist Georges Bernanas once wrote, the worst, the most corrupting, of lies are problems poorly stated. No doubt the root of much of the difficulties faced by the United States in Vietnam was the failure of the architects of that war to define the problem accurately. The problems were clearly political, but the response was military. The most important rural innovation, the strategic hamlet program, designed to give peasants protection and win their allegiance to the government, was given to Nhu, the brother of President Diem. Predictably, Nhu began to make the program his own personal fief and power base; hence the political approach to an essentially political problem was from the start vitiated.

Similarly, during the 1960s, the problems of poverty were construed largely in terms of inadequate performance in the individual or group. Accordingly, the solution was a services strategy, that is, the provision of specific services that would change the modes of behavior that were presumed to be the root of poverty. In time it became apparent that the cost-benefit ratios of service programs were, at the very least, depressing. An alternative way to look at the problem of poverty was in terms of a lack of money. This view was surely supported by social research: the one seemingly fixed correlation in the literature was that well-being rises with income. It was this new view of the poverty problem that led in 1969 to the development of the Family Assistance Plan (or guaranteed income).

But attention to the definition of problems must not replace attention to the discovery of opportunities. Actually, by consistently directing performance toward opportunity rather than toward problems, the administrator will tend to foster high morale. In contrast, the problem-focused organization is an organization on the defensive; it feels that it has performed well if things do not get worse. In short, administrators who want to create and maintain the spirit of achievement in their agencies therefore stress opportunity.

Policy Planning

The next major structural element in Figure 5–2 is policy planning. Policy planning is the process of determining goals and their priorities. It is at this point in the planning process that the influence of political leadership is especially important.

According to journalist David Halberstam (1969: 370–71), during the Vietnam War the highest level of American policy makers refused to accept the necessity for making decisions at this level. They tried to delay such decisions and thus buy a little more time. These policy makers "were above all functional, operational, *tactical* men, not really intellectuals, and tactical men think in terms of options, while intellectuals less so; intellectuals might think in terms of the sweep of history and might believe that 12 months would make little difference in Vietnam. . . ."

To no small extent, it was precisely this failure to distinguish properly between policy and program that undermined much of the extraordinary effort at social improvement in the 1960s. Daniel P. Moynihan (1973:272–73), who served in the subcabinets of Presidents Kennedy and Johnson and in the

Daniel Moynihan, who served in the sub-cabinets of Presidents Kennedy and Johnson and in the cabinet of Nixon, argues that too much American policy is defined in terms of program. In the picture above, Ambassador Moynihan prepares to argue in the United Nations. In late 1976, Professor Moynihan was elected Senator from New York.

United Press International

Cabinet of President Nixon, argues that one of the more important things about the structure of American government is that too much public policy is defined in terms of *program* rather than true *policy*.

> In simpler times a simple pragmatic approach was an efficient way to go about the public business. The problem comes . . . when society becomes ambitious and begins to seek to bring about significant changes in the operation of complex systems such as society itself.

The problem with the program approach is that it deals only with a part of the system; policy, on the other hand, seeks to respond to the system in its entirety. Moynihan continues:

> The idea of policy is not new. We have for long been accustomed to the idea of foreign policy, including defense policy. Since 1946 Congress has mandated an employment and income policy more or less explicitly based on a "general theory" of the endlessly intricate interconnections of such matters. Yet our ways of behavior resist this: only great crises, great dangers, seem to evoke the effort. Or have seemed able to do so in the past. I believe, however, that a learning process of sorts has been going on. Increasingly the idea of system-wide policies commends itself to persons of responsibility in public affairs as an approach both desirable and necessary. We can expect it to be one of the formative ideas of the 1970s.

Interestingly, political scientist James McGreger Burn (1974), believes that the failure to establish a guiding vision or, what is the same, to set up goals to inform everyday decisions was the one administrative failing that, above all others, brought about the Watergate crisis. In the past, there have been all sorts of crises, compromises, and concessions in the presidency. But with other presidents there was always a kind of guiding objective or vision they kept in mind. Not so, it would appear, with the Nixon White House. "The only vision was service to the president and helping him realize his ambitions. And I think when you don't have this kind of guiding vision, all sorts of other practical and impractical things come into operation, and people loose their way."

Contrast the situation Burns describes to the clear goals of the Apollo mission. Write Sayles and Chandler (1971:21):

> While both purposes and plans need to have a great deal of flexibility to allow for changes in sentiment, new information and unforeseen problems and opportunities, objectives need to be relatively fixed and highly specific. They become the emotional symbols, the universally visible target that attracts and holds political support. They can also become the catalyst that mobilizes resources and encourages whole new technologies by capturing the imagination, the commitment, and the dedication of both those who will support the program and those who will actually do the work.

Medium-Range Planning

The best policy is only a policy—that is, good intentions—unless it is transformed into action; medium-range planning is an important step in that direction. At this stage in the planning process, detailed, coordinated, and comprehensive plans are made for an agency to deploy the resources necessary to attain the goals laid down in the policy planning stage. We are concerned, in particular, with two aspects of this stage: (1) the design of alternatives and (2) the evaluation of each alternative in terms of its consequences.

1. Let us return for a moment to the issue of poverty. It can be said that in the last three years of the Johnson administration there was fairly wide agreement that the existing welfare system constituted a major problem. Further, there was even considerable consensus on the goals of welfare problem: to raise incomes of the poor; to narrow disparities among states in benefit levels; to reduce inequities in treatment of different kinds of poor people; to increase incentives to work; to remove incentives to break up families. But on the question of how to achieve these goals—that is, what the objectives should be—polarization was the rule.

According to Alice M. Rivlin (1971:19 ff), who served as Assistant Secretary for Planning and Evaluation during the Johnson administration, at least three alternative strategies on how to attain these goals were available and each had its spokesmen both within and outside the administration. One of these approaches was to improve the existing welfare system by a series of amendments to make it more uniform and more nearly adequate. Another was put forth by the advocates of a negative income tax. And the third was family or children allowance.

It would be a serious mistake to jump to the easy conclusion that the existence of such widely divergent alternatives is a bad thing. Consider the 1964 planning group headed by William Bundy. This group also presented President Johnson with a set of three alternatives—but these concerned the Vietnam War. The first alternative was light bombing with more reprisals and more use of covert operations. The second was very heavy massive bombing, including the Phuc Yen airfield at Hanoi and cutting the rail links with China. And the third was a moderate solution—a slow squeeze, which allowed the United States to put increasing pressure on Hanoi while "keeping the hostage alive" but still permitting it to pull back if it wished. What was significant about these proposals of course was that all three included bombing; there was, in other words, really no political option at all.

What lesson is to be derived from these two cases? Simply this: effective planning calls for a multiplicity of inputs. To achieve this multiplicity, the planner must studiously avoid becoming the captive of any one group of advisors or experts. To emphasize this point, we might cite one more example—this time from the Kennedy administration.

Shortly after the Bay of Pigs disaster, a number of members of the Kennedy circle became increasingly uneasy with decision-making processes of the administration. Arthur Goldberg, the new Secretary of Labor, finally asked the President why he had not consulted more widely, why he had taken such a narrow spectrum of advice, much of it so predictable. Kennedy said that he meant no offense, but although Goldberg was a good man, he *was* in labor, not in foreign policy.

"You're wrong," Goldberg replied, "you're making the mistake of compartmentalizing your Cabinet." The secretary then went on to point out— much to the president's surprise—that the two men in the Cabinet that should have been consulted were Orville Freeman, the Secretary of Agriculture, and himself. Freeman had been a Marine, made amphibious landings, and knew how tough such landings can be; and Goldberg had been in OSS during World War II and ran guerilla operations. (Halberstrom 1969:90)

2. After an adequate list of alternatives is developed, the next step is to consider their consequences. In this respect, the case of the Family Assistance Plan (FAP) is again instructive. In the first place, thanks to the development in early 1969 of a simulation model (discussed in Chapter 6), it was possible to actually test and cost-out the various versions of FAP. The use of this technique, probably without precedence in the development of major social legislation in the opinion of Moynihan, did much to discipline and inform debate.

In the second place, the case of FAP is instructive because it involved the use of experimentation. Hence, those wanting to know the consequences of the various versions of FAP merely had to examine the preliminary results from carefully designed negative income tax experiments in New Jersey, Iowa, and North Carolina.

The case of FAP involved the use of yet a third procedure to scrutinize the consequence of the alternatives: congressional hearings. While not as modern as computer simulation and social experimentation, it is, all in all, just as effective. In fact, it was this process more than the other two that proved most effective in exposing the undesirable consequences of FAP.

Significantly, such techniques to scrutinize consequences were certainly atrophed if not totally absent, in planning the war in Vietnam. Consider:

> Each time the question of the domino theory (that is, the theory that it was prudent to stop Communist agression in Vietnam rather than somewhere closer to home) was sent to intelligence experts for evaluation, they would send back answers that reflected their doubts about its validity, but the highest level of government left the theory alone. It was as if, by questioning it, they might have revealed its emptiness, and would then have been forced to act on their new discovery. (Halberstam 1969:152)

> Above all, Johnson believed in secrecy. He liked to control all discussions. . . . Thus by his very style Johnson limited the amount of intergovernmental debate, partly because debate went against his desire for consensus, whether a good policy or not, a wise one or not. The important thing was to get everyone aboard. . . . (ibid.:441)

> In early March 1965, a pessimistic Emmitt John Hughes, a former White House aide under Eisenhower, went to see McGeorge Bundy. What, Hughes asked, if the North Vietnamese retaliate by matching the American air escalation with their own ground escalation. Hughes would long remember the answer and the cool smile: "Just suppose it happens", Hughes persisted. Bundy answered, "We can't assume what we don't believe." (ibid.:640)

These three anecdotes bring to mind an aphorism by the German philosopher Nietzsche: "A very popular error: having the courage of one's convictions; rather it is a matter of having the courage for an *attack* on one's convictions!!!" Good philosophy, good administration.

Programming

The planning process began, it will be recalled, on a lofty plane, where goals are set and policy established. That stage then merged into a consideration of alternatives and their consequences. Now we arrive at the point where these alternatives must be divided into specific targets that need to be met and actions that need to be taken in order that the objectives are attained. A program is thus a governmental action initiated in order to secure objectives whose attainment is by means certain without human effort. The degree to which the predicted consequences take place we call *successful implementation.* To put it inelegantly, implementation is the nuts and bolts of the planning process. (Programming or implementation is similar to what private sector managers call control).

Consider policies with the objective of improving environmental quality. A variety of specific actions are available to give effect to environmental policies. These approaches to policy objectives fall into four general sets (Caldwell, 1972). In brief:

1. Self-executory: for example, the pricing of pollution and other forms of environmental degradation through taxes, licenses, and rebates.
2. Self-helping: for example, establishment of environmental rights which may be enforced through judicial action.

3. Technological: for instance, specifications regarding applications of technology; assistance for development of ameliorating technological innovations.

4. Administrative: for instance, air and water quality standards; controls over emissions, land use, water disposal, and other environment-affecting behaviors.

What, then, should those at "the top" do? Perhaps the most important rule to follow is: do not divorce programming or implementation from policy. Later we shall see that this rule is more than a homily. Chapters 7 and 8 stress the need for careful attention — early in the planning process — to the organizational structure for executing a program. Chapter 9, which is concerned largely with implementation, focuses on a number of specific steps that the planner can take to tie policy and implementation together. Among such steps, we shall consider the role of incentives, penalties, and rewards; the reduction of the length and unpredictability of necessary decision sequences; and the creation of an effective communication system.

Evaluation

The last stage in our basic model is evaluation. It is axiomatic that effective planning requires periodic review to insure not only that the plans are being carried out in the prescribed manner but also that they are achieving the expected results — an axiom of administration not always honored.

This task, in turn, requires that the output of public services be measured. A new and important area of social research, evaluation techniques are discussed in Chapter 9.

In this chapter, we have attempted to set forth a few basic planning terms and to get a bird's-eye view of the planning process. The picture offered by the basic model is admittedly oversimplified, but it does provide a means of unifying greatly the material of the next four chapters.

NAILING DOWN THE MAIN POINTS

1 The essence of planning is to see opportunities and threats in the future and to exploit or combat them by decisions taken in the present. More rigorously defined, a policy is a statement of goals and of the relative importance attached to each goal. It can be translated into a plan by specifying the objectives to be attained. A proposed set of specific actions intended to implement a plan is called a program.

2 The rational planning process goes thus: (a) Identify the problems to be solved; (b) Design alternative courses of action to solve the problem and forecast the consequences of each alternative; (c) Compare and evaluate

the alternatives and choose the one whose probable consequences would be preferable; (*d*) Design a plan of action for implementing the preferred alternative; and (*e*) Keep the plan current through a feedback and review.

3 Policy planning, the process of determining goals and their priorities, is often ignored in American government. Too much public policy is defined in terms of program; as such, it seeks to deal only with parts of the system. The influence of political leadership is perhaps greatest at this early stage in the planning process.

4 In the medium-range planning stage, policy begins to be converted into action. Here, in particular, we are concerned with the design of alternatives and the evaluation of each in terms of its consequences. Common errors in this stage: failure to consider enough alternatives and reluctance to question rigorously every alternative (and the assumptions upon which it is founded).

5 Implementation and evaluation are the final two stages in the planning process. They will be discussed more fully in Chapter 9.

CONCEPTS FOR REVIEW

city planning	policy, plan, and program
land-use plans	goals, objectives, and actions
zoning laws	rational planning model
comprehensive plan	planning premises
development planning	policy planning
Balanced Growth and Economic	medium-range planning
Planning Act	programming; implementation
fiscal policy making	evaluation

PROBLEMS

1. Public officials at all levels of government are frequently criticized for short-sighted decisions. Elected officials may be accused of looking forward only as far as the next election and of placing narrow, parochial interests above the general welfare. To what extent is such criticism justified? Do you see any solution?

2. The anecdote about Kennedy and Goldberg in this chapter illustrates the need for a chief executive to consult widely before important decisions. Discuss the problems that might arise if this approach to decision making is pushed too far.

3. Planning like other good things has its limitations. One authority on planning lists among the more important shortcomings the following:

   Environmental events cannot always be controlled.
   Internal resistance.

Planning is expensive.

Ineffective during sudden crises.

What might an agency do to overcome these shortcomings? Can you think of other limitations on planning?

4. Unlike several European countries, the United States does not have a full-fledged national planning body. Nonetheless, a number of institutions such as the Council of Economic Advisors, do have important planning functions. What other institutions would you say contribute to planning at the national level? Should the United States have a central planning body?

5. The Environmental Protection Agency routinely disseminates air and water pollution abatement requirements that virtually dictate state and local land use in many situations; this activity reflects a national awareness that in a complex industrial society many sorts of public regulation and planning are inescapable. It also poses a national dilemma. On the one hand, the federal government can tamper with a 200-year-old national tradition of land use being determined primarily by private initiative. On the other, it can do nothing. The second option allows communities all over the country, beset by growth troubles, to adopt growth plans. (In 1971, for example, Boulder, Colorado, called for a population limitation.) Do you think local governments can effectively influence growth and development? Since the national population is to increase at least 50 million people in the next 25 years, is growth control really just a fancy term for exclusionary policies? Will attempts to manage growth have a negative impact on the local economy?

6. Using back issues of local newspapers, survey the planning process in one urban area for one particular policy problem (e.g., mass transportation). Pay particular attention to when the need was first perceived, who the participants were, what the "leverage points" were, and where the sources of funds were. (The term leverage points refers to those participants who, at various times in the entire process, exhibited exceptional power or influence over the course of events.)

7. In his *Doomsday Syndrome,* John Maddox argues that forecasts, designed to influence public planners, are often so exaggerated and simplified that their effect is the very opposite of what their authors desire. Far from alerting planners to important problems, the doomsday syndrome may so condition them to disaster that it undermines the capacity of the human race to survive. Discuss.

6

Decision Making

INTRODUCTION

Decision making means selecting from various alternatives, one course of action. As such, it can not be divorced from the planning process described in the preceding chapter. Herbert Simon (1957:1) said that the "task of 'deciding' pervades the entire administrative organization quite as much as does the task of 'doing'—indeed, it is integrally tied up with the latter."

Melvin Anshen (in Steiner 1969:326) is quite explicit on the relationship between decision making and planning. According to Anshen, decisions can even be classified in terms of planning. For example, some decisions are agenda decisions *because they involve identifying problems and assigning priorities among problems. Other decisions,* search decisions, *are related to the selection of procedures for finding solutions.* Allocation decisions, *a third type, commit resources to specific actions to solve the problem.* Implementation decisions *involve determining who does what, when, where, and how. Finally,* evaluation decisions *concern the measurement of performance against some standard. Appropriately, then, we follow our chapter on planning with one on decision making.*

Below we begin by considering three models that attempt to explain how decisions are really made in the public sector. This discussion is followed by a detailed examination of one of the three, the rational model. As we shall see, rational decision making can be either quantitative or nonquantitative. Both approaches to rational decision making are noted. The chapter concludes with a critique of the rational approach in general and systems analysis in particular.

HOW DECISIONS ARE MADE

In recent years, a number of writers have attempted to develop better models to explain how decisions are actually made in the public sector. This section examines three explanatory models put forward by Graham Allison (1971).

The Rational Model

The rational model of decision making should not be entirely new to the reader, since the planning model described in the previous chapter uses most of the basic concepts that we associate with the rational model. To see what these concepts are, let us review how the rational decision maker analyzes a problem.

A classical formulation runs something like this. Faced with a problem, the rational actor first clarifies his *goals* or *objectives*. He then translates the goals or objectives into a "payoff" (or *utility*), which represents the value of alternative sets of consequences. Next, he lists all the possible ways of achieving his goals; these are his *alternatives*. Fourth, he investigates all the important consequences that would follow from each of the alternatives. Finally, the decision maker makes his *choice* by selecting that alternative whose consequences rank highest in light of his goals. In short, we say that the rational decision maker consistently maximizes his values.

In one of former Secretary of Defense Robert McNamara's most important policy addresses, a speech at Ann Arbor in 1962, we find a prime example of the application of the rational model of decision making. "Let us look at the situation today. First, given the current balance of nuclear powers, which we confidently expect to maintain in the years ahead, a surprise nuclear attack is *simply not a rational act for any enemy.* Nor would it be rational for an enemy to take the initiative in the use of nuclear weapons as an outgrowth of a limited engagement in Europe or elsewhere. I think we are entitled to conclude that either of these actions has been made highly *unlikely.*" (cited Allison 1971:19)

To see how deeply this rational model is engrained in our thinking, Allison (ibid.:28) suggests that we consider the language used in writing or speaking about international events: "We speak of occurrences not as unstructured happenings but rather as 'the Soviet decision to abstain from attack,' 'the Chinese policy concerning defense of the mainland,' and 'Japanese action in surrendering.'"

Since World War II, a rich assortment of tools, many of great power, have become available for managers in making decisions more easily and with more assurance that they are rational. A major portion of this chapter is devoted to them. But before we begin considering them, we must note two other models of how decisions are "really" made.

The Government Politics Model

Charles Lindblom (1968:Chapter 3) notes four shortcomings in the rational model. First, and most important, is the difficulty in identifying and isolating a given problem and its cause. Second, decision makers seldom have the time, the capacity, and the information necessary to make the in-depth studies that the rational method calls for. Third, the problem of values is especially nettlesome. Specifically, how does one identify values as required by the rational approach? If not all values can be considered, then some must be sacrificed. But which? Moreover, some values may be inconsistent with others. Fourth, the relationship between alternatives and consequences may be ambiguous.

Given these shortcomings, Lindblom suggests a method that he believes superior, *the incremental approach.* The administrator considers only a limited number of alternatives, which are only incremental modifications of (i.e., bit by bit additions to) past government activities. A good example of how this approach works is the budgetary process. Political scientist Richard Fenno (1966) finds that, over a 12-year period, appropriations of one third of the federal agencies were within 5 percent of the previous year's appropriation; in one half of all cases, appropriations were within 10 percent; and in three quarters of all cases, appropriations were within 30 percent. Thus it appears that decision makers do not annually review the whole range of existing and proposed policies but rather consider existing programs and expenditures as a base. This essentially conservative approach is taken not only because of the limitations to the rational approach but also because of the political expediency of incrementalism. That is, agreement comes easier in decision making when the items in dispute are only slight modifications to existing programs, when the consequences are already known (as in the case with on-going programs), and when heavy investments (*sunk costs*) can make radical change politically unwise.

While the incremental approach is not as neat as the rational approach, it does perhaps square better with reality—for decision making in the real world of public administration is generally a partial, sequential process rather than a spur of the moment affair. As Henry Fairlie (1965), a British journalist, points out, when decisions are made they emerge from a less than ideal process. He records the following observations by one of Britain's great prime ministers at the end of his career.

> I am not sure that there is really such a thing as "power" or "decision." I would certainly find it very hard to give you an example of when I have ever exercised power or taken a decision. Of course, I will try to make it all look very different in my memoirs: and if I am lucky, part of my vision will be accepted by historians, and I will be called a great statesman. But it all happens very differently. For one thing, there is just a build-up of big and small factors, and they may not be brought to your notice until the issue has already been decided; and, when you eventually have to decide, it may be in response to the smallest of them all. That is not "power" or "decision."

But to make the somewhat simplistic incremental model square even better with reality, we must fully appreciate its political dimension. In particular, we need to recognize that the participants in the decision process are highly partisan, that they differ in the values they think important, and that, consequently, they do not always act in unison. The picture that begins to emerge is probably not quite what an outsider might imagine.

Following Graham Allison we call this refined model of incremental decision making the *governmental politics model.* Decisions thus become the resultants of complex bargaining processes among governmental players. In this model, the governmental actors are viewed neither as rational actors nor as a conglomerate of organizations, but rather as individual players.

Organizational Process Model

According to our third model, public decision making is best understood as the "outputs of large organizations functioning according to standard patterns of behavior."

What are these "standard patterns of behavior"? Perhaps the best known is the rule-of-thumb; i.e., a judgment based on practical experience rather than the result of scientific inquiry. Recall J. Pierpont Morgan's famous rule-of-thumb: If you must think about the cost of your yacht, you shouldn't own one. Few organizations can operate without these labor-saving devices. They help expedite many aspects of the operation of an agency, from hiring personnel to replacing equipment.

Herbert Simon (1957) contends that a widely used administration rule-of-thumb is *satisficing.* Rather than maximize a value—as in the rational model—the organization merely finds a course of action that is "good enough." Organizations that satisfice are happy to find a needle in the haystack rather than searching for the sharpest needle in the haystack.

Simon also distinguishes between *programmed* and *nonprogrammed* decisions. In computer language, programmed decisions are those that can be programmed on a computer; nonprogrammed decisions can not. Broadly, the former are repetitive and routine; the latter, novel and unstructured. Frequently, large service agencies in the treatment of clients can use a programmed decision approach.

Standard Operating Procedure (SOP) is a well known standard pattern of behavior found in organization. The U.S. Navy's failure to anticipate the Japanese attack on Pearl Harbor illustrates how SOP can work. Since an extraordinary amount and quality of intelligence of Japanese movements was available, the rational model seems to suggest that conspiracy, incompetence, or both were involved in the Pearl Harbor tragedy. But this interpretation proves incorrect. Writes Allison (1971:88,93): "Instead the Navy's activity on December 7 was identical with its behavior on December 6, which differed imperceptibly from its behavior on December 5, and so on. Each of these details represents standard outputs of an organization functioning according to very established routines." Even when a breakthrough occurred when the Japanese codes were cracked, the question in the navy was not "What do these messages mean?" Rather, it was an organizational one: "Who would perform the task of serious evaluation of enemy intentions— the Office of Naval Intelligence or the War Plans Division?"

MAJOR TOOLS AND TECHNIQUES FOR RATIONAL DECISION MAKING

In the preceding section, we examined three models of public decision making and found each to have explanatory power within its own right. The remainder of this chapter, however, focuses on only one: the rational model. Because the tools and techniques associated with the rational approach appear likely to grow in effectiveness and increase in popularity, this focus seems justified. Administrators, particularly top administrators, do not need to have a specialist's understanding of the methodology of the newer quantitative techniques for rational decisions. But a conceptual understanding is useful, for administrators must be in a position to ask staff specialists the right questions about their assumptions, methods, and results. Steiner (1969:428) puts it well:

> Managers should have an understanding about where the tools can be most useful and what their limitations are in different parts of the planning process, for different problems, and in different time phases of planning. Managers should have some knowledge of the methods to be able to adapt the techniques to their own particular problems. Above all, managers must have a conceptual understanding to avoid, on the one hand, being captives of staff specialists or, on the other hand, blindly dismissing the techniques because they refuse to try to understand them.

Nonquantitative Methods

Rational decision need not be always quantitative. Effective decisions often require no more than a healthy dose of common sense laced with logic. In the next few paragraphs, we consider a couple of nonquantitative elements that any rational decision should contain.

First, decision makers should establish what kind of problem exists. More specifically, they need to ask if the problem is generic or unique? (See Drucker 1966:123.) Most of the problems an administrator faces are generic, though this is not always apparent.

Too often problems or events appear to be unique when actually they are symptoms of more basic problems. The decision maker should therefore attempt from the start to discover this underlying problem. Then he or she can make a decision that establishes a rule or principle. In this way, good administrators need not make many decisions.

In other words, good administrators avoid cosmetic solutions. But the temptation to treat symptoms can be strong, particularly in an age of technology. Consider the concept of the *technology fix*. The concept was defined by Dr. Alvin M. Weinberg (1966) as an innovation devised for the purpose of correcting a social defect. Admittedly, the device has its advantages sometimes; e.g., drugs taken orally to prevent unwanted conception as a measure of population control. But not always. Stronger locks, higher (perhaps electrified) fences, and more powerful police weapons can, for example, reduce the *symptoms* of crime without affecting the real causes. Even Weinberg admits that Hitler's machinery for the extermination of the Jews was itself a monstrous kind of technology fix.

But let us return to the distinction between generic and unique problems and ask, What does the decision maker do about truly unique problems? Drucker maintains that events that appear to be completely isolated events turn out to be, upon closer examination, the first manifestations of a new generic problem. Surely this was true of the free speech movement at Berkeley, the 1965 power failure in the whole northeastern North America, and the thalidomide tragedy. These three "isolated" events were actually bellwethers — to the campus turmoil of the late 1960s, the energy squeeze of the early 1970s, and the increased concern over assessing new technologies of the 1960s and 1970s.

Such events call not for unique but for generic solutions. Drucker (ibid.:166) argues that a major failure of the Kennedy administration was its tendency to treat generic situations as unique. In the name of pragmatism, its members refused to develop rules and principles and insisted on treating everything "on its own merits." Some would argue that bureaucracy does just the opposite — that is, treats the unique as the generic.

With the problem accurately defined, the administrator then turns to framing the response. Here careful attention should be given to what I shall term the upper and lower limits of the decision.

By *upper limits,* I refer to the ever-present limitations that determine how far the administrator can go. Sorensen (1963:22–42), in his lectures on decision making in the White House, notes five:

1. The limits of permissibility (is it legal? will others accept it?).
2. The limits of available resources.
3. The limits of available time.
4. The limits of previous commitments.
5. The limits of available information.

Though Sorenson's list is self-explanatory, his fifth point merits emphasis simply because administrators rely so much on past experiences in making decisions. The experienced administrator believes, often without realizing it, that past mistakes and accomplishments are an almost infallible guide in decision-making situations. Hardly, Sorenson seems to be saying. Rather, administrators must try to visualize the world as a whole and as a total system in which their own personal experiences are a very small and inadequate sample. A major corrective to this generalizing from personal experience is statistical analysis. Modern statistics is based on the concept of probability; it deals with the problem of making a probability judgment about a characteristic of the population (e.g., income) on the basis of information derived from a small sample of that population. Statistical analysis has come to play an increasingly important role among sophisticated administrators.

By *lower limits* I refer to what at least must occur for the problem to be solved. For example, Germany knew at the outbreak of World War I that it could win if and only if two minimum conditions were met. Germany would (Condition I) put up weak resistance against Russia thus allowing it to (Condition II) concentrate forces for a knockout blow to France. But as Russia began to penetrate deeper and deeper into East Prussia, the German general staff decided to pull forces from the Western front. Condition II was therefore not met and the chance for victory lost. (Drucker 1966:132)

Chester I. Barnard (1938:202–5) introduced an idea quite similar to that of lower limits which he calls the *limiting* (*strategic*) *factor* in decision making. It is the factor "whose control, in the right form, at the right place and time, will establish a new system or set of conditions which meets the purpose. Thus, if we wish to increase the yield of grain in a certain field and analyze the soil, it may appear that the soil lacks potash; potash may be said to be the strategic (or limiting) factor." If an administrator can discover the strategic factor—can exercise control at the right times, right place, right amount, and right form—then the decision becomes not only simpler (for other factors tend to work themselves out) but also more economical.

In the following subsections, the emphasis begins to shift increasingly to quantitative techniques. But before we begin, two points. First, the list of management tools that follows is not exhaustive. In fact, in later chapters, we shall have occasion to introduce additional ones. But even then, no more than a small sampling will have been presented. My second point is simply this: these tools provide no substitute for judgment and experience. Nor do they give us certainty. I have termed them management tools because they do what tools do: help.

Scheduling Models

Scheduling models facilitate the coordination of activities of an enterprise and help achieve a better utilization of resources. These models are useful for a wide range of activities, from a seemingly trivial task of scheduling of a field office tour for a high ranking official to a very complex job of scheduling activities in the space program. While a wide variety of such scheduling models are in use, we shall mention only three: Gantt chart, Critical Path Method (CPM), and Program Evaluation Review Technique (PERT). Fortunately, understanding the basics of these scheduling models requires no technical background.

The Gantt bar chart was developed in 1917 by Henry L. Gantt. Essentially, the bar chart describes progress by comparing work done against planned

FIGURE 6–1
Gantt Bar Chart

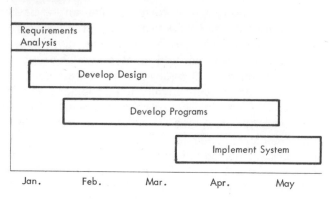

Jan.	Feb.	Mar.	Apr.	May

objectives. Figure 6–1 shows the application of the basic Gantt charting technique to a generalized project.

The Gantt chart might be redesigned as a CPM chart. This would have several advantages. First, because bars are replaced by a network of flow plan, the network shows how the events and activities are related. In CPM and PERT charts, events (e.g., "start testing") are often shown as circles.

Paris Match/Carone

Ever-present limitations determine how far decision making in the White House can go. One of John F. Kennedy's top advisors noted five: permissibility, available resources, available time, previous commitments, and available information (see text).

Activities are the time consuming elements of the program and are used to connect the various events; they are shown as arrows. Thus, the CPM chart reflects all significant program accomplishments and thus approximates the complexity of the program.

Since most events depend on one or more prior events, the charts show the interrelationship of events leading to the accomplishments of the ultimate objective. Within the project is a *critical path,* that is, the longest possible time span along the system flow plan. To determine the critical path, events are organized in sequence. The starting point for plotting the critical paths is the final event in the total network. From the final event, related events are placed sequentially backwards, until the starting point is reached. Next, all the expected elapsed times (t_e) are summed throughout the network paths to determine the total expected elapsed time for every path of the network. The completion date of the project is dependent on the path that takes the longest time. Because this path has the highest total elapsed time, it is called the critical path. (In Figure 6–2 the critical path is indicated by heavy arrows.)

Knowing the critical path can be very useful to the decision maker. If an activity is on the critical path, any slippage or delay for the activity will delay the completion of the entire project. Conversely, slippage in an activity not on the critical path will normally not affect the project deadline, since the difference between the lengths of time along the critical path and the non-critical paths is slack time.

To determine the elapsed time between events one must make estimates. When the decision maker has had some experience with the various activities in the project, he or she can use estimates based on this experience. This approach might be fine for public works projects such as street construction

FIGURE 6–2
PERT Network

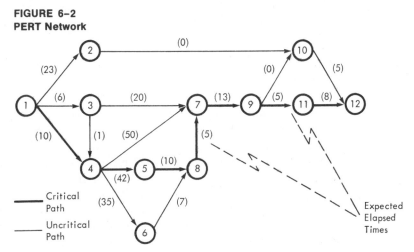

Source: Adapted from Air Force Systems Command (1963:11–18).

and repair, but when confronted with a nonregular project — e.g., the Polaris submarine project — estimation would be more difficult. In such cases, the decision maker needs a more systematic approach to estimation. PERT provides it.

With PERT, expected elapsed-time between events is based on three possible completion assumptions: Optimistic completion time (*O*), most likely completion time (*M*), and pessimistic completion time (*P*). Based on these three-time estimates, a simple formula can be derived that will give an estimation of how long the activity will take. Assuming $O = 6$ weeks, $M = 8$ weeks, and $P = 16$ weeks, the expected elapsed time can be computed using the formula:

$$\frac{O + 4M + P}{6} = t_e = \frac{6 + 32 + 16}{6} = 9$$

The estimation is then used in the flow diagram.

PERT can also assist the administrator in *cost accounting*. As used in this chapter, the term cost accounting refers to determining the cost to be associated with each benefit received by the public. The more usual approach is to merely record and report how much was spent. The term is defined more fully in Chapter 11.

In using PERT-cost, the administrator must now develop cost estimates for each activity. In Figure 6–2, only the addition of these cost estimates is necessary to adapt the basic PERT to handle costs. If we have costs as well as times for each activity, we are able to compare planned expenditures and time. For example, if a PERT computation showed that 20 percent of an activity was completed but 40 percent of the money budgeted for it had been spent, then the activity might be heading for a cost overrun. This trend should be of major concern to the administrator.

While PERT has obvious strengths — it forces careful planning, permits experimentation, encourages participation in the planning process, permits effective control, etc. — it is not without its limitations. Recent evidence points to decreased use by NASA and its contractors. Many capable administrators insist that one cannot wait for a problem to make itself known through such schedule control techniques: anticipating trouble requires closer observation.

Sapololsky (in Lambright 1976:54) suggests that PERT might have a political rather than management function. In his account of the development of the Polaris submarine (where PERT and a dozen other management techniques originated), he writes: "Whenever there was a question on Polaris's development status or the like, program officials always had a colored chart, a slide, or a computer printout which would demonstrate the effectiveness of the management team. Actually, this strategy might well be labelled the 'Slight of Hand Strategy' since few of these management techniques were ever used to manage the Polaris development. The use of PERT in the program, for example, was strongly opposed by those technical officers who

Saturn Program Control Center with a control chart in background. Do you think it is for "evaluation and review" or for show?

were in charge of the development effort and there never was a complete application of the technique in the program, but the illusion of PERT's use was carefully cultivated. During most critical stages of the Polaris development when PERT's role was minimal, the program held hundreds of briefings and prepared thousands of booklets describing how PERT was guiding the missile's progress. The message was that no one need be concerned about the quality of the program's development decisions as the program itself was the pioneer in perfecting management systems for complex projects. And since enough people who could influence policy believed this to be the case, the program was able to gain the independence and flexibility it needed to deal effectively with the missile's technological uncertainties."

Relevance Tree

The relevance tree is a structural analysis that can help the decision makers (a) insure that a program contains all the necessary elements and (b) allocate resources to maximize some utility. Both aims of a relevance tree appear in the generalized tree shown in Figure 6–3.

To make the concept clearer, let us consider a specific application in the

FIGURE 6–3
Relevance Tree

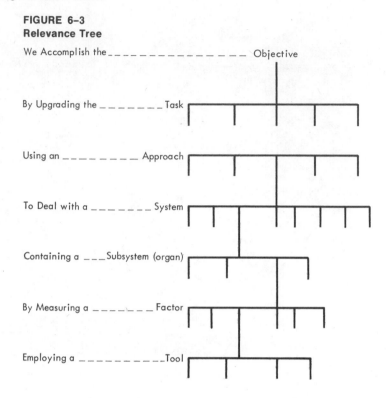

We Accomplish the _ _ _ _ _ _ _ _ _ _ _ _ _ _ _ Objective

By Upgrading the _ _ _ _ _ _ _ Task

Using an _ _ _ _ _ _ _ _ Approach

To Deal with a _ _ _ _ _ _ _ System

Containing a _ _ _ Subsystem (organ)

By Measuring a _ _ _ _ _ _ _ Factor

Employing a _ _ _ _ _ _ _ _ _ _ Tool

area of biomedicine (Bright 1972). A national biomedical objective might be "to maximize human life span with optimal health and activity in all environments." The six tree levels, in turn, might be defined as follows:

1. Task: The principal areas of activity devoted to the determination, treatment, and prevention of disease; the administration and efficient operation of hospitals and clinics; the education of future researchers and practitioners; and the application of biomedical science to military and space problems.

2. Approach: The general procedures to be applied to specific tasks (such as surgery under the treatment branch of level B).

3. System: A major (bodily) activity carried out by several units (organs) operating together under integrated control (e.g., reflex control of locomotion, circulation of blood).

4. Subsystem: A unit, either natural or artificial, that performs a specialized activity (things to be examined).

5. Factor: The parameters that need to be measured, analyzed, and/or controlled to evaluate or cause the normal or abnormal operation of an organ.

6. Tool: Devices in the form of hardware or software used to acquire or process data or to treat, cure, or prevent disease.

The task level of the tree might be charted as below:

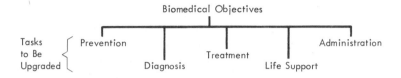

As used here, prevention refers to the reduction of the future incidence of abnormalities, arrest of the threatened onset of disease, and control of the population explosion. Diagnosis, to the means of determining the status of the whole organism. Treatment, to the means by which abnormalities of the organism are corrected or held static. Life support, to the enhancement of useful activity of the human being in space, undersea, or other non-earth-surface environmental conditions. And administration, to the means employed to manage directly and indirectly total patient care, education, and research programs in the field of biomedicine.

At the approach level, the tree begins to branch considerably. The diagnosis task for example, might be divided as follows:

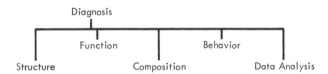

Each approach can, in turn, be divided in a similar manner. But the idea should be clear enough now: The relevance tree is designed to show what is required for a mission or system and to reveal the missing parts.

The relevance tree, in addition, provides a useful methodology for relating future spending to national needs. For example, the National Institute of Health spent over $1.6 billion in 1975 for support of research and development in human health. The relevance tree could help us distribute those funds more wisely. We begin by establishing the relative importance of improving each task (viz., prevention, diagnosis, treatment, life support, and administration) to the accomplishment of the overall objective.

But to do this, we must be more precise about our objective. Specifically we need to express it in terms of a set of criteria. For example, we could use the following:

C_1 Influence on population dynamics.

C_2 Implications for government-directed medical services.

C_3 Degree to which task contributes to increased age of modal death or reduction of disability time.

C_4 Psychological impact on world opinion if task not accomplished.

C_5 Effect on cost of medical care to the individual.

But, obviously, these five are not equally important. To account for this inequality, we need to "weight" them, that is, assign them numbers indicating their relative importance. So, let us say that the importance of C_1, C_2, C_3, C_4, and C_5 are 0.20, 0.10, 0.30, 0.15, and 0.25 respectively. Let us be clear on what this means. Among other things, it says that C_3 is three times more important than C_2 in attaining our overall objective.

Now we are in a much better position to suggest which tasks are the most important. In plain English, we want to assign the most dollars to those tasks that are most effective in terms of the more important criteria.

The matrix in Figure 6–4 provides a convenient framework for these calculations. The relevance number (R_N) for each task is computed by weighting each task against each single criterion in turn. For example, how much does prevention contribute to C_1 relative to the other four tasks? Say that its contribution is quite high, around 0.40. (This also tells us that somehow 0.60 must be proportional among the other four tasks.) Next, we multiply the weight of criterion 1 by 0.40. This gives us a 0.08 to put in the upper left-hand cell. Similarly, we multiply the weighted criterion 2 by the relative importance of prevention; we do the same with criteria 3, 4, and 5. Add the five products. This sum is the final relevance number for the task of prevention.

FIGURE 6–4
Form for Relevance Assignment at the Task Level

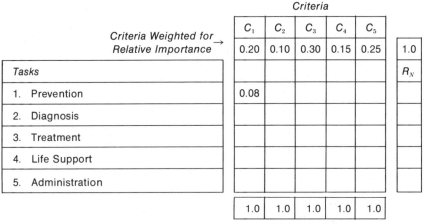

Tasks Weighted for Relative Importance to Each Criterion

Criteria

Criteria Weighted for Relative Importance →	C_1	C_2	C_3	C_4	C_5	
	0.20	0.10	0.30	0.15	0.25	1.0
Tasks						R_N
1. Prevention	0.08					
2. Diagnosis						
3. Treatment						
4. Life Support						
5. Administration						
	1.0	1.0	1.0	1.0	1.0	

Task Upgrading

Source: Adapted from Bright (1972, Exhibit 7.6).

Four more rows to go. So, we must do a similar calculation for each of the four remaining tasks. Final relevance numbers for all tasks should add up to one. In theory at least we would use these numbers to determine how much of the $1.6 billion would go to each task. Of course, the same procedure could be applied to approach level in the original relevance tree. For example, assume the R_N for Diagnosis was calculated to be 0.20. Using new criteria, 0.20 can be proportioned among structure, function, composition, behavior, and data analysis. Obviously, toward the bottom of the tree, the relevance numbers become quite small. Nonetheless, armed with this kind of information, we should be better able to answer the question of whether we are distributing our R&D resources appropriately against the vast range of research possibilities and future needs.

Decision Trees

Another network approach to structuring complex problems is the decision tree. In this approach, the decision is not viewed as an isolated decision because today's decision depends upon the ones we shall make tomorrow. Thus, the decision problem is examined in terms of a tree of decisions. The tree uses decision forks and chance forks to indicate the interrelationships of choice and possible events.

A typical decision problem that would benefit from this approach is the case of a community threatened with a landslide sometime during the next year, before reforestation is completed (adopted from Public Policy Program, 1972). The basic decision is whether to build a retaining wall. In Figure 6–5, this decision is represented by the small square at the far left. Emanating from the square are two forks—the upper one representing the decision to build; the lower one, the decision not to build.

Regardless of the decision, however, the landslide could occur. This possibility is indicated slightly to the right of the decision square by the two chances nodes. Emanating from each node are two forks—the upper ones representing the actual occurrence of a slide. Based on expert judgment or historical records, a probability is assigned that a slide will occur. In this case it is one-in-five or simply .2. Since retaining walls do not always hold, we must indicate the possibility of failure by yet another chance node even farther to the right. The probability of failure is estimated to be .3.

At the extreme right of Figure 6–5, we have calculated the probabilities of every possible outcome. Once we combine this information with certain costs figures, we are on the way to knowing whether to build. Basically, we need two costs figures. First, if a landslide occurs, we estimate that the only damages will be to property, valued at $3 million, since population can evacuate. Second, constructing a retaining wall will cost $200 thousand.

What is the cost of the decision to build? In addition to the outright cost of $200,000, we must figure the benefit from avoiding property damage. This would be 0.14 × $3 million or $420,000. The net benefit of the decision to build is, therefore, $420,000 minus $200,000 or $220,000.

FIGURE 6-5

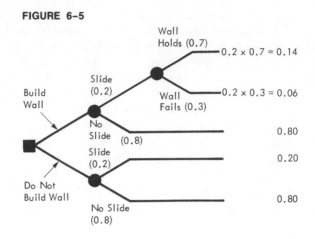

The problem could be made more complicated but more realistic by call-ing in experts to give their opinions. The occurrence of slides depends in part upon underlying geographical features. Having established what these features are, the experts can assess the likelihood of a slide better than they could without the tests. How would you set the problem up now?

Systems Approach

The systems approach is not easily defined. In fact, it has been compared to the geological phenomenon known as "Roxbury puddingstone" in both history and construction. "This formation, located in a suburb of Boston, Massachusetts, resulted from glacial movement, which over the miles and the centuries dragged with it, accumulated, and then incorporated a vast heterogeny of types of rock, all set in a matrix and solidified in an agglomerate mass. Many fragments still retain their original identity and character; some have undergone metamorphosis in varying degrees. In like manner, the sys-tems approach is kind of mosaic, made up of bits and pieces of ideas, the-ories, and methodology from a number of disciplines. . . ." (Hoos, 1972:27). Discernable among these disciplines are engineering, sociology, biology, philosophy, psychology, and economics.

Very broadly, the systems approach, or systems analysis, forces us to look at problems as systems, that is, assemblies of interdependent compo-nents. While this may sound commonsensical—even trite—it is often ig-nored. Consider this classic from Barry Commoner's *The Closing Circle* (1971:180).

A basic problem in sewage treatment is that, when organic sewage is dumped into a river or lake, it generates an inordinate demand for oxygen. But oxygen is needed as well for the bacteria of decay, which use the oxygen converting organic matter to inorganic breakdown products. "As a result,

this practice of dumping has commonly depleted the oxygen supply of surface waters, killing off the bacteria of decay and thereby halting the aquatic
cycle of self-purification." Enter the sanitation engineer. His solution is
simply to domesticate the bacteria of decay in a treatment plant, artificially
supplying them with sufficient oxygen to accommodate the entering organic
material. Thus what is released from the treatment plant is largely inorganic
residues. "Since these have no oxygen demands, the problem, as stated, has
been solved."

Unfortunately, the sanitation engineer did not recognize that he was dealing with a system, and that system includes nature's rivers and streams. The
treated sewage is now rich in the inorganic residues of decay — carbon diox-
ide, nitrate, and phosphate — which support the growth of algae. "Now heavily fertilized, the algae bloom furiously, soon die, releasing organic matter,
which generates the oxygen demand that sewage technology had removed."

In order to appreciate better the specifics of the systems approach, we
shall classify the methodology into four basic steps: (1) problem formulation, (2) modeling, (3) analysis and optimization, and (4) implementation.

1. Problem formulation is perhaps the most difficult step, sometimes requiring three fourths of the total effort. This step includes the detailed description of the task and identification of important variables and their relationships. Consider, for example, an investigation into some observed and
perceived difficulties in an urban transportation system. In the systems approach, one begins by deciding whether the prime objective is better service,
lower cost, less pollution, or something else. One must also decide what
data are necessary: passenger miles by mode of transportation; passenger
miles by sex, age, race, and income; passenger miles by time and place; etc.
Finally, one must identify key decision makers in the urban area and their
motivations.

2. The scene changes in the next step: one goes from the real world of
the problem to the abstract world of the modeler. The modeler's task is probably more artistic than rigorous, more creative than systematic. He must
strike a balance between including all relevant aspects of reality and keeping that model simple enough that it is in line with existing theoretical loads,
computation time, and data availability. Ultimately, of course, the test of a
model's quality is how effective it is in helping to solve the original problem.
Figure 6–6 shows a model for a criminal justice system.

To the uninitiated, a frequent cause of puzzlement is how models such as
the one shown in Figure 6–6 can be "quantified." In other words, how can
the analyst convert something as physical, as real as police and courts into
something as abstract as a set of mathematical relationships? While the
equations relating the different components in Figure 6–6 probably present
a level of sophistication far beyond the scope of this text, the idea behind this
mathematically representing a physical system involves no chicanery.

Take, for example, a simple inventory system. What would be some important variables in such a system? Among them would probably be:

C_O = The cost of ordering per unit.

C_H = The cost of holding per unit per time period.

D = The quantity of units used each time period.

A useful model, incorporating these variables, would be:

$$Q = \text{most economical quantity to order} = \sqrt{\frac{2C_O D}{C_H}}$$

FIGURE 6–6
Model of Criminal Justice System

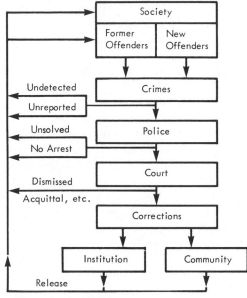

Source: Lapatra (1973:154).

3. During the analysis and optimization step, the model is studied to find the best strategy for resolving the problem given. Two options might be mentioned: computer simulation and sensitivity analysis.

Simulation models, for instance, allow users to replicate to a very great extent the actual dispatch and patrol operations of most urban police departments. (See Larson 1973.) The simulation works in the following way. Incidents are generated throughout the city and distributed randomly in time and space according to observed statistical patterns. Each incident has an associated priority number, the lower numbers designating the more important incidents. For instance, a Priority 1 incident would be an officer in trouble, a felony in progress or a seriously injured person; a Priority 4 incident could be an open fire hydrant, a lock-out, or a parking violation. As each incident becomes known, an attempt is made to assign (dispatch) a patrol unit to the scene of the incident. In attempting this assignment, the computer is programmed to duplicate as closely as possible the decision-making logic of an actual police dispatcher. In certain cases this assignment cannot be performed because the congestion level of the accumulated incidents is too high; then, the incident report (which might in actuality be a complaint ticket) joins a queue of waiting reports. The queue is depleted as incidents are assigned to available patrol units.

The model is designed to study two general classes of administrative policies—the patrol deployment strategy, and the dispatch and reassignment policy.

The patrol deployment strategy determines the total number of patrol units, whether units are assigned to nonoverlapping sectors, which sectors constitute a geographical command and which areas are more heavily patrolled than others. The dispatch and reassignment policy specifies the set of decision rules the dispatcher follows when attempting to assign a patrol unit to a reported incident. Included in the dispatch policy are the priority structure, rules about crossprecinct dispatching, the queue discipline, and so forth.

Environmental Protection Agency

Simulation of models does not always take place on computers. Nor need it always involve sophisticated mathematics. The Federal Environmental Protection Agency, for example, has designed a tank to find better ways to handle oil spills. The principle involved is no different than the one used in the text with criminal justice: Much time and money can be saved by first testing various alternatives on a model rather than in the real world.

The model tabulates several important measures of operational effectiveness. These include statistics on dispatcher queue length, patrol travel times, amount of preventive patrol, workloads of individual patrol units, the amount of intersector dispatches, and others.

In sum, simulation provides a tool to assist in answering a wide range of allocation questions. Police administrators should find simulation models valuable for the following purposes:

They facilitate detailed investigations of operations throughout the city (or part of the city).

They provide a consistent framework for estimating the value of new technologies.

They serve as training tools to increase awareness of the system interactions and consequences resulting from everyday policy decisions.

They suggest new criteria for monitoring and evaluating actual operating systems.

Perhaps the most ambitious application of simulation is the previously mentioned model by Dennis Meadows that treats the entire world as an interdependent unit (read: system). When the model was simulated, the computer projected that the level of world pollution would eventually skyrocket and population would plummet; following this catastrophe, however, the quality of life would rise rapidly, reaching previously unknown heights. (See Figure 6–7.)

FIGURE 6–7

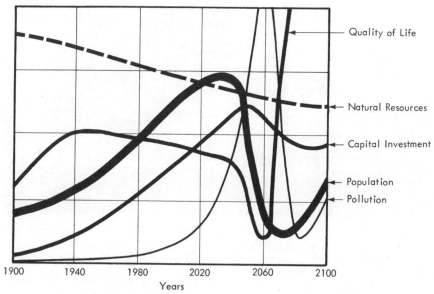

Sources: Adapted from Meadows et al. (1972).

One of the advantages of simulation derives from the *counter intuitive* nature of public systems. To call these systems counter intuitive is to say that they do not react in ways we think they should. The reason why intuition provides so little guidance in understanding a system's behavior is that the human brain cannot grasp the totality of relationships among all the variables. Thus, common sense tells us that wider highways reduce congestion, but as urban planners have learned, the reverse is often the case.

Still the accuracy of such long-range forecasting remains in doubt. Critics complain that the computer's hard numbers add a degree of precision and credibility that is totally undeserved. In rebuttal, the systems analysts argue that the data on which the national and global models depend are improving. Furthermore, they point out that the techniques of building and working with large complex models of urban, national, and global systems is very much in its infancy. As one of the pioneers in computer simulation points out: "Much of the criticism stems from comparing early work to a nonexistent perfection."

Another criticism was that the World III model ignored the world's vast regional differences. Significantly, a more recent model of Mesarovic and Pestel (1974) divides the world into ten regions based on socioeconomic levels. The authors maintain that a number of European Common Market planners and several research institutes have expressed interest in using it.

Not necessarily requiring the assistance of a computer, *sensitivity analysis* is another option which is available in analyzing the model to find the best strategy for solving the original problem. A sensitivity analysis process consists of making very small changes in the model to show the extent to which results may be importantly altered because of change in one or a few factors. To see how sensitivity analysis might work, let us reexamine Figure 6–6, which shows a model of an urban criminal justice system. Now assume that the mayor calls for a large reduction in the total operating expenses. Since one does not want to reduce the strength of the police force, the patrol on the line, one looks elsewhere for "fat." Assume, therefore, that the typing pool in the Probation Division is reduced. As a result, the typing of presentence reports of convicted defendants waiting to be sentenced is delayed. Defendants now must spend even more time in jails and the systems over all operating costs reach a new high.

Let us try a different tack: Discontinue night courts. But closing these courts adds substantial costs to the police, who will have to house, feed, and guard the defendants awaiting court action. Another suggestion might be to reduce the number of judges or prosecutors by 8 percent and the police by 3 percent. (Not entirely hypothetical, since this is precisely what New York City did in 1975). What results do you see from such a course of action? Do you see any effects on a city's tax base that might result from cuts in the area of criminal justice?

4. In this subsection, we have discussed the systems approach in terms of four steps, giving particular emphasis to the first three. The last step, imple-

mentation refers to the procedure by which the results determined from the model are translated as a set of actions to the real world. The four steps, however, seldom occur in perfect sequence; indeed, the systems approach is highly iterative. As such, it might easily move through a sequence of steps such as the following: Formulating the problem, selecting objectives, designing alternatives, collecting data, building models, weighting cost against effectiveness, testing for sensitivity, questioning assumptions, reexamining objectives, looking at new alternatives, reformulating the problem, selecting different or modified objectives, and so on. (Quade 1966:10)

Operations Research: The Tap Root of Systems Analysis

Preceding the arrival of the systems approach in the decision making centers of government was the use of operations research. The formal inception of operations research may, in fact, be traced to World War II. Faced with acute shortages of men and material and working against the clock, the military turned for assistance to the scientific and engineering community for help in resolving some knotty operations problems. These problems concerned for example, the most effective setting of the time fuse of a bomb dropped from an aircraft onto a submarine; the optimal formation of bombers as a function of a target shape; the best bomber-fighter combination to achieve maximum security and still accomplish the mission; the measurement of the effectiveness of arming merchant ships against enemy aircraft; and the optimal location of radar stations. And due to the revolution begun when electronic computers became commercially available and the increased demand for greater productivity on a large part of American industry, the use of operations research had by the early 1950s spread to industry.

While operations research, or management science as it is increasingly referred to, and the systems approach share many characteristics — e.g., use of interdisciplinary teams, modeling, and sophisticated mathematics — they are not the same. The scope of the former is narrower. It tends to be concerned with problems that can be represented by mathematical models that can be optimized. For example, a typical operations research problem would determine (subject to certain constraints) the optimal (i.e., the very best) location in terms of service for a new fire station or a new bus route in a city. Operations research tends, we might say, to be concerned with problems in the small. Indeed, it was because the World War II teams studied small, operational problems that the original (English) name was *operational research;* it was only later modified to operations research — with typical American unconcern for syntax.

The systems approach, on the other hand, is concerned with problems of greater complexity (recall the Club of Rome world models) and abstraction (hence: less emphasis on calculation). Actually, OR is one of the most important inputs to systems approach. The relationship then between the system approach and OR is much like that of strategy and tactics.

Of all the quantitative techniques that OR emphasizes, *linear programming* is one of the most widely used. Accordingly, we conclude our discussion of OR by considering linear programming.

Linear programming is a mathematical technique for deriving the optimal solutions to linear relationships. Any problem concerned with maximizing or minimizing some economic quality (e.g., cost) subject to a set of constraints (e.g., human resources, materials, and capital) is a linear programming problem. In general, the technique has been used with enormous success to solve a variety of administrative problems in areas such as the following:

Determining a product mix that meets certain established specifications at minimum cost. Examples are found in establishing the lowest cost for meeting the standard requirements of adult nutrition. In 1973, one could live on about $95 per year. (But what a product mix this implies: kidneys, cabbage, beans, buckwheat flour, and not much else.)

Determining optimum product lines and production processes. Examples are found in those situations where capacity limitations exist and decisions must be made as to optimal production of scarce resources.

Determining optimum transportation routes. For example, a railroad must move a number of freight cars about and wished to do it at the lowest cost. If there were three origins, ten distributions, and 100 cars to distribute, then the total number of feasible solutions would be in the millions.

Writes Spencer (1971:277):

> Although linear programming has been applied primarily to industrial situations, there have been widespread applications of it by governmental agencies. For example, the military services have employed elaborate programming techniques to achieve optimum allocations of men and materials. Various bridge, highway, and airport administrative agencies (e.g., the Port of New York Authority) have made major utilization of specialized programming methods to find optimal solutions to such problems as stacking aircraft over airports, queuing ships at docks, and easing the congestion of vehicles at toll booths of tunnels and bridges.

A simple example will help to clarify some of the ideas behind linear programming (adapted from Public Policy Program, 1972). A sewage treatment plant processes both raw sewage and garbage before dumping the remains into a nearby river. Since an extract obtained in the processing of the garbage is necessary in the treatment of sewage, it is essential to process two tons of garbage (G) for every three tons of sewage (S) treated. This is a linear relationship and can be shown as

$$\frac{G}{S} = \frac{2}{3} \quad \text{or} \quad 3G - 2S = 0$$

A state official has examined the plant and assessed pollution factors of 0.3 damage units per ton of treated sewage and 0.4 damage units per ton of

FIGURE 6–8
Simple Linear Programming Example

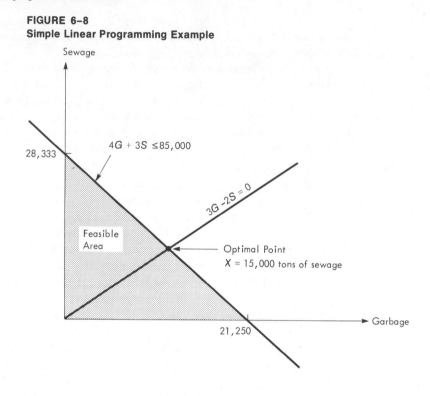

garbage. The state board of water control has ruled that the plant may not in any one day allow the product of the damage factors multiplied by their respective amounts of material treated to exceed 8,500 damage units. The linear relationship is a constraint and is shown in Figure 6–8.

If a county official calls up the plant manager and informs him that it is absolutely crucial that the plant process as much sewage as possible that day, what is the maximum that can be processed? Though this problem may be solved algebraically, a graphical solution is given in Figure 6–8.

A CRITIQUE OF SYSTEMS ANALYSIS

Public administrators should be clear regarding the pitfalls in each step of the systems analysis.

Analysis begins, it will be recalled, with problem definition. Significantly, one of the most distinguished practitioners of the systems approach, Charles Hitch (1960:11) maintains that RAND had never undertaken a major system study where satisfactory objectives could be defined. Where attempts were made, objectivity proved elusive. For example, in a classic systems study on water resources (McKean 1963), the goals read as follows: *Adequate* pollution control; *reasonable* irrigation development; *proper* erosion control and sediment reduction; *suitable* flood control; *optimum* contribution in alternation the impact of drought; *full* development of the basin's resources for recreational programs. Where did these goals come from? What do the italicized words mean?

Gathering information is also a part of the first step. Writes Ida R. Hoos (1973:162–63):

> Dear to the hearts of technically oriented analysts is the information gathering and processing state. In fact, so [agreeable] is the occupation with data that many systems designs, purported to deal with pressing social problems, never progress beyond that point. Displaying the ingestive propensities of a snake, the information system swallows up all the resources allocated to a given project and diverts attention from its larger purpose.

To buttress her point, Dr. Hoos cites the activity of the Bay Area Transportation Study Commission, which was instructed to prepare a master regional transportation plan. In the end, the experts "listed as their accomplishments a total of 10 million pieces of information, converted to 1.5 million punch cards, which were recorded on 1,100 reels of magnetic tape, which require one and one half hours of IBM 7094 time to reprocess."

In sum, too many analysts apparently think that, if only enough factual research is done, then somehow a valid generalization will automatically emerge. But such is not the case. What does frequently emerge are some very expensive price tags ($3 million in the case of BATSC).

Perhaps the first pitfall to note about the second step, modeling, is that the analyst structures the problem; that is to say, the analyst inevitably must view the problem through his own eyes and determine what the relevant variables are. Assuming one wants to wage war against poverty, then how does one go about establishing the poverty level? What does one base his calculations on? The U.S. Department of Agriculture's Economy Food Plan?

The system itself must also be determined. But how inclusive should it be? Clearly, Barry Commoner's sanitation engineer was not inclusive enough. Conceivably, the criminal justice system in Figure 6–6 was not inclusive enough. (It had no way of indicating the economic effects of crime rate; e.g., reduced tax base as residents move away from city due to increase in crime.) Hoos (1973:161) puts the issue concisely: "Systems experts have made a great show of addressing totality but have actually dealt with shreads and patches."

The third step in the system approach is analysis and optimization. Here the analyst runs the risk of becoming locked into attaining the originally stated objectives of the study. This is no paradox, for a good systems study should be a *heuristic;* that is, a method to help discover. Obviously, what we need to discover cannot be known in advance. A famous study of the location of military bases conducted by Albert Wohlstetter and his associates at RAND illustrates this nicely. (See Wohlstetter in Quade 1964:125–26)

In 1951 the air force asked RAND to help them select locations for new airbases to be built overseas in the 1956 to 1961 period. Wohlstetter's approach was not to try to answer the straightforward request (where should the bases go?) but to examine the assumptions inherent in the question itself. After a year and a half of analysis, he and his staff concluded that adding such bases was too risky, since aircraft positioned overseas closer to the Soviet Union were too vulnerable to surprise attack on the ground. They further concluded that overseas bases were more costly, less of a deterrent, and more of a problem for U.S. foreign policy than an alternative. The alternative was to build more bases in the United States and supplement them with small overseas installations for refueling.

A final pitfall in the systems approach is to let the method supplant the problem. In other words, some experts tend to begin with the question, What problems are available for my techniques? The proper initial question, of course, is, What is the problem?

Such experts are not unlike the drunk the policeman finds late at night under a streetlight. When asked what he is doing, the drunk replies that he is looking for his keys.

"Where did you loose the keys?" asks the policeman.

"In the alley."

"Then why are you looking for them here?"

"Because," replies the drunk, "this is where the light is."

Plain Talk about Computers

What effect do the more than 150,000 computers that have been installed throughout the world have on decision making in the public sector? The contribution of these glamorous machines is two-fold. First, they can improve the data base that the manager needs for making a decision. As a dutiful, rapid, and tireless slave in processing huge volumes of paper work—billing for public services, processing of traffic violations, developing a census (the U.S. Bureau of Census acquired a LINIVAC I in 1951), and on and on—the computer excells. The second contribution is more direct: dealing with problems so complex that they are practically insoluble by manual methods. Typical problems of complexity are the Viking landing on Mars, economic models for Council of Economic Advisors reports, and optimization of the air-defense system.

Let us call the first "payoff" from computers informational and the second one analytical. Now let us try a little more thoughtful answer to the question posed above: What effect do these payoffs have?

The Informational Payoff

One's first reaction to this payoff might be to wonder if the government really needs more information.

William D. Carey (1973:77), a former Assistant Director of the Budget, maintains that the resource potential of information technology should not be measured in the capacity to generate output per se, since we are already glutted with information. "In the government sector alone the volume of waste information is stupefying. In thousands of political jurisdictions each year, armies of public employees go through the motions of preparing and submitting "plans" of every description—comprehensive, functional, multistate, metropolitan, etc.—which pile up either unread or unbelieved. Tens of thousands of pages, charts, graphs, forecasts, and analyses are produced at great cost, as part of the alleged management process, to be looked at (maybe) but seldom studied. Government files are filled with thousands of consultant studies, with additional thousands of pages, unimplemented and unused. Copying machines proliferate millions of pages of information, untold quantities of moribund 'information.'" Once viewed in this light, the informational payoff of computers loses some of its glamour.

An argument often heard in favor of the computer runs like this. The computer came along just in time to avert a catastrophic crisis: were it not for the timely introduction of computers not enough people could have been found to staff bureaucracies such as the Internal Revenue Service, to guard millions of welfare clients against the temptation to cheat, and to handle the logistic problem of American armed forces spread all over the world. Joseph Weizenbaum (1976:27–28), Professor of Computer Science at MIT, does not buy this argument. As he notes, huge managerial, technological, and scientific problems had been solved without the aid of electronic computers in the decades preceding the Second World War and especially during the war itself. "The Manhattan Project produced the atomic bomb without using electronic computers; yet the scientific and engineering problems solved under its auspices required probably more computations than had been needed for all astronomical calculations performed up to that time. The magnitude of its managerial task surely rivaled that of the Apollo Project of the '60s. Most people today probably believe that the Apollo Project could not have been managed without computers. The history of the Manhattan Project seems to contradict that belief."

But the belief in the indispensability of the computer is not entirely mistaken. "The computer becomes an indispensable component of any structure once it is so thoroughly integrated with the structure, so enmeshed in various vital substructures, that it can no longer be factored out without fatally impairing the whole structure."

Weizenbaum (1976:30–31) further maintains that computers interject a conservative bias into governmental administration. "It may be that social services such as welfare could have been administered by humans exercising human judgment if the dispensing of such services were organized around decentralized, indigenous population groupings, such as neighborhoods and natural regions. But the computer was used to automate the administration of so-cial services and to centralize it along established political lines. If the computer had not facilitated the perpetuation and 'improvement' of existing welfare distribution systems — hence of their philosophical rationales — perhaps someone might have thought of eliminating much of the need for welfare by, for example, introducing negative income tax. The very erection of an enormously large and complex computer based welfare administration apparatus, however, created an interest in its maintenance and therefore in the perpetuation of the welfare system itself." In sum, "The computer . . . was used to conserve America's social and political institutions. It buttressed them and immunized them, at least temporarily, against enormous pressures for change."

Analytical

How much of a contribution can the computer make to human problem solving? While it would be flippant to regard the computer as just a big machine, the way the computer decides is a caricature of the qualitative considerations in human decision making which take the whole situation into account instead of mechanically totaling up the size of various factors.

In a fascinating essay on chess, Arthur Koestler (1974:206–31) takes a look at recent research on programming computers to play the game. He sums up the lessons learned from this research thus: "the machine does not really 'simulate' or reproduce processes in the human mind, any more than the motions of a marionette pulled by strings reproduce the processes of muscle-contraction; man and machine function according to different principles."

There are many reasons why this should be so. "One is that the human player is often guided, sometimes subconsciously, by the accumulated memories of similar situations encountered in the past; but although the computer also has a memory of stored data, it is unable to select and manipulate them in a way even remotely resembling the human way of learning from experience." But an even simpler reason for the inferiority of the computer is that the really important decisions in public affairs require as much art as science. The computer can laboriously compute a solution that seems to promise some economic benefit, but it cannot fit that solution into a pure general, policy framework. The broader issues are, so to speak, above its head. In contrast, an experienced public decision maker can take the total situation in at almost a glance. Picasso's dictum *"Je ne cherche pas, je trouve"* — I do not search, I find — applies to the human decision maker too.

The interaction of the computer with the systems analysis described in this chapter is also instructive. It is important to understand very clearly that strengthening a particular technique contributes nothing to its validity. "For example, there are computer programs that carry out with great precision all the calculations required to cast the horoscope of an individual whose time and place of birth are known. Because the computer does all the tedious symbol manipulations, they can be done much more quickly and in much more detail than is normally possible for a human astrologer. But such an improvement in the technique of horoscope casting is irrelevant to the validity of astrological forecasting. If astrology is nonsense, then computerized astrology is just as surely nonsense." (Weizenbaum 1976:35)

NAILING DOWN THE MAIN POINTS

1 Decision making means selecting from various alternatives one course of action. Thus, it cannot be divorced from the planning process described in Chapter 6; indeed, decision making pervades every facet of planning.

2 According to Allison, three models help explain how decisions are made in the public sector. The first, the rational model, is essentially the same as the rational planning model introduced in Chapter 6. Given the numerous shortcomings in the application of the rational model in the real world, Allison suggests a second model: governmental politics. What the rational model seems to ignore is that agreement comes easier in decision making when the items in dispute are only slight modifications to existing programs. In the governmental politics model, decisions thus become the resultants of complex bargaining processes among governmental players.

The third model, organizational process, views decision making as the outputs of large organization functioning according to standard pattern of behavior. In contrast to the second model, the importance of individual governmental players becomes secondary. In the organizational process model, it is the routines of the organization itself that are primary.

3 Rational decisions need not be always quantitative. For example, recognizing the kind of problem that exists (generic or unique) can significantly improve the quality of decision making.

4 Scheduling models facilitate the coordination of activities of an enterprise. Among the leading types are Gantt chart, Critical Path Method (CPM), and Program Evaluation Review Technique (PERT). Regarding PERT, some authorities have suggested that it might be as much window dressing as a real control technique.

5 The relevance tree is a structural analysis that can help decision makers (a) insure that a program contains all the necessary elements and (b) allocate resources to maximize some good. Like the relevance tree, the decision tree provides a network approach to structuring complex problems. With this approach, however, the decision to be made is not viewed as an isolated decision because today's decision depends upon the ones we will make tomorrow. Therefore, the decision problem is examined in terms of a tree of decision forks and chance forks to indicate the interrelationships of future choices.

6 The systems approach, or systems analysis, forces us to look at problems as systems, that is, assemblies of interdependent components. The four basic steps in this approach are: (a) policy formulation, (b) modeling, (c) analysis and optimization, and (d) implementation.

   During the analysis and optimization step, the model is studied to find the best strategy for resolving the problem. Among the options available here are computer simulation and sensitivity analysis.

7 While operations research (OR), or management science, shares many characteristics with the systems approach, it is not quite the same thing. The scope of OR is narrower; its nature, more mathematical. Of all the techniques that OR emphasizes, linear programming is one of the most widely used. Any problem concerned with maximizing or minimizing some economic quality subject to a set of constraints is a linear programming problem. For the mathematically inclined only:

$$\text{Objective:} \quad \text{Maximize } c_1x_1 + c_2x_2$$

$$\text{Subject to:} \quad a_{11}x_1 + a_{12}x_2 \leq b_1$$

$$a_{21}x_1 + a_{22}x_2 \leq b_2$$

8 Systems analysis is not without pitfalls. Satisfactory objectives are often hard to define; satisfactory variables, hard to select. Analysts can become enamored by data, tending to collect far more than necessary. And perhaps above all, analysts can let their techniques determine the problems they study—when the problems should of course come *first*.

CONCEPTS FOR REVIEW

decision making

rational, governmental politics, and organizational process models of decision making

incremental approach

sunk costs

satisficing

programmed and nonprogrammed decisions

standard operating procedure

technology fix

generic and unique problems

upper and lower limits of decisions
limiting (strategic) factor in decision
    making
scheduling models
Gantt chart
CPM, PERT
critical path
PERT-cost
relevance tree; decision tree
systems approach

four basic steps in systems approach
simulation
sensitivity analysis
counter-intuitive nature of public
    systems
operations research
linear programming
heuristic
"payoffs" from computers

PROBLEMS

1. "Decision making is the primary task of the administrator." Discuss.

2. Suppose you were to build a model that would forecast the nationwide demand for nurses 20 years from now. As a start, one must make assumptions about population growth and effects of new drugs. What else? Do you think the list of varibles is endless?

3. Read Leonard Mandlebaum's "Apollo: How the United States Planned to Go to the Moon," *Science,* 163 (February 14, 1969), pp. 649–53. Which of Allison's three explanatory models of decision making best applies? Can you apply one of the models to U.S. energy policy making?

4. In July 1976 the Israeli cabinet made a decision to attempt to rescue 105 hostages held by pro-Palestinian skyjackers at Uganda's Entebbe Airport. The 2,620-mile flight to Entebbe, the rescue, and return by 100 commandos was a spectacular success. What were the limiting (strategic) factors in the decision? What were the upper limits?

5. A disgruntled group member once defined a camel as a horse put together by a committee. Group decisions are often frustrating and inadequate, but there can be real strength in group problem solving. Jay Hall ("Decision," *Psychology Today* (November 1971), 51 ff.) provides some thoughtful suggestions on how. Read his article and then conduct his experiment, "Lost on the Moon," to see how effective his methods are.

6. Find the critical path in the following network. (Hint: begin by working backward, assigning cumulative numbers to each mode. You do not need to test all possible paths. Follow the Bellman principle: If the optimal path from X to F passes through Y, and if the optimal path from T to F passes through X, then the optimal path from T to F passes through Y.)

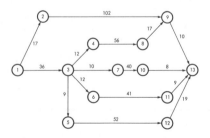

7. As the head of a city housing agency, you must decide whether to submit either plan A or B (but not both) to the mayor who, in turn, must submit it to the city council. You estimate that there is a 90 percent chance that the mayor would accept A but only a 50 percent chance the council will accept. The council likes B, indeed, you are certain they would accept it—if, that is, it ever got past the mayor (only 3-to-1 odds of this happening). You prefer A and evaluate its utility at 1.00. In fact, because you think it the most socially desirable, even if the mayor accepts and has it rejected by the council, you would assign a utility of 0.40 to these consequences. Of course, if the reject came first from your boss, the mayor, the utility would be somewhat less, say, 0.20. However, Plan B, if accepted by the city council, has a utility of 0.80 to you. But the worst situation is to have it rejected; there would be no utility in such a case. What should you do?

8. Conduct a systems analysis of your community. This may sound like an overwhelming job. Nevertheless, if you read the proposals Robert K. Lamb makes in "Suggestions for a Study of Your Hometown," *Human Organization* (Summer 1952), you will find ways and means for shortcutting and sampling.

9. Care must be taken in systems analysis to insure that the measures of effectiveness are appropriate. A classic example of how incorrect measures can throw off the analysis concerns the installation of antiaircraft guns on merchant vessels in World War II. While these guns made the crews feel safer, data on equipped and nonequipped ships showed that only 4 percent of attacking planes were shot down. Because the guns were expensive and needed elsewhere, their removal was proposed. Was percentage of planes shot down the correct effectiveness measure of the guns? If not, then what was? (See Morse and Kimball, 1951: 52–53).

10. Use the relevance tree to help you decide among four models of automobiles. Using a form similar to Figure 6–4, establish criteria and weight it. The final step in your analysis should be to divide the relevance number by the cost of the automobile; this will give you four benefit-to-cost ratios to compare.

11. Give several examples of recent nonincremental decisions in American government.

12. Gotham City has to dispose of 22,000 tons of refuse daily, an amount increasing by 4 percent a year. Currently, it has eight incinerators that have a usable capacity of 6,000 tons a day; residue and nonincinerated refuse must go to sanitary landfills that will be exhausted by within five years. Four superincinerators, with a capacity of 20,000 tons a day have been proposed. Unfortunately, they are quite expensive: $1 billion to build and $50 million a year to operate. Moreover, they would add substantially to hazardous air pollution by emitting thousands of tons of soot particulates a year. Outline and discuss an analytic model that could help the mayor of Gotham City decide what to do. What additional information would you need? What are the upper and lower limits of the decision? Is the decision simply one of whether to build the superincinerators or are alternatives available?

13. The town of Broken Arrow needs a fire department and you must make recommendations concerning its size and structure. What would be a good rule of thumb for the number of fire engines? (The fire chief of Gotham City suggested the number of fire engines should be proportional to the number of buildings.) Regarding structure, you have two basic alternatives: (a) one central department or (b) several decentralized stations. Discuss how you decide between (a) and (b).

14. Write a paper comparing the decision making—that is, the approach to decision making—of two or more recent presidents. Which is most effective? Why?

15. Apply Critical Path Method (see Figure 6–2) to some process with which you are familiar (e.g. building a boat or preparing a dinner).

16. "Experience is not only an expensive basis for decision making but also a dangerous one." Discuss.

INTRODUCTION

Planning and decision making, the subjects of the two preceding chapters, cannot be separated from organizing. If people are to work together effectively in implementing plans and making decisions, they need to know the part they are to play in the total endeavor and how their roles relate to each other. To design and maintain these systems of roles, write the authors of one of the most popular and respected management textbooks, is basically the managerial function of organization. (Koontz and O'Donnell 1974)

This definition is a good one. While many management theorists give loose and woolly definitions, Koontz and O'Donnell simply try to look at the organization as the "practicing manager" does. Organizing thus becomes the grouping of activities necessary to attain objectives, the assignment of each grouping to a manager with authority to supervise it, and the provision for horizontal and vertical coordination in the agency structure.

This chapter and the next will be in the same key, that is, looking at organization the way the practicing manager does. We should keep continually in mind, however, that in these two chapters we deal only with the formal structure of organization. How the people who fill the roles in these structures actually behave is the subject of Part IV.

Another Key

How does our key—namely, looking at organization the way a manager must—differ from the more conventional, more theoretical ones usually encountered in introductory texts? Probably the most obvious difference is simply in appearance,

7

Organizational Structure

for the latter can often look quite Byzantine—with concepts such as closed model, open model, and model synthesis taking the place of the longitudinal basilicas, circular domes, and large vaults. All in all, a bewildering experience the first time through. But conventional approaches involve more fundamental problems, and we may as well make them explicit least we too succumb.

First, conventional approaches to organization tend to be unrealistic. The proponents of these approaches have accepted too readily the rational model and dismissed, either consciously or unconsciously, the other two models presented to the last chapter—namely, the government politics and organizational process models. They also have ignored the major environmental forces noted in Part I. So their approaches start from the bogus assumption that managers can simply collect and weigh facts and probabilities, make an optimal decision, and see that it is carried out. Yet in large scale governmental projects, such a clear sequence of action is seldom possible because of their extended duration, the many technical and social unknowns, the continual discovery of new facts, and constantly changing pressures. Given these messy realities, what the manager needs is not an abstract model of other organizations to copy but rather an analytical discussion of the ways to design administrative systems that allow recommitment, reassessment, and redirection (cf. Sayles and Chandler 1971). The following chapter will attempt to provide such discussions.

Second, conventional approaches are unlikely to cover the newer kinds of organizational forms one finds in government and business today. What is sorely needed, it seems, is a more balanced discussion that covers not only the traditional organizational concepts but also the newer forms of organizations.

Third, conventional approaches separate the study of organization from the study of policy planning, while, as stated in the first sentence of this chapter, the two are really quite inseparable. Organization, in other words, should not be made an end in itself. If anything, the reverse is true: organization should *follow* policy. Otherwise our "practicing manager" might find himself in the same situation Halberstam (1969:635) found in the Vietnam War: "It was as if someone had ordered the greatest house in the world, using the finest architect, the best stone mason in the world, marble shipped from Italy, choicest redwood for the walls, the best interior decorator, but had by mistake overlooked one little thing: the site chosen was in a bog."

The discussion that follows is in three sections. The first attempts to provide as broad a perspective as possible on the subject of organizational structure. To do this, it surveys the five major ways in which people have worked together throughout history, namely, leader/follower clusters, mosaic organization, pyramids, conglomerates, and organic organizations. Since pyramidal organizations are the most common form found in the public sector, considerable time is devoted to them.

In fact, in the second section, we deal with the problems of this form. Our discussion builds around the four principles commonly associated with the pyramid. We conclude with a look to the not-too-distant future and, appropriately, that section is entitled Organizations of the Future.

FIVE TYPES OF ORGANIZATIONS

To the preceding list of shortcomings, we might add a fourth: conventional treatments of organization ignore the considerable variety in organizational forms—old as well as new.

Some time ago, Kenneth Boulding developed a fascinating hierarchy of systems concepts ranging from the simple atom to imponderables beyond the galaxies. More recently, Gerald J. Skibbins (1974) took this powerful organizing concept, narrowed the focus considerably, and constructed a comprehensive list of systems of which humans are components. They range from the system most often used in history ("leader/follower cluster") to the system Skibbins sees next in the evolution of organizations ("the organic organization").

Which brings us to an interesting paradox: to know the future we must know the past; that is, to grasp adequately the significance of the newer organizational forms referred to in point two above, we must have some grasp of organizational evolution itself. Figure 7–1, which presents a simplified version of Skibbin's list, is a means to that end.

The Leader/Follower Cluster

We can begin with the most natural of human relationships, that between leader and followers. The relationship, is, however, not as simple as it might appear at first blush.

The leader's authority, for instance, can seldom be satisfied with obedience based merely upon the grounds of common sense or respect. Rather, as the great German sociologist Max Weber (Gerth and Mills 1946: 51–55, 246 ff.) was to note, authority seeks to arouse something else (love, fear, even awe) in the followers. This line of inquiry lead Weber to the conclusion that there are three types of legitimate authority: legal, traditional and charismatic.

Legal authority we associate with constitutional governments; traditional authority with kings and parents. But it is charismatic authority that is most relevant to the leader/follower cluster. It is based on the members' abandonment of themselves to an individual distinguished by holiness, heroism, or exemplariness. The word itself, charisma, from the Greek means literally "gift of grace." All charismatic authority implies wholehearted devotion to the person of the leader who feels called to carry out a mission. Examples of

FIGURE 7-1
The Seven Organizational Concepts

Classification	Symbol	Image	Structure	Examples	Life Span	Ability To Adopt Technology and Systems Advances	Ability To Alter Own Organizational Structure
I Leader/Follower Cluster		Human	Leader at Center, Followers at Periphery	Leader/Tribe Model, Napoleon's Army, Hitler's Germany, Mao's China, Chiang's Taiwan, Most R&D Groups, Performing Arts Companies, the Military Squad	5.5 Million B.C. to Today	Low	Almost None
II Mosaic		Social Interdependence	Loosely Connected Assembly of Subsystems	Holy Roman Empire, United Nations, NATO, SEATO, European Common Market, Urban Communities, Voluntary Associations, IGY, ILO, Tribal Nations, HMO Groups, Law Partnerships, Colleges	9000 B.C. to Today	Low	Low
III Pyramid		Geometric	Hierarchy	U.S. Government Departments (HEW, Agriculture, etc.), Unions, Utilities, Banks, Transportation Companies, Public Education System, Religions, Foundations, Public Corporations such as N.J. Turnpike Authority, Military Establishments, Organized Churches, Courts of Law, Political Parties, Governments in General, Most Small and Middle-Sized Businesses	2600 B.C. to Today	Low	Fair
IV Conglomerates		Geometric (cluster of pyramids)	Assembly of Hierarchies United at Summits	The 1900 Trusts in the United States, Modern LTV, Litton Industries, Sperry Rand, Gulf & Western, ITT, the Pentagon	A.D. 1000 to Today	Moderate	Fair
V. Organic		Biological Growth with Man as the Model	Network	Possibly IBM, Xerox, NASA, Texas Instruments, Volvo, Battelle, and CSIRO (Australia); and Unknown Forms Yet to Be Developed	A.D. 1950 to 3050 (est.)	High With Unusual Potential	Highest With Capacities for Complete Metamorphosis

Source: Adapted by permission of the publisher from G. Skibbins, *Organizational Revolution*, end paper © 1975 by AMA COM, a division of American Management Association.

University of Heidelberg Museum

Max Weber

this special type of leader/follower relationship would be Hitler's Germany and the guru/novitiate in arcane religions. Needless to say, the bonds are very firm.

The strengths of this relationship are also its weaknesses. Too often a leader is unwilling to adapt to new challenges. One reason for this low capacity for adaptation is that change could affect the leader's absolute power.

The British historian Arnold J. Toynbee (1946: vol. 1, 307 ff.) suggests another reason—the *nemesis of creativity.* According to Toynbee, it is most uncommon for the creative responses to two or more successive challenges in the history of a group to be achieved by the same individual. Indeed, the party that has distinguished itself in dealing with one challenge—probably an act that brought it to power—is apt to fail conspicuously in attempting to deal with the next. The failures here seem to derive from an overconfidence acquired after the leader's first triumphs ("idolization of an ephemeral self").

Mosaic Organization

Writes Skibbins:

> As the name implies, the mosaic form involves the putting together of separate, distinct pieces, glued only at the edges, to form some pattern. Most mosaic organizations form random patterns because of the autonomy of the pieces. They are held together by the merest traces of adhesive. This organization form is a social interdependence concept. It involves connectedness only for a few particular purposes; in all other respects the parts are independent. . . ." (ibid.: 60–61)

As the examples in Figure 7–1 indicate, the key problem with the mosaic organization is precisely this tenuousness between parts. As Robert Hutchins is reported to have said of one mosaic organization, the University of Chicago, the only thing that held it together was its heating system.

Pyramidal Organization

The pyramid is a geometric figure and it symbolizes the structure of the hierarchy (described in Chapter 2). Interaction within a pyramid conforms to the hierarchical structure of the organization and emphasizes superior/subordinate relationships.

A closely related concept is that of *bureaucracy*. Most of us have a general idea of what a bureaucracy is and I have admittedly taken the liberty of using the term in earlier chapters without providing a formal definition. But now I must. Once again, our surest guide is Max Weber (Gerth and Mills 1946: 196–98), who in the early part of this century, spelled out in considerable detail the features of the bureaucratic structure. In simplified terms those features are: (*a*) a division of labor based on functional specialization; (*b*) a well-defined hierarchy of authority; (*c*) a system of rules covering the rights and duties of employment; (*d*) a system of procedures for dealing with work situations; (*e*) impersonality of interpersonal relations; and (*f*) promotion and selection based on technical competence.

The role of Weber and his bureaucratic model in relation to the pyramidal organizations, however, must be clarified in two respects. In the first place, the bureaucratic model was not a description of reality but an *ideal type;* i.e., what organizations to varying degrees approximate. Some organizations are more bureaucratic than others but none are perfect examples of bureaucracy. Second, Weber really represents a separate thread in intellectual development of the pyramidal concept. His ultimate interest was bureaucracy in its political and social context; those that followed largely ignored not only this link to the social structure but also the historical context of bureaucracy.

A far more important thread in the intellectual development of the pyramidal concept begins with the American engineer Frederick W. Taylor (1856–1915) and the scientific management movement (see Chapter 1) and ends with Luther Gulick and Lyndall Urwick and the administrative management movement. The thrust of both movements, and this is where they diverge from Weber, was to discover principles that would enable the manager to build up and administer an organization in the most efficient manner. Below we discuss four of the more important of these principles.

1. Without a doubt, the cornerstone of the four principles is the *division of labor* into specialized tasks. But how does the administrator do it? Begin by determining the necessary activities for the accomplishment of over all organization objectives. Then, divide these activities on a logical basis into departments that perform the specialized functions. In this way, the organization structure itself becomes the primary means for achieving the technical and economic advantages of specialization and division of labor.

But the procedure is hardly as simple as it sounds, for there are many ways by which the administrator can divide and place in separate departments (*departmentation*) the functions of the organization. The most common, of course, is by objectives. For example, the Department of Health, Education and Welfare organizes in Washington along health-education-welfare lines; similarly, NASA subdivides into the Office of Manned Space Flight and the Office of Space Science and Applications.

Such divisions by use or objective, we might note parenthetically, can present problems. For example, the interrelationship among components often turns out to be much more complicated than would appear at first. Increasingly, the interfaces become blurred as technology progresses. In nuclear power plants, for instance, one finds no neat dividing lines among the functions of fueling, heating, and power generation. And future developments in NASA such as the space shuttle suggest that a clear division of labor and function – say between the launch vehicle and payload – will no longer be possible, as the two appear to meld or blend into each other. (See Sayles and Chandler 1971:9.)

Another criterion the manager might use in making these structural decisions is geographic. In other words, administrative authority is distributed not by function but by area. In the national government only the Department of State, the Tennessee Valley Authority, and, to a lesser degree, the Department of the Interior have followed this criterion. Nevertheless, in other departments and agencies, division by geography does appear in modified form. In the case of HEW, referred to a moment ago, it could be added that the secretary also has regional representatives who try to shepherd into one flock the regional commissioner of Social Security, the regional offices for the U.S. Office of Education, the regional Public Health Service Offices, and the others.

Two other bases for division of labor are by process and client. Process-type departments have at their roots either a particular technology, a particular type of equipment, or both. Technology, as used here, refers not only to hardware technology (such as welding in a transportation maintenance

The scalar principle at work: A senior staff meeting helps the White House coordinate its work with that of the bureaucracy, Congress, and the world beyond.

work center) but also to software technology (such as accounting or operations research). Obvious examples of client based agencies include the Bureau of Indian Affairs and Veterans Administration.

2. The second principle of administrative management is hierarchy. It is based on *scalar principle,* which states that authority and responsibility should flow in a direct line vertically from the highest level of the organization to the lowest level. This flow is commonly referred to as the chain of command. In such an arrangement, a cardinal sin would be to fail to go through channels in trying to get an important message to the top. The hierarchical components in the national, state, and local administration are evident in the organization charts shown in Figures 7–2, 7–3, and 7–4.

3. Closely related to the principles of division of labor and hierarchy is *span of control.* This principle concerns the number of subordinates a superior can efficiently supervise. Traditional theory advocates a narrow span to enable the executive to provide adequate integration of all the activities of subordinates. According to James W. Fesler (1949:51), most federal agencies, apparently mindful of the span of control principle, have kept their principal subnational areas to less than 20. Referring to Figure 7–2, what is the span of control of the Assistant Secretary for Science and Technology?

4. The last principle we shall consider is *line and staff.* The simplest way to understand it is probably by military analogy: Soldiers with weapons stand

FIGURE 7-2
Department of Commerce

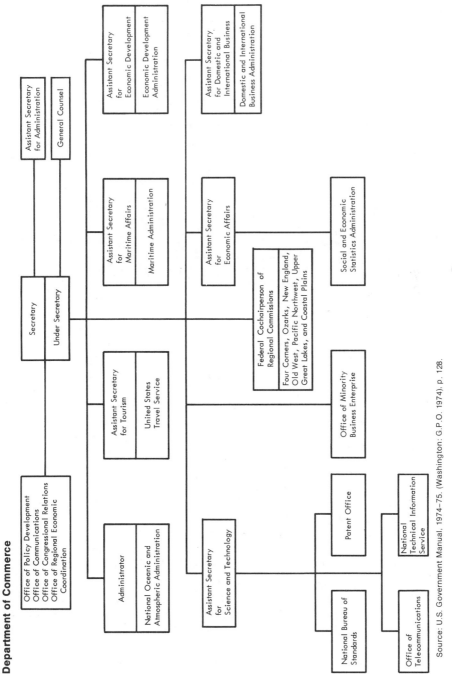

Source: U.S. Government Manual, 1974–75. (Washington: G.P.O. 1974). p. 128.

FIGURE 7–3
State Administrative Organization with "Strong" Executive*

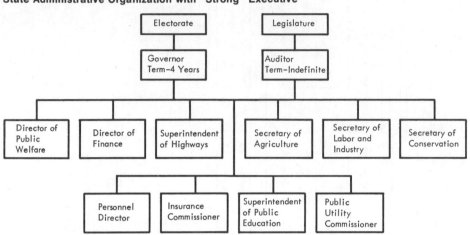

* A "weak" executive would be one who does not have the power to appoint his key subordinates. In such a system, many of these individuals would be elected directly.

in the line, carrying out a military organization's essential functions; meanwhile, usually somewhere behind the front lines, stands (or sits) staff to investigate, to research, and to advise the commanding officers to whom it reports. Only through the commanding officer can the staff influence line decisions.

As any organization—military or otherwise—becomes more complex, managers begin to need advice. Staffs aid managers in many ways. As Anthony Downs (1967:154) points out, a large staff can function as "a control mechanism 'external' to the line hierarchy, promote changes in opposition to the line's inertia, and act as a scapegoat deflecting hostility from its boss." The innovative advantage of a staff appears to result from (a) the technical orientation of its members, who are younger and better educated; and (b) the incentive structure of the staff, which is to help the top administrator improve the line's performance.

The importance of understanding the line-staff concept cannot be over emphasized. Superior and subordinate alike must know whether they are acting in a staff or line capacity. Lack of clarity on this point often causes friction. And here, the notion of *functional authority* can help. Functional authority is "the right that an individual or department has delegated to it over specified processes, practices, policies, or other matters relating to activities undertaken by personnel in departments other than its own." (Koontz and O'Donnell 1974:175) Thus in Figure 7–5, the functional authority of the personnel director might cover and only cover giving competitive examinations and conducting in-service training programs.

Why have we dealt at such length with pyramidal (or bureaucratic) or-

FIGURE 7-4
Two Forms of City Government

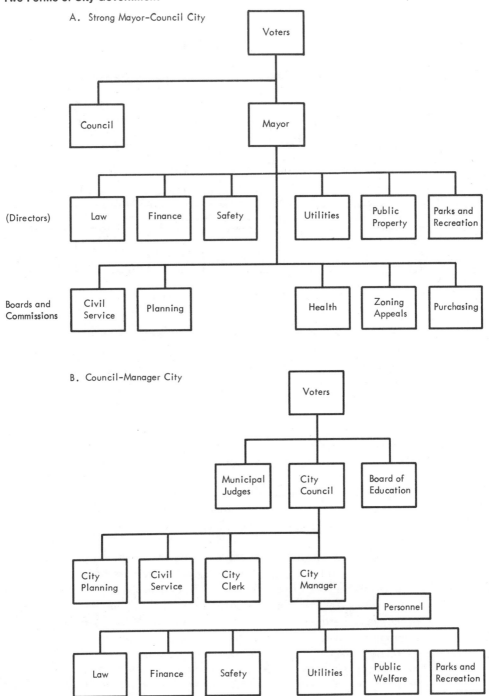

FIGURE 7–5
Line and Functional Authority

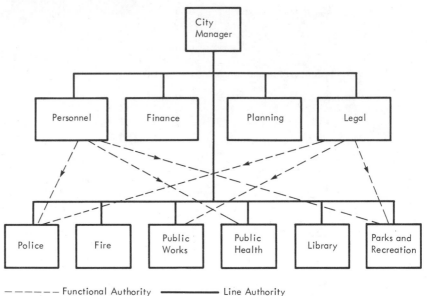

——————— Functional Authority   ————— Line Authority

ganization? Simply because it is most representative of the way in which government at all levels is today organized. Presently, we shall have more to say about it, but for now we must return to Skibbins's classification of organizations.

Conglomerates

To conglomerate anything means to bring together, to work into a ball various disparate materials. In conglomerate corporations, however, Skibbins (1974:68) argues that it is more likely that the organizations being clustered together are, as a rule, all pyramids. Authority over the entire structure is marked by a core management that prevails roughly over the authority structures of the pyramids, and "thus gradually erodes their spirit and drive."

Interestingly, in addition to the well-known commercial conglomerates of today (e.g., ITT, LTV, and Litton), Skibbins includes here the Pentagon. An unorthodox view but probably correct, I believe. In 1949, the army, navy, and air force—all pyramids, to be sure—were put under a single full-orbed executive department the present Department of Defense. The Defense Reorganization Act of 1958 further entrusted still greater authority to the secretary; specifically, it gave him power to transfer, abolish, or reassign defense functions and to assign new weapons systems among the various services and a new Director of Defense Research and Engineering. Beginning with Robert McNamara, centralization of control under the Secretary of Defense has proceeded energetically since 1961. Quite recently, some observers have suggested that the mammoth Department of Health, Education and Welfare adopt a similar design.

Skibbins maintains that, because conglomerate's core management (referred to by some as shark pens) on many occasions have torn up the managements of their component's pyramids, they have opened up opportunities to innovate by fiats. This certainly seems true in the case of the Pentagon. Consider how rapid racial integration was achieved (relative to society) and how easily new management techniques such as program budgeting were implemented (relative to other departments).

Organic Organizations

"It is provocative to learn that of all systems man can distinguish around him, the most advanced and complex are of a biological nature. Nature is far ahead of our comprehension in its ability to construct systems." (ibid.:69) With this mildly startling observation, we begin consideration of the fifth type of organization.

What characteristics of an organism could be possibly relevant to human organization? Consider these connections:

A loose network but a unified whole. As a result, individual parts tend to flower in this lively, growing environment that considers some of their needs.

Relative freedom of communication flow in many directions, especially from the environment that nurtures it.

Death. In contrast, the pyramidal form of organization seems to lack the biological notion of death. The consequences of this lack are seen most clearly in what, one hopes, is an extreme case. The Italian bureaucracy, as late as 1973, contained agencies to grant loans to persons who suffered damages in the 1906 eruption of Mount Vesuvius; to take care of war orphans, although the youngest of them must now be 28 years old; and to administer pensions for veterans of the Battle of Adewa, Ethiopia, in 1896.

If the analogy between organisms and organization seems somewhat fanciful, perhaps as if taken out of *Lord of the Rings,* then consider the analogy upon which most of today's organizations are based, the machine. While the machine analogy is perhaps most visible in the writing of Taylor and the scientific management school, it still remains the bedrock assumption upon which the pyramidal organization rests. Waldo (1948:173–74) described this view well: "people and organization parts are regarded more or less as though they were the interchangeable parts of modern machinery."

Some advocates of the organic model of organization go much farther than simply rejecting this machine model. They argue that the ultimate model for organizations should be homo sapiens rather than just any organism. But why? The crucial component that man possesses is his mind. But the concept of mind implies much: perfectability, changeability, analysis, learning and goal seeking. Writes Skibbins (ibid.: 71; cf. Deutsch 1963), "an organization built with the idea of man as its model would possess a many-sensed awareness of the realities of existence and of life which more rigid forms could never achieve. In such an organization we could blend human minds with an organization consciousness and work together to achieve goals hitherto thought impossible. Within such a symbiotic relationship, NASA took us to the moon. Tomorrow, such organization will take us to the stars as well." Table 7–1 summarizes some of the key differences between mechanistic and organic organizations.

To conclude this survey of organizational evolution—which stretched from primitive leader/follower clusters to futuristic self-directing models reaching for the stars—two points are in order. First, the survey should make the manager more sensitive to the rich variety of organizations as well as the capabilities and limitations of each form. Second, it should provide us with some basis for deciding where our inquiry into organization structure

TABLE 7–1
Characteristics of Mechanistic and Organic Organizations

Mechanistic		Organic
High; many and sharp differentiations	SPECIALIZATION	Low; no hard boundaries, relatively few different jobs
High; methods spelled out	STANDARDIZATION	Low; individuals decide own methods
Means	ORIENTATION OF MEMBERS	Goals
By superior	CONFLICT RESOLUTION	Interaction
Hierarchical based on implied contractual relation	PATTERN OF AUTHORITY CONTROL AND COMMUNICATION	Wide net based upon common commitment
At top of organization	LOCUS OF SUPERIOR COMPETENCE	Wherever there is skill and competence
Vertical	INTERACTION	Lateral
Directions, orders	COMMUNICATION CONTENT	Advice, information
To organization	LOYALTY	To project and group
From organizational position	PRESTIGE	From personal contribution

Source: Litterer (1973:339).

should go next. Based on the foregoing survey, it appears that the organizational form calling the loudest for more detailed study are the pyramidal — because it is most characteristic of government today — and the organic (human) type — because it is, apparently, the most attractive alternative to the former. These two topics constitute the remainder of the chapter.

THE PATHOLOGY OF THE PYRAMID

The Principles Revisited

Earlier we looked at the four principles of management — viz., specialization, hierarchy, span of control, and line-staff — that characterize the pyramidal organization. Now we need to reexamine the principles through a more critical lens. Despite this essentially critical approach, our intent is not to debunk. Rather, we want to point out a *few* important shortcomings in the pyramidal form of organization. Accordingly, we must also disavow any claims to a comprehensive critique.

And throughout it should be kept firmly in mind that, despite its flaws, the pyramidal form of organization, and its attendant principles, have often served the needs of government well. As a former top administrator of NASA noted, the systematization of these principles resulted in a body of doctrine, which, for all its publicized faults, still provided the building blocks from which parts of a large-scale endeavor could be constructed. "A hierarchical system of authority, the hallmark of the traditionalists, is in one form or another essential. Basic principles covering delegation of authority and 'division of labor' must be applied. The span of control must have some limit, and tasks must be structured so that there is a logical and consistent relationship between functions." (Webb 1969:64–65)

The rub, of course, comes when one tries to make this traditional doctrine into a system of management applicable to the large, complex undertakings so indicative of all levels of government today. For this reason, then, a critical look is in order. We begin as we did earlier with the doctrine of division of labor or specialization.

1. Litterer (1973:370–71) notes at least three drawbacks to the division of labor by function. First, a high degree of specialization may tend to make the occupants of these subunits more concerned with their specialty than with organization's goals. Selznick (in March and Simon 1958:40–44) refers to this phenomenon as the "internalization of sub goals." Second, because of their interest in their specialty, people may find it increasingly difficult to communicate with other organizational members. Coordination suffers, though its need has increased because of specialization. Third, "in many instances people who have risen through several levels of the organization within a functional specialty have advanced within a very unique professional environment and, consequently, may be poorly equipped eventually to as-

sume overall organization responsibilities. Hence, a company may have a very difficult time in finding presidents and key vice presidents within its own ranks."

Sayles and Chandler (1971:15) offer a fourth criticism of specialization: it conflicts with the interdisciplinary efforts required—almost by definition—in large mission or problem oriented programs. "The biologist is asked to conceive of the impact of a hard vacuum on genetics and to work with aerospace engineers on joint endeavors. The project manager is asked to move for six months to a distant location to be closer to a critical development team and to shift both his organizational identity and his family's home every several years. Specialists are asked to give up their specialties in favor of joining multidisciplinary teams and to learn from those whom they would normally ignore or consider beneath their dignity. University-based electrical engineers are asked to learn to work with geologists or chemists with whom they usually share only the common membership of a faculty club."

Hitler's master builder, Albert Speer (1970), adds a fifth criticism of specialization—one that surely has some points of reference with Chapter 4. In his memoirs, he noted that the ordinary party member was taught that grand policy was much too complex for him to judge. Consequently, one was never called upon to take personal responsibility. Indeed, the whole structure of the system was aimed at preventing conflicts of conscience from even arising. The result was the total sterility of all conversations and discussions among these like-minded persons. Further, the Reich's leaders explicitly demanded that everyone restrict his or her responsibility to their own field. "Everyone kept to his own group—architects, physicians, jurists, technicians, soldiers, or farmers. The professional organizations to which everyone had to belong were called chambers (Physicians Chamber, Art Chamber), and this term aptly described the way people were immured in isolated, closed-off areas of life. The longer Hitler's system lasted, the more people's minds moved within such isolated chambers."

2. Let us now consider the problems created by the second principle of management, hierarchy.

"I used to be in the government service," Dostoevsky tells us in *Notes from the Underground.* "I was a spiteful official. I was rude and took pleasure in being so. I did not take bribes, you see, so I was bound to find recompense in that, at least. When petitioners used to come for information to the table at which I sat, I used to grind my teeth at them, and felt intense enjoyment when I succeeded in making anybody unhappy. I almost always did succeed. For the most part they were all timid people—of course, they were petitioners." How do we account for this perennial difficulty that clients seem to experience with bureaucracies? One of America's foremost sociologists, Robert K. Merton (in March and Simon 1958), in a marvelous, though involved, analysis of bureaucracy traces it to, among other things, that fearful symmetry, hierarchy.

His analysis begins with a demand for control made by the top administrators: more specifically, they are concerned with increasing the reliability of behavior within the organization. The techniques used to secure reliability draw upon what we earlier called the "machine model." Standard operating procedures (SOP) are instituted and control consists largely in checking to ensure these procedures are followed.

Three consequences follow. First, the amount of personalized relationships is reduced. Second, the participants internalize the rules of the organization; in fact, rules originally devised to achieve organizational goals assume a positive value *independent* of the goals. Third, the categories used in decision making become restricted to a relatively small number. For example, when a specific problem arises, the bureaucrat tends to say that this problem is essentially a certain type of problem. And since the type has been encountered before, one knows exactly how to handle it. Never mind nuances. In this way, an increase in the use of categorization decreases the search for alternatives.

According to Merton, these three consequences—the reduction in personalized relationships, the increased internalization of rules, and the decreased search for alternatives—combine to make the behavior of members of the organization highly predictable. Which is a nice way of saying that the result is an increase in the *rigidity of behavior* of participants.

In addition to satisfying the original demand for reliability, one of the major consequences of rigid behavior is increased difficulty with clients of the organization and with achievement of client satisfaction. Yet client satisfaction is a near-universal organizational goal.

Let us continue our critique of hierarchy by turning from the question of unanticipated consequences to a more basic one: Is hierarchy ever an adequate description of the way in which decisions are made? Surely, the principle of hierarchy is unequivocal on how decisions are to be made: authority and responsibility for decision making flow in a direct line—follow a chain of command—vertically from the highest appropriate level to the lowest. But analysis by Willard Zangwill (in Sayles and Chandler 1971:174) of the large multimillion dollar procurement decisions at NASA seems to contradict this principle.

The organizational mechanism NASA uses is an ad hoc source evaluation board comprised of a small team of informed *middle-level* people. After an extensive assessment of the potential competency and efficiency of the industrial firms competing for a given contract, the board presents its findings to a panel consisting of the *top level* executives of the agency. The SEB process capitalizes upon an interesting division of labor between the top administrators and middle-level board members. The board members, having spent several months on the topic, are intimately knowledgeable about the specific procurement and understand in detail its cost, technical, and management aspects. Top management people, on the other hand, have a broader view of the entire agency, of the strengths and weaknesses of corporate management, and of the political-economic climate. But where exactly the locus of the decision is no one can say with certainty.

3. The principle that a manager can only supervise a very small number of people—i.e., the span of control principle—can lead to what Peter Drucker (1973:412) has termed the "deformation of management."

Actually, what really matters in determining the span of control is not how many people report to the manager but how many people *who have to work with each other* report to the manager. For example, the head of the Energy Research and Development Administration, who has reporting to him a number of top administrators, each concerned with a major function, should indeed keep the number of direct subordinates to a fairly low number— between eight and twelve is probably the limit. Why? Because these subordinates must work closely with each other. Consider the administrator of the Energy Research and Development Administration to whom six key assistant administrators report. Their areas of responsibility concern (a) fossile energy, (b) nuclear energy, (c) environment and safety, (d) solar, geothermal, and advanced energy systems, (e) national security, and (f) conservation. Clearly, they have to work closely and frequently with each other. Accordingly, a small span of control is called for since the problems of coordination are greater than say, a police sergeant, who supervises several patrols. Each patrol is discrete and autonomous, since there is usually little need for interaction between them. Hence a broad span of control is possible.

A second shortcoming of span of control should be apparent from our discussion in Chapter 2 of multiple hierarchies. The span of control concept assumes that a manager's main relationship is downward, but this direction, as we saw, is only part of the picture. The upward relationship to overhead authority is at least equal in importance to the downward relationship to the subordinates. Likewise, lateral relations with cognate agencies and interest groups are also important. What is needed, then, is to replace the concept of the span of control with a more relevant concept: the span of managerial relationships. The span of control, in short, is a terribly limited concept in public sector management.

4. The line-staff concept, likewise, needs rethinking. To state the problem more sharply, what is one to do about the ever increasing size of staff functions in comparison to line functions?

Some writers, such as Robert Townsend, former chief executive officer of Avis Rent-a-Car, take an iconoclastic approach. Regarding a company's personnel function, for example, Townsend (1970:144) says, "fire it." He continues: "Unless your company is too large (in which case break it up into autonomous parts), have a one-girl people department (not a personnel department). Records can be kept in the payroll section of the accounting department and your one-girl people department . . . acts as personnel (sorry, people) assistant to anybody who is recruiting."

Others, rather than seek solutions, have sought to explain why their staff functions seem, inexorably, to grow. Probably the most famous, and certainly the most witty, account comes from C. Northcote Parkinson.

Notes Professor Parkinson (1957), accurately but with mock scholarship, the number of ships and men in the British Navy between 1914 and 1928 decreased by 68 and 32 percent, respectively. Meanwhile, the number of officials in the admiralty *increased* 78 percent. He also notes, for the same period, that the dockworkers increased only 10 percent, while the dockyard officials and clerks increased 40 percent. (More recently, Senator Proxmire has detected the law at work in the Department of Housing and Urban Development. Since 1973, HUD spending has almost doubled, while HUD assisted housing starts have been almost halved.)

Parkinson attributes this kind of growth not to increased work but to the dynamics of staff operations. To begin with, officials tend to multiply subordinates. Thus, if a civil servant — call him A — thinks he is overworked, he will have B and C appointed under him. This act increases his importance and precludes any colleague from taking over some of his work. In time, Parkinson suggests, B will find himself overworked; when A allows him subordinates D and E, he must likewise allow C the same numbers: hence, F and G. (One might wonder why *two* subordinates are necessary in each case. One subordinate would result in a division of work with the original supervisor and, to that extent, the subordinate might assume almost equal status.)

Seven officials are now doing what one did before. How can this be? Parkinson offers another "proposition": officials make work for each other. For example, an incoming document arrives or comes to D, who decides it really falls within the province of E. A draft reply is then prepared to E and placed before B, who amends it drastically before consulting C, who asks F to deal with it. But F goes on leave at this point, handing the file over to G, who drafts an amendment that is signed by C and returned to B, who revises his draft accordingly and lays the new version before A.

Now, what does A do? This person is beset by many problems created by the new subordinates (e.g., promotions, leaves, domestic problems, raises, transfers, and office affairs). A could, of course, simply sign it unread. Parkinson (1957:20) thinks not: "A is a conscientious man beset as he is with problems created by his colleagues for themselves and for him — created by the mere fact of these officials' existence — he is not the man to shirk his duty. He reads through the draft with care, deletes the fussy paragraphs by B and G, and restores the things back to the form preferred in the first instance by the able (if quarrelsome) E. He corrects the English — none of these young men can write grammatically — and finally produces the same reply he would have written if officials B and G had never been born. Far more people have taken longer to produce the same result. No one has been idle. All have done their best. And it is late in the evening before A finally quits his office and begins the return journey home. The last of the office lights are being turned off in the gathering dusk that marks the end of another day's administrative toil. Among the last to leave, A reflects with bowed shoulders and a wry smile that late hours, like gray-hairs, are among the penalties of success."

The Bennis Critique

In the preceding subsection, we saw some of the shortcomings of the pyramidal or bureaucratic form of organization—a form, we must reemphasize, quite characteristic of the public sector today. Yet our critique was limited to four principles and this hardly does justice to the breadth of the problem. To appreciate better the range of criticisms consider the following sample (cf. Bennis 1966):

Bureaucracy does not adequately allow for personal growth and the development of mature personalities. (More on this in Chapter 12.)

Its systems of control and authority are hopelessly outdated.

It does not possess adequate means for resolving differences and conflicts between the ranks, and most particularly, between functional groups.

The full human resources of bureaucracy are not being utilized due to mistrust, fear of reprisals, etc.

It cannot assimilate the influx of new, complex technology.

But the major problem with bureaucracy in the last quarter of the 20th century is probably none of the above. Rather, suggests Warren Bennis, it is the lack of adaptability inherent in the pyramidal structure of authority. While this form of organization may have been suitable for the undifferentiated and stable environment of the Industrial Revolution (when Weber wrote), its value in a rapidly changing technological environment becomes highly questionable.

NASA is a classic example. In meeting the challenge of the moon landing, notes James Webb (1969:134), a flexible organization, within which procedures and responsibilities could be readjusted without major internal struggles, was essential. People could not be frozen into rigid assignments, for a fluid state allowed in time for a better match of men with work assignments.

The key word in describing the kind of organizational structure that Webb advocates for successful large scale endeavors and that Bennis views as the organizations of the future is "temporary." Organizations of the future therefore will be not hierarchies or pyramids but adaptive, rapidly changing temporary systems. Further, they will be organized around problems and based on an organic not a machine model.

If all this sounds like Skibbins's organic form of organization discussed earlier in this chapter, it should. Bennis clearly is in fundamental agreement with Skibbins. Writes Bennis (1968:74): "The language of organization theory reflects the machine metaphor: social engineering, equilibrium, friction, resistance, force-field, etc. The vocabulary for adaptive organizations requires an organic metaphor, a description of a process not a structural arrangement. This process must include such terms as open, dynamic systems, developmental, organic, adaptive, etc." Enough. Bennis is on the cutting edge of organization theory; and there we must leave him—trying to close what Webb calls the significant gap between management doctrine and management needs.

In the following section, we conclude our discussion of organizational structure by looking at several concrete examples of organizations that appear to be forerunners to what Bennis is talking about. These examples should not, however, be considered patterns that a public executive might use to "make" an organization. On the contrary, as we shall see in Chapter 8, organization structure is the last step in organization design.

ORGANIZATIONS OF THE FUTURE: FIVE FORERUNNERS

Organizations, like people, are hard to classify. Nevertheless, I have tried to catalogue below some of the organizational types that seems to be emerging and that are consistent with the broad characteristics Bennis cites.

The Systems Structure

The systems concept is much more widely discussed than understood. For purposes of this discussion, a *system* remains what it was in Chapter 6: simply an assemblage or combination of interrelated parts (components) forming a complex whole. Increasingly, organizations are being considered from a systems point of view. The systemic approach to organization is the antithesis of the bureaucratic one, with the latter's neatly defined areas of specialization and communication through the hierarchy. In contrast, the systems structure presumes that interaction at all levels supports the total system. The systems approach deemphasizes the parochial goals of the subunits (or, as Selznick called it, bifurcation of interest) but emphasizes total system performance.

The Systems Development Corporation, the Strategic Air Command, and Lockheed have used this concept to redesign major phases of organization. But probably no organization has pushed the systems approach further than NASA. For, in essence, NASA has built a team out of a wide variety of different units (contractors, subcontractors, universities, research laboratories, government offices, etc.) and insured that all these components work toward a common goal. NASA itself serves as a kind of mind or consciousness for the entire operation, attempting to integrate the functional units in a way that contributes to over all goals. NASA continually demanded system-wide performance and "used a large battery of techniques to attain it—data banks, [accounting systems], endless performance review meetings, and so on. It gave constant attention to the integration of widely separated efforts. It also nurtured an in-house capability that enabled it to know more about the total effort than any of the contracting parties." (Sayles and Chandler 1971:319)

But the systems structure is not without problems. It requires a truly astonishing amount of communication. Key NASA executives, for example, spend something like two thirds of their time in meetings, often dealing with matters only remotely related to their own tasks. It requires that each management unit take responsibility far beyond its own assignment. It requires exceptionally clear objectives (e.g., land a man on the moon)—and this is just the rock that can sink a systems structure as it sallies forth to confront the less technical problems of society. Sayles and Chandler observe:

> "The days of the clearly specialized . . . agency are numbered." "The purely operational mission is becoming a luxury item. Operations are more and more mixed with regulatory function. And to add further to the complexity, missions have become interrelated. Oceans, pollution, health, urban development, interact with one another." (ibid.:319)

> "Compared to some of the sociotechnical programs on the horizon, NASA had a simple life. NASA was a closed loop—it set its own schedule, designed its own hardware, and used the gear it designed." "Space was no one's territory." "As one moves into the sociotechnical area, this luxury disappears." (ibid.:320)

In any event, the record still remains clear on at least one point. NASA's system structure proves unequivocally that large, complex systems, both human and technical, can be managed.

Task Force

In 1973 the South Dakota village of Wounded Knee was seized by members of the militant American Indian Movement. The federal government was quick to respond by dispatching a 400-member group to the troubled area. This group had all the characteristics of a second type of organization that seems increasingly common in government, the task force.

What are its characteristics? It is formed on an ad hoc or project basis. (As Bennis would say, it is "temporary.") It is problem oriented. It is interdisciplinary. It is a team. Thus the task force at Wounded Knee was made up of elements of the Justice Department, the Bureau of Indian Affairs, the FBI, and the Department of Health, Education and Welfare.

When should an administrator turn to the task force device? While there are no simple rules of thumb, we suggest three guidelines (Stewart 1969:291–302):

First, it might be useful when faced with a one time undertaking that is (a) definable in terms of a single, specific end result and (b) requires more people, dollars, and organizational units than any other infrequent undertaking in the organizations experience. In short, (b) says that the undertaking would overwhelm any single office division.

Second, the problem being undertaken is unfamiliar and complex. Thus many new mayors and most recent presidents call upon task forces, rather than the existing bureaucracy, early in their administrations to generate policy initiatives.

Third, the unit of government must decide it has a stake in the outcome of the undertaking. In other words, would failure to resolve the problem— through, say, "benign neglect"—entail serious penalties for the unit?

Having opted for the task force device the administrator should be aware of the special sources of trouble associated with this organizational form. First, many task force leaders find that their working relationships with other agency heads have not been clearly defined by the top level political executives. Second, though political executives can seldom give the leader as much guidance and support as he might wish, they can easily jeopardize the task force's success by lack of awareness, ill-advised intervention, or personal whim. Third, there are innumerable possibilities for interagency conflict. Finally, the severe penalties of delay in resolving the problem often compel the task force leader to base his decisions on relatively few data, analyzed in haste.

These problems, however, are hardly insurmountable. Moreover, as long as administrators must face unfamiliar and complex problems, it seems safe to say that the task force form of organization will be a part of public administration for some time to come.

Matrix Organization

A kind of compromise between the task force and the pyramidal form of organization is the matrix organization. It gets its name from the fact that a number of project (team) managers exert planning, scheduling, and cost control over people who have been assigned to their projects, while other managers exert more traditional line control (e.g., technical direction, training, and compensation) over the same people. Thus, we see a shared responsibility for the subordinate, who, in turn, must please two supervisors.

A simple matrix arrangement is shown in Figure 7–6. The program manager is essentially a "contractor" who "hires" personnel from the line organization. The project manager is assigned the number of personnel with the essential qualifications from the functional departments for the duration of the project.

Again, the question arises, when should this particular form of organization be used? Let us approach the answer from the obverse side: A matrix organization should *not* be used when the work performed by an agency is applied to standardized services with high volumes (e.g., waste disposal). But it can be used effectively when the work performed is for specific, narrowly defined projects (e.g., antitrust cases). As specific projects end, they

FIGURE 7–6
Matrix Organization

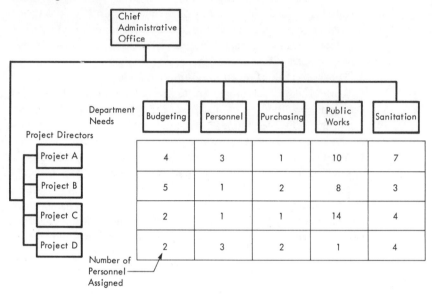

Department Needs	Budgeting	Personnel	Purchasing	Public Works	Sanitation
Project A	4	3	1	10	7
Project B	5	1	2	8	3
Project C	2	1	1	14	4
Project D	2	3	2	1	4

can be deleted from the organization, for the matrix organization is a fluid organization. A general rule then would be this: when an organization has a large number of specialists—and coordination is therefore difficult—the matrix organization might be a solution.

But project groups have their problems. They tend, for example, to narrow the training experience of personnel. Technical personnel, who are often shifted back and forth among projects, can feel isolated and rootless. Finally, with personnel constantly shifting from one project to another, an organization can find it difficult to build up a source of accumulated wisdom, such as is possible in functional departments.

System Four

Also somewhat removed from the pyramidal form of organization stands Rennis Likert's System 4 model. (Likert 1967) This structure consists of small, interacting groups drawn from various levels within the organization. The leader of the group at one level helps form the groups at the next. In this manner, each group leader is a leader of a group at one level and a member of a group at the next higher level (see Figure 7–7).

This arrangement might work in a municipal organization as follows. The first level team includes the mayor (team leader), council members, and the city administrator. The last-named individual, in turn, serves as the team leader for the second level team, which also includes all department heads.

FIGURE 7–7
Likert's Concept of Overlapping Groups and the Linking-Pin Function

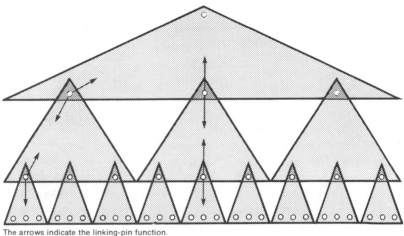

The arrows indicate the linking-pin function.

Source: From R. Likert (1961:113).

Each department head belongs to another team, which also includes his mid-level supervisory personnel. Obviously, this arrangement could be followed down the chain of command to the work force level.

The strength of this structure is that leaders function as *linking pins,* that is, they facilitate interaction among the various groups and promote an open style of communication—upward, downward, and laterally.

The advantages of the System 4 structure are numerous (Powers 1974:33–34):

By breaking the organization into small groups, relationship building and open communication are facilitated.

By linking staff and line functions horizontally and vertically, conflicts can be dealt with more effectively.

Contradictions are minimized, since policies at each level can be determined by groups responsible for carrying them out.

Greater satisfaction for all persons in the organization is generated, thus creating a higher level of morale and commitment.

The organization becomes much more responsive to demands placed on it from both internal and external sources.

The following disadvantages, however, should be kept in mind:

Certain emotionally insecure people might find it difficult to function effectively in small, open groups or without strong, autocratic leadership.

Certain individuals might dominate the groups. Communication might take the form of charisma, producing *group think,* where decisions are reached not because they are necessarily the best decisions but out of respect for the employee who is most personable, forceful, and persuasive.

Linking pins may abdicate their leadership role, thus producing a country club atmosphere.

Federal Decentralization

In a sense, this idea is only a variation on an old theme, namely, *delegation of authority.* In other words, to the extent that authority is not delegated, it is centralized. Absolute centralization in one person is conceivable only in the leader/follower cluster discussed earlier in this chapter; consequently, for most government organizations, we can safely say that some decentralization is inevitable. On the other hand, if *all* authority were delegated, the position of manager would cease to exist; indeed, we could hardly say an organization still existed. As Ulysses put it in *Troilus and Cressida:*

> Oh, when rank is shaked
> Which is the ladder to all high designs,
> The enterprise is sick! How could communities,
> Degrees in schools and brotherhoods in cities,
> Peaceful commerce from divided shores . . .
> Privilege of age, crowns, sceptors, laurels
> But by rank, stand in authentic place?
> Take but rank away, untune that string,
> And hark, what discord follows! Each
>   thing meets
> In utter conflict.

Fortunately centralization and decentralization (or delegation), like "hot" and "cold," are tendencies—not absolutes. But our concern is not, strictly speaking, with the general concept of decentralization but rather the organizational form of federal decentralization; that is, an organization based on decentralized operating authority *and* centralized policy control. Though quite characteristic of today's conglomerate type organization, federal decentralization was first worked out by Pierre S. Du Pont in 1920 in the reorganization of the family owned Du Pont Company. Shortly thereafter, General Motors, under the direction of Alfred P. Sloan, put into effect a far more polished version, which became the prototype of decentralization.

Drucker (1973: Chapter 46) holds that this organizational form has more advantages than any of the other new organizations we have examined:

> Both operating and innovative work can be done by decentralized units of the organization. Meanwhile, top management is free for top management tasks—especially policy control. In Drucker's words, "there must be a kind of supremacy clause reserving to central management the decisions that affect the business as a whole and its long-range fu-

ture welfare, and allowing central management to override in the common interest, local ambitions and pride."

It is easy for the autonomous subunits to understand their own missions as well as the missions of the total organization.

It focuses the vision and efforts of managers on performance and results. Thus it encourages manager development.

How might this form of organization work in the public sector? Two examples come to mind—the first suggested by Drucker (1973:576) himself, the second by the President's Departmental Reorganization Program (Office of Management and Budget 1972:62–63).

> The hospital of tomorrow may be reorganized in autonomous federal units. One such unit might, for instance, take care of the fairly small number of hospital patients—about a quarter to one third at any one time in a general hospital— who need intensive care or clinical care. Another unit might take care of the large load of ambulatory or short-stay patients who require neither intensive clinical care nor surgery. Yet another unit might take care of the large number of surgical patients who require no hospitalization or only a short stay of a day or two in a "hotel" bed rather than the far more expensive "hospital" bed. Another autonomous component might be a mental health unit, again mostly for ambulatory patients. Another unit might be a convalescent unit. There might further be a "hotel" unit—which in effect is all the healthy mother and her healthy baby need two days after the delivery of the child. All these units would, of course, share common services—laboratories, dieticians and the kitchen, social and maintenance workers, psychiatric case workers, physical therapists, and so on. But these services are organized as central services anyhow today.

One important aspect of President Nixon's aborted attempt to reorganize the executive department was the creation of a superagency, the Department of Community Development. In addition to the basic management structure, located in Washington, D.C., was a field organization, conforming to the ten Federal Regions established in 1969 by executive order. The following excerpt is taken from the report on the regional organization:

> . . . in implementing its program responsibilities, the Department of Community Development has a peculiar need to "decentralize." Programs must be coordinated at the state and local levels and the coordination and implementation of programs must be suited to the particular needs, problems, and opportunities of each community. Communities must be encouraged to create area-wide comprehensive development strategies and to fit categorical program assistance for planning, management, development, community services, housing, and transportation into these strategies.
>
> The organization contemplates a departmental field structure headed by strong regional directors. This is in keeping with the general objectives of the broad departmental reorganization—to strengthen responsible management and to base the internal organization of each department on major purposes.
>
> While the Department's leadership makes and interprets policy, establishes priorities, promulgates standards, criteria, and procedures for all levels of field operation, and provides for overall program administration, the regional director will be responsible for coordinating and integrating all programs and activities

of the Department in his assigned geographic jurisdiction. Most significantly, the regional director will control the allocation and distribution of funds to subregional offices in his jurisdiction.

Despite the optimism of Drucker, the future of federal decentralization is by no means certain. To be more specific, many agencies as well as businesses are finding pressure for recentralization now coming from two directions. First, organizations are finding that it is very difficult to segregate activities. NASA, for example, has moved in the direction of merging parts of its manned and its scientific programs. Second, the development of sophisticated computerized management information systems makes a tighter control of complex operations more feasible.

In this chapter, we began by classifying the five basic ways in which roles might be structured to attain the goals of public policy. Two of these—the pyramid and organic—seemed especially deserving of far closer attention; and both were assessed in terms of their strengths and weaknesses.

If this chapter had a theme, it must have been this: Yesterday's final solutions are inadequate to the storm and stress public organizations now face. If the following chapter has a purpose, it is this: to counterpoint this theme. Specifically, it will try to provide a systematic and consolidated account of today's best thinking on how to design more effective and efficient organizations. But it contains no final solutions.

NAILING DOWN THE MAIN POINTS

1 Organization follows policy. In other words, not until we have decided where we want to go, can we know the part people are to play in the total endeavor and how their roles relate to each other.

2 Roughly speaking, people have organized themselves throughout history in one of five ways: leader/follower cluster, mosaic, pyramid, conglomerate, and organic. The pyramid especially concerns us, since so many public organizations follow this pattern.

Closely related to the pyramidal organization is the concept of bureaucracy, which Max Weber defined in these terms: (a) a division of labor based on functional specialization, (b) a well-defined hierarchy of authority, (c) a system of rules, (d) a system of procedures, (e) impersonality of interpersonal relations, and (f) promotion and selection based on technical competence.

Also closely associated with the pyramidal organization is the administrative management movement, which sought to discover the "principles" of organization. Among these principles were: (a) division of labor, (b) hierarchy, (c) span of control, and (d) line and staff. In certain situations, these principles can be destructive to an organization's mission.

3 Quite unlike the mechanistic pyramidal model of organization stands the organic model. The organic organization is less rigid (hence: more flexible), more democratic, less authoritative, more project oriented, and more adaptive.

4 To not a few observers, the organic organization, because it adapts so well to a rapidly changing environment, might be termed the organization of the future. In fact, at least five forerunners are already visible: the systems structure, task force, matrix organization, System 4, and federal decentralization.

CONCEPTS FOR REVIEW

organizing
five types of organization
legal, traditional, and
   charismatic authority
bureaucracy
division of labor,
   departmentation
scalar principle,
   hierarchy
span of control

line and staff
functional authority
systems structure
task force
matrix organization
system 4 organization,
   linking pins
group think
federal decentralization

PROBLEMS

1. "People don't like teams; the longest games are only 60 minutes." Evaluate in terms of the team type organizations (e.g., task force).
2. What are the advantages and disadvantages of using charts to illustrate organization structure?
3. It has been alleged that one of the reasons that the sophistication of organization in government lags behind that of business is due to the lack of competition. Do you agree? If you agree, how might a small dose of competition be introduced?
4. A recent political cartoon by Bill Maudlin consisted of a light socket, labeled the presidency, with numerous extensions running out of it. These extensions were labeled Commander-in-Chief, The Bomb, Party Politics, Urban Affairs, Foreign Affairs, and Ceremonial Duties. Do you think the presidency is overloaded? Discuss in terms of span of control. What modifications might be made?
5. How might the following institutions look if they were restructured along the lines of the futuristic organizations discussed at the end of the chapter: garbage collection service, library, drug treatment clinic, state highway patrol, and university?

6. Select one specific government agency. Then list a few of the possible external changes that would effect its operation if they occurred. Assess the agency's capacity to respond to these changes.

7. To make the staff work better, it is suggested that the manager "make" the line listen to the staff and keep the staff informed. The staff, in turn, should strive to make sure its recommendations are as clear and complete as possible. What are some specific ways in which these abstract goals might be realized?

8. To see how complex large scale organizational efforts can become, see Walter Guzzardi Jr., "Management of the War," *Fortune* (April 1967), p. 134. What are the major organizational differences between the civilian and military chains of command?

9. How can the line-staff concept be viewed as a compromise between hierarchy and division of labor?

10. "Some adverse reactions to modern management stem from inadequacies in the person rather than in the organization." Do you agree or disagree?

11. "In the modern world," wrote Bertrand Russell in *Authority and the Individual,* "and still more, so far as can be guessed, in the world of the near future, important achievement is and will be almost impossible to an individual if he cannot dominate some vast organization." Do you agree or disagree? Why?

INTRODUCTION

New programs usually require new organizations. In the United States at least, this generalization certainly holds for the executive branch: the space program led to the creation of the National Aeronautics and Space Administration; new environment programs, the Environment Protection Agency; and new energy programs, the Energy Research and Development Administration. Likewise, at the state and local levels of government, new programs often mean new organizations.

But not all new organizations stem from new programs. The city of Lakewood, Colorado, is a case in point. In August 1969, as a result of a successful incorporation campaign waged by citizens, it became—literally overnight—the fourth largest city in the state. Lakewood's mayor and ten elected members of the city council were then faced with the initial objective of developing a form of government that could function decisively in dealing with the complicated problems that had developed because of growth.

How important is organizational design? Drucker's (1973:519) perspective on the issue is sound: "The best structure will not guarantee results and performance. But the wrong structure is a guarantee of nonperformance." The right organizational structure is, in short, a prerequisite of performance. I suspect that recognition of this point accounts for why a group of Master of Public Administration degree holders recently rated organization theory one of the most valuable courses they took, second only to the politics of administration. (Grode and Holzer 1975:403–12).

This chapter will survey a lot of important territory. In the first section, we return to a topic introduced early in Chapter 7, the organization

8

Organizational Design and Productivity Improvement

chart, in an effort to establish its limitations as a vehicle for either under-standing or designing organizations. How then one might go about design-ing organizations is the subject of the next two sections, "The Process of Organizational Design" and "Making Organizations More Effective." But the road to better organizations has on it a dragon called politics. In the fourth section, therefore, we shall note the political implications of reorganization.

The last section deals with an idea whose time has come: productivity improvement. We shall consider the meaning and importance of pro-ductivity; the barriers to its realization in the public sector; and, finally, specific techniques for its increase — barriers or no barriers.

THE ORGANIZATION CHART

Despite the importance of organizational design, most administrators approach it rather informally — indeed, one might almost say the approach amounts to little more than drawing boxes on a page. Eventually, a new or-ganization chart appears. The administrator can always defend the pattern in the public sector.

Organization charts are by no means useless in designing and under-standing organizations. The organization chart of most agencies shows — indeed is designed to show — at least two things: the division of work into components and who is (supposed to be) whose supervisor. Moreover, it implicitly shows several other things: the nature of the work performed by each component; the grouping of components on a functional, regional, or service basis; and the levels of management in terms of successive layers of superiors and subordinates.

Nevertheless, what the chart does not show is often the most interesting part — at least to someone interested in organization design (Stieglitz 1969:372–76). In the first place, the chart by itself can not tell us much about the degree of responsibility and authority exercised by positions on the same management level. Two persons on the same management level may have vastly different degrees of authority. In a word, the chart cannot show the degree of decentralization.

Second, attempting to determine line and staff positions from an or-ganization chart is an arduous academic chore. In some agencies, charting methods are used to attempt to make this distinction. For example, the so-called staff units are charted on one horizontal plane, line units on another. Other agencies use skinny lines to connect staff but robust ones to connect line units. To try to interpret these differences in terms of line-staff responsibilities, authorities, and relationships is as difficult as reading the degree of decentralization from the chart.

Third, some people view the linear distance from the chief executive officer as a measure of status or importance. But this interpretation may or may not be correct: it has the same limitations as trying to infer relative importance from size of office, files, parking lot space, etc.

Fourth, while the chart shows some major lines of communication, it does not show all. It is axiomatic that every organization is an intricate network of communication; if it were not, then nothing would get done.

Closely related to the preceding limitations to the organization chart is a fifth one. The chart fails to show the *informal organization,* that is, "those aspects of the structure which, while not prescribed by formal authority, supplement or modify the formal structure." (Gross 1968:238) The formal organization, therefore, encompasses all the relationships and channels of communication that people are expected to develop and use in order to meet organizational and, often, personal objectives. "It is informal," writes Harold Stieglitz (1969:375–76), "only in the sense that nobody has found it necessary to inundate the organization with memorabilia that fully spell out its workings."

In sum, we would do well to heed former Secretary of State Acheson's (1959) advice that "organization or reorganization in government, can often be a trap for the unwary. The relationships involved in the division of labor and responsibility are far more subtle and complex than the little boxes which the graph drawers put on paper with their perpendicular and horizontal connecting lines." In an effort to follow Acheson, and avoid the organization chart pit-fall, a process for thinking through a new organizational structure will be given in skeletal form. This process should facilitate the complex task of separating those things that must be taken into account so far as structure is concerned from those that have less bearing on organizational performance.

THE PROCESS OF ORGANIZATIONAL DESIGN

In designing the building blocks of organization, Peter Drucker (1973:Chapters 42–44) suggests that we consider four questions: (1) What should the units be? (2) What units should join together, and what units should be kept apart? (3) Where do decisions belong? And (4) What is the appropriate placement and relationship of different units? (The discussion that follows builds around these four questions and draws largely on Drucker, ibid.)

The analysis suggested by each question should always be kept as simple and brief as possible. In a small agency or office, they can often be done in a matter of hours and on a few pieces of paper. But in a very large and complex enterprise (e.g., Energy Research and Development Administration and the Executive Branch of the State of Texas), the job may well require months of study.

In either case, organization design begins not with a consideration of the principles of organization but with a review of the organization's goals. In fact, one could even define organization as the ideal, concrete reflection of an agency's goals. A review of goals enables us to begin to determine what are the *key activities.* That is, in what area is excellence required to attain the agency's goals? Conversely, in what areas would lack of performance endanger the results, if not the survival, of the enterprise? Finally, what are the values that are truly important to us?

This line of inquiry puts us in a better position to answer the question, What should the units be? Clearly, key activities require organizational representation.

Roughly, *all* activities in an organization fall into one of four categories. First, are *top management activities.* These, according to Drucker, include maintaining external relations, thinking through the mission of the agency, making decisions during major crises, and building the human organization. Second, are *results-producing activities.* These contribute most directly to performance of the entire enterprise. While results-producing activities are not hard to discover in the private sector (just look for those directly producing revenue), they are less obvious in the public sector. (Turn ahead to Table 8–1, which offers some examples of the output of these activities for local governments.) Third are *results-contributing* or *staff activities,* for example, advising, teaching, legal research, and training. Fourth are the *hygiene and housekeeping activities,* which range from the medical department to the people who clean the floor.

Why this classification? The answer Drucker (1973:534–35) gives is that "activities that differ in contribution have to be treated differently. Contribution determines ranking and placement." By suggesting a few tentative propositions, perhaps we can begin to see how this classification can help us better answer the question, what units should join together?

Irwin Gooen

Born in Vienna in 1909, Peter F. Drucker was educated as a lawyer. Today he is probably the world's best known management consultant. According to Drucker, organizational design must follow organizational purpose. In other words, we cannot properly design an organization until we are clear on its goals.

1. Results-producing activities should never be subordinate to non-results-producing activities.

2. Support activities should never be mixed up with results-producing activities. Halberstam reports, for example, that General Harkins, when commander of Military Assistance in Vietnam, kept his intelligence gathering activity in the same shop as his operations. Not surprisingly, intelligence reports were edited down by the operations people; rather than reflect what was happening in the field, Harkins's shop reflected Washington's hopes. The recent split of the Atomic Energy Commission into the Energy Research and Development Administration and the Nuclear Regulatory Commission might be viewed, on the other hand, as an effort to follow this proposition. Until this split, the AEC in effect combined rather closely a result-producing activity (the development of nuclear energy) with a support activity (the monitoring of safety standards).

3. Top management activities are incompatible with other activities. The emergence in recent decades of a "presidential establishment" provides, I think, proof. Robert C. Wood (quoted in Otten 1973), former Secretary of Housing and Urban Development for Lyndon Johnson and now political scientist at Massachusetts Institute of Technology, argues that a huge White House staff increasingly became involved in day-to-day decisions, spending less and less time on broad, long-range policy issues (the latter activity is of course what we have termed top management activity). Observes Wood: "Confusion is created when men try to do too much at the top . . . a curious inversion occurs. Operational matters flow to the top, as central staffs become engrossed in subduing outlaying bureaucracies, and policy-making emerges at the bottom."

4. Advisory staffs should be few, lean, and nonoperational. Further, advisory work should not be a career; that is, it is work to which a manager or career professional should be exposed in the course of his growth but not work that a person should do for long.

5. Hygiene and housekeeping activities should be kept separate from other work or else they will not get done. In a hospital where these activities are technically under the upper levels of management, they tend to be neglected. No "respectable" manager in a hospital wants to have anything to do with them. As a result, they are left unmanaged; and this means they are done badly and expensively. But what can be done? One way is to farm out these activities to somebody whose business is to provide these hotel services. The federal government's General Services Administration is an excellent example of this proposition's application. Drucker (1973:540) again: "For the senior soil scientist in the Department of Agriculture, managing the automotive fleet for his unit is a chore for which he has neither interest nor respect. Yet there obviously is a good deal of money at stake. . . . For the General Services Administration the administration of the government automotive fleet is its business and can be organized as such."

The third question was, Where do decisions belong? If we can successfully answer this question, we achieve two things. We gain a better idea of where the structural units, discussed above, belong and we reduce the risk that, in the new organization, decision will have to go looking for a home.

The crux of the issue is *delegation of authority;* that is, the determination of the proper level at which a decision should be made. Are any guidelines available? Robert Townsend, the business-executive-turned-writer we met in the last chapter, gives a forceful, but grossly oversimplified, one: "All decisions should be made as low as possible. The charge of the Light Brigade was ordered by an officer who wasn't there looking at the territory." We shall procede to essentially the same conclusion, only more circumspectly.

To begin, it seems safe to say that the level of a decision will depend on the nature of the decision. Specifically, the more a decision is characterized by these three factors, the higher the level at which it must be made:

Futurity; i.e., how long into the future the decision commits the organization.

Impact; i.e., how many other functions in an organization it affects.

Rarity; i.e., how distinct the event is.

Now, with some appreciation of the factors that *limit* how low in an organization a decision can be made, we might rephrase the Towsendian position: (1) a decision should be made as close to the scene of action as possible, yet (2) high enough to insure that all activities affected are fully considered. "The first rule tells us how far down it *can* be made. The second how far down it can be made, as well as which managers must share in the decision and which must be informed. The two together tell us where certain activities should be placed. Managers should be high enough to have the authority needed to make the typical decisions pertaining to their work, and low enough to have detailed knowledge and the first-hand experience. . . ." (Drucker 1973:345)

This rule explains why—contrary to traditional organization theory— functions are not bundles of related skills. If we followed that logic, we would probably, like the Office of Economic Opportunity once did, put the evaluation function into the Office of Research, Plans, Programs, and Evaluation, because it already had responsibility for budget preparation, analysis related to program planning, and basic research. But the Urban Institute (Wholey et al. 1973) found in a 1968 study that, when evaluation is formally assigned to a "planning and evaluation" unit that has many program planning and development responsibilities, "evaluation is never done or is done very poorly" (ibid.:69). Accordingly, the Institute recommended that the evaluation function be based on differences in the types of decisions made at different levels of an organization. They recommended that generally departments and agencies should assign major evaluation responsibilities roughly as follows (ibid.:70).

Evaluation Task	Level of Responsibility
Developing evaluation work plans (overall responsibility)	Agency level
Program impact evaluation	Agency level
Program strategy evaluation	Program level
Project rating	Program level
Monitoring	Program level
Disseminating significant results	All levels
Developing methodology	Agency levels

MAKING ORGANIZATIONS MORE EFFECTIVE

Upon completion of the design process one should then reexamine the final product in terms of three standards: clarity, simplicity, and flexibility. This short section attempts to highlight such a design criteria.

Clarity

"The failure to clarify relationships," write Koontz and O'Donnell (1974:221), "probably more than any other mistake, accounts for friction, politics, and inefficiencies." In other words, the members of an organization need a clear understanding of the authority and the responsibility for action; people in an organization need to understand their assignments as well as that of their co-workers.

But how does the administrator achieve this? One widely used vehicle is of course the organization chart. Despite the limitations noted earlier, the chart can, by mapping lines of decision-making authority, *sometimes* show inconsistencies and complexities and, thereby, lead to their correction. On the other hand, the administrator who believes that team spirit can be engendered by not clearly spelling out relationships is opening a Pandora's box of organizational ills: politics, intrigue, frustration, lack of coordination, duplication of effort, vague policy, and uncertain decision making. A second vehicle, to be discussed in greater detail in Chapter 13, is the position description. "A good managerial position informs the incumbent and others about what he is supposed to do and helps determine what authority must be delegated in order to carry out the job." (Ibid.:228–29)

Simplicity

"Simplify, simplify, simplify." This might well be the plaint of a modern administrator, as it was of the author of *Walden.* Most overorganization results from failure to realize that an organization is merely a framework for efficient performance of people.

Narrow spans of control and numerous levels of supervision are two signs that this criterion is probably being ignored. They were, however, not being ignored by Truman when he vetoed an early proposal by scientists for a

National Science Foundation. He took particular exception to the provisions insulating the director from the president by two layers of part-time boards and warned that "if the principles of this bill were extended throughout the government, the result would be utter chaos" (quoted in Seidman 1970:22).

Other signs of over organization include excessive procedures ("red tape"), too many committees and meetings, and unnecessary line assistants. The last named item comes in for especially harsh criticism by Townsend, who once remarked that the only people who thoroughly enjoy being assistants-to are vampires. "The assistant-to recommends itself to the weak or lazy manager as a crutch. It helps him where he shouldn't and can't be helped — head-to-head contact with his people" (Townsend 1970:23). No mercy for the executive assistant to the Principal Deputy Assistant Secretary of Defense for Program Analysis!

Adaptability

As noted toward the end of the previous chapter, one of the most obvious traits of postbureaucratic organizations is greater flexibility, greater adaptability. "Internal redesign," reports Alvin Toffer (1970:117–18) "has become a byword in Washington. When John Gardner became Secretary of HEW, a top-to-bottom reorganization shook that department. Agencies, bureaus, and offices were realigned at a rate that left veteran employees in a state of mental exhaustion. During the height of this reshuffling, one official . . . used to leave a note behind for her husband each morning she left for work. The note consisted of her telephone number for that *day.* So rapid were the changes that she could not keep a telephone number long enough for it to be listed in the departmental directory."

Let us now turn from the technical issues of organizational design to the political issues the process involves. As a kind of bridge between the two issues, I would like to pose the question, can reorganization be carried too far? The answer is, I think, "yes." And a word has even been coined for this chronic affliction, organizitis. The following section attempts to put the phenomenon in perspective.

THE POLITICS OF REORGANIZATION

Some (not all) attempts at reorganization are in reality efforts to escape rethinking the principles of sound management outlined above. At the first sign of trouble, the cry goes out for reorganization. As might be expected, the times when this kind of surgery is needed are limited.

Perhaps the most obvious occasion for reorganization is growth. Thompson (cited in Litterer 1973:656–57) colorfully illustrates this by pointing out that, if the giant in *Jack the Giant Killer* were to exist many times larger than normal man, he could not have the same form as man. In other words, if the giant were to have the same proportions as normal man but were a hundred times larger in size, his bone structure would be entirely inadequate. Biological design must conform to the square-cube law that says: if a giant were a thousand times the size of man, his volume would increase (10 × 10 × 10) and so roughly would his weight. But his area would increase only 10 × 10; hence, the cross-sectional area of his bones would increase at a far lower rate than the weight which they had to support. So, when the giant attempts to stand, his leg bone breaks. In short, the *form* of man is inadequate for a larger being. The square cube law explains why larger beings walk on four legs like the elephant or float in the ocean like the whale. And the law seems to hold for organizations: Larger organizations require different forms than the smaller ones.

Frederich C. Mosher (1967:494–97) notes five additional conditions to warrant reorganization: (1) changes in social needs that must be mirrored in organizational structure and responsibility; (2) a changing philosophy on the role of government in policy development and group regulation; (3) new management techniques, equipment, and technology that would modernize an agency's work processes; (4) increasing qualifications of personnel for policy analysis and administrative oversight, which can trigger administrative reorganization to utilize the rising talent of such individuals; and (5) the obsolescence of low-ranking organizations in the light of fundamental policy changes instigated within upper hierarchical echelons.

Assuming then that there are only select instances in which reorganization is called for, what can we say about its effectiveness; that is, does it increase economy and efficiency? At the national level, at least, its track record is poor: of the 86 reorganization plans transmitted to the Congress between 1949 and 1969, only three were supported by precise dollar estimates of savings.

These observations lead us to a second perspective by which to view reorganization process. No reorganization can be politically neutral. In one way or another, it must reflect certain political values and interests. The following examples, I think, support this position.

> Reorganization can be used to exclude billions in expenditures from the budget. In 1971 President Nixon proposed to Congress legislation that would reorganize the domestic executive departments and a number of independent agencies into four new major purpose departments— Human Resources, Natural Resources, Community Development, and Economic Affairs. As it turned out, his effort was unsuccessful; and by 1973, he had abandoned his plans. But should this abortive effort be viewed purely in terms of economy and efficiency? From a political perspective, it would appear that it was, as well, an attempt to abolish many of the programs and agencies that had become symbols of President Johnson's Great Society.

> Reorganization can also provide a means for dumping an unwanted official. This purpose certainly seems behind Secretary Rusk's plan to

abolish the State Department's Bureau of Security and Consular Affairs, a brainchild of Senator Joseph McCarthy. This ploy, which was not successful, would have allowed Secretary Rusk to shift the director to another post.

Reorganization can be used to bypass troublesome committee or sub-committee chairmen. The transfer in 1961 of civil defense activities from the Office of Civil and Defense Mobilization to the Secretary of Defense in 1961 was expected to remove the shelter program from the juris-diction of an unfriendly appropriations subcommittee chairman.

Reorganization may be necessary to save a program with little political support. "The frequent reorganization and renaming of the foreign aid agency," writes Seidman (1970:26), "reflect efforts to bolster congres-sional support . . . rather than to . . . improve management."

And let us not forget the iron cross in Chapter 2 that showed, among other things, that each agency had external clients. These clients can provide an agency threatened with reorganization support, especially when the clients perceive that the reorganization is not in their best interest. Quite clearly, labor unions perceived President Johnson's proposal to combine the Departments of Labor and Commerce as reducing their access to and influence on the president.

ORGANIZING FOR PRODUCTIVITY IMPROVEMENT

Thus far in this chapter, we have dealt with two topics, organizational design and reorganization. Now we need to focus attention on what might be called the nuts and bolts of management, that is, the problems and procedures that confront the public administrator on a day-to-day basis. Traditionally, these problems have been labeled economy and efficiency; today, they go by the name of *productivity*. And they have never been any more important to the public administrator. Before considering the impor-tance of productivity any further, we must be clear on its meaning.

The Meaning of Productivity

Simply put, productivity is a measure of the efficiency with which re-sources (land, labor, capital) are converted into products or services. In other words:

$$\frac{\text{output}}{\text{input}} = \text{productivity}$$

A productivity ratio could be expressed, therefore, as tons of garbage col-lected per hour.

Finding good measures such as this one for output is, in the public sector at least, a difficult task. Table 8–1 attempts to show a few of the measures

TABLE 8-1
Illustrative Set of Output Measures, Qualitative Factors, and Local Condition Factors in Local Government

Selected Service Functions	Illustrative Output Measures	Illustrative Qualitative Factors That Should Be Considered in Interpreting Output	Illustrative Local Condition Factors That Should Be Considered in Interpreting Output
Solid waste collection	Tons of solid waste collected	Visual appearance of streets "Curb" or "backdoor" collection Fire/health hazard conditions from solid waste accumulation Service delays	Frequency of collection Private versus public collection Local weather conditions Composition of the solid waste (including the residential-commercial-industrial mix; type of waste, etc.)
Liquid waste treatment (sewage)	Gallons of sewage treated	Quality level of effluent, e.g., "BOD" removed and remaining after treatment Water quality level resulting where dumped	Initial quality of waterway into which the sewage effluent is released Community liquid waste generation characteristics
Law enforcement (police)	Number of surveillance-hours Number of calls Number of crimes investigated	Reduction in crime and victimization rates Crime clearance rates, preferably including court disposition Response times Citizen feeling of security	Percentage of low income families in population Public attitude toward certain crimes
Law enforcement (courts)	Number of cases resolved	Number of convictions/no. of plea-bargain reduced sentences Correctness of disposition Delay time until resolution	Number and types of cases
Health and hospital	Number of patient-days	Reduced number and severity of illnesses Conditions of patients after treatment Duration of treatment and "pleasantness" of care Accessibility of low income groups to care	Availability and price of health care Basic community health conditions

TABLE 8–1 — *Continued*

Water Treatment......	Gallons of water treated	Water quality indices, such as for hardness and taste Amount of impurities removed	Basic quality of water supply source
Recreation..............	Acres of recreational activities	Participation rates Accessibility to recreational opportunities Variety of opportunities available Crowdedness indices Citizen perception of adequacy of recreational opportunities	Amount of recreation provided by the private sector Number of individuals without access to automobiles; and the available public transit system Topographical and climate characteristics Time available to citizens for recreation activities
Street..................... maintenance	Square yards of repairs made	Smoothness/"bumpiness" of streets Safety Travel time Community disruption: amount and duration Dust and noise during repairs	Density of traffic Density of population along roadway Location of residences, homes, shopping areas, recreational opportunities, etc.
Fire control.............	Fire calls Number of inspections	Fire damage Injuries and lives lost	Local weather conditions Type of construction Density of population
Primary and .... secondary education	Pupil-days Number of pupils	Achievement test scores and grade levels Continuation/dropout rates	Socioeconomic characteristics of pupils and neighborhood Basic intelligence of pupils Number of pupils

Source: Hatry (1972:779–80).

that have been developed to measure the output of services in an urban government. Note carefully the two right-hand columns, which indicate the multitude of variables that must be taken into consideration when interpreting these measures.

Productivity, it should be stressed, is not effectiveness. The latter is not a ratio but an attempt to estimate the consequences of a particular program or output. Suppose, for example, that the goal of a particular governmental program is to reduce the damage by fires in a given area. To accomplish this goal, additional fire hydrants are installed. A productivity measure may indicate that the hydrants are being installed very efficiently, but this measure of hydrants installed to manhours does not tell whether additional hydrants affect fire damage. This fact raises an important point: governments must sharpen their goals and priorities if greater productivity is to progress. They must, in other words keep asking "efficiency for what?" Otherwise, productivity becomes an end in itself and we find ourselves doing more and more efficiently what should never have been done in the first place.

The Importance of Productivity

Despite the persistent rise in productivity levels—increasing sixfold in the past eight decades—the United States has in the last decade experienced a considerable slowing down of this rise. Without digressing into economic theory, it can be said that this decline in the rate of productivity growth, to no small degree, is responsible for the rapid rise in inflation. Some authorities go further, calling productivity improvement the keystone to better environments and standards of living (see Newland 1972:739).

With nearly 20 percent of working Americans employed by government, growth of output per worker-hours in the public sector becomes, therefore, critical. In the average American's view, how well has the public administrator performed when faced with increased compensation to the labor force (such as in New York City) and a growing reluctance on the part of citizens to permit higher taxes? Perhaps a *Time* (March 23, 1970) essay, "America the Inefficient," provides a not unrepresentative answer: government "sets a particularly disastrous example." Government has "given the nation, among other questionable monuments to efficiency, the farm-subsidy program, the F-111 swing-wing jet, and urban renewal (sometimes referred to as 'Negro removal')." Among the other examples *Time* cites are these:

> In the name of efficiency, the Internal Revenue Service changes the income tax form, making them so complicated that millions of Americans for the first time must hire tax specialists. Sample instruction: "If line 15a is under $5,000 and consisted only of wages subject to withholding and not more than $200 of dividends, interest and nonwithheld wages, and you are not claiming any adjustments on line 15b, you can have IRS figure your tax by omitting lines 16, 17, 18, 20, 21, 22, 23, 24, 25 and 26 (but complete line 19)."

> The post office, meanwhile, takes 16 days to move a letter from Massachusetts to New Jersey.

> In the San Francisco area, the Bay Area Rapid Transit Authority (BART) manages to loose 100 lamposts, a total of 200,000 lbs. of metal costing $150,000.

> In Chicago, the Transit Authority opens a 5.2 mile new subway and

surface line. In the first ten days, there were four derailments and one collision. Chicago *Daily News* columnist Mike Royko was moved to write: "Everybody agreed that it had been a big event in transportation history, ranking right behind the voyage of the *Titanic* and the landing of the *Hindenburg.*"

Barriers to Productivity

In response to these kinds of problems, Senator William Proxmire and the Joint Economic Committee of Congress began in the early 1970s to focus on productivity and, about the same time, President Nixon established a National Commission on Productivity.

An outgrowth of the Commission was the Wingspread Conference, held in July 1973 to examine the issue of productivity at the state and local levels of government. One set of workshops at the conference concentrated on identifying obstacles to public sector productivity and means to overcome them. In what follows we shall attempt to summarize the abundance of ideas that derived from that workshop. (See National Commission on Productivity, 1973.) To help frame the discussion, the obstacles are grouped into four categories: (1) incentives, (2) information, (3) financial restrictions, and (4) organizational constraints.

1. Government management systems generally penalize bad performance more than they reward good performance. Thus, there is more incentive to avoid egregious failure than to achieve success.

A similar incentive problem might be labeled misdirection by the budget. In contrast to business (other than monopolies), government agencies are typically paid out of a budget allocation. The budget allocation is not directly tied to their performance. Being paid out of a budget allocation changes the incentive system: Performance often becomes the ability to maintain or to increase one's budget. In such an atmosphere, the successful manager is seldom the individual who, at the end of the year, returns large sums of his allocation saved through productivity improvements.

Governments, therefore, need to take a more positive approach to incentives. The Wingspread participants recommended explicit public recognition of good work, productivity bonuses, and bonuses tied to overall organizational success.

How do productivity bonuses work? A good example is found in the solid waste collection area, where collectors are permitted to go home as soon as they finish their collection routes without losing wages. Another example is found in the law enforcement area, where police are given an extra day off for every 90 days of perfect attendance. Using this approach, Plainville, Connecticut, was able to reduce sick leave to an average of five days per person per year. How does the public administrator tie bonuses (e.g., promotions) to overall organization success? One method is to install a management-by-objectives system; this approach, which requires a greater clarification of public objectives, is discussed in the next chapter.

Naturally, a large part of the responsibility for providing incentive belongs to the elected official, the politician. The realities of political survival, however, emphasize short-run results and this factor, quite clearly, militates against long-run efforts to achieve productivity improvement. Perhaps the day is not too far off when demonstrated productivity improvement will be the key to political success — after all, the mood of voters can shift suddenly.

2. Productivity does not necessarily require exotic new technology, but it does require the effective exploitation of existing technology and the timely dissemination of productivity improvement ideas. For example, when one city figures out a cheaper way to dispose solid waste, every city ought to hear about it; or, if letting policemen take cars home reduces crime, every police department ought to know about it. Significantly, a study of productivity improvements by the Urban Institute recommended, among other things, a national clearinghouse for the transference of such information.

3. Financial restrictions in public management systems are a third obstacle to productivity improvement.

Funds are not always as available as they seem. Some are earmarked for a given purpose and cannot be transfered to clearly related alternative purposes. Thus specifically committed highway funds cannot be transfered to a public transit system — even when the public might be better served by the latter.

Similarly, it is more efficient in the planning of long-range projects, which requires heavy capital investment, if the public administrator can know what funds will be available over the life of the project. Trying to plan such projects on a year-to-year basis can prove quite costly.

4. Organizational constraints on productivity improvement are not hard to identify. Statutory and constitutional constraints obviously limit the public executive far more than his business counterpart in making desirable organizational readjustments. Moreover, many purely administrative positions in local government are elective offices and, as such, often beyond the pale of the chief executive's jurisdiction. Political boundaries often clash, rather than coincide, with mutual economic interests. For example, rivers that provide economic and commercial unity to a region are frequently used as boundaries. The ideal solution in such situations would be consolidations or other joint arrangements to obtain what the economists call *economies of scale,* that is, savings that result from doing things on a larger scale than individual cities or towns. (A business example would perhaps serve best in clarifying this concept. An instance of economics of scale would be when an automobile manufacturer decides to make 100,000 rather than 500 of a new model and the cash per unit is thus reduced).

Finally, as we saw in Chapter 3, there are many problems between governments: the federal government's fiscal restrictions and reporting requirements—plain old red tape in many instances—often impede state and local productivity efforts. The availability of federal multiyear funding is always in question. And the uncertainties of the federal appropriations process create scheduling problems in any given year.

Opportunities for Improvement

In this section, we shall begin with (1) a general recommendation for increasing productivity and then move on to (2) specific recommendations in five program areas that urban government are concerned with. (For a more complete listing, see Hatry 1971.)

1. The general recommendation concerns the use of the private sector, which means individual citizens as well as business firms. Among the possibilities:

> Private firms may, in some instances, be able to provide services at lower costs and without sacrificing quality. Private firms are already doing solid waste collection. In fact, a 1970 New York City analysis indicated potentially large cost savings by switching part of its collection to private firms. Scottsdale, Arizona, meanwhile, has contracted with a private firm for fire fighting. A few school districts have begun to contract for some elementary educational services.

> Public funds can be used to attract citizen resources to, say, improve neighborhood conditions. Local governments can on a regular, systematic basis attempt to attract citizen volunteers for selected tasks such as recreational activities, health functions, social services, school aides, and even police functions.

> Citizens and businesses can be requested to do more on their own; e.g., improved preparation of waste and its collection at curbside, required burglar alarm systems for certain businesses, and antilitter campaigns for everyone.

2. The specific recommendations concern five urban government functions:

> Administration of criminal justice: relocation of policemen to assign them to times and locations more in accord with crime patterns; assignment of priorities to incoming calls; mailing of summonses in some misdemeanor cases rather than sending patrolmen; use of walkie-talkies to expand the scope of action; use of computer systems to provide data on suspects and automobiles; better scheduling of court cases; improved procedures to save police time by calling them only when needed; and setting time limits for cases (thereby forcing prosecution to act more quickly).

> Environmental management: using waste collectors on other collection

vehicles while loaded trucks and drivers go alone to disposal sites; and development of larger, more mechanized sanitation trucks.

Health care: use of paramedical personnel as substitutes for physicians; use of computers for monitoring, diagnosis, and prescription control; and greater use of the telephone to save patient visits to the physician's office.

Fire Protection: reallocation of existing fire fighting resources to increase productivity (here the operations research techniques discussed in Chapter 6 can be used); and use of chemical additives to reduce friction of water in a hose.

Education: use of schools 12 months per year and more hours per day; use of various types of computer-assisted instruction; and adoption of school accountability procedures to provide measurement of individual school performance.

Elements of Management Engineering

In this concluding section, we are concerned with the more quantitative, systematic approaches to management; here and only here, the practice of management begins to resemble science rather than art. We shall term this particular approach *management engineering.* This term, I think, is preferable to "industrial engineering," which in too many minds produces the image of a steely-eyed efficiency expert, prowling an assembly line armed with his stop watch and clipboard.

Regardless of the public, any public administrator with a real commitment to productivity improvement should be familiar with these techniques— either to use them himself or to interpret the finding of the experts. Below five basic techniques are discussed: (1) work sampling, (2) work distribution analysis, (3) flow process charting, (4) layout analysis, and (5) queuing theory.

1. Assume a manager wants to answer the question, How many people does it really take to do this job? The best means of making that determination is *work sampling.* This method, one of the most effective and frequently used in management engineering, is based on the fact that a small number of chance observations tend to give an accurate picture of the actual distribution of work. In a work sampling study, observations are taken at random intervals over, say, 15 days. During the observations, the types of activities observed are recorded in predefined categories (see columns A and B in Figure 8–1). From the distribution of random observations, the proportions of activity in each of the categories can be predicted for the particular work situation (see column C).

Knowing exactly what percentage of the day workers are engaged in productive work, the manager is in a better position to know how many people he needs in a particular work situation. Moreover, a hard look at

FIGURE 8–1
Work Sampling Record

WORK SAMPLING RECORD	COMMAND, LOCATION, ORGANIZATION LEVEL SAC, OFFUTT AFB, WING	DATES STARTED 8 May 72 / COMPLETED 26 May 72
FUNCTION Personnel	SUBFUNCTION/CODE Classification & Testing, 1634	WORK CENTER TITLE/CODE Classification & Testing

COMPUTATIONS

CATEGORY A.	NUMBER OF SAMPLES B.	PERCENT OCCURRENCE $\bar{P}$ C.	TIME MEASURED D.	TIME LEVELED E.	TIME ALLOWED F.
DIRECT					
1. Officer Classification	638	.255	318.75	321.94	359.29
2. Airman Classification	535	.214	267.50	270.18	301.52
3. Testing	353	.141	176.25	178.01	198.66
4. Occupational Analysis	82	.033	41.25	41.66	46.49
5. Proficiency Pay Program	50	.020	25.00	25.25	28.18
6. Classification Board	41	.016	20.00	20.20	22.54
7. Congressional Inquiries	10	.004	5.00	5.05	5.64
INDIRECT					
8. Supervision	150	.060	75.00	75.75	84.54
9. Administration	80	.032	40.00	40.40	45.09
10. Meetings	30	.012	15.00	15.15	16.91
11. Training	25	.010	12.50	12.62	14.08
12. Supply	13	.005	6.25	6.31	7.04
13. Office Equipment Maintenance	20	.008	10.00	10.10	11.27
14. Discussion and Receiving Instructions	60	.024	30.00	30.30	33.81
15. Clean-up	44	.018	22.50	22.72	25.36
16. Travel	75	.030	37.50	37.88	37.88
TOTAL PRODUCTIVE	2206	.882	1102.50	1113.52	1238.30
NONAVAILABLE	83	.033	41.25		
UNAVOIDABLE DELAY	0	0	0		
PERSONAL/REST	100	.040	50.00		
IDLE	111	.044	55.00		
TOTAL	N = 2500	.999	1248.75		
SAMPLES REQUIRED	N' = 844	ABSOLUTE ACCURACY FOR LARGEST $\bar{P}$			.0175

(left-margin labels: PRODUCTIVE spanning categories 1–16; OTHER spanning NONAVAILABLE through IDLE)

Source: Adapted from USAF (1973: Figs. 5–6 and 5–7).

how time is allocated among the categories might suggest areas for productivity improvements. (Why so much time for clean up? Why so many meetings?)

The manager should, of course, implement as many improvements as possible *before* work sampling, since his primary objective is to set a standard of how many people it takes to do the work efficiently, not just any way. Consequently, work sampling is usually preceded by techniques designed to ferret out areas of inefficiency. Work distribution analysis, flow process charting, and layout analysis are such techniques.

2. The logical method of procedure in *work distribution analysis* is, first, to prepare a list of activities and tasks. An *activity list* is a general inventory of the principal activities of the office being studied; listing of detailed activities should therefore be avoided. Tasks lists are prepared by each employee in the office to show jobs or duties performed. From this information, the work distribution chart is prepared. All three items are shown in Figure 8–2.

An analysis of the work distribution chart can help to answer a number of important questions: Is there misdirected effort? Are the employees' skills properly used? Are they doing too many unrelated tasks? Are the tasks spread too thinly among employees? Is work divided evenly among employees? (Parker 1971:264)

3. In order to see how a job is being done and to highlight further areas for productivity improvement, a *work flowchart* can be used. The basic elements are shown in Figures 8–3 and 8–4.

As should be apparent from these figures, flow process charts are pictures of the procedure charted. A chart may follow a procedure through several organizational units, or it may be limited to a part of the procedure. "The chart should show in detail just how the job is being done—not the way someone thinks it is being done or the way the office manual says it should be done. . . . The flow process chart must show every step that takes place in carrying out a procedure. When distance, quantity, or time have some significance, such information should be entered on the form. Forms, form letters, and individuals affected by or that affect any step in the procedure should be identified on the chart." (Bushey 1974:231)

Figures 8–3 and 8–4 are examples of a simple form used by some federal agencies to analyze procedures. (Note in particular the bottom of the form.) Figure 8–3 focuses on a specific form (10-P-10, Application for Hospitalization) and shows the 27 steps the old procedure required to process it. Figure 8–4 shows the 13 steps to which the old procedure can be reduced.

4. Closely tied to procedures analysis is *layout analysis,* which is simply a sketch of the work place, preferably indicating the flow of work. The particular advantage of the layout chart, like the floor plan for a house, is that it shows the relationships of a physical situation without requiring one to actually create that situation. The layout chart should: Make it possible to plot the walking distances involved in getting work done; show the flow of work from one location to another; identify poor arrangements of work sta-

FIGURE 8–2
Work Distribution Chart

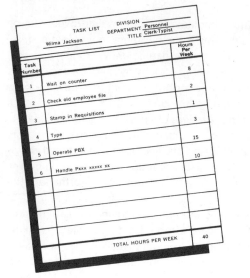

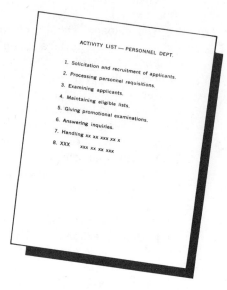

WORK DISTRIBUTION CHART

ACTIVITY	TOTAL MAN-HOURS	Wilma Jackson Clerk-Typist	MAN-HOURS	Jack Moody Personnel Assistant	MAN-HOURS	H. Melody Principal Clerk	MAN-HOURS	M. Dickson Clerk-Typist	MAN-HOURS	Daisy Hahn Clerk-Typist	MAN-HOURS	Mrs. Stern (Record Room) Principal Clerk	MAN-HOURS
Solicitation and Recruitment of Applicants	39	Wait on counter / Check old employee file	8 / 2	Write want ads / Wait on counter / Check old employee file	1 / 8 / 2	Write want ads	2	Type want ads / Wait on counter / Check old employee files	1 / 1 / 3	Wait on counter / Check old employee file	7 / 3		
Processing Requisitions	32	Stamp in Requisition	1	Check Requisition / Keep Requisition Register / Maintain Suspense File	2 / 2 / 2	Check requisition / Allocate / Keep Requisition Register / Certification	2 / 10 / 2 / 5	Assist Miss Melody	3	Assist Miss Melody	3		
Examining Applicants	1					Make request for needed examination to provide names for certification	1						
Fingerprinting New Employees	16	Type Fingerprint form	3	Fingerprint new employees / Maintain fingerprint file	10 / 2					Type fingerprint forms	1		
Giving Promotional Examinations	1					Request needed promotional examination	1						
Maintaining Eligible Lists	21					Supervise maintenance of Eligible and Promotional Lists	8	Maintain Eligible and Promotional Lists		Maintain Eligible and Promitional Lists			
Answering Inquiries	32	Operate PBX	15	Answer inquiries	5	Answer phone, letter, and personal inquiries	2	Answer Inquiries	2	Answer Inquiries / Relieve on PBX	6 / 2		
	240		40		40		40		40		40		

Source: Bushey (1974:228).

FIGURE 8-3
Flow Process Chart: Old Procedure

SUMMARY						FLOW PROCESS CHART
						WORK SIMPLIFICATION PROGRAM

FLOW PROCESS CHART — WORK SIMPLIFICATION PROGRAM

SUMMARY

ACTIVITY	PRESENT NO.	PRESENT TIME	PROPOSED NO.	PROPOSED TIME	DIFFERENCE NO.	DIFFERENCE TIME
○ OPERATIONS	19	7½ min	9		10	7½ min
⇨ TRANSPORTATIONS	4	1½ min	1		3	1½ min
☐ INSPECTIONS	3	½ min	2		1	½ min
D DELAYS						
▽ STORAGES	1		1			
DISTANCE TRAVELLED	75 FT.		0 - FT.		75 FT.	

PROCESS: Patients Control Clerk's handling of mailed VA Form 10-P-10 (Application for Hospitalization)—non-emergent, waiting list cases.
☐ MAN OR ☒ MATERIAL
CHART BEGINS: 10-P-10 received by Patients Control Clerk
CHART ENDS: After Filing 10-P-10 with authorizations to report.
CHARTED BY: John Doe (Patients Control Clerk)
DATE: Jan. 26, 1960
PAGE NO. 1 OF 1

DESCRIPTION OF EACH STEP (☒ PRESENT ☐ PROPOSED METHOD)	OPERATION / TRANSPORT / INSPECTION / DELAY / STORAGE	DISTANCE IN FEET	QUANTITY	TIME	NOTES	POSSIBLE ACTION (ELIMINATE / COMBINE / CHG. SEQ. / CHG. PLACE / CHG. PERSON / IMPROVE)
1. Take 10-P-10 from in-basket	●⇨☐D▽				10-P-10 previously processed by Eligibility Unit	
2. Check to see if legal and medical eligibility established	○⇨■D▽					
3. Determine that 10-P-10 must go on waiting list	●⇨☐D▽					
4. Prepare 3x5 card for alphabetical index kept on my desk	●⇨☐D▽		1 min	Record to assist in quickly locating 10-P-10		X
5. Prepare 3x5 card for chronological and priority file on my desk.	●⇨☐D▽		1 min	Record used in selecting applicants to authorize		X
6. Enter tally mark on waiting list report record I maintain.	●⇨☐D▽		½ min.	Running record of waiting list cases.		X
7. Enter veterans name on waiting list roster.	●⇨☐D▽		½ min.	Handy reference for telephone inquiries		X
8. Prepare waiting list letter to veteran and place in out-basket	●⇨☐D▽					
9. Attach copy of waiting list letter to 10-P-10	●⇨☐D▽					
10. Carry 10-P-10 and related material to file drawer	○⇨☐D▽	25 ft.	½ min.			X
11. Place 10-P-10 in file drawer	●⇨☐D▽			Filed Alphabetically		
12. 10-P-10 remains in file drawer until bed is available.	○⇨☐D▼					
13. Pull 3x5 chronologically filed index card.	●⇨☐D▽		½ min.	when bed is available		X
14. Go to file drawer—match 10-P-10 and index card.	●⇨☐D▽		1 min			X
15. Carry 10-P-10 back to desk	○⇨☐D▽	25 ft.	½ min.			X
16. Review file — to see if any pertinent correspondence added.	○⇨■D▽		½ min			X
17. Remove name from waiting list roster.	●⇨☐D▽		½ min			X
18. Indicate change on waiting list report record.	●⇨☐D▽		½ min.			X
19. Select reporting date and note bed control record	●⇨☐D▽					
20. Remove 3x5 card from waiting list alphabetical file.	●⇨☐D▽		½ min.			X
21. Prepare memorandum to travel clerk	●⇨☐D▽		1 min			X
22. Send 10-P-10 and instructions to Travel clerk	○⇨☐D▽					
23. Take 10-P-10 and travel authorization out of basket	●⇨☐D▽			When returned to my desk from Travel clerk		
24. Check travel authorization	○⇨■D▽		½ min			X
25. Attach copy of T/O to 10-P-10. Place original T/O in out-basket	●⇨☐D▽		½ min.			X
26. Carry 10-P-10 and related papers to file drawer	○⇨☐D▽	25 ft.	½ min.			X
27. File 10-P-10 with other authorized cases according to reporting date.	●⇨☐D▽					
	○⇨☐D▽					
	○⇨☐D▽					
	○⇨☐D▽					
	○⇨☐D▽			Note: Time has been estimated only for steps that may be eliminated		

ANALYZE - QUESTION EACH STEP. ASK *WHAT? WHERE? WHEN? WHO? HOW?* and follow each with *WHY?*

Source: Bushey (1974:230).

FIGURE 8-4
Flow Process Chart: New Procedure

SUMMARY						
ACTIVITY	PRESENT		PROPOSED		DIFFERENCE	
	NO.	TIME	NO.	TIME	NO.	TIME
○ OPERATIONS			9			
⇩ TRANSPORTATIONS			1			
☐ INSPECTIONS			2			
D DELAYS						
▽ STORAGES			1			
DISTANCE TRAVELLED FT.		FT.		FT.		

FLOW PROCESS CHART
WORK SIMPLIFICATION PROGRAM

PROCESS Patients Control Clerk's handling of mailed VA Form 10-P-10 (Application for Hospitalization)-non emergent waiting list cases

☐ MAN OR ☒ MATERIAL

CHART BEGINS 10-P-10 received by Patients Control Clerk
CHART ENDS After filing 10-P-10 with authorizations to report

CHARTED BY John Doe (Patients Control Clerk)
DATE Jan. 27, 1960
PAGE NO. 1 OF 1

DESCRIPTION OF EACH STEP ☐ PRESENT ☒ PROPOSED METHOD	OPERATION	TRANSPORT	INSPECTION	DELAY	STORAGE	DISTANCE IN FEET	QUANTITY	TIME	NOTES	POSSIBLE ACTION ELIMINATE	COMBINE	CHG. SEQ.	CHG. PLACE	CHG. PERSON	IMPROVE
1. Take 10-P-10 from in-basket	●	⇨	☐	D	▽										
2. Check to see if legal and medical eligibility established	○	⇨	☒	D	▽										
3. Determine that 10-P-10 must go on waiting list.	●	⇨	☐	D	▽										
4. Prepare waiting list letter to veteran and place in out-basket	●	⇨	☐	D	▽										
5. Note 10-P-10 to indicate waiting list letter sent	●	⇨	☐	D	▽				Save preparing copy of waiting list letter.						
6. Place 10-P-10 in file drawer (file chronologically)	●	⇨	☐	D	▽				File cabinet for this purpose to be relocated by my desk.						
7. 10-P-10 remains in file until bed becomes available.	○	⇨	☐	D	▼										
8. Pull 10-P-10 when bed is available.	●	⇨	☐	D	▽				10-P-10's are filed chronologically-come up in turn						
9. Review file - to see if any pertinent correspondence added	○	⇨	☒	D	▽										
10. Select reporting date-Stamp date on corner of 10-P-10 *	●	⇨	☐	D	▽				Stamped info. for Travel Clerk-replaces memorandum						
11. Send 10-P-10 to Travel Clerk	○	⇨	☐	D	▽				Travel Clerk prepares authorization-forwards orig for mailing						
12. Take 10-P-10 from in-basket	●	⇨	☐	D	▽				Following its return from Travel Clerk						
13. File 10-P-10 with other authorized cases-by reporting dates	●	⇨	☐	D	▽										
	○	⇨	☐	D	▽				Notes:						
	○	⇨	☐	D	▽				1. The number of steps will be reduced from 27 to 13						
*and on bed control record.	○	⇨	☐	D	▽				2. I will just turn around in my chair to file applications						
	○	⇨	☐	D	▽				3. Carrying 10-P-10's a distance of 25 feet on three occasions will be eliminated. (I walk 50 feet going and returning)						
	○	⇨	☐	D	▽				The proposed changes are to some extent made possible by the reduction in applications placed on the waiting list since the present procedure was installed. Very little time will be required to make a physical count of applications on the waiting list, or to locate an application for telephone or other inquiries						
	○	⇨	☐	D	▽										
	○	⇨	☐	D	▽										
	○	⇨	☐	D	▽										
	○	⇨	☐	D	▽										
	○	⇨	☐	D	▽										
	○	⇨	☐	D	▽										
	○	⇨	☐	D	▽										
	○	⇨	☐	D	▽										
	○	⇨	☐	D	▽										
	○	⇨	☐	D	▽										
	○	⇨	☐	D	▽										
	○	⇨	☐	D	▽										
	○	⇨	☐	D	▽										

ANALYZE - QUESTION EACH STEP. ASK *WHAT? WHERE? WHEN? WHO? HOW?* and follow each with *WHY?*

Source: Bushey (1974:232).

tions in relation to one another; and show improperly located equipment, such as files, telephones and machines.

5. Who has never had to wait in a government agency for service? Next time you must wait, think about the merits of *queuing theory*. This mathematical technique, sometimes called waiting theory, enables us to determine with precision how long clients will have to wait. Actually, how long they wait depends on three kinds of information: arrival rates (8:02 A.M., 8:05 A.M., 9:32 A.M., etc.), service time (12 minutes, 9 minutes, 10 minutes, etc.), and the number of clerks assigned to provide the service.

Given only arrival rates and service times, management could state a goal—say, to hold service times (that is, how long a client must remain in the office) to less than 5 minutes—and then calculate exactly how many clerks are required to attain it. Unfortunately, the mathematical methods of solving queuing theory problems are largely statistical in nature and presume a level of knowledge of statistics beyond the scope of our discussion. There are, however, a number of excellent illustrations available that indicate the mathematical formulation and solution to these problems. (For examples in the area of transportation planning and hospital practice, see Morse 1967:Chapters 5 and 6).

Conclusion

To some, no doubt, this nuts and bolts approach to better organization may seem pedestrian. To be sure, striving for productivity improvement is hardly as exhilarating an experience as, say, designing an entire city like Lakewood, Colorado.

But it matters. Consider, for instance, the fact that in 1973 the federal government used 5,298 different forms and that the cost of all this paperwork (enough to fill the Astrodome 50 times) amounts to more than $40 billion (in cost both to the government and the private citizens and businesses that have to fill out the forms and mail them back). Flow process charting helps streamline and thereby reduce this paper shuffling.

Let us bring the issue into sharper focus. In 1972, New York City's hospital corporation, with a budget of $800 million, had $43 million added to that budget simply from processing paper to get third-party repayments. But flow process charting streamlines this paper shuffling. To reduce an expense that almost equals total federal spending in 1976 for enforcement of environmental laws is not, I submit, pedestrian.

NAILING DOWN THE MAIN POINTS

1   Intelligent organizational design requires more than moving boxes around on an organizational chart; it demands careful attention to four

related questions: (*a*) What should the units be? (*b*) What units should join together, and what units should be kept apart? (*c*) Where do decisions belong? and (*d*) What is the appropriate placement and relationship of different units?

2   Upon completion of the four step design process, the results can be reexamined in terms of three standards, which form a kind of design criteria: clarity, simplicity, and adaptability.

3   Reorganization is radical surgery and should be undertaken only when truly warranted. No reorganization can be politically neutral.

4   Simply put, productivity is a measure of efficiency with which resources are converted into products or services. Or:

$$\frac{\text{Output}}{\text{Input}} = \text{Productivity}$$

And with nearly 20 percent of working Americans employed by government the importance of the growth of productivity in the public sector can hardly be overemphasized.

Yet barriers to increasing productivity exist: (*a*) lack of incentives, (*b*) lack of information on how to increase it, (*c*) legal and political restrictions on how public monies may be spent, and (*d*) jurisdictional restrictions that sometimes make economies of scale impossible.

5   Despite these barriers, opportunities for improvement are largely untapped. For example, contracting to private firms can in some instances result in the same output at less cost; public funds can be used to attract citizen resources; or, citizens and business can be requested to do more on their own and the possibilities for improvements in specific areas of public service (e.g., law enforcement) are virtually limitless.

Management engineering, moreover, provides a systematic approach to greater productivity in a wide variety of settings. Five techniques of management engineering seems especially relevant to the public sector: (*a*) work sampling, (*b*) work distribution analysis, (*c*) flow process charting, (*d*) layout analysis, and (*e*) queuing theory.

CONCEPTS FOR REVIEW

organizational design
limitations to the organizational
  chart
the process of organizational
  design
key activities

top management, results
  producing, results
  contributing (or staff), and
  hygiene and housekeeping
  activities
delegation of authority

design criteria
productivity
efficiency, effectiveness
barrier to productivity
economics of scale
management engineering

work sampling
work distribution analysis
flow process charting
layout analysis
queuing theory

PROBLEMS

1. Read Juan Cameron's "The Management Problem in Ford's White House" in *Fortune* (July 1975), pp. 74 ff. and John Hersey's "The President" in the *New York Times Magazine* (April 20, 1975). Based on the information in these articles, and the concepts discussed in Chapters 7 and 8, write a short report on how the White House operations could be improved or on how Carter has tried.

2. What do you think the drawbacks are to allowing advisory (staff) work to be a career?

3. In this chapter a number of governmental functions were noted that have been contracted to the private sector. What other possibilities can you think of? What problems can you see in this trend?

4. Critique the productivity factors indicated in Table 8–1; that is, show how they could give an inaccurate picture of actual productivity.

5. In response to articles in the *New York Times* about the New York State Education Department reviewing Ph.D. programs and recommending some be dropped, one reader wrote: "The trouble with this line of reasoning is that a university is not an industrial organization; it has different purposes, functions and commitments. A university has an organic quality about it. Drop a history department and you adversely affect every other department. Change or destroy one segment of the university and you affect all the other segments. To continue the metaphor, the thing to do with a weak part of the body is to work to strengthen it, not amputate." Do you agree or disagree? Are there other organizations to which these arguments might apply?

6. Can you think of any public organizations that would have benefited had they paid more attention to those areas where lack of performance could endanger results? What structural changes could have been made?

7. "Established organization doctrine, with its emphasis on structural mechanics, manifests incomplete understanding of our constitutional system, institutional behavior, and the tactical and strategic uses of organization structure as an instrument of politics, position, and power. Orthodox theories are not so much wrong when applied to the central issue of executive branch organization as largely irrelevant." Comment.

8. Analyze some recent decision by a public executive in terms of the three traits of a decision that determine where it should be made (viz., futurity, impact, and rarity). Was it made in the right place?

9. Some management theorist say build the organization around people. Quite clearly, this approach was not taken in Chapter 8. What weaknesses do you see in their approach? What do the most successful football coaches do?

10. Apply the design criteria (clarity, simplicity, and adaptability) to some organization with which you are familiar.

11. Write a review of Frederick C. Thayer's "Productivity: Taylorism Revisited (Round Three)" in *Public Administration Review* (November/December 1972), pp. 833–40.

12. In the latest edition of the *U.S. Government Organization Manual* read the section on the Department of Commerce, paying particular attention to its mission. Using the concepts of this chapter, what structural changes (if any) would you recommend?

13. Develop some *general* guidelines for the reorganization of an agency: How would you deal with outside interests groups? What sequence of steps should be followed in implementing the change? How would you minimize personal disruption?

14. Answer the three questions below for a university, a prison, a welfare office, and a church:
    (*a*) Where is excellence required to attain the agency's goals?
    (*b*) In what areas would lack of performance endanger the results?
    (*c*) What are the values that are truly important to us?
    Remember, you will need first to establish goals for each. Do you think you have made the key activities the central, load-carrying elements in your organizational structure? Have the organization's values been organizationally anchored?

INTRODUCTION

Half the business of thinking is knowing what one is after in the first place. Before we launch into the last chapter of Part II, it might help to try to cut through the great mass of incidental and, sometimes perhaps, obscuring details presented in the last four chapters in order to lay bear the structure of program management.

The key is Figure 5–1, which showed policy planning as a dynamic process. Good program management begins, we saw, with careful attention to goals and to the objectives for attaining these goals. Careful attention to objectives, in turn, certainly means that, at a bare minimum, the policy planner considers alternative strategies for their attainment as well as the consequences of each alternative.

Decision making pervades the entire process of program management. Based on the assumption that today's administrator should be acquainted with the tools and techniques of rational decision making, most of Chapter 6 was devoted to exploring this approach to decision making.

But plans and decisions are not made in some ethereal realm; much to the contrary, they must be firmly fixed within an organizational setting. Indeed, the keynote of Chapters 7 and 8 was that planning and decision making cannot be separated from organizing. If people are to work together effectively in implementing plans and making decisions, they need to know the part they are to play in the total endeavor and how their roles relate to each other. To design and maintain these systems of roles is basically the managerial function of organization.

The story does not end here, however. Two vitally important, exceedingly difficult, and fre-

9

Implementation and Evaluation

quently exciting steps remain—implementation and evaluation. Again, let us be crystal clear about what we are after. First, we want to know the potential problems the administrator faces when attempting to implement a program; then, too, we want to know the strategies available for overcoming such problems. It was no coincidence when, immediately after the election of Jimmy Carter, political cartoons began to appear showing the president elect standing, arms full of papers marked "programs," in front of a giant labeled "bureaucracy." In each cartoon, the giant had an unmistakable look of you'll-have-to-deal-with-me-first-fellow. Second, regarding evaluation, we need to know what it is and how it works. But this will not be easy, for few areas in the field of public administration are more neglected than evaluation.

The combination of two major subjects within one chapter can be, I think, justified to the extent they are closely related. Indeed, without decent evaluation, the administrator has little way of knowing how well implementation is going. A former Secretary of HEW put it well; not an original point, but a point stated with an unnervous simplicity: "Evaluation is a necessary foundation for effective implementation and judicious modification of our existing programs. At this point, evaluation is probably more important than the addition of new laws to an already extensive list of educational statues. . . . Evaluation will provide the information we require to strengthen weak programs, fully support effective programs, and drop those which simply are not fulfilling the objectives intended by the Congress when the programs were originally enacted" (Robert H. Finch quoted in Wholey et al. 1970:19).

Our approach will be to begin by clarifying why implementation is a vital concern to the administrator. Then a number of techniques are discussed that, in combination, should improve the chances of success in program implementation. In the third section, we shall pose the same question about evaluation that we did about implementation—namely, why is it so important to the public administrator? The fourth section amplifies the third by examining evaluation as an aid to better decision making. The chapter concludes on a rather practical note: How does one actually go about evaluating a program?

IMPLEMENTATION: THE ACHILLES' HEEL OF PROGRAM MANAGEMENT

We shall let implementation mean just what the dictionary says it means: to carry out, accomplish, fulfill, produce, complete. But what is it that is being implemented? A policy, yes; but, more exactly, that part of a policy that we defined in Chapter 5 as a program.

The distinction between policy and program is an important one when speaking of implementation. The great difficulty in government today is not so much determining what appears to be reasonable policies on paper as it is "finding the means for converting these policies into viable field operations. . . ." (Williams 1975:453) In short, we have more good solutions (i.e., policy) than appropriate actions (i.e., programs).

Pressman and Wildavsky (1973) note among the major difficulties in implementing new social programs or program modifications three in particular: multiplicity of participants, multiplicity of perspectives, and multiplicity of decision points. These three seismic forces converge to delay — and, in many instances, stifle — administrative efforts to secure the joint action required in program implementation. The following discussion draws on an analysis by Pressman and Wildavsky of the Economic Development Administration's efforts in Oakland.

Multiplicity of Participants

On the face of things, the effort in 1966 to help the black unemployed of Oakland, California, began brilliantly. There were dedicated and powerful officials in Washington who were concerned that, if the city did not receive meaningful help quickly, then it might be torn apart by riots. The officials were able to get a multimillion-dollar congressional appropriation to finance a program to provide jobs, while also enlisting Oakland businessmen and governmental officials in the effort. And many of the usual bureaucratic barriers to action were struck down. It would be hard to think of a more propitious beginning for a government program. Yet the program by 1969 was essentially a failure: not very much money had been spent and the number of new jobs obtained for hardcore unemployed was ridiculously small. Why?

One answer is that governmental programs, even when designed to be carried out in a direct and simple manner, eventually come to involve a large number of governmental and nongovernmental organizations and individuals. In the case of the Economic Development Administration's employment effort in Oakland, the authors (1973:94) admit to oversimplifying the situation by restricting the participants to only the EDA, the rest of the federal government, and the city of Oakland, each with their constituent elements. For the EDA this would mean the initial Foley-Brandford task force, EDA operating departments in Washington, the agency's leadership after Foley, the regional office in Seattle, and the field office in Oakland. Other federal agencies that became involved included the General Accounting Office; the Department of Health, Education and Welfare; the Department of Labor; and the navy. Participants in Oakland were the mayor, city administrators, the Port of Oakland, World Airways, and several of the city's black leaders, conservative groups, and tenants of the Port of Oakland.

Some of these participants (such as the departments of Labor and Health, Education and Welfare) became involved because they possessed jurisdictional authority over important parts of the project; others (like the navy) entered the process when they felt their interest being impinged on; and still others (such as black people in Oakland) were intentionally brought into the program by the EDA in order to build local support for the projects.

This story should help explain the failure of President Ford's conditional amnesty program. Given the depth of emotion generated by the Vietnam War and the resistance movement, it seems likely that no amnesty program — no matter how brilliantly conceived and run — would have worked perfectly. For all the more reason, then, the design of the program chosen should have been simple and direct, but such was not to be the case. The program actually involved *four* federal government agencies: the newly created Clemency Board, the Defense Department, the Justice Department, and the Selective Service. As the deadline for applications approached in early 1975, only 7,400 of an estimated 137,000 eligible men had chosen to participate in this Rube Goldberg contraption.

Multiplicity of Perspectives

To return to the Oakland case, Pressman and Wildavsky found that each participating group had a distinctive perspective and therefore a different sense of urgency — although they still agreed on the ends of policy (e.g., developing jobs for unemployed minorities) and the means of achieving it (e.g., creating jobs through grants for public works). But different perspectives make or break a program. Several reasons why participants can agree on the ends of a program and still oppose (or merely fail to facilitate) the means for effecting those ends might be given (ibid: 99–102):

1. Direct incompatibility with other commitments. Thus HEW came to view one of EDA's training proposals as competing for scarce funds with one of their own training institutions in the area.

2. No direct incompatibility but a preference for other programs. Many EDA employees viewed rural areas and small towns — not urban areas — as the proper focus of the agency.

3. Simultaneous commitments to other projects. The Port of Oakland's architect/engineer delayed his work on plans for the marine terminal because his staff was busy on other port projects. This reason also probably helps explain why law enforcement agencies have not regulated obscenity more strictly, despite the 1973 U.S. Supreme Court's ruling that they could. As Manhattan's District Attorney put it, "We've got more serious cases than we can handle already. When we have got more homicides, more rapes, and more assaults, prosecuting prostitution or pornography has to be low in priority" (*New York Times,* November 2, 1975).

4. Dependence on others who lack a sense of urgency.

5. Differences of opinion on leadership and proper organizational role.

6. Legal and procedural differences. Discussing the frustrations of the early days of public works program implementation, an EDA task force member remarked that, "There were all sorts of technical things that had to be decided. The job issue came later. There were a number of questions

about EDA policy—how you process these things, how much meddling EDA would do. . . . In September, October, and November of 1966, there was hostility between the EDA and the Port on construction issues." For example, regarding the quality of landfill, at every point, the port and EDA had their own engineering opinions. "There was hardening, but not over the right issues. They were fighting about landfill, but they *should* have been worrying about employment."

Multiplicity of Decisions

In their analysis of the relatively simple EDA Public Works Program, Pressman and Wildavsky were able to isolate 30 decision and clearance points, which involved a total of 70 separate agreements. As Table 9–1 shows rather dramatically, as the number of decision points increases the probability of agreement among all participants becomes terribly low.

TABLE 9–1
Probability of Program Completion as a Function of Participants' Level of Agreement

Probability of Agreement on Each Clearance Point (*in percent*)	Probability of Success after 70 Clearances	Number of Agreements that Reduce Probability below 50 Percent
80	0.000000125	4
90	0.000644	7
95	0.00395	14
99	0.489	68

Source: Pressman and Wildavsky (1973:107) The Table assumes of course that each decision is independent. Do you think that assumption is warranted?

Nevertheless programs do survive. They survive because they adapt themselves to their environments.

> In considering the sequence of events necessary to implement a program, we assumed that at each decision point the various participants would give a simple "yes" or "no." While this assumption may be met by some participants part of the time, it would rarely hold for all participants all of the time. However useful an all-or-nothing assumption may be to begin analysis, it is clearly insufficient to end our discussion. We know that a negative act by a participant at a decision point need not signify that the program is dead; it can be revived by going back later on and seeking a favorable verdict. Vetoes are not permanent but conditional. Accommodations may be made, bargains entered into, resistances weakened. (Pressman and Wildavsky, 1973:116)

But there is a price to be paid of the ultimate agreement: delay. And the more intense and stronger the opposition, the higher the delay.

TOWARD MORE EFFECTIVE IMPLEMENTATION

The most important lesson to be learned from the EDA experience in Oakland is that implementation needs more careful attention during the policy development. That is to say, when the broad objective of policy is being set, efforts should be made to keep the number of participants and decision points small. Policy statements should contain action commitments and answer several distinct questions: What action has to be taken? Who is to take it? And, Do these people have the capacity to do it?

Given the psychological makeup of policy makers, however, this lesson might not be an easy one to put into practice. Write Pressman and Wildavsky (1973:136–37): "The view from the top is exhilarating. Divorced from problems of implementation, federal bureau heads . . . think great thoughts together. But they have trouble imagining the sequence of events that will bring their ideas to fruition. Other men, they believe, will tread the path once they have so brightly lit the way. Few officials down below where the action is feel able to ask whether there is more than a rhetorical connection between the word and the deed."

Certainly an encouraging exception to this disdain for the problem of implementation is found in "A National Plan for Energy Research, Development and Demonstration," a report prepared by the Energy Research and Development Administration in response to the Federal Nonnuclear Energy Research and Development Act of 1974, which required ERDA to develop such a plan. In this report, ERDA carefully specified the actions necessary for the realization of each objective (two examples are shown in Table 9–2). Further, in Chapter VII, ERDA considered the roles of key participants, although apparently no attempt was made to limit the number. In Chapter IX, ERDA considered potential constraints to implementation. Among them were: (a) economic viability of the programs, (b) capital requirement, (c) industrial constraints with regard to manpower, equipment, raw materials, and transportation; (d) water resource constraints; and (e) negative environment, health, and safety.

Another ERDA (1975b) report, "National Solar Energy Research, Development and Demonstration Program," is also illustrative. The basic strategy for the program is to carry out research, development, and demonstration projects to determine the technical and economic viability of solar energy technologies. To *implement* this strategy requires a very extensive array of studies, institutions, projects, requirements, barriers, and constraints. Figure 9–1 is an attempt by ERDA's policy planners to diagram this array schematically.

In addition to paying closer attention to implementation during policy making, there are other ways of improving the effectiveness of implementation. One is to pay as much attention to the creation of organizational machinery for *executing* a program as for launching one. Again Pressman and Wildavsky (1973:145–46): "EDA leaders took great pains to design the best organization they could think of for approving application, committing funds, and negotiating initial agreements. But in most of the projects they did not spend as much time ensuring that the initial commitment would be followed up by the agency; in fact, the EDA itself seemed to lose its own in-

TABLE 9-2
Federal Energy Program Implementation

	Objective	Approach to Attainment
Geothermal	To develop and demonstrate technologies for the production of both electric power and nonelectric outputs from domestic geothermal resources to make possible an initial annual energy contribution by 1985 (under 1 quad) and a moderate to substantial contribution by 2000 (2.5–6 quads).	Give near-term priority to technologies utilizing moderate temperature, low salinity geothermal reservoirs with fluid reinjection in support of industry efforts. Investigate technologies for utilizing more advanced and extensive reservoir types: Geopressured. Hot dry rock. Conduct a comprehensive national geothermal resource assessment to establish, by 1980, reserves to support significant energy production in the 1985–2000 period. Complete environmental characterization and establish control technology requirements in parallel with technology programs. Provide incentives for commercial development through federal guarantee programs and leasing programs. Conduct jointly funded government/industry demonstration projects if appropriate for two 50 Mw(e) electric power plants in the 1979–82 period.
Oil shale	To develop and commercially demonstrate in situ technology for the economic recovery of shale oil to make possible a moderate annual energy contribution both in 1985 (up to 2.5 quads) and by 2000 (up to 4.5 quads).	Give priority of effort to in situ technology development; monitor industrial development of above-ground processes that are more advanced. Conduct small scale experiments and field tests to: Develop understandings of basic phenomena. Assess commercial potential Motivate industry participation in demonstrations. Develop environmental and socioeconomic impact assessments of all shale processes in parallel with technology development to resolve public acceptability issues. Conduct major field tests by: 1977: 25 ton/day gas production. 1978: True in situ oil processing.

Source: Adapted from Energy Research and Development Administration (1975a: VIII–2).

tense interest in the program after 1966. Although those who design programs might not generally enjoy the less exciting work of directing their implementation, a realization of the extent to which policy depends on implementation could lead such people to alter their own time perspectives and stay around for the technical details of executing a program."

A third way to make implementation more effective is to use the scheduling such as Gantt charts, CPM, and PERT discussed in the chapter on deci-

FIGURE 9–1
Implementation of the National Solar Energy Research, Development, and Demonstration Program

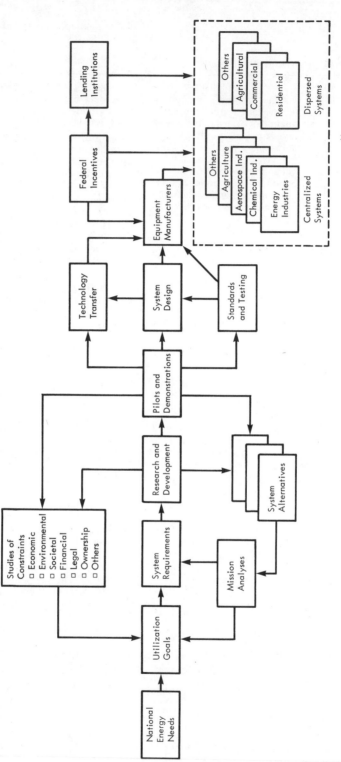

Source: Energy Research and Development Administration (1975b:II–4).

sion making. Figure 9–2 shows a highly ambitious application of another of the techniques discussed in Chapter 6, the relevance tree.

A fourth way is to use an "expediter." At the national level of government, it appears that OMB's Program Coordination Division—composed of a Program Implementation Branch and a Field Coordination Branch—fills this role. The Ash Council, which recommended the establishment of OMB, viewed the division as means by which the "president could demonstrate that things can work, that there is an expediter who can jump into the breach, representing the president's office and get something done."

For a fifth way of improving implementation, we turn neither to Washington nor Oakland but to Japan. When faced with policy decision, the top management in a Japanese organization refers it to a committee of "appropriate people." The decision-making process now becomes, to an American at least, excruciatingly slow, but finally a consensus is reached. What makes the resulting policy a good one is that the people who must participate in the implementation phase have participated in the policy making phase; they are already presold. Moreover, this process "makes it clear where in the organization a certain answer to a question will be welcomed and when it will be resisted. Therefore, there is plenty of time to work on persuading the dissenters, or making small concessions to them which will win them over without destroying the integrity of the decision." (Drucker 1973:470)

Governments have, of course, a wide range of mechanisms for encouraging proper behavior among those involved in a program. ("Proper behavior" simply means behavior that leads to attainment of the program's objectives.) These mechanisms range from political techniques such as persuading (discussed in the second chapter) to formal mechanisms such as those shown in Table 9–3. As indicated, the formal mechanisms are not without drawbacks when applied to an area of policy such as pollution control.

In addition to fully recognizing these drawbacks summarized in Table 9–3, the administrator should strive to build *incentives* into the program. Perhaps the most notorious examples of ignoring the incentive question are to be found in social-benefit programs. As a 1973 Joint Economic Committee report (cited in *New York Times,* July 8, 1973) put it, the combined benefits to recipients of New York City's welfare, Medicaid, and eight other programs "can make it extraordinarily unprofitable to work."

But the problem of incentives applies to the administrator as well as the recipient. The Small Business Administration is a case in point. Writes former federal budget director Charles L. Schultze (1969:208, 213) "Measures have not been developed which can be used to judge the performance of various regional loan offices in terms of overall program objectives. Defaulted loans, on the other hand, are easily identified, and a significant default rate is sure to invite congressional questions. Loan officials, therefore, tend to avoid risky loans. As a consequence, far from meeting their original objectives, the programs end up, in many cases, simply in making loans of commercial quality at less than commercial rates." Schultze also points to how federal

FIGURE 9–2
Evolutionary Paths to Far-Future Space Endeavors

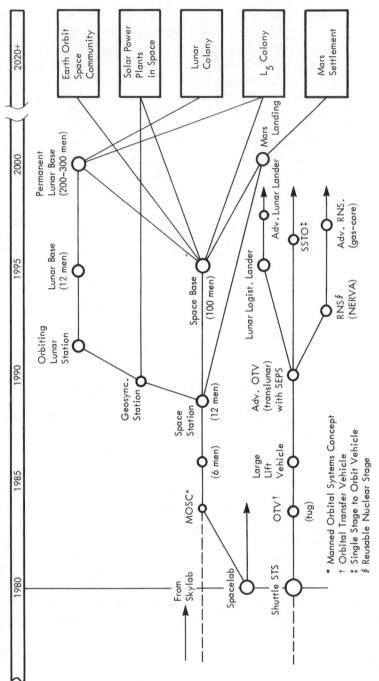

Source: von Putt Kramer (1975:38).

TABLE 9–3
Alternative Governmental Mechanisms for Pollution Control

Mechanism	Example	Difficulties
1. Prohibition	Full treatment of effluents and sewage required of all business and municipalities	An optimal solution to pollution does not require full treatment only "right amount," since the natural biological processes in lakes and streams give them a certain capability of cleansing themselves.
2. Directive	Government determines the *extent* to which municipalities bordering Lake Erie treat sewage	It is very difficult to determine just what percentage of organic matter and phosphorous to remove. And even if standard could be set, it must be translated into directives for each of the entities that emit pollutants
3. Taxes and Subsidies	Tax polluters; give subsidies to business that hire hard core unemployed	Immense information requirements necessary for the implementation of these schemes. Government must know the effect of pollution and unemployment so that a tax or subsidy could result in just the right amount of waste discharge or hiring.
4. Regulation	Require that all new cars be equipped with devices designed to reduce the level of pollutants in the exhaust	Regulation, to be effective, must be accompanied by the practice of periodically inspecting all cars. Expensive. Inflexible.
5. Payment..............	Federal subsidy for capital costs of improving regional sewage facilities	Crude: Does not easily provide proper coordination for all the relevant units in the system. Limited to problems where capital costs—rather than, say, operating expenses—are the block to improvement of the situation.
6. Action.................	Where the fish population of a lake is endangered by over fishing, the government continually stocks the lake	Limited applicability

Source: Adopted from Otto A. Davis and Morton I. Kamien (1969:67–86).

reimbursement formulae contribute to hospital inefficiency: "Essentially each hospital is reimbursed by the federal government for the 'reasonable costs' of delivering services to patients under medicare and medicaid programs. Payment is matched to the individual costs of each hospital. There are virtually no incentives for efficiency. Any savings from more efficient operations result in lower federal payments; any increased costs are fully passed on. To the extent that larger staffs bring prestige and promotion, there are positive incentives for inefficiency."

Two additional means of improving the effectiveness of implementation remain to be discussed, communications and management by objectives. Since these are rather broad topics, two subsections are devoted to them.

Communication

The sheer mass of communication that occurs during the implementation of a program is overwhelming. In an attempt to determine the time spent in communicating, one investigator (cited in Koontz and O'Donnell 1974:336) reported that 232 technical employees of a research organization spent 61 percent of their eight-hour workday in this activity, 5 percent in speaking and listening, 16 percent in writing, and 10 percent in reading.

Written and oral messages have their advantages and disadvantages. Written messages, for example, can be retained as permanent references to work off and guide action during implementation. Additionally, they have the advantage of providing a legal record, although, over time, the retention of voluminous written communications can be very expensive.

Of paramount importance in the use of the written message are clarity and simplicity. To insure that messages leaving his headquarters met this dual standard, Napoleon, it is said, kept on his staff an exceptionally ungifted captain. The officer's responsibility was to read all outgoing messages; if he was able to understand them, then presumably no officer in the Grande Armée would have any difficulty. While it is unlikely that any agency head today could get such a position established, one can at least try to keep the reader in mind when drafting a memorandum.

But, even then, the reader may still be uncertain as to the writer's fine meaning. Tone and nuance are not easily put into words. Accordingly, in certain instances, oral communication is preferable.

The biggest advantage of oral over written communication, at least during implementation, is that it is two-way. When the speaker's message creates ambiguity, the listener can ask follow-up questions (such as: "As I understand it, you mean so and so?"). At the same time the supervisor has the opportunity to *receive* as well as impart information.

One final point, closely related to oral communication: The importance of on-site inspections by top management during implementation of a program is hard to overemphasize. If we suffer from armchair generals, then surely we can suffer too from armchair administrators.

During these face-to-face encounters, the listener must resist the tendency to evaluate communication prematurely. According to Rogers and Roethlisberger (1952), those who would communicate should be listened to in noncommittal, unprejudiced fashion and thus be encouraged to state their full position before response is generated. Halberstam (1969:305–6) reports that this dictum was repeatedly ignored during the American involvement in Vietnam. For example, during his on-site visit, McNamara tended to look for the war to fit his criteria, his definitions. He went to Danang in 1965 to check on the marine progress there. A marine colonel in I Corps had a sand table showing the terrain and patiently gave the briefing: friendly situation, enemy situation, main problem. McNamara watched it, not really taking it in, his hands folded, frowning a little, finally interrupting. "Now, let me see," McNamara said, "if I have it right, this is your situation," and then he spouted his own version, all in numbers and statistics. The colonel, who was very bright, read him immediately like a man breaking a code, and without changing stride, went on with the briefing, simply switching his terms, quantifying everything, giving everything in numbers and percentages, percentages up, percentages down, so blatant a performance that it was like a satire. Jack Raymond of the *New York Times* began to laugh and had to leave the tent. Later that day Raymond went up to McNamara and commented on how tough the situation was in Danang, but McNamara wasn't interested in the Vietcong, he wanted to talk about that colonel, he liked him, that colonel had caught his eye. "That colonel is one of the finest officers I've met," he said.

Management by Objectives

A final way by which the implementation might be made more effective is the use of a highly touted management system called management by objectives (MBO). According to McConkey (1975), MBO has four features that make it especially well suited for contributing to program implementation. First, those accountable for directing the organization determine what they want to achieve during a particular period; that is, they establish overall objectives and priorities. Second, all key management people are encouraged to contribute their maximum efforts to attaining these overall objectives. Third, the planned achievement of all key management people is coordinated to promote greater total results for the organization as a whole. Fourth, a control mechanism is established to monitor progress compared to objectives and feed the results back to higher levels.

The system has been applied successfully in a variety of organizations. Among the nonprofit type organizations are hospitals, schools, police departments, nursing homes, defense departments, municipal governments, and federal agencies. Instrumental in bringing the system to 21 departments and agencies of the federal government in April 1973 was OMB Director Roy Ash. Now, as supervisors of the system, the OMB bosses have an excuse to drop in regularly on cabinet secretaries and other agencies to find out how well the work is being done.

Stripped of its business school jargon, the system works as follows (Brady 1973):

1. The annual MBO cycle begins when the department formulates its budget. Program managers are urged to accompany each request for funds with a list of measurable, specific, results oriented objectives. The secretary (or city manager) then compares these initial proposals with what he or she wants the department to accomplish during the coming year. During this stage, he or she works closely with the agency heads.

Here is a typical dialogue between former HEW Secretary, Elliot L. Richardson and an agency head as they formulated an objective. (Quoted in ibid.)

> AGENCY HEAD: One of our agency's most important initiatives this year will be to focus our efforts in the area of alcoholism and to treat an additional 10,000 alcoholics. Given last year's funding of 41 alcoholic treatment centers and the direction of other resources at the state and local level, we feel that this is an achievable objective.
>
> SECRETARY: Are these 41 centers operating independently or are they linked to other service organizations in their communities? In other words are we treating the whole problem of alcoholism, including its employment, mental health and welfare aspects, or are we just treating the symptoms of alcoholism?
>
> AGENCY HEAD: A program requirement for getting funds is that the services involved must be linked in an integrated fashion with these other resources.
>
> SECRETARY: I am not interested in just looking at the number of alcoholics that are treated. Our goal ought to be the actual rehabilitation of these patients. Do you have data to enable you to restate the objective in terms of that goal?
>
> AGENCY HEAD: As a matter of fact, Mr. Secretary, we have developed a management information and evaluation system in which each grantee will be providing quarterly data on the number of alcoholics treated, as well as on the number of alcoholics who are actually rehabilitated.
>
> SECRETARY: How do you define "rehabilitated"?
>
> AGENCY HEAD: If they are gainfully employed one year after treatment, we regard them as being rehabilitated.
>
> SECRETARY: Please revise this objective, then, to enable us to track progress on how effective these programs really are in treating the disease of alcoholism and in rehabilitating alcoholics.

2. The staff of the secretary draws up the department's budget and forwards it to the president for action.

3. The secretary then prepares for his agency heads and regional managers a list of the priorities determined during the budget preparation. In light of these priorities, the executives review and alter as necessary their preliminary objectives. Typically, they will select eight to ten objectives that represent the most important results expected of their programs. Just prior to the start of the fiscal year, they submit these objectives—along with milestones that must be reached (e.g., expand OEO projects to increase capacity by 25,000 patients by September) and resources that must be expended for their accomplishment—to the secretary.

4. The office of the secretary and his staff workers in each agency monitor progress in meeting the objectives. The success of the entire MBO system depends largely on the bimonthly management conferences attended by principal staff aids. Here managers seek advice or assistance in meeting their objectives. Prior to the conference, managers must submit an evaluation of the status of each objective.

The preceding four steps centered on the relationship between a secretary and agency heads. With only minor modifications, the system could, and should, be spread throughout the hierarchy. In other words, for MBO to work properly, managers at all levels should have objectives and milestones.

MBO delivers many benefits to the managers: a greater voice in determining his job, agreement on what is expected and appraisal based on results (not busyness or personality), better management of time by focusing on the priorities, and fewer surprises through continual monitoring. (McConkey, 1975:Chapter 9)

But the road to developing an effective MBO system is not without pitfalls (ibid.:Chapter 8). Given the increasing popularity of MBO, some organizations might be tempted to adopt the system without really understanding it. Or, organizations can overlook the fact that MBO takes time (3–5 years) before it can reach an effective level of operation. As should have been apparent from the dialogue between Richardson and the agency head, setting good, measurable objectives is no easy task. Finally, MBO can be dealt a lethal blow by omitting period reviews (such as the previously mentioned management conference) or failing to reward managers who achieve high performance levels.

To sum up, in the first part of this chapter we have seen that, while implementation is probably the most difficult part of program management, the public administrator is not without means to improve the effectiveness of implementation. But what I have to say next will surely sound strange. The very effectiveness of implementation can lead us into a serious trap: We can come to think that more is better. Of this euphoric state of mind, Elliot Richardson (quoted in Haveman 1973:787) once said, it suggests that "doing twice as many good things will . . . produce twice as many good results. In other words, if you don't know where you're going, run faster." Management by activity replaces management by objectives. But this management perversion need not take place. And few preventives outclass an effective program of evaluation.

WHY EVALUATION?

Program evaluation is the systematic examination of a program to provide information on the full range of its short and long term effects on citizens. (Hatry, Winnie, and Fisk 1973:8) In short, it asks: Is this program delivering?

The answer to that question should be of considerable interest to the administrator. Writes Carol H. Weiss (1972:16–17): "Evaluation can be asked to investigate the extent of program success so that decisions such as these can be made: (1) To continue or discontinue the program; (2) To improve its practices and procedures; (3) To add or drop specific program strategies and techniques; (4) To institute similar programs elsewhere; (5) To allocate resources among competing programs; and (6) To accept or reject a program approach." Examples follow.

When drug abuse became epidemic a few years ago, the federal government funded a multimillion dollar drug abuse education act. But by the mid-1970s, a number of members of Congress wanted to eliminate it, for several evaluative studies had been sharply critical of the program. Specifically, three scientists—who surveyed programs among high school, junior high, and grade school students—reported that such programs not only fail to decrease drug abuse but may, in some cases, cause them to experiment with illegal drugs.

In 1973, a report by the Government Accounting Office urged Congress to consider terminating aid to Brazil, which had become so prosperous that the $17 million in U.S. aid planned for fiscal 1974 would have no direct impact on the per capita income.

In 1975, the GAO found that, despite some beneficial results, the Adult Education Act of 1966 had, through 1973, "little impact on reducing illiteracy among adults." During the first nine years of the program, about 4.6 million adults were enrolled but only about one percent of the adult education program's estimated target population at 57 million adults (who never finished high school) have participated. Similarly, an Office of Education funded evaluation of the program in 1973 found that during a three-month period, one third of enrollees had either regressed or made no gains.

Evaluation thus forces decision makers to take a closer look at their programs. While this seems only fitting and proper, it is not a popular notion. During the 1960s, in fact, many administrators who had "done excellent work in measuring needs, existing sources, and community attitudes, in following the general steps for defining objectives, and in carrying out of the requisite public service activity, seemed unwilling to proceed with an evaluation of their efforts. If a particular service appeared to exist, then supplying that service in accord with the best available knowledge seemed to them to be sufficient justification in itself." (Suchman 1967). As late as 1971 a survey by the Urban Institute (Wholey et al.:1) concluded:

> "The most impressive finding about the evaluation of social programs in the federal government is that substantial work in this field has been almost nonexistent."
>
> "Few significant studies have been undertaken. Most of those carried out have been poorly conceived. Many small studies around the country have been carried out with such lack of uniformity of design and objective that the results rarely are comparable or responsive to the questions facing policy makers."
>
> "There is nothing akin to a comprehensive federal evaluation system. Even within agencies, orderly and integrated evaluations operations have not been established. Funding has been low. Staffing has been worse. . . ."

The 1970s did, however, usher in a period of program evaluation and public retrospection. The significance of this sea change did not escape Allen Schick (1971:57), who wrote in its early stages:

> The emphasis no longer is on building a record of program initiatives or on projecting the cost-effectiveness of prospective federal policies, but on looking

backward to measure what has been accomplished by means of the activities already undertaken.

The difference between analysis and evaluation is tied to the policy-making context within which social science operates. The uses of analysis are most in demand when underutilized slack resources are available, when there is a great deal of confidence in the efficacy of public action, and when policy makers want to forge new program initiatives. When these conditions change, the dominant tone of both social science and public policy shifts to evaluation. The drainage of resources, confidence, and the will to innovate thus account for the recent rise of evaluation.

Viewed from the late 1970s, the practice of evaluation remains very much in its formative stages. And despite the billions the federal government spends on new programs to improve society—many of which do not work very well—the White House and Congress still do not always insist on good procedures to evaluate new programs.

EVALUATION FOR DECISION MAKING

Decision making, as we noted earlier in Part II, pervades the policy planning process. Similarly, evaluation affects all stages in that process. For this reason, the feedback loop in Figure 5–1 connects with the policy planning process at not one but several points.

This section builds on these ideas. For here we consider the effect of evaluation on decision makers at two levels: (a) policy makers, concerned with legislative changes and budget levels; and (b) program managers, concerned more with implementation.

Evaluation for Policy Makers

Three major types of evaluation are of interest to policy makers: (1) national program impact evaluation, (2) demonstration projects, and (3) field experiments.

1. The Westinghouse-Ohio University evaluation of the national Head Start program provides a leading example of program impact evaluation. The study design was not perfect, writes Wholey (ibid.:362), "but the results of the study probably furnished a correct assessment of the impact of the national Head Start program. It revealed that one, two, and three years after children from low-income families had gone through the Head Start program, there was little or no improvement in their cognitive achievement or motivational attitudes (when compared with similar children in the same communities)." Despite these generally negative findings, the budget for Head Start was not significantly reduced.

Perhaps a more typical example of national program impact studies is the Department of Labor's $4 million per year evaluation of manpower programs. Writes Wholey (ibid.:363): ". . . the results of these studies play almost no part in the administration of Labor Department programs. Even if reliable and valid data were being generated in the national program impact studies being done, such studies are not appropriate support for the types of decisions actually made within the Labor Department. National program impact evaluation studies circulate from office to office in the Labor Department without being acted upon or in most cases even read, because Labor Department administrators do not make the types of decisions which these studies are designed to support."

Wholey is not against national program impact studies but does feel that too often it is done for people who need other types of information to help them make decisions. "While evaluators have always recognized the need to understand thoroughly the programs being evaluated, rarely if ever is evaluation preceded by an analysis of the decision-making process and the constraints on the options open to the decision-makers for whom the evaluation is being done." (ibid.:364)

2. *Demonstration projects* appear to have a better chance to influence decision makers. A good, straight-forward example of evaluation by a demonstration project is the Urban Institutes's study of the Indianapolis Police Fleet Plan. According to this plan, police are allowed to take their police cars home with them for their private use in off-duty hours—thus putting a lot more police cars on the city streets. The Urban Institute also worked with the city of Fort Worth, which had some interest in the possibility of adopting the Police Fleet Plan. The evaluation results were quite positive in favor of the Police Fleet Plan: auto thefts went down, auto accidents went down, outdoor crime, purse snatching, and robbery went down.

3. One of the best ways to evaluate is to use a randomized, controlled *field trial.* This means, first, that individuals or groups are selected to be included in the new program entirely by chance and, second, that the program is observed under actual operating conditions ("in the field"). Finally, the results obtained from the participating individuals or groups is compared with results from a similar randomly selected *control group.*

Outstanding examples of field experiments include the Office of Economic Opportunity's negative income tax experiment conducted in New Jersey; HEW's income maintenance experiments in Gary, Seattle, and Denver; and OEO's experiments with performance contracting in elementary education. Unlike program impact evaluations, which tend to be retrospective, the demonstration project and field trial may be introduced into public program either before a major operating program is started or simultaneously with a major operating program.

The principal difference between the field trial and the demonstration project is that in the former those responsible for evaluation exercise control over input variables (e.g., purpose, staffing, clients, length of service, location, size of program, auspices, and management) and carefully measure outputs to determine the extent to which the project reaches its objectives. In short, the conditions are a little closer to those of the laboratory.

How do these three approaches compare? An advantage of the field trial is that it has what social researchers call *internal validity,* that is, the results of the experiment accurately reflect the effect the program had on the participants. Since the major rationale for a social experiment is to examine the effect of a specific treatment, the importance of validity is obvious. But how does one insure validity? In field trials, for example, the nature of the treatment should be specified as closely as possible. Further, only a few significant variations should be allowed. Thus, OEO's negative income tax experiment in New Jersey varied only the level of income guarantee and the tax rate.

A disadvantage of the field trial concerns its limited *external* validity; i.e., the degree to which results of the experiment can be generalized to a broader population. Further, some critics charge that a field trial is unethical — it involves "fooling around with people" and giving benefits to one group (e.g., the poor of New Jersey) and not to another. A third disadvantage is that large social experiments like field trials often prove difficult to manage. For the team launching the negative income tax experiment, logistics become an almost overwhelming problem. They had to cope with legal details at the state and federal levels, as well as survey population before the experiment itself could begin (Roos 1975:252). It follows, fourth, that the costs of field experiments run relatively high; J. O. Wilson (cited in Roos 1975:254), for example, put the costs of six health insurance experiments he examined at $162 million. Yet, surely, these costs are paltry when compared with the costs of going ahead with programs that do not work. A final disadvantage is that the presence of an evaluator can itself affect the experiment. This phenomenon is sometimes referred to as the "Hawthorne effect" (see Chapter 12).

Impact evaluation, which is retrospective, has two major advantages. First, it is more promising than field experiments in external validity and, second, it is usually cheaper. The Westinghouse Head Start evaluation, for example, cost approximately $585,000 and this included a substantial amount of primary data collection. Naturally, when retrospective evaluation can rely upon secondary data, their costs are even lower.

But, selecting this data and designating the comparison groups presents severe methodological problems. For example, the results may be related more to the way the samples are chosen or the tests were carried on than to the worth of the program. Of course, in some instances, it might prove impossible to find before and after data.

Evaluation for Program Managers

Evaluative research is also useful to program managers at federal, state, or local levels who have responsibility for operating programs. According to Wholey (1972:365), "members of the evaluation groups at the Urban Institute have become more and more convinced that the primary evaluation payoff (in terms of decisions actually influenced) may be in evaluation that is done in enough detail to get at the effects of operational changes within operating programs. Many program managers really want to know what works best under what conditions." Wholey (ibid.:365–66) cites two examples of evaluation systems designed to help program managers.

In 1971 the District of Columbia Sanitation Department, in conjunction with the Urban Institute, developed a monitoring system for solid waste collection activities. Inspectors, armed with reference photographs and a tape recorder, drove along city streets and alleys rating the cleanliness of the block (by comparison with reference photograph). Writes Wholey: "This system . . . produces data on the *outputs* of services not simply inputs or estimates of outputs. One can imagine this system being used to assess the results of operational changes in sanitation department activities or to justify budget requests." In sum, the system helps the managers determine if particular additional inputs (e.g., increased services) does in fact produce differences in outputs (e.g., moving a neighborhood's street and alleys from an average rating of four to a rating of two).

Public school personnel are rarely provided with data relevant to decision making. The Urban Institute, therefore, attempted to develop a system for estimating the relative effectiveness of different public schools in Atlanta. In this project, schools were classified by the economic level of the students and by the amount of pupil turnover. The institute tested the notion that information on the relative effectiveness of schools running comparable student populations could be useful to the superintendent and staff.

We might also consider what is being done under the name of *performance auditing.* Harry P. Hatry (1974:20) defines performance auditing as the assessment by an *independent* group of the performance of a government program or service to determine its success in efficiently achieving its explicit and implicit objectives. What distinguishes it from program evaluation is "the independence of the activity, and the attempt to verify the performance finding for external use."

The General Accounting Office's 1972 report *Standards for the Audit of Governmental Organizations, Programs, Activities, and Functions* provides a good example of the performance audit. One of the forces that leads to the development of the GAO standards was the great increase in recent years in the flow of funds from the federal government to state and local governments. How these funds are being used, naturally, concerns GAO. In the words of Comptroller General Elmer B. Staats (1974:6): "It has been a basic GAO premise that different government levels should rely on each other's audit work to the maximum practicable extent. This premise is based on the belief that much duplication of effort by both auditors and those being audited can be avoided by making audits serve the needs of various government levels."

HOW TO EVALUATE

In the preceding section, we noted several types of evaluation. To set down a general procedure for carrying out each type is not easy. Perhaps the best approach to such a formulation is to say that evaluation research follows, ideally, a procedure reminiscent of the classical research experiment: (1) find out the goals of the program; (2) translate the goals into measurable indicators of goal achievement; (3) collect data on the indicators for those who have been exposed to the program and for those who have not (i.e., the control group); and (4) compare the data on program participants and controls in terms of goal criteria.

Find Goals

There are three points to keep in mind about goals. First, programs are likely to have multiple goals: to evaluate only one is to evaluate partially. A program to reduce air pollution, for example, might be concerned with the reduction of several types of air pollution at several sources. For purposes of evaluation, the sweeping goal of "reduce air pollution" might be broken into components, represented by this matrix (adapted from Cook and Scioli 1972):

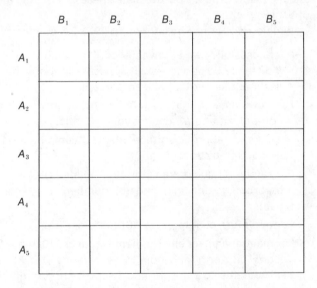

where the *A*s represent pollution types (*viz.,* carbon monoxide, sulfur oxides, hydrocarbons, nitrogen oxides, and particles) and the *B*s, pollution sources (*viz.,* automobiles, industry, electric power plants, space heating, and refuse disposal). Thus rather than consider air pollution in terms of one composite figure, the evaluator considers it in terms of several separate measures.

Second, many areas of public policy lack standards (or bench marks) by which a goal can be established. The Schlitz Brewing Company may have as its goal for next year to increase sales more than Coors increases its sales. But how does the public decision maker know the proper goals for reduction of poverty and illiteracy in the year ahead?

Third, programs not only move toward official goals. They accomplish other things, sometimes in addition and sometimes instead, as Weiss puts it (1972a:25). For example, programs that may increase the supply of workers in a particular occupation (intended consequence) may result in the exertion of downward pressures on the wages of existing workers in the occupation (unintended consequence). A good evaluator tries to look at all possible effects of program activity.

Translate Goals into Measurable Indicators

Program goals tend to be ambiguous, hazy. Consider this one for an urban transportation program: "To provide access to community services, facilities, and employment in a safe, quick, comfortable, and convenient manner for all segments of the community without causing harmful side effects." How would you translate these goals into measurable indicators of achievement?

Winnie and Hatry (in Hatry et al. 1973:27) suggest the following criteria:

For accessibility and convenience: (1) percentage of residents not within *x* distance of public transit service and more than one hour from key destinations; and (2) citizen perception of travel convenience.

For travel time: (3) time required to travel between key origin and destination points; and (4) congestion—duration and severity of delay.

For comfort: (5) road surface quality ("bumpiness") index; and (6) citizen perception of travel comfort.

For safety: (7) rate of transportation-related deaths, injuries, and incidents or property damage; and (8) numbers of transportation crime incidents.

For minimum cost to users: (9) costs per trip.

For maintenance of environmental quality: (10) noise level along transportation corridors and number of persons at risk; and (11) air pollution attributable to transportation sources and number of persons at risk;

For general public satisfaction: (12) citizen perception of adequacy of transportation services.

For monetary costs: (13) program costs.

For another interesting example of measurable indicators, we might turn to the work in the area of *social indicators*. In a seminal work on this subject, Professor Raymond A. Bauer (1966:1) described social indicators operationally as "statistics, statistical series, and all other forms of evidence that enable us to assess where we stand and are going with respect to our values and goals. . . ."

The social indicator movement has developed concurrently with evaluation research. And, given the dearth of respectable evaluation studies, some have argued for social indicators as a substitute for experimental evaluations. In my opinion, this substitution would be unfortunate because social indicators cannot tell *why* a program succeeds or fails. Yet the why is often as important as the how well.

In any event, the social indicator movement still provides us with ambitious attempts to translate goals and values into numbers. Michael J. Flax and Harvey A. Garn (1973) offer comparisons of major cities based on data available in yearly series for periods ranging from 1962 to 1970. The results, along with an explanation of the 14 indicators, is shown in Figure 9–3. The researchers say it is an attempt to reach leaders and concerned citizens with a simple set of measures to "help reduce the role of hearsay, intuition, and isolated bits of personal experience as the major criteria for citizen decision making."

The most "desirable" rating is numbered one and the least favorable is the highest number in each series. The 14 indications were described as follows:

Unemployment: in percentage of labor force out of work.

Poverty: in percentage of households with cash incomes under $3,000 a year.

Income: in terms of money income per person, adjusted for cost-of-living differences.

Housing: in costs for a moderate-income family of four, using 75 percent renters, 75 percent homeowners.

Health: based on deaths of infants under one year of age per 1,000 live births.

Mental health: in terms of the rate of reported suicides per 100,000 population.

Public order: in terms of rate of reported robberies per 100,000 population.

Racial equality: comparing white and nonwhite unemployment rates.

Community concern: measured by individual contributions to united fund charitable appeals.

Citizen participation: in terms of percentage of voting-age population that cast votes in presidential elections.

Educational attainment: measured by median school years completed by persons 25 years old or older.

Transportation: in terms of costs for a moderate-income family of four.

FIGURE 9–3

Indications of Some Major Aspects of the Quality of Life in 18 Metropolitan Areas

Metropolitan Area (by 1970 Population)	Unemployment	Poverty	Income Level	Housing	Health	Mental Health	Public Order	Racial Equality	Community Concern	Citizen Participation	Educational Attainment	Transportation	Air Quality	Social Disintegration
New York	9	9	4	17	9	1	18	1	18	14	9	1	10	7
Los Angeles/Long Beach	18	15	3	10	2	17	11	3	17	11	3	7	8	3
Chicago	2	5	5	13	18	3	14	6	15	2	7	13	16	1
Philadelphia	7	9	14	9	17	13	6	9	10	8	13	8	15	n.a.
Detroit	17	3	1	5	12	15	17	8	7	5	13	8	14	n.a.
San Francisco/Oakland	16	17	2	14	2	18	13	2	13	7	2	16	1	5
Washington	1	2	8	11	5	7	15	7	16	18	1	10	3	6
Boston	4	1	17	18	6	10	3	n.a.	12	2	6	15	5	4
Pittsburgh	14	12	13	3	11	11	5	5	12	2	13	14	17	n.a.
St. Louis	10	13	12	8	10	4	9	11	6	11	17	14	18	2
Baltimore	5	11	16	4	15	14	16	4	14	14	18	9	11	n.a.
Cleveland	12	7	9	15	8	16	10	12	1	9	9	6	13	n.a.
Houston	5	17	11	1	16	12	12	10	11	16	9	17	5	n.a.
Minneapolis/St. Paul	14	4	6	6	1	5	7	n.a.	5	1	3	11	2	n.a.
Dallas	3	16	7	2	14	6	8	n.a.	9	16	3	4	3	n.a.
Milwaukee	10	5	15	16	4	8	1	n.a.	8	5	7	11	11	n.a.
Cincinnati	7	14	10	7	7	9	2	n.a.	3	11	13	12	9	n.a.
Buffalo	12	8	18	12	13	2	4	n.a.	4	10	9	18	5	n.a.

n.a.: Not available.
Source: Flax and Garn (1973).

Air quality: measuring concentration of suspended particulates.

Social disintegration: in terms of estimated narcotics addiction rates per 10,000 population.

Collect Data

Data for evaluation research can come from a variety of sources and research techniques. To name but a few: interviews, questionnaires, observation, ratings, institutional records, government statistics, diary records, physical evidence, clinical examinations, financial records, and documents

FIGURE 9-4
Quasi-Experimental Analysis for the Effect of Specific Course Work, Including Control Series Design

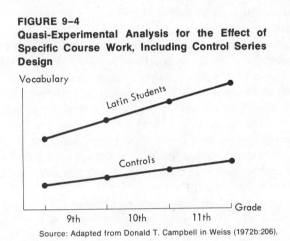

Source: Adapted from Donald T. Campbell in Weiss (1972b:206).

(e.g., minutes of board meetings, newspaper accounts of policy actions, and transcripts of trials.)

Data must be collected not only for those who participated in the program but also for those who did not; the latter is termed the control group. Figure 9-4 shows the measurable effect (vocabulary scores) of a program (course work in Latin) on the control group in comparison to the program participants.

Compare Data

The classic design for evaluation is the experimental model that uses experimental and control groups. Out of the target population, units (e.g., people, precincts, or cities) are randomly chosen to be in either the group that gets the program or the control group. Measures are taken of the relevant criterion variable (e.g., vocabulary scores) before the program starts and after it ends. Differences are computed, and the program is deemed a success if the experimental group has improved more than the control.

(Weiss 1972b:60–61) Or, in terms of the model below, the program is a success if $(b - a)$ is greater than $(d - c)$.

	Before	After
Experimental	a	b
Control	c	d

The model is deceptively simple. How can the evaluator always insure that nothing else caused the change but the program? For example, a few years ago, Washington, D.C., reported a drop in the crime rate. But to attribute this solely to the effects of one program would be exceedingly difficult. Writes Hatry (et al. 1973:66–67): "During the period, several major program actions occurred, including: major increases in the number of policemen, build up of a large drug addict treatment program, and the extensive new street lighting in some portions of the city. In addition, some believe that various social conditions had changed in the city. . . . Some of these effects could be partially isolated, e.g., street lighting effects presumably would occur in some areas and not others, but others would be extremely difficult, if not impossible, to extract."

The model simplifies in yet another way. Since experiments are only for a limited period of time, they may fail to allow for the cyclic fluctuation of time series data. (See Figure 9–5.)

Two final points. Regardless of the specific approach taken to evaluation, two final points need to be kept in mind; the first point applies mainly to the evaluator, the second applies more to the administrator to whom, presumably, the findings of evaluation studies go.

1. Evaluation, to be useful, must be viewed as a tool of management. Ideally, evaluators and the administrator cooperate. When the policy decisions about program design are to be made, the evaluator should ask the manager to specify the objectives of the program. The evaluator also determines the administrator's set of assumptions about what is believed to happen when money is spent and the intervention is made—tests cannot be designed for people who are unable to state their assumptions. Finally, the evaluator determines what kind of data would cause the administrator to act (i.e., make adjustments in the management of the program) and the kinds of action the administrator has the authority and willingness to implement. (See Horst et al. 1974:300–8.)

2. Evaluation should not be a "go or no-go" proposition, with one test determining whether a major social program is to be launched; rather, evaluation should be built into the new program, examining its strengths and weaknesses while it goes forward. Since most programs that work well usually produce only relatively small gains in their early stages, the "go or no-go" approach might force the administrator into a box where nothing is tried until we know it will work. Most social progress comes not in large leaps

FIGURE 9-5
Connecticut Traffic Fatalities

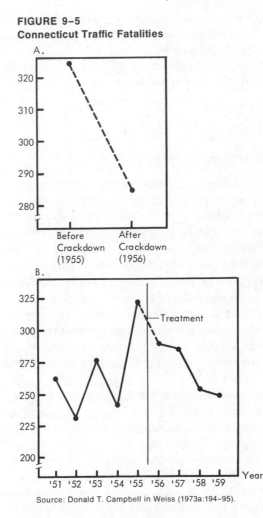

Source: Donald T. Campbell in Weiss (1973a:194–95).

but in small changes continued through time. These small changes, eventually, can lead to large ones. To discover that society's root problems are to be solved, especially in a massively successful way and in a short period of time, is just not a realistic objective for evaluation. (Mosteller, Light, and Gilbert cited in Olten 1975)

This chapter concludes Part II, "The Management of Governmental Programs." But this part cannot stand alone. As we saw in Part I, the environment of public administration has a decisive influence of program management. Presently, in Part III, we shall see that program management can*not* be thought of divorced from financial management. Indeed, scarcity of financial resources is a principal constraint in the public sector. Regardless of its financial position, no public enterprise can avoid looking at its programs in terms of these constraints.

To be sure, budget analysis, budget making, and financial planning involve areas of public administration that require significant long-term professional training. Nevertheless, it is essential to good management in the public sector that all administrators must have a full appreciation and understanding of financial management.

NAILING DOWN THE MAIN POINTS

1   With the organizational structure decided upon, the process of carrying out, accomplishing, or fulfilling the objectives of a program can begin. In short, we say implementation can begin. In the public sector, however, this task can be exceedingly difficult. Chances are the participants are heterogeneous and many. Chances are their perspectives on and priorities for a given program or project vary.

2   Given these difficulties, it becomes especially important to consider implementation at the start of the planning process—and that means during the policy planning stage (see Figure 5–1). Additionally, certain management techniques can increase the probability of success. Among these are scheduling models (see Chapter 6), expediters, incentives, good communication, and management by objectives.

3   Program evaluation is the systematic examination of activities to provide information on the full range of the program's short- and long-term effects. Based on this information, the decision maker can know whether to continue the program, to modify its procedures, or to expand its application. In short, evaluation forces managers to take closer looks at their programs. Unfortunately, as late as 1971, it appeared that evaluation of social programs in the federal government was "almost nonexistent." While evaluative activity today remains a much underdeveloped activity, it is at least receiving increasing attention.

4   Three major types of evaluation in particular concern policy makers: national program impact evaluation, demonstration projects, and field experiments (using a control group). It appears that the second and third types of evaluation have the best chance of influencing policy makers. The principal difference between the field trial and the demonstration project is that in the former those responsible for evaluation exercise greater control; conditions, in other words, are closer to those of a laboratory. One advantage of the field trial is internal validity; one disadvantage, limited external validity.

But evaluative research is useful to middle level program managers as well as the policy makers at the top. Wholey thinks, in fact, that the primary evaluation, pay-off— in terms of decision actually influenced—is evaluation that is done in enough detail to get at the effects of operational changes within operating programs. Performance auditing can also be quite important at this level.

5 One of the best approaches to carry out an evaluation is reminiscent of the classical research experiment: (*a*) Find out the goals of the program; (*b*) Translate the goals into measurable indicators of goal achievement; (*c*) Collect data on the indicators for those who have been exposed to the program and for the control group; and (*d*) Compare the data on the program participants and controls in terms of goal criteria.

6 Evaluators must remember that, above all, evaluation is a management tool. At the same time, managers need to remember that evaluation should not be a "go or no-go" proposition, with one test determining whether a major social program is to be launched; rather, evaluation should be built into the new program, examining its strength and its weaknesses while it goes forward.

CONCEPTS FOR REVIEW

implementation
multiplicity of participants, multiplicity of perspectives, and multiplicity of decision points
expediter
Japanese decision making
incentives in public policy
premature evaluation of communication
management by objectives

analysis and evaluation
national program impact evaluation
demonstration projects
field experiments
control group
internal and external validity
performance auditing
steps in an evaluation
social indicators

PROBLEMS

1. What are the implications of Table 9–1 for citizen participation?

2. Crucial to the success of an MBO system is the writing of objectives. The objectives should tell *what* (the end result), *when* (a target date or period), and *who* (who is accountable for the objectives). Further, objectives should meet several criteria: cover only priority matters; be specific (no weasel words like "reasonable" or "highest"); be realistic yet set a level of difficulty that stretches the manager; and be supportive of the objectives of other departments. (McConkey, 1975:52–59) Now, in light of this criteria, develop several objectives for a specific administrative position (e.g. director, division of criminal investigation; executive director of mental health center; and training director).

3. What weaknesses can you find in each of the measures of quality of life in Table 9–3? Can you think of better measures? How would you weigh each aspect to get an overall figure for the quality of a city?

4. Discuss the advantages and disadvantages of setting up a *new* agency to carry out a program.

5. The objectives of a city's recreation program are these: "To provide all citizens, to the extent practicable, with a variety of leisure opportunities that are accessible, safe, physically attractive, and enjoyable. They should contribute to the mental and physical health of the community, to its economic and social well-being and permit outlets that will help decrease incidents of antisocial behavior such as crime and delinquency." Establish some measurable evaluation criteria for these objectives.

6. Prepare a paper on recent evaluative research on the U.S. criminal justice system. You may want a narrower topic: "Does punishment cut down on crime?" "Do work-release programs boost a convict's chance of getting a job?" etc.

7. "Paradoxically, field offices often complain that they receive too many communications at the same time that they complain that they are insufficiently informed on new developments. The attempt of the central office to supervise closely the operations in the field often results in a steady flow of procedural regulations, instructions, bulletins, and whatnot to the field offices. If too much of this material is trivial, detailed, or unadapted to local problems—and the field office will often feel that it is—it may remain unread, undigested, and ineffective. This problem is not one of geographical separation alone, but applies generally to organization communications." (Simon, Smithburg, and Thompson 1950) Do you agree? Can you think of instances where this has occurred? What concrete steps could the central office take to overcome this problem?

8. Read Michael Aron's "Dumping $2.6 Million on Bakersfield (or How *Not* to Build a Migratory Farm Worker's Clinic)," *Washington Monthly* (October 1972), pp. 23–32. What are the lessons here for program implementation?

9. Read Herbert E. Meyer's, "How Government Helped Ruin the South Bronx," *Fortune* (November 1975), pp. 140 ff. What are the lessons here for program implementation in general and the use of incentives in particular?

PART III

Financial Management

INTRODUCTION

The subject of this chapter and the next is commonly referred to as public finance. *By public finance we mean the package of problems and issues that involve the use of tax, borrowing, and expenditure measures for public purposes.* Sometimes it is asserted, sometimes by students of public administration, that public finance is a dull subject—perhaps best left to experts in accounting and bookkeepers with green eyeshades. But this claim goes soft on detailed investigation.

Many of the most significant political questions of the day are, essentially, questions of public finance. Is the problem of poverty best approached through a negative income tax? What is the proper balance between defense spending and domestic spending? How is unemployment reduced without increasing inflation? What effect do taxes have on economic growth? What is the best way to finance education and other local services? Are tax loopholes just? Do the benefits from pollution control measures exceed their costs?

And, what approach to budgeting best insures that governmental activities and societal goals coincide? For as we shall see in Chapter 11, a budget is more than a mere document containing words and figures. Rather, it is the translation of financial resources into human purposes. It is, in Wildavsky's (1964) words, a series of goals with price tags attached.

The preceding series of questions serves not only to expand our earlier definition of public finance but also to preview the kinds of issues with which we shall be grappling in these two chapters. While considerable emphasis is placed on financial administration at the local level, it is perhaps best that we begin our discussion at the top. In par-

10

Revenues and Expenditures

ticular, we shall note the three major objectives of federal government spending and taxing. Since many administrators at all levels of government become involved in the issue of how to tax, the second section below will focus on revenues. We shall be especially interested in understanding the full implications of each possible source.

Administrators spend, too. Not surprisingly, a major portion of this chapter focuses on how governments spend. The capstone of the chapter is the final section on cost-benefit analysis—the preeminent technique of policy analysis (see Chapter 1).

FUNCTIONS OF FEDERAL FISCAL POLICY

In 1651, the English philosopher Thomas Hobbes maintained that the sole reason for the institution of government is to provide security: *Salus populi suprema lex* ("The safety of the people is the supreme law"). While such a statement has a certain aphoristic resonance, it seriously misrepresents the economic role of modern government.

In this section we examine one important part of that economic role, *fiscal policy.* Thus our concerns center on government spending, tax rates, and, consequently, the size of budget surplus or deficit; other aspects of economic policy—regulation of competition, the operation of public corporations, and changes in the supply and cost of money by the federal reserve system (i.e., *monetary policy*)—are kept very much in the background.

The effects of federal tax and spending measures on the economy are varied, but Musgrave and Musgrave (1973:6) managed to distinguish at least three more or less distinct functions:

1. Allocation: the provision of various government goods and services to society and thus involving the allocation of resources to the production of these goods and services rather than to the private sector.

2. Distribution: adjustments to the distribution of income and wealth in society.

3. Stabilization: efforts of the government to use fiscal and monetary policy to get rid of inflation, unemployment, or both and to maintain an appropriate rate of economic growth.

While other breakdowns might be made, this division suffices to set the stage for a general orientation to government fiscal policy. Following this overview, we shall examine taxation, expenditures, and cost-benefit analysis.

The Allocation Function

How does a nation determine the way in which resources will be used? The set-up is called *economic system* and it comes in a variety of types.

At one extreme is the command system in which the government makes all major decisions regarding what goods and services will be produced and who will get them. At the other extreme is the market system in which these decisions are determined by the supply and demand among many firms and individuals, casting their "dollar votes" in the market place. All advanced industrial societies (which includes the Soviet Union as well as the United States) contain an admixture of both the command and market systems.

Which brings us to some rather warmly debated questions of ideology or, if you wish, economic philosophy—the difference between those two concepts probably being no more than Leonard Silk (1975) said it was: "the false ideas held by your opponents" and "what *you* believe." Lovers of the market system contend that it is the most efficient. The critics counter: "Markets do not take account of wider social impacts—such as filth, contamination of water, congestion or depletion of resources—nor provide necessarily for wider social benefits—schools for the poor, parks for city folk, preservation of wildlife, growth of knowledge, beauty, love" (ibid).

Critics of the market system further assert that markets are stacked in favor of *private goods* (e.g., food, autos, cigarettes, hair sprays, and socks) and against *public goods* (e.g., public television, public beaches, clean streets, and clean air). Perhaps no one stated the imbalance with more verve than John Kenneth Galbraith (1958:199–200) in his influential *The Affluent Society:* "The family which takes its mauve and cerise, air conditioned, power steered, and power braked automobile out for a tour passes through cities that are badly paved, made hideous by litter, blighted buildings, billboards, and posts for wires that should long since have been put underground. They pass on into a countryside that has been rendered largely invisible by commercial art. They picnic on exquisitely packaged food from a portable icebox by a polluted stream and go on to spend the night at a park which is a menace to public health and morals. Just before dozing off on an air mattress, beneath a nylon tent, amid the stench of decaying refuse, they may reflect indeed, the American genius?"

But Professor Galbraith was writing in 1958 and, while the societal problems he notes have not been eliminated, the balance between the public and private goods has changed. Whereas the U.S. government took about 25 percent of the gross national product (GNP; i.e., the value of all goods and services produced in a year) in 1955, by the early 1960s it was taking 27 percent. The Great Society boosted the plateau to about 32 percent. And, by the mid 1970s, it reached an all-time high of 37 percent. Still, this figure is far below the British level of about 60 percent.

Distribution Function

Critics of the market system also argue that, if left alone, it would produce an income distribution that is socially undesirable. In particular, it appears that a pure market system would provide inadequate income to the very young, the very old, the sick, and the disabled.

Several techniques of income redistribution are available. Musgrave and

Musgrave argue that the *tax-transfer* schemes—such as Social Security and unemployment benefits—are the preferable devices. But redistribution may also be affected by implementation of *progressive taxation;* that is, a policy whereby the fraction of income paid increases as income rises. Thirdly, redistribution may be implemented by the government directly financing public services, such as public housing, that are available only to low-income groups.

Those with a conservative economic philosophy (or ideology) look with alarm on the rise in transfer payments; i.e., direct payments to individuals with no goods and services provided to the government in return. These payments have been increasing at the rate of nearly 9 percent a year. Assuming a constant dollar GNP continues to rise 3.5 percent a year and all other federal spending is held to only a 1 percent annual growth, some economists point out that the federal budget for the year 2000 would be $1.4 trillion, in current dollars, or four times the present level and nearly 40 percent of the then GNP. Furthermore, transfer payments would in the not-too-distant year make up 80 percent of all federal dollars spent, compared to 20 percent in 1950 and over 50 percent in 1975. Figure 10–1 shows this trend not only for transfer payments but also for *grants-in-aid;* i.e., expenditures programs designed to help state and local government provide services and money for the needy.

FIGURE 10–1
Composition of Federal Sector Expenditures

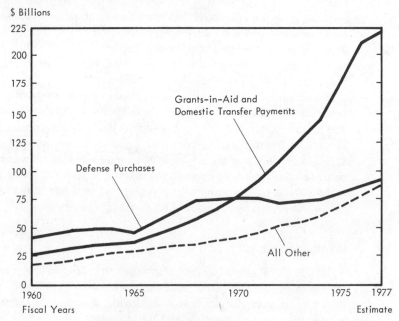

Source: U.S. Office of Management and Budget (1976:16).

How much redistribution really occurs? Though all income groups experienced truly massive gains in real income for a generation after World War II, the disparity in income remains basically unchanged. In 1947, the wealthiest fifth of American families accounted for 43 percent of the total received by all families, while the poorest fifth accounted for just 5 percent. Twenty-seven years later in 1974 the top fifth received 41 percent of total income and the bottom fifth got slightly under 5.5 percent.

One possible explanation for this paradox of rising transfer payments combined with relatively stable income distribution is that insufficient attention is paid to who gets the money. The Council of Economic Advisors recently analyzed the role federal transfer payments have played in reducing income inequality. The council found that only 16 percent of the people who get Social Security are classified as poverty victims, although, to be sure, the chief aim of Social Security is not income redistribution but insurance. For other kinds of transfer payments, the percentage is much higher—92 percent of the people who get food stamps were on the poverty level, as were 76 percent of the people on welfare and 70 percent of those who get medicaid. The CEA study, however, also showed that even those programs specifically designed for poor people do not reach all of them. Public assistance payments reached only 24 percent of the families with incomes in 1970 of $1,000 to $1,999, only 19 percent of those with incomes of $2,000 to $2,999, 12 percent of those with incomes of $3,000 to $3,999 and 9 percent of those with incomes of $4,000 to $4,999 (see Balz 1975:249.)

Stabilization Function

The three components of the stabilization function are (1) price stability, (2) full employment, and (3) economic growth.

1. When the total demand of people, business, and government exceeds the capacity of the nation's total resources to supply them—when too many dollars are chasing too few goods—we have *price instability or inflation.* Since the mid-1960s, this condition has been common in the United States. Writes Galbraith (1975) "A central feature of modern economic society is the rejection by subordinate social classes of the prescriptive limits on their income and consumption. With this rejection go claims on production that cannot be met; from these claims comes inflation."

2. In the opposite case, where the quantity supplied exceeds the quantity demanded, the result is a surplus and businesses will be forced to use less labor. This, of course, leads to increased *unemployment.* (But unemployment also results from other factors: lack of education or skills, job discrimination, pay scales set above the productive value of some member of the labor force, and urban decay.)

3. Today *economic growth* has become an uncertain concept. Many advocate zero growth; others, the substitution of quality of life for economic growth as the proper goal (recall the social indicator movement discussed

in the preceding chapter). This concept is a big, important one. We shall return to it in Chapter 15.

Now that we have some idea of what is meant by stabilization—namely, price stability, full employment, and economic growth—we can ask how fiscal and monetary policy attempt to achieve it. The orthodox answer, derived (some would say erroneously) from the great British economist John Maynard Keynes, was the soul of simplicity (see McCracken 1961).

As the depression of the 1930s made clear, the market system could not, by itself, insure growth or high employment. To combat depressions, Keynes suggested that government actively stimulate demand levels. When growth is slow and employment low, government should reduce taxes in order to stimulate purchasing and production. Government expenditures produce similar effects. So, during periods of economic decline, governments should increase its expenditures, which, in turn, will stimulate production.

But the Keynes prescription has two sides. In inflationary periods, when the economy is growing rapidly and employment is high, government should increase taxes to lessen the dollars available for purchasing. Cuts in governmental expenditures, which reduced demand, also help slow down inflation.

Until the 1930s the government rejected these unconventional ideas. For the government to spend more than it received—to engage in *deficit spending*—would, it was feared, wreck the economy. But after World War II, Keynesian manipulation of spending level to stabilize the economy became *de rigueur.* This obligation was reflected in the passage of the Full Employment Act of 1946, which created the Council of Economic Advisors and authorized the president to deliver the annual economic report to Congress. *The Economic Report of the President* recommends actions to achieve high levels of employment. In recent years, with the economy suffering from both unemployment and inflation, these recommendations require considerable economic artistry and sorting out of values.

MEETING THE COSTS OF GOVERNMENT

The subject of this section is taxes. And the problem it presents to the administrator and legislator, as the French finance minister J. B. Colbert once said, resembles the problem of plucking a goose: Getting the largest amount of feathers with the fewest squawks.

We begin by taking a quick look at the structure of revenues at the federal, state, and local levels of government. This survey is followed by a discussion of the pros and cons of each source of revenue. We conclude by attempting to answer the question, who bears the tax burden?

Tax Structures

Figure 10–2 provides a useful summary of not only the size of the revenues generated by the federal and state and local governments in the United

FIGURE 10–2
Total Revenue by Major Financial Sectors for the Federal Government and for State and Local Governments: 1973–1974

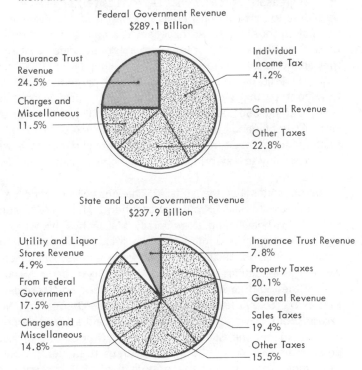

Federal Government Revenue
$289.1 Billion

Insurance Trust Revenue 24.5%

Charges and Miscellaneous 11.5%

Individual Income Tax 41.2%

General Revenue

Other Taxes 22.8%

State and Local Government Revenue
$237.9 Billion

Utility and Liquor Stores Revenue 4.9%

From Federal Government 17.5%

Charges and Miscellaneous 14.8%

Insurance Trust Revenue 7.8%

Property Taxes 20.1%

General Revenue

Sales Taxes 19.4%

Other Taxes 15.5%

Source: Bureau of the Census (1976).

States but also the distribution of sources at both levels. Before considering the individual merits of these sources, let us note three pragmatic concepts with which a financial manager in the public sector should be acquainted when developing a tax system: (1) tax equity, (2) tax efficiency, and (3) tax overlapping. (The following discussion of these three concepts draws on Slinger, Sharp, and Sandmeyer 1975.)

1. A fair tax would be, first, one that treated equally people in equal economic circumstances. A tax distribution that adheres to this principle provides for what is technically known as *horizontal equity*.

A fair tax should also treat unequals unequally; this principle is called *vertical equity* and is in turn founded on two related principles of taxation: The ability-to-pay principle and the benefit received principle. The former simply says that taxes should be distributed among taxpayers in relation to their financial capacities. For example, those with higher incomes should, the principle holds, pay a higher proportion of their income in taxes. If they do, then the tax is progressive. Some American conservatives have advocated, however, an income tax that takes the *same* proportion of taxes at each income level. For example, everyone pays 30 percent of their income in taxes, regardless of what the income might be; this kind of tax we call, for obvious reasons, *proportional*. A *regressive tax* means that ratio of tax payments to income *declines* as income rises: the more you earn, the less you pay proportionally. An excellent example of this type is a sales tax on food. Consider a family of four with an annual income of $5,000. Assuming they spend $2,000 on food and that the sales tax on it is 5 percent, they are paying a $100 per year tax on food, or 2 percent of their annual income. Now contrast this hypothetical family with a professional couple (no children) making $60,000 a year. They eat well, spending $4,000 a year. But what percentage of their income goes to taxes on food? Less than the Waltons, for sure. Of these three kinds of taxes, therefore, we generally say that the ability-to-pay principle is most closely associated with *progressive taxation.*

Which states tax the stiffest? The answer depends on one's income bracket. According to Professor Stephen E. Lile (1976), some states consistently tax heavily (e.g., New Jersey, Massachusetts, Wisconsin, Maryland) and others lightly (Florida, Louisiana, Mississippi, Nevada), but within both groups, some go easier on low-income families, while others spare the well-off. Connecticut, the second-stiffest taxer at the $5,000 level, ranked 27th at the top bracket. By contrast, New York was toughest at the top, but 21st at the $5,000 level. In only two states—Oregon and New York—were taxes "progressive": The $5,000 bracket paid a lower percentage of its income than did the $50,000 bracket. (In Oregon, 6.6 percent versus 10.6 percent; in New York, 11.6 percent versus 15 percent). Washington's taxes were most "regressive": the bottom paid 10.4 percent and the top, 3.5 percent.

The second underpining of the concept of tax equity is the benefit received principle. In a sense, the principle attempts to apply a free market approach to the distribution of taxes. Direct charges (e.g., user fees) for government goods force individuals to reveal their willingness to pay for these goods. While this principle faces many practical limitations at national level (how do you apply it to a social good such as national defense?), local governments are able to apply it to many services—parking, recreation, garbage collection, libraries, utilities, etc. Yet even at the local level there are limitations to the application of this principle. Many benefits, such as fire and police, accrue collectively and are difficult to measure. Or, sometimes the objectives of government are in direct opposition to the principle, public assistance being a case in point. Note Slinger, Sharp, and Sandmeyer (1975:44): "In spite of these limitations, in those cases where it is possible to measure individual benefits with reasonable accuracy and where the purpose of the government service is not to redistribute income, many economists hold that taxes should be selected in such a fashion that they can be defended by reference to the benefit received principle. Such procedure, it is held, is more likely to result in an equitable and efficient distribution of taxes."

2. Another useful concept in developing a tax system is *tax efficiency.* This concept involves basically two things, economic efficiency and administrative efficiency. The former concerns the effect the tax has on the public sector; that is, does it disturb the relative prices of private goods, the pattern of consumption and saving, and the pattern of leisure? Ideally, all these effects would be minimal. The latter concerns how easy the tax is to collect. In some cities, for example, it is necessary for city agents to raid those businesses that have been remiss in paying the selected sales tax. Nor should the costs of compliance by the taxpayer be overlooked. In this respect at least, a flat rate national income tax would appear superior to a progressive tax coupled with multitudinous loopholes and exemptions.

3. The concepts of *tax overlapping* and *tax coordination* are not difficult. In a federal system like that of the United States, two or more levels of government frequently use the same tax base. In New York City, for example, all three levels tax personal income. At the same time, in a highly mobile society like that of the United States, it is not uncommon for businesses and individuals to carry out economic activities that make them liable to taxes in many different taxing jurisdictions at the same level of government, e.g., in different cities.

While total elimination of these types of overlap is probably impossible, the administrator, if concerned with economic efficiency and taxpayer inequities, cannot ignore them. It is therefore necessary to try to *coordinate* taxing efforts at one level of government with those at the other two.

Fortunately, each level tends to rely mainly on one type of tax. Accordingly, we can properly characterize the federal fiscal system as one marked by *tax specialization.* According to Slinger, Sharp, and Sandmeyer (1975:55): "The federal government obtains 84.4 percent of its tax collections from individual and corporate income taxes; indeed, the federal government collects no less than 89.4 percent of the total income taxes collected by all levels of governments. State governments, on the other hand, obtain the largest portion of their tax revenue—56.9 percent—from general and selective sales taxes. Approximately 59 percent of all the general and selective sales taxes collected go to state governments. Finally, local governments still rely quite extensively upon the property tax—84.9 percent of local tax collections come from this source."

Source of Revenue

Knowledge of these three concepts—tax equity, tax efficiency, and tax overlapping—can help an administrator and legislator appreciate the advantages and disadvantages of selecting different sources of taxes. But they must also know the characteristics of each source. In an introductory text, however, we can hope to do no more than summarize them (see Table 10–1).

Taxes are not the only source of revenue. Actually, nontax revenue of cities in recent years increased in relative importance, reaching close to one half the general revenue of cities by the end of the 1960s. In general,

TABLE 10-1

Type	Pro	Con
1. Personal Income Tax	1. Ease of collection (withheld) 2. Progressive 3. Stable source of revenue	1. Unpopular with public 2. Difficult to collect if not withheld 3. Tends to be borne more by middle income groups due to law loopholes for higher income groups 4. Reduces monetary rewards of greater effort and risk taking
2. Corporate Income Tax	1. Ease of collection 2. Popular with general public 3. Progressive 4. Tends to redistribute wealth	1. Depress rate of return on invested capital 2. Is displaced to consumers of corporate products or services 3. Reduces capital available for reinvestment 4. Double taxation— shareholder's dividends are taxed after corporation is taxed
3. Property Tax	1. Very stable source of revenue 2. Revenue increases as value of property and improvements increases 3. Constantly expanding tax base	1. Difficult to collect delinquent amounts except by foreclosure 2. Are very regressive at low income level 3. Resources and needs are unequally distributed through society; e.g., some communities have high public needs but little taxable property 4. Difficult to assess property
4. Estate, Inheritance, and Gift Tax..............	1. Progressive 2. Burden not easily displaced	1. Difficult to collect 2. Unpopular with general public

TABLE 10–1 (*continued*)

Type	Pro	Con
	3. Tends to redistribute wealth and create equality of opportunity among new generation	3. Tends to reduce large family fortunes that might be used for capital investments 4. Double taxation from federal and state levels
5. Sales Tax	1. Ease of collection 2. Relatively stable source of revenue 3. Less visible — paid pennies at a time 4. Reaches nonresidents	1. Regressive 2. Difficult to enforce

municipal nontax revenue is composed of user charges and state and federal aid. Since the latter was discussed in Chapter 3, we limit our remarks below to user charges.

The use of the price system offers significant advantages in terms of both resource allocation and equity. As William Vickrey (in Mushkin 1972) notes, if prices are closely related to costs, there are "substantial possibilities for better utilization of resources, reduced levels of charges on the average, and improved service, all of which are inherent in pricing policies that are imaginatively concerned in terms of economic efficiency." A few examples should serve to make concrete Vickrey's remark.

Imposition of user charges can prevent excessive, wasteful use of electric power or water within an urban area.

Imposition of a price charge can ration facilities among users. A park or outdoor concert has a limited capacity; excessive demand, therefore, can bring demand into line with supply.

Imposition of fees and charges can help control activities that damage air and landscape or cause pollution or congestion. This is the rationale for what some think excessive taxes on downtown parking lots. User charges also have advantages in terms of equity. Due and Friedlaender (1973:100) put the case in a nutshell: "Except where special circumstances dictate otherwise, usual standards of equity dictate the persons pay for what they get."

Who Bears the Tax Burden?

Let us conclude this survey of taxes and other revenues with a particularly difficult question: Who ultimately pays a particular tax? The question is not as easily disposed of as might be imagined at first blush. Taxes placed on a producer or a retailer may be shifted forward, in the form of lower wages, rents, interests, and profits. Hence, one cannot assume that a person, who the law *says* a tax is levied on, will end up paying the tax.

A collateral problem concerns how progressive or regressive our *overall* tax and expenditure system actually is. Personal income tax is a function of the definition of income, allowable deductions, personal exemptions, and tax rates. Given the numerous exclusions and deductions, the income tax base in the United States is "eroded." Table 10–2 shows the practical effect of erosion.

TABLE 10–2
Who Bears the Tax Burden?

	Percentage of Income		
Family Income	Required to Be Paid by Tax Law	Paid in Actual Taxes after Using Loopholes	Saved by Loopholes
$2,000–3,000	1.9%	0.5%	1.4%
$5,000–6,000	7.5	2.8	4.7
$10,000–11,000	12.4	7.6	4.8
$20,000–25,000	20.8	12.1	8.7
$75,000–100,000	46.0	26.8	19.2
$200,000–500,000	58.0	29.6	28.4
$500,000–$1 million	60.5	30.4	30.1
Over $1 million	63.1	32.1	31.0

Source: Peckman and Okner (1974).

FIGURE 10–3
Total Tax Burden as Percentage of Income

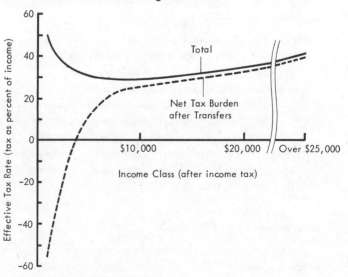

Source: Herriot and Miller (1971: 40).

In Figure 10–3, two additional variables are introduced, transfer payments and state and local taxes. Thus the top curve shows total tax burden, which roughly approximates the actual effective rate curve in Figure 10–2. The bottom curve in Figure 10–3, which shows taxes as a percentage of income, has been adjusted for transfer benefits. Note that there is little progression of total tax burden at middle-income levels.

HOW GOVERNMENT SPENDS

Expenditure Structure

Figure 10–4 summarizes not only the size of federal and state-wide expenditures in fiscal year 1976 but also the composition of expenditures at each level. The most important change no doubt is the rapid decline in the share of defense expenditures, notwithstanding the inclusions of large sums for the Vietnam War. Note that this decline in the relative importance of defense is almost exactly matched by the increasing share of budget allocated to transfer payments. In the 1960s, this use could be attributed to Great

FIGURE 10–4

Expenditure by Major Financial Sectors for the Federal Government and for State and Local Governments: 1973–1974

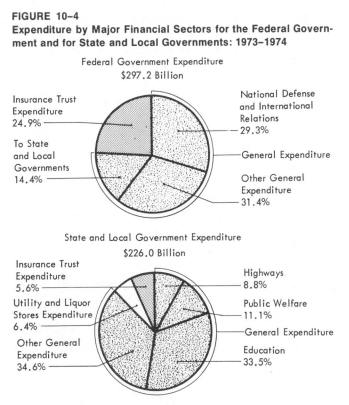

Federal Government Expenditure
$297.2 Billion

Insurance Trust Expenditure 24.9%

To State and Local Governments 14.4%

National Defense and International Relations — 29.3%

General Expenditure

Other General Expenditure — 31.4%

State and Local Government Expenditure
$226.0 Billion

Insurance Trust Expenditure 5.6%

Utility and Liquor Stores Expenditure 6.4%

Other General Expenditure 34.6%

Highways — 8.8%

Public Welfare — 11.1%

General Expenditure

Education — 33.5%

Source: Bureau of the Census (1976).

Society programs in education, manpower, social services, and health; in the 1970s, to income security and public assistance (Figure 10–1 shows these trends).

What can we say about the size and composition of state and local expenditures in recent years? Cities and states are spending more and more money with every passing year. The percentage of local government expenditures as a proportion of the gross national product crept up from 7.5 percent of the late 1950s to about 10 percent in the early 1970s. But, by the mid-1970s, these increases appear to be slowing or even disappearing. Payroll costs continue to be the most rapidly rising expenditure.

Tax Expenditures

These two words seem to resist conjoining, like magnets of similar pole. Yet, the term tax expenditure provides a concise way of drawing attention to the many tax subsidy provisions in the present federal income tax. Our discussion of expenditure structure would be incomplete without noting this increasingly popular approach to national problems. Let us begin with a few examples:

National defense: The supplements to salaries of military personnel, including provision of quarters and meals on military bases and quarters allowances for military families, and virtually all salary payments and reenlistment bonuses to military personnel serving in combat zones, are excluded from tax.

Agriculture: Farmers, including corporations engaged in agriculture, may deduct certain costs as current expenses even though these expenditures were for inventories on hand at the end of the year or capital improvements.

Natural resources, environment, and energy: State and local governments issue bonds, the interest income from which is exempt from federal tax, to finance pollution control facilities used by private firms. Certain capital costs necessary to bring a mineral deposit into production may be deducted as current expenses rather than spread over the useful life of the property.

Community and regional development: Taxpayers may, under certain conditions, select to compute depreciation on rehabilitation expenditures for low- and moderate-income rental housing over a five-year period.

Education, training, employment, and social services: Taxpayers may elect to amortize over a five-year period expenditures incurred in acquiring, constructing, reconstructing, or rehabilitating child care or on-the-job training facilities. Recipients of scholarships and fellowships may exclude such amounts from taxable income, subject to certain limitations. The exclusion of educational benefits under the GI bill is included in veterans benefits and services. Taxpayers may claim personal exemptions for dependent children 19 or over who receive income of $750 or more per year only if the children are full-time students.

Health: Payments by employers for health insurance premiums and other medical expenses are deducted as business expenses by employers and excluded from income by employees.

Income security: Most forms of government transfer payments to individuals, such as Social Security and unemployment benefits, are excluded from taxable income.

According to professor Stanely S. Surrey of Harvard Law School, these tax preferences really should be viewed as subsidy payments to preferred taxpayers. Such subsidies include efforts to assist particular industries, business activities, or financial transactions and to encourage nonbusiness activities considered socially useful, such as contributions to charity. For fiscal year 1971, Surrey found that these items totaled between $55 to $60 billion or, roughly, one fourth of the regular budget.

During hearings before the Joint Economic Committee, Surrey (1973:83) cut to the heart of the problem created by tax expenditures:

> It can generally be said that less critical analysis is paid to these tax subsidies than to almost any direct expenditure program one can mention. The tax subsidies tumble into the law without supporting studies, being propelled instead by clichés, debating points, and scraps of data and tables that are passed off as serious evidence. A tax system that is so vulnerable to this injection of extraneous, costly, and ill-considered expenditure programs is in a precarious state from the standpoint of the basic tax goals of providing adequate revenues and maintaining tax equity. It is therefore imperative that the process and substance of these tax subsidies be reexamined.

Encouragingly, the Congressional Budget and Impoundment Control Act of 1974, which we shall hear more of in the next chapter, requires that OMB submit an annual statement of tax expenditures so that they can be subjected to congressional and administrative review. Thus, for the first time, the president's budget presents a systematic listing of this serious drain on the treasury.

The remainder of this chapter explores one major analytical tool that public decision makers can use in reviewing not just tax expenditures but, indeed, any public expenditure.

EVALUATING EXPENDITURES: COST-BENEFIT ANALYSIS

Why Cost-Benefit Analysis?

During the early 1970s, requirements for improved data on the costs and benefits of environmental activities became a major concern of Congress. The following incident, which occurred while the House considered the

Federal Water Pollution Control Act Amendment of 1972, illustrates rather dramatically this new concern.

Sometime earlier the Senate had passed a similar bill that established a "zero discharge goal" for 1985, with interim goals for 1976 and 1981. The House bill, however, attempted a different approach: rather than set a goal of zero discharge of pollutants, it called for a goal of "best practicable technology available" of effluents by 1976. In the floor debate on the House bill, Representative Harsha (R-Ohio), ranking minority member of the House Public Works Committee, argued for a cost-benefit study before the 1981 and 1985 goals were implemented. Said Harsha (quoted in Blodgett 1972): "What would be the impact of such requirements on other environmental problems? Would we create air pollution problems? Are there deleterious effects of large-scale land disposal? Ask yourself: Do you know the economic costs? The other environmental impacts? I must admit I do not: the committee does not."

Mr. Harsha then quoted from the Senate debate where Senator Muskie was asked "whether some estimate of judgment has been made as to the cost of achieving zero discharge by 1985." Muskie replied, "There are no estimates of that kind that, in my judgment, have any validity." "Well," concluded Mr. Harsha, "I say to my colleagues that I would not want today to have to stand before you and state that we have recommended a no-discharge requirement without knowing the cost to this nation and its taxpayers of such legislation."

Interest in weighing cost against benefits has not abated. In fact, in November 1974, President Ford ordered a recalcitrant federal bureaucracy to start filing such assessments on all major government actions that drive up cost and prices. Now the federal government must do more than assess the benefits of goals such as a cleaner environment, safer products, healthier working conditions, and better mass transit—it must also weigh the cost and other side effects of such action.

The methodology for these kinds of assessments has been around at least since 1936. That was the year that cost-benefit analysis became a requirement with the Flood Control Act, which established the policy that "the federal government should improve or participate in the improvement of navigable water . . . for flood-control purposes if the benefits to whomsoever they may accue are in excess of the estimated costs. . . ."

Most cost-benefit analysis involves familiarity with certain common elements: the measurement of costs and benefits, the discount factor, and decision rules. The paragraphs below examine each of these elements.

Measurement of Costs and Benefits

The Federal Water Pollution Control Act Amendments of 1972, referred to above, provided that a National Academy of Sciences–National Academy of Engineering study would examine "all aspects of the total economic, social, and environmental effects of achieving or not achieving the effluent limitations and goals" set forth in the bill. To look at such a wide range of effects, the analyst must proceed systematically. In dealing with the various types of costs and benefits, Musgrave and Musgrave distinguish several major categories. (These are shown in Table 10–3 with examples.)

Let us begin with the distinction between real and pecuniary costs and benefits. *Real benefits* are the benefits derived by the final consumer of the public project and, as such, represent an addition to the community's total welfare; they must, however, be balanced against the *real costs* of resources withdrawn from other uses.

TABLE 10–3
Major Categories of Costs and Benefits for Irrigation Project

Category	Costs	Benefits
Real		
Direct		
Tangible............	Costs of pipes	Increased farm output
Intangible..........	Loss of wilderness	Beautification of area
Indirect		
Tangible............	Diversion of water	Reduced soil erosion
Intangible..........	Destruction of wildlife	Preservation of rural society
Pecuniary................		Relative improvement in position of farm equipment industry

Source: Musgrave and Musgrave (1973: 142).

Pecuniary benefits and costs, on the other hand, "come about due to changes in relative prices which occur as the economy adjusts itself to the provision of the public service. As a result, gains accrue to some individuals but are offset by losses which accrue to others. They do not reflect gains to society as a whole." (Musgrave and Musgrave 1973: 141) For example, say that earnings of roadside restaurants increase because of a highway project. Such gains do not reflect a net gain to society, since they are offset by costs to others; i.e., restaurants and grocery stores elsewhere. Consequently, in cost-benefit analysis, we can ignore these benefits.

Real benefits and costs can be either direct or indirect. Direct benefits and costs are those closely related to the main project objective. *Indirect benefits and costs* — sometimes called "externalities" or "spillovers" — are more in the nature of by-products. The line between direct and indirect costs and benefits is, however, sometimes fuzzy, requiring a judgment call by the analyst. Finally, the term *tangible* is applied to benefits and costs that we can measure in dollars; those we cannot — e.g., gain in world prestige from Moon shot projects — are referred to as *intangible*.

The following items illustrate some of the problems in and techniques for measuring costs and benefits.

Some argue that a military force staffed partly by conscripts would "meet our military requirements at a comparatively lower cost" than an all-volunteer force. While it is true that compulsory service can be used to lower budgetary costs of the military, not all costs are reflected in the budget. Consider a young man who would volunteer for the military at a wage of $10,000 per year or more. If he were conscripted and paid $6,000 per year, he would bear a $4,000 cost of defense that would not show up in the defense budget. Since World War II, conscription has thus disguised the true costs of defense. It was recognition of these hidden costs—as well as benefits inherent in an all-volunteer military (e.g., lower turnover rates, reduced training costs, more efficient use of manpower and better trained forces)—that prompted the Gates Commission to report in 1970 that "the cost of an all-volunteer armed force is unquestionably less than the cost of a force of equal size and quality manned wholly or partly through conscription."

A frequent undesirable side effect in government programs is red tape. For example, a new federal law designed to safeguard employee pension rights is causing small firms to terminate their plans because of paperwork requirements. Moreover, firms are required to retain an actual and certified public accountant. With reference to Table 10–3, how would you clarify these costs? Remember: The distinction between direct and indirect cost—or benefits—cannot be defined rigorously. Probably the most useful guide in these matters is to look to legislative intent.

Likewise, it is difficult to measure costs and benefits with rigor. In its second annual report in 1971, the Council on Environmental Quality found that dangers from air pollution were the least known and it reported an EPA estimate that the annual toll from air pollution, health, vegetation, materials, and property values was $16 billion. But the figures used in reading this estimate were called "crude approximations." And if these are crude approximations, what would you call estimates for, say, esthetic costs and human discomfort?

The study of pollution control costs reveals another important aspect of cost-benefit analysis: controlled costs can be documented as benefits. For example, assume that the annual nationwide bill for pollution is $481 per family and that an annual investment of $170 per family can reduce in pollution damages by $370 per family. Thus we can say that a direct benefit of the pollution control policy is $370 per family. What controlled costs could be documented as benefits for an urban transportation project that reduced automobile ridership?

Not all cost-benefit studies reveal benefits exceeding costs. A study prepared for the Office of Science and Technology on the benefits and costs of pollution control and safety devices added to autos in compliance with federal laws revealed that estimated costs of emission controls exceeded savings from the abatement of pollution caused by auto emissions. For the "conversion decade" of 1976–85, investment plus maintenance and operation costs were estimated at $95.1 billion, while benefits from reduced pollution were estimated at $18.3 to $46.3 billion, or a net excess of costs over benefits of $48.8 to $76.8 billion ($4.9 to $7.7 billion per year). After the conversion decade, the annual costs of emission control would run $10.1 billion per year and benefits from $3.5 to $9.1 billion, giving a net excess of costs over benefits of $1.0 to $6.6 billion per year.

Distributional Impacts of Public Programs

In addition to trying to measure costs and benefits, some thought should be given in cost-benefit analysis to the distribution of the costs and benefits resulting from a public program. (Bonnen 1969:425–26)

For benefits:

1. What is the purpose or objective of the public program or legislation, part of which is the question, Who should benefit?

2. Who actually benefits? What groups? It is sometimes not easy to identify beneficiary groups clearly.

3. How much are the total benefits of the program? Placing a value on the benefits of many programs is also not an easy analytical proposition.

4. What is the distribution of program benefits among beneficiaries?

5. What is the current distribution of incomes and assets or other relevant dimensions of welfare among (a) actual beneficiaries and (b) intended or potential beneficiaries?

For cost:

6. Who should pay the program costs?

Sometimes the nature of the program contains strong implications as to whom the burden should be given; at other times this is almost an unanswerable question.

7. Who actually does pay the cost of the program? Identification of the burdened groups should consider not only the tax structure, but direct price and income effects and the indirect effects of major factor and product substitution caused by the program.

8. What are the total program costs? Many times this includes, as it does in Question 7, economic and social costs not reflected in federal budget expenditures but market and non-market costs generated through the operation of the program itself. Thus, these are not simple questions.

9. How are program costs distributed among the burdened groups?

10. What is the current distribution of incomes and assets among (a) the actual burdened groups and (b) the intended or potential burdened groups.

Discount Factor

Most public projects and programs take place over time. How the analysis treats this time element is the subject of this subsection.

For sake of simplicity, let us think of time divided into years and of future benefits and costs accruing in specific years. Table 10–4 shows, in column B, the dollar benefits over an interval of eight years: Since two years are required for construction, no benefits accrue until the third year. Column C

TABLE 10-4
Hypothetical Cost-Benefit Study
(dollars in millions)

Year (A)	Benefits* (B)	Costs* (C)	Net Benefits (D)	Discount Factor ($i = 5\%$) (E)	Present Value of Net Benefits (F)
1..............	$ 0	$ 4	−4	.9524	$−3.8
2..............	0	4	−4	.9070	−3.6
3..............	1	1	0	.8638	0.0
4..............	2	1	1	.8227	0.8
5..............	3	1	2	.7835	1.6
6..............	4	1	3	.7460	2.2
7..............	4	1	3	.7107	2.1
8..............	4	1	3	.6768	2.0
Total........	$18	$14	4		$ 1.3

*Generally, in cost-benefit computations, only the *direct* costs and benefits are used. The overall study should, however, include a discussion of indirect costs and benefits.

shows the costs, which are initially higher but then level off. Column D simply shows the net benefits (benefits minus costs) for each year.

But is the one million dollar net benefit occurring in the fourth year really worth one million dollars in present dollars? No, these future proceeds must be adjusted to allow for the fact that future benefits are less valuable than present ones. The reason is that today's one million could be invested and certainly return more than one million to the investor four years later. Cost must be adjusted in a like manner. We call making these adjustments — that is, reducing future dollars to be comparable to today's dollars — *discounting.*

To find the value of a dollar in any future year, one need only multiply by a discount factor. The formula is

$$\text{Discount factor} = \frac{1}{(1 + i)^t}$$

where i is the interest rate and t is number of years. Equipped with this formula (or, more likely, a table of discount factors for different rates and years), we return to the question posed a moment ago: How much is $1,000,000 four years from today worth today? Assuming a modest interest rate of 5 percent, we first calculate the discount factors and then multiply the $1,000,000 benefit by it. Thus,

$$\text{Present value} = \frac{1}{(1 + .05)^4} \times \$1,000,000 = 0.8227 \times \$1,000,000 = \$822,700$$

Column E, Table 10-4, gives the discount factors for the first eight years of the project. Now we can adjust the net benefits in column D to reflect their present values and show them in column F. If we sum column F, we shall see that by the eighth year the project's benefits outweigh its costs.

Parenthetically, I cannot help but wonder how many college football players who sign $100,000 professional contracts *to be paid over a five year period* understand discounting. What is the present value of their income for the fifth year?

Decision Rules

It does not necessarily follow that we should go ahead with our hypothetical project. What we do depends on our decision rule.

First, we might be faced with a simple project that involves a yes-no decision; that is, the decision is between doing the project and not doing the project. The criterion we wish to use is the net *benefit criterion.* Define net benefit (*NB*) as

$$NB = B - C$$

and use the following decision rule: A simple project should be done if and only if its net benefits exceed zero. Thus, in our example, the net benefit is $400,000, so the project should be undertaken. While this approach might seem obvious, it is an important one since it is frequently used by the Corps of Engineers in evaluating whether to approve funds, say for widening a ship channel.

This decision rule is similar to *break-even analysis,* a well known management concept that has been used for many purposes. Essentially, the break-even model is a comparison over time of the costs of inputs to the benefits from outputs. Figure 10–5 shows a break-even analysis for a hypothetical project. As soon as the Area A (total net costs) equals Area B (total net benefits), the break-even point has been reached.

Second, we might be faced with a choice between two mutually exclusive projects. For example, we might have the choice of building four different types of bridges, but we can fund only one. If so, then the general rule is: When choosing one project from a set of mutually exclusive projects, choose the one with the greatest net benefit.

Another criterion, which turns out to be the equivalent of the net benefit criterion mentioned earlier, is the benefit-cost ratio (BCR) criterion. It is defined as

$$BCR = B/C$$

Is the benefit-cost ratio of any use in choosing among mutually exclusive projects? Unfortunately, the answer is no. In the case of the four bridges, one could be a rather modest footbridge, suitable only for light traffic. Because only a small investment is required, the benefit-cost ratio is likely to be relatively high. But in comparison to a bridge designed for trains and trucks, the net benefits might appear meager indeed.

Third, we might be faced with a case involving nonefficiency objective. For instance, the distributional consequences of the projects in terms of regional economic development and unemployment might be of central

FIGURE 10–5
Hypothetical Break-Even Analysis

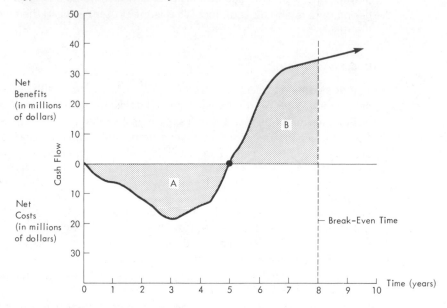

concern; in such cases, pecuniary changes become relevant. Thus, larger contractors, such as the Defense Department and NASA must be concerned not only with the costs and benefits of a project but also with which state gets the contract, what size business gets the subcontracts, and what kinds of jobs (i.e., skill levels) are involved.

Fourth, we might have to select the *level* at which several projects are to be operated under a budget constraint. In such cases our rule is to push expenditures for each project to that point where the benefit of the last dollar spent is equal to the last dollar spent on any similar project. As the economists put it, the *marginal* net benefits should be equal. In other words, as government continues to invest in a program (e.g., disease control), total benefits (e.g., lives saved) increase. After a certain point, however, with each successive new dollar, total benefits will grow at a slower and slower rate.

Robert N. Grosse (1969:1197–1223) provides us with a clear example of how the marginal net benefit criterion might be used to determine the preferred mix of disease control programs. Assume that we can determine as in the following table the number of lives saved by different expenditures on disease A and disease B:

	Expenditures	Lives Saved (cumulative)
Disease A	$ 500,000	360
	1,000,000	465
Disease B	$ 500,000	200
	1,000,000	270

Writes Robert N. Grosse: "If we only knew the effect of spending $1 million, we might opt for a program where all our money was spent on controlling disease B. Similarly, if we only knew the effects of programs of half million dollars, we would probably prefer A, as we'd save 360 rather than only 200 lives. But if we knew the results for expenditures of both half a million and $1 million dollars in each program, we would quickly see that spending half our money in each program was better than putting it all in one assuming we have $1 million available. Our calculations would be:

Expenditures	Lives Saved
$1,000,000 on A	465
$1,000,000 on B	270
$1,000,000 { $500,000 on A............ 360 } .... { $500,000 on B............ 200 }	560

Opportunity Cost: A Digression and Preview

Related to the above discussion of cost-benefit analysis is an even broader notion about cost. Unlike the man in the street, the administrator looks beyond the actual cash payments in evaluating the costs of public programs and projects. He realizes that some of the most important costs attributable to doing one thing rather than another stem from the foregone opportunities that have to be sacrificed in doing the one thing.

What is the opportunity cost of taking a course in public administration? In addition to registration fee, one must consider the implicit cost of the highest foregone alternative to the individual. This alternative might be income from a job, or it might be other available opportunities: playing tennis, taking another course, swimming, etc. This alternative cost economists term opportunity cost. Since public administrators must operate in a world of continual and eternal scarcity, it is a useful concept — indeed, it pervades the entire next chapter.

NAILING DOWN THE MAIN POINTS

1 Public finance concerns the package of problems and issues that involve the use of tax, borrowing, and expenditure measures for public purpose.

2 The three functions of federal fiscal policy are allocation, distribution, and stabilization. The first function essentially refers to the federal government's efforts to overcome the inherent bias of a market type economic system to ignore public goals in favor of private goods. The second function refers to the government's efforts to provide adequate income to the very young, the very old, the sick, the disabled, and other disadvantaged. While several techniques of income distribution are avail-

able, Musgrave and Musgrave maintain that tax-transfer schemes are the preferable devices. Since 1970 these payments have grown quite rapidly. The third function, stabilization, contains three components: price stability, full employment, and economic growth.

3   Three important concepts that a financial manager ought to keep in mind when developing a tax structure are tax equity, tax efficiency, and tax overlapping. A fair or equitable tax would: (a) treat equally people in equal economic circumstances and (b) treat unequally people in unequal economic circumstances. Tax equity further implies that, when feasible, people will be charged according to benefit received.

   Tax efficiency means that the tax will neither disturb the public sector too much nor prove difficult to collect. Lastly, tax overlapping refers to the coordination of taxing effort by various levels of government.

4   Among the leading sources of revenue for governments are personal income tax; corporate income tax; property tax; estate, inheritance, and gift tax; and sales tax.

5   Personal income tax, the leading source of federal revenue, is a function of the definition of income, allowable deductions, exemptions, and tax rates. Given the numerous exclusions and deductions, the income tax in the U.S. is "eroded" at upper levels. In a sense, these exclusions and deductions are examples of a larger phenomenon: tax expenditures. Stanely S. Surrey thinks these tax preferences really should be viewed as subsidy *payments* to preferred tax payers.

6   In recent years, as the costs of government became a greater concern to the taxpayer as well as to political leadership, cost-benefit analysis grew in popularity. Now, virtually all costly governmental programs are subjected to some type of cost-benefit analysis.

   This analysis does basically three things. First, it attempts to measure *all* the costs and benefits from a program. Second, since most programs or projects take place over extended periods of time, the flow of future cost and benefits must be converted into their present values. We call making these adjustments discounting. Finally, we must decide by one of several decision rules whether the benefits justify the cost.

CONCEPTS FOR REVIEW

public finance

fiscal policy, monetary policy

three functions of federal fiscal policy

economic system

private and public goods

transfer payments

price instability or inflation

economic growth

deficit spending

tax equity

tax efficiency

tax overlapping, tax coordination

horizontal and vertical equity

progressive and regressive taxation

tax specialization

sources of revenue

tax expenditure

cost-benefit analysis

direct and indirect costs and benefits, spillovers, and externalities

real and pecuniary costs and benefits, tangible and intangible costs and benefits

discounting

decision rules for cost-benefit analysis

break-even analysis

opportunity cost

PROBLEMS

1. What are the shortcomings in using "lives saved" as a measure of benefit?

2. Use the concept of opportunity cost to explain why lawyers and housewives are more likely than medical doctors to get involved in politics.

3. Given the following data, how would you spend $1 million? What idea is expressed in this exercise?

Disease A		Disease B	
Expenditures	Lives Saved	Expenditures	Lives Saved
$ 100,000	100	$ 100,000	50
$ 200,000	180	$ 200,000	50
$ 300,000	250	$ 300,000	135
$ 400,000	310	$ 400,000	170
$ 500,000	360	$ 500,000	200
$ 600,000	400	$ 600,000	225
$ 700,000	430	$ 700,000	240
$ 800,000	450	$ 800,000	255
$ 900,000	460	$ 900,000	265
$1,000,000	465	$1,000,000	270

4. One of the most vexing problems in the distribution of benefits is that similar benefits do not necessarily have similar values to the recipients. Some scholars have, therefore, suggested that the total value of a project be the *weighted sum* of its incomes. In the Table below, seven alternative weighting functions are presented along with the values placed on additions to incomes to persons at various income levels. Which function comes closest to reflecting your own views to the weights society should place on increments to income generated by public expenditure? For example, if you think that benefits to poor ($1,000 per year) persons is at least 30 times more valuable than income to middle class ($10,000 per year) persons, then (a) may come closest to reflecting your value judgment. (Freeman 1969:576)

Form of Social Welfare Function: Marginal Social Welfare =	Value Placed on One Extra Dollar of Income to a Person With Income of			
	$I = \$1{,}000$	$I = \$10{,}000$	$I = \$100{,}000$	$I = \$1{,}000{,}000$
a. $I^{-1.5}$	$31.62	$1	$0.03	$0.001
b. $I^{-1.0}$	10.00	1	0.10	0.01
c. $I^{-0.5}$	3.16	1	0.32	0.10
d. I^0	1.00	1	1.00	1.00
e. $e^{-\left(\frac{I}{10{,}000}\right)}$	2.46	1	0.0001	Nil
f. $\left(\dfrac{I}{5{,}000}+1\right)^{-1}$	2.50	1	0.14	0.01
g. $\left(\dfrac{I}{5{,}000}+1\right)^{-2}$	6.25	1	0.02	0.0002

5. Milton Friedman (1969), Nobel prize-winning conservative economist at the University of Chicago, offers eight broad guidelines for governmental activities:

   a. The basic function of government is to make and enforce general rules governing individual behavior. Changes in such rules are frequently the most effective way to resolve problems without further government intervention.

   b. When in doubt whether to go farther, stay out and let private actions prevail.

   c. If government does go farther, the least harmful measure is generally to finance specified activities, openly and directly, without administering them, directly or indirectly.

   d. When government does finance, it is best to finance intended beneficiaries, not producers.

   e. If government not only finances but also administers an activity, it should always permit competition in order to have a private yardstick.

   f. Also, it should buy the resources it uses on the market and not commandeer them.

   g. Whenever government produces a product or service, it should if possible charge the user his pro rata cost, i.e., not give the item away.

   h. Only as a last resort should government finance, administer, and deliver free of charge.

   How many of these guidelines do you agree with? How might they be applied to activities such as education, post office, welfare, oil, and rent control?

6. Explain this statement: "The American political process probably leads to provision of public goods in excess of the optimum because of its logrolling nature."

7. Are defense and domestic spending really transferable? In other words, do you see any fallacy in comparing a new navy destroyer to so many new hospitals or new schools? What other factors might make a dollar-for-dollar comparison difficult?

8. Plot the data in Table 10–4 on a graph similar to Figure 10–5.

9. "The full impact of major new technological development efforts may not be known for a decade: most predictions and forecasts as to the more enduring effects of new technology tend to be wrong. This raises serious questions about some of the underlying assumptions of [cost benefit analysis] at very early planning stages, particularly when the uncertainties resulting from multiple purposes and shifting emphases are considered. Further debate and acrimony are maxi-

mized when one seeks a clear definition of ends; these are the most controversial, the most shifting of sands." (Sayles and Chandler 1971:20–21) Discuss.

10. One of the most critical issues in public finance is how to distribute the goods of our system more equally without undermining the efficiency of the system. The problem, essentially, is to continue efficiency with greater equality — even at some cost to efficiency. To crystalize the issue, Arthur M. Okun (1975), who was chairman of the Council of Economic Advisors under President Lyndon B. Johnson, invites us to participate in what he calls "the leaky-bucket experiment." Suppose that you could transfer $4,000 from each of the 5 percent of families at the top of the income distribution to the 20 percent of families at the bottom. Each family at the bottom would then get $1,000. But there's a hitch — the bucket in which you transfer this income leaks. Some of the money carried from the rich to the poor will leak out of the bucket and never reach the poor — as a result of a loss of efficiency. Some, like John Rawls (see Chapter 4), would give a clear, crisp answer: make the switch to increase equality, unless an unequal distribution of income would definitely be to everyone's advantage. Equality should have priority. But others, like Milton Friedman, give an equally clear, crisp, and opposite answer: efficiency should have priority. What if 10 percent — $100 — leaked out so that each poor family got only $900? Would you still make the switch? What if $500 leaked out? What if $999?

INTRODUCTION

Budgeting is a common practice to the extent that everybody—households, corporations, clubs, agencies, etc.—must anticipate income and expenses. Historically, the word "budget" referred to a leather bag in which England's Chancellor of the Exchequer carried the statement of the government's needs and resources to Parliament. In time, however, the budget came to refer to the papers within the bag rather than to the bag itself.

Today, budgets are not carried in bags but are bound in volumes that, for at least the major units of government, contain an extensive array of data in standardized formats. The massiveness and the formatting of major budgets are generally so intimidating that one wonders if those responsible have purposefully made budget-reading unappetizing. In any case, the public administrator must be able to understand the development and functioning of budgets if he or she is to perform effectively.

The last chapter began by looking at the three functions of fiscal policy. We start here in much the same way—by looking at three functions of the budget. We shall further note how each of these functions can be loosely associated with certain historical periods.

The core of the chapter, however, is the second and third sections. The former will take us through the four phases of the federal budget cycle; the latter, through the nine steps of a typical budget cycle for a local government. Many of the ideas introduced in this chapter will be crystalized in the case study of New York City's financial problems found at the end of the chapter. The case study also contains certain new ideas essential to effective financial management.

11

The Budgetary Process

THE CHANGING ROLE OF THE BUDGET

The generally accepted purposes of budgeting are, according to Allen Shick (1966), control, management, and planning. Control he identifies as legislative concern for tight control over executive expenditures. The most prevalent means of exerting this type of expenditure control has been to appropriate by object of expenditure; financial audits then are used to insure that money has in fact been spent for the items authorized for purchase. This focuses information for budgetary decision making upon the things government buys, such as personnel, travel, and supplies, rather than upon the accomplishments of governmental activities. In other words, responsibility is achieved by controlling the input side.

The management orientation emphasizes the efficiency with which ongoing activities were conducted. Historically, this orientation is associated with the New Deal through the First Hoover Commission (1949). Emphasis was placed upon holding administrators accountable for the efficiency of their activities through such methods as work performance measurement.

Finally, planning is reflected in the budget message for fiscal 1968: "A federal budget lays out a two part plan of action: It proposes particular programs, military and civilian, designed to promote national security, international cooperation, and domestic progress. It proposes total expenditures and revenues designed to help maintain stable economic prosperity and growth." Here we see an obvious emphasis on programs and the relationship between revenues and expenditures in order to accomplish objectives.

The overall development just outlined should, however, be viewed not in terms of three separate phases but in terms of accretion. Thus, the function of the budget today is really a combination of all three purposes. Table 11–1 emphasizes this aspect of the budget's development.

Line-Item Budgeting

The first image that generally comes to mind with the utterance of the word "budget" is a list of items and their associated costs. Indeed, a *line-*

TABLE 11–1
The Budget's Changing Role

Function		Budget Type	Time Period
Control	1.	Listing of revenues and expenditures	1700s to early 1900s
Control and Management	2.	Line item budget	1915–35
	3.	Performance budget	1935–60
Control, Management, and Planning	4.	Program-planning budget	1960–70
	5.	Zero-base budget	1970–present

Source: Suggested to the author by Norman Weed.

item budget used for projection and control of expenses remains at the heart of the budgeting process. The line-item budget is designed to keep spending within the limits set by the legislative body. Cost categories are established for recording of all expenditures and back-up bookkeeping systems contain sufficient detail to insure that all disbursements (i.e., expenditures) are made in accordance with law. The makers and keepers of line-item budgets rely on accounting skills — the ability to keep track of revenues and expenses in a systematic way. They focus on answering the question, "How was the money spent?" While tabulations of line-item costs are still fundamental to any budgeting process, the concept of budgeting has generally been extended beyond the strict definition of expenditure control.

Performance Budgeting

Oscar Wilde once defined a cynic as "a man who knows the price of everything and the value of nothing." Perhaps, then, President Franklin Roosevelt was trying to battle cynicism in government when his second administration introduced the concept of performance budgeting. In 1939, the Bureau of the Budget was transferred from the Treasury Department to the newly formed Executive Office of the President with the directive to "keep the president informed of the progress of activities by agencies of the government with respect to work proposed, work actually initiated, and work completed, together with the relative timing of work between the several agencies of the government; all to the end that the work programs of the several agencies of the executive branch of government may be coordinated and that the monies appropriated by the Congress may be expended in the most economical manner possible to prevent overlapping and duplication of effort."

Thus began the search at the federal level for an answer to the question that, almost 40 years later, still haunts government at all levels: Is the public getting its money's worth? As the end result of line-item budgeting, government should be able to tell the public that an agency spent, say $19,872,-403.91, with so much going to salaries and wages and fringe benefits, so much spent on various materials and supplies, and so much paid out under each of numerous contracts. As a result of performance budgeting, on the other hand, government should be able to tell the public how much public services was delivered for this $19,872,403.91. If the agency is a city sanitation department, performance measures could be given to show how many tons of trash were collected; the cost per ton and the cost per pick-up; and comparative unit costs to indicate efficiency of the department against previous years, comparable departments in other cities, and comparable services provided by private sanitation companies.

As can be surmised, the development of valid performance measures for public agencies ranges from the difficult to the impossible. Unique problems are encountered in each field of public endeavor (national defense, education, health, transportation, public safety, etc.) at each level of government.

Currently, most government budgets include an aspect of performance budgeting, often in the form of a narrative describing the accomplishments and work in progress of the agency or department. But objective, quantitative evaluations of governmental units — evaluations that attempt to answer the question, "Is the public getting its money's worth?" — are rarely done either within the budgetary process or outside of it.

In the preceding paragraphs, I have gently tried to point out a few of the limitations that an administrator must face when using the budget as a management tool. Drucker (1975:141–47), however, is not so gentle: he attacks the management orientation of budgets with a vengeance. Since ferocity of attack is no grounds for dismissal, the thoughtful administrator might give Drucker a hearing.

The basic difference between business and government concerns the way they are paid. The former are paid for satisfying customers, the latter, out of a budget allocation. "Being paid out of a budget allocation changes what is meant by performance. Results . . . mean a larger budget. Performance is the ability to maintain or increase one's budget. Results . . . that is . . . achievement toward goals and objectives, are, in effect, secondary."

Here efficiency becomes sin. "The importance of a budget-based institution is measured essentially by the size of its budget and the size of its staff. To achieve results with a smaller budget or a smaller staff is, therefore, not performance."

Counterstrategies, however, are available. To change for a moment the setting — but not the principle — let us consider how a university president might conduct his annual planning session. Due to a mandate from the governor, he announces that the total budget for all units under his direction will be reduced by 10 percent from the previous year's level. (Congress or OMB could seek a similar across the board reduction.)

Further, the university president provides the following ground rules to his vice presidents: emphasis is to be placed on increased productivity; standards of quality are to be maintained; budgetary allocations, both in total and by individual units are fixed; and final budgets are due on September 1.

Each of the vice presidents submits his budget when the deadline falls. Not surprisingly, it reflects exactly what the president had called for; he is ebullient in commending his staff for their planning expertise.

Is anything wrong in this approach? Certainly, on the surface at least, the president's desire to cut old programs is not wrong. But what is questionable is his approach. First, this approach precludes real participation by the managers; he deliberately refuses to establish any competition among his managers for the available capital. In contrast, the Department of Defense has five committee members on a resource allocation committee who each heads units competing for the same resources.

Second, inefficient as well as the efficient are rewarded (or penalized) with equal severity.

Third, the president puts the budget at the wrong end of the planning process: he should consider first his priorities and then make cost allowances.

The lesson then is simply this. Top administrators, as well as congressmen, can cut programs, but they need, as far as possible, to establish competition *within* the organizational units for the resources.

Planning-Programming-Budgeting

Without ever having really mastered performance budgeting, the federal government proceeded to develop an even broader view of budgeting in the early 1960s. Robert McNamara, as Secretary of Defense in the Kennedy administration, introduced the Planning-Programming-Budgeting System (PPBS) into the Defense Department. Where line-item budgeting is limited to funding *accountability* and performance budgeting extended only to the realm of funding *efficiency,* PPBS attempts to stretch budgeting into issues of funding *allocation* among various competing agencies and programs. It was not as if funding allocation had never before taken place—legislative bodies had historically performed this function based on inputs from constituents and from affected agencies. What the proponents of PPBS hoped to accomplish was the injection of greater rationality into the process, by first planning *goals* and *objectives,* then developing *programs* to achieve these goals, and finally budgeting for projects within each program.

After a reasonably successful debut in the Department of Defense (see Hitch and McKean, 1960, for the "more bang for the buck" story), PPBS helped to tone down inter-service competition for weapons systems by analyzing expenditures under such categories as "strategic forces" rather than army/navy/air force.

President Johnson then began, in 1965, requiring other federal agencies to implement PPBS. But nondefense agencies found their domains to be far less quantifiable, so that goals and objectives did not easily translate into programs, then projects. Meanwhile, some state governments switched to PPBS but did not find the system workable. Many state and local governments, after review of PPBS, decided to keep what they had. While much of the terminology of PPBS remains at the federal level, the PPBS process, like Hamlet's opinion of drinking, is more honored in the breach than the observance.

Zero-based Budgeting

A recent variation of PPBS is zero-based budgeting. Here the basic objectives of a program are examined by taking an if-we-are-to-start-all-over-again look; that is to say, each program is challenged for its very existence each budget cycle. In 1962, at the same time the Defense Department was developing and refining PPBS, the U.S. Department of Agriculture engaged in a zero-based budget experiment. More recently, Georgia (under Jimmy Carter) and New Mexico have attempted to use it.

Zero-based budgeting involves three basic steps. First, all current and proposed programs must be described and analyzed in documents called decision packages. These documents are designed to help top management evaluate the programs in terms of purpose, consequences, measures of performance, alternatives, and costs and benefits. Next, the program packages are ranked through cost-benefit analysis. Finally, resources are allocated in accordance with this ranking.

Advocates of zero-based budgeting cite these advantages:

It allows managers throughout the entire organization to participate in the formulation and determination of the budget, since managers at all levels are responsible for either creating or evaluating the decision packages (see Pyhrr 1971).

It identifies duplication.

It assists managers, directors, legislators, and governors in identifying the costs and benefits associated with each decision package.

It facilitates adaptation to changes in expenditure levels that may occur in the budget cycle, since the list of ranked decision packages can be used by managers to identify those activities that ought to be expanded or curtailed. (Boss 1976)

It provides administrators a management tool with which they can evaluate the performance of their employees.

It insures continued evaluation of programs.

It actually strengthens control of expenditures by the use of the traditional line-item method as well as program and performance methods. (Pyhrr 1971)

Critics, however, point to these weaknesses:

It pays little attention to political realities or the administrator's biases within which the budget system must operate.

It is time consuming.

It buries the decision maker in information.

It presents massive methodological problems. (How do we identify cost and benefits? the objectives of a program? the degree to which these objectives are attained?)

Perhaps then it is asking too much of the budgeting process to attempt to answer (as PPBS and zero-based budgeting do) the question, "Why is a government program needed?" But beyond this issue of feasibility, critics see yet another: Should budgeters be devising an ersatz decision-making process of their own or should they really be implementing the decision of the political leadership? To fully answer this question, requires, first, some familiarity with the phases of the budgetary cycle, and, second, an appreciation of the attendant politics. The next two sections, which deal respectively with the federal and local budgetary cycles, attempt to provide both.

THE FEDERAL BUDGET CYCLE

The connection between governmental programs, the focus of Part II, and the budget, the subject at hand, is fast. One might even be so bold as to suggest the priority of the latter. That is, strictly speaking a program is really no more than a statement of purpose, a piece of paper, a mere shadow. Not until it appears in the budget does it take on life, begin to matter. In this sense, the budget animates a program.

And more. Because the budget must reveal how funds are allocated among many and varied programs, it provides us with probably the most clear cut way of determining the president's or Congress's priorities. Thus, presidential budget briefings seldom solicit from reporters questions about large economic issues. Rather, the questions reflect deep concerns over who gets what and the rightness of the president's choice of priorities. And perhaps the most important of these concerns centers on the issue of defense spending versus individual benefits (see Figure 10–1).

Remember the concept of opportunity cost first introduced in Chapter 2 and later in Chapter 10? This concept can help us see more clearly what we mean by choice of priorities. Opportunity cost represents the implicit cost of the highest foregone alternative to an individual or group; in short, it is the true cost of choosing one alternative over another. The president each year is confronted with a multiplicity of such choices; he soon learns that spending in one area is viewed by certain groups as money not spent in their area of special interests. Part of the opposition to the war in Vietnam, it is safe to say, can be explained as much in terms of opportunity cost (viz., reduced spending for urban programs) as in terms of morality. Today, space programs come in for similar criticism — not only by groups of urban activists but also groups of certain scientists. A case in point is the American Miscellaneous Society, a group, which despite its whimsical title, is composed of quite serious oceanographers and other less space-oriented scientists. Their slogan: "The ocean's bottom is at least as important as the moon's behind."

Keeping these ideas in mind, we now turn to what the Office of Management and Budget (1976) calls the four identifiable phases of the budget process: (1) executive formulation and transmittal; (2) congressional authorization and appropriation; (3) budget execution and control; and (4) review and audit. But two things need to be kept in mind in studying the budget process. First, each phase of the process interrelates and overlaps with the other; and second, the issues of priorities and opportunity cost are at the very heart of the process.

Executive Formulation and Transmittal

As stressed above, the budget sets for the president's financial plan of operations and thus indicates national priorities for the coming year. The president's transmittal of his budget proposals to the Congress early in January climaxes many months of planning and analysis throughout the executive branch. Formulation of the budget for fiscal year 1977, for example, began in the spring of 1975.

This is the way it works. In the spring, agency programs are evaluated, policy issues are identified, and budgetary projections are made, giving attention both to important modifications and innovations in programs and to alternative long-range program plans. In early June, preliminary plans are presented to the president for his consideration. At about the same time, the president receives projections of estimated receipts, prepared by the Treasury Department, and projections of the economic outlook, prepared jointly by the Council of Economic Advisors, the Office of Management and Budget, and the Treasury Department.

Following a review of both sets of projections—that is, of expenditures and receipts—the president establishes general budget and fiscal policy guidelines for the fiscal year that will begin about 15 months later. Tentative policy determinations and planning *ceilings* are then given to the agencies as guidelines for the preparation of their final budget requests during the summer.

Agency budget requests are reviewed *in detail* by the Office of Management and Budget throughout the fall and are presented, along with OMB recommendations, to the president for decision. Overall fiscal policy issues—relating to total budget receipts and outlays—are again examined. The actual budget data from the most recently completed fiscal year provide an essential reference base in this review and decision process. Thus, the budget process involves the consideration simultaneously of the resource needs of individual programs and the total outlays and receipts that are appropriate in relation to the outlook for the national economy. In sum, the federal budget, like any well managed household budget, reflects the results of both income and expense considerations.

The president hardly has a free hand in allocating resources. In fact, OMB classified about 75 percent of the 1976 budget as "uncontrollable"; that is, as impossible to cut through appropriation bills. Thus, the only way this part of the budget could be reduced is if Congress passed other kinds of legislation cutting these programs. Table 11–2 shows the kinds of budgetary items that fall into this category. Note also the steep rise since 1967 in the percentage of the budget that is uncontrollable.

For purposes of analysis, we can put the various uncontrollable items on a continuum, running from those most beyond the reach of congressional action to those easiest to control (see Havemann 1975). Legal commitments made by the government in previous years—such as interest on the national debt—are naturally uncontrollable. Next, along the continuum might come payments to meet contracts for weapons systems, spacecraft, highways, and sewers. In sharp contrast to these contracts are programs that guarantee individuals that they will receive benefits if they meet certain qualifications (e.g., old age and poverty). To reduce the costs of these programs, Congress need only change the laws authorizing them—which is hardly a way to win votes.

Yet, it is clear that these artificially uncontrollable programs require fundamental change. For example, in 1972 the formulas used to compute Social Security benefits were modified in an attempt to make incomes keep pace automatically with the cost of living. Now benefit payments for those working are rising faster than wages; after the turn of the century, a beneficiary's pensions could exceed his other preretirement wages. Moreover, the system's financing problems will then be intensified by the increasing proportion of aged in the population. Not surprisingly, growth in uncontrollable spending, such as that seen in this example, has led to some dire warnings. As James T. Lynn (quoted in Havemann 1975: 1620), President Ford's Director of OMB, told the House Appropriations Committee: "Were the growth of domestic assistance programs to continue for the next two decades at the same rates as in the past 20 years, total government spending (federal, state, and local) would grow to more than half our national output."

Can anything be done? Murray L. Weidenbaum (1969: 357–68) recom-

TABLE 11–2
"Uncontrollables" in the Federal Budget
(all figures in billions of dollars)

	1967	1975	1976
Payments for individuals			
Social Security and railroad retirement.....................	$ 22.5	$ 66.6	$ 76.6
Federal workers' retirement and insurance	3.8	13.5	15.7
Unemployment assistance......................................	2.8	15.2	18.6
Veteran benefits..	5.0	11.9	11.9
Medicare and medicaid...	4.6	20.9	24.1
Housing payments...	0.3	2.1	2.6
Public assistance	2.9	14.2	15.6
(Subtotal, payments for individuals)	(41.8)	(144.4)	(165.1)
Spending from prior-year contracts			
National defense	21.2	22.3	23.5
Civilian programs..	15.8	26.8	30.5
(Subtotal, spending from contracts)	(37.0)	(49.1)	(54.0)
Interest payments..	10.3	23.6	26.1
General revenue sharing	—	6.2	6.3
Farm price supports	1.7	0.9	0.7
Other programs...	3.0	7.9	8.6
Total uncontrollable spending	93.7	232.1	260.7
Total spending...	158.3	313.4	349.4
Percentage of spending that is uncontrollable..............	59.2	74.2	74.7

Source: Havemann (1975a: 1626).

mends four changes that might help to improve the allocation of public resources. He recommended, first, a review of the necessity for the numerous trust funds (such as the federal-aid highway program) that have been established; second, a reevaluation of the need for the various permanent and indefinite appropriations (such as $50,000 paid to each state and Puerto Rico for A&M colleges); third, a reexamination of the fixed changes in the budget with the hope of letting the appropriations committee determine annually the amount to be voted in light of current conditions; and, fourth, focusing greater attention on new starts of construction and other long-term programs.

As we shall see in the following section, the 1974 Congressional Budget and Impoundment Control Act attempted to implement at least one of these recommendations. We shall also see how this important act affects the *content* of the budget as it is formulated in the executive branch.

Congressional Authorization and Appropriation

Congressional review begins when the president transmits his budget to the Congress. The Congress can change programs, eliminate them, or add programs not requested by the president. It can increase or decrease the amounts recommended by the president to finance existing and proposed new programs. It may also act upon legislation determining taxes and other means of raising revenues.

Congressional consideration of requests for appropriations and for changes in revenue laws has traditionally followed an established pattern. They are considered first in the House of Representatives. The Ways and Means Committee reviews proposed revenue measures; the Appropriations Committee, through its subcommittees, studies the proposals for appropriations and examines in detail each agency's performance. Each committee then recommends the action to be taken by the House of Representatives.

As parts of the budget are approved by the House, the appropriation and tax bills are forwarded to the Senate, where a similar process is followed. In case of disagreement between the two houses of Congress, a conference committee (consisting of members of both bodies) meets to resolve the issues. The report of the conference committee is returned to both houses for approval, and the measures are then transmitted to the president in the form of an enrolled bill, for his approval or veto.

The 1974 Congressional Budget and Impoundment Control Act changes the congressional budget process in several significant ways. Before considering these, let us note the new information the act requires the executive to submit to Congress by November 10.

The new act requires submission to Congress by November 10 of each year five-year projections of estimated outlays, budget authority, and receipts. The most straightforward of these projections is the *Current Serv-*

Alice M. Rivlin's appointment as the first head of the Congressional Budget Office caused some raised eyebrows. Nevertheless, Mrs. Rivlin rapidly assembled a staff to start providing the kind of analysis of the federal budget never before available to members of Congress.

David Vick/New York Times Pictures

ices Budget that details the costs of continuing the current fiscal year's programs at the same level in subsequent years. The executive is further required to spell out its economic assumptions (inflation, unemployment, real economic growth, program caseloads, and pay increases) as part of the current services report. It seems likely that this document will become the "baseline budget." By separating the cost of continuing current programs from additions to the budgetary base, Congress is able to separate out critical issues for decision.

In addition to these projections, the executive must also submit estimates of tax expenditures (see Chapter 10) for the budget year.

How is Congress affected by the new act? Perhaps the most apparent change is that the Congressional Budget Act establishes (*a*) one new legislative agency, the Congressional Budget Office (CBO), to serve both houses, and (*b*) a Committee on the Budget in each house. The new office and committees have substantial responsibilities.

In past years the president would send his budget to Congress each January and then Congress would pass a series of bills authorizing various programs and appropriating the money to pay for them. But these bills were enacted on a piecemeal basis, with no over-target on either income or expenditure and no emphasis on how one spending bill related to another. As one authority put it, "legislators become unhappy with the collective consequences of their individual choices."

Consequently, several new budgetary controls were established:

Within 15 days after Congress convenes in January, the president submits his annual budget message to Congress. The Congressional Budget Office analyzes it and suggests alternatives. Says Alice Rivlin (1975), CBO's first director, the office is going to be "laying out issues and options that make clear what the choices are. . . . We will pick the major budgetary issues and work on these. . . . Example: Social Security and retirement programs. Those seem to me to be very high priority. There is a lot of confusion about where Social Security is going. So we will say: Here is the way it is, here are some options. You can either raise benefits. You can make these shifts. You can finance it in different ways. Here is what it will cost."

By April 15 Senate and House budget committees draft a tentative budget, setting target for revenue and 14 areas of spending.

By May 15, after debate and revisions, Congress fixes budget goals. The results of this first concurrent resolution are shown in Table 11–3 in comparison to President Ford's budget proposal of February 1975.

From May through September, appropriations committees act on various bills.

By September 15, Congress takes a second look at the budget. If the appropriations have exceeded targets, Congress decides whether the projected deficit is acceptable. If not, a "reconciliation" bill is passed cutting spending or raising taxes.

On October 1 the new fiscal year begins.

Since 1975 was the first year of these budget reforms, a full assessment

TABLE 11–3
Presidential and Congressional Budget Levels
(billions of dollars)

Functional Area	President	Congress
National defense	$ 93.9	$ 90.7
International affairs	6.3	4.9
General science, space, and technology	4.6	4.6
Natural resources, environment, and energy	10.2	11.6
Agriculture	1.8*	1.8
Commerce and transportation	14.7	17.5
Community and regional development	6.0	8.65
Education, manpower, and social services	16.7	19.85
Health	28.4	30.7
Income security	120.9	125.3
Veteran benefits	16.2	17.5
Law enforcement and justice	3.3	3.4
General government	3.2	3.3
Revenue sharing and general fiscal assistance	7.2	7.2
Interest	34.4	35.0
Allowances	8.1	1.2
Undistributed offsetting receipts	−20.2	−16.2
Total outlays	$355.6	$367.0
Total revenue	$295.9	$298.2
Deficit	$ 59.8	$ 68.8

The Table compares President Ford's April 4 revision of his budget proposal with outlay and revenue targets adopted by Congress in its first budget resolution.

Source: Havemann (1975b: 762).

must wait. But, in the short run, one vital sign certainly worth monitoring is the degree to which the budget committees exercise their power to seek cuts in spending legislation already enacted by Congress. If the budget committees remain content for the most part to endorse the individual spending and revenue bills that Congress already passed, then they are likely to be dismissed as window dressing.

One observation regarding the first and second phases of the budget process needs underscoring. To be effective in the budgetary process, the administrator should understand the various strategies that are available. Aaron Wildavsky (1964), in a masterpiece of analysis, inventories several that have been used by agencies when defending their budgetary requests before Congress. The strategies might just as well be used by federal, state, and local agencies when presenting their initial request before the central budget office.

> Find, serve, expand, and use a clientele. As noted in Chapter 2, interest groups can be a valuable, indirect vehicle for the furtherance of agencies aims.

> In order to maximize support, rearrange administrative units. The decision of the National Institutes of Health to have separate institutes for heart research and cancer research, observes Wildavsky, "has helped mobilize more support than lumping them together under a general title with which it would be more difficult for individuals to identify."

> Inform the public of the good the agency does and, in some instances, create a climate of opinion that will influence Congress. Thus, one administrator replies to a student who requested a summer job: "Because of our inadequate funds at this critical time many students, like yourself, who would otherwise receive the professional training that this work provides, will be deprived of that opportunity. . . . Only prompt action by Congress in increasing these funds can make the success of our mission possible."

> Build confidence. The more confidence the appropriations subcommittee has in an administrator, the more he can accomplish. But how does the administrator build confidence?

> Before the hearing, visit members of Congress or invite them to the agency. Sargent Shriver, when head of Peace Corps, called on at least 450 of the then 537 members in their offices.

> At the hearings, display candor, supportive analysis (e.g., cost-benefit studies), and mastery of detail. To insure mastery of details, rehearsals in the agency are frequently held to uncover weak spots in the administrator's defense of his budget. And the fruits of careful preparations are quite evident. After listening to an airtight case by one chief administrator, Representative Rooney could only say, "We are stymied. What can we do to prevent giving you any of the taxpayer's money?" "You can-

not do very much, Congressman," the administrator replied with evident satisfaction.

Guard against cuts in old programs. When the NIH wants to start, say, a new dental research program, it has been known to begin by cutting one or all of the more popular institutes (e.g., heart, cancer, and mental health). Presumably, these cuts will generate citizen complaints. Complaints, in turn, lead Congress not only to restore the funds but also to approve the whole package, which includes the dental research program.

Inch ahead with existing programs. The more new spending looks as if it is really a part of the agency's base, the easier come new appropriations. Thus the National Institutes of Health reduces the number of its research grants while increasing their size. For the same reason, when the air force is faced with the choice of (a) renovating 100 units of old equipment or (b) keeping the old and buying 50 new ones, it prefers to renovate the old equipment. The alternative looks too much like an increase in force size even though it is the less expensive alternative.

Herman Kahn (cited in Wildavsky 1964: 111) provides the *reductio ad absurdum* of this "make do" principle. In the early days of the Republic, Congress proved unwilling "to retire old naval ships and replace them with new ones, so the navy disguised its replacement program as a repair and maintenance program. They took old ships, tied them up at the docks and let them deteriorate. The money was saved, and as soon as it amounted to enough a new ship was bought and given the same name as the old ship."

Add new programs. Every effort is made in the agency to make new programs appear old, or temporary, or insignificant ("the wedge or the camel's nose"), or relevant (related to defense, energy, etc.). But the ability of enterprising administrators to downplay the future implications of current budgetary decisions, however small, is expected to be reduced by the Congressional Budget Act of 1974. In particular, a number of observors think that the emphasis on projections, provided by the act is occasion for hope. As Rivlin (1975) put it before the Joint Economic Committee:

Projecting the consequences of alternative budget decisions has to become the first, not the last step, in Congress's decision process. Indeed, little will have been accomplished if the Congress retains its traditional focus on current year decisions (even with the new budget procedures), making current year decisions first and then asking "Let's see what these decisions mean for the future?" If, however, Congress starts with forward projections, asking itself "What do we want to see happen five years from now?"; debates these questions, and then translates its desires back into current budget decisions, the process will have significantly altered for the better.

Try salesmanship. It is no secret that on more than one occasion, congressmen have been irritated by the use of "Peter Rabbit" presentations with graphs, brochures, flashy pictures, and warnings of cures. Sales-manship, notes Wildavsky, runs the gambit from cops-and-robbers appeal—e.g., agents of our Narcotics Bureau engaged in a 45-minute gun battle with Mexican smugglers—to the agony sessions at the NIH hearings. The effect on a congressman of these drama-ridden hear-ings—including vivid descriptions of disease—is revealed by one representative (cited in Wildavsky 1964: 120): "A week ago, Mr. Chair-man, after this hearing about cancer, I went home and checked all the little skin flecks and felt for bumps and bruises. And then more recently I lay awake listening to my heart after hearing the heart-trouble talk. I listened to see if it went too fast or if it was too weak or if it was irregular or whether it was pumping too hard. . . . And here I am listen-ing to all this mental health talk . . . and I wonder what I am going to dream about tonight."

But ultimately, how well an agency fares in the budgetary hearings de-pends on how well it performed in the execution of its programs. Ac-cordingly, *tangible* results are most desirable; not surprisingly, the temptation is great to devise a criterion that will enable a program's supporters to say that it works. We might note too that the temptation is sometimes great to make extreme, even absurd, claims of success—even when such claims lack common sense. Such is the unhappy tale Wildavsky tells of the State Department official "who, at a time we had no diplomatic relations with China, refused to admit that a Chinese language program would have a deferred payoff."

REPRESENTATIVE ROONEY: I find a gentleman here, an FSO-6. He got an A in Chinese and you assigned him to London.

MR. X: Yes, sir. That officer will have opportunities in London—not as many as he would have in Hong Kong, for example—

REPRESENTATIVE ROONEY: What will he do? Spend his time in Chinatown?

MR. X: No, sir. There will be opportunities in dealing with officers in the British Foreign Office who are concerned with Far Eastern Affairs. . . .

REPRESENTATIVE ROONEY: So instead of speaking English to one another, they will sit in the London office and talk Chinese?

MR. X: Yes, sir.

REPRESENTATIVE ROONEY: Is that not fantastic?

MR. X: No, sir. They are anxious to keep up their practice. . . .

REPRESENTATIVE ROONEY: They go out to Chinese restaurants and have chop suey together?

MR. X: Yes, sir.

REPRESENTATIVE ROONEY: And that is all at the expense of the American taxpayer?

Few would deny that Wildavsky's treatment of the politics of the budgetary process lacks color or, more important, insight. But let us not conclude that the process is all politics and no analysis: Several of the analytical, quantita-tive approaches discussed in earlier chapters can help sell a committee on a program's worth. A case in point is the study made by the Soil Conservation Service that found that any money spent on soil erosion research would soon be repaid by reduced costs in dredging channels and reservoirs. But we can go further and cite the increasing influence of the analysis conducted by the Office of Technology Assessment, the Congressional Research Service, the National Academy of Science, and, of course, the Congressional Budget Office. Let us note too the increasing effect environmental impact statements, technology assessment, forecasting, microeconomic analysis, and cost benefit analysis are having. Significantly, many of these institutions and techniques bloomed only after Wildavsky's book appeared.

Budget Execution and Control

Once approved—whether by salesmanship, analysis, or a little of both—the budget eventually is passed and becomes the financial basis for the operations of the agency during the fiscal year.

Under the law, most budget authority and other budgetary resources are made available to the executive branch through an apportionment system. Under authority delegated by the president, the Director of the Office of Management and Budget apportions (distributes) appropriations and other budgetary resources to each agency by time periods (usually quarterly) or by activities. Obligations may not be incurred in excess of the amount apportioned. The objective of the apportionment system is to assure the effective and orderly use of available authority and to reduce the need for requesting additional or supplemental authority.

Whenever the president proposes to defer (i.e., temporarily withhold or *impound*) all or part of any budget authority provided by the Congress, he transmits a special deferral message to the Congress. Either House may pass a resolution disapproving this deferral of budget authority, thus requiring that the funds be made available for obligation. If Congress takes no action deferrals may remain in effect until the end of the fiscal year.

Review and Audit

This step is the final one in the budget process. The individual agencies are responsible for assuring—through their own review and control systems—that the obligations they incur and the resulting outlays are in accordance with the provisions of the authorizing and appropriating legislation, as well as other laws and regulations relating to the obligation and expenditure of funds. The Office of Management and Budget reviews program and financial reports and keeps abreast of agency programs in attainment of program objectives. In addition, the Comptroller General, as agent of the Congress, regularly audits, examines, and evaluates government programs. His findings and recommendations for corrective action are made to the Congress, to the Office of Management and Budget, and to the agencies concerned.

Why audit? In 1975, it was reported that HEW paid out more than $800 million on contracts without auditing them to find out if refunds are due the government. According to Defense Department auditors, an average of 1.13 percent of all money spent on defense contracts can be recovered. Using that yardstick, HEW could have conceivably recovered $8 million from its backlog of unaudited contracts. HEW auditors estimate that it would take 18 years to catch up on the backlog of unaudited contracts. Examples could, of course, be found throughout the federal bureaucracy.

STATE AND LOCAL BUDGETING

While the federal budget process might appear mindboggling, with its extended cycle, series of deadline dates, multiyear outlook, and intermittent congressional involvement, state, local, and institutional budgeting is much simpler to comprehend. It will be even easier if, at the outset, we clear away some features which are peculiar to certain governments, leaving a common-core budgeting process to describe. (With certain modifications, much that follows applies equally to service institutions such as universities and hospitals.)

While most states vest budgeting responsibility solely with the executive, some established a budget commission that has legislative representation. In one state, Arkansas, budgeting is entirely a legislative function. Virtually all local budgets are prepared by the executive, although this distinction is blurred under the commission form of municipal government.

State and local fiscal years vary. In the Northeast, the calendar year is common at the local level. The old federal fiscal year (July 1–June 30) has been common, especially in the West. Presumably this will change with the change of the federal fiscal year to the October 1–September 30 cycle. A large number of municipalities, including those in Florida, budgeted on an October–September fiscal year prior to the federal switch. This is fortunate for the localities. The commonality of federal, state, and local fiscal years eliminates cumbersome budget reformulations for those agencies that participate in intergovernmental transfers.

Leaving aside peculiarities in budget responsibility and reporting cycles, the state and local budgeting process can be readily conceptualized. The nine-step process shown in Figure 11–1 summarizes the public sector budgeting effort. Each of the nine steps will be briefly discussed.

Perception of Public Needs

This should be the start of any governmental budgeting process. Public perceptions are almost always felt, at least implicitly. For example, if a law-and-order candidate is elected mayor, it is likely that the voters' choice will be manifested in proportionately higher public safety expenditures. In some jurisdictions, the perception of public need is more formalized. In Lower Merion Township, Pennsylvania, for example, an annual survey of residents

FIGURE 11-1
State and Local Budget Process

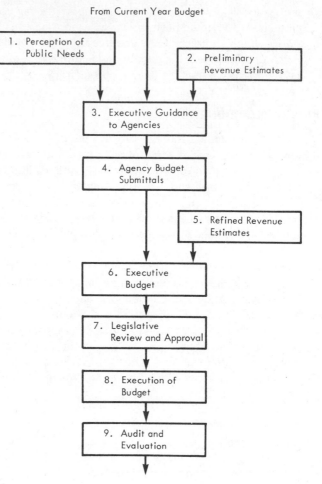

is taken, asking: "Do you feel more, less or the same tax dollars should be spent in the following areas?" The survey results for 1976 are shown in Table 11-4.

Of course, it is very difficult for typical residents to assess whether too much or too little is being spent on a particular public service. Even if the public service is perceived as inadequate, the problem could be one of inefficiency rather than underallocation of resources. And once the problem is identified, the solution may not necessarily be increasing the budget of the involved agency. For example, higher summer crime rates might be attacked by a program of summer employment in city parks. Notwithstanding these difficulties, if government's job is to maximize public benefits using

TABLE 11-4
Lower Merion Township, Pennsylvania, Budget Preference Survey

Do you feel more, less, or the same tax dollars should be spent in the following areas?

	1975 Township Budget	More	Less	Same	*Not Answered
				Percent	
35. Police	$3,425,000	24.5	4.1	53.9	17.5
36. Fire	430,000	21.9	1.6	58.4	18.0
37. Parks, recreation, and shade tree	975,000	15.5	10.9	55.5	18.2
38. Street maintenance	1,150,000	19.9	4.4	57.4	18.3
39. Libraries	630,000	12.8	12.4	55.4	19.5
40. Health	150.000	10.9	7.6	58.1	23.4
41. Zoning, planning and building regulations	360,000	7.8	12.1	58.1	22.0
42. Sanitation (refuse and sewage disposal)	2,560,000	13.0	6.3	61.2	19.4
43. Street lighting	405,000	25.4	4.7	51.4	18.6
44. Storm drainage	135,000	20.4	2.8	54.4	22.4

Source: *Lower Merion Township Report* (1975).

available resources, then public needs and priorities must be the starting point for budgeting.

Preliminary Revenue Estimates

In this step, the executive through the controller or the finance office makes an overview of revenue sources to establish expenditure guidelines for the following year. For each major category of revenue—tax proceeds, fees and user charges, and intergovernment transfers—growth estimates are made. The resultant gross revenue projection is compared against the current budget level to see what kind of growth in public services can be sustained.

As a result of this step, the public executive may find in a healthy economy that a significant increase in government expenditures can be supported within the existing tax rates. Or, the public executive may find in a weak economy that tax rates will have to be raised just to support a budget at the previous year's level, despite inflation's erosion of purchasing power.

Executive Guidance to Agencies

With a perception of public needs and preliminary revenue estimates, the public executive is prepared to provide guidance to each agency in its budget preparation. Usually, this guidance is incremental—a certain percentage change in expenditure from the previous year is specified. Sometimes, however, the executive may require an agency to prepare a zero-based budget, which must provide justification for both existing and new elements of the program.

Not only must established public services compete for government funds, but new proposals for public involvement must also be weighed. In some cases, these new public ventures carry the allure of matching federal grant money. Public transportation is a case in point. As private local bus operators threatened shutdown in community after community, local subsidies for transit became commonplace, encouraged by federal grant programs.

It is extremely difficult for a "newcomer" public service candidate, such as public transportation, to gain admission to the select list of long-standing public services. And even after entry, they have a tough time competing against entrenched agencies such as police and fire protection, road construction and repair, sanitation services, and the like.

One can sense quite different priorities for spending among the various U.S. cities. Minneapolis, for example, spends significant sums on snow removal (as could be expected), and also, perhaps not as predictably, has a relatively large traditional commitment to the park board. Houston, on the other hand, must spend considerable amounts on storm drainage due to its low topography, but it spends nothing on municipal zoning because, uniquely among large U.S. cities, it does not have a zoning code.

Agency Budget Submittals

There are four basic categories of expenditures to be forecast in an operating budget—personnel, materials, service contracts, and direct client payments. Of these, personnel is the most important.

In economic terms, government is a labor-intensive industry. To emphasize this point, sometimes executives will set personnel ceilings as the single quickest way to hold the line on expenditures. While it is true that many government services are difficult to automate, the intensive use of labor in government may have a political as well as a technical component. The following story illustrates such a circumstance.

A central city in the state of New York had just built a new municipal services building. One of its modern features was an electrical snow-melting system. On the day after the first snowfall, however, a team of men could be seen shoveling the sidewalks. A friend of the mayor asked him what problems he was having with the snow-melting system. The mayor replied: "Oh, the snow-melting system works fine. Only it don't vote."

Personnel costs are determined by the number of employees and by the remuneration paid to each. The importance of labor arrangements in promoting or retarding government efficiency cannot be overemphasized. To the fundamental consideration of base wages and salaries must be added the increasingly important issues of work rules (hours of work, responsibilities, manning levels, etc.) and fringe benefits (holidays, vacations, hospitalization and life insurance, etc.). Public pension benefits are coming under increasing scrutiny now that the Pension Reform Act of 1974 requires private companies to adequately finance pension funds as liabilities are incurred. Overly generous pension provisions, which have resulted in personnel continuing to receive a large portion of their government salary after "retirement" as early as age 40, have driven some cities to the edge of bankruptcy (see the New York City case study, which follows).

Costs of materials, while a secondary aspect of the total government budget, can be of major importance for specific agencies and projects. The cost of asphalt is a principal component of street repair cost, for example, and the cost of food usually has high visibility in hospital administration. The cost of fuel for transportation, heating, and power, is gaining increased attention as fossil fuels become more scarce. With materials, the key thrust should be *conservation*—limiting use to essentials and reusing where possible.

Service contracts can be used either to support government services or to actually provide the service. Examples of service support are contracts for insurance and for computer maintenance; examples of service contracts for delivery of public services are contracts with private sanitation companies and with private schools featuring special education programs. Service contracts should be used when the private sector offers something that government cannot provide for itself. They should also be used when, over the long term, contracting will secure the service more efficiently than government.

The last major category of agency expenditure is *direct client payments.* These are primarily found in welfare and unemployment departments but can be identified to a lesser extent in other areas. For example, when a school district, which is obligated to provide pupil transportation, cannot economically commit a school bus, it may pay the parent directly for transportation of the youngster. Welfare and unemployment expenditures are extremely difficult to budget, since they are primarily a function of economic conditions. A poor economic climate can devastate even the most carefully devised government budget, through the dual effect of decreasing tax receipts and increasing direct client payments.

Refined Revenue Estimates

At the same time that each agency is calculating next year's personnel, materials, service contract, and direct client payment expenditures, the central budget office is refining revenue estimates. Not all revenues come under the purview of the central office, however. Those user chargers that derive from the performance of a public service (transit fares, university tuition, and public hospital payments, for example) are generally budgeted by the agency responsible for the service, so that their budgets are for *net* public subsidies.

The central budget office must refine estimates for those revenues coming directly to the government's general fund. Taxes are the largest source of general fund revenue. At the city and county level, the property tax is generally the principal revenue source. At the state level, sales and income taxes are the major common tax sources. Gasoline taxes and auto license fees, while yielding considerable revenue, are often specifically designated *earmarked* for road expenditures. While there is a certain logic behind each earmarking (such as a proposal to earmark liquor taxes to support alcoholic rehabilitation centers), an earmarked tax reduces the latitude of both the executive and legislative branches to shift spending priorities.

Intergovernmental transfers (see Chapter 3), particularly federal payments to states and localities, have been increasingly important revenue sources. It has been said that the federal government is the most efficient level for revenue collection and that the locality is the most efficient level for direct public service expenditures. If this is the case, then the trend of increasing intergovernmental transfers is a good one. General revenue sharing is a transfer of the purest sort, with such funds available to support most local activities. Categorical grants are also offered by the federal government to support programs that are directed toward achievement of national goals. Federal grants, particularly categorical grants, present a special problem to the state and local budget maker: When is the grant receipt assured so that the money can be counted as revenue? Governments have found in some cases that due to failure to meet all requirements, categorical grants that have been budgeted did not arrive. On the other hand, if the requirement that federally supported projects could not be undertaken without the cash in hand were strictly adherred to, state and local services would be sharply curtailed in many functional areas.

Executive Budget

With the budget requests from departments and revenue estimates from the budget officer in hand, the chief executive officer (governor, mayor, or city manager) is now in a position to prepare the budget document. Essentially, the purpose of this document is "to present to the legislative body a comprehensive picture of proposed operation for the budget year, expressed in both verbal and statistical terms." (Moak and Killian 1974: 216)

The term "budget document" refers either to a single document, or as in the case of larger local governments, and states, to several documents. Regardless of its size, the important elements of the budget document generally include the following:

The *budget message* of the chief executive officer, which sets forth in broad outline the aims of the proposed budget and an overall explanation of the major elements of the proposed budget.

The official estimate of revenue. This section of the budget document gives the recent history of revenue by major categories and also includes the recommendation of the chief executive officer for specific revenue measures to finance the proposed budget of expenditures.

A summary of the proposed expenditures for the budget year, with appropriate comparisons between the expenditures of one or more prior years and the current year.

Detailed expenditures estimates, which present and justify overall expenditure needs in terms of perceived requirements. Presentation may be by activities, by administrative department, or by both. Moak and Killian (ibid.: 234) suggest the inclusion of the following items: (a) a narrative explanation of the function of each department, suborganizational unit, and activity, and a separate section for comments on the major changes proposed in each activity; (b) a listing by major objects of expenditure or the overall cost of conducting each department and suborganizational unit and a detailed listing of the costs required to carry out each activity and identification of proposed change; (c) the personnel complement assigned to each department, listed by position title within the various activities, showing the changes proposed; and (d) identification of the workload volume being undertaken in connection with each activity.

Legislative Review and Approval

The budget is now ready for presentation to the legislative body and, through the mass media, to the people.

In local governments, initial consideration of the budget by the legislative body is ordinarily in public session. Heads of departments and agencies are invited to explain their requests for funds; the finance officer, the revenue measures called for to balance the budget. At this time, citizens are offered an opportunity to present their views on any aspect of the budget that interests them.

At the conclusion of these public hearings, the legislative body holds executive sessions to consider components of the budget and the proposed revenue measures. A budget officer may be invited to provide additional information — but not to advocate the administration's point of view. Acting on the determinations of the executive session, the legislature makes amendments as it deems fit to the executive's expenditure and revenue recommendations. The final product is reported, in public session, to the legislature. Adoption in the presented form is likely. (Moak and Hillhouse 1975: 90)

Some cities and states provide for the possibility of executive veto and legislative reconsideration of the budget as adopted. The veto comes in several varieties: The entire budget, an entire item, and reduction of an item.

According to Moak and Hillhouse (1975: 91), the most desirable variety is the reduction of an item.

Execution

In this step of the budget cycle, financial management and day-to-day program management intertwine. A fair statement of the administration's job at this point would be, I think, this: to attain program goals within monetary limitations. Since this step covers really the entire fiscal year, it is treated in greater depth than the preceding six.

Patterns of budget execution vary widely from government to government. In some, execution amounts to little more than establishing budgetary accounts and recording the expenditures as they are processed for payment. More frequently, however, responsibility for execution rests primarily with the chief executive. "By delegation from him, the central staff agencies and operation heads assume portions of this responsibility. Operating heads, in turn, share segments of their responsibility with their subordinates. . . ." Moak and Hillhouse (ibid.) In short, budget execution encompasses management at all levels.

Allocation and Allotment of Appropriations. The first step in execution, at least in more advanced budgetary systems, is the allocation of elements of the appropriation. The legislative appropriation, in other words, is subdivided according to programs, minor organizational units, or classes of expenditures; e.g., motor fuel. The basic aim of the allocation process is to assign elements of larger appropriations to specific categories of expenses in order that money may be reserved for that category.

The most common and systematic scheme by which the money is allocated is a numerical one in which a number is assigned to every fund; each fund, in turn, is divided into accounts. The National Committee on Governmental Accounting (1968: 7–8) suggests eight types of funds:

1. The general fund is normally the most important fund of a municipality. It accounts for all resources not otherwise devoted to specific activities and finances many of the basic municipal functions. This fund might be assigned the number 001; its accounts might then be classified by the following system:

```
001–01000............................. City Council
001–11000............................. City Secretary-Treasurer
001–11100............................. Corporation Court
001–11200............................. Elections
001–12000............................. Legal
001–13000............................. Tax Office
001–14000............................. Street Department
001–15000............................. Police Department
001–16000............................. Fire Department
001–17000............................. Health Department
```

2. Special revenue funds account for the receipts from revenue sources that have been earmarked for specific activities; for example, a city with a special property tax levy for parks might have a park fund.

3. Debt service funds account for the financing of the interest and the retirement of the principal of general long-term debt.

4. Capital projects funds account for the acquisition of capital facilities, which may be financed out of bond issues, grant-in-aid, or transfers from other funds. This type of fund is most closely related to the capital budgeting process, which is discussed in the final section of this chapter.

5. Enterprise funds account for business-type activities. Municipal utilities, golf courses, swimming pools, toll bridges, and other activities supported largely by user changes and accounted for by this type of fund.

6. Trust and agency funds account for assets held for others or for nontax resources held by the government under specific trust instructions. Taxes collected for (and to be forwarded to) other governmental units are accounted for in agency funds. The most important municipal trust funds are those associated with retirement systems. Another example of a trust fund is the money donated to the city to buy park equipment as a commemoration. Such a donation would be accounted for as a trust fund although it partakes of a special revenue fund.

7. Intergovernmental service funds are similar to enterprise funds except that the services are not rendered to the general public but to other governmental organizational units within the same governmental jurisdiction.

8. Special assessment funds account for the financing and construction of those public improvements that benefit a specific group of properties. The costs of a street-paving project or a sewer extention may be assessed against the abutting properties rather than be charged against the taxpayers as a whole.

After the appropriations have been allocated to the proper fund, the next step in the execution of the budget is to allot the money for a specified period of time, usually by quarters. The aim here is to ensure not only that the money is spent properly but also that its expenditure is timed to meet requirements that may vary widely for some activities (for example, summer playground supervisor and snow removal).

Not surprisingly, accountants play a major role in both of these steps and, indeed, in the conduct of government in general. But what is *accounting*?

The Role of Accounting. Simply stated, accounting is the art of recording and summarizing the activities of an organization in terms of money and of interpreting the results. No organization – public or private – can function effectively without a good accounting system. Why? Because expenditures must be kept within the approved budget totals; because what has been paid must be available for legislative audit, the last step in the budget cycle; and, as we shall see in the study that closes this chapter, because accounting systems can serve as excellent management tools, promoting greater efficiency and better control.

Let us take a brief look at how the accounting permits us to record and summarize the activities of an organization in terms of money. All financial transactions of a government require an entry into a *journal.* The journal stores information such as which accounts are affected by the transactions, whether it is to be debited (reduced) or credited (increased), the date of the transactions, the amount of change in each affected account, and a brief description of the transaction.

Next, the transaction is posted into a *ledger,* which is a summary of transactions, according to the accounts affected. The ledger records all changes in the balance of each account. Some transactions of government involve a great amount of detail; these transactions are kept in special or subsidiary ledgers. For example, an *encumbrances ledger* is used for funds committed but not spent to date. Similarly, an *assets ledger* is used for the larger physical assets and equipment.

Figures 11-2 and 11-3 show examples of a journal and a ledger. Note how the journal entry is tied to the ledger by account number. Note too how both forms use the account numbers. Note, finally, the heading of Figure 11-3. In governmental accounting, each fund must have its own general ledger.

Funds and accounts, ledgers and journals provide the data base for the monthly financial reports that aid the administrator in insuring that the city is spending money in accordance with the budget. They also help him or her answer these kinds of questions: Are city services being provided at the level planned? Are actual expenditures in accord with the estimated expenditures and appropriation? Is the flow of revenue coming into the city's coffers — from taxes, licenses, permits, fines, etc. — at the expected level.

FIGURE 11-2

CITY OF X
General Fund
General Journal

Month of _____ , 19 _____

Day	Account Title and Explanation	Account No.	Subsidiary Ledger			General Ledger		
			✓	Dr.	Cr.	✓	Dr.	Cr.

FIGURE 11–3

GENERAL LEDGER					
_____ Fund					
Account Title _____		Account No. _____			
Date	Explanation	Reference	Debit	Credit	Balance

In this subsection we have noted two facets of the execution of the budget; namely, the allocation and allotment of appropriations. We further noted how important a role accounting has in each. We now round out our discussion of budget execution with a brief discussion of the purchasing function.

Purchasing. Generally, within a government or large organization, requests (requisitions) to purchase equipment or other items involve approval by the central budget office. These requests generally require *vouchers* similar to the one shown in Figure 11–4. Managers, with some justification, consider this requirement an intrusion upon their freedom to conduct the affairs of their agencies within the overall framework of the appropriations made available. Write Moak and Hillhouse (1975: 93): "It is in this area that the 'art' of budgeting perhaps reaches its fullest development. Obviously, no competent department head wants all of the decisions regarding his operations second guessed by the central budget office—frequently by lower-grade budget examiners. On the other hand, left without the discipline of central review, some departmental officials would pursue a path that was contrary to their own justification of funds and, simultaneously, embarrass the administration in its relations with the governing body and the public." Given this apparent necessity for a central review process, what are the essentials of an effective purchase and supply system?

First, of course, is the establishment of a central purchasing agency. An important responsibility of the central purchasing agency is to stimulate competition among bidders. The procedure is to require the vendors to submit sealed bids and then to order from the lowest bidder. The procedure is not quite that clear cut, however. Most legal promises are flexible enough that the lowest bid can be rejected. Moreover, based on past experiences, the

FIGURE 11-4

CITY OF X
Voucher

Date _____

To Whom Payable _____ Voucher No. _____

Address _____

Invoice No.	Invoice Date	Items	Amount
			Total

Requisition No._____   Purchase Order No._____

Terms of Payment_____   Due Date _____

Audited by _____   Approved by _____

(Front)

purchasing agency may lack confidence in the vendor's integrity, merchandise, or both. Finally, a not uncommon practice is to write the specifications for the item in such a way that only one vendor can bid.

What makes a good central purchasing agent? According to A. Wayne Corcoran (1975: 270), the agent should: (a) be familiar with the sources of supply; (b) understand pricing, business practices, and market conditions; (c) know the statutes and ordinances with respect to bidding; (d) establish a system that ensures that discounts are taken, that quality is tested, that ordered items are properly received and stored, and that deliveries are prompt; (e) deal effectively with sales representatives and contractors as well as with municipal service departments; and (f) have authority to obtain bids based on the precise specifications that the agent has helped formulate.

One final point about central purchasing. Bulk orders save money. For this reason, local governments not only establish central purchasing agencies but also form cooperative arrangements for joint purposes.

But centralization has its exceptions. In some cases, authority is delegated from the central agency to the using department to save time (the item, for example might be perishable). In other cases, the sheer size of government leads to delegation; thus, the federal government's central purchasing agency, the General Services Administration, delegates some purchasing authority to administrative agencies. For this reason, the Department of Defense has its own agency for purchasing and supply, the Defense Supply Agency—although GSA has the responsibility for all DOD's nonmilitary supply. Nevertheless, one should not think delegation of purchasing the wave of the future. Quite the contrary. In 1974, OMB established an Office of Procurement Policy to ride herd on the purchasing policies of all federal departments and agencies. (Executive branch procurement in recent years has averaged about $60 billion.)

In addition to a centralized purchasing agency, a purchasing and supply system requires efficient supply management procedures. Such procedures, for example, help keep inventory at an optimum level. Figure 11–5 shows the flow of an inventory over time. As the inventory is drawn down, the quantity reaches the reorder point, which triggers the placing of a replenishment order. The time between the placing of the order and the arrival of the material is known as *lead time*. The reorder point is set so that the usage rate during lead time does not drive the inventory below the safety stock level.

How do we determine best safety stock level? The basic approach, which is all we shall mention, is to balance the costs of holding various inventory sizes against the costs of lacking the item. The costs of lacking an item could

FIGURE 11–5
Inventory Flow over Time from Starting Level to Reorder Point, and Lead Time to New Starting Level

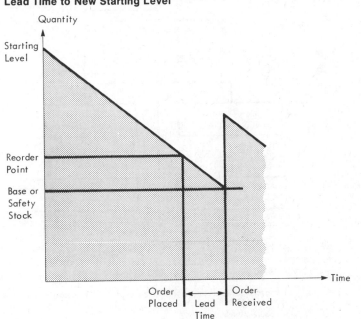

be the costs of delaying a project or suspending services until the needed supplies arrive.

How important are these matters? Commission on Organization of the Executive Branch of the Government (1955) provides an answer: "The government has mountainous accumulations of property which it would not have bought if it had a good inventory system. It is estimated that with proper inventory control and more realistic stock levels from $10 billion to $25 billion of supplies now in government warehouses could be eliminated." Indeed, in some military depots, the commission found supply items—easily obtainable from the manufacturers—in quantities sufficient to meet needs for 20, 30, and in one case, even 128 years.

We conclude our discussion of the execution of the budget with a story that happens to be true. There is a medium-sized city in the Midwest that

FIGURE 11–6
General Organization Chart, Department of Finance

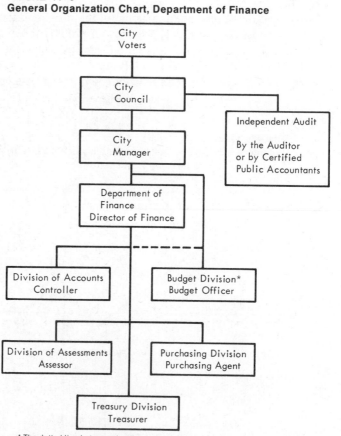

* The dotted line between the director of finance and the budget officer indicates that the latter is often primarily responsible to the chief administrator, being physically located in the finance department to prevent the duplication of records. In many cities the finance director handles the budget job.

Source: Ruchelman (1975: 19).

suffers briefly but regularly from ice formation in its streets. Thus the sight of many cars blocking intersections and facing at odd angles, because their drivers had not begun sliding to a halt soon enough, was common. The streets were neither sanded nor salted. When the mayor was asked about the icy condition, the mayor responded, "What God has given, God can take away." He was not reelected.

This story illustrates nicely the importance of considering all community needs. Clearly, the mayor was not; he thought only "sand and salt cost money and require storage space." He was, in short, considering only budgetary restrictions. As Corcoran (1975: 262) observes: "Efficiency . . . must always be considered in a total community context." I think this should be borne in mind at all times during the execution of the budget.

Audit

The National Municipal League suggests a model of a fully integrated financial system. An adaptation of that model is presented in Figure 11–6. As that Figure indicates, auditing — or, more accurately, postauditing — is done by a unit *outside* of the finance department. The audit may be performed (a) by a city's internal audit staff, provided it is removed from operating responsibilities; (b) by auditors from higher levels of government such as the state; or (c) by independent professional accountants.

At the state level, the postauditing function is not entirely satisfactory. Only a minority of states have legislative auditors. The majority have either an elected auditor, who is independent of both legislative and executive, or one within the executive branch.

FINANCING NEW YORK CITY: A CASE STUDY

Background

In the mid 1970s, New York City faced the worst fiscal crisis since the depression. And certainly, adds Steven R. Weisman (1975), "the most melodramatic crisis in memory, as the city careened from the threat of default to a last-minute bail-out by the state, its first massive layoffs in a generation, a garbage strike and slowdowns by cops and firemen, then back to the brink again, with the hope that a municipal wage freeze could stave off the unthinkable — insolvency, or even bankruptcy."

How did the city become involved in this fiscal nightmare? In the following section, I shall argue, with no claim to originality, that unsound financial management is, partly at least, the answer. The rest of the answer is to be found in external changes that affected the city after World War II. The first of these changes was an influx of impoverished blacks, Puerto Ricans, and other immigrants. The second was the outflux of tax- and revenue-producing industries.

Thus, as New Yorkers began to demand a greater and greater range of services (more than any other city provides; see Table 11–5), the tax base that could generate the money for those services grew weaker. As a result, in recent years the New York budget grew at a rate of 15 percent annually while revenues grew only 5 percent annually.

TABLE 11–5
City Government Finances, 1973–1974

	Net Debt per Capita
New York	$1,012
Chicago	314
Los Angeles	626
Philadelphia	536
Houston	385
Detroit	421
Baltimore	546
San Francisco	473
Boston	524
48 cities	553

Source: Bureau of Census (1975).

Financial Mismanagement

Whipsawed by the increasing expenditure demands and decreasing sources of revenue, the city's leaders turned to a bag of budget tricks. As Dick Netzer (quoted in Weisman 1975), dean of the Graduate School of Public Administration at New York University, put it: "The tradition in New York is that the budget is a fake piece of paper from the start of the fiscal year. There's confusion, lack of knowledge, obscurity and use of stealth. The people who make up the budget feel defenseless, somehow, if anybody can figure out what's going on."

No doubt part of the reason for the budget's phantom numbers is the fact that New York State law requires city budgets to be balanced. And, in an article titled "How New York Became a Fiscal Junkie," Weisman (1975) gives us a look at some of the fiscal magic that helped "balance" it. Weisman notes four "fixes": (1) the expense fix, (2) the revenue fix, (3) the capital fix, and (4) the outright deficit fix.

1. The basic rule with the expense fix appears to be this: Treat this year's costs as next year's costs. In 1971, for example, Controller Beame suggested that Mayor Lindsay balance his budget by charging $25 million in end-of-the-year teachers' salaries to the following year by simply having the checks go out July 1 instead of June 30.

2. To use the revenue fix, treat next year's revenues as this year's revenue. A few years ago, the city decided to begin to count big chunks of education aid, due in the fall, as revenue to its fiscal year ending the previous June 30.

Writes Weisman: "It has to borrow against the future revenues to pay its bills. The city also borrows against sales taxes and other revenues that come in as cash during the first quarter of the following year but are generated in the fourth quarter of the current year."

3. New York, like most cities, has two budgets. One is the *capital budget,* intended for changes in the physical plant of the city like new schools and subway lines. It is financed through borrowing. The other is the *expense budget,* intended for day-to-day operations such as the payment of salaries and, supposedly, financed through revenues. We must digress for a moment from our New York story to make these differences clear.

Although important relationships exist between the two types of budgets, there are special characteristics of capital projects that justify a separate budget. The following characteristics of capital projects have contributed to the segregation (Moak and Hillhouse 1975:98–99):

Because of their life span, capital projects have a long-range effect upon the community; therefore, they need to be planned within a long-range (five or six years) perspective.

"Since capital projects affect land use, traffic circulation, the density of population, and the future physical look of the municipality, they require a special expertise, namely, that of the architect-city planner. In application of the principle of a division of labor, the programming of capital improvements has been assigned to those especially equipped to do the job."

Many current operating decisions are subject to reversal, in whole or in part, at the end of (or even during) the current budget. New York City's budget is changed about 5,000 times during its July 1 to June 30 lifetime, as funds are shifted about through "budget modifications." In contrast, capital decisions are irreversible for an extended period; mistakes last longer and are apt to be more costly.

The ability to postpone most capital projects (usually much more easily than current services) means that, without a separate budget, important capital expenditures would often be neglected by cities.

Even though some of these characteristics may now be open to question, all in all, a strong rationale for the separation remains. Nevertheless, over the years, the distinction has blurred in New York City. A few capital items are tucked away in the expense budget, but more important, numerous expense items have loaded down the capital budget. For example, not only does the paint used on city bridges come from the capital budget but so also do the salaries of the men who do the painting. In fact, the Controller's Office calculates that 52 percent of the capital funds goes for expense items. Not surprisingly, the Chairman of the City Planning Commission called the capital budget as "a listing of money that will never be spent for projects that will never be built."

4. The outright deficit fix refers to borrowing to balance the budget. The borrowing is supposed to be paid off by revenues that actually arrive. Except·that the minute they arrive, there are other expenses that have to be met by borrowing. Weisman (1975) continues: "In no other major city has the short-term borrowing grown by such leaps and bounds. In no other city is the ratio of debt to the value of taxable real estate so high. The cost of servicing the city's debt has exploded from $644 million in 1969 to $1.8 billion this year; debt service—the cost of principal and interest on loans— amounts to nearly 17 percent of its budget, more than it spends on police, fire, and environmental protection."

Learning from New York City

One of the lessons to be learned is that the state can provide an early detection of financial problems in order to prevent local financial crisis. The financial controls that Albany wanted to exert over New York City in return for helping it avert a financial crisis were significantly less than those that some other states had over their municipalities.

By far, the most comprehensive local budget control law is New Jersey's. Indeed, under the criminal provisions of that state's law, city officials can go, and in at least one instance have gone, to jail for falsifying budget estimates. Michigan also has a strong law and, like New Jersey, a tradition of staffing local budget offices with professionals who are reasonably free of politics. In the opinion of some municipal finance experts, this combination of a strong law and its administration by professionals goes a long way toward explaining how cities like Detroit and Newark, despite high unemployment rates, have avoided the New York City fiscal emergency.

Yet even New Jersey and Michigan's laws fail to come close to the fiscal restrictions that were recommended by the Advisory Commission on Inter-governmental Relations in a 1973 study entitled *City Financial Emergencies*. Among the dozens of proposals in the report were the following:

> Funds must automatically be included in the current year's budget for the payment of any short-term operating debt that was not liquidated at the end of the previous fiscal year.

> States should enact laws that would establish, in advance, the conditions under which the state can move in and take over much of the financial management of a municipality or county. Some of the conditions that might trigger such interventions would be default on debt payments, failure to pay taxes collected for other jurisdictions, failure to pay salaries or to fund pension obligations, and the existence of unpaid obligations totaling 10 percent or more of the total budget.

Another lesson is to recognize that short-term operating loans—what Weisman called outright deficit fixes—are clear indication of trouble. The administrator should make certain that with or without state law, any unliquidated short term debt at the end of the fiscal year is automatically included in the next year's budget.

Municipal debt administration is a complicated technical process, so we shall limit our remarks to two points. Be aware (a) that one of the best indicators of the health of a municipality is its short term borrowing policy and (b) that state and municipal short term general obligation loans have increased sharply since 1968, exceeding sales of bonds for the first time in 1971.

A third lesson that might be derived from New York City's situation is the desirability of having an accounting system more like business firms have. The budget maze that characterized New York in the past made it virtually impossible to measure agency heads' performance in dollar-efficiency terms each month; rather, vagaries such as press released announcements of alleged progress and new programs had to be relied on.

Somehow modern accounting forms such as *cost accounting* just never infiltrated the city's government. Cost accounting is closely related to performance budgeting, which was mentioned earlier in the chapter. Without reference to methods, we can say, following R. M. Mikesell (1956: 407), that cost accounting refers to

> ascertaining the cost of units of services or goods produced or, when applied to general government, of benefits received by the public. Cost accounting may be described as that portion or form of accounting activity which endeavors to evaluate the production of goods or services in terms of the cost of measurable units. To a large extent, governmental expenditure accounting and statements have been confined to recording and reporting how much was spent; unit cost accounting, on the other hand, is an endeavor to record, measure, and report how much was accomplished and at what price. It is a system for measuring output, as compared with general expenditure accounting, which measures input.

The Texas Highway Department, for instance, receives computer printouts that show to the penny operating cost—and the per-mile or per-hour costs—of every vehicle and piece of heavy machinery on inventory. Some printouts show when costs for a particular item are running above normal so that someone can start finding out why.

Admittedly, this type of accounting is easier to implement for a highway department than, say, an office. Although much remains to be done in the latter area, some progress has been made in establishing work units for office operations. Examples follow:

Office	*Work Unit Basis*
Public recorder............	Number of documents or number of lines recorded.
Treasurer	Number of tax bills prepared.
	Number of tax bills collected.
	Number of bills, notices, and receipts mailed.
	Number of parking meters serviced.
	Amount of money collected.
	Number of licenses and permits issued.
	Number of checks or warrants written.

Office	*Work Unit Basis*
Accounting	Number of claims examined and approved.
	Number of tax bills computed and recorded.
	Number of cases investigated or otherwise handled.

A final lesson is that city governments might do well to consider keeping their books on an *accrual* basis. The lesson is not new: the first Hoover Commission recommended in 1949 that the government adopt the accrual basis of accounting and Congress in 1956, by amendment to the Budget and Accounting Procedures Act of 1950, required it of agency heads. Nor is the lesson esoteric.

When the accounts are on an accrual basis, revenues are posted in the period in which they are earned, even though some time might pass before they are actually collected. Similarly, expenditures should be recorded in the period in which the obligation is incurred, even though actual payment is deferred to a subsequent period. Is this not the way a well managed household operates? The head of the household might operate superficially on a cash-flow basis—"how much money is on hand and how much must be paid today"—but have in mind a kind of accrual account. For example, the head of the household understands that if a commitment is made, when Mary is born, to send her to college when she is 18, at some point this person must begin diverting current income away from current expenses into saving. Corporations also keep their books on an accrual basis. And in early 1976, Treasury Secretary William Simon told the House Appropriations Committee that his department plans to begin this accounting procedure in 1978. Putting governmental accounts on the accrual basis, Simon said, would help thwart the natural tendency to want to claim revenues too early and expenditures too late, thereby postponing the day of reckoning.

But in general governments—and New York City is not unique—tend to operate on a cash-flow basis. As a result, they have a less than accurate picture of the total costs and total revenues for future periods. Like Dickens's Mr. Micawber, the city's leaders can go to bed making calculations "in case anything turned up."

Accrual accounting makes such wishful thinking more difficult. In the first place, it might force them to acknowledge that taxes cannot always be raised to meet future liabilities, since tax increases tend to reduce revenues by eroding the tax base.

Equally important, accrual accounting would bring into better focus the gargantuan proportions of those future liabilities such as pension funds. A study by Data Resources, Inc., concludes that many of the 2,400 state and local retirement systems are "deteriorating," since "expenditures will overtake receipts from contributions in the next decade." In the aggregate, these pension funds are adding an estimated $3.5 billion a year to future liabilities.

Perhaps something will "turn up." But it is not likely that the federal government will be able to come to the rescue. In an interesting exercise, the accounting firm of Arthur Anderson & Co. (1975) developed a chart showing incomes and expenses for the federal government on an accrual basis for the year 1973. Instead of the $3 billion deficit reported that year on a cash-flow basis, the accrual account turns up a $95 billion deficit. In that year, the government promised to pay $75 billion in Social Security benefits and $20 billion in military, civil service, and veteran pensions over and above projected employee contributions. For 1974, the firm estimated a deficit of $150 billion on an accrual basis.

In sum, it appears that if, in the years ahead, states and cities cannot find the taxes or borrow what they need, they may find themselves sliding into New York City's dilemma: either cut spending—something interest groups resist fiercely—or see their increasingly shaky financial scaffolding collapse. Richard Ravitch is a New York developer who spent six months working out a rescue operation for the state's mammoth housing and development agency when it defaulted (that is, failed to meet its financial obligations). Mr. Ravitch (quoted in *Business Week*, September 22, 1975) sees the dilemma as a major challenge: "The business of government in the 1970s will be to pay for the decisions of the 1960s." The cynic might ask whether the governments of the 1980s will be able to pay for them at all.

NAILING DOWN THE MAIN POINTS

1   The generally accepted purposes of budgeting are control, management, and planning. Significantly, emphasis on each purpose has shifted over the years, but today the function of the budget is really a combination of all three.

Further, we can associate with each function certain specific types of budgets. For example; line-item and performance budgeting go with the control and management functions; planning-programming and zero based budgeting, with the planning function.

2   The federal budget cycle, which was changed considerably by the Congressional Budget Act of 1974, consists of four phases: (a) executive formulation, (b) congressional authorization and appropriation, (c) budget executive and control, and (d) review and audit.

3   The Congressional Budget Act, which establishes the Congressional Budget Office to serve both houses and a committee on the budget in each house, substantially changes (b) under point two. In the past the president would send his budget to Congress each January and then Congress would pass a series of bills authorizing various programs and appropriating the money to pay for them. But these bills were enacted on a *piecemeal* basis. Under the new act, however, over-all targets are set on income and expenditures (in broad categories); how one spending bill relates to another is emphasized. The new Congressional Budget Office, meanwhile, helps analyze the president's budget and suggest alternatives.

4 State, local, and institutional budget processes, of course, vary. Nevertheless, we can generally characterize it as a nine-step process: (*a*) perception of public needs, (*b*) preliminary revenue estimates, (*c*) executive guidance to agencies, (*d*) agency budget submittals, (*e*) refined revenue estimates, (*f*) executive budget, (*g*) legislative review, (*h*) execution of budget, and (*i*) audit and evaluation.

5 The first step in execution of state, local, and institutional budgets is the allocation of elements of the appropriation. The most common and systematic scheme by which money is allocated is a numerical one in which a number is assigned to every fund; each fund, in turn, is divided into accounts. The next step in the execution of the budget is to allot the money for a specified period of time.

Accounting plays a major role in both these steps. Indeed, no organization—public or private—can function effectively without a good accounting system. Why? Because expenditures must be kept within the approval budget totals; because what has been paid must be available to legislative audit; and because accounting systems (such as cost and accrual) serve as excellent management tools.

CONCEPTS FOR REVIEW

budgeting
purposes of budgeting
line-item budget
performance budget
planning-programming-budgeting system
zero-based budgeting
four phases of federal budget cycle
fiscal year
"uncontrollables" in federal budget
authorization and appropriation
Congressional Budget and Impoundment Control Act of 1974
Congressional Budget Office

political strategies in the budget process
audit
state/local budget process
funds and accounts
accounting
journal, ledger
encumbrances ledger, assets ledger
vouchers
central purchasing agency
capital budget, expense budget
cost accounting, accrual accounting
impounding

PROBLEMS

1. "The environment of financial decision makers includes a complex mixture of interest, desires, and claims, plus economic resources, political commitments, and governmental structures. Some actors in the decision maker's environment are overtly self-seeking, and some garnish their claims with statements about the national interest or objective economic realities. To cope with their highly charged

environment, policy-makers have created institutions [and procedures] that help to isolate decisions about taxes and expenditures from much of the controversy that surrounds them." (Sharkansky 1969:6) Discuss.

2. Write a paper on one of the following topics: zero-based budgeting, controlling "uncontrollable" spending, or the CBO's emerging role. Be sure to take a position on each issue and support it.

3. "Some students of the federal system argue that our budgetary procedures should be so adjusted as to free large and complex endeavors from the uncertainties and vagaries of the annual authorization-appropriation process. They say that once a major undertaking like the space program or an urban renewal program is under-way, too much is at stake to risk a loss in momentum or serious change in direc-tion every 12 months. . . ." Do you agree? James Webb (1969: 100–1), who made the statement, continues: "On the other hand, considering the great concentration of resources and power that the large-scale endeavor represents and the far-reach-ing consequences that would follow from absences, there must be effective means to protect the interest of society." Do you still agree with the original statement?

4. Common Cause has prepared a series of questions on budget priorities for presi-dential candidates to address themselves. (See "Budget Priorities Questions" below.) Such questions will enable candidates to level with voters as to the costs, the sacrifices, the hard trade-offs involved in setting and realizing national priori-ties.

Where appropriate, the questions that follow are accompanied by official federal spending and revenue estimates to guide candidates in formulating their responses. The questions are stated in sufficient detail to elicit the basic policy assumptions underlying candidate's budget approaches without unduly burdening candidates with minutia. How would you fill it out?

Budget Priorities Questions

1. The Office of Management and Budget projects that, with no changes in spending laws and priorities, the simple continua-tion of existing federal programs in FY 1977 will cost $414.5 billion distributed among the major functional categories set forth below. Given these categories and their important subprograms (de-scribed in the attached appendix), and given total FY 1977 outlays of $414.5 bil-lion, or less if you so choose, what would your spending goals be for each functional category? Candidates need comment only on those categories where they would pro-pose distinctive changes, using the at-tached appendix in such cases to indicate which subprograms would be affected by the change. [Candidates should indicate their spending priorities within the ceiling set above even if they believe higher total spending should occur. An opportunity to change the ceiling is afforded by the next question.]

	Amount in Billions*	
Function	Spending if No Existing Programs are Changed	Proposed Change
Income Security	$146.1	_____
National Defense	103.1	_____
Health	37.7	_____
Education, Manpower, and Social Services	18.4	_____
Commerce and Transportation	18.1	_____
Veterans Benefits and Services	18.0	_____
Natural Resources, Environment and Energy	14.1	_____

	Amount in Billions	
Function	*Spending if No Existing Programs are Changed*	*Proposed Change*
Revenue Sharing and General Purpose Fiscal Assistance............	7.3	_____
International Affairs..................	6.4	_____
Community and Regional Development.........	6.2	_____
General Science, Space and Technology...........	4.6	_____
General Government..........	3.5	_____
Law Enforcement and Justice	3.3	_____
Agriculture...............	2.2	_____

*Amounts do not total $414.5 billion because interest ($41.9), Allowances ($4.8), and Undistributed offsetting receipts (−$21.2) are omitted.

Source: *Current Services Estimates for FY 1977*, Office of Management and Budget, November 10, 1975, p. 22.

2. OMB's *Current Services Estimates for FY 77* projects a federal deficit of $42 billion, with a spending level of $414.5 billion. If you believe a bigger deficit for FY '77 is acceptable, how large a deficit would you target and how would you distribute the implied additional spending among the functional categories listed above?

3. The Office of Management and Budget projects that by FY 1980, federal revenues will exceed expenditures by $25 billion, assuming continuation of present taxing and spending policies, and by $61 billion if the economy is operating at full capacity (i.e., 4% unemployment rate). How would you generally allocate this excess revenue among existing spending programs, new programs you endorse, tax relief, and/or federal debt reduction?

Source: *The Budget of the U.S. Government—FY 1976*, Government Printing Office, pp. 42–46.

4. The administration estimates that $260.7 billion or 75%, as described below, of the FY 1976 budget is "uncontrollable." Expenditures are considered to be relatively uncontrollable in any one year when government decisions in that year can neither increase nor decrease them without changing existing substantive laws that, for example, require contract fulfillment or specify eligible beneficiaries and benefit formulas. In addition, federal government personnel costs amount to $63.1 billion. Given such base or fixed costs, some budget experts argue that executive branch policymakers have little discretion in developing their budget priorities. Which, if any, of the so-called "uncontrollable" expenditures listed below do you consider alterable and what proposals would you make to modify them over the course of your administration?

	Amount in Billions	
Description	*Present Cost*	*Proposed Change*
Social Security and railroad retirement	$76.6	_____
Payments due under contracts for procurement or construction signed in prior years		
Defense................	23.5	_____
Nondefense	30.5	_____
Interest on the debt.....	26.1	_____
Medicare and Medicaid..................	24.1	_____
Unemployment assistance	18.6	_____
Public assistance and related programs including food stamps....................	15.6	_____
Veterans' benefits	11.9	_____
Civil service retirement	8.8	_____
Military retirement.......	6.9	_____
General revenue sharing	6.3	_____
Housing subsidies and insurance..........	2.6	_____

Description	Amount in Billions	
	Present Cost	Proposed Change
Farm price supports..................	.7	_____
Personnel costs*		
Military....................	24.0	_____
Civilian....................	39.1	_____

* Special Analyses, p. 134.

Source: *The Budget of the U.S. Government — FY 1976*, Government Printing Office, p. 354.

5. In the current 1976 Fiscal Year, each of the 16 tax preferences listed below will cause a federal revenue loss of $2 billion or more. If you believe that tax fairness could be improved or government revenues increased by eliminating or modifying tax preferences, which, if any, of *these* tax preferences would you change and by how much? Are there other tax preferences you would modify?

Description	Amount in Billions	
	Present Cost	Proposed Change
1. Deductibility of nonbusiness state/ local taxes (other than on owner-occupied homes and gasoline)........	$10.0	_____
2. Investment credit....................	8.8	_____
3. Deductibility of mortgage interest on owner-occupied homes ...	6.5	_____
4. Net exclusion of pension contributions and earnings.....................	6.4	_____
5. Deductibility of property taxes on owner-occupied homes	5.3	_____
6. Deductibility of charitable contributions (other than education)	5.1	_____

Description	Amount in Billions	
	Present Cost	Proposed Change
7. Exclusion of interest on state/ local debt.............	4.8	_____
8. Exclusion of capital gains transferred at death	4.6	_____
9. Capital gains: individual (other than farming and timber)................	4.2	_____
10. Exclusion of unemployment insurance benefits ...	3.8	_____
11. Exclusion of employer contributions to medical insurance premiums and medical care.........	3.7	_____
12. Exclusion of Social Security benefits...............	3.7	_____
13. $25,000 corporate surtax exemption............	3.6	_____
14. Deductibility of interest on consumer credit.........	3.5	_____
15. Deductibility of medical expenses................	2.6	_____
16. Excess of percentage standard deduction over minimum standard deduction.............	2.1	_____

Source: *Estimates of Federal Tax Expenditures*, prepared by the Treasury Department and Joint Economic Committee.

(Appendix begins on page 328.)

APPENDIX: Federal Budget Categories and Important Subprograms*

The Office of Management and Budget projects that, with no changes in spending laws, the simple continuation of existing federal programs will cost the following in FY 1977:

Function	Amount (in Billions)
Income Security	$146.1
Social Security	84.5
Federal employee retirement and disability	10.3
Unemployment insurance	19.4
Supplemental security income	5.9
Public assistance	6.5
Housing assistance	3.2
Food stamps	7.3
Child nutrition and other food programs	3.0
National Defense	103.1
Military personnel	26.0
Retired military personnel	7.7
Operation and maintenance	30.0
Procurement	18.3
Research and development	10.1
Military construction	4.1
Military assistance	.3
Health	37.7
Medicare	21.7
Medicaid	9.1
Health research and education	3.0
Prevention and control of health problems	.9
Education, Manpower, and Social Services	18.4
Elementary, secondary and vocational education	4.9
Higher education	2.6
Comprehensive manpower assistance	2.8
Temporary employment assistance	2.3
Social services	3.7
Commerce and Transportation	18.1
Federal aid highways	7.3
Urban Mass Transit Administration	1.8
Other ground transportation	1.2
Air transportation	2.7
Shipping	.8

Function	Amount (in Billions)
HUD mortgage insurance and related programs	1.4
Postal Service	1.8
Veterans Benefits and Services	18.0
Income security for veterans	8.4
Education, training, rehabilitation	5.1
Hospital and medical care	4.0
Natural Resources, Environment, and Energy	14.1
Energy	3.2
Pollution control and abatement	5.1
Water resources and power, including TVA and Corps of Engineers	3.9
Conservation and land management	1.2
Revenue Sharing and General Purpose Fiscal Assistance	7.3
International Affairs	6.4
International development assistance	2.1
Food for Peace	1.1
Conduct of foreign affairs	.9
International financial programs; e.g. Export-Import Bank	1.7
Community and Regional Development	6.2
Community development grants	2.1
Urban renewal and model cities	1.0
Area and regional development; e.g. Appalachia and Indians	1.5
Disaster relief and insurance	.5
General Science, Space, and Technology	4.6
Space research and technology, manned space flight	3.4
General science and basic research	1.1
General Government	3.5
Legislative functions	.7
Central fiscal operations	1.8
Law Enforcement and Justice	3.3
Federal law enforcement and prosecution	1.8

Federal correctional and
   rehabilitative activities 2
Law enforcement assistance,
   e.g. LEAA and Legal
   Services Corporation 9
Agriculture 2.2
   Farm income stabilization 1.3
   Agricultural research and
     services............................   .9

* The subprograms listed are illustrations only; they do not include every federal spending program in each functional category.
  Source: *Current Services Estimates for FY 1977,* Office of Management and Budget, November 10, 1975.

PART IV

The Management of People

INTRODUCTION

This chapter is animated by a single question: How does the administrator motivate people within an organization?

The critical importance of employee motivation to good management is the subject of the first section. The second section relates the story of how the behavioral sciences have increased our understanding of how a manager can motivate. Today the manager has a number of theories to choose from in seeking a better grasp of human behavior in organizations. Rather than to skim over this embarrassment of riches, I have decided to treat in some depth only three. Broadly speaking, these are: the process of leadership, transactional analysis, and organizational development. While these three terms might at this point sound strange, by the end of the chapter they should not. Indeed, the aim of the chapter is not just to define them but to present them in such a manner that they can be used.

MOTIVATION: A CRITICAL MANAGEMENT CONCERN

In his research on motivation, the eminent American psychologist and philsopher William James found that employees maintain their jobs — that is, avoid being fired — by working at only 20 to 30 percent of their ability. But, if highly motivated, employees work at 80 to 90 percent of their ability. Figure 12–1 illustrates both of these levels of motivation; obviously, if motivation is low, employee's performance will suffer as much as if ability were low. For this reason, motivating is an extremely important function of management and, indeed, essential to society. Writes John W.

12

Human Behavior in Organizations

FIGURE 12–1
Potential Influence of Motivation on Employee Performance

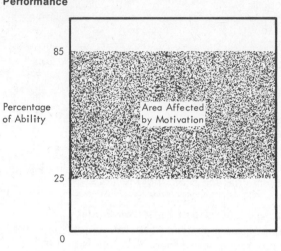

Gardner (1961), "When an institution, organization or nation loses its capacity to evoke high individual performance its great days are over."

But how much enthusiasm for work does one find in the United States today? A recent book by Studs Terkel, *Working,* offers us valuable, fresh insight into the present condition of the work ethic. Although scholars, editorialists, management experts, and sociologists have long made the case for the importance of motivation, *Working* clinches the point by letting the employees themselves argue it in a manner that is hard to deny. Any administrator who thinks that employee alienation and the need for more attention to motivation are issues created by academics and other nonadministrative types should at least consider the following two interviews (Terkel 1972:458, 460–61, 448, 450). They are quite real.

For the administrator, perhaps the most important collective outlook on work to come from the 133 interviews Terkel collected is a common desire to work and to gain satisfaction from a job. Not one person talked seriously about not working. In fact, many expressed fear of retirement, while others said their daydreams were often about work (e.g., the fantasy of getting a better job or restructuring the jobs they now have).

The task of motivation is therefore not an impossible one. People have *not* resigned themselves to aim only for the 20 to 30 percent James found to be the bare minimum to avoid dismissal. In the next section, we explore what we have learned in the decades since James about motivation.

Speaking Freely

Diane Wilson is an OEO clerk who processes grants to organizations of the poor. She speaks: "Life is a funny thing. We had this boss come in from Internal Revenue. He wanted to be very, very strict. He used to have meetings every Friday— about people comin' in late, people leavin' early, people abusin' lunch time. Everyone was used to this relaxed attitude. You kind of went overtime. No one bothered you. The old boss went along. You did your work.

"Every Friday, everyone would sit there and listen to this man. And we'd all go out and do the same thing again. Next Friday he'd have another meeting and he would tell us the same thing. (Laughs.) We'd all go out and do the same thing again. (Laughs.) He would try to talk to one and see what they'd say about the other. But we'd been working all together for quite a while. You know how the game is played. Tomorrow you might need a favor. So nobody would say anything. If he'd want to find out what time someone come in, who's gonna tell 'em? He'd want to find out where someone was, we'd always say, "They're at the Xerox." Just anywhere. He couldn't get through. Now, lo and behold! We can't find him anywhere. He's got into this nice, relaxed atmosphere . . . (Laughs.) He leaves early, he takes long lunch hours. We've converted him. (Laughs.)

"We had another boss, he would walk around and he wouldn't want to see you idle at all. Sometimes you're gonna have a lag in your work, you're all caught up. This had gotten on his nerves. We got promotion and we weren't continually busy. Anytime they see black women idle, that irks 'em. I'm talkin' about black men as well as whites. . . .

"One day I'd gotten a call to go to his office and do some typing. He'd given me this handwritten script. I don't know to this day what all that stuff was. I asked him, 'Why was I picked for this job?' He said his secretary was out and he needs this done by noon. I said, 'I can't read this stuff.' He tells me he'll read it. I said, 'Okay, I'll write it out as you read it.' There's his hand going all over the script, busy. He doesn't know what he's readin', I could tell. I

know why he's doing it. He just wants to see me busy.

"So we finished the first long sheet. He wants to continue. I said, No, I can only do one sheet at a time. I'll go over and type this up. So what I did, I would type a paragraph and wait five or ten minutes. I made sure I made all the mistakes I could. . . .

"I took him back this first sheet and, of course, I had left out a line or two. I told him it made me nervous to have this typed by a certain time, and I didn't have time to proofread it, 'but I'm ready for you to read the other sheet to me.' He started to proofread. I deliberately misspelled some words. Oh, I did it up beautifully. (Laughs.) He got the dictionary out and he looked up the words for me. I took it back and crossed out the words and squeezed the new ones in there. He started on the next sheet. I did the same thing all over again.

"I'm gonna see what he does if I don't finish it on time. Oh, it was imperative! I knew the world's not gonna change that quickly. It was nice outside. If it gets to be a problem, I'll go home. It's a beautiful day, the heck with it. So 12:30 comes and the work just looks awful. (Laughs.) I typed on all the lines, I continued it anywhere. One of the girls comes over, she says, 'You're goin' off the line.' I said, 'Oh, be quiet. I know what I'm doin'. (Laughs.) Just go away.' (Laughs.) I put the four sheets together. I never saw anything as horrible in my life. (Laughs.)

I decided I'd write him a note. 'Dear Mr. Roberts: You've been so much help. You proofread, you look up words for your secretary. It must be marvelous working for you. I hope this has met with your approval. Please call on me again. I never heard from him. (A long laugh.)

Steve Carmichael is a twenty-five year old project manager for the Neighborhood Youth Corps. "I doubt seriously if three years from now I'll be involved in public administration. One reason is each day I find myself more and more like unto the people I wanted to replace.

"I'll run into one administrator and try to institute a change and then I'll go to someone else and connive to get the change. Gradually your effectiveness wears down. Pretty soon you no longer identify as the bright guy with the ideas. You become the fly in the ointment. You're criticized by your superiors and subordinates. Not in a direct manner. Indirectly, by being ignored. They say I'm unrealistic.

"The most frustrating thing for me is to know that what I'm doing does not have a positive impact on others. I don't see this work as meaning anything. I now treat my job disdainfully. The status of my job is totally internal: Who's your friend? Can you walk into this person's office and call him by his first name? It carries very little status to strangers who don't understand the job. People within the agency don't understand it. (Laughs.)

"Success is to be in a position where I can make a decision. Now I have to wait around and see that what I say or do has any impact. I wonder how I'd function where people would say, 'There's hotshot. He knows what he's talking about.' 'And what I say became golden. I don't know if it would be satisfying for me. (Laughs.) That might be more frustrating than fighting for everything you want. Right now I feel very unimportant.

THE BEHAVIORAL SCIENCES MAKE THEIR MARK

For at least the last 50 years, behavioral scientists and administrators have had at least one common interest: identification of the ways in which the effectiveness of an organization can be improved. The story of this question is a fascinating one and it begins in the 1920s, when the Harvard Business School under the supervision of Elton Mayo (1933) conducted a series of experiments in the Hawthorne, Illinois, plant of Western Electric.

Hawthorne Studies

In 1924, Western Electric efficiency experts designed a research program to study the effects of illumination on productivity. The assumption was that increased illumination would result in higher output. Two groups of employees were selected: A test group, which worked under varying degrees of light, and a control group, which worked under normal plant illumination. As expected, when lighting increased, the output of the test group went up. But something else happened—and it was entirely unexpected. The output of the control group also went up.

At this point, Western Electric turned for help to Mayo and his associates. Mayo's researches then began to implement a variety of changes, behavioral as well as physical. Rest periods were scheduled. Work hours were altered. Hot snacks were served. But no matter what was done to the workers, output continued to soar.

Baffled by the results, the researchers took a radical step: They restored the original conditions. This change was expected to have a tremendous negative psychological impact and most certainly reduce output. But output jumped to an all-time high. Why? The answer was fairly simple, but the implications were catastrophic, bringing an almost precise reversal of the whole line of management thought and practice since the Industrial Revolution. In a nutshell, what the Harvard team found—after further investigation, including interviews of over 20,000 employees from every department in the company—was this. The worker's productivity went up because the attention lavished upon them by the experimenters made them feel that they were important to the company. No longer did they view themselves as isolated individuals. Now they were participating members of a congenial, cohesive work group.

The general lesson was patent: the significant factor affecting organizational productivity was not the physical conditions or monetary rewards derived from work but the interpersonal relationships developed on the job. Mayo found that when informal groups felt that their own goals were in opposition to those of management and their control over their job or environment was slight, productivity remained low.

In a word, the new goal for management, the golden key, seemed to be *morale*. To maintain a high level of output, the administrator had only to develop ways to satisfy the worker, to make him feel good about his work, his boss, and his organization. Dr. Feelgood had replaced the grim efficiency expert.

Behavioral science was making progress. The discovery of the informal group—and, in a larger sense, the humanity of the worker—was, as we said, a real breakthrough in management thought. But the same cannot be said for the concept of morale. As subsequent research began to show, morale was no panacea. Given happy employees, it by no means follows with iron logic that they will feel an urge to work harder and harder. So, disillusionment set in and the scientists began to look for a new tack to improving the effectiveness of organizations.

Hierarchy of Needs

The next scene in our story opens with a question, much as the Hawthorne affair did. Money, presumably, was a great incentive to work hard, but when people were asked what was most important to them in their jobs, it often rated third, fourth, or even fifth place. Factors like "full appreciation for work done," "feeling in on things," "sympathetic understanding of personal problems," and "job security" ranked higher. Why?

Speaking roughly, we might say that human motives or needs form a more complicated pattern than one is likely to suppose. In the early 1950s U.S. psychologist Abraham Maslow (1954) did much to limn this pattern by suggesting the existence of a hierarchy of needs. According to Maslow, the behavior of an individual at a particular moment is usually determined by his strongest need. If this is so, then it would seem useful for administrators to have some understanding about the needs that are commonly most important to people. Maslow notes five (see Figure 12–2).

1. In his formulation, the physiological needs (e.g., food, clothing, and shelter) are at the bottom of the hierarchy. The satisfaction of these needs is usually associated in our society with money. But as these basic needs

Abraham H. Maslow, who died in 1970, was one of the foremost spokesmen of humanistic psychology. In order to pursue the truth of things, to discover a way of experiencing the highest levels of human awareness, and to research the best social conditions in which man might bring himself to a "full humanness," he found he could not separate the empirical methods of science from the aesthetics of philosophical inquiry. "Experiencing is only the beginning of knowledge," he said, "necessary, but not sufficient." He introduced the hierarchy of needs, which included self-actualization. In 1965, he described in *Eupsychian Management* the interrelations between psychological theory and an enlightened, modern management.

Photograph by William Carter

begin to be fulfilled, other levels of needs become important and motivate and dominate the behavior of the individual.

2. Above physiological needs, Maslow places the need for safety or security. As with other motives, security can be either above the surface and apparent to the individual or largely subconscious and not easily identified. The latter form can be developed during early childhood through

FIGURE 12–2
Maslow's Hierarchy of Needs

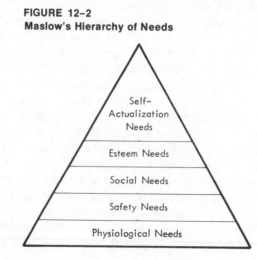

identification with security-minded parents who are willing to accept whatever fate comes along.

Do you want a job that offers a challenge to imagination and ingenuity and that penalizes failure? Or, do you find real satisfaction in the precision, order, and system of a clearly laid out job? (Remember Sinclair Lewis's Babbitt, from whom "a sensational event was changing from the brown suit to the gray the contents of his pockets.") How you answer these questions is a good indication of how important the security motive is to you. Some organizations, it has been suggested (Gellerman 1963), tend to overemphasize the security motive by providing elaborate programs of fringe benefits; e.g., medical insurance and retirement plans. While this emphasis can make employees more predictable, it cannot necessarily make them more productive. And if creativity is necessary in their jobs—which is often the case in the public sector where a high percentage of employees are knowledge workers—overemphasis on security can actually thwart creativity.

3. Once physiological and safety needs are fairly well satisfied, social needs become dominant. Considerable sophistication is required to deal effectively with these needs.

In the first place, the administrator needs to recognize that the social needs of decision makers in the organization can lead to *groupthink.* This mode of thinking is regularly encountered in studies of group dynamics when concurrence-seeking becomes so dominant that it tends to override realistic appraisal of alternative courses of action. And no level of decision making is immune to this strain of social conformity.

An important symptom of groupthink is pressure. "Victims of groupthink apply direct pressure to the individual who momentarily expresses doubts about any of the group's shared illusions or who questions the validity of the arguments supporting a policy alternative favored by the minority. This gambit reinforces the concurrence-seeking norm that loyal members are expected to maintain." James C. Thompson Jr., a historian who spent five years as an observing participant in both the State Department and the White House, reports that whenever a member of President Johnson's ingroup began to express doubts about Vietnam, the group made subtle social pressure to "domesticate" him. The dissenter was made to feel at home provided he did not voice his doubts to outsiders and kept his criticism within the bounds of acceptable deviation. Thompson tells us when one such "domesticated dissenter," Bill Moyers, arrived at a meeting, the president greeted him with, "Well, here comes Mr. Stop-the-Bombing." (Cited in Janis 1971.)

One behavioral scientist concludes, after pouring over hundreds of relevant documents, that social need is the only explanation of why groupthink continues to occur in the corridors of power. Writes Irving L. Janis (ibid), "My belief is that we can best understand the various symptoms of groupthink as a mental effort among group members to maintain . . . emotional equanimity by providing social support to each other. . . ."

A second thing that the administrator needs to recognize about social needs concerns not the corridors of power but the informal work group. Administrators are often suspicious of informal groups that develop in organizations because of the potential power these groups have to lower productivity. Recall how Diane Wilson's group was able to maintain a lax work schedule, despite the efforts of the new supervisor from the Internal Revenue Service. But why are such work-restricting groups formed? Studies show that they sometimes form as a reaction to the insignificance and impotence that workers tend to feel when they have no control over their working environment. In fact, the situation is made worse when, at the same time, workers are closely supervised but have no clear channels of communication with the top. (See Schachter 1959.) In this type of environment, which is not unlike Diane Wilson's, work restriction becomes a means to preserve the identification of individuals within the group. Yet, informal groups *can* be an asset to administration.

But how? To answer that question we might first note a cardinal insight of recent studies on informal groups: an inherent conflict exists between the social needs of the individual and the requirements of the organization. Social psychologists draw a useful distinction here: the social needs of the individual are called *primary needs* and the requirements of the organization *secondary needs.* One need not spend much time in public organizations to find out that the vocabulary of bureaucracy abounds with avowals of secondary needs at the expense of primary ones. Consider: "Nothing personal, but. . . .", "I'm sorry to have to do this, but. . . .," "I have my job to do too, you know. . . ."

In contrast, the effective administrator not only tries to avoid this officious approach but also *tries to integrate primary and secondary relationships.* But how does one go about this integration? The successful administrator, according to Katz and Kahn (1966: 325–56) "mediates and tempers the organizational requirements to the needs of persons." But this mediating is done in ways that are not damaging but actually enhancing to the organization. Further, the administrator "promotes group loyalty and personal ties. He demonstrates care for persons as persons." In trying to influence the people in the organization, the administrator seldom relies on formal powers, such as found in rules and regulation, but on (a) *referent power;* i.e., influence based upon liking or identification with another power, or (b) *expert power;* i.e., influence based upon the expertise of the administrator that is relevant to the task.

Write Katz and Kahn (ibid): "He encourages the development of positive identification with the organization and creates among his peers and subordinates a degree of personal commitment and identification. He does these things by developing a relationship with others in the organization in which he introduces what might be termed primary variations on the secondary requirements of organization. Within limits he adapts his own interpersonal style to the needs of other persons. In so doing, he generates among mem-

The need for esteem and prestige is fourth on Maslow's hierarchy. The French government distributes each year a bewildering array of awards, which the model above displays. According to one sardonic French saying, half the riders in the Paris metro wear the Legion of Honor, while the other half have applied for it. Apparently, Maslow's hierarchy applies cross-nationally.

Picherie—Paris-Match

bers of his group a resultant strength of motivation for the achievement of group and organizational goals which more than compensates for occasional bureaucratic irregularities. The secondary role requirements remain the dominant figure in his behavior, but they appear on a background of, and are embellished by, an attention to primary interpersonal consideration.''

4. Assuming then that the individual social needs are met within the organization, a fourth need comes into prominence: esteem. Failure to understand this need often lies behind the administrator's complaint: ''We've given our people everything—good salary, pleasant working conditions, even affection—and yet some are still dissatisfied.'' In other words, it is precisely because employees have had the three basic needs sufficiently satisfied that a fourth need emerges. And, like social needs, it can cause

organizational problems unless the administrator finds ways of satisfying it.

While the need for esteem appears in a variety of forms, we shall discuss only two, recognition and prestige. But with each form, the message for the public administrator remains the same: Do things to make employees feel important.

William James (1952: 189) gave an especially gripping explanation of the importance of recognition:

> We are not only gregarious animals, liking to be in sight of our fellows, but we have an innate propensity to get ourselves noticed, and noticed favorably, by our kind. No more fiendish punishment could be devised, were such a thing physically possible, than that one should be turned loose in society and remain absolutely unnoticed by all the members thereof. If no one turned round when we spoke, or minded what we did, but if every person we met . . . acted as if we were nonexisting things, a kind of rage and impotent dispair would be a relief; for these would make us feel that, however bad might be our plight, we had not sunk to such a depth as to be unworthy of attention at all.

In an organizational setting, what this means is that people look for support from their supervisors. Studies show, for example, strong relationship between an administrator's supportiveness and the self-esteem of his subordinates (see Bowers 1964). Further, studies by members of the Institute for Social Research at the University of Michigan have shown that supervisors who exert pressure for production *but do not support their people* end up with a low production organization.

Despite the importance of recognition, most contemporary organizations are deficient in it. This is evident, says Harry Levinson (1968: 183) of Harvard's Business School, in the repetitive response to a simple question. "If one asks people in almost any organization, 'How do you know how well you are doing?' 90 percent of them are likely to respond, 'If I do something wrong, I'll hear about it.'" According to Levinson, what people are really saying is that they do not feel sufficient support from their supervisors.

The power to gain ascendency over the minds of men and to command their admiration for distinguished performance is prestige. To be sure, some tend to seek only the material symbols of status. Salary, to the extent it carries social value, can certainly be included here as well as under physical needs. Michael Korda's book *Power!* would hardly merit our attention except that its very popularity evidences how widespread (one might say even pathological) this need for people to have their importance clarified has become. In a chapter entitled "Symbols of Power," Korda offers detailed advice on how shoes, typewriters, telephones, office furniture, briefcases and clocks can all increase status. Sample: "A full calendar is proof of power, and for this reason, the most powerful people prefer small calendars, which are easily filled up, and which give the impression of frenetic activity, particulary if one's writing is fairly large. One of the best power symbols is a desk diary that shows the whole week at a glance, with every available square inch of space filled in or crossed out. It provides visible evidence that one is busy—too busy to see someone who is anxious to discuss a complaint or a burdensome request." The author even suggests, if necessary, filling the diary up with entries such as "gray suit at cleaners" or "Betsy's birthday." "The effect from a distance is awe-inspiring." (Korda 1975: 208)

5. According to Gellerman (1963), the need for prestige is more or less self-limiting. Once people have gained the level they think they deserve, the strength of this need declines. Prestige now becomes a matter more of maintenance than of further advancement. At this point, too, we witness the emergence of Maslow's fifth and final need: self-actualization.

What exactly is self-actualization? In *The Farther Reaches of Human Nature,* a book light-years removed from Korda's, Maslow (1971: 43) provides us an answer: "Self-actualizing people are, without one single exception, involved in a cause outside their own skin, in something outside of themselves. They are devoted, working at something, something which is very precious to them—some calling or vocation in the old sense, the priestly sense. They are working at something which fate has called them to somehow and which they work at and which they love, so that the work-joy dichotomy in them disappears."

Admittedly, this explanation lacks the rigor indicative of good social and behavioral science; and there is no gainsaying the fact that the concept of self-actualization is difficult to pin down. But we must try. (I harbor the belief that the great undiscussed paradox in management literature is that in discussions of Maslow's hierarchy of needs the most underdeveloped part, self-actualization, is the most important.)

An especially well-researched motive, closely related to self-actualization, is the urge to achieve. By considering this phenomenon, perhaps we can better understand self-actualization.

Adapting a simple example from David McClelland (1961) can help us distinguish the achievement motivated person from the social motivated and esteem motivated. Given the task of building a boat, the achievement motivated person would obtain his gratification from the making of the boat. This intense interest in the work is, of course, quite consistent with the above quote from Maslow. The socially motivated person would have fun in playing with others and with the boat but would be little concerned about its seaworthiness. Finally, the esteem oriented person would be concerned with the specific role he had in the project and the rewards of success.

Achievement motivated persons set moderately difficult but potentially surmountable goals for themselves; they prefer situations where they can obtain tangible information about their performance; and they habitually think about how to do things better. Maslow tells an anecdote about Brahms that illustrates the last point. Somebody had been fiddling around at the piano and was idly playing notes and chords and, in the middle of playing, left the piano. Brahms had to get up and finish the progression. He then said, "We cannot let that chord go unresolved forever."

From the various achievement studies, we have learned that this motive can be taught and developed in people. But how? Levinson (1968:243) provides these guidelines: The administrator "should make demands on people, expect them to achieve reasonable goals, and even some that border on the unreasonable. He should respect their capacity to chart their own course toward those goals if they are adequately protected and supported, acknowledge what they have to contribute toward reaching collective goals and, following Diogenes's dictum, 'Stand out of their light.'"

After Maslow

To summarize: Maslow contended that human needs could be classified on five levels, each succeeding need becoming more pressing as the more primitive ones were satisfied. In ascending order these are physical needs, safety needs, social needs, esteem needs, and self-actualization needs. Subsequent research — such as that by Herzberg, discussed in Chapter 14 — would discover that certain lower level needs, while not exactly motivations, could, if ignored, lead to job dissatisfaction. (See Figure 14–2 for a complete listing of what the "dissatisfiers" and "motivators" are.)

To my mind, this theory was a remarkable contribution, for Maslow was saying — with far more precision than any of his predecessors — that different people require different treatment by management (in the vernacular: different strokes for different folks). And more: that the same person may over time require different treatment and that management should never expect a cessation of complaints but only different ones.

How Maslow's theory gave rise in subsequent years to some quite contrary theories I must leave for others to sort out. Since the purpose of this chapter is not to review all the existing theoretical, empirical research, and case studies, we can safely skip over these behavioral mastodons and proceed immediately to consideration of what we know today about motivating employees.

Specifically, we shall be concerned with three topics, each of which, I think, represents a real contribution to our understanding of human behavior in organizations. First is the shift in behavioral research away from a concern with identifying the leader (as opposed to the follower) or the effective leader (as opposed to the ineffective one), and toward the study of the process of leadership itself — that is, how the leader, group, and situation all interact. The second topic, now only in its infancy, stems largely from psychoanalytic conceptions. In contrast to the humanistic, self-actualizing theory of Maslow, these more complex theories of motivation are derived from insights originally based on clinical work with individuals. While several major theorists share this point of view, below we shall deal with only one, Eric Berne, the originator of transactional analysis and author of the well known *Games People Play* (1964). The third topic, the management of change, stems from the openness of the organization as a system and from the fact that it functions in a changing environment. These changes are multifarious: technological, legal, cultural, economic, climatic, etc. Not surprisingly, they generate demands on the public organization that the patterns of behavior within it change. In the final section of this chapter, therefore, we shall be concerned with the problems of change in general and the new technique of *organizational development* in particular.

THE QUEST FOR LEADERSHIP

A Problem Recognized

Americans today are especially sensitive to the problem of leadership in government. The acuity of the sensitivity was reflected in the opening litany of complaints *Time* (July 15, 1974) assembled for a special story on leadership in the United States:

> The pop cosmologist Erich Von Daniken conjures up primordial heroes from the plain of Nazca and the temples of Palenque—extraterrestrial astronauts who strayed to this planet long ago and then vanished. Today heroes and leaders bred on the earth seem almost as scarce. "There is a very obvious dearth of people who seem able to supply convincing answers, or even point to directions toward solutions," says Harvard President Derek Bok. "Leadership," observes Northwestern University Political Scientist Louis Masotti, "is one of those things you don't know you need until you don't have it." In the U.S. and round the world, there is a sense of diminished vision, of global problems that are overwhelming the capacity of leaders. As Journalist Brock Brower wrote three years ago, if Martian spacemen were to descend and demand, "Take me to your leader," the earthlings would not know where to direct them.

Meanwhile, the behavioral scientists, as well as thoughtful executives (public and private), have become more sensitive to the problem of leadership, though for somewhat different reasons. First, they have begun to express concern within recent years that more than a few of the motivational theories and techniques were manipulative. The danger no longer was that organizational life would come to resemble totalitarian *1984* but that it would resemble technocratic *Brave New World.* Thus, they argued, management should stop looking upon employees as merely a problem to be solved and start thinking about the leadership of people.

Scientist and managers have had a second revelation. Leadership can provide the influential increment over and above the level of motivation normally expected when many routine needs have been met. In other words, when the administrator thinks in terms of *leadership*—in contrast to establishing a pleasant work environment, giving generous recognition, etc.— he or she may be able to more fully realize the potential of a group.

But What Is It?

Leadership can be spoken about in at least two ways. The first is sweeping. It conjures up visions of an indefatigable Washington crossing the Delaware and echoes of the message that went out to the fleet in 1939 when

Churchill was reappointed to his old post in charge of the Admiralty: "Winston is back." The French critic Henri Peyre (cited in ibid) defined it lucidly:

> A broad ideal proposed by the culture of a country, instilled into the young through the schools, but also through the family, the intellectual atmosphere, the literature, the history, the ethical teaching of that country. Will power, sensitivity to the age, clear thinking rather than profound thinking, the ability to experience the emotions of a group and to voice their aspirations, joined with control over those emotions in oneself, a sense of the dramatic . . . are among the ingredients of the power to lead men.

In this section, however, we are concerned more with a second meaning of leadership. While its definition is less sweeping than the first, its presence in administration is more pervasive. Leadership, in this second sense, we define as the process of influencing the activities of a group in efforts towards goal attainment in a given situation. The key elements in this definition are leader, followers, and situation. Leadership, then, is a function of three variables. Symbolically,

$$L = f(l,f,s).$$

For convenience, we term this approach to the study of leadership *situational*.

From the Trait Approach to the Situational Approach

In the past (especially from 1930 to 1950), the most common approach to the study of leadership focused on traits; it sought to determine what makes the successful leader from the leader's own personal characteristics. These inherent characteristics—such as intelligence, maturity, drive, friendliness—were felt to be transferable from one situation to another. The list of traits grew and grew, but no clear cut results appeared. Finally, Eugene E. Jennings (1961) did for trait approach to leadership what Glenden Schubert did for the concept of public interest (see Chapter 4)—conduct a careful and extensive review of the literature. Jennings concluded, "Fifty years of study have failed to produce one personality trait or set of qualities that can be used to discriminate leaders and nonleaders."

Empirical studies do, however, support the situational approach. Moreover, the situational approach has an important practical advantage: by emphasizing behavior and the environment, more encouragement is given to the possibility of training individuals. In other words, people can increase their effectiveness in leadership through training in adapting their leadership style to the situation and the followers. Needless to say, this approach does require that the administrator be a good diagnostician to identify clues in an environment and be flexible enough to vary his own behavior. The following two subsections should provide useful frameworks for helping an administrator know how to adapt leadership style to the environment.

With apologies to Eugene E. Jennings, who concludes that 50 years of study have failed to produce any set of qualities that can be used to discriminate leaders, here is Jefferson's assessment of Washington: "His mind was great and powerful, without being of the very first order. . . . Perhaps the strongest feature in his character was prudence, never acting until every circumstance, every consideration was maturely weighed; refraining when he saw a doubt, but, when once decided going through with his purpose whatever obstacles opposed. His integrity was most pure, the justice the most inflexible I have ever known. . . . He was indeed, in every sense of the word, a wise, a good and a great man." Unlike the French model who appeared earlier in the chapter, the general wears no medals. How might Maslow explain their absence?

Courtesy the Pennsylvania Academy of Fine Arts

Toward the Life-Cycle Theory of Leadership

Dorwin Cartwright and Alvin Fander (1960) claim that all group objectives fall into one of two categories: (1) the achievement of some group goal, or (2) the maintenance or strengthening of the group itself. The first, which we shall call *task behavior,* refers to "the leader's behavior in delineating the relationship between himself and members of the work group and in endeavoring to establish well defined patterns of organization, channels of communication, and methods of procedure." When the leader assigns group members to a particular task, asks the group members to follow the rules, and lets the group members know what is expected of them, we can say that he is exhibiting task behavior.

The second dimension of leader behavior, which we shall call *relationship behavior,* refers to "behavior indicative of friendship, mutual trust, respect, and warmth in the relationship between the leader and the members of his staff." When the leader finds time to listen to group members, is willing to make changes, and is friendly and approachable, we can say that he is exhibiting relationship behavior.

Using only various combinations of these two kinds of behavior, Blake et al. (1964) note five fairly distinct leadership styles:

Impoverished: Exertion of minimum effort to get required work done is appropriate to sustain organization membership.

Country Club: Thoughtful attention to needs of people for satisfying relationships leads to a comfortable friendly organization atmosphere and work tempo.

Task: Efficiency in operations results from arranging conditions of work in such a way that human elements interfere to a minimum degree.

Middle-of-the-road: Adequate organization performance is possible through balancing the necessity to get out work while maintaining morale of people at a satisfactory level.

Team: Work accomplishment is from committed people: interdependence through a "common stake" in organization purpose leads to relationships of trust and respect.

Figure 12–3 plots these five styles.

FIGURE 12–3
Managerial Grid Leadership Styles

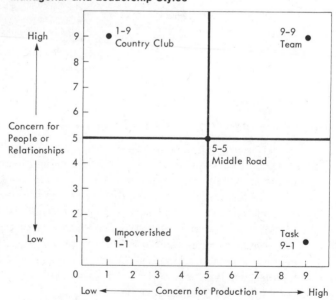

Source: Adapted from Blake and Mouton (1964: 10).

Now recall the earlier statement that leadership effectiveness is a function of the leader, the group, and the situation. This tells us that we cannot ignore the dynamic quality of leadership style; in other words, the best leadership style is not frozen in stone but varies with the situation. But how?

Maturity we may define as willingness and ability to take responsibility. The nature of this relationship tends to be curvilinear (see Figure 12–4). This theory we call the life-cycle theory of leadership. But what does it tell the administrator? In a nutshell, this: as the maturity of one's followers continues to increase, appropriate leader behavior requires initially less structure (i.e., task behavior) but more socioemotional support (i.e., relationship behavior). Eventually, as the group approaches full maturity, the socioemotional support may be decreased, too.

Since not all groups are necessarily immature to begin with, the manager —especially the new one—must first size-up the maturity level of his subordinates. The untoward effects of failing to do so are well illustrated in the following case described by Hersey and Blanchard (1972:138–39):

> Normally, in basically crisis-oriented organizations like the military or the police, the most appropriate style tends to be high task, since under combat or riot conditions success often depends upon immediate response to orders. Time demands do not permit talking things over or explaining decisions. For success,

FIGURE 12–4
Life-Cycle Theory of Leadership

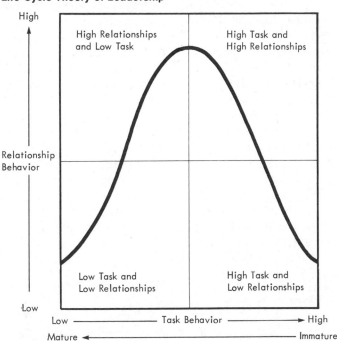

Source: Adapted from Hersey and Blanchard (1972: 135).

behavior must be automatic. While a high task style may be effective for a combat officer, it is often ineffective in working with research and development personnel within the military. This was pointed out when line officers trained at West Point were sent to command outposts in the DEW line, which was part of an advanced-warning system. The scientific and technical personnel involved, living in close quarters in an Artic region, did not respond favorably to the task-oriented behavior of these combat-trained officers. The level of education, research experience, and maturity of these people was such that they did not need their commanding officer to initiate a great deal of structure in their work. In fact, they tended to resent it. Other experiences with scientific and research oriented personnel indicate that many of these people desire, or need, a limited amount of socioemotional support.

An additional point to keep in mind in the application of this theory is that on occasion it may be necessary for a leader using low task-low relationships style to deviate from this style. For instance, during the early stages of implementing a new program, a certain amount of structure as to the requirements and limitations of the project must be established. Then, once these are understood, the program manager can move rapidly through the cycle back to low task-low relationship style.

Leadership and Decision Making

The life-cycle theory is not the only situational approach to leadership. Vroom and Yetton (1973) also maintain that no one leadership approach applies to all situations. They, therefore, provide a normative model (i.e., a model that tells how a manager *should* act) for the analysis of situational requirements that can be translated into prescriptions of leadership styles.

Classifying leadership styles is a popular endeavor among behavioral scientists. But most classifications boil down to making subdivisions between two extremes, autocratic leadership and laissez-faire leadership. Thus we can think of every leadership style as falling somewhere along the continuum between these two extremes. Figure 12–5 shows such a continuum.

The big question is how do managers know which leadership style is appropriate? Well, the life-cycle theory provided us with one answer: in a word, the style depends on the maturity of subordinates. But the normative model provides a different one: style depends on the type of decisions to be made. And, since decisions change, the leadership style used in response to one should not constrain the style used with other decisions.

To determine the feasible set of leadership styles Broom and Yetton (1973:145–47) present the following seven rules. The numbers in parenthesis after each rule is the probability that it will be violated in actual practice:

1. The information rule: If the quality of the decision is important and the leader does not possess enough information or expertise to solve the problem by himself, AI (see Figure 12–5) is eliminated from the feasible. (0.02)

2. The trust rule: If the quality of the decision is important and subordinates cannot be trusted to base their efforts to solve the problem on organizational goals, GII is eliminated from the feasible set. (0.11)

FIGURE 12–5
Continuum of Leadership Behavior in Terms of Decision Processes

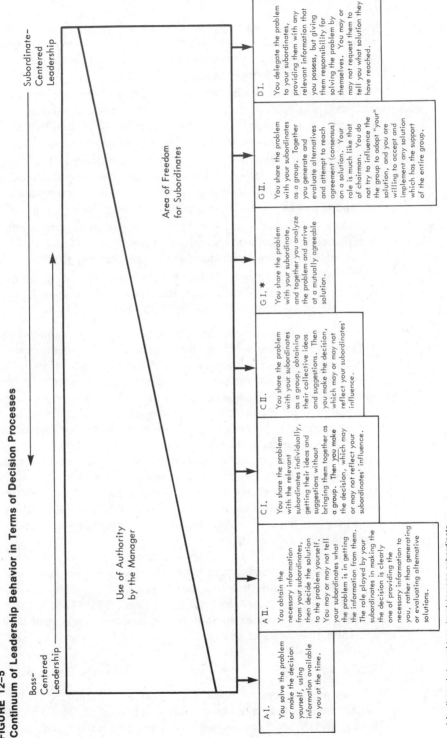

Boss–
Centered
Leadership

Subordinate–
Centered
Leadership

Use of Authority
by the Manager

Area of Freedom
for Subordinates

A I.

You solve the problem or make the decision yourself, using information available to you at the time.

A II.

You obtain the necessary information from your subordinates, then decide the solution to the problem yourself. You may or may not tell your subordinates what the problem is in getting the information from them. The role played by your subordinates in making the decision is clearly one of providing the necessary information to you, rather than generating or evaluating alternative solutions.

C I.

You share the problem with the relevant subordinates individually, getting their ideas and suggestions without bringing them together as a group. Then you make the decision, which may or may not reflect your subordinates' influence.

C II.

You share the problem with your subordinates as a group, obtaining their collective ideas and suggestions. Then you make the decision, which may or may not reflect your subordinates' influence.

G I. *

You share the problem with your subordinate, and together you analyze the problem and arrive at a mutually agreeable solution.

G II.

You share the problem with your subordinates as a group. Together you generate and evaluate alternatives and attempt to reach agreement (consensus) on a solution. Your role is much like that of chairman. You do not try to influence the the group to adopt "your" solution, and you are willing to accept and implement any solution which has the support of the entire group.

D I.

You delegate the problem to your subordinates, providing them with any relevant information that you possess, but giving them responsibility for solving the problem by themselves. You may or may not request them to tell you what solution they have reached.

* Applies only to problems involving one subordinate.
Source: Adapted from Tannenbaum and Schmidt (1958:96) and Vroom and Yetton (1973:13).

3. The unstructured problem rule: When the quality of the decision is important, if the leader lacks the necessary information or the expertise to solve the problem by himself, and if the problem is unstructured, AI, AII, and CI all are eliminated from the feasible set. (0.10)

4. The acceptance rule: If the acceptance of the decision by the subordinates is critical to its effective implementation, and if it is not certain that an autocratic decision made by the leader would receive that acceptance, AI and AII are eliminated from the feasible set. (0.12)

5. The conflict rule: If the acceptance of the decision is critical, and an autocratic decision is not certain to be accepted, and if subordinates are likely to be in conflict or disagreement over the appropriate solution, AI, AII, and CI are eliminated from the feasible set. (0.30)

6. The fairness rule: If the quality of the decision is unimportant and if acceptance is critical and not certain to result from an autocratic decision, AI, AII, CI, and CII are eliminated from the feasible set. (0.78)

7. The acceptance priority rule: If acceptance is critical, not assured by an autocratic decision, and if subordinates can be trusted, AI, AII, CI, and CII are eliminated from the feasible set. (0.50)

The superiority of the life cycle theory and the Vroom and Yetton normative model over most earlier treatments of leadership derives chiefly from the clarity with which they predicate the dynamic quality of the relationship among leader, group, and situation. But still, I am inclined to think of them as somewhat like the Venus de Milo: what is *there* is very good indeed.

What then is missing? As the series of pressures, social forces, and cultural crosscurrents have begun to ferment in the last generation, it has become increasingly difficult to motivate people in terms of the variables— leader, group, and situation. Unconscious motivations—drives, defenses, problems of identity, mastery, dependency, attitudes toward power—need to be taken into account. At the same time managers need to learn more about psychological man, they need to learn much more about themselves than they do; but as Drucker puts it, "most managers are action-focused rather than introspective."

Sensing these gaps in traditional modes of understanding human behavior in organizations, a number of people have tried to eliminate these problems. The major theorists who have tried are Elliot Jaques (1970), Abraham Zaleznik (1966), and Harry Levinson (1968; 1973). In the following section, however, we examine only one particular version of this general approach, transactional analysis.

TRANSACTIONAL ANALYSIS

In an introductory textbook, transactional analysis (TA) enjoys at least two advantages over alternative theories of psychological man. First, it is already widely used in business, industry, and government (certainly far more than the theories of Jaques, Zaleznick, and Levinson). Second, it is relatively easy to *apply* — that is, once the basic vocabulary is grasped. This section, which draws on Albano 1974, James 1975, and Meininger 1973, is essentially expository, that is, it attempts to explain TA as it applies to management in much the same manner as its proponents would. While this approach seems the most effective way of getting across these new ideas, the reader should be aware that what follows does not stand above criticism. And, if the reader adopts a critical attitude towards the material presented, so much the better.

The Vocabulary of TA

While the theoretical exposition of TA is complex, its application requires an esoteric vocabulary of only six words.

According to Eric Berne (1973), our psyche — that is, the totality of one's self or, in short, one's personality — is actually tripartic: exteropsyche, neopsyche, and archaeopsyche. Each psychic organ manifests itself as an *ego state:* exteropsychic (e.g., identificatory), neopsychic (e.g., data processing), and archaeopsychic (e.g., regressive). Fortunately, Berne provides us with colloquial expressions for these types of ego states: *parent, adult,* and *child.*

When people, including the administrator, feel and act as their parent once did, we say they are in their parent ego state. Let us be quite clear on this point: When someone is in a parent ego state, they will be acting just as their mother or father (or any other significant older person in their early life did). Not only will they speak as the parent did, they will also carry themselves as the parent did. In short, they are acting automatically on the basis of an old tape. But when people are thinking and acting rationally — gathering facts, estimating probabilities, and evaluating results — we say that they are in their adult ego state. And when people are feeling and acting as they did in childhood, we say that they are in their child ego state. Table 12–1 summarizes how each ego state contributes to behavior.

In using TA to deal with people, one should try to *recognize* which ego state they are in. Equally important, one should try to recognize his or her own ego state. Table 12–2 lists several indications for each of the three states.

What do these three ego states mean for the administrator? Ideally, an administrator should be able to shift from one ego state to another at will. But this is difficult. In the first place, many administrators are nearly frozen into their parent state, despite all their university degrees and administrative experience. The administrator who is the constant parent will treat employees as children and try to run everything.

Another common problem is contamination of adult thinking. The administrator believes he or she is thinking rationally but actually the feelings left over from childhood and prejudices absorbed from parents interfere in subtle, almost inperceptable ways. When one begins to express opinions on

TABLE 12-1
Ego States and Behavior

What the Parent Does	What the Adult Does	What the Child Does
Nurtures	Processes information	Invents
Criticizes	Takes objective action	Expresses curiosity
Restricts	Thinks, then acts	Acts on impulse
Judges	Organizes	Acts selfishly
Blames	Plans	Loves
Encourages	Solves Problems	Imagines—brainstorms
Supports	Estimates Risks	Acts belligerently
	Ferrets out assumptions	Complains
Source—the relationship between you and your parents	Source—the emergence of independent thinking in early life and its subsequent development	Source—the best and worst of your young self

Source: Albano (1974: 7).

TABLE 12-2
Recognizing Ego States

	Body Language	Expressions	Vocal Tone
Parent indicators	Looking down over rim of glasses; pointing an accusing finger; hands on hip, the head leaning or straining forward; patting on the back	"You should . . ."; "You ought. . . ."; "You must"; "Why don't you . . ." "Stay loose"; "Be cool"; "Don't tell me . . ."; "You disappoint me"; "You always . . ."; "Poor thing"; "I'll protect you"	Harsh; judgmental; soothing; indignant; commanding; comforting
Adult indicators	A straight, relaxed stance; slightly tilted head; appearance of active listening; regular eye contact; confident appearance	They offer alternatives and options; use of the 5 Ws in questioning; "Aha, I see"; "I see your point"; "I recognize . . ."; "How do you feel about . . ."	Relaxed; assertive; somewhat deliberative; self-assertive
Child indicators	Forlorn appearance; drooping shoulders; withdrawal; pursed lips; scowling; skipping; hugging; twinkle in eyes	"I want"; "I wish"; "Wow"; "I should"; "If only"; "Did I do okay?"; "One of these days"; "It's not fair"; "It's; not my fault"; "Oh, boy!"	Appealing; complaining; nagging; indignant; cheerful; protesting; grumbling; mumbling

Source: Albano (1974: 8).

how a program "should be" run and to speak on why women (or people of a different ethnic background or mode of dress) could not possibly be good managers, then transactional analysis suggests that the parent is contaminating the adult. On the other hand, when one begins to let feelings of inadequacy lead to overcomplying with rules; to let feelings of anger, to bullying; and of conceit, to meretricious behavior, then the analyses suggest that the child is doing the contaminating.

In addition to parent, adult, and child ego states, the vocabulary of TA attempts to identify certain repetive sets of social maneuvers. Such maneuvers are colloquially called *pastimes* and *games.* More complex operations are based on an elaborate unconscious life plan or *script.*

Pastimes, Games, and Scripts

As the name implies, pastimes are comfortable almost ritualistic ways in which people pass the time by talking to each other. Many transactions in a bureaucracy can be identified as pastimes. Some examples are "Why don't they" (change things around here), "Did you hear" (the latest gossip), "What became of" (good old Bill), and "Ever been" (to New York, L.A., Chicago). To the extent such games are judgmental and indignant, they are early parent-parent, that is, take place between two or more people in the parent ego state.

But pastimes are only preludes to games. In TA a game is defined as a sequence of transactions with a definite pattern. Two things in particular need to be noted about such games. First, the transactions have a surface meaning as well as a secret meaning. And, second, games always end with a *stroke,* which is a kind of payoff. Strokes can be either verbal or nonverbal; they can also be either positive (and produce good feelings) or negative (and produce bad feelings). According to TA, people throughout life play games to produce the strokes—positive *or* negative—that produce the feelings they have become accustomed to. These strokes give meaning to existence. Examples follow.

> In the game called Kick Me, the player attracts others who are willing to be critical and give a kick. For example, a secretary who asks her supervisor to sign an important rush letter with several typing errors is inviting a put-down. When the secretary hands the letter to the supervisor, her secret message is "Kick me for my carelessness." The supervisor responds, "It's got two errors, but it has to be in the mail now." This, however, is his only surface message. By his frown while reading, he delivers the kick.
>
> The game called NIGYSOB ("Now I've Got You, You S.O.B.") results in confirming the player's conviction that the other player is unreliable. In the following exchange (adapted from Meininger, 1973:81) notice how A sets up B so that he can entrap him.

A: "A very interesting thing happened. Someone said he left a message for me earlier this morning. Isn't that strange: No one told me about the message!"

B: "Was it Mr. C who left the message?"

A: "Yes, it was. How did you know?"

B: (Beginning to feel trapped): "Because I talked to him."

A: "Ah ha!" (Pausing triumphantly.) "Can't you even take a message without bungling it?" (Zap.) "Can't you even do that right?" (Zap, zap.)

Who receives this payoff? Is it positive or negative? (Remember: positive payoffs produce good feelings.)

A popular game in an office setting is Yes, But. It may be played as follows (adapted from Albano, 1975:26–27):

A: "I'd like you to do an article on training for the agency newsletter."

B: "I wish I could help you, but I'm awfully busy on this project."

A: "Mr. C told me you could put it aside."

B: "Yes, but if I did that I'd never meet the deadline."

A: "I'll get some temporary help for you."

B: "The last thing I need is those dumb temporary people who don't know which end is up."

A: "You can show them how you want things done."

B: "Yes, but if I do that I won't have any time to do your article."

Although the surface transaction in this example is adult-adult, at the secret level a parent-child transaction is in progress. A is coming on parent, trying to instruct B's stubborn child, which is replying, secretly, "Nothing you say is going to influence me."

Such games as these appear to be segments of larger, more complex sets of transactions called scripts. The idea of scripts, like the idea of strokes, is not unique to TA. Indeed, the notion that certain elements of a person's early life influence the way he acts in latter life is surely the message of such classics of behavioral science as *Psychopathology and Politics* by Harold Lasswell, a political scientist, and *Young Man Luther* by Erik Erickson, a psychologist.

In TA the critical element in early development of an individual are the transactions that originate with members of his immediate family. Later in life, he will attempt to select new people to immortalize in his life certain family members; hence, the many parent-child relationships in the world of administration.

An especially important element in an individual's development is early stroking experiences, for how one learns to get strokes influences his life script decisively. For example, a person raised on strokes for performing well (i.e., according to rules set by his parents) finds that the major interest in life is "doing a good job." Such a person is depressed by failure and, consequently, seeks out people to play achievement-oriented games (like

"Look How Good I'm Doing" or "I'm Staying Late"). In short, this person follows a performance-oriented script. On the other hand, a person who learned to get strokes when young, by stroking other people first, finds that the major interest is "being nice to people." This person follows an accommodation-oriented script.

Another useful way of looking at scripts is in terms of life positions. Of all the aspects of early childhood that influence our later lives, none is more significant than the child's conclusion about self and others, for that conclusion becomes the life position. In TA terms, there are four life positions (some of life themes suggested by James, 1975:139–40):

1. I'm OK, You're OK. A person with this life position is confident and gets along by being trustworthy. The life script might have themes such as "from one success to another," "acquiring friends not enemies," and "being responsible and fun."

2. I'm OK, You're not OK. This person has a haughty attitude and tends to belittle associates.

3. I'm not OK, You're OK. This person is depressed; themes include "never doing anything quite right," "always getting the short end of the stick," and "trying hard on the unimportant."

4. I'm not OK, You're not OK. This person tends to give up on people by not expecting anything positive—either from other people or from themselves. Life scripts include "giving up" and "missing the boat."

Motivation, Leadership, and TA

With some grasp of the basic vocabulary of TA, we take up its implication for motivating and leading people.

1. Effective administrators avoid games. Once they recognize a game—and it is impossible to avoid being caught up, from time to time, in one's own and other people's games—they attempt to stop it by not offering the expected payoff. For example, in the game Kick-Me, the obvious payoff is for the supervisor to put the employee down, but effective administrators simply refuse to do this. Actually, if an administrator continues to use the adult ego state, the employee might begin to feel uncomfortable in the child state and start transacting from the adult.

Of course one of the most effective ways to end a game is to recognize what is happening, describe it to your fellow players, and then express your desire to withdraw.

2. But the effective administrators do not always act from the adult ego state. Emerson was correct: "Nothing great was ever achieved without enthusiasm." Rather, they use the adult to filter, assemble and weight thoughts *before* acting. Action, then, can be from any ego state.

The importance of the adult in decision making cannot be overemphasized. Research on low-IQ students seems to indicate that some of their problem in thinking derives from personality. In particular, Benjamin Bloom and Lois Broder (cited in Whimbey 1976) have found that these students tend to engage in one-shot thinking. "Low-aptitude students seem mentally careless and superficial. They often rush through instructions or even skip them. They select wrong answers because they fail to comprehend what is required. When asked to reread the instructions more carefully, they frequently understand them and proceed correctly." In TA terms, we could say that their child, rather than their adult, controls.

3. Finally, the effective administrators recognize that different persons require different strokes. Recall the example from a moment ago of the employee who attempted to engage his supervisor in a Kick-Me game. The effective supervisor here would not only refuse the payoff but also attempt to see what deep need underlies the game playing. In this instance, it is likely that the employee really seeks recognition, attention. The supervisor might, therefore, attempt to swing the employee over to a cycle of positive strokes.

Similarly, the supervisor recognizes that hard-driving self-starters need to have their parent satisfied. Clearly established standards of sufficiency in work performance can reduce some of their (unnecessary) striving for perfection. Giving timely recognition for achievement also becomes important. In fact, in TA a prime test of good administrators (an OK boss) is that they can establish a system in which unconditional, positive strokes are given frequently (just because people are people) and jobs are designed to provide people with the opportunity for receiving conditional strokes for good performance. And they do not tell employers they did a good job when the job was trivially easy.

How does one deal with the child? On the positive side, an administrator might consider assigning a person in his ego state projects that offer an opportunity to express creativity (e.g., special report, membership on special task-force committee, or research on new operating producers). Yet, the administrator must also be able to counter the evasive strategy of an employee's child. For example, deliberately misinterpreting comments to evade the real issue. In such cases, the administrator should require the employee to repeat back his or her understanding until it is clear they understand.

In reprimanding, TA advocates separating the person from the act, that is, addressing the behavior involved not the personality or presumed attitude of the employee. This approach, notes Albano (1975:51), disarms the employer's child "by making it easier for him to focus on the behavior in question rather than brood on the threat to his self-esteem."

Further, TA dictates that the administrator be a good listener. Undivided attention helps to make employees feel they matter (the child says, "Gee, my supervisor really cares about my feelings); it also allows the employee to ventilate feelings (the parent says, "It was good that you told it like it is").

The greatest benefit of TA, some contend, comes when an administrator develops skill in actively helping subordinates identify where they are and becomes capable of helping them get where they would like to be. In effect, the administrator is helping employees rewrite their scripts, to become more aware of themselves, and to gain greater autonomy over their own lives.

ORGANIZATIONAL DEVELOPMENT

Like TA, the last of the three approaches to understanding human behavior, organizational development, deals with changing people in organizations. Only with this approach, the theme of change must be played fortissimo.

Government bureaucracies, it was argued in Chapter 7, grow old and stale; disciplined neither by profit nor by competition, they are particularly prone to the sclerotic process, which is epitomized in the following story (told by Morrison in Bright 1964:100). In the early days of World War II, the British army was forced to use some rather old artillery pieces. These guns, hitched to trucks, served as useful mobile units in the coast defense. In order to increase the rapidity of their fire, a time-motion expert was called in. Studying the slow motion pictures of the soldiers performing the loading, arming, and firing routines, he noticed something odd: a moment before the firing two crew members ceased all activity and came to attention for the duration of the discharge of the guns. Puzzled, the expert summed an old colonel of artillery. What did it mean? After reviewing the films, the colonel was finally able to say, "Ah, I have it. They are holding the horses."

This story, which I understand is true, suggests nicely how the solutions and management practices of today can be out of date tomorrow. And, to the extent we are more than ever before a society committed to change, the story's message is especially timely. As John Gardner observed in *Self-Renewal,* innovation within organizations should be viewed no longer as unique, shattering events but rather as necessary, continuing processes.

How do you develop this in a bureaucracy? The suggestion in Chapter 7 was essentially structural: To cope with rapidly altering circumstances, the pyramidal organization needs to be replaced by the organic model. The suggestion still stands, but now we want to add to it a careful consideration of the human problems involved in change. Our thesis, then, is this. A society committed to change requires adaptive public organizations. Such organizations, in turn, require not only certain modifications in their structure (as discussed in Chapters 7 and 8) but also careful attention to the attitudes of its members. The latter desideratum is the subject of the next three subsections.

Recognizing Resistance to Change

Professor Elting E. Morrison (ibid.:100–15) did an intriguing case study of the stubborn resistance of the American naval establishment at the turn of the century to an important innovation in gunnery that would improve firing accuracy by some 3,000 percent. In explaining this resistance, Morrison concluded that a primary source of conflict and tension was, in a word, identification:

> It cannot have escaped notice that some men identified themselves with their creations—sights, guns, gear, and so forth—and thus obtained a presumed satisfaction from the thing itself, a satisfaction that prevented them from thinking too closely on either the use or the defects of the thing; that others identified themselves with a settled way of life they had inherited or accepted with minor modification and thus found their satisfaction in attempting to maintain that way of life unchanged.

In other words, intuitively and quite correctly, these men felt that a change in a weapon portended a change in the arrangements of their society (i.e., their organization). Thus, a major factor in resistance to change is the fact that new situations—whether derived from a new project, technology, or otherwise—almost invariably bring with them a redistribution of power and influence.

Research also indicates that there are certain types of individuals who are particularly likely to resist change. These people rely heavily on their own personal experience ("mind-forg'd manacles," Blake called it) and have little propensity to take risks. And, as the Hawthorne study showed, people can have strong affinities for their work group. This desire to remain in the group can also result in resistance to a change.

Organizational Development

In response to such resistances, a process of planned, organization-wide change has appeared. This new approach to change in organization, which has been used in government considerably less than in business, lacks a clear definition. It sometimes goes by the name of "applied behavioral science," sometimes "planned change," and sometimes "organizational development" or OD. Essentially, what OD attempts to do is alter values, attitudes, and beliefs of a significant number of organizational members. Once the value structure has been revised, it is assumed by its proponents, structural modification will follow.

Although there is no simple formalized procedure for OD, a typical effort might include the following stages (Eddy, 1970):

1. A problem recognition stage in which the organization recognizes the fact that productivity is being hampered by ineffective interpersonal relations or other kinds of socially related variables, and calls in outside consultants or addresses its own members to exploring these problems.

2. A data-gathering stage in which interviews, observations, meeting-analysis techniques, or other approaches are utilized to pinpoint difficulties involved in the organization's operation and provide suggestions for reasons for these difficulties.

3. A data analysis and feedback stage in which members of management are brought together and involved in reviewing the findings, diagnosing problem areas, and planning strategies for improvement and change.

4. The intervention programs, which are designed to bring about desired changes, may include meetings (on-site or at retreats) at which organizational members are helped to participate in developing new programs or new approaches to existing situations.

5. The responsibility for helping the organization come to grips with change problems and to work its way through the difficulties encountered is often assigned to someone in a *change agent role.* This individual (who is either a member of the organization or an outside consultant) usually does not play the role of the expert advisor but uses clinical skills and knowledge to help facilitate the problem-solving process of the group.

6. Members of the organization collaboratively develop procedures, policies, and norms to reinforce and implement the new ways of operating developed in the previous change efforts.

7. Training is an important component of OD. Ongoing programs integrated into the change process are made available to employees. Training methods tend to be participatory and experience based. The laboratory approach of the National Training Laboratories (T-Groups or sensitivity training) is frequently used to help employees develop interpersonal competence and teamwork skills such as group problem solving and decision making.

The training component of OD is not without its critics. Harry Levinson (1973:160,162) in particular makes a couple of points worth noting, since (I suspect) they help explain the relatively lack of success of OD in the public sector. First, OD practices are more intuitive than systematic and focus too much on specific problems. They "concentrate largely on having people talk to each other about their mutual working interests and problems; on working together on the resolution of common problems; and on having people weigh, out loud and with each other, their organizational aspirations and goals."

Further, much OD "seems to hinge on one device, namely, confrontation, which, when it is the single technique for all problems, necessarily becomes merely a gimmick. With respect to organizational development, we are at that point in time comparable to the use of leeches in medicine. Just as they served the purpose of drawing bad blood, so the single technique in organizational development seems to be justified in terms of serving the purpose of drawing out bad feelings or emotions."

Beyond OD: A Case Study

If OD is not the panacea for the human problems involved in changing organizations, then what can the administrator do? Below we attempt to answer that question by examining a method used to revitalize the Department of State that seems applicable to many other types of organizations. (See ibid.: chapter 9.)

By the end of the 1960s reform of the State Department and its international career component the Foreign Service, was long overdue. For example, the largely academic-intellectual "diplomat" types who staffed the Foreign Service had a traditional aversion toward the management of operational programs (as contrasted with the making of policy). The new leadership, acting on a charge from the president to do something, called in Drs. Alfred Marrow and Harry Levinson.

Both psychologists spoke of the need to "open up" the department, to create a problem-solving atmosphere. Levinson felt that the crucial need was to create avenues through which the ego motivation of people of the department could quickly be turned into creative action; he therefore suggested that a series of task forces be established to study the department's problems. Significantly, these task forces would be made up of department personnel across all levels. What Levinson recognized was that top management could not by itself change internal arrangements; they needed the cooperation of those who would be closest to the changes. Recalls Levinson (ibid.:149), "My underlying assumption was that those on the inside knew their problems and probable solutions better than anyone else. Further, when significant numbers of people in the department were involved in self-criticism and adaptive change, a new attitude would be developed about the bureaucracy; namely, that it was a structure amenable to change by those who worked in it in order to serve its own and their need better."

Acting on this recommendation, the new deputy under secretary for administration appointed 13 task forces to address themselves to 13 specific topics (e.g., promotion policies, personnel training, recruitment, stimulation of creativity, reorganization of the Foreign Service Institute, and management tools). "It was clearly understood that this was an effort by the Foreign Service and not by the management of the department. The task force chairmen were chosen from the ablest and most experienced officers of the department." (Ibid.:150) Levinson frequently met with the skeptics and cynics to reassure them that the effort was a serious one and that there was a need to legitimize dissent and turn it to constructive ends.

In about five months, the task forces had completed their work. Now, the change process moved into its next phase. Extensive discussions were scheduled with personnel at all levels of management. Subsequently, task force draft reports were circulated. Finally, after employees had been given adequate time to review the draft reports, the chairmen of the task forces and members met with all levels of the organization to answer questions. The comments that arose from these consultations were carefully reviewed and many were incorporated into the final report. At last, the total report was ready for submission to the secretary of state. The implementation process consisted of assigning each recommendation to one of four categories: those approved for immediate implementation, those to be implemented within 90 days, those requiring further study, and those disapproved (a quite small category).

And what is the lesson? Simply this: behavioral science can revitalize organizations provided that the approach is well thought out, systematic (no one-shot talk session here) and that all layers of management are brought into the process.

To summarize a relatively long chapter is a difficult but necessary task. And, if summarize I must, perhaps the best place to begin is with the concept of motivation.

As I tried to make clear with the opening quotations from Studs Terkel's *Working,* motivation is a real problem and not something invented by tender-minded academicians. On that assumption, we proceeded to examine in some detail two milestones in the story of how behavioral science helped management get closer to the core of the motivation issue. These milestones were, of course, the Hawthorne studies and Maslow's hierarchy of needs. The remainder of the chapter was devoted to three of the more promising contemporary approaches to that core: life cycle theory of leadership, transactional analysis, and organizational development (in a somewhat modified form).

When pressed to nail their subject down to its quintessence, some economists have been known to reply, "TINSTAAFL" (There is no such thing as a free lunch). Can students of organizational behavior do the same? I know of no instances. But I think if I were so pressed, and free to let my bias come into play, I would look to leadership as the key to motivation. Now, by leadership I do not necessarily mean the kind of star quality recorded in the mass media, though it certainly has a measure of greatness in it. And, while I can not describe it in eight words I can come close by quoting the sixth century B.C. Chinese philosopher Lao-tzu: "Of a good leader . . . When his work is done . . . They will all say, 'We did this ourselves.'"

NAILING DOWN THE MAIN POINTS

1 Because of its profound influence on employer performance, motivation is a subject that no manager can afford to ignore. In this century, the behavioral sciences have helped to expand the manager's understanding of motivation. First, the Hawthorne studies revealed that organizational productivity was the result not only of physical condition or monetary rewards (as perhaps Frederick Taylor would have it) but also of interpersonal relationships developed on the job. In particular, the researchers

found that, when informal groups felt their own goals were in opposition to those of management and their control over their job or environment was slight, productivity remained low. In short, morale affects productivity.

2   In the early 1950s, Abraham Maslow suggested that human motives or needs formed a more complicated pattern than generally thought. Behavior of an individual is actually determined by his or her strongest need; that is, by the need in the following hierarchy that has not been, as yet, satisfied:

3   In the past, a popular approach to the study of leadership was to list traits. Unfortunately, this approach leaves little room for considering such important variables as the maturity of the followers and the nature of the situation.

Thus, the life-cycle theory of leadership tells us that as the maturity of one's followers continues to increase, appropriate leader behavior requires initially less structure (i.e., task behavior) but more socioemotional support (i.e., relationship behavior). Eventually, as the group approaches full maturity, the socioemotional support may be decreased, too. Similarly, Vroom and Yetton provide normative models for the analysis of situational requirements that can be translated into prescriptions of leadership styles.

4   Transactional analysis is especially effective in one-to-one relationships with subordinates. Among other things, it tells the managers to try to recognize ego states—not only in subordinates but also in themselves. Further, it tells them to recognize—and avoid—games. Finally, transactional analysis suggests some ways in which the manager helps to develop their subordinate's full potential (or, as Maslow might say, help them self-actualize).

5   Organizational development attempts to alter values, attitudes, and beliefs of a significant number of organizational members. Once the value structure has been revised, say its proponents, structural modifications will follow. Presumably, as the environment of public administration becomes more turbulent, the capacity for organizational change becomes more important.

CONCEPTS FOR REVIEW

motivating

Hawthorne studies

morale

hierarchy of needs

groupthink

primary and secondary needs

referent and expert power

leadership

situational leadership

trait approach to leadership

life-cycle theory of leadership

task behavior, relationship behavior

normative model (Vroom and
    Yetton)

transactional analysis

ego states

pastimes, games, and scripts

stroke

organizational development

stages of organizational
    development

change agent

PROBLEMS

1. "Most theories about human behavior in organizations say the same thing only with different language." Using only the ideas in this chapter, can you support this assertion?

2. Reread the excerpts from Terkel's *Working* found at the beginning of this chapter. Does transactional analysis offer you any insight on how a supervisor might motivate these individuals?

3. Energy can shift from one ego state to another, shown in the diagram below.

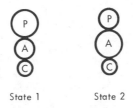

State 1   State 2

Recall some recent situations in which you have been. Try drawing ego-state diagrams for them. Draw one for what you perceive to be your management style. Draw one for a recent supervisor or instructor you have had.

4. Do you see any similarity between the life-cycle theory of leadership (Figure 12–4) and the child-parent relationship as the child matures.

5. What organizational problems could result if a supervisor had too rigid a performance script?

6. Think of specific ways in which a supervisor could motivate through the prestige needs of employees. Are they meaningful?

7. Do you find a connection between the ideas of Walter Kaufmann (in Chapter 4) and the concept of the adult ego state?

8. What generalizations can you make from Levinson's study of the State Department about organizational change?

9. Consider and discuss these points by Katz and Kahn (1966:390–91): "The major error in dealing with problems of organizational change, both at the practical and theoretical level, is to disregard the systemic properties of the organization and to confuse individual change with modifications in organizational variables." "With respect to the supersystem of the nation-state the same confusion of individual and system functioning is often apparent. It was conspicuous, for example, in the objections to changing Negro-white relations by law. A common point of view was that individuals would have to change their attitudes and habits first. The fallacy in this position has been demonstrated by the revolution created by changes at the top of the legal structure, specifically the Supreme Court decision of 1954" . . . "Yet we persist in attempting to change organizations by working on individuals without redefining their roles in the system, without changing the sanctions of the system, and without changing the expectations of other role incumbents in the organization about appropriate role behavior."

10. In terms of Maslow's hierarchy, what motivates you? How would you determine what motivates employees?

11. John Gardner says that when people even in a democratic organization develop sacrosanct rights, the organization itself rigidifies. Indeed, the more democratic an organization is, the more the vested interests of its members will be reflected in its policies. Thus a democratic organization may be especially resistant to change. Do you agree with this analysis? Can you think of any examples that either prove or disprove it?

12. Though rarely discussed in the management literature, protection might be considered a part of good leadership. In other words, it is expected that those who have leadership power will be protective in varying ways. Discuss.

13. Katz and Kahn (1967:302) consider the essence of organizational leadership to be the "influential increment over and above mechanical compliance with the routine directives of the organization." Despite the fact that all supervisors at a given level in the hierarchy are created equally, they do not remain equal. Why? In thinking through this question, French and Raven's (1968) five types of power might prove useful.

INTRODUCTION

Regardless of the particular leadership style, the administrator can and should turn to others for help with certain people related activities. What kind of help might this be?

Some managerial concerns, which might require expert assistance, are basic. For example, the work to be performed in the organization must be broken down into jobs; each job in turn should have a clear description of the work it entails. At the same time, a plan must be developed to assure equal pay for equal work, that is, the compensation scale should be based on the skills required by the job. These two areas of concern, position classification *and* compensation, *provide the basis for effective* recruitment.

Recruitment, or staffing, is the process of matching individual skills and aptitudes with job specifications. It is another area of managerial concern in which help might be desirable. Too often administrators agonize over termination decisions when a wiser investment of time would have been in the selection decision. Closely associated with the staffing concern are the procedures used to recognize accomplishment and to use individual abilities to greatest advantage. In particular, the public executive frequently needs assistance in such critical areas as examination, performance evaluation, and promotion.

For help in the never-ending task of motivating employees, the administrator might turn to others for help with training and counseling. Similarly, in those difficult cases of individual suspension and dismissal, the prudent administrator might seek assistance.

The foregoing concerns—classification and compensation, staffing, training, and separation—

13

Public Personnel Management: Traditional Concerns

are the traditional concerns of public personnel management. They form the body of this chapter.

But to these traditional concerns we must add a second cluster, which can be called the "new concerns" of public personnel management. One of the better publicized of these concerns is affirmative action, that is, increasing the employment opportunities of minorities and women.

Another important concern to emerge in the last decade is job redesign. By creating work situations where the employee is more productive and content to be so, the sometimes elusive problem of the last chapter—motivation —can be solved. Some management authorities even argue that it is not human nature but the structure of the job that determines how people will act.

In addition to equal employment opportunity and job redesign, we might also include among the newer concerns of the personnel function participative management (i.e., sharing power and decision making with lower levels of the organizational hierarchy) and management development (i.e., providing the managers with the skills that they might need for future, and more important, duties). Some scholars would—correctly I think—also include among the newer concerns several of the techniques discussed in Chapter 12 as well as the productivity improvement efforts discussed in Chapter 8. Not surprisingly, these newer concerns of public personnel management frequently require full-time attention.

We shall examine these newer concerns in Chapter 14. There too we shall examine labor relations. While labor relations is not, strictly speaking, a new concern in public personnel management, it has undergone in recent years profound quantitative and qualitative changes. Indeed, the task of handling relations with employee organizations and unions has in some instances become so intricate, so pervasive that it requires full-time experts. To call this task "traditional" seems a worse assault on English than to call it a "new concern."

IMPORTANCE OF THE PERSONNEL FUNCTION

Government on the Move

The importance of the "people" factor in government cannot be overestimated. Today more than one out of every six Americans work for a government either at the federal, state, or local level. And about one out of every eight in the total labor force is a state or local government employee. State and local employment has tripled to more than 12 million since 1955, while federal employment has risen modestly to 2.8 million from 2.4 million. Salary costs (not counting fringe benefits) came to almost half of every state and local dollar spent. Thus, the way federal, state, and local administrators recruit, select, and develop their employees will be crucial to the quality of government and the effective use of the tax dollars.

This point has not been lost on the federal government. And the most clear cut evidence is the passage of three significant new federal laws.

First was the Intergovernmental Personnel Act of 1970 (IPA). It provides principles for personnel systems, which will contribute to improved public services. These principles include hiring and promoting on the basis of relative ability, providing equitable compensation, retraining employees on the basis of performance, providing training, assuring equal opportunity in all aspects of personnel administration, and protecting against political coercion.

The major features of the act are: grants for personnel administration improvement and training, technical assistance in personnel management, advice on maintaining merit standards, temporary intergovernmental assignments, admission to federal training, and cooperative recruiting and examining. All of these are designed to foster a closer working relationship and sharing among governments.

A second law with an important impact on government personnel management was the Emergency Employment Act of 1971. Thousands of state and local government agencies participated in the public employment program under that act to provide employment to meet unfilled needs for public services. The act required jurisdictions receiving funds to analyze job descriptions and skill requirements. They also had to assure that their public employment programs would contribute to the elimination of artificial barriers to employment and occupational advancement.

Shortly after implementation of the public employment program, the U.S. Civil Service Commission issued "Guidelines for Reevaluation of Employment Requirements and Practices Pursuant to the Emergency Employment Act." In addition, through a cooperative agreement with the Department of Labor, the commission has provided direct, onsite technical assistance to participating jurisdictions on all aspects of personnel administration. The commission provided its technical assistance in a manner consistent with the Intergovernmental Personnel Act because it provides a statement of fundamental principles for sound public personnel systems, encourages innovation, and provides for diversity in the design and administration of personnel systems to meet the needs of the particular jurisdiction.

During the past year, the commission made over 3,000 contracts with more than 3,800 state and local jurisdictions. Field personnel noted over 7,000 personnel systems changes — completed, in process, or under consideration.

The third law is the Comprehensive Employment and Training Act of 1973. The act requires participating jurisdictions that implement public service employment provisions to:

eliminate artificial barriers to employment and occupational advancement, including civil service requirements, which restrict employment opportunities for the disadvantaged; and

undertake analysis of job descriptions and reevaluations and, where shown necessary, revisions of qualification requirements at all levels of employment, including civil service requirements and practices relating thereto, with a view toward removing artificial barriers.

While government shows its increasing concern for the "people" factor in management through laws such as these, business and industry has demonstrated perhaps an even greater concern. The rationale behind this concern was stated well by Ted Mills (1975:121), a former television executive and now director of the nonprofit National Quality of Work Center in Washington, "As capital grows scarcer, managements across the country may have begun to suspect that the potential extent of human contribution to output (as distinct from capital contribution) could and should be far more fully understood and developed than it has traditionally been in more affluent times. The classic business cliché that any worker will be productive if you put enough capital behind him suddenly seems to be undergoing a sea change. And almost all of this has happened within the present decade."

The Concept of Human Resources

But what should one call this crazy quilt of people related concerns? In most governments today, this emerging field still hides behind the old, comfortable office doors of "personnel," "employee services," or "training and development." In too many cases, these offices were never conceived or organized to become involved in the range of concerns outlined above.

Although in this chapter we use the term public "personnel management," the term that more accurately portrays these basic concerns as a single field of study is *human resources development* (HRD). Mills (ibid.) again: "One discerning, if homiletic, definition of it by an auto parts worker proudly involved in a Tennessee experimental project in this field was simply 'the people part of getting the work out right again' (with the emphasis on the "again"); the Swiss playwrite, Max Frisch, may have synthesized its concerns eloquently when he wrote that 'we sought workers, and human beings came instead.'"

But why refer to human beings as *resources?* Because to make employees achieve, the manager needs to look upon them not as a problem, a cost, or an enemy but as a resource. Human resources development can provide a high potential rate of return on a relatively low cost, low investment of resources. In this sense, it is simply sound management. Its proponents suggests that serious public executives are turning more and more to HRD, not so much for remedial action against various troubling socioeconomic disorders, but rather for action toward better management of a conspicuously underdeveloped resource: its people. Such is this and the next chapters' approach to public personnel management.

In the sections that follow, we take a closer look at how an effective public personnel system can help the manager develop human resources. To set the stage for that look, we must begin by clarifying what we mean by public personnel systems.

PUBLIC PERSONNEL SYSTEMS

Framing a satisfactory typology of personnel systems is, as Frederick C. Mosher (1968:135–175) correctly notes, a challenge. "American governments have displayed almost unlimited ingenuity in developing different kind of arrangements for the employment of personal services, ranging from compulsion (selective service) to volunteers (Peace Corps, Vista, etc.) and without compensation (WOC), with a great variety of categories in between." Nevertheless, for purposes of description, analysis, and comparison, Mosher is able to classify the public service into four main types of personnel systems: (1) political appointees, (2) general civil service, (3) career systems, and (4) collective system. But he warns us: the boundaries around each are not clear-cut and, as we shall see presently, they are moving.

1. The political appointees are those public officials appointed to an office without tenure, who have policy-making powers and are outside the civil service system. When Carter took office in 1977, approximately 2,200 jobs outside the civil service system were potentially available for him to fill. These jobs ranged from cabinet officials to confidential secretaries. Judicial positions are not included as part of this calculation.

Appointive positions that fall outside both the civil service system and professional career systems (the two are discussed below) are classified as "schedule A, B, C," or "noncareer executive." Some of these positions are highly political.

Schedule A positions are those for which examinations are impractical. Approximately 1,300 such appointive jobs are available, most of which are filled by various types of attorneys. Schedule B employees are appointed after a noncompetitive examination to highly specialized positions. For example, tax specialists for Treasury Department positions are given such examinations in order to determine their qualification. Schedule C posts are of a policy-making or confidential character, such as upper ranking staff assistants or secretaries to policy-making officials.

At the state and local level, civil service law and practice vary so widely that generalization is hazardous; but, as Mosher (ibid.:166) notes, "it is safe to assume that most of the larger governments in industrialized areas have political executives in approximately parallel capacities and roles. Some have a great many more proportionately than the federal government; some have many fewer."

Mosher suggests that the political executives may be the crucial element in the maintenance and democratic control over an increasingly professional and career oriented public service. Nevertheless, recent trends in the type of person tapped for political appointments might undermine the effectiveness of this control. In particular, as Mosher himself points out, more emphasis is put on intellect than political experience, more reliance is placed on prior experience in government. In short, appointees are becoming increasingly professional in their backgrounds and orientations.

2. The *general civil service* system is, in the federal government, composed of white collar personnel, mostly nonprofessional, who have tenure. Their employment is administered in accordance with traditional civil service practices.

That tradition is easily traced back to the 1870s, when the obvious abuses of the *spoils system* (i.e., the right of elected officials to reward their friends and supporters with government jobs) had produced demands for reform that could not be ignored. By 1883, the first civil service law, the *Pendleton Act,* passed. This legislation, also known as the Civil Service Reform Act, established the bipartisan Civil Service Commission to choose the federal employees from lists of those who had passed competitive examinations (the so-called *merit system*).

The examinations under the civil service system are practical rather than scholarly. Each available position is described in detail and the examinations are geared to the needs of each. After passing a written test, the candidate might take an oral examination if the job warrants it. If successful with both, the person's name is placed on an eligibility list, which is set up on the basis of examination scores. Federal law requires that the agency choose from among the top three to five scores on the list, without passing over veterans. In many merit systems there are further job requirements, such as height and weight requirements for policemen, high school or college graduation for particular occupations, and certifications or licenses for many civil service positions, such as those for the position of attorney or physician. Such requirements, however, must be clearly job related.

Merit systems can be organized many ways. The arrangement adopted and where it fits into the framework of government will depend on such factors as the size of a jurisdiction, the authority of the chief executive, the political tradition and climate, and the influence of citizen and employee groups. In many jurisdictions, a nonpartisan or bipartisan commission or board is charged with general program direction and appellate functions, leaving to a personnel director (appointed by the board or the chief executive) the responsibility for day-to-day program administration. In others, a personnel director reporting to the chief executive is responsible for general program direction, with a civil service commission or board serving in a watchdog, advisory, or appellate role (or all three.) All kinds of variations on these arrangements are possible.

The central personnel agency for the federal government is the Civil Service Commission (CSC), composed of three members, not more than two of whom could be members of the same political party. They serve for overlapping terms of six years. The president designates the chairman and a vice-chairman, who serves as chairman in the former's absence. The chairman has administrative powers in his own right and acts as the executive head of the agency. Most state and local systems have similar—though more independent—agencies. The reaction to the commission, as we shall see shortly, has been mixed.

In recent years the actual operating activities of the commission—recruiting and classifying—have been performed on a decentralized basis by the line agencies themselves and by components of the commission in the field. Hence the CSC serves chiefly as kind of advisor to the agencies that administer their own programs according to general guidelines set down by the commission.

For example, the Program Planning Division of the Bureau of Programs and Standards acts as a broker for ideas on the improvement of personnel administration. The division attempts to stimulate progressive thinking throughout the service. Similarly, the Bureau of Inspections and Classification Audits sends out inspection teams from the commission's regional offices to provide liaison between the commission and the agencies and to advise the agencies how to improve their operations. Critics maintain that these audits have at times been rather lenient.

Although 33 states have also adopted comprehensive merit systems and, at the local level, about 75 percent of the employees are hired on a merit system, the system is under heavy attack. Ironically, the attack is being mounted in the name of good government (Laing, 1975):

> Chicago and Minnesota have abolished their civil service boards and switched such functions as hiring, firing, and promotions back to elected officials.

> About 100 other state, county, and local governments, while not abandoning the system, have overhauled it extensively. Many, for example, have replaced written hiring and promotion tests—the bedrock of the merit system—with more general selection standards (e.g., job experience and educational qualifications).

> The National Civil Service League, which had played a key role in the adoption of the civil service concept, officially renounced the system in in 1970. The league now recommends that personnel functions be vested in the executive branch of government and that civil service commissions be relegated to a minor watchdog role. Says the former director of the league, Jean Couturier (cited in ibid.): "The gut issues today . . . are the productivity and efficiency of government and not patronage. On those scores, civil service has obviously failed." Later in the chapter, we shall take a closer look at some of the reasons for this "failure."

3. Government jobs outside the civil service system are not necessarily appointive, for many agencies have developed their own *career systems.*

These systems are composed of white-collar personnel, generally professionals and paraprofessionals, who are tenured in the agency and occupation though not in the position. Their employment is administered as a progressive, preferably planned development. In such a system, repeated failure to attain promotion—being "passed over" too many times—can result in dismissal; hence, the expression "up or out."

The model of the career system is that of military officers. In fact, the military system has been copied in or adapted to a number of other federal activities—for example, the Foreign Service, the Public Health Service, the Federal Bureau of Investigation, the Central Intelligence Agency, and the Tennessee Valley Authority. In varying degrees, it has also been a model for state and local police systems and local fire departments.

Unlike the civil service system, a career system emphasizes the individual rather than the position. Thus, as Mosher points out, a "nonprofessional civil servant working in the Department of the Navy is most likely to respond, 'I work for the Navy Department'; an officer, 'I am an officer (or an admiral or captain) in the navy.'"

Career systems possess several challenges to the manager. For example, members of a career personnel system, such as the naval officer in the preceding paragraph, must work with other personnel within the organization who lack comparable career status. Obviously, when personnel are working together on the same project but under two distinct systems of employment, the possibility of friction is great. This is especially true when (a) one system claims a near monopoly of the top jobs and determines agency policy; or (b) "the personnel under the two different systems have comparable *levels* of education and experience but in different fields and bring to bear different orientations on the same problems and different views of organizational purpose" (Mosher 1968:150–51).

4. The *collective system* is composed of blue collar workers whose employment is governed primarily through bargaining between union or association and governmental jurisdiction. This system is discussed in the first section of Chapter 14.

One final word. As noted earlier, Mosher sees the boundaries between these four personnel systems moving. For example, as labor organization accelerates among white-collar workers, general service and career systems begin to show characteristics of the collective system. On the other hand, as high level occupational specialties develop standards, coalesce, and become recognized, the general service system looks more like a career system.

TRADITIONAL PERSONNEL CONCERNS

Classification and Compensation

At all levels of government, the basis of the civil service is the *position classification system.* Simply stated, position classification involves identifying the duties and responsibilities of each position in an organization and then grouping the positions according to their similarities. A good system can help the administrator make better decisions regarding the relationship of duties and responsibilities to the other concerns of personnel administration. After all, a fair compensation plan does require an understanding of the duties and responsibilities of each position ("equal pay for equal work"); effective examination and recruiting do require knowledge of what the agency is examining and recruiting for; and determining the qualifications necessary for performing the job does require an understanding of what the job entails.

Though position classification evolved as a convenient and useful tool, today the concept is frequently under attack. First, the procedures for classification can be a paperwork maze in which job incumbents have considerable influence, though they often view the process with trepidation. See Figure 13–1 for a typical questionnaire distributed to all employees to determine their duties. Observes Arch Patton (1974a:34), chairman of the recent Presidential Commission on Executive, Legislative, and Judicial Salaries: "For all practical purposes, the technicians evaluate the jobs in the government system, and the line or functional management must accept their judgments. Industry reverses the process. The line or functional managers — who certainly know the jobs best — evaluate the various positions and tell the technicians in personnel where they should be valued in the structure."

While evaluating the difficulty of duties may not cause too many problems, evaluating and comparing *responsibilities* often does. How many subordinates are supervised? How much time is spent in actual supervision? Who is supervised? How much innovation is expected? To attempt to weigh these factors objectively is no easy task.

In the federal service, authority for classifying positions rests primarily with the individual agencies, although the Civil Service Commission may audit the classifications before they become effective and it is required to review existing classifications on a recurring basis. At state and local levels, the usual arrangement is to have a central personnel office responsible for classification as well as review of its implementation. This central office review can help to reduce at least one abuse in agency (overclassification).

Some attack position classification as being obsolete. Although it once provided a way of treating people equitably and eliminating spoils, position classification is not always relevant to activities performed by the more sophisticated organizations discussed at the end of Chapter 7. In such organizations, the work situation becomes too collegial, too free-form for rigid position classifications. In such an organization, position classification (or rank-in-job approach) might be replaced with the *rank-in-person-approach,* which uses the abilities and experience of the individual as the basis for making various personnel decisions (e.g., setting of compensation). Examples of this kind of system include the military and college faculties. The rank-in-person concept, therefore, means that a person carries a rank regardless of the duties performed at a particular time.

FIGURE 13-1

POSITION CLASSIFICATION

QUESTIONNAIRE

| 1. Mr.   Last Name   First   Middle Initial | 4. Commission, Board, or Department |

2. Official Title of Position

5. Division or Institution

Usual Working Title of Position

6. Section or Other Unit of Division or Institution

3. Regular Schedule of Hours
   of Work

7. Place of Work or Headquarters

	From	To	Total Hrs. per Wk. _____
Mon.	_____	_____	Explain rotation of shifts if any:
Tues.	_____	_____	
Wed.	_____	_____	
Thurs.	_____	_____	
Fri.	_____	_____	
Sat.	_____	_____	Hrs. of "On-Call" Time
Sun.	_____	_____	per Wk. _____

Length of Lunch Period _____

8. Is your work ☐ Full-Time? ☐ Part-Time? ☐ Year-round?

☐ Seasonal? ☐ Temporary?

If work is *seasonal, temporary, or part-time*, indicate part of

year or proportion of full-time: _____

9. Do you receive any maintenance (room, meals, laundry, etc.) in

addition to your cash salary? ☐ Yes ☐ No

10. Describe below in detail the work you do. Use your own words, and make your description so clear that persons unfamiliar with your work can understand exactly what you do. Attach additional sheets if necessary.

TIME	WORK PERFORMED	LEAVE BLANK

11. Name and Title of Your Immediate Supervisor:

12. Give the names and payroll titles of employees you supervise, if five or fewer. If you supervise more than five employees, give the number under each title. If you supervise no employees, write "none."

13. Machines or equipment used regularly in your work. Give per cent of time spent in operation of each:

	%		%
	%		%
	%		%

Source: Texas Municipal League (1975).

FIGURE 13-1 (*continued*)

14. What are the nature and extent of instruction you receive regarding your work?

15. What are nature and extent of the check or review of your work?

16. Describe your contacts with departments other than your own, with outside organizations, and with the general public.

CERTIFICATION: I certify that the above answers are my own and are accurate and complete.

Date_____   Employee's Signature_____

STATEMENT OF IMMEDIATE SUPERVISOR

17. Comment on statements of employee. Indicate any exceptions or additions.

18. What do you consider the most important duties of this position?

19. Does this position involve typing?

☐ No

☐ Yes—Give % of time spent in typing _____ %

20. Does this position involve shorthand?

☐ No

☐ Yes—Give % of time spent in typing _____ %

21. Indicate the qualifications which you think should be required in filling a future vacancy in this position. Keep the position itself in mind rather than the qualifications of the individual who now occupies it.

	Basic Qualifications	Additional Desirable Qualifications
Education, general:		
Education, special or professional:		
Experience, length in years and kind:		
Licenses, certificates, or registration:		
Special knowledges, abilities, and skills:		
Age, sex, physical requirements, or other factors:		

Date_____   Immediate Supervisor's Signature_____

STATEMENT OF DEPARTMENT HEAD OR OTHER ADMINISTRATIVE OFFICER

22. Comment on the above statements of the employee and the supervisor. Indicate any inaccuracies or statement with which you disagree.

Please comment on the qualifications suggested by the supervisor _____

Date_____   Department Head's Signature_____

Further, position classification plans are difficult to keep current. Yet to be an effective management tool, job classification must be as dynamic as the many systems it supports. The responsibility for keeping a classification plan up-to-date is usually assigned to the personnel director of the jurisdiction. This responsibility will include reviewing and making or recommending necessary policy or technical adjustments in the plan. Information collected through job analysis is useful in developing and keeping the plan current. The classification of each position under the plan should be reviewed regularly to ensure its continued accuracy.

Like position classification, compensation of public employees is a very important and often a very controversial part of public personnel administration. Based on our discussion of motivation in the preceding chapter, the importance to the employee of an adequate and equitable compensation schedule should be apparent. If the employee perceives that the plan is unfair, conflict is likely.

But how does one establish a good pay plan? The general rule is this: Pay according to differences in levels of duties and responsibilities. To develop an appreciation for the variety of elements that must be taken into consideration, we shall consider the provocative arguments Arch Patton levels against the federal pay system. Many of his generalizations apply with equal force to state and local systems. (The following discussion draws from Patton 1974a–e.)

To Mr. Patton the most impressive thing about the federal pay system is not its size, although it has 2.7 million nonmilitary employees and a $33 billion payroll; not its growth, although the federal payroll has expanded three times faster than the gross national product in the past decade; not even its complexity, although it has "developed administrative rituals that are quite different from anything to be found in industry." Rather, what is most remarkable, in his view, is the enormous difficulty a student finds in developing evidence to prove or disapprove the effectiveness of the system.

Any assessment of the federal pay system should perhaps start with a description of the government's five major salary structures, the executive structure and the general schedule (the civil service structure). The former includes all members of the executive branch subject to presidential appointment, Supreme Court judges and members of both houses of Congress. The executive structure is therefore the apex of the federal pyramid. A sampling of the position in each of its five "levels" and the 1974 salary paid is as follows.

Level I: $60,000
  Cabinet Secretaries/Supreme Court justices
Level II: $42,500
  Representatives/Major agency heads; e.g., Veterans Administration, Comptroller General/Judges, circuit and claims courts
Level III: $40,000
  Under Secretaries; e.g., Labor, Commerce/Assistant Comptroller General/Judges, district and customs courts

Level IV: $38,000
   Assistant Secretaries; e.g., Air Force, Agriculture, Interior/Capitol Architect/
   Librarian of Congress
Level V: $36,000
   Heads of minor agencies; e.g., Panama Canal, Renegotiation Board, Indian
   Claims Board/Deputies of Capitol Architect and Librarian of Congress

As this tabulation clearly shows, the pay differentials from Level II through Level V average less than 6 percent and the number two person in the typical government organization stands only one level below his boss. Writes Patton, "Both conditions would be motivationally disastrous in most industry situations. Who would want the vastly greater responsibility of the top job if he were only paid a 6 percent premium for the greater responsibility and risk?" Moreover, the structure violates one of the cardinal principles of compensation, namely, equal pay for equal work. All cabinet officials for example, are paid the same, but some have substantially greater responsibility than others. The story is told that after Nixon "promoted" George Schultz from Secretary of Labor (at $60,000) to Director of the Office of Management and Budget (at $42,500), Mrs. Schultz commented, "One more promotion like this, George, and we'll have to borrow money to live."

Inflation itself adds another problem. By law, no salary in the general schedule may exceed the lowest salary in the executive structure. Since the executive structure tends to change slowly, by 1974 the top GS grades— 18, 17, and most of those in 16—were paid $36,000, which was of course the lowest level in the executive structure. Writes Patton, "Even today, three to four echelons of executives reporting one to the other are paid the same. Three years hence, if the ceiling is not removed, five reporting levels, all paid $36,000, are likely to be fairly common. This would, of course, be a motivational nightmare."

And yet, with all these problems, the executive schedule is, in comparison with the general schedule, the soul of simplicity. To begin with, the GS structure has 18 grades—ranging from the unskilled messengers in Grade I and moving up to executives in Grade 18, who may supervise thousands of subordinates and spend billions of dollars annually (on military hardware, for example). But the structure contains really two structures. First are ten clerical grades: GS 1 through GS 10. Second, and partially interspersed, are 11 professional grades: GS 5, 7, 9, 11, 12, 13, 14, 16, 17, and 18.

According to Patton, writing in 1974, this dual structure is unique because as the job responsibilities increase, the pay differentials decrease. For example, a promotion from GS 11 to GS 12 brings a 19.2% pay increase, while a promotion from GS 16 to GS 17 brings only a 15.7% increase. Today, the differences between the top levels are even less. But does it make any difference? Yes, if we are concerned with motivation. Because promotion is so much more rapid in the lower grades, it would appear that a smaller differential between grades would provide adequate financial motivation.

In developing a pay schedule such as the general schedule, positions are assigned to particular salary ranges. Within each salary range are usually several steps so that an employee in one range may move through a number of steps before reaching the top pay of the range. Each grade in the general schedule, except GS 16, 17, and 18, has 10 steps. Theoretically, these steps are for two purposes: for rewarding performance and for continuing to work for the government. In practice, however, reward for performance is rare— less than 4 percent of the civil service employees receive such merit increases each year (and less than 1 percent had pay increases withheld for inadequate performance!). The step rate appears to reward getting older, not how well a job is done.

In recent years, government at all levels has become increasingly aware of public employee compensation relative to the private sector. Today pay comparability studies are commonplace. The purpose of such studies is to determine what pay level is appropriate for a particular skill (lawyer, chemist, engineer) in a given region. Despite the plethora of comparability studies, Patton argues that government salaries are out of line with the pay patterns of private industry. In particular, government tends to pay "too much at the lower level and middle level where the majority of its 2.7 million nonmilitary employees are found." In contrast, at the top, government salaries are well below what private industry pays for jobs involving comparable responsibility for decision making (see Figure 13–2). "The most important reason some industries compensate executives well above the average is that the quality of executive decisions is what makes profit in that business."

Fringe benefits are considered part of the total compensation package.

FIGURE 13–2
What Top Executives under 40 Can Expect to Earn in the Private Sector

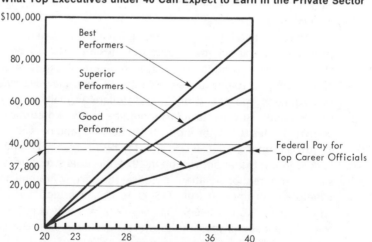

Source: Data, Korn/Ferry *International, based on salaries of candidates placed.* Chart 64, adapted from the October 6, 1975, issue of *Business Week* by special permission. © 1975 by McGraw-Hill, Inc.

Legislation or civil service rules will usually spell out provisions on vacations, paid holidays, sick leave, education leave, time off for military service, jury duty, retirement, group health insurance, group life insurance, disability benefits, unemployment compensation, relocation expenses, etc.

How do these fringe benefits compare with those offered employees by private industry? A Bureau of Labor Statistics survey of fringe-benefit costs reports that the government spends 10 percent of its payrolls on civil service retirement annuity plan, while industry pay 9.5 percent of the payroll into retirement plans. But pensions are but one fringe benefit; other benefit costs as a percent of payroll are as follows:

	Federal	Industry
Vacations	8.1%	5.3%
Holidays	2.9	3.2
Personal leave	0.6	0.3
Sick leave	3.3	1.1
Health, life, accident insurance	1.8	4.4
Totals	16.7%	14.3%

Staffing

The term staffing refers to the process of recruiting, selecting, and advancing employees on the basis of their relative ability, knowledge, and skill.

Merit recruiting means more than just posting an examination announcement on a bulletin board. Every possible source of qualified candidates within the appropriate labor market must be reached in a positive way. The U.S. Civil Service Commission (1974) suggests that a program of positive recruitment include elements such as the following:

Writing examination announcements in clear, understandable language.

Advertising in publications that circulate to the various segments of the population, and using other media such as radio and television.

Establishing easily reachable job information centers.

Visiting colleges, high schools, and community organizations.

Using mobile or storefront recruiting centers.

Developing continuing contacts with minority and women's organizations.

Selection on the basis of "relative ability" presumes being able to draw distinctions among the qualifications of competing candidates fairly and objectively. Recent court decisions have made it clear that all selection tools must be valid and job-related. In other words, performance on a test had to match performance on the job.

On March 8, 1971, the Supreme Court ruled in *Griggs* v. *Duke Power Co.* that psychological tests given to job applicants had to be job-related. "What Congress has commanded," ruled Chief Justice Warren Burger in what many lawyers consider his finest opinion to date, "is that any tests used must measure the person for the job and not the person in the abstract."

The particulars of the case vividly illustrate this point. Prior to the date the Civil Rights Act of 1964 went into effect, Duke Power Company openly discriminated against blacks. After July 2, 1965, any black employee could become a coal handler provided he had a high school diploma and passed the Wonderlic Personnel Test and the Bennett Mechanical Comprehension Test. Not surprisingly, the company's lawyers were hard pressed to prove what these two tests or a high school diploma had to do with measuring how well a person could shovel coal. The Supreme Court voted eight to zero that the screening devices were illegal. As we shall see in the next chapter, this greater emphasis on evaluating the relevance of entry requirements has lead to a greater opening up of opportunity in the public service to all groups — and, in particular, minorities and women.

Employers have, of course, other methods besides written tests to evaluate candidates for initial employment or advancement: performance tests, panel interviews, ratings of relevant training, and experience, or any combination of these with each other or with written tests. For most jobs, a combination of job-related testing devices, rather than any single one, provides a better measure of the knowledges, skills, and abilities needed for successful job performance.

David McClelland (1973) proposes testing for competence rather than intelligence. He attacked the circular reasoning that links psychological tests to our credential happy society. The basic problem with many proficiency measures for validating ability tests is that they depend heavily on the credentials — the habits, values, accent, interests, etc. — that the man brings to the job and that make him acceptable to management and to clients. Employers have a right to select bond salesmen who have gone to the right schools because they do better, but psychologists do not have a right to argue that it is their (white bond salesmen's) intelligence that makes them more proficient in their jobs.

McClelland is also interested in getting away from multiple-choice tests. A. N. Whitehead once wrote that these tests require only one level of mental activity beyond being awake: recognition. In any event, according to McClelland, sorting out the trivial from the absurd is hardly a good way for a person to prove his capabilities. McClelland therefore wants tests that measure, for example, capacity to learn.

Peter Koening (1974) tells about a screening program McClelland set up for the U.S. Information Agency that used the PONS (Profile of Nonverbal Sensitivity) Test. McClelland played short tape segments to job applicants and then asked them what emotion was being expressed. Presumably, this kind of sensitivity would be important to diplomats. The State Department, however, vetoed the program: "Too experimental." A more traditional graphite-pencil-on-standardized-form tester was called.

Ironically, in China, where the Mandarins first set up a civil-service testing program around 2200 B.C., the job test no longer exists. Reports Koenig (1974:102): "In 1949 Mao Tse-tung fundamentally rearranged the hierarchy of test developers, test publishers, test users, and test takers. Today in China, peers select peers for jobs."

Once a competitive examination is completed, an employment list based on the examination results is established and the names of the highest ranking eligibles are *certified* to the appointing official for selection. According to merit concept, only a limited number of qualified eligibles should be certified. To do otherwise, such as certifying a whole list of eligibles, for example, would change the basis for hiring from competitive merit to a "pass-fail" system.

Personnel systems usually follow the *rule of three,* which permits the appointing official to choose among the top three individuals certified to him, without passing over veterans. The purpose is two fold. First is to overcome the objection that written tests cannot appraise personality factors adequately, that the examining process can produce individuals who may qualify intellectually but have serious personal problems. Second is to appease appointing officers by bringing them more into the process.

Significantly, the Hoover Commission recommended instead that applicants be grouped into several categories such as "outstanding," "well-qualified," and "unqualified," and that appointing officials select individuals from the higher categories, moving down as each list was exhausted. Today, as the crucial issues in public administration become productivity and efficiency—not patronage, which the civil service system was designed to eliminate—these recommendations are more acceptable than ever.

An increasing number of critics claim that state and local civil service commission—usually appointed by successive mayors and governors and removable only for cause—can not easily be controlled by a single elected executive. Because elected officials have little control over the selection of their employees, they are obviously hampered in instituting the programs they were elected to carry out.

In short, civil service commissions are, critics maintain, archaic and inflexible. Denver police officers, for example, are still required to have a minimum of four molar teeth, an apparent holdover of "bite the bullet" to remove the wax the bullets used to be encased in. And until only recently, Denver police regulations stipulated that Civil War veterans be given preference for job vacancies. (Laing 1975)

Regardless of the process by which candidates are certified, the managers eventually face the decision of selecting one individual to fill the vacancies. This decision is perhaps the heart of staffing. But what should the manager look for?

In a word, strength. Writes Drucker (1966:Chapter 4): "Whoever tries to place a man . . . in an organization to avoid weakness will end up at best with mediocrity. The idea that there are "well-rounded" people, people who have only strengths and no weaknesses . . . is a prescription for mediocrity . . . strong people always have strong weaknesses, too. Where there are peaks, there are valleys. And no one is strong in many areas." "There is no such thing as a 'good man.' Good for what? is the question."

Drucker relates the familiar story of how Lincoln learned this lesson the hard way. Before Grant came a string of generals whose main qualifications were their lack of major weaknesses. "In sharp contrast, Lee . . . had staffed from strength. Every one of Lee's generals, from Stonewall Jackson on, was a man of obvious and monumental weaknesses." "Each of them had, however, one area of strength, and only this strength, that Lee utilized and made effective."

One story about Lee captures especially well the meaning of making strength productive. After learning that one of his generals had, again, disregarded his orders, Lee, who normally controlled his temper, became furious. Finally, an aide asked, "Why not relieve him?" Lee turned in complete amazement, looked at the aide, and said, "What an absurd question—he performs."

Most jurisdictions provide that a new employee must serve a probation period for a limited time, usually six months. During this period, the manager should give him or her special attention in matters of instruction, indoctrination, and general adjustment to the job. In theory, probation is the last phase of the testing process, for at this time the individual may be discharged without the right of appeal and reinstatement. Unfortunately, very few dismissals occur during probation. Apparently, few managers have the fortitude to judge others when careers are at stake.

Former NASA administrator Webb (1969:162) is, however, a happy exception. Webb sees little use in attempting to select an executive scientifically through a long complex matching and testing. Through experience, he found that to spend months seeking just the right executive could be counterproductive. "When you put an undue effort into a selection and persuasion process and a man fails, you find yourself committed to him. Furthermore, the failure rate is not greatly lessened by such an arduous process. Today, in NASA, we search until we find a man who seems to be qualified, and then we put him to the test. If he works out, well and good. If not, we try another."

A career service must provide opportunity for advancement. But this does not preclude filling positions from outside as well as from within the service to keep an organization from becoming too inbred, or to obtain especially outstanding persons for positions above the entry level. To maintain an organization's vitality and competence, without harming employee morale, many jurisdictions provide for filling positions from within unless a better qualified person is available from outside. Using the same approach, some jurisdictions turn to the outside only when there is an insufficient number of well-qualified persons for consideration within the organization.

In state and local jurisdictions, a competitive promotional examination—covering general administration, psychology, personnel, etc.—is often required of employees. Supporters maintain that the open competitive pro-

Casting about for a College President

Everyone seems to believe, in private, that the presidency of a college can agree on the job description, but at the same time they are convinced that (a) whoever they pick will be unworthy of the institution and (b) they do not want anyone who will ever appear on campus.

Typically, the job description does not acknowledge what everyone knows: no one connected with the institution wants a president to do the job described. The faculty does not want a leader in curriculum reform; the trustees do not want better management if it threatens such pet programs as intercollegiate athletics; and the students do not want to be straightened out by the president—which is what the alumni want him to do.

The characteristics mentioned in the typical job description divide into two clusters, those that would qualify the candidate for canonization and those that would make him a multimillionaire in the business world. However, if no one wants the president to appear on campus except for occasional visits, the second cluster of qualities, the management skills, are irrelevant to the job. That leaves as the crucial qualities required of a new president the humane gifts—sensitivity, awareness, appreciation, flexibility—that make for an effective spokesperson for higher education but have no practical consequence for the day-to-day running of an institution. We may go further and argue that even these qualities are not important for the presidency; here we can follow the advice of Machiavelli that "a prince . . . need not necessarily have all the good qualities . . . but he should certainly appear to have them."

A search committee that accepts the logic of this argument has its job immeasurably simplified: hire an actor as president. The job description might read something like this: "Wanted, character actor with wide experience playing professorial roles. Should be six feet or taller, have slim athletic build, look good in tweeds and casual sport clothes. Some skill in tennis, squash, skiing helpful. Most be able to read aloud with understated deep conviction, memorize parts quickly, have good memory for names, faces, quotations from Shakespeare, enjoy touring. Some possibility of improvisational and ad lib performances after first year."

There are drawbacks to the plan. One is that with so clear a job description for the president, it would be harder to blame him for the inadequacies of the faculty, administration, and student body and harder to keep him happy in uncongenial working conditions. A good actor with a strong script could move from the provinces to the big time very easily.

Also, some colleges might actually recognize that they *need* leadership from a president, that their need is vision rather than appearance. If an institution looking for a president should come to the conclusion that it needs more than a persuasive front man, it will have to eschew the beauties of this plan and try to find someone who genuinely has vision, energy, drive, and capacity to lead. And to persuade such a person to be president, the college will have to explain why anyone with all the required qualities should think of wasting them on a presidency. To demand all those management skills, the institution will have to demonstrate that it is willing and able to be managed; to expect all those good humane qualities, it will have to demonstrate that it knows how to treat its leaders humanely, that its faculty, students, trustees, and alumni have a modicum of that sensitivity, openness, and understanding being demanded of the new president. And before being able to make demands of the new president, the institution's members will have to answer his question. "What's in it for me?"

On balance, it is probably easier to hire an actor.

Source: Lacey (1975).

motion helps motivation and combats inertia. But most federal agencies have avoided competitive promotion by examination in favor of a merit promotion plan that establishes "the methods to be followed in selecting employees for promotion to positions grouped together for promotion purposes by certain common features which allow for like treatment. Each plan identifies the position covered, minimum area of consideration, methods of locating candidates, qualification standards, evaluation procedures." (U.S. Civil Service Commission 1971)

In addition to examination, performance ratings can take the form of measurement of output (such as in management by objectives system, discussed in Chapter 9), rating characteristics, or narratives. The check-off or objective evaluation consists of rating employees on a scale concerning such qualities as writing ability, initiative, and promptness. The narrative approach allows managers to be more flexible in discussing the good and bad points of subordinates; but because they are difficult to compare and more time consuming, they are less popular than the objective form.

Two criticisms of performance evaluation as practiced in government might be cited. First, most evaluations fail to give adequate weight to the truly important. In this sense, a management by objectives based system can have a salubrious effect. But even MBO does not go really far enough: it fails to give adequate weight to a manager's working relationship with elements in the environment—e.g., clients, universities, legislature, cognate agencies, and industry—but outside his span of control.

The second deficiency of performance evaluation is even more basic: the process is periodic rather than continuous, which is to say the manager should not wait until, say, the end of the year to tell an employee he is not performing but rather discuss the good and bad aspects of performance as they occur. An excellent vehicle for the latter is the conventional interview. If an administrator is squeamish about expressing judgments regarding subordinates, then he or she should at least stay away from managing large nonroutine public programs.

On this point Webb (1969:166) deserves a careful hearing: "As NASA administrator it became my practice to meet privately once each week with each of NASA's eight top executives for an hour of face-to-face, structured discussion that amplified and expanded the feedback process that had been continually going on between us. Inputs from all sources were brought into focus in these meetings, where no holds were barred. There were no intermediaries and no agreed ground rules. There were just two men, each charged with heavy responsibilities and vested with substantial powers, sitting face-to-face, probing each other's minds on problems, possible solutions, and how we and our other associates were doing our jobs. These were not staff meetings; we had staff meetings, too. The face-to-face evaluation and discussion meeting was a penetratingly personal confrontation on many matters that neither would have wanted to bring up in meetings with broader attendance.

Training

How important is training? The consequence of a slipshod training program were dramatically revealed in the early 1970s by a series of raids by federal narcotics officers against innocent people. Threats and abusive language were common. Eventually, Justice Department officials were forced to admit that many narcotics agents had little enforcement experience and went to the agencies right out of college. Although the Bureau of Narcotics and Dangerous Drugs operated a national training institute for its agents — which provided eight weeks of training on searches, seizures, and constitutional rights — attendance was not required. Investigation revealed that quite a few of the officers involved in the mistaken raids had not taken the training.

Proper training can, of course, do much more than reduce the possibility of such indelicacies as midnight raids in the bedrooms of innocent citizens. In the first place, by providing employees with the opportunity to improve themselves, specific training and development programs help to reduce the number of dead-end jobs in an agency. Reducing such jobs, providing opportunity for advancement can, in many instances, increase motivation. Further training programs can help to remedy a situation faced by many

Source: NASA.

James Webb, shown above conferring with former Chief Justice Earl Warren, was picked by President Kennedy in 1961 to head the U.S. Space Program. He served in the role until 1969. An extremely able administrator himself, Mr. Webb thinks administrators should not be squeamish about expressing judgments regarding subordinates.

minority groups, namely, the difficulty of attaining government position because of skill deficiencies. Indeed, as the result of a presidential memorandum in 1969, a provision in the Equal Employment Opportunity Act of 1972 (discussed in Chapter 14), and the Labor Department's Public Service Careers Program, the Civil Service Commission and all federal agencies have begun to develop in-service training programs designed to encourage the upward mobility of lower-echelon personnel, with special emphasis devoted toward assuring the advancement opportunities of minority groups.

And, finally, training helps prepare employees for certain jobs that are unique to the public sector. As government continues to serve as the armature of technological progress as well as the champion of social progress, the number of these unique jobs will, very likely, increase.

For these reasons, then, managers should not prejudge training programs as time-consuming frills. On the contrary, they should look to their agency's employees development branch as a key ally in their own tasks of employee motivation and program management.

A manager should also be aware of the types of training program available. The orientation program is perhaps the most elementary, but it is not unimportant. When well conceived, an orientation program can make employees more productive more quickly. On-the-job training (OJT) is a second type. Basically, an individual without all the needed skills or experience is hired and then learns the job from another employee.

For administrative, professional, and technical (APT) personnel, a wide variety of development programs are available, inside and outside the organization. For example: workshops and institutes (such as the Federal Executive Institute at Charlottesville, Virginia), professional conferences, university and college programs, management development programs, internships, and sabbaticals. The previously mentioned Intergovernmental Personnel Act of 1970 opened up federal in-service training programs to state and local employees and authorizes grants to them. Similarly, the Labor Department's Public Service Careers Program and the Justice Department's Law Enforcement Assistance Administration also attempt to foster state and local programs. Since the development of in-service training programs at these levels has lagged that of the federal government these trends are to be applauded.

Nor should *rotation* — that is, transfer from unit to unit — be neglected as a method of providing for employee development. Herbert Kaufman (1960) furnishes an excellent example of how this type of training works. Transfers in the Forest Service, he found, do not wait for vacancies; rather, they are made every three or four years to acquaint employees with the various perspectives of duties of employees at all job levels and with a variety of specialties. According to the service, such a practice seeks "the development, adjustment, and broadening of personnel." The advantages of such a program for developing a pool from which top management can be drawn are obvious. Compare it to an agency that allows its top management to progress up the ranks within one functional specialty.

Discipline and Grievances

Two of the more sensitive concerns of public personnel management are disciplining employees and listening to their complaints. Reprimands, suspensions, demotions, reassignments, and dismissals can obviously have an adverse effect on the career (read:life) of an employee; accordingly, few managers enjoy situations that call for such forms of discipline. And yet, the public expects, quite rightly, efficient service from those paid by its taxes.

Nor do managers usually enjoy the complaints of subordinates. Even administrators who pride themselves with their open door policy usually become unhappy when an employee begins to complain. The complaint seems to indicate that somehow they have failed to a degree as a manager. Whether an administrator finds discipline and grievances sensitive matters or not, he or she needs to keep several points in mind about each.

In disciplinary matters, the administrator should strive for improvement in employee performance. This improvement is only possible if disciplinary policy and standards of performance are clearly understood by all and impartially applied. Further, disciplinary actions should always be based on a careful assessment of the facts. Failure to do so can result in considerable embarassment for the administrator if the employee decides to refute the charges and have the disciplinary action reviewed by an impartial body.

Discipline in an organization takes many forms, oral and written reprimands being the most common. And if the administrator can make it clear (a) that the objective of the reprimand is solely to correct employee action and (b) that mutual respect exists between the two, then these forms should work. Still, the administrator should not turn to them too readily. Is the employee's action sufficiently important to require a reprimand? If the answer is yes, then are more indirect, less formal approaches available? A well thought out hint or joke might suffice for the moderately perceptive employee.

If reprimands continue to prove ineffective, then more severe forms of discipline need to be considered: suspension, demotion, reassignment, and dismissal. In such cases, the administrator will probably need to turn to the personnel office for assistance.

Suspension and demotion are less than satisfactory, except when an employee has demonstrated lack of ability in a particular position. Suspension often creates hostility. Demotion, or reassignment, by reducing motivation, can hamper agency performance, as the following interview by Terkle (1972:454) indicates:

> "When management wants to get rid of you, they don't fire you. What they do is take your work away. That's what happened to me. They sent somebody down

> to go through my personnel file. "My God, what can we do with her?" They had a problem because I'm a high-grade employee. I'm grade 14. The regional director's a 17. One of the deputy directors told me, "You're going to be an economic development specialist." (Laughs.)
>
> I'm very discouraged about my job right now. I have nothing to do. For the last four or five weeks I haven't been doing any official work, because they really don't expect anything. They just want me to be quiet. What they've said is it's a 60-day detail. I'm to come up with some kind of paper on economic development. It won't be very hard because there's little that can be done. At the end of 60 days I'll present the paper. But because of the reorganization that's come up I'll probably never be asked about the paper.

Dismissal means being fired for cause; it does not refer to those employees who must leave government because of economic measures. Actually, more employees are dismissed from government service than might be thought. The annual dismissal rate ranges from slightly less than 1 percent to about 1.5 percent, depending on the jurisdiction. These rates are comparable to those found in the private sector.

Nevertheless, public administrators, like their counterparts in industry, avoid dismissal as long as possible. And for good reason: the process is difficult and even unpleasant. Even when the dismissed employee has no right of appeal for reinstatement, the administrator may suddenly face strong external pressure from legislators, influential friends, and professional groups. Internally, he might face displeasure from other employees.

To guarantee fair play in personnel actions most agencies provide for appeals. The following excerpt is from Iowa's Merit System Act:

> Any employee who is discharged, suspended, or reduced in rank or grade, except during his probation period, may appeal to the appointing authority and if not satisfied, may, within thirty (30) days after such discharge, reduction, or suspension appeal to the commission for review thereof. Upon such review, both the appealing employee and the appointing authority whose action is reviewed shall, within thirty (30) days following the date of the filing of the appeal to the commission, have the right, to a hearing closed to the public, unless a public hearing is requested by the employee, and the present [evidence]. Technical rules of evidence shall not apply at any hearing so held. If the commission finds that the action complained of was taken by the appointing authority for any political, religious, racial, national origin, sex, age or nonmerit reasons, the employee shall be reinstated to his former position without loss of pay for the period of the suspension. In all other cases the merit employment commission shall have jurisdiction to hear and determine the rights of merit system employees and may affirm, modify, or reverse any case on its merits. The employee or the state may obtain judicial review of the commission's decision. . . .

What this excerpt does not and can not convey is how grueling a hearing can be for the administrator. The employee's lawyer naturally tries to discredit the administrator's motives. At times, an observer might wonder if the administrator is on trial.

And yet, much can be said in favor of the hearing procedure: it helps forward not only individual rights but also administrative responsibility.

How the procedure does the former is, I trust, self-evident; how it does the latter, evident in the case that follows.

By 1969, Mr. A. Earnest Fitzgerald had risen to a $31,000 GS-17 ranking in the federal bureaucracy before top level White House officials decided to dismiss him. He had become their target after appearing before Congress and disclosing a multibillion-dollar cost overrun in the now-obsolete C-5A transport. At the time of his testimony, Mr. Fitzgerald was a civilian cost analyst in the office of the Secretary of the Air Force.

He had told a joint congressional subcommittee on the economy in government how the military and the Defense Department bureaucracy let the aerospace and munitions industry drive up the costs of weapon systems through various accounting schemes. Although the accuracy of the testimony was not challenged, President Nixon's chief of staff, H. R. Haldemen, received a memorandum from a lower-level White House aide, who advised that the administration should "let him (Fitzgerald) bleed" because "he must be given very low marks in loyalty; and after all, loyalty is the name of the game." Shortly thereafter, Mr. Fitzgerald was dismissed from his job.

He then turned to the Civil Service Commission, arguing that he was the victim of retaliation. Since the commission did not order his reinstatement, Mr. Fitzgerald obtained two lawyers. Despite the delaying tactics of a small army of government lawyers, his lawyers kept up the pressure and finally, nearly four years after the dismissal, the Civil Service Commission ordered Mr. Fitzgerald reinstated. While he received more than $100,000 in back pay, he still faced legal fees of more than $400,000—far more money than a middle-level civil servant could expect to have.

Then, in December 1975, a federal judge ordered the commission to pay the costs of Mr. Fitzgerald's fight. This ruling has far-reaching effects, for without it, the heavy legal costs incurred by Mr. Fitzgerald in fighting his dismissal would strongly tend to silence civil servants aware of governmental errors. Administration would, in other words, become a little less responsible.

Therefore, I suspect that in the future we shall see much more of the whistle-blowing the Fitzgerald case had inspired even before the 1975 ruling. Indeed, since the Fitzgerald disclosure, other federal whistle blowers have:

Accused the Internal Revenue Service of planning to spend hundreds of thousands of dollars on office furniture and filing cabinets it does not need.

Tipped off the press and congressional investigators to possible conflicts of interest and questionable contracting practices on the part of a former postmaster general.

Forced the General Services Administration to back away from unpublicized plans for a vast federal computer network. The proposed system, touted as a way to cut costs, could have compiled financial and other confidential information on millions of citizens.

Provided information about negotiated Air Force contracts for maintenance manuals that the General Accounting Office confirmed would have cost taxpayers millions less under competitive bidding. (Schorr 1975)

In contrast to appeals, grievance procedures are designed more for hearing employee complaints about working conditions and other aspects of employment (e.g., job evaluation) and resolving them. While such procedures obviously benefit the employee, they also promote better management. Most administrators think they are fair, equitable, considerate, and sensitive to their employees. And perhaps they are, but the power and authority of their position can keep employee grievances from surfacing directly. Consequently, the effects of unresolved grievances begin to surface in other, more indirect ways such as higher turnover figures, reduced motivation, and more union organizing.

Grievance procedures are generally prescribed in civil service rules or regulations rather than in laws; but regardless of jurisdiction, for a grievance to work, certain elements are essential. First, the procedures should specify the steps to be followed by employees and supervisors to resolve differences. Established lines of authority should normally be followed—the immediate supervisor first and then up the line. Some jurisdictions provide a final avenue of review to an impartial panel when all else fails. Finally, employees filing grievances must be protected from reprisal.

The Hatch Act

We cannot conclude this chapter without mentioning one of the oldest concerns in public personnel administration: the notion that public employees should be removed from partisan politics. This notion was embodied in the Political Activities Act of 1939, commonly referred to as the Hatch Act. Over time, the act was broadened to cover state and local employees working on federally funded projects. Several states have enacted similar legislation.

What does the Hatch Act try to do? The Hatch Act was provoked in 1939 by rampant corruption, by party pressures on job holders. During the depression, some Works Progress Administration (WPA) officials used their positions to win votes for the Democratic party among the legion of WPA workers. Democratic Sen. Carl Hatch of New Mexico, therefore, introduced the bill to end such corrupt practices in national elections.

The Hatch Act today forbids bribery or intimidation of voters and limits political campaign activities among federal employees—no ringing door bells in someone's election campaign, running a political fund-raising operation, and so forth. Such activities on behalf of an incumbent congressman or a winning challenger would presumably magnify the political influence of the civil servant and make Congress more beholden to him and his union.

Advocates of the Hatch Act argue that those on the payroll of the federal government can still vote and express their personal opinions and that the act protects them from pressure by politically appointed bosses. When he signed the bill, President Franklin Roosevelt pronounced the law an essential complement to the basic civil service law. He saw it as a protection for the merit system and for federal employees. But he warned then that a time would come when efforts would be made to repeal or weaken the law.

That time came. In 1976 both houses of Congress voted for legislation that would allow the government's civilian employees to take an active part in political campaigning, solicit and make political contributions, and run for federal, state, and local office. While the legislation was vetoed, the argument for it merits consideration. The crux of the argument is that the Hatch Act turns public officials into second-class citizens by denying them the rights of political expression common to all citizens. The Supreme Court, however, disagrees. In a 1973 opinion (*U.S. Civil Service Commission v. Letter Carriers*), the Court stated that the "restrictions so far imposed on federal employees are not aimed at particular groups or points of view, but apply equally to all partisan activities . . . They discriminate against no racial, ethnic or religious minorities nor do they seek to control political opinion or beliefs."

NAILING DOWN THE MAIN POINTS

1 Public personnel management (or, more accurately, human resources development) can provide public administrators specialized help in managing people. The federal government has clearly recognized the importance of human resources through the passage of such legislation as the Intergovernmental Personnel Act, Emergency Employment Act, and Comprehensive Employment and Training Act.

2 Frederick C. Mosher classifies personnel systems into four main types: (*a*) political appointees, (*b*) general civil service, (*c*) career systems, and (*d*) collective system.

3 At all levels of government, the basis of the civil service is position classification; that is, identifying the duties and responsibilities of each position in an organization and then grouping the positions according to their similarities. Nevertheless, today the concept is frequently under attack. Like position classification, compensation is a very important and controversial part of public personnel administration. The general rule for establishing a good pay plan is to pay according to differences in levels of duties and responsibilities.

4 Staffing refers to the process of recruiting, selecting, and advancing employees on the basis of their relative ability, knowledge, and skill. Drucker says staff for strength.

5 In disciplinary matters, the administrator should strive for improvement in employee performance.

CONCEPTS FOR REVIEW

public personnel management

Intergovernmental Personnel Act of 1970

Emergency Employment Act of 1971

Comprehensive Employment and Training Act of 1973

human resources development

four types of public personnel systems

spoils system

Pendleton Act

merit system, merit recruiting

Civil Service Commission

rank-in-person approach

compensation

staffing

Griggs v. *Duke Power Co.*

certification

rule of three

performance evaluation

OJT

job rotation

reprimands, suspensions, demotions, reassignments, and dismissals

whistle-blowing

Hatch Act

PROBLEMS

1. "There's no such thing as individual performance on the job. It's a myth. People aren't free to operate according to their full ability. Productivity is a function of technology and agreement—formal and informal—among workers and between workers and managers." Discuss.

2. Thomas Jefferson once wrote that "there is nothing I am so anxious about as good nominations, conscious that the merit as well as the reputation of an administration depends as much on that as on its measures." Do you think this is more true or less true today? Why?

3. "Since personnel decisions using the rank-in-person approach tend to be more subjective than position classification approach, supervisors experience more anxiety in making their decision. Subordinates find it difficult to accept another as 'better' when they cannot see the whole picture." Discuss.

4. Select a public sector job and then decide from among the following what the examination used to determine the fitness and ability of the applicants should consist of: (*a*) a written test, (*b*) a performance test, (*c*) an evaluation of education and experience as shown on the application, (*d*) oral examination, (*e*) interview, (*f*) physical test, and (*g*) health examination. How would you weigh each part? Be prepared to defend your choices.

5. Should employees know each others' salaries? Discuss.
6. Write a paper on one of the following topics: (*a*) repeal of the Hatch Act and (*b*) the British and American public personnel systems compared.
7. As noted in this chapter, Alan Patton thinks that the most important reason some industries compensate executive well above the average is that quality of executive decisions is what makes profit in the business." What do you think? If you agree, does this mean public sector pay scales need radical alteration?

INTRODUCTION

The preceding chapter introduced some of the traditional concerns of public personnel management. In this chapter, we continue our treatment of the subject by considering some of the newer concerns. The first of these is labor relations. While not, strictly speaking, a new concern, labor relations, as we shall see, has grown quite rapidly importance in recent years. Today few administrators at any level of government can afford to ignore it.

Nor can many administrators afford to ignore affirmative action, the second new concern of public personnel management.

The chapter concludes by considering three concerns that, as much as anything, explain what we mean when we say, as we did early in Chapter 13 that personnel management might better be called human resources development. These three concerns are management development, participative management, and job design. Together they represent, in theory and in practice, a formidable effort to realize the full potential of the men and women that work in the public sector.

A brief word of caution. Unlike most of the chapters that have come before, this chapter does not attempt to present a systematic framework for studying the subject. I really doubt one exists. Our approach therefore resembles a Dutch lunch.

14

Public Personnel Management: New Concerns

LABOR RELATIONS IN THE PUBLIC SECTOR

The Growth of Collective Bargaining

One of the most visible concerns of public personnel management is labor relations—after

The New York Times

Uncollected garbage in New York's Greenwich Village, during a 1968 strike by municipal workers, conjures up a vision of an urban wasteland.

all, garbage, transit, and police strikes effect virtually everyone. Accordingly, labor relations warrants separate discussion. Yet, the intent of this section is not to consider the field in any depth. Topics such as labor law, union organization, and contract terms, which typically are covered in detail in more specialized treatments of personnel, are not of concern here.

Not too long ago few public sector employee belonged to labor unions — at least relative to private sector employees. This balance began to shift in 1962, when President Kennedy signed Executive Order 10,988. Going beyond the Lloyd La Follette Act of 1912, which had permitted federal employees to organize but had not confirmed their bargaining right, Executive Order 10,988 guaranteed public employees union recognition and bargaining rights.

Since 1962, the membership in unions and professional associations at the federal, state, county, and local levels has soared from slightly more than one million to 4.5 million, an increase of 350 percent. Among the largest unions are the 1.2 million-member National Education Association and the 700,000-member American Federation of State, County and Municipal Employees, which claims to be the fastest growing union in the nation. A merger of the two is under consideration and the resulting union would approach in size the 2.2 million-member Teamsters Union, now the largest in the country. Thus, in less than a decade of intensive organizational activity, unions in the public sector have succeeded in organizing a higher proportion of employees than have been organized in the private sector in 35 years of protection and encouragement under the National Labor Relations Act.

Arguments Against Collective Bargaining

Despite this extraordinary growth, the arguments used against public unionism have been even more involved and, some would say, persuasive than those used against collective bargaining in the private sector. Essentially, four arguments are heard.

1. Collective bargaining violates governmental sovereignty. Since the people have selected certain representatives to govern for them, those representatives cannot in turn share their sovereignty with any group such as a union. Proponents of this argument maintain, in short, that the public cannot be bound by decisions made by elected officials *and* union representatives.

2. Collective bargaining interrupts essential services. Calvin Coolidge said it long ago, when governor of Massachusetts, in replying to AFL leader Samuel Gomper's plea for leniency toward striking Boston police. The normally cryptic Coolidge declared, "There is no right to strike against the public safety by anybody, anywhere, anytime." The rationale for this position centers on the fact that many public employees are hired for functions considered vital to public health and safety. Striking employees of General Motors or U.S. Steel can inconvenience but not also endanger. Yet the issue becomes less clear cut when medical doctors, nurses, milkmen, and airline pilots decide to strike.

3. Collective bargaining interferes with the budgetary process; more specifically, it leads to ever-increasing budgets. In the private sector, proponents of this view maintain, both union members and employers are disciplined by the workings of the market, but in the public sector, employees, protected by civil service rules, never come face to face in any responsible manner with the taxpaying and employing public.

As Professor Sylvester Petro (1975) points out something called the "Hanslowe Effect" comes into play. Kurt L. Hanslowe of Cornell was first to describe the mutual backscratching inherent in public sector bargaining laws: Public employees and politicians reinforce the other's interest and domain. The citizen remains helpless, unless able to persuade other taxpayers to refuse a bond issue or, even more unlikely, stage a tax strike. But by then, the union usually has its contract. Taxpayers, in effect, are presented with a ukase; if they fail to accept it, government simply ceases.

New York City provides an example of the Hanslowe effect at its worst. The city's crumbling tax base and years of deficit financing, which were discussed in Chapter 11, coupled with rising labor costs, compelled Mayor Beame in summer 1975 to request a pay freeze. The unions refused and he was then forced to lay off 20,000 workers. As a result, sanitation workers refused to work; hundreds of laid-off policemen staged a raucous demonstration; laid-off roadworkers blocked traffic; and many fire fighters reported sick.

Under this kind of pressure, key state politicians granted Beame an additional $330-million in taxing power. The mayor was now able to rehire 10,000 workers—although the additional taxes raised the threat that more business would leave the city. The union's refusal of a pay freeze as a trade-off for unemployment was viewed by the public as the kind of intransigence that would be less likely to happen in the private sector. "We've faced bankruptcies many times and have done many things to keep the companies in business," said a union leader in private industry. In contrast, the municipal union claimed that by giving up a scheduled 6 percent raise scheduled they would destroy the sanctity of their contracts. (See *Business Week,* July 21, 1975, p. 53.)

Can the bargaining process be better integrated with the budgetary process? Can the continual dipping into the taxpayer's pocket to finance wage increases be halted? Fortunately, some state governments are experimenting in this area. For example, Wisconsin has enpowered a committee of the legislature to reject state employee contracts negotiated by the executive branch. If rejected, the contract goes back to the bargaining table; if ratified, the state is bound to the contract.

4. Collective bargaining is inconsistent with the merit system. Mosher (1968:197–98) highlights several of the issues of the actual and potential

Subject	Collective Bargaining	Merit Principles
Employee participation and rights	Union shop, closed shop, or maintenance of membership Exclusive recognition	Equal treatment to each employee Open shop (if any recognition)
Recruitment and selection	Union membership and/or occupational license Entrance at bottom only	Open competitive examination Entrance at any level
Promotion	On basis of seniority	Competitive on basis of merit (often including seniority)
Classification of positions	Negotiable as to classification plan, subject to grievance procedure as to allocation	Intrinsic as to level of responsibilities and duties on basis of objective analysis
Pay	Negotiable and subject to bargaining power of union	On basis of analytically balanced pay plan and, for some fields, subject to prevailing rates

Subject	Collective Bargaining	Merit Principles
Hours, leaves, conditions of work...	Negotiable	On basis of public interest as determined by legislature and management
Grievances...	Appealed with union representation to impartial arbitrators	Appealed through management with recourse to civil service agency

collisions between collective bargaining and the traditional merit principles.

In considering these collisions between collective bargaining and the merit principles, a couple of points should be kept in mind. First, in many instances, unions have been involved in gaining training and improvement programs. Second, unions can improve communications between employees and managers. Unions hold the manager's feet to the fire. What this means is expressed quite well in the following remarks by George P. Schultz (1961:4). While his remarks concern the private sector, his point applies with equal force to the public sector.

> We have a tremendous stake and a great interest in the vitality of private parties and private processes. If you have management that is moribund and is not doing anything, or if you have a union that is lazy and is not representing its workers adequately, you really do not have a healthy situation at all. We want, instead, companies and unions who are alert, energetic, driving—who are analyzing their interests and representing them vigorously. So we have a great stake, as the public, in having private parties who are vital in this sense. And if, because of our abhorrence of strikes, we take action that in effect takes the play away from private parties, we will sap their vitality, and wind up with a peaceful stagnant inefficiency on both sides.

THE COLLECTIVE BARGAINING PROCESS

Despite these four arguments, in recent years the scope of union organization and negotiating rights has extended beyond those granted by the previously mentioned Kennedy order. Of particular significance was Nixon's Executive Order 11,491 of 1969, which attempted to deal with a growing number of negotiating problems that had emerged since 1962. In brief, the Nixon order emphasized the need for (a) secret ballots in the selection of representatives for federal civil servants and (b) resolution of labor-management disputes by third party machinery.

Fortunately, we need not go through a name-the-parts exercise here. What does seem useful, however, is a general discussion of the collective bargaining process, one applicable to all jurisdictions. In the venerable tradition of medieval theologians, we divide our discussion of the process into three parts: preparation, negotiation, and impasse.

Prologue to Negotiations

Not all administrators face negotiating with unions. Many areas of the federal civil service still remain outside the jurisdiction of collective agreements. In fact, less than one third of all federal employees (excluding the Postal Service) work under collective agreements. And the proportion of union membership for state and local employee is even less, though the rate of membership growth at those levels is greater.

Assuming then the administrator will face a recognized union, what is the first step in preparing for negotiations? Clearly, one of the earliest decisions must be who will lead the bargaining, who will be on the team, and how the team will relate to other interested governmental parties. The chief negotiator should possess empathy, patience, articulateness, and a knowledge of labor relations and law; these traits help create a climate of trust and integrity. In his *How Nations Negotiate,* Fred Charles Ikle (1964) noted an even higher standard: "The compleat negotiator according to 17th- and 18th-century manuals on diplomacy, should have a quick mind but unlimited patience, know how to dissemble without being a liar, inspire trust without trusting others, be modest but assertive, charm others without succumbing to their charm, and possess plenty of money and a beautiful wife while remaining indifferent to all temptation of riches and women."

In local government, the chief negotiator may be from the chief executive's office or from the personnel, legal, or finance departments. While this person will be the government's principle spokesman, he or she might want to engage outside help such as an experienced negotiator, attorney, or management consultant. One of the chief negotiator's most difficult tasks will be to establish a unified management position. Political processes can make this task difficult. In the private sector, management is generally answerable only to itself; but, in the public sector, the negotiator is answerable to elected officials, who, in turn, are answerable to the public. The result is that public bargaining is not a two-sided affair, but a multifaceted one, with the "management team" split into the chief executive, the legislature, and relevant administrative heads. Consensus does not always come easy.

Prior to actual negotiations, the management team should (a) try to anticipate union demands and (b) prepare responses as well as develop support for its own position. More specifically, Sam Zagoria (1974: 272–73) suggests that during this period management should:

Review contracts of comparable jurisdictions. Such data can often be obtained from the contract files maintained by the U.S. Department of Labor.

Review unmet union demands from previous negotiations. Past grievances should be examined for subject, frequency, and unit involved to see if they can be reduced through changes in the contract language. At the same time, all supervisors should be solicited for suggestions on contract language that would help them carry out their management responsibilities.

Review cost-of-living data for current costs and for trends.

Assemble a great deal of data about the work force involved, so that the effect of various union proposals can be assessed. Included should be age distribution charts; length of service distribution charts; pay step distribution charts showing the number at each step; pay escalation charts showing improvement over various numbers of years; data on turnover, absenteeism, and average overtime; and the average wage rate for hourly employees.

Once the union proposals are received they should of course be explained thoroughly; union negotiators should be expected to explain each proposal. "In the process," writes Zagoria, "management members will begin to separate those proposals which are really meant from those which are 'eyewash' to placate only a few employees or to be used as trade-offs."

During this period prior to the start of face-to-face negotiations, management should develop its own proposals. In recent years, considerable attention has been given to productivity. In 1971, for example, New York City implemented its first major productivity improvement in welfare. A top official in the Human Resources Administration explains (quoted in Zagoria 1973:15): "We replaced our caseworkers with specially trained income maintenance clerks, and switched from a field investigation system to a declaration system. No longer did one $10,000-a-year caseworker have to go out and visit 60 clients. Now 1,200 clients came to the welfare center to be serviced by a group of five $7,000-a-year income maintenance specialists. This program yielded a $67 million productivity savings." Of course much of this change involved labor-management relationships. The mayor's director of labor relations lay the groundwork for the change by declaring: "No salary increase is justified when it is not necessary to offset inflation *or is not tied to corresponding increases in worker productivity.*" At the same time, the city encouraged union leadership to make productivity suggestions. The assumption is that, without union cooperation, management's productivity improvement program has little chance.

Each new city contract includes language along these lines (Zagoria 1973:16):

Delivery of municipal services in the most efficient, effective and courteous manner is of paramount importance to the city and the union. Such achievement is recognized to be mutual obligation of both parties within their respective roles and responsibilities.

The union recognizes the city's right to establish and/or revise performance standards or norms notwithstanding the existence of prior performance levels, norms, or standards. Such standards, developed by usual work measurement procedures, may be used to determine acceptable performance levels, prepare work schedules and to measure the performance of each employee or group of employees.

Employees who work at less than acceptable levels of performance may be subject to disciplinary measures in accordance with the applicable law.

As the labor relations director sees it, such language puts employees on notice that their union acknowledges management's right to define the job, judge the performance, and hold employees accountable.

The Negotiations

The initial session, because it is likely to set the tone of the whole relationship can be crucial. A few of the things to keep in mind during this part of the process:

In the early stages, sessions should be spaced so that there is adequate time to consult with affected departments, gather facts, and analyze and propose responses. "Later, as the climax approaches, sessions tend to be more frequent and occasionally go around the clock. A good general rule is to bargain as long as progress is being made and recess when it is not. Tired people tend to become hostile people, and that is not the road to agreement."

Since negotiations provide an opportunity for employers to let off steam, the negotiators should be prepared for disruption and even name calling.

The negotiator should not be pressured into developing provisions on the spot. I believe it was Cardinal Richelieu who once said, "Give me six lines written by the most honest man, I will find something there to hang him." And, while today's negotiator might not run the risk of hanging, important management rights can be yielded if the negotiator does not exercise caution and insist on clarity during this period. Further, the negotiator should make it clear that each provision is approved conditionally, subject to agreement on the entire contract.

During this period, it is also useful to think through an overall plan with possible trade-offs based on an analysis of management's and the union's priorities; when trade-offs are not possible, compromises might work. Bacon—a lawyer who knew something about imprisonment if not hanging—offered this advice on the art of negotiating: "If you would work any man, you must either know his nature and fashions, and so lead him; or his ends, and so pursuade him; or his weakness and disadvantages, and so awe him; or those that have interest in him, and so govern him. In dealing with cunning persons, we must ever consider their ends, to interpret their speeches; and it is good to say little to them, and that which they least look for. In all negotiations of difficulty, a man may not look to sow and reap at once; but must prepare business, and so ripen it by degrees."

Eventually, management may decide to make its final offer. As much as possible, it should be a united view. If management does stand firm, charges of failure to bargain in *good faith* are likely. In general, "good faith" refers to "a willingness to sit down at reasonable times, to confer about appropriate matters, and to put into writing any agreement reached."

Impasse Procedures

In the event that negotiations end in a stalemate or impasse, four alternative outcomes are possible.

Since *mediation* is essentially voluntary, it is one of the first steps in attempting to resolve an impasse. In mediation, an impartial third party attempts to persuade the parties to come to agreement. Mediators are usually supplied by either a state government agency or the Federal Mediation and Conciliation Service.

A second method employs an impartial third party to gather data on the issues in controversy and make a report on their recommendation. The rationale behind this fact finding is that, because the report is by neutrals, public support will be behind it. Since both parties retain final control over whether to accept the recommendations, fact finding is sometimes referred to as *voluntary arbitration*. Nevertheless, states like New York and Wisconsin have had remarkable success with this approach to impasses.

A third method is *arbitration*. Because the arbitrators hold formal hearings, weigh evidence, and hand down an award, it is essentially a judicial process. The decision, however, can be either advisory or binding.

Finally, the impasse might result in a strike. Most experts contend that this alternative is the worst: nobody gains by a strike and the sooner the parties get back to the bargaining table the better. But is a strike really worse than arbitration? In many instances, binding arbitration can provide employees with higher benefits *at less cost to the employees* than a strike would. For this reason, some government officials regard the strike as preferable to third-party decisions on wage increases. At a minimum, allowing strikes would rationalize the bargaining process and prevent the delegation of budget-making to an outside body responsible to nobody.

Another argument for allowing strikes is that laws against them are rather ineffective. Only a half dozen states grant a limited right to strike. Yet Texas, which has one of the strongest antistrike laws in the nation, had more public employee strikes in 1972 than all but 11 states. Then, too, there is the nonstrike strike. Policemen conduct mass ticket writing campaigns for minor parking violations—such as being an inch over the legal distance from the curb—and fill out long forms on such normally ignored incidents as the finding of a penny on a city sidewalk. (In 1974 Baltimore police were even calling in the photo unit for help with identification of the recovered lucre.)

THE EXPANDING ROLE OF PERSONNEL: HUMAN RESOURCES DEVELOPMENT

As indicated early in this chapter the role of public personnel management has, in recent years, expanded far beyond such traditional—but still important—concerns as classification and compensation, staffing, training, and separation. What are these newer concerns? Some authorities would no doubt list topics discussed in earlier chapters: organizational changes, productivity improvement, and motivation; and I have no quarrel with this inclusion. But here we shall limit ourselves to only four topics: affirmative action, management development, participative management, and job redesign.

From Equal Opportunity to Affirmative Action

The road to equal opportunity in America has been a tortuous, uphill one that eventually led to a great national consensus expressed legislatively in the Civil Rights Act of 1964. Its meaning was clear: no longer would there be any discrimination on the ground of race, color, religion, or national origin in voting, public education, public accommodation, or employment.

No sooner had the civil rights act seemed to fulfill old promises at last, than President Johnson was observing at his historic commencement address at Howard University in June 1965:

> But freedom is not enough. You do not take a person who, for years, has been hobbled by chains and liberate him, bring him up to the starting line of a race and then say, "You are free to compete with all the others" and still justly believe that you have been completely fair.
>
> Thus it is not enough just to open the gates of opportunity. All our citizens must have the ability to walk through those gates.
>
> This is the next and the more profound stage of the battle for civil rights. We seek not just freedom but opportunity. We seek not just legal equality but human ability, not just equality as a right and a theory but equality as a fact and equality as a result.

The outgrowth of that promise for positive approaches is that affirmative action efforts have been developed at all levels of government. Affirmative action plans require employees to demonstrate good faith in their efforts to increase opportunities for "deprived groups"—a term inclusive of blacks, chicanos, native Americans, Asian-Americans, and women. The Equal Employment Opportunity Commission is only one of many federal agencies administering the Civil Rights Act in general or the "affirmative action" programs in particular. There are overlapping jurisdictions of the Labor Department; the Department of Health, Education and Welfare; the Justice Department; the EEOC; and the federal courts. When one federal agency approves or requires a given practice, this in no way protects an employer from being sued. Indeed, federal agencies have sued one another under this act.

And so the environment of public administration becomes an increasingly tangled skein of lawsuits, guidelines, and racial quota. Consider the case of one college president who in 1975 wrote to lawyers at the Equal Employment Opportunity Commission that "Colby (College) is prepared, as we have always tried to do, to comply with the law of the land, but first it would be helpful to know what the law of the land is." The cause of Colby's befuddlement was the position the EEOC had taken on retirement plans, namely, that men and women employees of equal status should get the same monthly pension. But women live longer than men on the average; therefore, equal monthly benefits mean that contributions to pension funds would have to be higher for women than men. Enter a second federal agency: the Office of Federal Contract Compliance of the Department of Labor, which says that monthly contributions for men and women should be equal. Whose definition of equality is to prevail?

An overriding objective in all affirmative action plans is to increase public employment for minorities and women. Harry Kranz (1974: 435–36) contends that a more representative bureaucracy is desirable for political, economic and social reason; moreover, it would benefit not only minorities, but also clients, bureaucratic organizations, and the American governmental system:

"For minorities and women, increased public employment would provide greater income, job security, and living standards, as well as increased power, influence, and participation in government decision making. Increased economic and political status would lead to increased social status, both in their own eyes and in the eyes of others, within the organization and outside it."

"A more representative bureaucracy would benefit the recipients of public services, particularly members of minority groups, whether those services were directly furnished by minority staff or not." "... we ... expect that minority and female 'representatives' as a group will more closely mirror the needs and wishes of their group, whether overtly or subconsciously, than nonminorities do, and that on most decisions and services, a bureaucracy with 'ideal-type' representation of minorities and women will govern 'better' than one which is unrepresentative. The decisions will be 'better' because we subjectively believe democracy is 'better' than oligarchy."

"Equitable minority and female representation would be beneficial for the bureaucratic organizations themselves. By increasing the opportunities for decision making by a broader cross section of the population, it would tend to dilute the discretionary power and influence currently vested in unrepresentative elites. Propinquity reduces ignorance and rejection; increased bureaucratic understanding of minority views

The New York Times/Roger Neville Williams

Two of the still-rare women park rangers—in 1976, there were a total of 76—at ruins in Mesa Verde National Park. As one female bureaucrat put it, "We've still got to deal with the resistance that comes from the 'strong man in uniform image.'"

and feelings would lead to greater responsiveness to minority problems and needs. Moreover, the infusion of new blood should increase
internal democracy by stimulating diversity, egalitarianism, conflict,
and change."

"A more representative bureaucracy would increase the legitimacy of the
entire American system by making the predominant arm of government—the nonelected bureaucracy—a closer reflection of the diverse
population it represents, both actually and symbolically." Further, a
representative bureaucracy would provide a more efficient use of
America's human resources and would increase domestic tranquility
by reducing alienation, apathy, and antisocial behavior.

Not every one shares Kranz's optimism about the implications of affirmative action. Indeed, today the charge of reverse discrimination is commonplace. But what are the facts? For the federal government at least, we have
fairly good statistics (see U.S. Civil Service Commission, *Study of Minority
Group Employment in the Federal Government, 1974* and *Study of Employment of Women in the Federal Government, 1973*). Blacks, with 11 percent
of the American population according to the 1970 census, held 16.1 percent
of the jobs in 1974; Spanish surnamed, with 5.0 percent of the population,
held 3.3 percent of the jobs; native Americans and Orientals, with .9 percent
of the population, held 1.7 percent of the jobs; and women with 51.0 percent
of the population, held 34.0 percent of the jobs. Significantly, total minority

employment in the federal government increased from 18.9 to 21.0 percent between 1967 and 1974.

But, as the advocates of affirmative action are quick to point out, these statistics do not tell the entire story. As can be seen from Tables 14–1 and 14–2, minorities and women are poorly represented in the higher levels of civil service. The analysis must, however, be pressed one step further. As indicated in the right hand columns of Tables 14–1 and 14–2, the percentage change in the 1967–74 period was far greater in the *higher* levels of civil service than in the lower.

The crux of the argument against affirmative action seems to be idea of setting quotas and goals. In other words, because hiring or promoting a woman or minority person is often accepted as proof of nondiscrimination, employers may be inclined to accept less qualified applicants. For example, Guy Alitto, Ph.D. in Chinese history from Harvard under Professor John Fairbank with dissertation completed and under consideration by a university press, was interviewed in 1975 for two jobs. Both jobs ultimately went to women who were just starting their dissertations—prima facie instances, it appears, of individuals less qualified than he being hired on the basis of affirmative action. Meanwhile, the courts, while disavowaling outright quota systems, have ordered several state and municipal agencies to follow rather specific hiring practices (e.g., one black for every newly hired white) until given percentage is attained, (e.g., 25 percent black.)

The line between quotas and goals, which are less rigid requirements

TABLE 14–1
Minority Group Employment in Federal Government

Pay Grade	Percent of Total		Percent Change
	1967	1974	
GS 1–4.............	25.2	28.5	+13
GS 5–8.............	15.0	21.1	+41
GS 9–11	6.8	10.8	+59
GS 12–18...........	3.3	6.0	+81

Source: Derived from U.S. Civil Service Commission, *Study of Minority Group Employment in the Federal Government, 1974.*

TABLE 14–2
Female White-Collar Employment in the Federal Government

Pay Grade	Percent of Total		Percent Change
	1970	1973	
GS 1–6.............	46.1	46.6	+ 1
GS 7–12	20.7	23.4	+13
GS 13–18...........	3.9	4.5	+15

Source: Derived from *U.S. Civil Service Commission, Study of Employment of Women in the Federal Government, 1973.*

than quotas, is exceedingly thin. Yet, as I think the National Civil Service League's *Model Public Personnel Administration Law* illustrates, an effective affirmative action plan does not necessarily require quotas. Consider the following two recommendations that can do much to help break down artificial barriers to minority group employment.

Offer preferential treatment to disadvantaged persons and minority group members. This recommendation means that a jurisdiction will take affirmative action to remedy the results of past discrimination and increase its employment of minorities. Specifically, preferential treatment includes aggressive recruiting for minorities, selective certification for certain positions, and training programs to allow the disadvantaged to become fit for merit system jobs.

Establish selection systems based on job-related, culture-fair evaluations. In the last chapter, we discussed the Griggs case and little more needs to be said here about making the examinations related to the job: The essential point is that we need not find coal shovelers who can scan Virgil correctly, but coal shovelers who are properly qualified for shoveling.

Likewise, the examination should not be culturally biased. An obvious example of cultural bias is an overly sophisticated English vocabulary on a written test for a chicano. Similarly, individuals that have spent the majority of their lives in a low income, urban setting might find that some examinations favor a more middle class, suburban background.

Fortunately, the problem of cultural bias is not insurmountable. If the tasks to be performed can be recorded through careful job analysis, any one of three selection methods can be used to determine relative ability: (1) competitive performance tests of a sample of the job to be done (e.g., typing or driving); (2) bio-data forms to determine and rate experience and training relevant to the specific job and obtain accurate appraisals of the candidate's qualifications from past employers, trainers, and associates; and (3) structured oral interviews by selection boards containing minority and female representatives, particularly where, as in telephone switchboard and receptionist positions, public speaking is a job requirement. On the other hand, if it is not feasible to determine relative ability to perform the job, other methods are available for use where minorities and women are under-represented. Recognizing that all tests are subject to a statistical margin of error (even if the test is valid) and that there is no sanctity to "passing marks" or relative rankings, the pass-fail test might be used. Only the minimum essential requirements for the job are established, and priority in appointment from among all those with "pass" grades goes to those individuals whose group (race, sex, nationality, etc.) is most under-represented in the particular position. (Kranz 1974:438)

The principal problems with affirmative action efforts, as I see it, are three. First, what is to prevent more ethnic groups from demanding to be included? Why include blacks, chicano, and orientals, but not Polish-Americans,

Italian-Americans, and Armenian-Americans? In the respect, as Sheila K. Johnson (1975:33) points out, it is an important precedent that Executive Order 11,246 has already been amended once to include women. "There is no reason why the executive order could not be amended to include gays, spastics, paraplegics, blind and deaf individuals, persons over 50, and any number of other groups that have often been discriminated against in the labor market." Furthermore, how does, say, HEW determine whether an individual is black, oriental, or American Indian. One grandparent? One great grandparent?

Second, many agencies might be suffering from society's traditional assignment of male and female roles rather than overt discrimination. The Interior Department quotes a 1970 survey showing that "one woman of every nine fished . . . compared with one man in three; and the count of hunters included only one woman in 94, compared with one man in five." That helps explain, the department said, why "men still clearly predominate in management of fish and wildlife programs." (Hyatt 1976:32)

A third problem is suggested by Nathan Glazer (1976), a sociologist at Harvard. In brief, Glazer argues that affirmative action has failed to help the mass of working class blacks. In fact, he makes clear that he has no principled opposition to preferential job treatment, if he thought it would actually work. But, he contends, by the time hiring quotas came into being in the early 1970s, they were no longer needed. The laws against discrimination had already opened doors to jobs, and blacks were making "marked" economic progress. The black middle class (in which Glazer includes, vaguely, "the black worker") did not need preferential treatment. On the other hand, he contends, poorly educated, low-income black families—especially those headed by women—were out of reach of antidiscrimination programs because they were largely unemployable.

It would be nice to end our discussion of affirmative action on an affirmative note. I can not. I see no way to determine the meaning of "affirmative action." All that can be done is what was done, namely, to examine the particulars—the concepts, intentions, effects, and trends.

But studying the trends can be more confusing than edifying. On the one hand, we have fairly clear cut data on EEOC activities; we know that they are on the increase, as shown in Figure 14–1. On the other, we have the June 25, 1976, Supreme Court decision that held, 9 to 0, that the Civil Rights Act of 1964 bars discrimination against whites "upon the same standards as would be applicable were they Negroes." While the full meaning of the court's decision is not yet clear, it does appear, indirectly at least, to cast doubt on some hiring and promotion quotas favoring blacks and women.

Management Development

According to Raymond Pomerleau (1974), the explicit purpose of management development programs in the public sector is "to extend the span of utility for those managers who may be confronted with the imminence of

FIGURE 14–1
Equal Employment Opportunity Commission Activities

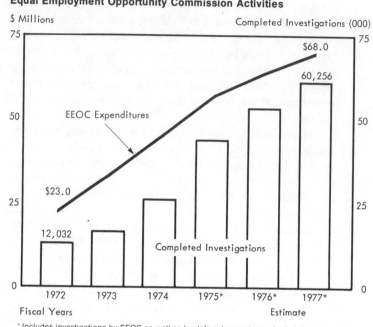

* Includes investigations by EEOC as well as by deferral agencies and administrative closures.
Source: U.S. Office of Management and Budget (1976a:234).

premature obsolescence; and to prepare high potential mid-managers whose past performance has been outstanding for assuming higher managerial functions." Because management development is a way of increasing the supply of managerial talent, it is at the heart of public personnel management today.

An organization can take a number of approaches to management development; Saul W. Gellerman (cited in Pomerleau 1974) notes three. First is the jungle theory. Once placed in the organization, talented individuals distinguish themselves by outperforming colleagues. They are, in other words, identified by natural selection. Gellerman, however, contends that the notion that talent always rises to the top has been almost universally discredited. Recognizing these inadequacies, many organizations hold to an education theory of management development. The basic idea behind this theory is that management consists of skills that can be deliberately developed by an educational program, which may include formal classroom experiences or rotational assignments. The third is the agriculture theory. The idea here is "that effective managers are grown not born; and since most of this growth takes place outside the context of formal training programs, it is important that managers work is a job environment that is as growth-conducive as possible."

Clearly, organizations have diverse approaches to management development. Nevertheless, a careful examination reveals certain commonalities. Many of these common elements can be seen in NASPAA's Matrix of Professional Competencies, referred to in Chapter 1. In other words, the objectives of management development programs tend to emphasize (a) the impartation of job relevant information such as new regulations; (b) the development of new analytical skills; (c) the inculcation of new values, that is, new ways of thinking and feeling about things; and (d) the broadening of the individual perspective. The final component is concerned with jarring loose managers from conventional thinking and from their narrow job specialties. It can even result in increasing the managers capacity to deal with a wider range of problems. Fundamentally, it seeks to change the managers' behavior.

A concrete example of how these components can appear in a management development program is provided by the objectives of the Federal Executive Institute (FEI) in Charlottesville, Virginia. The program at the institute is concerned with promoting the educational needs of career executives within the supergrade structure (GS 16–18 and equivalents). The specific objectives toward which these executives work include these:

Improved understanding of executive roles. The behaviors expected of executives serve as standards for action. Role prescriptions in the literature of business and government executives and in actual practices of federal executives are compared and contrasted with individual perceptions and behaviors.

Strengthened individual capabilities. FEI programs are designed to help strong people become stronger—to help individual executives assess existing strengths, interests, and needs, and to develop knowledge, skills, and programs for continued learning based on that assessment.

An aerial view of the Federal Executive Institute reveals the attractiveness of the setting.

Increased knowledge of management systems and processes. Knowledge of current theories and practices of management and of their historic contexts in government and in business provides a framework for individual executive assessment, learning, and improved management behavior on the job. Consequently, this is an area of major emphasis in individual objective setting at FEI.

Understanding of national needs and priorities. Effectiveness as an executive means doing the right things, and that requires a profound understanding not only of agency goals and objectives but of the needs and priorities of the entire governmental system. Because of the interagency character of FEI programs and the high quality of executives selected as institute participants, it is possible to probe deeply into current and future problems and prospects for the United States and the world and to relate general developments to specific situations which confront government executives. Because of these considerations, it is important that the participants at the institute share approximately the same high levels of responsibility.

The management development coin has two sides. In addition to the essentially "training" side we have thus far been discussing is the "selection" side. Jay Shafritz (1974:735) writes, "The range of experience . . . that managers are exposed to over the years leaves records in terms of specific scores or subjective evaluations upon which future advancements may be based. While it is not overly difficult to make promotional decisions based on this array of information, what criteria should an organization use in selecting relatively inexperienced managers in whom to invest its development resources?"

The use of the *assessment center* method is one answer. This method involves multiple evaluation techniques (see Table 14–3) selected to bring out behavior related to the qualities identified by research as important to job success in the jobs for which the participants under consideration. By observing, over a one to three day period, a participant's handling of the simulated problems and challenges of higher level jobs, assessors are able to get a feeling for a participant ability before the promotion. (Byham and Wettengal 1974)

While the first recorded use of assessment procedures was by the German Army to help select officers during World War I, the first major use of it in the federal government was by the Internal Revenue Service in 1969. The last few years, however, have witnessed increasing application by government jurisdictions in the United States and Canada. Byham and Wettengal (1974) note several reasons for the recent popularity: its great flexibility in adapting to different jobs and job levels; its inherent potential for higher validity than available from tests or interviews alone; and its enthusiastic acceptance by involved participants and managers."

TABLE 14–3
Description of Exercises Used at the Assessment Center

Assigned Role Group Discussion

In this leaderless group discussion, participants, acting as a city council of a hypothetical city, must allocate a $1 million federal grant in the time allotted or make other judgments on the varying proposals offered. Each participant is assigned a point of view to sell to the other team members and is provided with a choice of projects to back and the opportunity to bargain and trade off projects for support.

Nonassigned Role Group Discussion

This exercise is a cooperative, leaderless group discussion in which four short case studies dealing with problems faced by executives working in state government agencies are presented to a group of six participants. The participants act as consultants who must make group recommendations on each of the problems. Assessors observe the participant's role in the group and the handling of the content of the discussion.

In-basket Exercise

Problems that challenge middle- and upper-level executives in state government are simulated in the in-basket exercise. These include relationships with departmental superiors, subordinates and peers, representatives of other departments, representatives of executive and legislative branches, the public, and the news media. Taking over a new job, the participant must deal with memos, letters, policies, bills, etc., found in the in-basket. After the in-basket has been completed, the participant is interviewed by an assessor concerning his or her handling of the various in-basket items.

Speech and Writing Exercises

Each participant is given a written, narrative description of a policy, event, situation, etc., and three specific situational problems related to the narrative, each requiring a written response. The participant is also required to make a formal oral presentation, based upon the background narrative description, before a simulated news conference attended by the Capitol Press Corps and interested government officials and citizens (assessors).

Analysis Problem

The analysis problem is an individual analysis exercise. The participant is given a considerable amount of data regarding a state agency's field operations, which he or she must analyze and about which he or she must make a number of management recommendations. The exercise is designed to elicit behaviors related to various dimensions of managerial effectiveness. The primary area of behavior evaluated in this exercise is the ability to sift through data and find pertinent information to reach a logical and practical conclusion.

Paper and Pencil Tests

Three different commercially-available objectively scoreable tests are included in the assessment: a reading test used for self-development purposes, a reasoning ability test, and a personality test. The latter two are being used experimentally at present, and as with the reading test, are not made available during assessor discussions.

Source: Byham and Wettengal (1974). Reprinted by permission of the International Personnel Management Association, 1313 East 60th Street, Chicago, Illinois 60637.

Participative Management

Warren Bennis, who was mentioned in Chapter 7 during our discussion of future organizations, argues that democracy in an organizational context is inevitable. In Bennis's view, the nature of work in the future in both the public and private sectors, will be increasing scientific and technological. Today we are already aware that this type of work leads to a more free-form, democratic organization. A chain of command inhibits the quick and cross-cutting flow of information required in scientific-technological enterprises.

Certain social forces are also pushing organizations toward a more democratic form. Workers today, public and private, are less docile; they are less likely to passively accept the edicts of management and more likely to want to have their say in decisions that affect them. In the decades ahead, few concerns of public personnel management will be less critical than participatory management. And, as there are diverse approaches to management development, so too are there diverse approaches to achieving worker participation in management. In this subsection, we shall consider the two main ones, leadership style and formal plan.

A participative leadership style, according to Richard E. Walton (1967), "involves sharing more information with subordinates, eliciting their ideas, encouraging interchange among them, employing general rather than close supervision, and engaging in a supportive interpersonal pattern." The Forest Service has developed several participatory management programs. Headquarters personnel regularly poll field officers for opinions on major decisions and constructive dissent is encouraged. Headquarters inspection of field operations also gives field employees a chance to speak on agency policies. Participation of field officials is of course more natural in the Forest

Drawing by Whitney Darrow Jr.: ©1972, *The New Yorker Magazine Inc.*
Employee participation can take many forms.

Service, with its regional organizational base, than it would be with many other agencies. A notation in the Forest Service manual that the agency "is dedicated to the principle that resource management begins — and belongs — on the ground," and that "the ranger district constitutes the backbone of the organization" makes the agency's mission naturally conducive to participation. (Kaufman 1970:332)

A formal plan, on the other hand, allows workers to "participate through joint union-management or worker-management committees that encourage, collect, and pass on suggestions for improving productivity. In most cases, there is some explicit scheme for sharing between workers and management the fruits of increased productivity." Thus, "the formal approach does not rely exclusively upon the same hierarchical channel for downward instructions and allocation of individual rewards and penalties and also for upward communication of ideas and influence." (See Figure 14–1.) Since 1933, TVA has been a pioneer in this approach to employee participation.

Through collective bargaining, employees negotiate agreements regarding classification of positions, work schedules, salary schedules, promotion, transfer, suspension, reduction in employment, grievances, employee-management cooperation, and employee training. And more: through the program of employee-management cooperation, they contribute suggestions for improving communications between employees and management; eliminating waste; correcting conditions making for grievances and misunderstanding; improving working conditions; and conserving manpower, materials, and supplies.

The cooperative program, sponsored jointly by TVA management and the unions, is composed of approximately 98 employee-management committees in the units of the TVA system. "The top executives of each unit represent management, and eight to ten employees are selected by the nonmanagerial employees in the unit as their representatives. The employee representatives are union members, but usually not officers. Since TVA has approximately 12,000 employees, less than 10 percent participate directly in the program at any one time. Those who are not committee members contribute their ideas through their representatives." (A. A. Thompson 1967)

Walton (1967) argues persuasively for the formal plan approach over the leadership style approach. First, it can be quite difficult for both first line supervisors and workers to initiate and maintain a pattern of open participation when this runs counter to all of their previous experience. While at higher levels in the organization, the leadership style approach might work well, Walton thinks that at the lower levels a committee structure and prescribed procedures are more realistic. Second, a parallel hierarchy (see Figure 14–2) gives workers more independence: they do not have to rely exclusively upon their immediate supervisor for upward communication of their ideas. Third, the explicit linking of bonuses with improvements in productivity encourages worker participation in higher organizational activities. Finally, "since the formal plan officially covers all groups and provides for participa-

FIGURE 14–2
Formal Approach to Worker Participation in Management

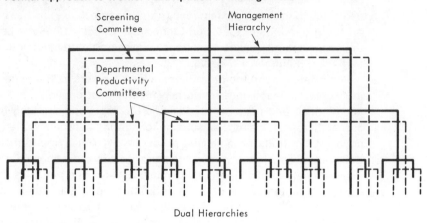

Source: Walton (1967).

tion mechanism in addition to the worker-supervisor relationship, a worker can participate in spite of a reluctant supervisor." Conversely, it allows each worker to choose their own level of participation.

Job Design

Early in Chapter 13, we noted that the importance of the public personnel function has in, recent years, expanded considerably. And this expansion concerns the private as well as the public sector. Witness the article that appeared in *Fortune* in early 1976, "Personnel Directors Are the New Corporate Heroes," telling how a number of big companies have learned that it pays to put especially capable executives in charge of human resources. In this final part of Chapter 14, we examine a topic that does much to explain this new importance.

Actually, job design is closely related to two topics previously covered, position classification and motivation. But in an era of intensive specialization, the tendency is often to make position description very narrow. Narrowness may result in greater expertise; it may also result in more boredom. Fortunately, through careful job design, employee apathy and alienation can be avoided. But the question is, How?

A good place to start looking for an answer is Frederick Herzberg's ground-breaking *The Motivation to Work* (1959). Figure 14–3 shows the results of Herzberg and his associates' empirical investigation of motivation. Essentially, what they found were five factors that determined job satisfaction: achievement, recognition, work itself, responsibility, and advancement. In addition, they found five factors that were associated with job dissatis-

FIGURE 14–3
Comparison of Satisfiers and Dissatisfiers

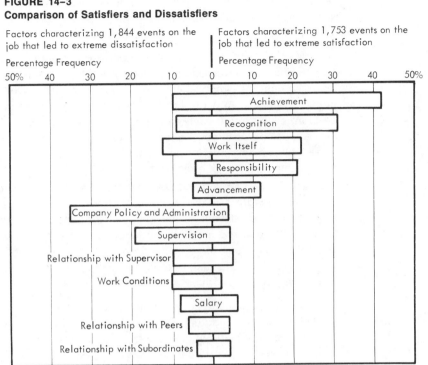

Source: Herzberg et al. (1959).

faction: company policy and administration, supervision, salary, interpersonal relations, and working conditions. Significantly, *the satisfying factors were all related to job content.*

This finding is most suggestive. It tells us that jobs should be designed to be challenging and provide ample opportunity for worker recognition. It tells us that employees should be given as much discretion as possible. It tells us that employees should be able to diversify activities, which is not the same thing as merely taking on more work. Finally, it tells us that employees should be able to witness some of the result of their output.

How well does job enrichment work? According to Roy W. Walters (1972): "The best proof of any theory is the hard, fast results which occur when the theory becomes practice. Job enrichment efforts in a number of cases over the last few years have produced excellent results, both for the companies and for the individual workers. In one organization, job enrichment saved $300,000 for the company by increasing production per employee. This was done by expanding job responsibilities and by reducing verification of the work. In another organization, the savings were $100,000, realized through increased production and reduction in the number of employees. In still another company, quality of output improved 35 percent."

One further point. Effective job design does not apply solely to workers. Drucker (1966:78–92) offers these guidelines for designing executive and professional jobs:

> Do not start out with the assumption that jobs are created by nature or God. Know they have been designed by highly fallible men. Therefore, guard against the "impossible" job, the job that simply is not for normal human beings." "Any job that has defeated two or three men in succession, even though each had performed well in his previous assignment, must be assumed unfit for human beings." Examples of such "undoable," man-killer jobs include the presidency of a large university and the ambassador of a major power.

> Make each job demanding and big. "It should have challenge to bring out whatever strength a man may have. It should have scope so that any strength that is relevant to the task can produce significant results." Survey of physicians in the Army Medical Corps, chemists in the research lab, nurses in the hospital produce the same results: "The ones who are enthusiastic and who, in turn, have results to show for their work, are the ones whose abilities are being challenged and used."

Here is hardly the place to begin a comparative analysis of the public and private sectors—which is actually the subject of the following, concluding chapter. Yet I can not help but note the fact that many of the nations largest and most successful corporations—AT&T, Texas Instruments, General Foods, Monsanto, Polaroid, etc.—have long had vigorous job design programs. Meanwhile, the public sector has again been found guilty of trailing far behind in an important area of management.

In this area, however, the consequences are especially costly. Albert Camus put it accurately and briefly when he wrote: "Without work all life goes rotten; but when work is soulless, life stifles and dies."

NAILING DOWN THE MAIN POINTS

1 One of the most visible concerns of public personnel management is labor relations. The growth in public sector employee unions really got underway in 1962 when President Kennedy signed Executive-Order 10,988, which guaranteed them recognition and bargaining rights.

2 Arguments against collective bargaining include these: It violates governmental sovereignty, interrupts essential services, interferes with the budgetary process, and conflicts with the merit principle. While each of these arguments needs qualification—if not rejection—we need also to keep these points in mind. First, unions have been involved in gaining training and improvement programs. Second, as George P. Schultz notes, unions can keep management on their toes, can help to prevent "a peaceful stagnant inefficiency."

3 Not all administrators face negotiating with unions. Many areas of the federal service still remain outside the jurisdiction of collective arguments. In fact, less than one third of all federal employees work under collective agreement. But, assuming the administrator does face a recognized union, he or she should give careful attention to the three parts of the collective bargaining process: preparation, negotiation, and impasse.

4 In 1965, President Johnson said that it is not enough just to open the gates of opportunity. "All our citizens must have the ability to walk through those gates." The outgrowth of that promise was that affirmative action efforts developed at all levels of government. Affirmative action plans require employers to demonstrate good faith in their efforts to increase employment opportunities for deprived groups.

5 Three topics on the frontiers of human resources development are: management development, which attempts to extend the utility of those managers who may be confronted with premature obsolescence; participative management, which, some would argue, is inevitable and which can be achieved through either new leadership styles or a formal plan; and job design, which aims to increase motivation by building more satisfying jobs.

CONCEPTS FOR REVIEW

Executive Orders 10,988, 11,246, 11,491
American Federation of State, County, and Municipal Employees
arguments against collective bargaining
Hanslowe effect
the collective bargaining process

impasse procedures
equal opportunity, affirmative action
management development
assessment center
participation management
job design
Herzberg's job satisfiers and dissatisfiers

PROBLEMS

1. "Thanks to machinery, air conditioning, and noise control, work has become much less nasty—only in the civil services, the police and fire departments, and the imagination of sociologists has work become more degrading and unpleasant in recent years." (Mayer 1976:55) Discuss.

2. Take a specific administrative position in the public sector and, using Table 14–1, design your own assessment center exercise. Be prepared to defend your design.

3. O. Glenn Stahl, a past high official in the Civil Service Commission, states that the logic of making special concessions to members of deprived groups discourages achievement and puts a premium on an attitude that effort is unnecessary to win a job. He adds that other society-wide changes must come first. Discuss.

4. Compare and contrast the approaches to participation found in *New Patterns of Management* by Rensis Likert (1961) and *The Scanton Plan* by F. Leiseur (1958).

5. Write a paper on the right to strike in the public sector.

6. The public sector is becoming increasingly co-ed, particularly at the higher administrative levels. This generates dilemmas for both men and women in an organization. Some are trivial, but others are quite serious affecting both careers and agency operations. Slowly, case by case, pragmatic solutions are evolving. In a sense, they constitute a series of do's and don'ts. The following series was suggested for corporate women and their male associates (*Business Week*, March 22, 1976). Which do you find appropriate? Inappropriate? What would you add?

For Men Executives	*For Women Executives*
Do:	Do:
Be as supportive or critical of a woman as of a man.	Plan your career and take risks.
Practice talking to her if you are self-conscious.	Stress your ambition. Ask "What can I do to get ahead?"
Let her open the door if she gets there first.	Speak at least once in every 10-minute meeting.
Tell your wife casually about a woman peer.	Take the chip off your shoulder.
	Don't:
Don't:	Say "I worked on . . ." when you wrote the entire report.
Make a fuss when appointing the first women.	Imitate male mannerisms — or do needlepoint at meetings.
Tune her out at meetings.	Hang on to the man who trained you.
Say "Good morning, gentlemen — and lady."	Leap to serve coffee when someone suggests it's time for a break.
Apologize for swearing.	

7. Could participation management be a form of co-optation?

INTRODUCTION

The preceding 14 chapters dealt with the four major themes—the environment of public administration, program management, financial management, and the management of people. These four themes, I maintain, pretty much make up the study of public administration. But, in an introductory textbook, a final chapter on the future of American public administration would hardly be supernumerary, for the advice of the Greek historian Thucydides still holds: those who must be thought the causes of events have reason to foresee them. So, in this concluding chapter, rather than luxuriate in grand summations, we shall be very much in the realm of the future.

We can add muscle to our reconnaisance of the future if we employ, as much as possible, the tools of futures research—a new and surprising rapidly growing field of study. So, the objective of this chapter becomes really two-fold: (1) to introduce a few of the basic concepts of futures research and then (2) to outline what the future of public administration might be with respect to political institutions and managerial behavior.

15

Looking Ahead

FORECASTING FOR THE ADMINISTRATOR

What Is a Forecast?

Erich Jantsch (1967:15) provides us with this definition of a forecast: a probabilistic statement, on a relatively high confidence level, about the future. A prediction, in contrast, is a nonprobabilistic statement (*X will* occur). Jantch also distinguishes between two types of forecasts. *Exploratory forecast* starts from today's knowledge and attempts to say what is likely to occur in the future. The Club of Rome simulation of world growth, noted in Chapter 6, is such a forecast. *Normative forecast,* however, start in the future, assessing goals, needs, desires, and so forth. They then work backward to the present, attempting to spell out what should be done to attain, at some time in the future, the desired goal. The relevance tree, also in Chapter 6, could be considered a normative forecast. (See Figure 9–2.)

So much for definitions. How does this relate to the task of the administrator? In brief, forecasting (or, futures research) provides a means of discovering and articulating the more important opportunities and problems in the future. Further, it provides a systematic method for estimating the trajectory likely to be produced by contemplated or existing governmental programs.

The number of forecasting methods available is vast. Below we discuss only six of the more basic methods: expert forecasting, consensus methods, cross-impact analysis, trend extrapolation, scenario, and leading indicators.

Expert Forecasting

The expert forecast is the oldest and most intuitive of the methods. Here, if one wants to know what is likely or unlikely to happen, one simply goes to the expert. The science fiction writer Arthur C. Clarke (1963) documents the limitations to this approach by citing numerous failures by experts.

Lord Rutherford, for example, was certainly an expert on the atom — more than any other scientist he helped to lay bare its internal structure. But, as Clarke (ibid.:14) notes,

> Rutherford frequently made fun of those sensation mongers who predicted that we would one day be able to harness the energy locked up in matter. Yet, only five years after his death in 1937, the first chain reaction was started in Chicago. What Rutherford, for all his wonderful insight, had failed to take into account was that a nuclear reaction might be discovered that would release more energy than that required to start it. To liberate the energy of matter, what was wanted was a nuclear "fire" analogous to chemical combustion, and the fission of uranium provided this. Once that was discovered, the harnessing of atomic energy was inevitable, though without the pressures of war it might well have taken the better part of a century.
>   . . . The example of Lord Rutherford demonstrates that it is not the man who knows most about a subject, and is the acknowledged master of his field, who can give the most reliable pointers to its future. Too great a burden of knowledge can clog the wheels of imagination; I have tried to embody this fact of observation in Clarke's law, which may be formulated as follows: When a distinguished but elderly scientist states that something is possible, he is almost certainly right. When he states that something is impossible, he is very probably wrong.

Consensus Method

To help overcome such limitations in forecasting by individual experts, consensus methods were developed. By far, the best known of these is the

Delphi technique. Generally, a Delphi exercise asks a group of experts on a certain subject—economics, medicine, automation, population, education, etc.—to state *anonymously* when a future event might occur. Their answers, with their reasons, are summarized and fed back to the entire group for a second round. This process may be repeated several times with the hope that eventually a narrowing of the initial spread of opinions will occur.

Cross-Impact Analysis

While in many respects a vast improvement over single expert forecasts, the Delphi techniques still has its disadvantages. For example, it tends to treat each component of the analysis as an independent variable. Cross-impact analysis attempts to correct this situation by evaluating each component of the forecast *in relation to each other.* For example, factors A and B may have a relatively low probability of occurrence. But the probability of factor A may be increased if factor B occurs. Cross-impact techniques try to account for such increases in probability.

Trend Extrapolation

If one buys the assumption that trends established in recent history will continue, then *trend extrapolation* might be used. A parameter—e.g., U.S. population, maximum aircraft speed, or even the world record in the mile run (see Figure 15–1)—is plotted on a graph against time. The analyst then extends the curve either by an "eyeball" extension or by a quantitative

FIGURE 15–1
Progress in the Mile Run

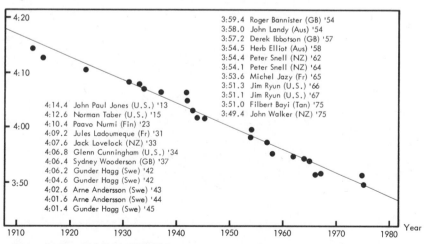

Source: Hopkins and Edwards (1976:45).

TABLE 15–1
Extrapolating World Records in Track

	Present	Projections	
Distance	Record	1976	2000
100m	9.9	9.8	9.5
400m	43.8	43.7	42.1
800m	1:43.7	1:42.1	1:40.4
1,500m	3:32.2	3:30.6	3:20.8
5,000m	13:13.0	13:09.0	12:20.0
10,000m	27:30.8	27:10.0	25:17.0
Marathon	2:08:33	2:06:30	1:55:00

Insufficient data available on 200m and hurdle events to make calculations.
Source: Hopkins and Edwards (1976:44).

curve fitting method. Table 15–1 shows the results this method gives when applied to track records.

As I see it, the biggest limitation to this method is the assumption that past trends hold, that we *know* what the curve is. Say that an analyst has the plot of historical data shown in Figure 15–2. How does this person know whether A or B is the proper extension? The first curve, represented by A, shows an exponential increase with no flattening in the time-range considered. For our purposes, we may think of an exponential growth curve as one that shows a constant *rate* of change; that is, the increase in December was greater than in November which, in turn, was greater than the increase in October and so on. This characteristic is exhibited by a number of parameters (e.g., maximum transport aircraft speed and energy conversion

FIGURE 15–2
Trend Extrapolation Dilemmas

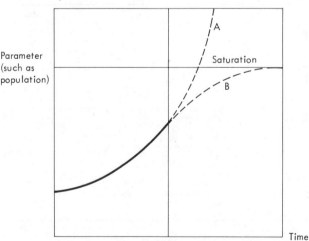

efficiency in illumination technology) at least until certain limits are hit (e.g., Concorde and the gallium arsenide diode).

But not all trends are exponential. And when one ignores the possibility of an *S*-shaped curve, such as represented by B, ludicrous forecasts can sometimes result.

For example, the growth in the number of scientists between 1850 and 1950 was very steep and probably followed roughly the path of the solid line in Figure 15–1. Someone who ignored the possibility of saturation might be lead to the mind boggling conclusion that, by the end of the century, all the Earth's inhabitants over the age of six would be holding doctorates in science. One also should be open to the possibility of certain external events or breakthroughs. In London in the latter part of the 19th century, with the horse as the principle means of rapid intracity transportation, the accumulation of manure in the streets was cause for no little concern. Naive extrapolation, ignoring the possibility of the technological breakthroughs such as the automobile, would have forecasted a city in 30 years buried.

Scenario

This method attempts to provide a narrative description of a potential course of developments—in a sense, it is a "future history." Now, most public administrators will admit that their organization's planning is usually done against a single set of assumptions about the future, or what Kahn and Wiener (1967) call "surprise free" futures. A few years later these plans prove to have been ineffective because of naive and incomplete consideration of the future that actually emerged. Most of us, after all, find it rather unpleasant to think about undesirable events that might occur.

But constructing alternative scenarios—pessimistic as well as optimistic —forces us out of this complacency. Considering a wide range of scenarios exposes events that could have a powerful effect and thus require new actions. Plans then can be modified to take into account these possible events.

Leading Indicators

One of the newest and most fascinating methods is Graham T. M. Molitor's (1975:204–10) schema of forecasting public policy change through leading indicators. Basically, Mr. Molitor suggests that by monitoring events, intellectual elites, literature, organizations, and political jurisdictions, the policy analyst can develop a better idea of what to expect in the future. The premise upon which this method builds goes something like this. Issues of public policy are almost always the result of unusual events that give rise to abuse or excess so extreme that public action eventually is required. Between the occurrence of the first, isolated event and the creation of public policy, Molitor thinks a fairly consistent pattern of behavior unfolds. The analyst's job, then, is one of monitoring this pattern as it unfolds. For example, we know that intellectual elites, who analyze and articulate social problems, tend to emerge around issues. Similarly, the victimized express their feelings and thus become powerful symbols for change. "By monitoring these . . . vanguards, whose ideas ultimately are diffused widely, early indications of change can be forecasted." (ibid.:206)

Meanwhile, the sequence by which different types of literature build up and provide a permanent written analysis and wider publicity of the new

FIGURE 15–3
Leading Political Jurisdictions

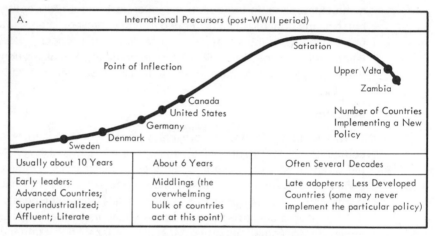

A.	International Precursors (post–WWII period)	
Usually about 10 Years	About 6 Years	Often Several Decades
Early leaders: Advanced Countries; Superindustrialized; Affluent; Literate	Middlings (the overwhelming bulk of countries act at this point)	Late adopters: Less Developed Countries (some may never implement the particular policy)

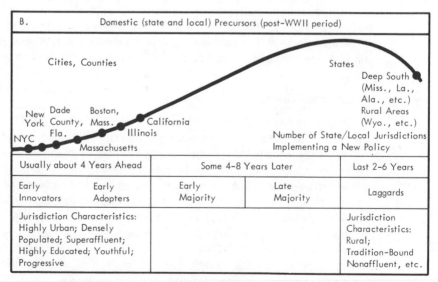

B.	Domestic (state and local) Precursors (post–WWII period)			
Usually about 4 Years Ahead		Some 4–8 Years Later		Last 2–6 Years
Early Innovators	Early Adopters	Early Majority	Late Majority	Laggards
Jurisdiction Characteristics: Highly Urban; Densely Populated; Superaffluent; Highly Educated; Youthful; Progressive				Jurisdiction Characteristics: Rural; Tradition–Bound Nonaffluent, etc.

Source: Molitor (1975:210).

ideas and concepts follows a rough pattern. The sequence, which might cover over 100 years, could go like this. At first, the early warnings about emerging problems appear in the more visionary classes of literature. (For example, it would appear that the poet Blake was one of the first to recognize the arrival of the Industrial Revolution and its social implications.) Then, the idea is rendered into specifics in monographs and speeches in specialized journals. Next, these phases: corrobation of details; institutional responses through journals for the cause; consideration in the mass media; and politicization of the issue in governmental reports and a diffusion of the idea among opinion leaders.

For a cause to be translated into public policy requires, however, more than advocates and articles—it requires organizational support. "Growth of institutional backing for a cause—whether measured by number of organizations, persons involved, or resources committed—follows exponential increases which tend to force serious consideration of the issue by public policy makers." (ibid.:209)

Ultimately, political power intercedes with certain leading political jurisdictions invariably among the first to implement new policy solutions. These early innovators and experimenters show the way to others; then, after the idea is proven, other jurisdictions emulate. As Figure 15–3 indicates certain jurisdictions "invariably are the first to innovate by implementing new public policy ideas."

Limitations to Forecasting

By definition, even the most sophisticated forecast yields only a probabilistic estimate of what will happen. Moreover, because some scientific and technological breakthroughs represent such large steps beyond the current state of knowledge, anticipation becomes exceedingly difficult. This difficulty can be seen from the two columns of concepts below (Clarke, ibid.:20). The concepts on the left were entirely unexpected. Perhaps even more interesting is the column on the right. These concepts have been around for hundreds, even thousands of years. "Some have been achieved, others will be achieved: others may be impossible. But which?" asks Clarke.

The Unexpected	*The Expected*
X rays	Automobiles
Nuclear energy	Flying machines
Radio; TV	Steam engines
Electronics	Submarines
Photography	Spaceships
Sound recording	Telephones
Quantum mechanics	Robots
Relativity	Death rays
Transistors	Transmutation
Masers; lasers	Artificial life
Superconductors;	Immortality
superfluids	Invisibility

The Unexpected	The Expected
Atomic clocks	Levitation
Determining composition	Teleportation
of celestial bodies	Communication with
Dating the past	the dead
(carbon 14, etc.)	Observing the past,
Detecting invisible	the future
planets	Telepathy
The ionosphere;	
Van Allen belts	

Despite such limitations in the art of forecasting, the fact remains that it has become a part of governance. How and where forecasting can and does fit into the governmental process will be discussed later. For now, let us concern ourselves with a more difficult question: What might the future of public administration in the United States look like?

Most answers to the preceding question begin with a listing of "significant trends" that will "shape the future." Now, this approach is not necessarily disreputable — although sometimes it seems a little too easy, like hunting from a helicopter. More to the point, in taking this approach we run two risks. First is the danger of selecting not a manifold (in the sense of operating on several things at once), long-run trend but what I shall call a pseudo-trend. Second is the failure to make explicit *how* these trends are going to affect the future of the public services.

TWO TRENDS

This section and the following one outline what are, in my judgment, three trends expecially important to the future of public administration: the politics of scarcity, the revolution of rising entitlements, and the integration of business into the political and social order.

The Politics of Scarcity

Around 1973, historians might one day note, the 19th century vision of Utopia — where all could indulge their appetites — was replaced by the specter of Doomsday. The passion for declivity ran high as plans for a "no growth" economy were anxiously put forward. Soon, public opinion polls were reporting that, by 51 percent to 34 percent, respondents agreed that the "times have changed and we must cut way back on the amount and kind of things we use." And, when respondents were asked in one poll to pick which of 13 possibilities are likely to be serious threats to our society and life as we know it in the United States, "the most frequently chosen responses" was "rapid depletion of natural resources."

Today, fortunately, we are beginning to get a more intelligent discussion of our situation with reference to energy availability, to potential food pro-

One of the world's leading futurist, Herman Kahn pioneered the use of the scenario in the early 1960s. More recently, he along with his associates at the Hudson Institute have argued that many of the doomsday prophecies of the early 1970s do not allow for qualitative changes in the system.

duction, to other raw materials, and to the pollution threat. The Hudson Institute (Kahn, Brown, and Martel 1976) explicitly analyzed many of the doomsday prophecies of the early 1970s. In brief, they found that these prophecies fail to allow for qualitative changes in the system. For example, through either existing or future technology, materials (e.g., copper) can be recycled and new sources of energy (e.g. solar) can be tapped. They further point out that the world has already adjusted—without catastrophe—to the increase in oil prices (which, after all, did not result from any physical shortages of crude oil but from a cartel).

Nevertheless, it is doubtful that scarcity can ever be eliminated. To do the kinds of things Herman Kahn and his colleagues at the Hudson Institute suggest will itself require a far more sophisticated application of technology and management of existing resources than ever before imagined.

And new technology brings problems as well as benefits. Man-induced climatic change to increase agricultural output certainly poses a long term threat. Similarly, genetic research to eliminate birth defects could lead to the creation of devastating new diseases. And nuclear safety needs no comment. These technological problems, in turn, lead to *the necessity for greater coordination, participation, planning, and regulation.* These administrative and political necessities—resulting from efforts to deal with physical scarcity—will not come cheaply. The custodial costs of managing our sources become enormous.

"Georgescu is a remarkable man," says his friend and fellow economist Paul Samuelson, a Nobel prize winner who shares with Georgescu credit for certain refinements in the theory of production. "Like vintage burgundy, he's appreciated by economic connoisseurs all over the world." In a review of Georgescu's book, *The Entropy Law and the Economic Process*, another leading economist, Kenneth Boulding, wrote that if the right 500 people read it, "science and economics perhaps would never be the same again."

Vanderbilt University

Few thinkers have thought through these problems with greater care than Nicholas Georgescu-Roegen, a Romainan by birth, statistician by training, and gadfly economic professor at Vanderbilt University. The starting point of his thinking is the entropy law, or second law of thermodynamics. Basically, the law tells us that certain processes are irreversible, that is, they go in one direction only and can never be repeated except at far greater cost on the whole. Thus, once you consume energy, it cannot be used again—it is not recyclable.

For example, a lump of coal can only be burned once. Of course, the resulting heat, smoke, and ashes have the same amount of energy as the lump but the energy in these products is so dissipated that it is, for all intents and purposes, unavailable for use. So, the entropy law says that the natural state of things is to pass from order to disorder. But, Georgescu finds little in human behavior that lead him to think that people know this.

According to Georgescu, the entropy law rules supremely over the economic process. While in the short run this might make little difference, in the long run it does. Georgescu, therefore, argues that we can not ignore what happens to our grandchildren or our great-grandchildren if we are to maintain any concern for the human species. Georgescu (1975:374) writes: "There is an elementary principle of economics according to which the only way to attribute a relevant price to an irreproducible object, say, to Leonardo's Mona Lisa, is to have absolutely everyone bid on it. Otherwise, if only you and I were to bid, one of us could get it for just a few dollars. The bid — i.e., that price — would clearly be parochial. This is exactly what happens for the irreproducible resources. Each generation can use as many terrestrial resources and produce as much pollution as its own bidding alone decides. Future generations are not, simply because they cannot be, present on today's market."

What does this imply in terms of public policy? Here we must limit ourselves to only three items from his purposed "minimal bioeconomic program." First, Georgescu contends that the Sun should become our chief energy source. Second, we need to get rid of the "circumdrome of the shaving machine," which is "to shave oneself faster so as to have more time to work on a machine that shaves still faster, and so on *ad infinitum*." (Ibid.:378) Third, we also need to get rid of the old form of wealth that was courted by the industrial society, namely, a type of wealth wherein there is a tyranny of quantity. Georgescu proposes that it be replaced by an economics of quality.

The Revolution of Rising Entitlements

The title of this subsection comes from Daniel Bell's book, *The Cultural Contradictions of Capitalism.* Professor Bell maintains that the American promise of equality has been transformed into a revolution of "rising entitlements"; that is, claims on the government to implement an array of newly defined and vastly expanded social rights. "This may take the form of a demand for a basic minimum family income, to give each family the floor of a modest standard of living; or a demand for "educational drawing rights" in which each person would be entitled to 12 or 14 or 16 years of free education, the times to be taken at the option of the individual; or a demand for the assurance of lifetime employment through a combination of private and public guarantees. The particular demands will vary with time and place. They are, however, not just the claims of the minorities, the poor, or the disadvantageous; they are the claims of all groups in the society, claims for protections and rights — in short, for entitlements." (Bell 1976:233) According to Bell, just about all grievances are today getting dumped into the lap of the government.

Not surprisingly, the revolution of rising entitlements leads to an extraordinary variety of social welfare programs (at last count over 1,100 at the federal level and, recalling Figure 3–2, this figure does seem possible). Bell notes parenthetically an even more remarkable fact from an article in the February 22, 1974, issue of *Science:* "In the state of California, on any particular day, about 7.2 million of the state's 19.5 million people were under some institutional care, in day care centers, schools (but not colleges), hospitals, prisons, old age homes, and the like. The total was nearly as large as the state's entire civilian labor force that year."

In his *Cultural Contradictions of Capitalism,* Daniel Bell maps a difficult terrain. He finds more and more Americans demanding that the government make them "equal" to other Americans. These demands, he suggested, may endanger the political system. Earlier, Bell coined the phrase "postindustrial society" to describe the new social structures evolving in modern societies. In his post-industrial society, the dominant institution will be service institutions like governments, hospitals, and universities.

Harvard University News Office

Bell's ideas seem consistent with what George Cabor Lodge (1975) calls the New American Ideology. The traditional American ideology breaks down into five great ideas. These most clearly articulated in the 17th century by the English philosopher John Locke, follow:

Individualism: the notion that the community is no more than the sum of its parts.

Property rights: the guarantee that the individual will be free from the predatory powers of the government.

Competition: the means of controlling the uses of property to serve individual consumer wants.

The limited state: a government lacking authority to plan or interfere significantly in economic life but capable of responding to crises or interest group pressures.

Scientific specialization and fragmentation: the theory that "if we attend to the parts, as experts and specialists, the whole will take care of itself." (Ibid.:10–11)

The new American ideology that Mr. Lodge sees emerging has five quite different elements:

Communitarianism as the replacement for individualism. "For most people today, fulfillment occurs through their participation in an organic social process." (Ibid.:17)

Rights of membership in the community: rights to survival, income, health, and other basic needs—replacing property rights. (This element, in particular, is reminiscent of the idea of rising entitlements.)

Community needs and purposes substituting for competition as a method
of controlling or justifying the use of property.

The state as planner—that is, as the setter of community goals and the
arbiter of community needs.

Holism: the theory that nature groups units of whatever kind into wholes
and indeed into a single, great unified whole. Scientific specialization
is giving way to a new sense of the crucial interdependence of things,
such as the fragility of the life supporting biosphere.

A THIRD TREND: INTEGRATION OF BUSINESS INTO THE POLITICAL AND SOCIAL ORDER

The preceding two trends—namely, the politics of scarcity and the revolution of rising expectations—should increase the likelihood of (i.e., cross
impact) a third. This third trend we call the integration of economic activity
(i.e., business) into the American political and social order. Neil H. Jacoby,
founding dean of UCLA's Graduate School of Management, agrees. Jacoby
(1973) argues that today's loud debate about corporations derives from the
fact that the American people are in the process of writing a new "social
contract" to govern corporate–societal relationships in which they expect
more of the corporation than in the past.

The Corporation as a Social Invention

But why is not this trend more widely recognized? One of the reasons, I
submit, is that we tend to think of invention only in terms of technology. Yet,
the corporation is surely as much an invention, as much a product of human
ingenuity, as the automobile. And, like technology, social inventions evolve.

The birth of the corporation might be traced to two events. The first was
the chartering of foreign trading companies by the Tudor monarchy in
England at the end of the 15th century. Chartered companies could, however, engage only in those activities specified in their charters. The second
event was when men of property began to pool resources for a common
enterprise. These unchartered companies, while able to set their own goals,
still faced a dual check—competition and individual liability.

In the United States, at first, states chartered companies. In time, however, the competition among states for corporations (which of course meant
more prosperity) led to significant modifications on the original design—
in particular, extremely broad goals and limited individual liability. Another
modification came from the judiciary: the concept of the corporation as a
"legal person." Thus the corporation acquired all the rights and privileges
of individual citizens.

Today we see another modification in the corporation: ownership is
separated from control; that is, managers control the corporations while the
owners hold tokens of ownership in the form of shares. In addition, we see

an immense growth in corporate scope and power. Professors Berle and Means (1932) were among the first to see this change when they pointed out that the corporation, "involves a concentration of power in the economic field comparable to the concentration of religious power in the medieval church or of political power in the national state."

Yet, we have not attempted to control corporations in the same way that we have controlled the powers of government. Federal regulation of the corporation has proceeded by attempts to prohibit specific acts through regulatory agencies, an expensive approach to be sure. (See Table 15–2.) But despite the cost, the record of these agencies has been something less than a complete success. Consider (examples drawn from Mayer 1976; *U.S. News,* June 30, 1975; and *New York Times,* June 29, 1975):

TABLE 15–2
Size and Cost of Federal Regulators

Number of Employees with Regulatory Functions		*Additions to the Cost of What People Buy: Estimated Yearly Costs of Government Regulations and Restrictions to Consumers*	
Agriculture Department Animal, Plant Health Inspection Packers Stockyards Administration	14,054	Economic regulation includes regulation of transportation, financial institutions, foreign and domestic trade practices, among other things	$45 to $60 billion
Environmental Protection Agency	9,203		
Food and Drug Administration	6,405		
Labor Department Employment Standards Occupational Safety	4,715	Environmental regulation	$50 to $60 billion
Treasury Department Bureau of Alcohol, Tobacco, and Firearms	3,760	Health, safety, product regulations	More than $10 billion
Federal Energy Administration	3,125	Total	$130 billion (estimated), or $2,000 for each American family
Interior Department Mine Safety	2,851		
National Labor Relations Board	2,454		
Equal Employment Opportunity Commission	2,189		
Securities and Exchange Commission	2,086		
Transportation Department Highway Safety Rail Safety	2,079		
Interstate Commerce Commission	2,061		
Federal Communications Commission	1,971		
Federal Trade Commission	1,569		
Federal Power Commission	1,320		
Other Agencies	3,602		
Total Federal Regulators	63,444		

Source: *U.S. News and World Report,* June 30, 1975.

The Federal Communications Commission delayed for ten years the operations of the domestic communications satellite.

The Federal Power Commission encouraged overconsumption of natural gas—our cleanest fuel—by setting the price at a level far below the likely market price.

The Interstate Commerce Commission created great expenses for trucking firms by insisting on its authority to set every route and rate for every category of freight. Thus, in some instances, trucks are not permitted to take the most direct route to their destination and must return empty even if cargoes are available to be carried.

The Federal Drug Administration's regulations are so heavily biased to keep drugs off the market that Victor Fuchs of Stanford observes that "penicillin and fluorexene, two valuable drugs, are both lethal to some laboratory animals." Thus if these drugs were just being developed today, clear evidence of their toxicity in animals would probably result in their rejection long before approval was sought to market them.

A General Accounting Office report on effects of environmental and land-use regulations found that more than 6 billion board feet of mature timber in national forests die every year because federal rules prohibit its harvest.

Mandatory safety standards for power lawn mowers being developed for the Consumer Product Safety Commission could increase the cost of a $100 lawn mower to $186 and might put 25 manufacturers out of business, according to a Stanford Research Institute study.

A tire-quality grading system being developed by the National Highway Traffic Safety Administration could cost consumers as much as $150 million a year and yet be too confusing to be of use of tire buyers, according to a report by the Rubber Manufacturers Association.

In contrast to this regulatory—almost ad hoc—approach to the control of business activity, the U.S. Constitution provides for a much more general approach to the control of government: distribution of power, creating checks and balances; assignment of responsibilities; etc. Perhaps it would not be unreasonable to expect in the coming decades a similar (that is, more general) approach taken towards the corporation.

What form might a more general approach to the control of the corporation take? One possibility is through taxation. William J. Baumol (1973) of Princeton University's Department of Economics suggests a plan whereby a firm's effluence would be metered and it would pay a certain amount for every unit of pollution. The regulatory approach currently in use says, in effect, "You can pollute up to a certain point free of charge; after that, you pay a fine. That is, provided the police catch you and a court finds you guilty." Under Baumol's plan, a firm simply pays a bill at the end of each month for its pollution of air and water. The police and courts—already overloaded—are not involved.

Another form that a general approach control of the corporation might take is hardly new: federal chartering. Lodge (1975:291–92) explains how it might work:

> This charter—not the ideas of property and ownership—would be the fundamental legitimizer of the corporation. It would establish that Exxon, for example, is not an individual with rights of privacy but a public collective chartered by the community to serve certain functions, and that all its activities are susceptible to public inspection. The corporate charter should stipulate certain conditions of legitimacy and set forth general rules of corporate organization and conduct. Most important, it should detail the information that the corporation is required to disclose regularly. . . .
>
> . . . The national charter should be relatively brief, general, and flexible, enabling corporations to invent and to experiment as far as possible. It should also leave room for supplementary legitimization by the various communities which the corporation affects and by the internal membership of the corporation. The corporation must be seen as a part of the several communities it touches, and essential to the design and development of the communities in which it is actually located. . . .

A New Public Private Balance

To attempt to spell out the exact relationship that will emerge would require another book at least the length of this one. Moreover, it would be too speculative for my taste. In place of a second volume I present Figure 15–4, which attempts to show in broadest strokes the kind of public-private balance likely to emerge at the national level in the United States within the next two decades.

FIGURE 15–4
A Possible Future Structure of U.S. Government at the National Level

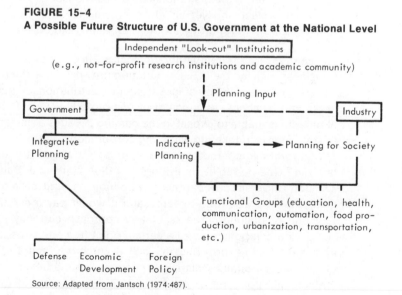

Source: Adapted from Jantsch (1974:487).

As shown, industry is a *partner* of government in the attainment of societal goals in all functional areas except defense, economic development, and foreign policy. In these three areas, government engages in what might be called integrative planning; that is, involving all concerned parties (the State Department, for example, would be intimately involved in defense planning). Integration planning is the opposite of piecemeal planning or incrementalism (see Chapter 6).

Indicative planning and the complex of relationships represented by the dashed line connecting government and industry will be discussed in some detail in the cases ahead.

The other dashed line, connecting "look-out" institutions with both government and industry, represents the flow of analytical studies into the planning process in both sectors. These studies provide, in particular, information on problems of the future and consequences of current programs and regulatory policies. Critics, however, argue that sometimes the scope of these studies goes too far, beyond the providing of input for public decision makers to the setting of public policy. For this reason, critics see these institutions as forming a kind of shadow government and becoming a threat to democratic morality (see, for example, Guttman and Sillner 1976).

In any event, if government is to make the crucial decisions regarding the growth of the economy and its balance, then sponsorship of these kinds of analytical studies will become increasingly important. Because of the intricately linked nature of these studies, a prime concern of government will be to husband this analytical talent.

The kinds of studies we are talking about here include decision and system analysis (discussed in Chapter 6), cost-benefit analysis (in Chapter 11), and futures research (earlier in this chapter). Included here also are two more broad gauged types of studies heretofore not discussed.

The first of these is the *Environmental Impact Statement*. EIS is a document prepared either by a governmental agency or private concern that outlines how a proposed action (e.g., construction of a new dam or highway) might affect the quality of the human environment. The requirement for EISs began with the passage of the National Environmental Policy Act (NEPA) of 1969. Section 102 (2) (c) of the act sets forth the EIS requirement. The significance of this requirement was not initially apparent to most government agencies or to private industry. Today the number and variety of EIS required at all levels of government is enormous.

A basic framework for an EIS might be something like the following: (1) describe present conditions; (2) describe proposed action (e.g., new highway or housing project); (3) describe probable impacts of each alternative to soil conditions, wildlife, climate, existing pollution, transportation congestion, aesthetics and so forth; (4) identify the alternative chosen; (5) describe probable impacts of proposed action in detail, and (6) describe techniques to be used to minimize harm.

Similar to the writing of an EIS is *technology assessment*. Joseph T.

Coates (1971:225) defines technology assessment as "the systematic study of the effects on society that may occur when a technology is introduced, extended, or modified, with a special emphasis on the impacts that are unintended, indirect, and delayed." Technology assessment became firmly established as a decision making tool in 1972 when Congress created the Office of Technology Assessment. Figure 15–5 shows the seven major steps in technology assessment; Table 15–3, just how far reaching these impacts can be and how wide a technology assessment exercise must cast its net.

FIGURE 15–5
Seven Major Steps in Making a Technology Assessment

Step 1	DEFINE THE ASSESSMENT TASK Discuss Relevant Issues and Any Major Problems Establish Scope (breadth and depth) of Inquiry Develop Project Ground Rules
Step 2	DESCRIBE RELEVANT TECHNOLOGIES Describe Major Technology Being Assessed Describe Other Technologies Supporting the Major Technology Describe Technologies Competitive to the Major and Supporting Technologies
Step 3	DEVELOP STATE-OF-SOCIETY ASSUMPTIONS Identify and Describe Major Nontechnological Factors Influencing the Application of the Relevant Technologies
Step 4	IDENTIFY IMPACT AREAS Ascertain Those Societal Characteristics That Will Be Most Influenced by the Application of the Assessed Technology
Step 5	MAKE PRELIMINARY IMPACT ANALYSIS Trace and Integrate the Process by Which the Assessed Technology Makes Its Societal Influence Felt
Step 6	IDENTIFY POSSIBLE ACTION OPTIONS Develop and Analyze Various Programs for Obtaining Maximum Public Advantage from the Assessed Technologies
Step 7	COMPLETE IMPACT ANALYSIS Analyze the Degree to Which Each Action Option Would Alter the Specific Societal Impacts of the Assessed Technology Discussed in Step 5

Source: Mitre Corporation (1971).

TABLE 15–3
Selected Impacts of the Automobile, 1895 to Present

Values

Geographic mobility

Expansion of personal freedom

Prestige and material status derived from automobile ownership

Over-evaluation of automobile as an extension of the self—an identity machine

Privacy—insulates from both environment and human contact

Consideration of automobile ownership as an essential part of normal living (household goods)

Development of automobile cultists (group identification symbolized by type of automobile owned)

Environment

Noise pollution

Automobile junkyards

Roadside litter

Social

Changes in patterns of courtship, socialization and training of children, work habits, use of leisure time, and family patterns

Created broad American middle class, and reduced class differences

Created new class of semiskilled industrial workers

Substitution of automobile for mass transit

Ready conversion of the heavy industrial capability of automobile factories during World War II to make weapons

Many impacts on crime

Increased tourism

Changes in education through bussing (consolidated school versus "one room country schoolhouse")

Medical care and other emergency services more rapidly available

Traffic congestion

Annual loss of life from automobile accidents about 60,000

Increased incidence of respiratory ailments, heart disease, and cancer

Older, poorer neighborhood displacement through urban freeway construction

Institutional

Automotive labor union activity set many precedents

Decentralized, multidivisional structure of the modern industrial corporation evident throughout the auto industry

Modern management techniques

Consumer installment credit

Unparalleled standard of living

Emergence of U.S. as foremost commercial and military power in world

Expansion of field of insurance

Rise of entrepreneurship

Basis for an oligopolistic model for other sectors of the economy

Land usage for highways—takes away from recreation, housing, etc.

Land erosion from highway construction

Water pollution (oil in streams from road run-off)

Unsightly billboards

Air pollution—lead, asbestos, HC, CO, NO_x, SO_x

Demography

Population movement to suburbs

Shifts in geographic sites of principal U.S. manufacturers

Displacement of agricultural workers from rural to urban areas

Movement of business and industry to suburbs

Increased geographic mobility

Economic

Mainstay and prime mover of American economy in the 20th century

Large number of jobs directly related to automobile industry (one out of every six)

Automobile industry the lifeblood of many other major industries

Rise of small businesses such as service stations and tourist accommodations

Suburban real estate boom

Drastic decline of horse, carriage, and wagon businesses

Depletion of fuel reserves

Stimulus to exploration for drilling of new oil fields and development of new refining techniques, resulting in cheaper and more sophisticated methods

Increased expenditure for road expansion and improvement

Increased federal, state, and local revenues through automobile and gasoline sales taxes

Decline of railroads (both passengers and freight)

Federal regulation of interstate highways and commerce as a pattern for other fields

Highway lobby—its powerful influence

Source: Strasser (1973).

A Contract State?

Now, to the heart of Figure 15–3 — the relationship between government and business. In an effort to meet the revolution of rising expectations, yet at the same time avoid further expansion, government will increasingly farm out a very large number of governmental activities to businesses that agree to render those services for a profit.

Contracting itself is not new. All levels of government have hired contractors to construct public office building, dams, airports, sewers, schools, barracks, government-owned utilities, and similar projects. But, as can be seen from Table 15–4, in recent years the scope of public sector contracts have moved far beyond capital projects.

Contracting explains the melancholy paradox of how the federal budget could increase from $70 billion a year to nearly $370 billion in 20 years without any significant increase in the number of full-time federal civil servants. In 1946, 30 percent of the federal administrative budget was spent on civil service payroll; by 1966, only 22 percent on full-time government employees but 34 percent on contractors. Since 1966, the government employee-private contractor breach has widened considerably. According to Guttman and Millner (1976), it today takes nearly 80,000 full-time government employees merely to administer the almost $60 billion we spend annually on such contractors and the more than $50 billion we spend each year in grants to state and local governments and such nonprofit organizations as universities. In an effort to bring order from chaos of government purchasing policies and practices generated by an undertaking of this size, the federal government in August 1976 established the Procurement Policy Office as a semiautonomous wing of OMB. As the first administrator of the new office put it, "we are the interface between the executive branch and industry."

The contract should not be confused with *public-private partnerships* and *governmental corporations.* The former are business-like corporations that are permitted to make a profit while performing some specific function desired by government. The Federal National Mortgage Associations and Communications Satellite Corporation are cases in point. Such organizations operate in close cooperation with the government. For example, in housing and other urban developments, the government partner might condemn land and convey it on an advantageous basis to the private partner.

A governmental corporation, on the other hand, is a totally different corporate form for accomplishing assigned public purposes. Such corporations are totally owned by the government; operated not-for-profit; staffed by civil service employees; and have been in operation for as long as 40 years, whereas public-private corporations have become significant only within the last dozen years. The TVA and Port Authority of New York and New Jersey are examples of governmental corporations.

But what are the advantages and disadvantages of contracting? Among the advantages, we might note, first, is a higher probability of efficiency. For example, in 1970 New York City found that it cost its department of sanitation almost three times as much to collect a ton of garbage as it costs the private

TABLE 15–4

Subject	Governmental Customer	Corporate Contractor
Auto safety	New York State	Fairchild-Hiller
Campus design	St. Louis junior colleges	McDonnell-Douglas
Classroom scheduling	St. Louis junior colleges	McDonnell-Douglas
Desalinization plant design	U.S. Department of Interior	Lockheed
Education information system	City of Philadelphia	Philco-Ford
Education information system	State of California	Aerojet-General
Educational reference center	U.S. Office of Education	North American Rockwell
Educational technology	U.S. Department of Education	Lockheed
High speed ground transportation	U.S. Department of Transportation	Hughes Aircraft
High speed ground transportation	U.S. Department of Transportation	TRW, Inc.
Information system	State of Alaska	Lockheed
Information system	State of California	Lockheed
Information system	State of Massachusetts	Lockheed
Instrumentation research	U.S. Department of Transportation	Melpar
International development	Agency for International Development	Lockheed
Medical information system	State of Vermont	TRW, Inc.
Parcel sorter	U.S. Post Office	Aerojet-General
Power management system	U.S. Department of the Interior	North American Rockwell
Regional development	Department of Commerce	Litton
Satellite communications	Comsat Corporation	Northrop
Supersonic transport aircraft	U.S. Department of Transportation	Boeing
Supersonic transport engines	U.S. Department of Transportation	General Electric
Systems analysis of poverty	State of Colorado	Philco-Ford
Traffic control system	New York City	Sperry-Rand
Transportation system design	State of California	North American Rockwell
Turbines for ground transportation	U.S. Department of Transportation	United Aircraft
Waste management	State of California	Aerojet-General
Waste management	U.S. Public Health Service	Aerojet-General
Zip code reader	U.S. Post Office	Philco-Ford

Source: Weidenbaum (1969:81)

entrepreneurs. Furthermore, the average sanitation truck is out of commission more than 30 percent of the time; the private truck, only about 5 percent of the time. E. S. Savas (1971:56), who served as First Deputy City Administrator in the Office of the Mayor, offers this explanation: if you own a mere one or two trucks, as most cartmen do, and your livelihood depends on them, you make sure they stay in working order. Another explanation of the three-fold difference in collection costs is also simple and derives from such embarrassingly old-fashioned concepts as close supervision and good managements, motivated by the lure of profits. The more refuse a private cartment picks up in a day, the more money he makes. In the municipal monopoly, there is absolutely no connection between the two.

The efficiency issue, however, might not be as clear cut as Savas views it. Evidences of business inefficiency range from confused charge accounts to the questioned quality of steel plates in U.S. Navy submarines to the reliability of home appliances. And the transit and construction industries are notoriously inefficient. Meanwhile there are instances of sustained good performance by government bureaus. The Processed Products Inspection Service of the U.S. Department of Agriculture, for example, has been solely supported for over 40 years by its own fee earning.

In Chapter 2, we noted the tendency for bureaucracies sometimes to disturb legislative intent. Under the contract system, where performance specification can be written in fairly specific language, such distortion becomes less likely.

A third advantage of contracting is that it reduces the opportunity for empire building within government.

A fourth advantage of contracting is that it would help free government from routine details. In the long run, perhaps, government could become a learning system (see Schon 1971). As a learning system, the federal government's role would be to detect significant shifts in society and in particular, to the emergence of ideas in good currency. (According to Donald A. Schon, problems of public policy are not given: they depend on whether they are seen; whether they are in good currency. For example, in early 1964, the Congress was focusing on competition with the Russians and pursuit of "excellence." If one went into Congress speaking of cost-benefit analysis, program budgeting, or productivity, one would surely be ignored.)

The federal government's role would also include learning from the periphery of society what works and does not work. In the past, Schon argues, government learning has been confined to efforts to induce localities to behave in conformity to *its* policy. As a learning system, however, the federal government comes to function as facilitator of society's learning, rather than as society's trainer.

But contracting has its disadvantages. Perhaps the most obvious is that too cozy relationships between business and government contracting personnel might develop. The immediate result of such relationships is graft. But some observers, looking further ahead, see totalitarian tendencies as the result. Government contracting officers and the contractors could simply begin to bypass both the legislative and executive branch, enrich themselves, and build a syndicate state, responsive to hardly anyone.

Another fairly obvious disadvantage is that, in certain areas of public policy, contracting seems inappropriate. Should, for example, Westinghouse be responsible for the education of third graders? The implications of a corporation shaped curriculum for young minds are staggering.

Which leads us to a final disadvantage: How does the government control the quality (as opposed to cost) of public interest services? Lyle C. Fitch (1974:511) writes: "For goods and services which can be identified, weighed, and measured, or tested as to performance and use, tests concentrate on how well the product meets specifications." But, he continues, "Where the product is not easily measurable as to quality *or* quantity, the apparatus of control involves product inspections, investigations of complaints (as of faulty service), and monitoring of production processes. Internal controls are subject to various intramural pressures—for example, hostility of administrative agencies toward auditors. External controls are vulnerable to friendly relationships between representatives of contracting agencies and contractors' representatives, political pressure, and outright bribery. In this respect, contracting out has no clear advantages over government in-house account production; in fact, the difficulties of quality control in many cases may be greater with private contractors."

Still, the contract system does not necessarily diminish the government's ability to incorporate political objectives such as small business preference, fair employment practices, labor regulation, and safety standards—into their contracts.

The Future of U.S. Government: The Search for the Middle Path

Despite the foregoing limitations to contracting, the U.S. government will continue to farm out its activities. I think the revolution of rising entitlements makes this more likely than ever. For if the government attempts to answer the clamor for more subsidies and entitlements by itself, independent of the private sector, it runs the risk of becoming a cumbersome, bureaucratic monstrosity. And worse: the revolution of rising entitlements could lead to system overload, ending in the total paralysis of state management.

For a number of reasons, however, contracting may help prevent such unsavory situations. Decentralization through contracts disperses responsibility for decisions and their effects. At the same time, we have good, empirical evidence that performance by the private sector can be just as effective and efficient as government in attaining societal goals. As government begins to get out of the "doing," it becomes freer to concentrate its efforts on differentiating public needs from public wants; to sort out who can do what most effectively in society; to consider new approaches to long-standing problems; and to discover and disclose inconsistencies or overlapping among all its interacting parts. In short, government becomes better focused.

In much the same way as rising entitlements increases the likelihood of contracting, the politics of scarcity increases the likelihood that national government will engage in planning on a much more systematic basis than in the past. But in speaking of planning in the United States, we must choose

Henry Ford II has few rivals for candor. Unlike some of his business colleagues, he does not shudder at the idea of a national planning group. "Some would worry," he says, "that over the years this kind of group would tend to be giving orders, deciding who gets what or when. That's not what I'm talking about. A timetable, cost effectiveness—those kind of things—a look at population growth; usages of raw materials, their availability, where they come from; what the price situation is going to be over a long period of time; other things that any one organization can do for itself only in a very limited way. Take a certain number of people and a certain gross national product, and how much steel do you need in a year? What kind of growth do you expect? We're going to need all kinds of plans."

our words with care. As Robert V. Roosa (1976) points out: "Much of the confusion and heated anxiety evident in the current debate stems from an ambiguity of language, not of objectives. We have not yet invented a descriptive word to distinguish a moderate concept of planning from a rigid, centralized economic plan. Yet there surely is a zone, somewhere along the spectrum between a collectivist economic plan and a renunciation of all planning, in which an optimum relationship—a planning compatibility—between governmental influence and private initiative can be found."

Significantly, we have already begun to see some leading indicators that more systematic planning is probably likely in the coming decade. For example, on May 21, 1975, Senators Jacob K. Javits and Hubert H. Humphrey introduced the previously mentioned Balanced Growth and Economic Planning Act of 1975. The act would establish a three member Economic Planning Board in the executive office of the president "to reform the government's management of its own economic policies and to enable it to better coordinate and cooperate with the private sector in the achievement of agreed upon national goals," (Humphrey 1975).

Regardless of what specific mechanisms and procedures might be established, a national planning group would probably attempt to meet the following five needs (Roosa, ibid.): (1) the need for better data—more accurate, more comprehensible and more usable; (2) the need for an early warning service, capable of locating at least some of the emerging problems within the economy and focusing appropriate attention upon them, (3) the need to trace through the long-range implications of the actions of present government agencies and to sort out inconsistencies among them, (4) the need to identify probable long-range economic needs that are not being met by existing programs, and (5) the need to formulate long-range goals for the national goals that reflect the need to compromise between concern for the quality of life and the hard economics of real cost. (For example, what effect did aesthetic and environmental constraints on the Alaskan pipeline have on unemployment among the black teenagers in New York City? On starvation among brown men in Bangladesh?)

How does the private sector view this trend towards planning? Apprehensively, would not be an unfair one-word characterization. And the root of this apprehension is clear enough: the danger that this moderate approach to planning, once begun, could be transformed into the rigid, centralized variety.

But some business leaders are less apprehensive than others. Henry Ford II, who has been head of the firm that bears his name for 30 years, is one. In an interview that appeared in *Time* (February 10, 1975), he made these points: "The U.S. has problems, and one of them is that it is always swinging one way or the other like a pendulum. We never plan anything. Take air- and water-pollution control, for instance. Suddenly there is a great big flap, and everybody gets excited, and all of a sudden some law is passed; it's got to be done within a very short time frame and it costs you a fortune to do it. You can't clean up the country in four years. I think there's got to be more central planning. Not the kind of central planning the Russians have, where they order the whole damned economy from a central plan. I'm talking about a federal planning organization that collects and disseminates information."

Other students of business contend that this type of indicative planning and specification of community goals would probably reduce the need for government interference in the economy. By giving guidance and coherence, government would have less occasion to stumble in to pick up the failures.

Parenthetically, we might note that local governments will not be immune to the trend toward more planning. Indeed, sudden industrialization and growth (especially in the South and West) have pushed *growth management* well toward the top of the local administrator's list of concerns. But, again, this challenge does not necessarily mean centralized control of economic activity. Growth management does, however, involve generating enough cooperation among the groups and persons involved to develop the economic, political, and social tools needed to use them to implement solutions to these questions: Where should growth be located? What should the rate of growth be? How should the benefits of growth be shared? How would the costs of growth be paid for, and who should pay for them? How can the parties-at-interest to growth be brought together to manage growth? (Gilmore and Duff 1975)

These, to be sure, are important questions, but unfortunately we lack the space to give them an adequate airing. I must, accordingly, limit myself to recommending John S. Gilmore's "Boom Town May Hinder Energy Resource Development," (*Science,* February 13, 1976) and Luther J. Carter's "Dade County: The Politics of Managing Urban Growth" (*Science,* June 4, 1976) as excellent introductions to the subject.

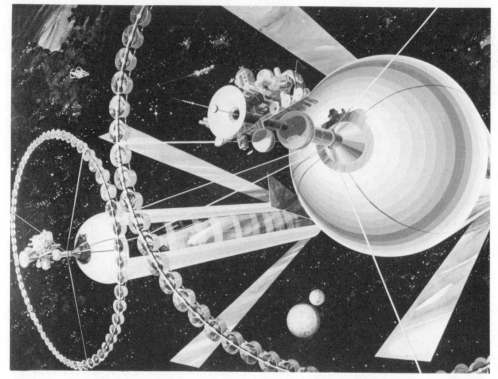

National Aeronautic and Space Administration

What kind of managers will space colonies need? In this photo, the reader must imagine himself or herself as a 21st century resident of a space colony returning home after a holiday on Earth. The 32 kilometer (19 miles) long, 6,400 meter (4 miles) diameter cylinder at right and its twin at left are seen as they would appear from an approaching spaceship some 32 kilometers (20 miles) away. The concept of a space colony orbiting between the Earth and Moon is suggested by Dr. Gerald K. O'Neill of Princeton University. He is part of the group of university and NASA experts who will study space colonization at the Ames Research Center during a 10-week period beginning this month. The colony designs depicted in this artist's rendering represent the largest of four types of space habitations outlined by Dr. O'Neill and could accommodate a population of 200,000 to several million, depending on how the interior is planned. Each cylinder would rotate around its axis once every 114 seconds to create Earth-like gravity. Solar energy would be the source of power and lunar or asteroid raw materials would be used for construction. All manufacturing processes would be carried on in space. The cylindrical portion is the living area and the interior could be fashioned to resemble an Earth landscape. The teacup-shaped containers ringing the cylinder are agricultural stations and the cylinder is capped by a manufacturing and power station. Large moveable rectangular mirrors on the sides of the cylinders, hinged at the lower end, would direct sunlight into the interior, regulate the seasons, and control the day-night cycle.

TOMORROW'S ADMINISTRATOR

It would be hard to imagine the foregoing trends having no effect on administrative behavior in the decades ahead. By way of conclusion—not only to this chapter but also to the entire work—let me suggest four traits that may go a long way toward characterizing tomorrow's administrators, public or private.

First, they will need to be generalists. Only generalists can provide the kind of leadership necessary in large, complex undertakings that have numerous direct as well as indirect — and often unintended — consequences for society. They must not only be politically astute but also be able to grasp the analytical work of their staffs.

Second, they will need to be low-keyed. And once more the reason is that large, complex undertakings seem to necessitate it. As Harlan Cleveland (1972:81) put it: "Complexity of operation magnifies small errors and makes the whole system vulnerable. People who get too easily excited are likely to get in the way, and will be asked to simmer down regardless of rank." And this applies not only in the control room of a modern aircraft but also in the office of a city manager or a hospital administrator.

Another reason for this trait can be derived from what was said in Chapters 7, 8, and 11: collegiate management — with an emphasis more on steering than on controlling — requires a low-keyed administrative style.

Third, tomorrow's administrator will tend less and less to see only one side of each issue. Recall the earlier example of the Alaskan pipeline: What is the "proper" solution, the proper trade-off between aesthetics and ecology on the one hand and unemployment and starvation on the other? One thinks here of that ferocious American journalist H. L. Mencken: for every knotty problem, there is a solution: neat, simple, and wrong.

So, increasingly, tomorrow's administrators must become skilled in analyzing issues in terms of trade-offs and reconciling what now often seem irreconcilable conflicts between the interests of different groups.

Finally, they will accept the ever increasing difficulty and challenge of managing the public sector. Maslow had something of this in mind when talking about the choice between being a hero or a worm. "So many choose wormhood. They have a hopelessness, a lack of regard for what one person can do, an adolescent disillusionment because the whole world doesn't change when one new law is passed. . . . It is this disillusionment that has so often taken the heart out of social reformers and men of good will generally, so that as they grow older they get tired and hopeless and glum and go into privatism instead of conscious social betterment."

And Maslow sees only one alternative for tomorrow's managers: they "must learn . . . to thrill with pride, to get excited, to have a strengthened feeling of self-esteem, to have a strong feeling of accomplishment when [just] one particular little reform or improvement takes place. . . ." But, alas, there are things books cannot teach.

NAILING DOWN THE MAIN POINTS

1 Unlike predictions, which attempt to make absolute statements about what *will* happen, forecasts offer probabilistic statements about what *may* happen. In recent years, the number of forecasting techniques has

grown quite rapidly, but most are related to six of the more basic methods: expert forecasting, consensus methods, cross-impact analysis, trend extrapolation, scenario, and leading indicators. Properly used, these methods can provide us with a little less murkey glimpse of the future of public administration.

2   Three trends seem especially important to the future of public administration in the U.S. The first trend is the politics of scarcity. This means not that we are "running out of everything" but that a more careful husbanding of existing resources and a more intelligent planning for future technology are imperative. The second trend is what Bell calls the revolution of rising entitlements. Quite possible, this revolution is only a part of the larger shift in American ideology noted by Lodge. These two trends, scarcity and rising entitlements, conspire to make a third, the integration of business into the political and social order, more likely than ever. While no one can say the precise form that this integration will take, we can at least conjecture about its broad characteristics.

Critics aside, the powers of government have been relatively well controlled in the United States for the last 200 years. And the approach has been a general one, outlined in sweeping strokes by the Constitution. In sharpest contrast, attempts to control the corporation have been piecemeal, specific. Therefore, it seems quite possible that, in the coming decades, as the search for effective control becomes more intense, general solutions will be sought. Taxation of certain actions and use of national charters would, in this context, be possible solutions.

3   What institutional changes might these three trends lead to? One possibility is a new public-private balance in which industry is a partner of government in the attainment of societal goals in all functional areas except defense, economic development, and foreign policy. Government would become more oriented toward the future and involved in contracting.

4   What changes in managerial behavior might these trends lead to? Tomorrow's managers, as I see it, will need to be broadly educated, low-keyed, open-minded, and self-actualized.

CONCEPTS FOR REVIEW

forecasts, predictions
exploratory and normative forecasts
expert forecasting
Delphi technique
cross-impact analysis
trend extrapolation
S-curve

scenario
leading indicators
entropy law
revolution of rising entitlements
traditional American ideology,
    the New American ideology
    (Lodge)

federal chartering
integrative and integrative planning
environmental impact statement
technology assessment

contracting
public-private partnerships,
    government corporations
growth management

PROBLEMS

1. Using Molitor's technique of leading indicators, what public policy innovations seem likely in the decades ahead? How did you arrive at your forecast; that is, what indicators did you use?

2. Cross-impact analysis is "based on the concept that the occurrence or nonoccurrence of a possible event or the enactment of a particular policy may affect the probability of occurrence of a host of other events and policies. The method requires that such interactions be defined and their strength estimated. In the absence of hard data about these future interactions, opinion and judgment are used." (Gordon and Becker 1972) Fill in the following cross-impact matrix by placing a zero in those cells where the probability of an event occurring remains the same and plus in those where it increases.

3. Government corporations are often formed when private industry finds the task to be undertaken either too risky or unprofitable. The chartering of Amtrak clearly falls into this pattern. Describe the circumstances concerning its formation, the powers it was given, and its record of performance thus far. What prognosis would you make concerning its likelihood of success? See *Congressional Quarterly Almanac, Congressional Quarterly Weekly Report,* and the *New York Times Index.*

4. Discuss the social and political implications of the "expected" technologies in the A. C. Clarke's list that appeared earlier in the chapter.

5. How to achieve a more responsive bureaucracy is a major theme in the literature of public administration. Prepare a paper that assess the potential of marketing

If This Event Were to Occur	Then the Probability of This Event Also Occurring Would Become			
	A	B	C	D
A. One-month reliable weather forecasts				
B. Feasibility of limited weather control				
C. General biochemical immunization				
D. Elimination of crop damage from adverse weather				

techniques for improving responsiveness. See, for a start, Philip Kotler, *Marketing for Nonprofit Organizations* (Englewood Cliffs, N. J.: Prentice-Hall, 1975).

6. In the last decade or so national planning in Japan and France has received considerable attention from American observers. Prepare a paper that discusses the role of government in the planning process in either or both countries. What are the lessons you find for the United States?

7. "Schools of public administration generally do not train managers, focused as they are on the relatively abstract conceptualization of policy problems and only slightly concerned with the function of the executive. The merger of business schools and public administration schools would be an excellent thing, right in step with the movement to synthesis. Clearly, the old distinctions between what is private and what is public have less and less meaning; in many areas they are merely artificial remnants of the old ideology, figments of the old notions of property, competition, and the limited state. The management problems of Consolidated Edison, the oil companies, General Electric, IBM, ITT, AT&T, savings and loan associations, and the like are as inseparably involved with public questions of community need as are those, let us say, of the TVA, COMSAT, the Port of New York Authority, and HUD. The management of garbage disposal, health systems, land use, and welfare is equally complex and in many ways quite similar to the management of the so-called private sector. There may be different measures of efficiency, different sources of capital, different allocation of profit, different problems of incentive, but these differences are closing and they do not detract from the overall similarities. Yet consolidation of the business school and the public administration school is hindered by traditional academic bureaucratization and deeply felt loyalties to old specializations. In consequence, both sets of school are in danger of obsolescence." (Lodge 1975:335–6) Discuss.

8. Review the list of traits for tomorrow's manager. Which would you eliminate? Which traits need to be added?

9. How would you explain this paradox: the public mistrusts government, yet wants more.

Bibliography

Bibliography

Acheson, D. 1959. "Thoughts about thoughts in high places." *New York Times Magazine,* October 11.

Adrian, C. R. 1976. *State and local government.* New York: McGraw-Hill.

Albano, C. 1974. *Transactional analysis on the job.* New York: Amacom.

Allison, G. 1971. *Essence of decision.* Boston: Little, Brown.

American Academy. 1973. *Education for urban administration.* Philadelphia:American
Academy of Political and Social Science.

Anderson, J. E. 1975. *Public policy-making.* New York:Praeger.

Anderson, W. 1960. *Intergovernmental relations in review.* Minneapolis:University of
Minnesota Press.

Appleby, P. H. 1952. *Morality and administration in democratic government.* Baton
Rouge:L.S.U. Press.

Arthur Andersen & Co. 1975. *Sound financial reporting in the public sector.* New York.

Ash, R. L. 1975. Looking beyond the budget deficit. *Wall Street Journal,* July 28.

Atcheson, G., and Neubauer, M. 1975. Committees power bases for special interest.
Houston Post, July 10.

Bagley, E. R. 1975. *Beyond the conglomerates.* New York:Amacom.

Bailey, S. K. 1966. *The office of education and the education act of 1965.* Syracuse:
Inter-University Case Programs.

————. 1968. "Objectives of the theory of public administration." In *Theory and
practice of public administration.* Philadelphia:American Academy of Political
and Social Science.

Baker, R. J. S. 1972. *Administrative theory and public administration.* London:Hutchin-
son University Library.

Balz, D. J. 1975. Economic focus/how much is enough and for whom? *National Journal,* February 15.

Barnard, C. I. 1938. *The function of the executive.* Cambridge, Mass.:Harvard University Press.

Bauer, R. A., ed. 1966. *Social indicators.* Cambridge:MIT.

Baumol, W. J. 1973. Interview. *Princeton Quarterly,* Winter.

Bennis, W. 1966. *Changing organizations.* New York:McGraw-Hill.

————. and Slater, P. E. 1968. *The temporary society.* New York:Harper & Row.

Benveniste, G. 1972. *The politics of expertise.* Berkeley:The Glendessary Press.

Bell, D. 1967. Notes on the post-industrial society. *Public Interest,* Winter.

————. 1973. *The coming of post-industrial society.* New York:Basic Books.

————. 1976. *The cultural contradictions of capitalism.* New York:Basic Books.

Berle, A. A. 1968. What GNP doesn't tell us. *Saturday Review,* August 31.

Berle, A. A., and Means, G. C. *The modern corporation and private property.* New York: Macmillan.

————. and Means, G. C. Eds. 1969. *The modern corporation and private property.* New York:Harcourt, Brace, and Jovanovich, Inc.

Berne, E. 1964. *Games people play.* New York:Grove Press.

————. 1973. *Transactional analysis in psychotherapy.* New York:Ballantine Books.

Black, A. 1968. The comprehensive plan. In *Principles and practices of urban planning.* W. I. Goodman and E. C. Freund. Washington:ICMA.

Blake, R. R., et al. 1964. Breakthrough in organization development. *Harvard Business Review,* November–December.

Blechman, B. M., Gramlich, E. M., and Hartman, R. W. 1975. *Setting national priorities: the 1976 budget.* Washington:Brookings.

Blodgett, J. 1972. Costing out pollution:the state of the art. *SPPSG Newsletter,* May.

Blumenthal, R. 1969. The bureaucracy:antipoverty and the community action program. In *American political institutions and public policy.* A. P. Sindler. Boston:Little, Brown, and Co.

Bonnen, J. T. 1969. The absence of knowledge of distributional impacts. In Joint Economic Committee, *The analysis and evaluation of public expenditure.* Washington:G.P.O.

Boss, R. W. 1976. Decision making:Theories and applications to the budgetary process. In *Public administration.* R. T. Golembiewski, et al. Chicago:Rand McNally.

Boulding, K. E. 1966. The economics of the coming spaceship earth. In *Environmental quality.* H. Jarrett. Baltimore:John Hopkins Press.

Bowers, D. G. 1964. Self-esteem and supervision. *Personnel Administration,* July–August.

Bowman, D. M. and Fillerup, F. M. 1963. *Management: organization and planning.* New York:McGraw-Hill.

Boyer, W. W. 1964. *Bureaucracy on trial: policy making by government agencies.* Indianapolis:Bobbs-Merrill.

Brady, R. 1973. MBO goes to work in the public sector. *Harvard Business Review,* March–April.

Bright, J. 1964. *Research, development and technological innovation.* Homewood, Ill.:Irwin.

————. 1972. *A brief introduction to technology forecasting.* Austin, Texas:Pemaquid Press.

Broder, D. S. 1975. Governor Brown: an honest approach. *Washington Post,* May 31.

Burnham, D. 1974. A.E.C. files show effort to conceal safety perils. *New York Times,* November 10.

Burnham, J. 1942. *The managerial revolution.* New York:John Day.

Burns, J. M. 1974. Interview. *Meet the press,* NBC, July 15, 1974.

Bushey, H. T. 1974. "Work analysis and work environment." In *Developing the municipal organization.* S. P. Powers et al. Washington:ICMA.

Buskirk, R. H. 1976. *Handbook of managerial tactics.* Boston:Cahners Books, Inc.

Byham, W. C. and Wettengel, C. 1974. "Assessment centers for supervisors and managers." *Public Personnel Management,* September–October.

Caiden, G. E. 1971. *The dynamics of public administration:guidelines to current transformations in theory and practice.* Hinsdale, Ill.:Dryden Press.

Caldwell, L. K. 1972. "Environmental quality as an administrative problem." In *The Annals.* Philadelphia:American Academy of Political and Social Science.

Carey, W. D. 1973. "New perspectives on governance." In the Conference Board's *Challenge to leadership:managing in a changing world.* New York:Free Press.

Carmichael, S. 1971. "Black power and the third world." In *Readings in U.S. imperialism.* K. T. Fenn and D. C. Hodges. New York:Herder & Herder.

Cartwright, D. and Alvin F. Eds. 1960. *Group dynamics:research and theory.* Evanston, Ill.:Row & Peterson.

Centron, M. J. and Bartocha, B. Eds. 1973. *Technology assessment in a dynamic environment.* New York:Gordon & Breach, Science Publishers, Inc.

Cervantes, A. J. 1973. "Memories of a businessman-mayor." *Business Week,* December 8.

Churchill, W. S. 1959. *Memoirs.* Boston:Houghton Mifflin Company.

Clarke, A. C. 1963. *Profiles of the future.* New York:Harper & Row.

Cleaveland, F. 1973. "The Changing Character of the Public Service and the Administrator of the 1980s." *Public Administration Review,* July–August.

Cleveland, H. 1972. *The future executive.* New York:Harper & Row.

———. 1975. "How do you get everybody in on the act and still get some action?" *Public Management,* June.

Coates, J. F. 1971. "Technology assessment." *Futurist.* December.

———. 1974. "Some methods and techniques for comprehensive impact assessment." *Technology Forecasting and Social Change,* June.

Commoner, B. 1971. *The closing circle.* New York:Knopf.

Cook, T. J. and Scioli, F. P. 1972. "A research strategy for analyzing the impact of public policy." *Administrative Science Quarterly,* September.

Corcoran, W. A. 1975. "Financial management." In *Management policies in local government finance.* J. R. Aronson and E. Schwartz. Washington:ICMA.

Coulam, R. F. 1975. "The importance of the beginning:defense doctrine and the development of the F-111 fighter-bomber." *Public Policy,* Winter.

Davis, O. A. and Kamien, M. I. 1969. "Externalities, information, and alternative collective action." In Joint Economic Committee, *Analysis and evaluation of public expenditures.* Washington:G.P.O.

Deutsch, K. 1963. *Nerves of government.* New York:Free Press.

Downs, A. 1967. "A realistic look at the final payoffs from urban data systems." *Public Administration Review,* September.

Drucker, P. 1973. *Management:tasks, responsibilities, practices.* New York:Harper & Row.

———. 1966. *The effective executive.* New York:Harper and Row.

Due, J. F. and Friedlaender, A. F. 1973. *Government finance.* Homewood, Ill.:Irwin.

Dwight, J. S. 1973. "The four 'Ds' of the new federalism." In *The administration of the new federalism.* L. E. Grosenick, ed. Washington: American Society for Public Administration.

Eddy, W. B. 1970. "Beyond behavioralism? Organization development in public management." *Public Personnel Review,* July.

Elazar, D. 1972. *American federalism.* New York:Crowell.

Ellul, J. 1964. *The technological society.* New York:Knopf.

Etzioni, A. 1973. "The third sector and domestic missions." *Public Administration Review,* July–August.

Fairlie, H. 1965. "Johnson and the intellectuals." *Commentary,* October.

Farney, D. 1975. "Is the nation ready to be baroodied?" *Wall Street Journal,* February 25.

Farrell, W. E. 1976. "Decentializations of control over use of U.S. funds." *New York Times,* March 8.

Fenno, R. 1966. *The power of the purse.* Boston:Little, Brown, and Company.

Fesler, J. W. 1949. *Area and administration.* Tuscaloosa:University of Alabama.

Finer, H. 1941. "Administrative responsibility in democratic government." *Public Administration Review,* Summer.

Finney, J. W. 1975. "Rickover." *New York Times,* July 13.

Fitch, L. G. 1974. "Increasing the role of the private sector in providing public services." In *Improving the quality of urban management.* W. D. Hawley and D. Rogers. Beverly Hills, Calif.:Sage Publications.

Flax, M. T. and Garn, H. A. 1973. *A study in comparative urban indicators: conditions in 18 large metropolitan areas.* Washington:Urban Institute.

Fowles, A. M. 1974. "Public information." In *Developing the municipal organization.* S. P. Powers, F. G. Brown, and D. S. Arnold. Washington:ICMA.

French, Jr., T. R. P. and Raven, B. H. 1968. "The bases of social power." In *Group dynamics:research theory.* D. Cartwright and A. Fander, eds., 3d. ed.

Friedman, M. 1969. Statement. In U.S. Congress, Joint Economic Committee, *Economic Analysis and the Efficiency of Government.* Hearings of the Subcommittee on Economy in Government, Part 3, September–October.

Galbraith, J. K. 1958. *The affluent society.* Boston:Houghton Mifflin.

———. 1967. *New industrial state.* Boston:Houghton Mifflin.

———. 1975. *Money:Whence it came, where it went.* Boston:Houghton Mifflin.

Gardner, J. W. 1961. *Excellence:can we be equal and excellent too?* New York:Harper & Row.

Georgescu-Roegen, N. 1975. "Energy and economic myths." *Southern Economic Journal,* January.

Gellerman, S. W. 1963. *Motivation and productivity.* New York:American Management Association.

Gerth, H. H. and Mills, C. W. Eds. 1946. *From Max Weber:essays in sociology.* New York:Oxford University Press.

Gilbert, C. E. 1959. "The framework of administrative responsibility." *Journal of Politics,* May.

Gilmore, T. S. and Duff, M. K. 1975. *Boom town growth management.* Boulder, Colo.:Westview.

Glazer, N. 1976. *Affirmative discrimination.* New York:Basic Books.

Golembiewski, R. T. 1974. "Public administration as a field:four developmental phases." Georgia Political Science Association *Journal,* Spring.

Gordon, T. J. and Becker, H. S. 1972. "The use of cross-impact matrix approaches in technology assessment." In *The methodology of technology assessment.* M. J. Cetran and B. Bartocha. New York:Gordon & Breach, Science Publishers, Inc.

Greenberg, D. S. 1967. *The politics of pure science.* New York:New American Library.

Grode, G. and Holzer, M. 1975. "The perceived utility of MPA degrees." *Public Administration Review,* July–August.

Grodzins, M. and Elazar, D. J. 1966. *The American System.* Chicago:Rand McNally.

Gross, B. M. 1968. *Organizations and their managing.* New York:Free Press.

———. 1970. "Friendly facism:a model for America." *Social Policy,* November–December.

———. 1971. "Planning in an era of social revolution." *Public Administration Review,* May–June.

Grosse, R. N. 1969. "Problems of resource allocation in health." In U.S. Congress, Joint Economic Committee, *The analysis and evaluation of public expenditures.* Washington:G.P.O.

Gulick, L., and Urwick, L., eds. 1937. *Papers on the science of administration.* New York:Augustus M. Kelley.

Guttman, D. and Willner, B. 1976. *Shadow government.* New York:Pantheon Books.

Halberstam, D. 1969. *The best and the brightest.* Greenwich, Connecticut:Fawcett Crest Books.

Hall, T. 1976. "How Cultures Collide." *Psychology Today,* July.

Hatry, H. P. 1972. "Issues in productivity measurement for local governments." *Public Administration Review,* November–December.

Hatry, H. P. and Fisk, D. M. 1971. *Improving productivity and productivity measurement in local governments.* Washington:Urban Institute.

Hatry, H. P., Winnie, R. E., and Fisk, D. M. 1973. *Practical program evaluation for state and local government officials.* Washington:Urban Institute.

Haveman, J. 1973. "White House Report/OMB's 'management by objectives' produces goals of uneven quality." *National Journal,* August 18.

———. 1975a. "Budget Report/Ford, Congress seek handle on 'uncontrollable spending.' " *National Journal,* December 29.

———. 1975b. "Budget Report/first fiscal resolution." *National Journal,* May 24.

Heller, W. 1966. *New dimensions of political economy.* Cambridge, Mass.:Harvard University Press.

Helmer, O. 1968. *Report on the future of the future—state-of-the-union reports.* Report R-14. Middleton, Conn.:Institute for the Future.

Hemenway, G. D. 1973. *Developer's handbook—environmental impact statements.* Berkeley, Calif.:Associated Home Builders of the Greater East Bay, Inc.

Henry, N. 1975. *Public administration and public affairs.* Englewood Cliffs, N.J.:Prentice-Hall.

Herriot, R. A. and Herman, P. M. 1971. "The taxes we pay." *The Conference Board Record,* May.

Hersey, P. and Blanchard, K. H. 1972. *Management of organization behavior.* Englewood Cliffs, N.J.:Prentice-Hall.

Hewlett, R. and Duncan, F. 1974. *Nuclear navy, 1946–1962.* Chicago:University of Chicago.

Herzberg, F., et al. 1959. *The motivation to work.* New York:Wiley.

Hill, G. 1970. "Pollutors sit on anti-pollution boards." *New York Times,* December 7.

Hitch, C. J. and McKean, R. N. 1960. *The economics of defense in the nuclear age.* Cambridge, Mass.:Harvard University Press.

Hitch, C. J. 1960. *On the choice of objectives in systems studies.* Santa Monica, Calif.: RAND.

Hoos, I. R. 1972. *Systems analysis in public policy:a critique.* Berkeley, Calif.:University of California Press.

————. 1973. "Systems technique for managing society:a critique." *Public Administration Review,* March–April.

Hopkins, B. and Edwards, D. 1976. "Where does the time go?" *Runner's World Magazine,* July.

Horst, P., et al. 1974. "Program management and the federal evaluator." *Public Administration Review,* July–August.

House, K. E. 1976. "Energy agency spend much energy to insure a long life, foes say." *Wall Street Journal,* March 9.

Houston-Galveston Area Council. 1975. "H-GAC project review tests impact of funding proposals." *HGAC Spectrum,* July.

Humphrey, H. H. 1975. "Points of view/national economic planning." *New York Times,* December 21.

Huntington, S. P. 1952. "The marasmus of the ICC:the commission, the railroads, and the public interest." *The Yale Law Journal,* April.

Hyatt, J. C. 1976. "In the federal garden of Eden, Eve is taking more bites from the apple—but not getting half." *Wall Street Journal,* February 24.

Ikle, F. C. 1964. *How nations negotiate.* New York:Harper & Row.

Irwin, R. 1975. "Carla Hill gives 'the woman's touch' a brand-new meaning." *Fortune,* December.

Jacoby, N. H. 1973. *Corporate power and social responsibility.* New York:Macmillan.

James, M. 1975. *The ok boss.* Reading, Mass.:Addison-Wesley.

James, W. 1952. *Principles of psychology.* Chicago:Encyclopaedia Britannica.

Janis, I. L. 1971. "Groupthink." *Psychology Today,* November.

Jantsch, E. 1967. *Technology forecasting in perspective.* Paris:OECD.

————. 1969. *Perspectives of planning.* Paris:OECD.

Jaques, E. 1970. *Work, creativity, and social justice.* New York:International University Press.

Jennings, E. E. 1961. The anatomy of leadership. *Management of Personnel Quarterly,* Autumn.

Johnson, S. K. 1975. "It's action, but is it affirmative?" *New York Times Magazine,* May 11.

Kahn, H. and Wiener, A. J. 1967. *The year 2000.* New York:Macmillan.

Kahn, H., Brown, W., and Martel, L. 1976. *The next 200 years.* New York:William Morrow and Company.

Kahn, R. L. et al. 1975. "Americans love their bureaucrats." *Psychology Today,* June.

Karr, A. 1975. "The 'wild man' of transportation." *Wall Street Journal,* October 27.

Katz, D. and Kahn, R. L. 1966. *The social psychology of organizations.* New York:Wiley.

Kaufman, H. 1960. *The forest ranger:a study of administrative behavior.* Baltimore:John Hopkins Press.

Kaufmann, W. 1973. *Without guilt and justice.* New York:Peter H. Wyden.

Koening, P. 1974. "They just changed the rules on how to get ahead." *Psychology Today,* June.

Koestler, A. 1974. *The heel of Achilles.* New York:Random House.

Koontz, H. and O'Donnell, C. 1974. *Essentials of management.* New York:McGraw-Hill.

Korda, M. 1975. *Power!* New York:Random House.

Kotler, P. 1975. *Marketing for nonprofit organization.* Englewood Cliffs, N.J.:Prentice-Hall.

Kotz, N. 1969. *Let them eat promises:the politics of hunger in America*. Englewood Cliffs, N.J.:Prentice Hall.

Kranz, H. 1974. "Are merit and equity compatible?" *Public Administration Review*, September–October.

Krause, E. 1968. "Functions of a bureaucratic ideology:citizen participation." *Social Problems*, Fall.

Lacey, P. A. 1975. "Casting About for a President." *Science*, vol. 187, pp. 1153, March 28, 1975. Copyright 1975 by the American Association for the Advancement of Science.

Laing, J. R. 1975. "Civil service setup; born as a reform idea, now hit by reformers." *Wall Street Journal*, December 22.

Lambright, W. H. 1967. *Shooting down the nuclear plane*. Indianapolis:Bobbs-Merrill.

———. 1976. *Governing science and technology*. New York:Oxford.

Landau, M. 1962. "The concept of decision making in the 'field' of public administration." In *Concepts and issues in administrative behavior*. S. Mailick and E. H. Van Ness. Englewood Cliffs, N.J.:Prentice Hall.

———. 1969. "Redundancy, rationality, and the problem of duplication and overlap." *Public Administration Review*, July–August.

Lapatra, J. W. 1973. *Applying the systems approach to urban development*. Stroudsburg, Pennsylvania:Dowden, Hutchinson, and Ross.

Large, A. J. 1975. "Federal agencies fight bill to open meetings to screening by public." *Wall Street Journal*, September 23.

Larson, R. 1973. "Resource allocation in public safety services." In *Proceedings of the first symposium:research applied to national needs*. Washington:NSF.

Lasswell, H. 1951. "The policy orientation." In *The policy science*. H. Lasswell and D. Lerner. Stanford:Stanford University Press.

Lesieur, F. G. 1958. *The scalon plan:a frontier in labor management cooperation*. New York:Wiley.

Levinson, H. 1968. *The exceptional executive*. Cambridge, Mass.:Harvard University Press.

———. 1973. *The great jackass fallacy*. Cambridge, Mass.:Harvard paperback.

Levitt, T. 1976. "Management and the 'post industrial' society." *The Public Interest*, Summer.

Lewis, A. 1975. "When government works." *New York Times*, October 27.

Lewis, W. A. 1968. "Development planning." In *The international encyclopedia of social sciences*. New York:Macmillan.

Likert, R. 1961. *New patterns of management*. New York:McGraw-Hill.

———. 1967. *The human organization:its management and value*. New York:McGraw-Hill.

Lile, S. E. 1976. "Tax report." *Wall Street Journal*, January 21.

Lindblom, C. E. 1968. *The policy making process*. Englewood Cliffs, N.J.:Prentice-Hall.

Lindsay, J. 1973. "Interview." *New York Times*, December 3.

Lippmann, W. 1955. *The public philosophy*. Boston:Little, Brown, and Company.

Litterer, J. A. 1973. *The analysis of organizations*. New York:Wiley.

Lodge, G. C. 1975. *The new American ideology*. New York:Knopf.

Long, N. 1949. "Powers and administration." *Public Administration Review*, Autumn.

Lower Merion Township. 1975. *Report*, Winter. Ardmore, Pa.

McClelland, D. 1961. *The achieving society.* Princeton:D. Van Nostrand.

————. 1973. "Testing for competence rather than for 'intelligence.'" *The American Psychologist,* January.

McConkey, D. D. 1975. *MBO for nonprofit organizations.* New York:AMACOM.

McCracken, H. L. 1961. *Keynesian economics in the stream of economic thought.* Baton Rouge:L.S.U.

McElheny, V. K. 1975. "States competing for solar centers." *New York Times,* November 9.

McGregor, D. 1960. *The human side of enterprise.* New York:McGraw-Hill.

McKean, R. H. 1963. *Efficiency in government through systems analysis.* New York: Wiley.

Mailer, N. 1959. *Advertisements for myself.* New York:G. P. Putnam.

Malcom, A. 1974. "The modern sheriff:a new breed." *New York Times,* October 3.

March, J. G. and Simon, H. A. 1958. *Organizations.* New York:Wiley.

Marini, F. ed. 1971. *Towards a new public administration:the minnowbrook perspective.* Scranton:Chandler.

Maslow, A. H. 1954. *Motivation and personality.* New York:Harper & Row.

————. 1965. *Eupsychian management.* Homewood, Ill.:Irwin.

————. 1971. *The farther reaches of human nature.* New York:Viking.

Mayer, M. 1976. *Today and tomorrow in America.* New York:Harper & Row.

Mayo, E. 1933. *Human problems of an industrial civilization.* New York:Viking.

Meadows, D. L., et al. 1972. *The limits to growth.* New York:Universe Books.

Meininger, J. 1973. *Success through transactional analysis.* New York:Grosset & Dunlap.

Mesarovic, M. and Pestal, E. 1974. *Mankind at the turning point:the second report of the club of Rome.* New York:E. P. Dutton.

Mikesell, R. M. 1956. *Governmental accounting.* Homewood, Ill.:Irwin.

Milgram, S. 1974. *Obedience to authority:an experimental view.* New York:Harper & Row.

Mils, T. 1975. "Human resources—why the new concern." *Harvard Business Review,* March–April.

Mitre Corporation. 1971. *A technology assessment methodology.* Office of Science and Technology. Washington, D.C.

Moak, L. L. and Killian, K. W. 1974. *A manual of techniques for the preparation, consideration, adoption, and administration of operation budgets.* Springfield, Mass.: Merriam.

Moak, L. L. and Hillhouse, A. M. 1975. *Concepts and practices in local government finance.* Chicago:Municipal Finance Officers Association.

Molitor, G. T. T. 1975. "Schema for forecasting public policy change." In *The next 25 years.* A. A. Spekke, ed. Washington, D.C.:World Future Society.

Morrow, W. 1975. *Public administration: politics and the political system.* New York: Random House.

Morse, P. M. and Kimball, G. E. 1951. *Methods of operations research.* New York:Wiley.

Mosher, F. C. (ed.). 1967. *Governmental reorganization:cases and commentary.* Indianapolis:Bobbs-Merrill.

————. 1968. *Democracy and the public service.* New York:Oxford.

Morse, P. M. 1967. *Operations research for public systems.* Cambridge:MIT.

Morstein, M. F., ed. 1959. *The elements of public administration.* Englewood Cliffs, N.J.:Prentice-Hall.

Moynihan, D. P. 1970. Policy vs. program in the 1970's." Reprinted with permission from *The Public Interest,* No. 20, Summer 1970. Copyright © 1970 by National Affairs, Inc.

———. 1973. *Coping:essays on the practice of government.* New York:Random House.

Musgrave, R. A. and Polinski, A. M. 1971. "Revenue sharing:a critical view." *Harvard Journal Legislation,* January.

———, and Musgrave, P. B. 1973. *Public finance in theory and practice.* New York: McGraw-Hill.

Mushkin, S., ed. 1972. *Public prices for public products.* Washington:Urban Institute.

Muskie, E. 1975. Interview. *Wall Street Journal,* March 6.

National Association of Schools of Public Affairs and Administration. 1974. *Guidelinea and standards for professional masters degree programs in public affairs/public administration.* Washington:NASPAA.

National Commission on Productivity. 1973. *Productivity in state and local govern-ment—the wingspread conference.* Washington:G.P.O.

National Committee on Governmental Accounting. 1968. *Governmental accounting, auditing, and financial reporting.* Chicago:Municipal Finance Officers Association.

National Training and Development Service. 1975. *Urban management curriculum development projects.* Washington:NTDS.

Neustadt, R. D. 1960. *Presidental power.* New York:Wiley.

Newland, C. A. 1972. "Introduction, a symposium on productivity in government." *Public Administration Review,* November.

Okun, A. M. 1975. *Equality and efficiency.* Washington:Brookings.

Otten, A. L. 1973. "Bureaucracy in the White House." *Wall Street Journal,* August 23.

———. 1975. "Learning what works." *Wall Street Journal,* April 17.

Ozbekhan, H. 1965. "The ideal of a 'look-out' institution." *Systems Development Cor-poration.* Santa Monica, Calif., March.

Parker, J. K. 1971. "Administrative analysis." In *Managing the modern city.* J. M. Banovetz. Washington:ICMA.

Parkinson, C. N. 1957. *Parkinson's law and other studies in administration.* Boston: Houghton-Mifflin.

Patton, A. 1974a. "To reform the federal pay system." *Business Week,* March 9.

———. 1974b. "Government's pay disincentive." *Business Week,* January 19.

———. 1974c. "Fallacies in federal pay standards." *Business Week,* January 26.

———. 1974d. "The hidden costs of federal pensions." *Business Week,* April 27.

———. 1974e. "The new look in civil services pay." *Wall Street Journal,* November 21.

Pechman, J. A. 1971. *Federal tax policy.* New York:W. W. Norton.

———. and Okner, B. A. 1974. *Who bears the tax burden?* Washington:Brookings.

Peter, L. J. 1967. "The Peter principle, or the incompetent shall inherit the earth." *West Magazine,* April 16.

Petro, S. 1975. *Sovereignty and compulsory public sector bargaining.* Wake Forest, N.C.:Wake Forest Law Review Association.

Pomerleau, R. 1974. "The state of management development in the federal service." *Public Personnel Management,* January–February.

Powers, S. P. 1974. "Management concepts and organization models." In *Developing the municipal organization*. S. P. Powers, F. G. Brown, and D. S. Arnold. Washington:ICMA.

Pressman, J. L. and Wildavsky, A. 1973. *Implementation*. Berkeley:University of California Press.

Price, D. K. 1965. *The scientific estate*. Cambridge, Mass.:Belknap Press.

Public Policy Program. 1972. *Teaching and research materials, public policy 210 problem sets*. Cambridge, Mass.:Kennedy School of Government.

Pyhrr, P. A. 1971. "Zero-base budgeting." *Harvard Business Review*. May.

Quade, E. S. 1966. *System analysis techniques for planning-programming-budgeting*. Santa Monica, Calif.:Rand.

————, ed. 1964. *Analysis of military decisions*. Chicago:Rand McNally.

Rawls, J. 1971. *A theory of justice*. Cambridge, Mass.:Belknap Press.

Rendon, A. 1971. *Chicano manifesto*. New York:Macmillan.

Richardson, E. 1973. "The maze of social programs." *Washington Post*. January 21.

Riker, W. H. 1962. *The theory of political coalitions*. New Haven, Conn.:Yale University Press.

Rivlin, A. 1971. *Systematic thinking for social action*. Washington:Brookings.

————. 1975. *Statement before the Joint Economic Committee*, April 3.

Rogers, C. R. and Roethlisberger, F. J. 1952. "Barriers and gateways to communications." *Harvard Business Review*, July–August.

Roos, N. P. 1975. "Contrasting social experimentation with retrospective evaluation." *Public Policy*, Spring.

Roosa, R. V. 1976. "Economic planning:a middle way." *New York Times*, February 8.

Roszak, T. 1973. *Where the wasteland ends*. Garden City, N.Y.:Anchor Books.

Rourke, F. E. 1972. *Bureaucratic power in national politics*. Boston:Little, Brown and Company.

————. 1969. *Bureaucracy, politics and public policy*. Boston:Little, Brown and Company.

Ruchelman, L. I. 1975. "The finance function in local government." In *Management policies in local government finance*. J. R. Aronson and E. Swartz. Washington:ICMA.

Safire, W. 1973. "The new federalism." *New York Times*, November 15.

Samuelson, P. A. 1973. *Economics*. New York:McGraw-Hill.

Sanford, T. 1967. *Storm over the states*. New York:McGraw-Hill.

Savas, E. S. 1971. "Municipal monopoly." *Harper's Magazine*. December.

Sayles, L. R. and Chandler, M. K. 1971. *Managing large systems:organizations for the future*. New York:Harper & Row.

Schachter, S. 1959. *The psychology of affiliation*. Stanford, Calif.:Stanford University Press.

Schlesinger, A. M. 1965. *A thousand days*. Boston:Houghton-Mifflin.

Schon, D. A. 1971. *Beyond the stable state*. New York:Random House.

Schorr, B. 1975. "More federal workers take on a second job:assailing government." *Wall Street Journal*, June 16.

Schubert, G. 1962. "Is there a public interest theory?" In *The public interest*. C. T. Friedrech. New York:Atherton Press.

Schultz, G. P. 1961. "Strikes:the private stake and the public interest." In *Report of *the president's task force on employee-management relations in the federal service.* Washington:G.P.O.

Schultze, C. L. 1969. "The role of incentives, penalties, and rewards in attaining effective policy." In The Joint Economic Committee, *Analysis and evaluation of public expenditures.* Washington:G.P.O.

Seidman, H. 1970. *Politics, position, and power:the dynamics of federal organization.* New York:Oxford.

Selznick, P. 1949. *TVA and the grass roots.* New York:Harper & Row.

Seyler, W. C. 1974. "Interlocal relations:cooperation." *Annals,* November.

Shafer, R. G. 1975. "Revenue-sharing versus raised tempers as law comes up for renewal." *Wall Street Journal,* March 27.

———. 1976. "More cities sign up a 'man in Washington' to help them win grantsmanship game." *Wall Street Journal,* January 15.

Shafritz, J. (ed.) 1975. *A new world:readings on modern public personnel management.* Chicago:IPMA.

Sharkansky, Ira. 1972. *Public Administration.* Chicago:Markham.

Sharkansky, I. 1969. *The politics of taxing and spending.* Indianapolis:Bobbs-Merrill.

Sherrill, R. 1974. *Why they call it politics.* New York:Harcourt, Brace, and Jovanovich.

Shick, A. 1966. "The road to PPB:the stages of budget reform." *Public Administration Review,* December.

———. 1971. "From analysis to evaluation." *Annals,* March.

Silk, L. 1975. "Economics for the perplexed." *New York Times Magazine,* March 21.

Simon, H. A. 1957a. *Administrative behavior.* New York:Macmillan.

———. 1957b. *Models of man.* New York:Wiley.

Simon, H. A., Smithburg, D. W., and Thompson, V. A. 1950. *Public administration.* New York:Knopf.

Skibbins, G. J. 1974. *Organizational evolution.* New York:AMACOM.

Slinger, B. F., Sharp, A. M., and Sandmeyer, R. L. 1975. "Local government revenues." In *Management policies in local government finance.* J. R. Aronson and E. Schwartz. Washington:ICMA.

Sorensen, T. C. 1963. *Decision making in the White House.* New York:Columbia University Press.

———. 1965. *Kennedy.* New York:Harper & Row.

Speer, A. 1970. *Inside the third reich.* New York:Macmillan.

Spencer, M. H. 1971. "Administrative science." In *Management of the urban crisis.* S. E. Seashore and R. J. McNeil. New York:Free Press.

Stahl, O. G. 1971. "Summary and prospects." In Public Personnel Association, *Personnel dialogue for the seventies,* Personnel Report 712, Chicago.

Steiner, G. A. 1969. *Top management planning.* New York:Macmillan.

Stewart, J. M. 1969. "Making project management work." In *Systems, organization analysis, management.* D. I. Cleland and W. R. King. New York:McGraw-Hill.

Stieglitz, H. 1969. "What's not on the organizational chart." In *Systems, organization, analysis, management.* D. I. Cleland and W. R. King. New York:McGraw-Hill.

Suchman, E. A. 1967. *Evaluative research.* New York:Basic Books.

Surrey, S. S. 1973. "Tax expenditures and tax reform." In *The political economy of federal policy.* R. H. Haveman and R. D. Hamrin. New York:Harper & Row.

Tanenhaus, J. 1960. "Supreme court attitudes toward federal administrative agencies." *The Journal of Politics,* August.

Terkel, S. 1972. *Working.* New York:Pantheon Books.

Texas Municipal League. 1975. *Handbook for administrators in small Texas cities.* Austin:Texas Municipal League.

Thompson, A. A. 1967. "Employee participation in decision making:the TVA experience." *Public Personnel Review,* April.

Thompson, F. 1976. "Types of representative bureaucracy and their linkage." In *Public administration,* R. T. Golembienski, et al. Chicago:Rand McNally.

Time. 1974. "The quest for leadership." *Time,* July 15.

Time. 1975. "The truth about Hoover." *Time,* December 22.

Toffler, A. 1970. *Future shock.* New York:Random House.

Townsend, R. 1970. *Up the organization.* New York:Knopf.

Toynbee, A. J. 1946. *A study of history,* abridged ed. New York:Oxford.

U.S. Advisory Commission on Intergovernmental Relations. 1965. *Federal-state coordination of personal income taxes.* Washington:G.P.O.

———. 1970. *Eleventh annual report.* Washington:G.P.O.

U.S. Air Force. 1973. *Management engineering manual AFM 25-5.* Washington:USAF.

U.S. Air Force Systems Command. 1963. *PERT-time system description manual.* Washington:Headquarters AFSC.

U.S. Bureau of Census. 1974. *Current population reports,* series P-25, No. 533. Washington:G.P.O.

———. 1975. *City government finances 1973-1974.* Washington:G.P.O.

U.S. Civil Service Commission. 1971. *Federal personnel manual.* Washington:U.S.C.S.C.

———. 1974. *Guide to a more effective public service:the legal framework.* Washington:U.S.C.S.C.

U.S. Commission on Organization of the Executive Branch of the Government. 1975. *Surplus property.* Washington:G.P.O.

U.S. Congress, House Committee on Ways and Means. 1971. *Hearings on general revenue sharing.* Washington:G.P.O.

U.S. Congress, House. 1973. Representative Craig Homer's extension of remarks, *Congressional Record,* E 6500-1, October 15.

U.S. Congress, Joint Economic Committee. 1975. *Hearings on the economic impact of environment regulations.* Washington:G.P.O.

U.S. Energy Research and Development Administration. 1975a. *A national plan for energy research, development and demonstration.* Washington:G.P.O.

———. 1975b. *National solar energy research, development and demonstration program,* Definition Report. Washington:G.P.O.

U.S. Office of Management and Budget. 1972. *Papers relating to the president's departmental reorganization program.* Washington:G.P.O.

———. 1975. *Strengthening public management in the intergovernmental systems.* Washington:G.P.O.

———. 1976a. *The budget of the U.S. government, FY 1977.* Washington:G.P.O.

———. 1976b. *Special analysis, FY 1977.* Washington:G.P.O.

Von Puttkamer, J. 1975. *Developing space occupancy:perspectives on NASA future space program planning.* Paper presented at conference on "Space Manufacturing Facilities," 7-9 May 1975, at Princeton, N.J.

Vroom, V. H. and Yetton, P. W. 1973. *Leadership and decision making.* Pittsburgh:University of Pittsburgh Press.

Wald, E. 1973. "Toward a paradigm of future public administration." *Public Administration Review.* July–August.

Waldo, D. 1948. *Administrative state.* New York:Ronald Press.

———, ed. 1971. *Public administration in a time of turbulence.* Scranton, Pa.:Chandler.

———. 1975. "Education for public administration in the seventies." In *American public administration:past, present, future.* F. C. Mosher. University of Alabama: University of Alabama Press.

Walters, R. W. 1972. "Job enrichment isn't easy." *Personnel Administration Review,* September–October.

Walton, R. E. 1967. Contrasting designs for participative systems. *Personnel Administration Review,* November–December.

Webb, J. 1969. *Space age management.* New York:McGraw-Hill.

Weidenbaum, M. 1969a. *The modern public sector.* New York:Basic Books.

———. 1969b. "Budget 'uncontrollability' as an obstacle in improving the allocation of government resources." In Joint Economic Committee, *Analysis and evaluation of public expenditures.* Washington:G.P.O.

Weinberg, A. M. 1966. "Can technology replace social engineering?" *Bulletin of the Atomic Scientists,* December.

Weisband, E. D. and Frank, T. M. 1975. *Resignation in protest.* New York:Grossman.

Weisman, S. R. 1975. "How New York became a fiscal junkie." *New York Times Magazine,* August 17.

Weiss, C. H. 1972. *Evaluation research.* Englewood Cliffs, N.J.:Prentice-Hall.

——— ed. 1972. *Evaluating action programs.* Boston:Allyn and Bacon.

Wizenbaum, J. 1976. *Computer power and human reason.* San Francisco:W. H. Freiman and Co.

Whimbey, A. 1976. "You can learn to raise your IQ score." *Psychology Today,* January.

White, L. D. 1927. *The city manager.* Chicago:University of Chicago Press.

Whitehead, A. N. 1929. *The aims of education.* New York:Macmillan.

Wholey, J. S., et al. 1970. *Federal evaluation policy.* Washington:Urban Institute.

———. 1972. "What can we actually get from program evaluation?" *Policy Sciences,* March.

———. 1973. *Federal evaluation policy.* Washington:Urban Institute.

Wildavsky, A. 1964. *The politics of the budgetary process.* Boston:Little, Brown, and Company.

Williams, W. 1975. "Special issue on implementation:editor's comments." *Policy Analysis,* Summer.

Wilson, W. 1941. "The study of administration." *Political Science Quarterly,* December.

Wise, D. 1973. *The politics of lying:government deception, secrecy, and power.* New York:Vintage Books.

Wolfe, T. 1970. *Radical chic & mau-mauing the flak catchers.* New York:Farrar, Straus, and Giroux.

Wright, D. S. 1974. "Intergovernmental relations:an analytical overview." *Annals,* November.

Zagoria, S. 1973. "Productivity bargaining." *Public Management,* July.

———. 1974. "Labor relations management." In *Developing the municipal organization.* S. P. Powers, F. G. Brown, and D. S. Arnold. Washington:ICMA.

Zangwell, W. 1969. "Top management and the selection of major contractors at NASA." *California Management Review,* Fall.

Zalenznik, A. 1966. *The human dilemmas of leadership.* New York:Harper & Row.

INDEX

INDEX

*This book has been set in 9 point Helvetica, leaded
3 points, and 8 point Helvetica, leaded 2 points.
Part numbers and chapter titles are 24 point, and
16 point Helvetica. Part titles are 18 point Helvetica
Bold and chapter numbers are 42 point Weiss
Series II. The size of the type page is 27 picas (text
area) by 46½ picas.*